SECOND EDITION

CONTEMPORARY DIRECT & INTERACTIVE MARKETING

Lisa D. Spiller
Christopher Newport University

Martin Baier

Prentice Hall

Upper Saddle River   Boston   Columbus   San Francisco   New York
Indianapolis   London   Toronto   Sydney   Singapore   Tokyo   Montreal
Dubai   Madrid   Hong Kong   Mexico City   Munich   Paris   Amsterdam   Cape Town

Library of Congress Cataloging-in-Publication Data

Spiller, Lisa.
  Contemporary direct and interactive marketing / Lisa D. Spiller, Martin Baier.—2nd ed.
    p. cm.
  ISBN 0-13-608610-1
  1. Direct marketing. I. Baier, Martin. II. Title. III. Title: Contemporary direct and
interactive marketing.
  HF5415.126.S65 2010
  658.8'72—dc22   2008055856

Acquisitions Editor: James Heine	Senior Operations Specialist: Arnold Vila
Editorial Director: Sally Yagan	Operations Specialist: Ben Smith
Product Development Manager:	Creative Director: Jayne Conte
Ashley Santora	Cover Designer: Anne Marie Sole
Editorial Project Manager: Melissa Pellerano	Cover Photo: iStockphoto
Editorial Assistant: Karin Williams	Manager, Cover Visual Research &
Media Project Manager: Denise Vaughn	Permissions: Karen Sanatar
Director of Marketing: Patrice Lumumba	Composition: TexTech International
Jones	Full-Service Project Management:
Senior Marketing Manager: Anne Fahlgren	Satishna Gokuldas
Permissions Project Manager:	Interior Printer/Binder: Hamilton Printing
Charles Morris	Cover Printer: Lehigh-Phoenix Color/
Senior Managing Editor: Judy Leale	Hagerstown
Production Project Manager: Clara Bartunek	Typeface: 10/12 Times

Credits and acknowledgments borrowed from other sources and reproduced, with permission, in this textbook appear on appropriate page within text.

If you purchased this book within the United States or Canada, you should be aware that it has been wrongfully imported without the approval of the Publisher or the Author.

Pearson Education Ltd., London	Pearson Education North Asia, Ltd., Hong Kong
Pearson Education Singapore, Pte. Ltd	Pearson Educación de Mexico, S.A. de C.V.
Pearson Education, Canada, Inc.	Pearson Education Malaysia, Pte. Ltd
Pearson Education–Japan	Pearson Education Upper Saddle River, New Jersey
Pearson Education Australia PTY, Limited	

Prentice Hall
is an imprint of

www.pearsonhighered.com

10 9 8 7 6 5 4 3 2 1

ISBN-10:   0-13-608610-1
ISBN-13:   978-0-13-608610-9

BRIEF TABLE OF CONTENTS

TABLE OF CONTENTS

FOREWORD

It has been apparent, especially since the advent of the interactive medium of the Web, that those engaged in direct marketing require expanded knowledge in certain aspects of marketing as these have been traditionally taught. It is these elements of direct marketing with which this textbook, *Contemporary Direct and Interactive Marketing, Second Edition,* is concerned.

The elements of special interest to students aspiring to careers in direct marketing, as well as professional direct marketers already there, include customer relationship management and recognition of the lifetime value of a customer, market segmentation and customer profiling, database development and utilization, research and testing, measurement and accountability which emphasizes response, offer creation, benefit-oriented promotion, interactive multimedia planning as well as fulfillment strategies. All of these concepts are expanded herein, as an *extension of*—not as an *alternative to*—basic marketing instruction.

The utilization of direct marketing methods has shown spectacular growth, to the point that its tools and techniques are now employed by virtually every organization, for-profit as well as not-for-profit. A major deterrent to continued explosive growth, though, is a dearth of trained talent.

That is why the positioning of this textbook and expanded curriculum dealing with direct marketing, already happening at some universities, is so vital. I am in accord with that.

Philip Kotler
Professor at the Kellogg School of Management,
Northwestern University

PREFACE

Welcome to the second edition of *Contemporary Direct Marketing* . . . now more relevantly titled *Contemporary Direct and Interactive Marketing*!

FOCUS OF THE BOOK

We developed this textbook to combine the theory and practice of modern direct and interactive marketing. It is written as a comprehensive examination of direct and interactive marketing concepts, methods, techniques, tools, and applications. It is designed as a college textbook for a core course in direct and interactive marketing or a second-semester course following an introductory traditional marketing course. It is designed to stimulate interactivity and creative discussion both in and out of the classroom. Its objective is to provide practical relevance for those interested in, about to enter, or already involved in marketing.

A century ago, mail-order merchants gathered customer names and addresses, created mailing lists, established relationships with logical prospects, and then sold their goods and services on a one-on-one basis to customers via mail and telephone. Today, much has changed and much has remained the same. Direct marketers are still concerned with creating relationships with each customer and then maximizing customer value by serving individual customer needs on a personal basis. However, computer technology and new high-tech digital media have dramatically changed the speed and effectiveness of these activities. More and more companies and organizations are using the direct and interactive model as their primary method for business transactions. This second edition recognizes the growth of various online Internet-oriented promotional strategies as the newest format for conducting direct and interactive marketing today. E-mail marketing is similar to direct mail in that it targets messages one-on-one with great precision and effectiveness, doing this with much greater speed of transmission and enabling an immediate customer response.

Direct marketing has always been accountable and measurable, and now with the various digital media formats and computer technology, it is more interactive and precise than ever before. This second edition builds on the traditional foundations of mail-order marketing that are still applicable today, and it extends into the future where continuous innovations in high-tech media are transforming the marketing landscape. The new media of yesterday—telephone and television, as examples—have become mainstream media today. We cannot begin to envision what changes are ahead. But one thing is certain: traditional direct and interactive marketing principles will still apply. This edition builds on these traditional foundations, captures the new media and methods, and explores the future innovations of direct and interactive marketing.

Recent American Association of Collegiate Schools of Business standards state that faculty members are expected to "use content and activities that are" current and relevant to their areas of instruction. Many practitioners and scholars are suggesting that a paradigm shift in marketing is under way, fueled by the growth of use of direct and interactive marketing. Today's marketers must know how to leverage new information, communication, and distribution technologies to more effectively create and communicate customer value in this digital age. For many companies, direct and interactive marketing—especially with its most recent transformation, Internet marketing—constitutes a complete business model. This new direct model is quickly changing the way companies attempt to build and strengthen relationships with customers. Given the many technological advances, marketers are increasingly using direct marketing applications to reach and interact with consumers on a personal basis. Students must be equipped with the knowledge and skill set to guide firms to achieve direct and interactive marketing success. This second edition will assist them in doing so.

ORGANIZATION OF THE BOOK

This textbook edition contains four major sections dealing with (1) The Foundations of Direct and Interactive Marketing; (2) Integrated Marketing Communications: The Message and Media Decisions in Direct and Interactive Marketing; (3) Response, Measurement, and Metrics of Direct and Interactive Marketing; and (4) Applications and Future Directions of Direct and Interactive Marketing. Individual chapters within these four major sections deal with such subjects as database marketing and customer relationship management, developing lists and profiling customers, planning value propositions, creating compelling message and media strategies, fulfilling the offer, serving the customer, conducting research and testing, understanding environmental, ethical, and legal issues, exploring international strategies, and applying direct marketing measurement and math. These sections can easily be adapted to any school's semester or quarter schedule. Each chapter identifies the key terms with margin definitions, end-of-chapter summaries, review questions, exercises, and cases.

LIST OF CHANGES TO THE NEW EDITION

The second edition is fully updated with an emphasis on database marketing, customer relationships, high-tech digital media formats, such as search engine marketing, blogs, social networking, and mobile marketing. Each chapter features an opening vignette that provides a glimpse of the material that will be covered in the chapter in addition to many new end-of-chapter cases, which directly apply the material covered, and many new chapter examples and figures.

The second edition includes two comprehensive direct and interactive marketing cases for detailed discussion, analysis, and quantitative evaluation. The second edition also provides two new appendixes. Appendix A features The Martin Agency. It takes you through the step-by-step process of developing a direct and interactive marketing campaign for a client. Appendix B features a detailed report on careers in direct and interactive marketing.

Two new chapters include Chapter 13, Applying Direct and Interactive Marketing Math and Metrics, and Chapter 14, Examining Direct and Interactive Marketing Applications in a Variety of Sectors. Chapter 13 provides an examination of many detailed quantitative concepts associated with the conduct of direct and interactive marketing, such as market penetration analysis, customer lifetime value, break-even analysis, response rate analysis, budgeting, and return on investment. Each mathematical concept is presented and discussed in an easy-to-read-and-understand fashion with numerous examples provided along the way. Chapter 14, the new chapter on *applications,* explores business-to-business, nonprofit, governmental, political, and sports direct and interactive marketing activities, and provides numerous examples for each sector.

In summary, the second edition contains state-of-the-art direct and interactive marketing content, many pictures and images, and numerous applications and examples to drive home important concepts.

INSTRUCTOR SUPPLEMENTS

The instructor supplements to accompany this textbook, available online at www.pearsonhighered. com/spiller, include an Instructor's Manual complete with chapter outlines, detailed chapter summaries, chapter learning objectives, key terms, review questions, exercise completion guides, and case discussion question guides. In addition, the Instructor's Manual features PowerPoint slides for each chapter containing many of the textbook images as well as valuable Web links to related resources and material. The Instructor's Manual also contains teaching notes for both of the comprehensive cases. The Test Item File contains essay questions, multiple-choice, and true/false questions for each chapter.

Adopting professors will also have free access to NextMark's List Research system. The Instructor's Manual will detail various exercises and projects that can be used in association with Chapter 3, Developing Lists and Discovering Markets, and the NextMark List Research system. The system is designed to enhance students' learning experience by providing a tool for completing class exercises, cases, and/or projects that involve list selection. Both of the comprehensive cases include a component where NextMark List Research system can be utilized in the case analysis. Finally, textbook adopters may gain access to updated material and valuable Web links for second edition chapters by visiting the Instructor's Resource Center online at www.pearsonhighered.com/ spiller.

ACKNOWLEDGMENTS

We are the authors and personally responsible for this comprehensive textbook in direct and interactive marketing, but we hasten to acknowledge lots of input and assistance from many individuals. Much has been derived from our direct marketing career experiences: from the firms that provided us with the opportunities and field laboratories, from our work colleagues at these firms, as well as from literally hundreds of other direct marketers who have shared their own successes and failures with us. In college classrooms, many seeds were planted by those who taught us. Our own presentations of concepts and theory have been considerably enriched by challenging and perceptive interaction with students.

We are grateful to the following two Christopher Newport University professors who have contributed information to select chapters of our textbook and who are coauthors of the Instructor's Manual and Test Item File: Dr. Elizabeth Young for coauthoring the Direct and Interactive Math and Metrics chapter and for her excellent review and editing assistance; and Professor Michelle Carpenter for her contributions to the High-Tech Digital Media and Creative Message Strategies chapters and for her editing assistance. Our special thanks to colleague and research partner Dr. Carol Scovotti of the University of Wisconsin, Whitewater, for coauthoring the two comprehensive cases and for her contributions to both the introductory and the international chapters.

We are grateful to the talented and dedicated people at The Martin Agency for allowing us to feature their agency in Appendix A and for their contributions to and assistance with Appendix B and several opening vignettes and cases featuring their clients. Our special praise goes to Barbara Joynes, J. P. LaFors, Terry Thompson, Sydney Norton, Britta Dougherty, and Andy Azula for their generosity of time and talent and firm belief in direct marketing education.

We also extend great appreciation to the kind and creative people at MindZoo, including Kelly Hill, Liz Weaver, Robynann Burkett, and Jim Kirby. We offer special thanks to and praise MindZoo's chief zookeeper, Randy Jones, for providing many excellent contributions and examples throughout the second edition and for his great sense of humor.

We owe special thanks to John Buleza of Lillian Vernon, for his assistance and important contributions and dedication to the second edition in many areas. We recognize and appreciate the research efforts of three former students: Mallory Martin, Nicholas Fletcher, and Caroline Hallum. We are truly grateful for the administrative and secretarial support of Lee Ann Wise, Clare Maliniak, Dianne Williams, and Crystal Kernan.

Very special appreciation goes to Sylvia Weinstein of the *Oyster Pointer* for her editorial assistance with this edition and for constant inspiration. Special thanks to Dana Marshall for his contributions to the Instructor's Manual and Test Item File.

We owe thanks to Dr. Hamed Shamma for contributions to the international chapter, Chuck George for contributions to the High-Tech Digital Media chapter, Katherine McPhaden for networking assistance, Suzanne Spiller for work on the definitions of key terms, and Anne Marie Sole for the cover design.

The authors owe a debt of gratitude to the Direct Marketing Association and the Direct Marketing Educational Foundation for the wealth of information and assistance provided over the years in keeping up with this dynamic field. Special thanks go to Jeff Nesler, Charles Prescott, Nilda Castillo, Anne Frankel, Anna Chernis, Pat Kachura, and Marsha Goldberger for their personal assistance with this second edition.

We are indebted to the many business professionals who kindly assisted in providing case information and textbook examples. These business executives include:

- Meredith Hines, TreadMoves
- Van Rhodes and Neil O'Keefe, Spiegel Brands
- Sherry Connell and Pat Overton, McDonald Garden Centers
- Mark Sarrett, Coldwell Banker Professional, Realtors
- Deborah McNeil, Kelly Carson, and Brad Beck, DuPont
- Jim Schloss, Eric Esch, Wendy Roth, and Yelena Shekhovtsova, Smithfield Foods
- Kurt Ruf, RUF Strategic Solutions
- Joe Pych, NextMark
- Peg Kuman, Telematch
- Fran Laura and Stephen Moore, Claritas, A Nielsen Company
- Cheryl Krueger, Mary Eckenrode, and Denise Meine-Graham, Cheryl&Co.
- Michael Sparling, 1-800-FLOWERS.com
- Rachel Vaness, GEICO
- Adam Brown, Tidewater Exterminating
- Lisa Box, Smart Space Enterprises
- Kirk Adams, Lillian Vernon
- Wendy Weber, Crandall Associates
- Pam Kiecker and Anne Schaeffer, Interactive Marketing Institute of VCU
- Robert DelGenio and Chad Williamsen, ShipShapes
- Pam Lingle, Virginia Beach Convention and Visitor's Bureau
- Vicki Rowland, Peninsula SPCA
- Whitney Owens, Junior League of Hampton Roads
- Angela Bumbrey, U.S. Navy
- Amy Nasir, Campbell-Ewald
- Mary Ellen Keating, Barnes and Noble
- Melissa Fischer and Chip Booth, ValPak
- Randy Yocum, Express Employment Professionals
- Amy Franks Hart, Hauser's Jewlers
- Marco Mori, Euro Intermail
- Heather McKeating, Norfolk Tides Baseball Club
- Scott Carl, Tricision
- Mike Downs and Doug Downs, The Clearwater Group
- Walter Cordiner, Norfolk Admirals Hockey Club
- Dave Abbott and Lisa Kuehl, Oriental Trading Company
- Dan Shaw, Direct Marketing Creative Strategy and Copy

Many reviewers at various institutions provided valuable comments and suggestions for this and the first edition. We are grateful to the following colleagues for their thoughtful inputs and recommendations:

Second Edition Reviewers

- Robert M. Cosenza, University of Mississippi
- Dale Lewison, University of Akron

- Mark A. Neckes, Johnson and Wales University
- Carol Scovotti, University of Wisconsin, Whitewater

First Edition Reviewers

- Dennis B. Arnett, Texas Tech University
- Bruce C. Bailey, Otterbein College
- Dave Blackmore, University of Pittsburgh at Bradford
- Deborah Y. Cohn, Yeshiva University
- John J. Cronin, Western Connecticut State University
- Wenyu Dou, University of Nevada, Las Vegas
- F. Robert Dwyer, University of Cincinnati
- James S. Gould, Pace University
- Richard A. Hamilton, University of Missouri, Kansas City
- Susan K. Harmon, Meddle Tennessee State University
- Sreedhar Kavil, St. John's University
- Barry Langford, Florida Gulf Coast University
- Marilyn Lavin, University of Wisconsin, Whitewater
- Paula M. Saunders, Wright State University
- Donald Self, Auburn University, Montgomery
- Carmen Sunda, University of New Orleans
- William Trombetta, St. Joseph's University
- Ugur Yucelt, Pennsylvania State University, Harrisburg

The authors wish to thank the many people at Pearson-Prentice Hall who helped develop this book. Our sincere thanks to Melissa Pellerano, editorial project manager; Sally Yagan, editorial director; James Heine, editor; and Clara Bartunek, production project manager.

Finally, we owe many thanks to our families for their constant support and encouragement—James "Dooley," Suzanne, Chad and Jack Spiller, and Dorothy Baier and Donna Baier Stein. To them, we dedicate this book.

Lisa Spiller

Martin Baier

ABOUT THE AUTHORS

As a team, Lisa Spiller and Martin Baier provide a blend of experience uniquely suited to writing a direct marketing text. Professor Spiller is an award-winning teacher with 25 years of experience teaching direct marketing to undergraduate business students. Martin Baier, a legendary member of the Direct Marketing Association's Hall of Fame and author of the very first direct marketing textbook, was a highly successful direct marketing professional who has dedicated more than 35 years to academia in an attempt to bridge the gap between what is learned in the classroom and what is practiced in the business world. In 1984, the two met at the University of Missouri, Kansas City, where Baier taught the graduate direct marketing classes and Spiller taught the undergraduate direct marketing classes. The rest is history . . . and their years of teaching experience and knowledge of direct marketing are captured in this text.

LISA D. SPILLER

Lisa Spiller is a professor of marketing in the Joseph W. Luter III College of Business and Leadership at Christopher Newport University in Newport News, Virginia. She has been teaching direct marketing courses to undergraduate business students for 25 years and has helped her university pioneer a major in direct and interactive marketing. Dr. Spiller's marketing students have won the coveted Collegiate Gold ECHO Award from the Direct Marketing Association in 2003, 2005, and 2007 and the Collegiate Silver ECHO Award in 2002. Her students have also received the Gold Collegiate Marketing Award for Excellence and Innovation (MAXI) from the Direct Marketing Association of Washington Educational Foundation (DMAW-EF) in 2004, 2005, 2006, and 2007; the Collegiate Silver MAXI Award in 2002 and 2003; and the Guy Yolton Creative Direct Mail Award in 2002, 2004, 2005, and 2007.

Dr. Spiller was named the Direct Marketing Educational Foundation (DMEF) Robert B. Clark Outstanding Direct Marketing Educator in 2005. She was the inaugural recipient of the DMAW-EF O'Hara Leadership Award for Direct and Interactive Marketing Education in 2008. Professor Spiller has received awards for her teaching, including the inaugural CNU Alumni Society Faculty Award for Excellence in Teaching and Mentoring in 2007; Faculty Advisor Leader Awards from the DMA in 2002, 2003, 2005, and 2007; a Distinguished Teaching Award in 1997 from the DMEF; and the Elmer P. Pierson Outstanding Teacher Award in 1987 from the University of Missouri, Kansas City. Her research studies, the majority of which have been related to some aspect of direct and database marketing, have been published in numerous journals. Dr. Spiller served on the Abstract Editorial Board of the *Journal of Interactive Marketing* for ten years, was an Academic Representative on the DMEF Board of Trustees for two years, and has been a member of the Academic Advisory Board of the DMAW-EF since 1996.

Professor Spiller received her B.S.B.A. and M.B.A. degrees from Gannon University and her Ph.D. from the University of Missouri, Kansas City. Prior to joining academia, Spiller held positions as a marketing director with an international company and as an account executive with an advertising agency. Through the years, she has served as a marketing consultant to many organizations.

Professor Spiller possesses a true passion for teaching and has been a strong advocate of direct and interactive marketing education throughout her entire academic career.

MARTIN BAIER

Martin Baier has been a direct marketing consultant and educator since retiring in 1987 as executive vice president of the marketing group at Old American Insurance Company. He is founder of the Center for Direct Marketing Education and Research in the Henry Bloch School of Business and Public Administration of the University of Missouri, Kansas City (UMKC), where he served for 25 years as adjunct professor. He has consulted with a variety of organizations now involved in or adopting the discipline of direct marketing. His education includes an M.A. in economics (1970), a B.A. in business administration (1943), and a B.S. in economics (1943)—all from UMKC. His *Elements of Direct Marketing,* the first college textbook on the subject, was published by McGraw-Hill in 1983. A Japanese edition was published by Nikkei in Tokyo in 1985; an international student edition was published in Singapore in 1986. His *How to Find and Cultivate Customers through Direct Marketing* was published by NTC Business Books in 1996. *Contemporary Database Marketing: Concepts and Applications,* coauthored with Kurtis Ruf and Goutam Chakraborty, is an interactive college textbook/CD, published by Racom Books in 2001.

Martin Baier has been affiliated with many professional organizations and listed in *Who's Who in Finance and Industry* and in *Who's Who in Advertising.* He has taught direct marketing at many universities and has conducted numerous seminars throughout the United States and in Europe, Australia, New Zealand, and Asia. His presentation of "ZIP Code—New Tool for Marketers" in the January–February 1967 *Harvard Business Review,* created substantial interest and caused the *Kansas City Star* to name him the "Father of ZIP Code Marketing."

He was inducted into the Direct Marketing Association Hall of Fame in 1989. The DMEF presented him its Ed Mayer Award and the Direct Marketing Insurance Council named him Direct Marketing Insurance Executive of the Year, both in 1983. The Mail Advertising Service Association honored him with its Miles Kimball Award in 1990. The Ed Sisk Award for Direct Marketing Vision was presented to him by the Direct Marketing Association of Washington Educational Foundation in 1994. The Andi Emerson 1995 Award, for contribution of outstanding service to the direct marketing creative community, was awarded by the Direct Marketing Creative Guild and the John Caples Awards Board. In 1995, he was elected International Fellow of the Institute of Direct Marketing (U.K.) in recognition of exceptional services to the profession. The New England Direct Marketing Association honored him with a Lifetime Achievement Award in 1996.

1

···

Examining the History and Processes of Direct and Interactive Marketing

Opening Vignette: Peace Frogs

Like most college students, Catesby Jones needed some extra cash, so in 1985 he decided to create beach volleyball shorts to sell around campus at the University of Virginia. He wanted an unusual design that would appeal to his target market, so he arranged an eye-catching assortment of national flags all over the boxer shorts. To put flair into his design, Catesby added a frog holding two digits in the air, forming a peace sign. After receiving numerous orders, he began manufacturing and selling the unique boxer shorts from his dorm room.

Catesby saw the potential in his creation, so he and a few buddies decided to place a $15,000 direct marketing advertisement in *Rolling Stone* magazine. The advertisement generated a total of 1,000 orders. By the time Catesby finished his degree in international relations, he was already four years into what would become his passion and a very successful business (Figure 1-1).

Peace Frogs began to dispense products through multichannel distribution using a mail-order catalog, retail stores—company-owned and licensed (from wholesale to department stores and specialty retailers)— and on the Internet at www.peacefrogs.com. These channels allowed the company to distribute its products to a vast number of consumers and save resources through cross-marketing. They also helped create brand recognition and loyalty because the consumer could see the merchandise at many different outlets.

Now a million-dollar company, Peace Frogs operates a 37,000 square feet distribution center at its home office in Gloucester, Virginia. This multipurpose facility houses Peace Frogs' merchandise, ordering systems, and a retail store. The 25 employees who work in the distribution center try to ensure that customers are completely satisfied.

The company not only has unique clothing, it has also found a distinctive way to distribute merchandise—psychedelically painted VW vans driving the roads and highways of the United States. Peace Frogs chose this vehicle both as a means of transportation and as a marketing statement, a representation of "reliability and freedom." As it did with its products, the company has taken something ordinary and transformed it into a unique message that leaves a distinct impression and has a positive impact on its customers. The peace frog and its related "positively peaceful thinking" message have become a significant symbol to which many can relate.

The company's line now includes T-shirts, sweatshirts, hats, boxer shorts, lounge pants, jewelry, accessories, and school supplies. In the process of building a business through direct marketing, Catesby Jones showed that with dedication, hard work, and daring to be a little different, people can make an impact (Figure 1-2).

FIGURE 1-1 Occupy the Nation of Your Choice.
Source: Used with permission of Crispies Co., Inc., d.b.a. Peace Frogs.

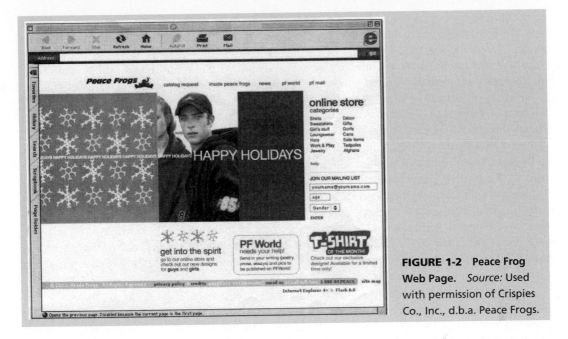

FIGURE 1-2   Peace Frog Web Page.   *Source:* Used with permission of Crispies Co., Inc., d.b.a. Peace Frogs.

What is direct and interactive marketing? What are its objectives, and how is it carried out? What is its history? What makes it different from traditional brand marketing? How and why have direct marketing and brand advertising converged? In this chapter, we'll find the answers to these (and many other) questions commonly raised about the exciting and dynamic field of direct and interactive marketing. Welcome to the wonderful world of "Modern Day Marketing 101!"

THE SCOPE OF DIRECT AND INTERACTIVE MARKETING

The use of direct and interactive marketing in today's business world is booming! Direct and interactive marketing is now at the center of the communications revolution and is being used by businesses, organizations, associations, and individuals across the world with great fervor. Over a decade ago, Roland Rust and Richard Oliver foretold the rise of direct marketing at the expense of traditional advertising. They claimed:

> Mass media advertising as we know it today is on its deathbed. . . . Advertising agencies are restructuring to accommodate a harsher advertising reality, . . . direct marketing is stealing business away from traditional advertising, and the growth of sales promotion and integrated marketing communications both come at the expense of traditional advertising.[1]

Practitioners and scholars suggest a paradigm shift in marketing is under way, fueled by the growth in use of direct marketing techniques. New digital and other high-tech marketing developments are dramatically changing how marketers create and communicate customer value. Today's marketers must know how to leverage new information, communication, and distribution technologies to connect more effectively with customers in this digital age.[2] For many companies, direct marketing—especially in its most recent transformation, Internet marketing and e-commerce—constitutes a complete business model. This new direct model is quickly changing the way companies think about building relationships with customers.[3] Given the many technological advances, marketers are increasingly using direct marketing applications to reach and interact with consumers on a personal basis.

Today, direct marketing is a fundamental marketing tool in a growing variety of businesses. Direct marketing grew faster than almost every other marketing activity for the latter part of the twentieth century.[4] In the United States, sales attributed to direct marketing media, methods, and channels rose from $1.8058 trillion in 2005 (10.3 percent of U.S. gross domestic product [GDP])[5] to the most recent figures available, $2.03 trillion in 2007 (10.2 percent of U.S. GDP). Almost 51 percent of advertising expenditures in 2007 were related to direct marketing. In fact, overall media spending for direct marketing reached $173.2 billion in 2007, up 4.4 percent over 2006 expenditures. In 2007, 10.6 million workers were employed as a result of direct marketing activity.[6] While the annual compound growth of U.S. employment from 2006 through 2011 is expected to be 1 percent, direct marketing employment growth is projected to be almost double, at 1.8 percent. Recent research revealed that in 2006, most companies hired between one and five new employees in direct marketing positions—31.1 percent at entry level.[7]

These statistics strongly suggest that direct marketing is becoming an integral element in the marketing manager's arsenal worldwide. The economic impact of direct and interactive marketing is simply mind-boggling! With this much emphasis being placed on direct and interactive marketing, it is important to understand what it is and how it is used.

CHARACTERISTICS OF DIRECT AND INTERACTIVE MARKETING

Despite its growth, there is no agreement about what direct marketing is. Both practitioners and academicians grapple with a contemporary conceptual definition. Unquestionably, the concept known as direct marketing continues to evolve. However, its definition provides a framework from which we can improve our understanding and determine the critical elements of its process. The definition you are about to read is the result of years of scholarly research involving a content analysis of direct marketing definitions published in direct marketing, principles of marketing, integrated marketing communication, and advertising textbooks.[8]

Definition and Description

Direct marketing *is a database-driven interactive process of directly communicating with targeted customers or prospects using any medium to obtain a measurable response or transaction via one or multiple channels.* This definition identifies database, interactivity, direct communications, target customers, any medium, measurable, response, and one or multiple channels as key dimensions in direct marketing activities. It encompasses not only what direct marketing is but the characteristics that make it unique.

Direct marketing is characterized by:

- Customer/prospect databases that make one-to-one targeting possible
- A view of customers as assets with lifetime value
- Ongoing relationships and affinity with customers
- Data-based market segmentation
- Research and precise experimentation (testing)

- Benefit-oriented direct response advertising
- Measurement of results and accountability for costs
- Interactivity with customers on a personalized individualized basis
- Multimedia direct response communication
- Multichannel fulfillment and distribution

Direct marketing is *database-driven* marketing. It is a process, a discipline, a strategy, a philosophy, an attitude, a collection of tools and techniques. In summary, its goal is to *create* and *cultivate* customers, regardless of whether these customers are themselves consumers, buyers for industrial organizations, or potential donors or voters. It is a way to market a for-profit business or a not-for-profit organization. Its principles apply to marketing activities targeting both business consumers (B2B) and final consumers (B2C). Today, direct marketing is being used by many traditional brand advertisers, and many experts believe that all marketing is converging.

The Convergence of Direct Marketing and Brand

Historically, direct marketing and traditional brand advertising were two separate disciplines. **Brand marketing** was mass marketing, and direct marketing was niche marketing. Brand marketers primarily used broadcast media (television and radio) to get products or services recognized and preferred by masses of consumers, whereas direct marketers predominantly used direct mail and catalogs with customized offers designed for individual customers to motivate a specific response that could be tracked and measured to determine its effectiveness and resulting sales. Figure 1-3 overviews the inherent differences between these two disciplines.

According to the Direct Marketing Association, the clear distinction between direct marketing and brand marketing has blurred with the digital revolution. Most companies now have a virtual storefront in the form of a Web site. Companies have the ability to store, track, and target information

Direct Marketing	Traditional Marketing
Direct selling to individuals with customers identifiable by name, address, and purchase behavior	Mass selling with buyers identified as broad groups sharing common demographic and psychographic characteristics
Products have the added value of distribution direct to the customer, an important benefit	Product benefits do not typically include distribution to the customer's door
The medium is the marketplace	The retail outlet is the marketplace
Marketing controls the product all the way through delivery	The marketer typically loses control as the product enters the distribution channel
Advertising is used to generate an immediate transaction, an inquiry, or an order	Advertising is used for cumulative effect over time for building image, awareness, loyalty, and benefit recall; purchase action is deferred
Repetition of offers, promotional messages, toll-free numbers, and Web addresses are used within the advertisement	Repetition of offers and promotional messages are used over a period of time
Customer feels a high perceived risk—product bought unseen and recourse is distant	Customer feels less risk—has direct contact with the product and direct recourse

FIGURE 1-3 Comparison between Direct Marketing and Traditional Brand Marketing.

about consumers like never before. Direct marketing strategies, such as URLs, toll-free numbers, e-mail addresses, and calls to action, have found their way into TV and radio spots, print ads, and almost every other type of media. Direct marketing's versatility, measurability, and undeniable return on investment have gradually garnered the respect of even the most traditional brand advertisers and agencies.[9] Direct marketers are also recognizing the importance of creating and reinforcing brand strategies at the individual level. Therefore, direct marketing and brand strategies are now viewed as complementary, and when applied correctly, they can create a synergistic marketing effect. Although these two disciplines have come from vastly different origins, they are indeed converging, with many companies recognizing the value of their combined marketing strategies.

Today, companies and organizations of all different sizes and types are integrating branding with their self-promotional direct marketing strategies. An excellent example is a creative boutique in Leesburg, Virginia, called MindZoo. This direct marketing agency, specializing in the development of highly customized direct marketing programs for newspapers, retailers, and consumer product and service providers, began in the basement of President Randy Jones's home in 2001. Jones's background included 10 years with Gannett, selling everything from classified advertising to database marketing services. The name MindZoo, intended as a whimsical description of Jones's nonconformist creative process, allows him and his staff an almost unlimited number of ways to integrate the zoo-branded theme into his direct response materials. MindZoo's brand begins with a distinctive logo with embedded animal eyes. As shown in Figure 1-4, MindZoo's creative

FIGURE 1-4 MindZoo's Promotional Materials.
Source: Used with permission of MindZoo, LLC. Photo by Kim Kirby, www.jimkirbyphoto.com.

materials have run the gamut from a customized Zoo Map on the homepage of the company's Web site to the inclusion of stuffed animals placed in zebra-lined gift bags in its direct mail packages and media kits.

Jones and the Zoo Crew strategically incorporate branding into all of the agency's direct marketing activities. Prospective clients get a taste of MindZoo's creative talent long before they begin to use its services.

Today, direct marketing is used by virtually any organization in any sector, including political, governmental, and sports. Its history is rich, and its future is seemingly unlimited!

HISTORY AND GROWTH OF DIRECT MARKETING

The first mail-order catalogs are said to have appeared in Europe in the mid-fifteenth century, soon after Gutenberg's invention of movable type.[10] There is record of a gardening catalog, the predecessor of today's colorful seed and nursery catalogs, issued by William Lucas, an English gardener, as early as 1667. By the end of the eighteenth century, there was a proliferation of such catalogs in England, and William Prince published a catalog in 1771 in colonial America. It is reported that George Washington visited Prince's gardens in 1791 and that Thomas Jefferson was a mail-order buyer in both America and England.

Benjamin Franklin, America's first important printer, published a catalog of "near 600 volumes in most faculties and sciences" in 1744. That catalog is especially notable, in a direct marketing sense, in that it contained a guarantee of customer satisfaction along with this statement on its cover: "Those persons who live remote, by sending their orders and money to said B. Franklin, may depend on the same justice as if present."

A Connecticut custom clockmaker, Eli Terry (whose neighbor and sometimes adviser was inventor Eli Whitney), deserves mention in the evolution of direct marketing in that he is credited as being the creator of the free trial offer. A Yankee peddler (a direct seller), Terry would pack his custom-made clocks in his saddlebags and would leave them, on trial, with the farmers on his route, collecting for them, in installments, during ensuing trips along the route.

The Birth of Mail-Order Catalogs

From these beginnings there followed a proliferation of catalogs during the post–Civil War period when agrarian unrest, through the National Grange, fueled the popular slogan "eliminate the middleman." Then, as now, mail-order catalogs reflected social and economic change. Beginning as books featuring seed and nursery products, mail-order catalogs of the late nineteenth century included sewing machines, dry goods, medicines, and musical instruments. Most sellers were product specialists, and mail order was an alternative mode of distribution. During this period in 1872, Aaron Montgomery Ward produced, on a single unillustrated sheet of paper, a mere price list of products, offering the rural farmer savings of 40 percent. Just 12 years later, in 1884, Ward's single sheet of prices had been expanded to a 240-page catalog containing 10,000 items. He, too, featured a "guarantee of satisfaction or your money back."

Two years later came the forerunner of what became by 1893 Sears Roebuck & Company. Young Richard Warren Sears, a telegraph operator in the remote location of North Redwood, Minnesota, acquired a shipment of undeliverable gold-filled watches. He reasoned that the best prospects for the purchase of these watches would be other railroad agents, like him, and he had a mailing list of 20,000 of them. By 1897 his original offer of a fine watch to a specific market segment had expanded to a catalog of more than 750 pages with 6,000 items.

By 1902 the sales of Sears Roebuck & Company exceeded $50 million annually. Ward and Sears were followed in 1905 by Joseph Spiegel, who introduced credit terms with catalog copy reading: "We are willing to trust you indefinitely . . . and to receive our pay by the month, so that no purchase is a burden."

Mail Order Diversifies

While mail-order merchandise catalogs were becoming more accepted, new cultural, social, and economic phenomena were breeding another form of mail order. Magazines reflecting these changes, such as *Time,* the *New Yorker,* and the *Saturday Review of Literature,* appeared during the early 1920s, with subscriber prospects solicited by direct mail. In 1926, Harry Sherman and Maxwell Sackheim, direct marketers who had earlier noted how few bookstores there were relative to the number of post offices capable of delivering direct mail ads as well as books, created the Book-of-the-Month Club. Sherman and Sackheim innovated the "negative option" offer, where books were sent to subscribers on a regular basis, unless the publisher was advised against it. Today, majority of books are sold by mail order, aided and abetted by the Internet.

In 1947, Maxwell Sackheim & Company hired Lester Wunderman as a copywriter. By 1959, Wunderman had started Wunderman, Ricotta & Kline, an agency specializing in mail-order marketing in 1959. The first agency he'd started with his brother had gone under in 1939, but he apprenticed himself to mail-order gurus and quickly revolutionized the advertising industry. He's credited for first using bound-in subscription cards, launching the American Express credit card, creating the Columbia Record Club, and boosting *Time*'s circulation through the use of toll-free numbers.

Direct marketing has played a major role in the evolution of business-to-business distribution, too. John H. Patterson, founder of the National Cash Register Company, was the first to use direct mail to get qualified leads for follow-up by salespeople. Today, his basic method of sales prospect qualification, augmented by direct response advertising media other than mail, plays a role in the total scheme of industrial direct marketing.

Print Media

The versatility of laser printing, personalization possibilities of inkjet printing, advances in press technology, and computerized typesetting are important examples of how the printing process is becoming more conducive to the "demassification" of the printed word. Further enhancing the growth of direct marketing, during the 1960s and to this day, has been the increasing availability of advertising media (other than direct mail) suitable for direct response advertising, especially those geared to highly defined market segments. The readers of selective publications, such as the magazines *Sports Illustrated* and *Organic Gardening* as well as the *Wall Street Journal* newspaper, are not only mailing lists in and of themselves but also provide an audience for direct response print advertising geared to specialized market segments.

Broadcast Media

The same evolution has been occurring in the broadcast media, television and radio, through special programming geared to market segments. Cable and satellite transmissions, now appearing with interactive capabilities, offer an array of channels appealing to special interests like news, sports, food, and home shopping.

Electronic Media

AT&T introduced Wide Area Telephone Service (WATS) in 1961, providing direct response promotions the convenience of toll-free telephone calling. This has been a tremendous stimulus to response. The phone itself has become another major medium for direct marketers, enhanced by cellular and wireless technologies.

The proliferation of phone usage (wired and wireless) has been augmented by access via computers to the Internet and its World Wide Web. Though its originator, Tim Berners-Lee, developed the Web in 1989 to enable information to be shared among particle physicist researchers, it subsequently grew into a huge virtual marketplace. It has become an exciting environment for targeted, measurable, response-generating direct marketing.

There have been advances as well in other electronic communications involving cable, satellite, and interactive television. Certainly a major media breakthrough has been the technology of the Internet and World Wide Web. Especially in tandem with print and broadcast media, direct response advertising entices buyers to well-structured Web sites.

High-Tech Digital Media

High-tech digital media are hot and growing rapidly for direct and interactive marketers. The Internet has surely changed the way most consumers make purchases and the way most companies conduct business today. Most companies and organizations not only have a Web site but are actively employing interactive online marketing strategies. There are many applications of high-tech digital media—e-mail marketing, online market research, Web advertising, and e-branding are some of the chief applications. There are new high-tech digital formats and strategies emerging daily. Some of the most recent ones include blogging, search engine marketing (SEM), online social networking, and mobile marketing. Modern marketing is high-tech and able to generate huge amounts of information for marketers. Although information has become a key business resource, the ability to access, understand, and effectively use that information is a necessity for success in today's economy. Yet many companies do not know what to do with all of this information. It is often as futurist John Naisbitt once said, "We are drowning in information but starved for knowledge."

Database-driven direct marketers using the Internet are obtaining that knowledge, enabling them to profile their customers and determine their prospects. At the same time, they are predicting future behavior and using promotional strategies that will not only drive prospects to their Web sites but also engage them in meaningful and ongoing transactions once there. Amazon.com is a great example. At its core is a database of customers and their transactions for continuity selling (which encourages customers to make a repeat purchase at a regular interval of time—monthly, quarterly, etc.) while diversifying product lines to music and video and more, which provides cross-selling opportunities (where related and unrelated products/services are sold to an existing customer base). Continuity selling and cross-selling to Amazon.com visitors enhance customer relationships in a variety of ways. The company does this by pointing out

- "Customers who bought this book also bought: . . ."
- "Our auction sellers recommend: . . ."
- "Look for similar books by these subjects: . . ."
- "This book is especially popular in these places: . . ."
- "We've included the top five titles for your browsing pleasure below. (At least these were the top five as of when we sent this message.)"

In summary, the emergence of different media has dramatically affected the history of direct marketing and in some ways has chartered its course. However, beyond media, several other factors have influenced the growth and direction of direct marketing. The next section details these factors.

Factors Affecting the Growth of Direct Marketing

The social and economic changes that have given impetus to the burgeoning rise of direct marketing since the mid-twentieth century have been coupled with equally impressive advances in the technology used in various elements of direct marketing. A few of these technological and social advances are worth mentioning.

PRINTING TECHNOLOGY   The versatility of laser printing, personalization of inkjet printing, advances in press technology, and computerized typesetting are important examples of how the printing process is becoming more conducive to the demassification of the printed word. Desktop publishing enables businesses to create newsletters, brochures, and other print materials that can have a highly professional look at a fraction of former costs. Graphic capabilities have also taken major strides. Compare, for example, the carnival cover design of the 1976 Oriental Trading Company catalog with its present carnival catalog cover design shown in Figure 1-5. Indeed, much has changed!

CREDIT CARDS   Since the advent of credit cards during the 1950s, there has been enormous growth of mail order as a selling method. Credit cards greatly enhanced and expedited transactions, which up to that time had been mainly cash with order. The ready availability of worldwide credit systems, together with rapid electronic funds transfer, has contributed to the feasibility and viability of direct marketing by simultaneously offering convenience and security.

PERSONAL COMPUTERS   Perhaps nothing has revolutionized direct marketing more than computing technology. Personal computers have made possible the recordkeeping, work operation, and model building that are so much a part of the art and science of direct marketing. The complex maintenance of lists and the retrieval of data associated with them are just two examples of the computer's contribution. The processing of orders and the maintenance of inventories are others. Of

FIGURE 1-5   Oriental Trading Company Catalog Covers.
Source: Used with permission of Oriental Trading Company.

course, the use of highly sophisticated analysis can mean the difference between direct marketing success and failure. The computer's contributions of great speed, lower-than-human error, and low cost have made it indispensable to users of direct marketing.

CHANGING CONSUMER LIFESTYLES   As travel becomes more expensive and communication becomes less expensive, there is further impetus to the use of mail, telephone, and Internet. Mailed catalogs, Web sites, and toll-free telephone numbers provide the convenience of shopping from home. Furthermore, as more women have entered the workforce, families are placing a greater emphasis on time utilization. Once a leisurely pastime, shopping has become more of a chore, especially for the majority of households in which both spouses work. The advent of mail order and the Web have made anytime day-or-night shopping even more convenient for these working spouses.

NEGATIVE ASPECTS OF RETAILING   Many consumers enjoy shopping in traditional retail stores. However, there is a strong belief that traditional retail shopping has a number of negative aspects associated with it. Some of these include inadequate parking facilities; concerns about safety; long walking distances; uninformed sales clerks; difficulties in locating retail sales personnel; long waiting lines at check-out; in-store congestion; difficulty in locating certain sizes, styles, or colors of products; and the hassle of juggling packages out of the retail stores. For these consumers, direct marketing, with all of its modern methods and conveniences, has been a welcome alternative.

The foregoing social and technological factors have served to not only popularize the use of direct and interactive marketing over the years but also affect the way direct and interactive marketing activities are carried out today. If the logic of direct and interactive marketing has become the logic of all marketing, its process must be explored and mastered. Let's investigate the process involved in conducting direct and interactive marketing.

THE PROCESSES OF DIRECT AND INTERACTIVE MARKETING

Direct marketing guru Edward Nash once said: "Direct marketing is somewhat like laser surgery; a powerful, precise, and very effective tool in the hands of professionals, but a potential disaster in the hands of amateurs. We must approach it as if we are surgeons, not butchers, as if we are cabinetmakers, not carpenters."[11] The process of direct and interactive marketing is presented in the model featured in Figure 1-6. This model is parallel with the definition of direct marketing provided earlier in this chapter. The model recognizes the importance of responses that are measurable and the value of customer data in driving direct marketing strategies. It also encompasses the strategic use of multiple channels—a topic that is of emerging importance to direct marketers.

First and foremost, direct marketing activities are based on their historical foundations. Inherent to the effectiveness of the direct and interactive marketing process is the constant focus on customers. *Customers* are the life-blood of an organization.[12] Enterprise thrives on customers. They are the reason for its existence. The creation and cultivation of customers is what direct marketing is all about. Much has been written in recent times about **customer relationship management (CRM)**. We examine *interactive customer relationships,* as well as the related subjects of customer affinity and loyalty, pointing to the need for determining the lifetime value of a customer in greater detail in Chapters 2 and 13.

Although new media like the Internet change the mechanism by which direct marketing activities are performed, its cornerstone database-driven direct response communications remain in effect today. In addition, the quality of the targeted list or database segment is critical to direct marketing success. That success is determined by measuring response rates. The formula for success

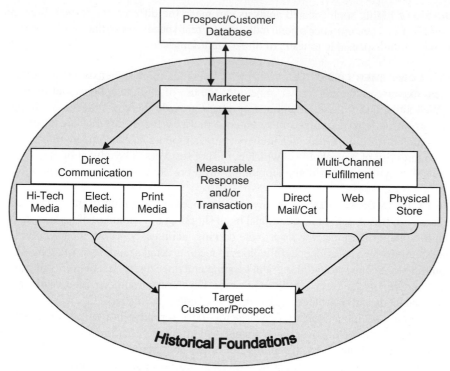

FIGURE 1-6   Direct and Interactive Marketing Model.   *Source:* Model created by Lisa Spiller and Carol Scovotti. Used with permission.

remains constant—reaching the *right* people with the *right* offer using the *right* creative approach. Now let's itemize the process of direct and interactive marketing.

A brief overview of the direct and interactive marketing process is as follows. The marketer sends out customized direct response communication via any type of media to customers or prospective customers on the basis of the information the marketer has about that customer or prospect. In the case of prospecting efforts, because customer data do not yet exist in the company's database, the company often rents a list of prospective customers based on specific selection criteria. The targeted customer or prospect receives that communication and responds directly to the company or organization via multiple channel options. The customer response, which could take many different forms (inquiry, transaction, donation, visit, vote, etc.), is entered into the company database and is processed. Once processed, the customer's response is fulfilled and delivery of the requested product, service, or information is provided directly to that customer. Then, the entire process begins again with the direct marketer using the data contained in its database to distribute more customized messages to select recipients and the process continues. Let's examine each component of the process in greater detail.

Direct Communication 1:1 The goal of direct marketers is to interact with customers on a one-to-one basis, with reference to the information obtained and stored about each customer in the customer database. Direct marketers then provide the customer with information and product/service offers that are relevant to each customer's needs and wants. This, too, is different from the activities of traditional marketers, who normally attempt to communicate with customers on a mass or segmented basis but not normally on a personal individual basis. Direct marketers actively seek out and identify those target customers to whom they will send a catalog.

Multiple Media While direct mail and direct response advertising are items within the historical foundations, direct marketing is not dependent on any specific form of media. In fact, it demonstrates that any media may be used to directly communicate with prospects and customers. Thus, media are placed into three categories: high-tech, electronic, and print media. High-tech media includes Internet, e-mail, search engines, blogs, online social networking, mobile marketing, and whatever new digital formats emerge in the future. This dimension stresses the importance of interactivity and acknowledges that direct marketing will continue to evolve with technological advances. In addition to the Internet, practitioners also consider electronic media like telemarketing and direct response television to be powerful vehicles for directly communicating with customers. Just because it's old doesn't mean it has lost its value. Finally, print media like catalogs and mail order round out the media options for direct marketing practitioners.

Measurable Response The single most notable differentiating feature of direct marketing is that it always seeks to generate a *measurable response*. This response can take the form of an order, an inquiry about the product or service, or traffic brought into a store. The activities of direct marketing are *measurable,* and the direct marketer must be *accountable,* always relating results to costs. Unlike most of the activities of traditional brand advertising—creating awareness for a product, service, or organization or enhancing the image of a product, brand, or a company—direct marketing activities can always be measured by the response of targeted customers and/or prospects.

Database The key technological tool that enables the building and maintenance of long-term relationships is the database. One of the most important tasks of direct marketing is capturing these customer responses and storing them in a database. The creation of a database enables direct marketers to target their best prospects and best customers, build customer relationships, and maintain long-term customer loyalty—the hallmarks of CRM. Thus, the goal of direct marketers is not just to make a sale but to *create a customer!* Although traditional marketers have a long history of building relationships with customers, their activities and interactions with them are not normally measurable, accountable, or captured and recorded in a database.

Customer Relationships Successful direct marketing relies on building strong customer relationships. While relationship building is referred to in many different ways (e.g., relationship marketing, one-to-one marketing, permission marketing, and CRM), the end result is the same—mutually beneficial long-term bonds between buyer and seller. The success of that relationship is measured in terms of lifetime customer value. Successful relationships also require respect for and protection of personal information shared by customers. Customer bonds with the seller strengthen when he or she trusts that the information shared is protected. Direct marketers have long known the long-term value of customers and have exercised CRM strategies to retain them.

Multichannel Fulfillment Direct response communication is intended to generate a measurable action (such as order, inquiry, charitable donation, or vote for a candidate) via multiple channels. Of course, each customer response generates information that is stored in the organization's database and is used by the direct marketer in future marketing activities. The customer selects the desired channel, such as a visit to a Web site or store or a phone call. Direct marketers must process or fulfill each customer's response, regardless of whether it is an inquiry or an order. These are the customer service and fulfillment activities, which are often called "back-end" marketing. They include delivery of information or order shipment directly to the target customer. Multichannel fulfillment is also called **multichannel distribution** because it refers to a marketer using several (two or more) competing channels of distribution to reach the same target consumer. By practicing multichannel distribution, direct marketers may incur greater expense but normally yield greater customer satisfaction by enabling customers to select their preferred shopping channels. Some customers prefer product delivery to their doorstep, and others won't purchase the product without careful personal examination of it, including trying it on for size and style decisions.

For example, Victoria's Secret, the well-known marketer of women's fashions and lingerie, uses three competing channels of distribution. First, its catalogs are mailed to its database of customers and prospective customers and contain both its toll-free number and Web address for consumers to place direct orders; second, its Web site permits consumers to shop online at www.VictoriasSecret.com; and third, its retail stores are located in most major shopping malls, enabling consumers to come into the store to browse and purchase the merchandise in person. These three channels of distribution may compete with one another for the same target customer's order, and yet if the company didn't offer all of these options, it might lose potential customers to other marketers. Multichannel fulfillment or distribution offers multiple options for today's increasingly demanding consumer. The bottom line: Consumers want choices! Multichannel fulfillment gives them exactly that.

The Peruvian Connection is another example of the many direct marketers using multichannel fulfillment. It obtains inquiries for its catalog from its Web site, direct mail, and magazine ads. It has retail stores in selected locations, where it sells surplus stock. A good many new sales now originate at its Web site, the home page of which appears in Figure 1-7.

Now that we have examined the process of direct and interactive marketing, you might be wondering: how does the marketer carry out these processes for each individual customer on a one-to-one basis? The answer lies in precise measurement and analysis and proper targeting. The marketer follows each direct and interactive marketing campaign with a response analysis that examines the results for effectiveness. He or she can then initiate future communication designed specifically for each target customer by using the customer information stored in the database. The process begins again: each direct response communication builds on the relationship the direct marketer has with each individual customer and reinforces that customer's loyalty to the company or organization. We'll expand on each of these characteristics of direct marketing and interactive marketing in subsequent chapters in this textbook.

FIGURE 1-7 Peruvian Connection Home Page.
Source: Used with permission of the Peruvian Connection.

WHO USES DIRECT AND INTERACTIVE MARKETING AND HOW

You can immediately recognize a direct response advertisement, regardless of the medium used, by noting whether the reader, listener, or viewer is requested to take an immediate action: mail an order form, call a phone number, go to a Web site, come to a store or event, fill in a coupon, ask for a salesperson to call, send a contribution, vote for a particular candidate, or attend a meeting. If there is such a request, it is an example of direct marketing.

Users of Direct and Interactive Marketing

At some time or another, virtually every business and every organization—charitable, political, educational, cultural, and civic—and every individual uses direct response advertising and, indeed, has a database for doing so. As individuals, we use direct mail whenever we send greeting cards, wedding invitations, and birth or graduation announcements. Job hunters find the mail is an excellent way to get their résumés to prospective employers. Businesses, especially small businesses, use a variety of media for direct response advertising and employ many of the other elements of direct marketing. This is true of giant corporations as well as small retailers and industrial service organizations. The leading enterprises using many of the elements of direct marketing include, among others:

- Periodical publishers
- Food stores and distributors
- Mail-order houses
- Department stores
- Book and music publishers
- Automotive manufacturers
- Pharmaceutical manufacturers
- Book and stationery stores
- Newspaper publishers
- Home furnishing stores
- Insurance companies
- Credit card companies
- Financial institutions

Among nonprofit organizations—civic, charitable, political, educational, and cultural—the list of users of the elements of direct marketing is virtually endless. Religious organizations, PTAs, colleges, and universities, as well as charities use direct marketing techniques to keep members informed, solicit funds, and promote understanding. Political organizations use direct response advertising to change public opinion, inform constituents, and raise campaign funds.

The range of businesses/organizations that have embraced direct marketing is diverse. The exploits of Aaron Montgomery Ward and Richard Warren Sears now range from the sophisticated and expensive products of Neiman Marcus, Gump's, and Saks Fifth Avenue to the fine sporting goods of L. L. Bean and Eddie Bauer to the art products of the Metropolitan Museum of Art and Lincoln Center to the specialty products of Omaha Steaks and Vidalia Onions. Today, most companies are realizing the great value direct and interactive marketing brings. For example, over the past few years, DuPont has increased its direct marketing activities, particularly e-mail and other e-marketing initiatives, to take advantage of this very popular and cost-effective communication channel. See Figure 1-8 for the DuPont Direct Web page.

FIGURE 1-8 DuPont Direct Web Page. *Source:* Used with permission of DuPont.

DuPont enjoys the fact that direct responses enable faster lead qualification and follow-up by sales, and the quantifiable results allow for calculation of return on investment for these activities. DuPont's most significant challenge continues to be finding the right target e-mail lists. DuPont has had the most success in North America and Europe, although it has increasing activity in Asia, where mobile devices and electronic media are widely used in the major cities. Although DuPont has increased its direct and e-marketing activities, it finds that it is still necessary to maintain a balance with other more traditional marketing activities, including advertising, public relations, and participation at key trade shows and industry events to maintain its global brand leadership position.

Applications of Direct and Interactive Marketing

Let's look at a sampling of the many applications of the tools and techniques of database-driven direct marketing in use.[13]

- ***Traffic-building at the seller's location:*** Retailers like Bloomingdale's, Neiman Marcus, Macy's, and Saks use direct mail, Web sites, and telemarketing—in addition to traditional print and broadcast media—to drive store traffic. They build databases in the process, as do very many specialty stores, like Radio Shack. Countless manufacturers, Hewlett-Packard among them, do the same for their resellers.

- *Lead generation at the buyer's location:* Business-to-business (industrial) direct marketers like IBM and Pepsi-Cola Bottlers use direct mail, Web sites, and telemarketing to generate leads so as to enhance their personal sales forces.
- *Mail order (remote location):* The term "mail order" is really a misnomer as consumer and industrial organizations go beyond traditional direct mail and catalogs. They now use telephones, Web sites, broadcast, and print media. They solicit responses via the Web. Then the United Parcel Service and FedEx, as well as the U.S. Postal Service, fulfill the responses. "Mail" often never enters the picture!
- *Multichannel distribution:* Williams-Sonoma, Abercrombie & Fitch, Talbot's, and Laura Ashley are just a few examples of enterprises whose roots are in mail-order catalogs but who now populate shopping malls and the Web. From catalog shopping to buying via the Internet and from personal selling to mail order and telecommunication, the channels have become blurred. What is the common denominator of all of these? A *database* and *customer relationship*!

The list of organizations that can benefit from a database and direct marketing is virtually all-inclusive:

- *Product and service enterprises*

  American Express builds customer relationships with financial services, travel services, and related products.

  IBM offers hardware and software products through its Web site. It generates leads for its sales staff. Gateway and Dell sell direct in a variety of media. Apple and Compaq sell direct and support resellers too.

  Bland Farms uses the tools and techniques of direct marketing as a purveyor of its Vidalia onion products.

  So do travel agents, stockbrokers, and banks.
- *Consumer and industrial enterprises*

  Packaged goods companies harness the power of coupons, whether mailed, in newspapers, in store, or on the Internet. One company built a database from coupons redeemed for fitness foods and used this to develop ongoing customer relationships for their other products appealing to fitness lifestyles.

  Manufacturers of heavy cranes or earth-moving equipment find prospective customers through various construction and building-permit databases.
- *For-profit and not-for-profit organizations*

  The U.S. Treasury encloses order forms for U.S. Mint Liberty Coins with income tax refunds.

  The University of Missouri's Repertory Theater uses databases to get prospects to a single performance and then upgrades them to season ticket buyers.
- *Fundraising organizations*

  Mother's Against Drunk Driving (MADD) developed a direct mail package containing a teddy bear to request funds from a list of potential donors.

  City Union Mission puts together a list of 4,000 prior contributors from which it gets contributions of $350,000 from a single letter. Sisters of Mercy do likewise.
- *Political action groups*

  Do you want to be elected president, governor, or mayor? Do you want to be elected to a school board?

Do you want to build support or raise funds for the National Women's Political Caucus or Planned Parenthood?

Do you want to overcome objections of legislatures to conversion of railroad rights-of-way to Rails-to-Trails?

Do you want to garner political and financial support for environmental causes like the Nature Conservancy, World Wildlife Fund, American Rivers, and starving elk?

If you answered "yes" to any of the above questions, you will rely on direct marketing activities to obtain votes and financial support!

TRENDS IN DIRECT AND INTERACTIVE MARKETING

There has been a major increase the in diversity of *nonstore retailing.* Direct and interactive marketing has become a way of life, especially since the advent of online shopping. Not only has there been a proliferation of mail-order catalogs, but now more than ever catalogs are generating transactions at both store locations, called "bricks," and other nonstore, online retailers, called "clicks" retailers. Catalogs have been responsible for generating a great deal of Internet traffic and phone orders too. It is clear that the advent of the Internet, together with its Web, has ushered in a whole new type of store.

Many of the traditional store retailers capitalized on their recognizable brands and images and expanded their distribution with mail order. A multimedia synergy also has developed, embracing all forms of advertising: broadcast TV and radio, printed publications, direct mail, and telephones. Most recently, personal computers have provided electronic access to what may become the most powerful medium of all: the Internet. The Internet has driven several recent trends in direct marketing, such as the interaction of bricks and clicks. Rapid advances in technology have encouraged this as have changing lifestyles. More and more, direct marketing has become characterized as multimedia and multichannel.

Creating In-Store Traffic

Direct marketing plays a major role in boosting store traffic and not just remote ordering. Many retailers, however, have tended to view catalogs (and Web sites) as an *alternative,* rather than as an *adjunct* that can create store traffic at the same time it generates added direct sales.

Customers, especially those at some distance from stores, are offered the convenience of shopping by mail, phone, or Web sites for items featured in promotions in a variety of media. Many also like to shop from catalogs or on the Internet but prefer to make their purchase in the store, where they can see and feel the merchandise, check colors, get a proper fit, and then take immediate delivery.

Oil companies have justified inclusion of circulars with their monthly billing that offer merchandise to promote traffic to their service station retail locations. Knowing that they are already receiving a monthly billing for their gasoline purchases, customers will be inclined to favor the company from which they purchase gas with extended-payment merchandise purchases, such as power tools or luggage, to be added to their monthly gasoline bill and thus avoid a second bill from another company. The oil companies have found that such regular monthly billing also encourages future loyalty for gasoline purchases.

Manufacturers, too, have used the tools and techniques of direct marketing to create retail traffic for their products. Many have built databases from warranty cards returned by recent purchasers of their products.

Coupons, mass distributed through direct mail, newspapers, magazines, and the Internet, have been used to promote retail store traffic. One major packaged goods manufacturer compiled the names of those who had redeemed coupons for fat-free and sugar-free foods. It used this to develop a database to send a quarterly nutrition newsletter to these calorie-conscious users to identify and build brand relationships. Coupons sent with the newsletter to a segmented market were redeemed at a rate five times that of coupons sent at random.

Directing Online Traffic

A major consideration for Internet retailers is generating traffic to their Web sites. A good many techniques have been developed to accomplish this for traditional "bricks-and-mortar" retailers who have opted to also sell online. These typically involve SEM and optimization strategies.

Web sites make available an endless array of information for those who want it and for those who prefer to shop at their leisure and convenience, just as they have been doing for some time with mail-order catalogs and direct-mail offers. A notable example of this is Internet pioneer Amazon.com, which has mastered the art and science of direct marketing in a way that has demonstrated the lifetime value of a customer. Amazon.com has built great market valuation in the form of a database with millions of active customer records. Its major asset seems to be its database of customers, coupled with its ability to continuity-sell and cross-sell new product lines in a manner that provides added benefits to its customers.

Membership (Affinity) Clubs

Following the success of airline frequent flyer programs, scores of businesses have created frequent buyer programs. Usually, like Hallmark Cards' Gold Crown Card program, these programs encourage store traffic and continuity of customer relationships with reward points that can be redeemed for future purchases. Whereas a TV presentation like the *Hallmark Hall of Fame* does much to promote its brand among those "who care enough to send the very best," dealers laud the Gold Crown Card, which generates store traffic that results in measurable sales.

Such membership programs are very much in evidence now. They register customers in a database and thus provide promotion opportunities together with an identification card entitling the customer to substantial discounts. Retailers scan purchases at checkout and record them in a database so they can recognize buying patterns as well as develop customer profiles. These buyer continuity programs, like those for frequent flyers, provide an air of exclusivity and affinity with the store. Some, like those of large-volume, high-discount retailers such as Sam's Club and Costco, even charge annual membership fees for the privilege of spending money with them. Membership programs also have proliferated among food stores; examples are the Kroger Plus Card, the Giant BonusCard, the Food Lion MVP Card, and the Harris Teeter VIC Card (as shown in Figure 1-9). Going hand in hand with these membership or loyalty club marketing activities is the issue of information privacy. Although privacy issues will be discussed in greater detail later in this book, their importance merits a brief overview here.

Issues of Privacy and Security

The important issues of privacy and security will be discussed in greater detail in Chapter 11; however, a brief overview is provided here to help you put into perspective the uncontrollable and ever-changing legal developments affecting direct marketers. With regard to the issues of privacy and security, one thing is certain—the privacy policies are changing, and they will have a great impact

FIGURE 1-9   Loyalty Program Card.

on direct and interactive marketing. With that in mind, let's look at a few of the key issues surrounding privacy and security.

The use of data culled from interactive customers and their transactions alarms privacy advocates. Will these concerns about information privacy affect the future of database-driven direct marketing? Databases provide opportunities to fulfill customer preferences through targeting of relevant messages and media. This minimizes intrusive or "junk" advertising—that which is not relevant to the interests of the recipient. In reality, though, people do not always react favorably when what they buy triggers further solicitations.

Privacy advocates also point to potential harm or injury to individuals as a result of data disclosure. It thus behooves the direct marketer to be responsible in both the acquisition and the use of data. Certainly not the least of the reasons for this is that it is inefficient as well as costly to send irrelevant direct mail advertising to those not interested. Some customers, of course, continue to view any promotion as an intrusion or a nuisance and feel it is an invasion of their privacy. Others, seeking to minimize the time they spend reviewing advertising for things they will never buy, welcome the database-driven offers they receive because of their relevance.

A few facts about information privacy are clear. Opinions about information privacy vary depending on the type of consumer. Governmental regulations and privacy legislation are on the rise. Information privacy is an area on which direct marketers must keep a close watch. It is a nebulous area that is changing rapidly.

Also changing are the laws governing Internet security. Direct marketers must constantly monitor the legal policies affecting interactive media—especially online marketing activities.

Summary

Direct marketing is a database-driven interactive process of directly communicating with targeted customers or prospects using any medium to obtain a measurable response or transaction via one or multiple channels. Almost all types of business can and do conduct direct and interactive marketing activities, including organizations and individuals whose goal is to establish long-term relationships with their customers. Direct and interactive marketing uses many different types of media and formats, including direct mail, catalogs, newspaper, magazine, radio, television, phone, Internet, hand-held devices, and mobile. The industry has a long history and has experienced rapid growth primarily due to credit cards, computers, advances in the printing industry, changing lifestyles of consumers, and the negative aspects of in-store retailing.

Customers are at the heart of the direct and interactive marketing process. The main goal of the direct and interactive marketing process is to develop and strengthen long-term relationships with customers. Many direct marketers are finding great success in using membership clubs to enhance customer loyalty. These are becoming very popular among direct marketers and among consumers. However, as with any area of marketing, there are many uncontrollable variables affecting the way direct marketing activities can be carried out. The issues of privacy and security are the most pertinent at the moment and will require direct marketers to constantly seek ways to satisfy consumer needs and wants while adhering to the regulations governing their industry.

Key Terms

direct marketing *4*
brand marketing *5*

customer relationship
management (CRM) *11*

multichannel fulfillment *13*

Review Questions

1. Name and elaborate on the characteristics that distinguish *direct* from *traditional* brand marketing.
2. What is meant by measurability of and accountability for marketing decisions?
3. What is the difference between a list and a database?
4. Write an overview of the components of the direct and interactive marketing process and model.
5. "Direct marketing is an aspect of marketing characterized by *measurability* and *accountability* with reliance on *databases*." Explain this statement.
6. Discuss the historical roots and the emergence of direct marketing; how has it been influenced by technological, economic, and social change?
7. Compare and elaborate on the changes in graphic design between the 1947 and 2008 catalog covers of Oriental Trading Company shown in Figure 1-6.
8. How does the Internet fit into the total marketing scheme of things and the distinguishing characteristics of direct marketing?
9. What is direct response advertising and how does it relate to direct mail as well as print, broadcast, and Web sites?
10. Describe the use of direct marketing by a business. Describe its use by a nonbusiness organization. Describe how it fits into the political scheme of things.

Exercise

Think of your favorite cuisine. Pretend you have just opened a restaurant featuring all of your favorite foods.

a. How will your marketing plan use direct marketing techniques to build your business?

b. Pretend a year has gone by and you have been successfully operating your restaurant. How will your direct marketing activities change over the next few years?

CASE
Cheryl&Co.

Overview

This case is an example of how a company effectively uses multichannel marketing in growing a business. It demonstrates how a new entrepreneurial venture was successfully launched on a very small budget by concentrating on direct-response communication channels, CRM, and measurement. The case specifically details how a company manages multiple channels in serving its customers. It is proof that direct and interactive marketing can work for any company, organization, or entrepreneur—regardless of size.

As a learning experience, the student should focus on the basic elements of direct marketing, including marketing research, database development, CRM, measurability and accountability, and multichannel distribution. Then, examine how direct and interactive marketing strategies and techniques play an integral role in the development and execution of a successful twenty-first-century business. Let's see what you can learn from this inspiring tale of a successful entrepreneur.

Case

In 1981, together with her college roommate, Caryl Walker, and equipped with an old-fashioned cookie recipe from her grandmother Elsie, Cheryl Krueger (Figure 1-10) launched her entrepreneurial business venture. What began as a single cookie store has now evolved into a multimillion-dollar business. Cheryl&Co., headquartered in Westerville, Ohio, is a multichannel marketer with retail stores, catalog, a growing Internet business, and a business gift division. How did she do it? What was her secret ingredient in building this successful business?

Cheryl has built this company from scratch, starting with $40,000, a degree in home economics/business, and seven years of retail experience. She began by opening one retail store. For the first five years, Cheryl worked two jobs to support the business. In 1985, she came on board full-time, and the company began to broaden its offering to include gifts and desserts along with an expanded dessert line, which now includes brownies, cheesecake, pies, and cakes. This business growth inevitably led to the change of the company name to Cheryl&Co.

Today, Cheryl&Co.'s team of 450 associates strives to be the best. Its mission statement reads: "Our mission is to be the best gourmet food and gift company, ever." That includes having a customer-centered focus throughout the entire business. Cheryl prides herself in putting the customer first, and this priority permeates throughout the Cheryl&Co. team. If a customer has a less than ideal experience, they will receive a personal letter from Cheryl. An overall philanthropic ethos exists throughout the company culture, from free shipping to military (APO/FPO), involvement with cancer research (see cookies online), Make A Wish products, and so on. Customer relationships are the key to any successful business. That is especially true for food and gift companies because of the large number and wide variety of competitors that exist in the industry. Therefore, building and maintaining customer relationships has been a focus of Cheryl&Co. right from the beginning.

In 2005, Cheryl&Co. merged with 1-800-FLOWERS.COM. 1-800-FLOWERS.COM is an enterprise of fine, individually branded companies that includes The Popcorn Factory, Plow & Hearth, Fannie May, Magic Cabin, HearthSong, Wind & Weather, Ambrosia, and many others. (Visit Cheryl&Co.'s Web site at www.cherylandco.com for a complete listing.) This family of

FIGURE 1-10   Cheryl Krueger.

brands offers opportunities for Cheryl&Co. to build relationships with many new customers across the entire 1-800-FLOWERS.COM enterprise.

Building and Maintaining Customer Relationships

Customer relationship management is made possible through the development and use of a customer database. Cheryl&Co.'s preferred customers receive certain offers and benefits that are not available to other customers. These special benefits are presented as a "surprise and delight" to the preferred customers. The special offers are most often delivered to individual customers via direct mail or e-mail communication.

Cheryl&Co. currently works with a third-party vendor that hosts its customer database; however, the company is in the process of transitioning to an in-house enterprise-wide customer data warehouse that will enable them to better understand and market to all enterprise customers. Therefore, any customer who has interacted with any of the 1-800-FLOWERS.COM brands will be listed in the enterprise-wide customer database. For example, someone who asks to receive a catalog from Plow & Hearth, makes a purchase from 1-800-FLOWERS.COM, or receives a gift from

Cheryl&Co. will be housed in the central database. There are many benefits to this system for both the individually branded companies and for all enterprise-wide customers. For example, wouldn't it be great for HearthSong to know how many recipients of "new baby" products Cheryl&Co. had so they could send these customers a timely HearthSong catalog? This is just one example of the potential benefit of understanding a customer's place in life, so to speak. This type of customer lifestyle data will lead to the delivery of more appropriate and timely need-satisfying offerings from all enterprise-wide businesses.

Some important considerations when maintaining a customer database include data hygiene—ensuring that the information contained in the database is current, accurate, and not duplicated. Customer data hygiene involves basics such as employing National Change of Address (NCOA) and Address Standardization on the database, as well as on direct mail campaigns, to save considerable marketing dollars lost when mailing to invalid addresses. Also, customer identification and matching are important parts of data hygiene to avoid duplicate records, which would potentially result in a customer receiving multiple or irrelevant marketing communication. For example, when Cheryl&Co. is able to identify that Customer Record X and Customer Record Y are actually the same person, the company can combine that customer's order history, contact preferences, and so on to optimize the profile of that customer, which will lead to more efficient and effective marketing contact(s).

Database analysis is also important to Cheryl&Co. The company tracks several customer metrics such as buyer file size, retention rate of existing and new customers, number of new customers, purchase frequency, average order value, net promoter score, and so on to be able to market more effectively with its customers. Cheryl&Co. is currently developing customer personas. A customer comes to "life" through this process—she gets a name, a face, a personality. Every decision the company will make will be viewed through the eyes of this fictitious customer.

Seeking New Customers

Prospecting efforts include cross-promotions with its enterprise-wide "family of brands." Cheryl&Co. actively seeks out new customers via catalog prospecting both within the family of brands and through list rental and exchange agreements with competitors as well as other retailers who have a similar customer profile. The best prospecting methods for Cheryl&Co. are when prospective customers have an opportunity to view or sample its products. Cheryl&Co.'s products are awesome, and the company consistently achieves high marks from its current customers via BizRate surveys. The company's frosted cookie is certainly what many consumers consider its "best foot forward" both from a visual presentation and a taste standpoint. Consumers also attest to the beautiful presentation of Cheryl&Co. products, which is why catalog mailings are important prospecting methods. However, with environmental concerns and the increasing cost of postage, it is difficult to get a catalog that showcases Cheryl&Co. products into every potential customer's hands! The company has met this challenge by including an online catalog on the Web site that is available for anyone to browse and by increasing its online marketing activities including paid search engine optimization and affiliate marketing. Figure 1-11 shows Cheryl&Co.'s online catalog.

In addition, Cheryl&Co.'s philanthropic focus often means the company is featured on charitable Web sites, such as Make A Wish Foundation, which generates awareness for the company. Cheryl&Co. also participates in public relations events, such as the events at three children's hospitals in Indianapolis along with the NBA Pacers. These events are perfectly aligned with Cheryl&Co.'s philanthropic initiatives and also result in excellent publicity for the company, which can lead prospective customers to purchase from one of Cheryl&Co.'s multiple channels.

FIGURE 1-11   Cheryl&Co.'s Online Catalog.   Source: Used with permission of Cheryl&Co®.

Multichannel Marketing Methods

Cheryl&Co. retail stores now account for about 11 percent of business sales, with telephonic and Internet (driven primarily by catalog and online marketing) accounting for 56 percent, the business gift services (driven primarily by the team of account managers via telephone and marketing efforts including catalog and online activities) generating 23 percent, and the remaining 10 percent coming from miscellaneous sources, including wholesale. Today, the most rapidly growing channel is its Internet business. Certainly a portion of these orders are driven by consumers receiving the Cheryl&Co. catalog.

Cheryl&Co. strives to align the customer experience regardless of what channel they choose to use. For instance, when a catalog is mailed out, often the company will feature the items that are on the catalog cover or on pages two or three in the catalog on the home page of its Web site. This same product line will also be "center stage" in Cheryl&Co. retail stores. This provides a consistently branded image and message to those customers who shop via multiple channels.

Summary and Conclusion

Today, Cheryl&Co. is a tremendous business success. Why? It is due to a combination of several things. First, it is because of the excellent quality products and strong focus on serving its customers. Second, its success is because of the application of savvy direct and interactive marketing strategies to maintain customers and reach out to new ones. Third, business success is due in part to offering customers multiple channels from which they can purchase products. Fourth, Cheryl&Co. is a member of the well-known 1-800-FLOWERS.COM family of brands, which provides excellent cross-branding and cross-selling opportunities. Finally, a portion of the success of this company is surely due to the drive and determination of Cheryl Krueger. Her creativity, passion, and sense of civic duty have earned her numerous awards and titles, as well as a national reputation as a successful female entrepreneur. And finally, as the saying goes, the proof is in the pudding (or in this case, in the cookies). Bon appetit!

Case Discussion Questions

1. What was the single most important direct marketing technique that Cheryl and her team employed early on?

2. What other ways could Cheryl&Co. work with its "family of brands" to increase its business?

3. Taking into consideration the limited budget of this entrepreneur, what else could be done to increase the size of Cheryl&Co.'s customer database?

Notes

1. Roland T. Rust and Richard W. Oliver (1994), "The Death of Advertising," *Journal of Advertising,* 23(4), 71–77.

2. Philip Kotler and Gary Armstrong (2008), *Principles of Marketing,* 12th ed. (Englewood Cliffs, NJ: Prentice Hall).

3. Gary Armstrong and Philip Kotler (2007), *Marketing: An Introduction,* 8th ed. (Englewood Cliffs, NJ: Prentice Hall).

4. Herbert Katzenstein and William S. Sachs (1992), *Direct Marketing,* 2nd ed. (New York: Macmillan).

5. *The Power of Direct Marketing, 2006–2007* ed. (New York: Direct Marketing Association, 2007), pp. 22–23.

6. *The Power of Direct Marketing, 2007–2008* ed. (New York: Direct Marketing Association, 2008), p. 22.

7. *The DMA 2007 Hiring Needs, Strategies and Compensation in Direct Marketing Report: An Employer's Perspective* (New York: Direct Marketing Association, 2007), xv.

8. Carol Scovotti and Lisa D. Spiller (2006), "Revisiting the Conceptual Definition of Direct Marketing: Perspectives from Practitioners and Scholars," *Marketing Management Journal,* 16(2), 188–202.

9. *The Integration of DM & Brand, 2007* ed. (New York: Direct Marketing Association, 2007), p. xxiii.

10. Many of the early historical references contained in this section are based on documentation prepared by Nat Ross for the Direct Marketing Association.

11. Edward L. Nash (1993), *Database Marketing: The Ultimate Marketing Tool* (New York: McGraw-Hill).

12. Martin Baier (1996), *How to Find and Cultivate Customers through Direct Marketing* (Lincolnwood, IL: NTC Business Books), p. 3ff.

13. Adapted from Martin Baier, Kurtis M. Ruf, and Goutam Chakraborty, *Contemporary Database Marketing: Concepts & Applications* (Evanston, IL: Racom Communications, 2002).

2

...

Building Databases, Selecting Customers, and Managing Relationships

Customer Database
Database Development
Customer Loyalty Programs
Examples of Loyalty Programs
Source Data
Recency/Frequency/Monetary Assessment
Database Maintenance
Match Codes and Merge-Purge
Multibuyers
Keeping Records Current
Database Security
Information Privacy
Proper Database Storage
List Seeding
Database Uses and Applications
Using a Customer Database
Performing Database Analytics

Database Enhancement
Internal Data Enhancement
External Data Enhancement
Customer Relationship Management
Customer Value
Lifetime Customer Value
One-on-One Personalized Marketing
Partner Relationship Management (PRM)
Summary
Key Terms
Review Questions
Exercise
Case: Smithfield Foods

Opening Vignette: Tidewater Exterminating

There isn't another industry that relies on the development, maintenance, and use of a customer database more than the services industry. Customer relationship management (CRM) is critical to the survival and success of most service organizations. This is the case for Tidewater Exterminating, a small family business located in the Tidewater area of Virginia that serves its customers with extra special care. Meet Adam Brown

FIGURE 2-1   Adam Brown.

(Figure 2-1). When Adam graduated from college, he joined the family business and began applying the database marketing concepts he learned while completing his business degree program.

Adam knew that the secret to success in this competitive industry was to establish and maintain strong relationships with his customers. He also knew just how to do that—a customer database. The database system Tidewater Exterminating used was designed specifically for companies in the pest control industry. Adam chose an online-based service with off-site auto backup for regular database maintenance. This type of secure database system is upgraded on a monthly basis so that the company can immediately implement technological upgrades as needed. With the database system in place, Adam was ready to get started. He began using the database daily to manage all aspects of his family business—accounts receivable, scheduling, technician tracking, customer penetration mapping, marketing communications, vehicle servicing, partner communication, partner and customer referrals, cross-selling activities, and, of course, the single most important use of a database—CRM. By using the transactional data to profile its customers, Tidewater Exterminating is able to effectively time its communication to the needs of each customer. Attractive offers are mailed to select customers, and the response is overwhelming. Adam is thrilled that the direct marketing strategies he has employed have consistently generated more than a 50 percent response rate on each mailing and nearly a 100 percent conversion rate from response to sale.

Though creating and maintaining relationships with homeowners who are regular users of the services of Tidewater Exterminating is Adam's main priority, he also uses the database for building and maintaining other relationships as well. Fostering long-term relationships with its industry regulators and suppliers is also extremely important to Tidewater Exterminating. Adam uses his database for partner relationship management (PRM) with people who directly influence purchasing decisions for real estate. This is a wide category with a number of segments, including developers, builders, real estate agents, property managers, attorneys, loan officers, and fellow service companies. These people are not necessarily direct consumers of Tidewater Exterminating's services but need its services to complete their jobs. These partners directly influence the purchasing decisions of property owners; therefore, maintaining strong relationships with these partners is imperative. Adam regularly sends new real estate agents a congratulatory letter and a "Bug Bucks," shown in Figure 2-2, to introduce the services of Tidewater Exterminating and encourage their referrals.

According to Adam, "When I first joined the family business, I was told by one of our largest competitors that if you take care of your customers, your customers will take care of you. I believe this is the key principle to growing a service company. Our customer database enables us to take care of our customers and

FIGURE 2-2　Bug Bucks.
Source: Used with permission of Tidewater Exterminating Inc.

partners in a highly efficient and effective manner." One of the best measures of success is customer retention or renewal. Tidewater Exterminating's customer renewal rate is higher than 90 percent. This is especially impressive because the longer customers remain with a company, the greater their lifetime value.

Adam's family business illustrates the value of building databases, selecting customers, and maintaining relationships—and that is the topic of this chapter.

All direct marketers seek to maximize the profits of their business. Two ways to achieve this are attracting new customers and encouraging your current customers to buy more from you. However, it is very well established that a new customer acquisition program may *not* be as profitable as a customer retention program. Did you know that it costs (on average) about eight to ten times as much money to acquire a new customer than it does to keep a current one?[1] Thus, direct marketers may be better served by directing their marketing efforts toward retaining the customers they already have. This is the concept behind database-driven direct marketing, which is the focus of this chapter.

We also discuss what a customer database is, its importance in developing customer loyalty, and how to build, maintain, secure, and use a customer database. In addition, this chapter discusses database enhancement and data analytics. Finally, we discuss the importance of CRM and PRM.

CUSTOMER DATABASE

A **customer database** is a list of customer names to which the marketer has added additional information in a systematic fashion. Just as a house list contains active as well as inactive customers, inquirers, and referrals, so does an organization's customer database. Thus we can think of a customer database as a computerized house list that contains more than merely a listing of customer names.

A customer database is the key to developing strong customer relationships and retaining current customers. The customer database is the vehicle through which a company documents comprehensive information about each customer. This information could include the consumer's past purchases (buying patterns), demographics (age, birthday, income, marital status, etc.), psychographics (activities, interests, and opinions), and much more. Marketers use this information to direct all future marketing activities with each customer on an individual basis. For example, the customer database is used for such purposes as lead generation, lead qualification, sale of a product or service, and promotional activities. Armed with this information, marketers are able to develop a closer relationship with each customer on a personalized basis. The stronger the relationship with each customer, the more likely that customer will continue purchasing from the company. That is why current customers, with whom the direct marketer already has an established relationship, are more likely to be retained as future customers.

How does a company retain its customers? By keeping the customer satisfied and happy. Highly satisfied customers tend to be loyal customers, and loyal customers generate greater profits for an organization over their lifetime of patronage. This is due to the following reasons.

1. Loyal customers tend to increase their spending over time. These customers are better to have and more profitable than other customers.[2]
2. Loyal customers cost less to serve than new customers. Repeat customers have greater familiarity with an organization's processes and procedures and therefore are more quickly and easily served.
3. Loyal customers are normally happy customers who tell others about the organization, commonly referred to as word-of-mouth advertising, which in turn generates additional business.
4. Loyal customers are less price sensitive than are new customers. They see value in their relationship with the organization and may spend more freely because of their high level of satisfaction with the firm.

In addition, according to Frederick Reichheld, author of *The Loyalty Effect,* a five-percentage-point increase in customer retention in a typical company will increase profits by more than 25 percent—and growth by more than 100 percent.[3]

The task of creating and maintaining loyal customers is what CRM is all about. In an attempt to retain current customers, marketers invest in programs and activities to create and enhance customer loyalty. The development of a customer database is the first step in this process.

DATABASE DEVELOPMENT

Developing a customer database for marketing purposes is an ordered process. It begins with obtaining basic data about customers. This is followed by the task of converting that data into relevant information for the company. Then the company uses that information to produce knowledge about its customers and their preferences. Armed with that knowledge, a company can develop strategy to better communicate with and serve its customers. Finally, customer interaction will likely yield additional valuable customer data for the company. Figure 2-3 provides a flowchart of the process.

However, in building a customer database, the management must first determine the company's primary goals. For example, an organization might want to get to know its customers better to develop more effective future promotional activities. Other objectives may include selling them different products/services, thanking them for their patronage, encouraging referral business, introducing a new product or service, distributing information about an upcoming event or sale, or introducing a new staff member or employee . . . the list goes on! Customer loyalty programs are commonly used in the process of creating a customer database.

Customer Loyalty Programs

Customer loyalty programs are programs sponsored by an organization or firm to encourage customer repeat purchases through program enrollment processes and the distribution of awards and/or benefits. Airlines, hotels, cruise lines, retail stores, and many other organizations have rewarded customer loyalty through structured programs for years.

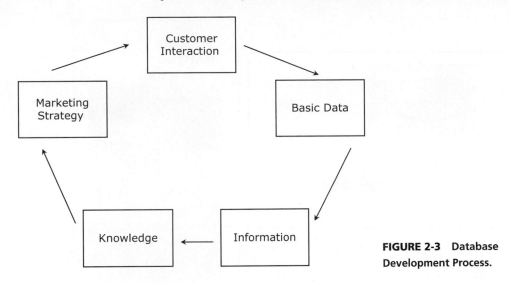

FIGURE 2-3 Database Development Process.

Organizations primarily offer customer loyalty programs to strengthen customer relationships. Loyalty programs are also used to develop or provide additional information to a company's customer database. The beauty of customer loyalty programs is that you can obtain information about customers on a direct basis and use this information to more effectively target customers' future needs and wants.

Examples of Loyalty Programs

Many people participate in frequent flyer programs or have at least heard about the program. American Airlines began their frequent flyer program 26 years ago and have teamed up with hotels, rental car companies, and credit cards to generate hundreds of millions of dollars per year.[4] Frequent flyer miles generate revenue and succeed at making a profit because the airline is basically selling a seat that would have probably been empty anyway.

Figure 2-4 provides an example of how McDonald Garden Center, with three retail locations in Virginia, rewards customer loyalty via its Garden Rewards Program. The Garden Rewards Program was established to allow McDonald Garden Center to know its customers and communicate with them based on the value of the relationship. It enabled the company to improve customer loyalty while reducing long-term marketing expenses through more precise market segmentation and tailored communication. The program quickly became a success. In less than six weeks from the launch date, the number of customers enrolled in the Garden Rewards Program totaled 15,375—which was almost 60 percent of the customers on the company's house list. Of the reward program cards issued, 70 percent were used at least one time during that same six-week period; 42 percent were used two or more times.[5]

Once managers have determined the objectives of the database and the method by which they will gather customer information, they can identify the data they need to collect from their customers.

Source Data

The information contained in a customer database is called **source data.** Each direct marketer must determine the particular source data needed for their customer database—which often varies based on the specific products or services or the competitive situation of the direct marketer. Collecting

FIGURE 2-4   Garden Rewards Program.   *Source:* Used with permission of McDonald Garden Center.

data that will not be used simply drives up the organization's marketing costs. Within their house records, direct marketers usually capture certain key data, such as product preferences or credit experience, if relevant.

Some of the basic data marketers should collect for a customer database are the customer's name and address including ZIP code, telephone number, and e-mail address. Many direct marketers document how the customer first learned about the product or service. Additional data called **transactional data** include what products each customer has purchased, how recently (recency) and how often (frequency), and how much the customer spends (monetary). This information provides an avenue to analyze each customer through some variation of the **recency/frequency/monetary (R/F/M)** assessment. By carrying the date and volume of purchases in the master list record over a period of time, marketers can determine the transaction record of each customer in a given period, which helps determine the future potential of that customer. Many direct marketers, such as Lillian Vernon and Newport News, use this approach in determining who will receive catalogs and how often. It relates the cost of promotion to the potential benefits to be derived from each customer.

R/F/M Assessment

The exact R/F/M formulation for each direct marketer naturally varies according to the importance given to each of the variables in relation to each other. For some promotions, marketers might need to manipulate their calculations by weighting one of the factors, so that, for example, the results will

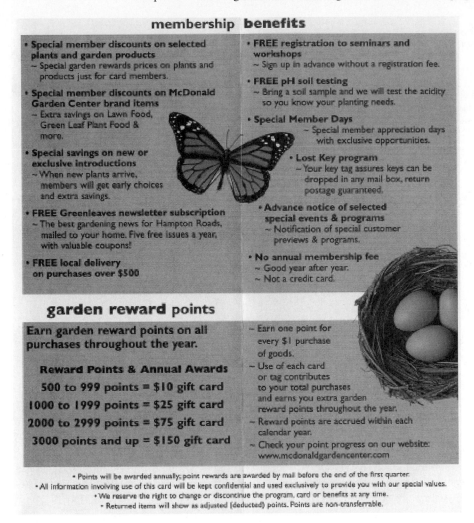

FIGURE 2-4   (continued)

show those customers who had purchased most recently. More sophisticated direct marketers use multivariate statistical techniques to mathematically determine the R/F/M weights and use them with greater reliability.

Figure 2-5 shows how to evaluate customers on a mailing list according to the combined R/F/M values of their transactions over time. For purposes of this example, the following weights are assigned to the variables: recency ($\times 5$), frequency ($\times 3$), and monetary ($\times 2$).

In the example in Figure 2-5 three customers (identified as A, B, and C) have a purchase history calculated over a 24-month period. We assigned numerical points to each transaction, according to the derived R/F/M formula and further weighted these points. The resulting cumulative point calculations, 202 for A, 79 for B, and 280 for C, indicate a potential preference for customer C. C's R/F/M history, and perhaps A's as well, justifies a greater amount of promotion dollars. Customer B might be an unlikely promotion dollar risk. To apply R/F/M assessments, marketers must keep the customer database—especially the transaction data—current by means of continuous database maintenance.

ASSUMPTIONS:

Recency of Transaction:	20 Points If within Past 3 Months 10 Points If within Past 6 Months 5 Points If within Past 9 Months 3 Points If within Past 12 Months 1 Point If within Past 24 Months
Frequency of Transaction:	Number of Purchases within 24 Months Times 4 Points Each (Maximum: 20 Points)
Monetary Value of Transaction:	Gross Dollar Volume of Purchases within 24 Months Times 10% (Maximum: 20 Points)
Weighting Assumption:	Recency = 5 Frequency = 3 Monetary = 2

EXAMPLE:

Cust.	Purchase #	Recency	Assigned Points	(x5) Wght. Points	Frequency	Assigned Points	(x3) Wght. Points	Monetary	Assigned Points	(x2) Wght. Points	Total Wght. Points	Cum. Points
A	#1	3 Mths.	20	100	1	4	12	$ 30	3	6	118	118
A	#2	9 Mths.	5	25	1	4	12	$100	10	20	57	175
A	#3	24 Mths.	1	5	1	4	12	$ 50	5	10	27	202
B	#1	12 Mths.	3	15	2	8	24	$500	20	40	79	79
C	#1	3 Mths.	20	100	1	4	12	$100	10	20	132	132
C	#2	6 Mths.	10	50	1	4	12	$ 60	6	12	74	206
C	#3	12 Mths.	3	15	2	8	24	$ 70	7	14	53	259
C	#4	24 Mths.	1	5	1	4	12	$ 20	2	4	21	280

FIGURE 2-5   R/F/M Values.

DATABASE MAINTENANCE

A database is a perishable commodity that needs constant oversight and maintenance. Direct marketers must establish maintenance schedules and adhere to them rigorously. An initial requirement for proper list maintenance is that the list be compiled and developed in a uniform manner. Only when such uniformity exists within a computerized list is it possible to use match codes with any assurance of control.

Database maintenance activities include identifying and eliminating any duplicate records, identifying consumer names that appear on a number of different direct marketing response lists, and keeping the customer records current. Let's look more closely at each of these activities.

Match Codes and Merge-Purge

A serious and often cumbersome problem in compiling and maintaining lists is the potential for duplicating the same individual or organization, not only within house lists but also within and between response and compiled lists and even between these lists and house lists. Given that most lists are computerized, marketers can extract from a name/address record abbreviated information about this record. This abbreviation is called a **match code,** and it is constructed so that each individual record can be matched with each other record. Because such matching requires a tremendous amount of computer memory, the match code is abbreviated to minimize the need for such storage. The match code abbreviation should be designed so that it addresses each area where errors are likely to occur within key parts of a record, such as transposition within a street address number as shown in the example here.

Ann Stafford 9330 West Arlington Road Alexandria, VA 22301	Ann Stafford 3930 West Arlington Road Alexandria, VA 22301

Position	Item	Description
1	State	A unique alpha-numeric code assigned to each state
2-5	ZIP code	Last 4 numbers of 5-digit ZIP code
6-8	Surname	1st, 3rd, and 4th alpha characters of surname or business name
9-12	Address	House or business number
13-15	Address	1st, 3rd, and 4th alpha characters of street name
16	Surname	Alpha-numeric count of characters in surname
17	Given name	Alpha initial of first name
18	Given name	Alpha-numeric count of characters in first name

EXAMPLE ADDRESS

Ann Stafford
9330 West Arlington Rd
Alexandria, VA 22301

DERIVED MATCH CODE

8 2 3 0 1 S A F 9 3 3 0 A L I 8 A 3
1 2 3 4 5 6 7 8 9 10 11 12 13 14 15 16 17 18

FIGURE 2-6   Match Codes.

An example of a simple 18-digit match code derived from the name/address is shown in Figure 2-6. Quite often, direct marketers add other data to the match code, such as a unique identification number or an expiration date for a magazine subscription. Mailing labels for catalogs or periodicals often demonstrate match codes of this type. An example is the ten-digit customer number used by the Newport News catalog of Spiegel Brands. This unique customer number reveals information about the particular market segment to which each customer belongs, their credit card status, whether they are a member of the Newport News Discount Club, and more.

An alternative to match codes is a unique identification number, such as a Social Security number, which identifies only one individual, but the customer or prospect has to provide this number for the marketer to be able to use it. Today, many consumers are not willing to provide their Social Security numbers due to privacy protection considerations.

Using the abbreviated match codes, the computerized **merge-purge process** identifies and deletes duplicate names/addresses *within* house lists. It can also eliminate names on house lists from outside response or compiled lists the marketer is using for new customer solicitation. Thus, the organization's own house list will not be duplicated within that promotion effort to prospects. The merge-purge process can eliminate duplication between these outside response and compiled lists as well.

Merge-purge is a highly sophisticated and complex process, but essentially it generates a match code for each name/address on each list, and these match codes, potentially many million of them at a time, are matched with every other name on the list in sequence. Duplications are identified for special handling (which we discuss later).

It is doubtful that a "perfect" match code could be developed, one that would compensate for *all* the idiosyncrasies and potential errors inherent in a name/address record. However, the one shown in Figure 2-6 has a pretty good track record. As demonstrated in the direct mail example shown in Figure 2-7, even a 5 percent "hit" rate, eliminating the need to mail 5 percent duplications, can result in substantial savings. This is especially true when several million name/address records

% DUPLICATION (OR MULTI-BUYERS)	TOTAL NUMBER OF NAMES/ADDRESSES MERGED					
	100,000	500,000	1,000,000	2,500,000	5,000,000	10,000,000
5%	$1,000	$ 5,000	$10,000	$ 25,000	$ 50,000	$100,000
10%	$2,000	$10,000	$20,000	$ 50,000	$100,000	$200,000
15%	$3,000	$15,000	$30,000	$ 75,000	$150,000	$300,000
20%	$4,000	$20,000	$40,000	$100,000	$200,000	$400,000
25%	$5,000	$25,000	$50,000	$125,000	$250,000	$500,000
30%	$6,000	$30,000	$60,000	$150,000	$300,000	$600,000

Assumption: Mailing cost is $200 per thousand names mailed (or not mailed).

FIGURE 2-7   Economic Value of Merge-Purge.

are merged and purged. With reference to Figure 2-7, identifying a duplication of 15 percent of the names, when one million names on various lists are merged and purged, would eliminate 150,000 pieces of unnecessary mail. At an assumed cost of $200 per thousand names mailed, this would result in a savings of $30,000. Against this savings, of course, would be the cost of the merge-purge itself, possibly as much as $10 per thousand names examined or $10,000 for a one million name/address input.

The merge-purge process can also effectively remove names of individuals who have expressed a desire not to receive solicitation as well as those who are poor credit risks or otherwise undesirable customers. Figure 2-8, adapted from an actual merge-purge procedure, displays the manner of showing duplicate names/addresses on two or more lists. Both name and address variations are shown.

Name	Address	City	State	Zip
Samantha Fox	12353 N. Oak Drive	Arlington	VA	22301
Samantha Fox	12353 N. Oak Drive	Arlington	VA	22301
Christina Smith	250 Elders Drive	Arlington	VA	22301
C Smith	250 Elders Drive	Arlington	VA	22301
Jerry Matthis	9372 Nasaw St	Arlington	VA	22301
Jerry Matthis	9372 Nasaw St	Arlington	VA	22301
Dale Armstrong	700 Mosac Ln	Arlington	VA	22301
Nancy Armstrong	700 Mosac Ln	Arlington	VA	22301
Steven Samson	3662 S 11th St	Arlington	VA	22301
Steve Samson	3662 S 11th St	Arlington	VA	22301
Regina Jones	251 12th Ave	Arlington	VA	22301
Regina Jones	252 12th Ave	Arlington	VA	22301
Elaine Lowell	261 N Second St	Arlington	VA	22301
Claire Lowell	261 N 2nd St	Arlington	VA	22301
Carson Snyder	690 42nd St	Arlington	VA	22301
Carson Snyder	690 42nd St	Arlington	VA	22301
Catherine Marlin	Apt 963 561 N 5th St	Arlington	VA	22301
Catherine Marlin	561 N 5th St	Arlington	VA	22301
Elizabeth Parks	68 Waverly Lane	Arlington	VA	22301
Elizabeth Parks	68 Waverly Ln	Arlington	VA	22301
Elizabeth Parks	68 Waverly Ln N	Arlington	VA	22301
Elizabeth Parks	68 Waverly Ln N	Arlington	VA	22301

FIGURE 2-8   Duplicate Records.

Multibuyers

Eliminating duplicate names/addresses, saving costs, and minimizing irritation to those receiving duplicate mailings all are obvious advantages of the merge-purge process. But there is another, possibly even greater advantage. If the same name/address is found on two or more response lists simultaneously, that individual may be a better prospect for a direct marketing offer because he or she is a **multibuyer.** Experimentation has shown, in fact, that those whose names appear on three lists have a higher response rate than those appearing on two lists. Likewise, names appearing on four lists are even more responsive.

In addition to identifying multibuyers, direct marketers perform database maintenance activities to keep their customer records current and accurate. These activities are discussed in the next section.

Keeping Records Current

If incorrect addresses or phone numbers result in misdirected advertising promotions, the cost is twofold: (1) the wasted contact, and (2) the sacrifice of potential response. That is what is at stake if the direct marketer does not keep his or her records current. In an effort to keep customer records current and accurate, direct marketers regularly perform change of address investigations, nixie removal, and record status updates. Let's examine each of these activities in greater detail.

Whenever possible, direct marketers request address corrections through the postal service. The U.S. Postal Service assures that mail prepaid with first-class postage is automatically returned if undeliverable or else forwarded without charge if the new address is known. In the latter instance, for a fee, the change of address notification can be sent back to the direct marketer. In the case of advertising mail, the use of the "address correction requested" legend on the mailing envelope guarantees prepayment of any return postage and service fees. There are many variations of this particular list correction service relative to either individual mail or catalog mail, concerning forwarding or return postage guarantees.

Additionally, direct marketers encourage the recipient of mail to inform them of any change of address or phone number. If available, customers are encouraged to reference a unique account code when requesting changes. If the account number is unavailable, customers are asked to provide both the old and new address—the former for entering into the system and removing the old record, and the latter for future addressing.

Using the "address correction requested" service on each and every customer mailing is not necessary; once or twice a year should suffice to clean the database. Using the legend more frequently, because of lags in handling times, could result in duplication of returned mail and unnecessary duplication of costs. The term **nixie** refers to mail that has been returned by the U.S. Postal Service because it is undeliverable as addressed, often due to a simple error in the street address or the ZIP code. Possibly, the person to whom the piece is addressed is deceased or has moved and left no forwarding address. The marketer will remove such names from the mailing list; unless the list owner can obtain updated information, they cannot be reinstated. Approximately 20 percent of U.S. households change addresses each year. Perhaps this is why e-mail addresses are quickly becoming the preferred address—because they do not necessarily change each time the person moves to a new geographical location. However, some Internet service providers are local, and if you move to a new location, you have to change your e-mail address. Also, keep in mind that a lot of consumers switch Internet providers due to personal preferences, and many more prefer to change their screen names.

Changes in telephone numbers should be made periodically to house lists that are accessed by telephone. Customers who have changed to unlisted numbers should be contacted by mail or an effort should be made to obtain these numbers.

The U.S. Postal Service, for a nominal handling fee, will provide direct marketers with correct address information, if available. Often, however, mail addressed to a deceased person will go to the surviving spouse. Business mail to an individual who has changed positions or even left an organization will go to the replacement in that position. Although the U.S. Postal Service will not send notifications in such instances, some direct marketers correct their lists in other ways. Special notices might periodically be sent with mailings requesting list correction. Additionally, sales representatives may request consumer information changes each time he or she calls on a customer. In some cases, the mail recipient sends such notice directly. Other ways list owners can update their lists include news items, periodic updates from telephone and other directories, and public records such as birth and death notices and marriage and divorce proceedings.

It is important to perform database maintenance not only from the perspective of nixie and otherwise undeliverable mail but also to keep the record status of customers up to date. List owners should enter new orders from customers into the database promptly because they have a major impact on the R/F/M formulation described earlier. Such prompt record keeping also avoids unnecessary mailings, telephone calls, or e-mails to customers who already have what the direct marketer is offering.

DATABASE SECURITY

Customer databases are assets, much the same as buildings, equipment, and inventories. Because their value is intangible, however, databases are not easily insurable (except for replacement or duplication costs) even if we can determine their future value. Unlike other assets, they're portable, especially when an entire database can be placed on a single computer disk.

For these reasons, marketers must take special precautions to prevent theft, loss, or unauthorized use of the database and to guarantee the information privacy rights of all consumers.

Information Privacy

As we address in greater detail later in Chapter 11, organizations that maintain a customer database also have a responsibility to safeguard the personal information contained in it. Direct marketers must use the information only in a highly ethical manner and honor any consumer requests to have their personal information kept confidential—which means not sharing it with other direct marketers. For example, the authors of this book asked numerous organizations for permission to reprint their marketing materials. Many agreed. Some refused. One organization, the Christian Foundation for Children and Aging (CFCA), was not able to grant the request to reprint a letter written from one of their volunteers to one of the authors, a sponsor of the CFCA. Their reason: the fact that the organization wanted to protect the privacy of the volunteer, the sponsored child, and the donor. Although you won't be viewing the CFCA volunteer letter when you read about how nonprofit organizations use direct marketing later in this text, you may be able to better appreciate the actions of many organizations to safeguard information privacy. Therefore, regular database maintenance should include activities to protect the information privacy rights of consumers, as well as to ensure that the information in each database record is accurate and kept up to date.

Proper Database Storage

A logical first step in database security is the provision of adequate storage. Usually, such storage protects against natural hazards of fire and water damage, as well as theft or unauthorized use. To discourage theft, marketers should limit and control access to database files at all times. This often involves certain passwords used to protect the database and permit only select individuals access to the information stored in the database. Should records become lost, adequate backup should be available in the form of duplicate records at a remote location.

List Seeding

Direct marketers have developed a variety of marking techniques to ensure that their customer lists are not misappropriated or misused, especially when rented to outside parties. One commonly used technique is called salting or seeding a list. **Seeding (salting)** a list is when the direct marketer places decoys, which are either incorrect spellings or fictitious names that appear nowhere else, on the customer list so as to track and identify any misuse. Although a seeded list may reveal such misuse, it may not lead to the guilty person. Marketers should construct identification programs like seeding so that the decoy names will not be removed through match coding. Of course the decoy names should be confidential and access to them limited.

Direct marketers discourage list theft by placing seeds on lists. Direct marketers must communicate their use of list seeds to all parties involved in the list industry. By fully disclosing the actions to protect their lists, direct marketers may discourage list theft.

DATABASE USES AND APPLICATIONS

Once we have captured and stored data, we can convert it into real information to better serve customers and maximize profitability. The uses of a customer database are virtually endless; we discuss some of the more common ones in this chapter. Keep in mind that the real beauty of a customer database is that it enables direct marketers to communicate with small market segments or individual customers without other customers knowing. This kind of communication secrecy, also called **stealth communications,** enables direct marketers to extend different types of offers to individual customers on the basis of their customer information. For example, Harris Teeter, a regional grocery store, sends elaborate gifts on a regular basis to its *very best* customers. These customers also receive a $10 Harris Teeter gift card at Thanksgiving along with a personally signed thank-you letter from the store manager. Gifts of lesser value and thank-you letters not containing the gift card may be sent to those regular customers who are not as *valuable* to Harris Teeter, based on the amount spent. Furthermore, Harris Teeter may send other direct mail letters containing coupons encouraging other customers (those even less valuable) to shop more often at Harris Teeter. This kind of one-on-one communication is made possible by analyzing the source data contained in a customer database. This is critical to successful direct marketing because building customer relationships is most effectively carried out on a one-to-one basis. The ability to know one's customers and communicate with them individually is the basic premise of a customer database for direct marketers.

Using a Customer Database

Though there are a million ways to use a database, let's explore eight of the more common uses.

1. *Profile customers.* By developing a geographic, demographic, social, psychological, and behavioral profile of their customers, direct marketers can better understand the various consumer market segments they serve. For example, Carnival Cruise Lines's passenger database of more than two million households includes information on prior travel habits.[6] Carnival collects information regarding passenger anniversaries and birthdays, what cruises passengers took, what they paid, their sailing date, how many people traveled in their party, and whether they traveled with children. This information enables the company to better understand the needs of their typical customers.

2. *Retain the best customers.* According to the well-known 80/20 principle, approximately 80 percent of an organization's business is generated by 20 percent of its customers. Thus, it is critical that direct marketers analyze their customer database to determine who their best customers are and to spend more effort (and promotional dollars) in keeping these customers satisfied and coming back for more! Just think of the Harris Teeter example. Harris Teeter can afford to spend more money in terms of promotional dollars to keep those customers who spend more money in groceries satisfied and coming back on a regular basis. Harris Teeter cannot justify sending its occasional shoppers gifts and personally signed thank-you notes from the store manager.

3. *Thank customers for their patronage.* All customers deserve to be recognized and thanked for their decision to purchase from a given organization. This is especially true when the direct marketer has a number of competitors from whom the customer could have purchased. Customers expect to be satisfied with their purchase decisions; however, follow-up activities can often provide an avenue for future dialogue with each customer to ensure that satisfaction. Thanking customers is also an effective way to both reinforce purchase decisions and promote future purchases. An example is the thank-you letters containing bumper stickers that are mailed to individuals who make donations to the various state and local police associations. Donors take pride in displaying those bumper stickers, which state, "I Am a Proud Supporter of the Virginia State Police."

4. *Capitalize on cross-selling and continuity selling opportunities.* **Cross-selling** refers to selling your current customers products and services that are related (and even unrelated) to the products/services they currently purchase from your organization. By analyzing the products and services your customers have purchased from you, you can identify and capitalize on numerous cross-selling opportunities. **Continuity selling** has also been referred to as "club offers"; here consumers purchase on a regular basis—either weekly, monthly, quarterly, or annually. *Time* magazine, for example, cross-sells its other publications—*People, Sports Illustrated, Fortune*—to certain current subscribers.

5. *Develop a customer communication program.* As mentioned earlier, the real beauty and power of a customer database is that it enables the direct marketer to communicate on a one-to-one basis with each customer. Thus, the company can segment its promotional strategies based on the customer group and individual with whom it is communicating. For example, newer customers could receive "welcome" letters, while established customers might receive "thank you for your loyalty" letters. Of course, each customer does not know what is being communicated to other customers. Unlike general advertising, a customer database also enables customized marketing communications to occur between the company and its customers without the competition knowing. This is another powerful use of the customer database. As Figure 2-9 reveals, customer communication plans or programs are targeted, tailored, and timed communications with select members or segments of the customer population. These are planned communications and most models depict a 12-month communication program.

In addition, a direct marketer can afford to spend more promotional dollars to communicate with regular customers who generate a substantial amount of business for the organization, spending less on new customers who may or may not purchase from the organization a second time. Therefore, a firm may distribute an annual newsletter to some customers, while communicating on a quarterly or monthly basis with others with whom it has a stronger relationship.

Finally, a customer communication program implies two-way communication. Direct marketers use customer feedback to revise and improve their marketing activities to better serve the customer and maximize profitability. Examples of customer communication programs are numerous.

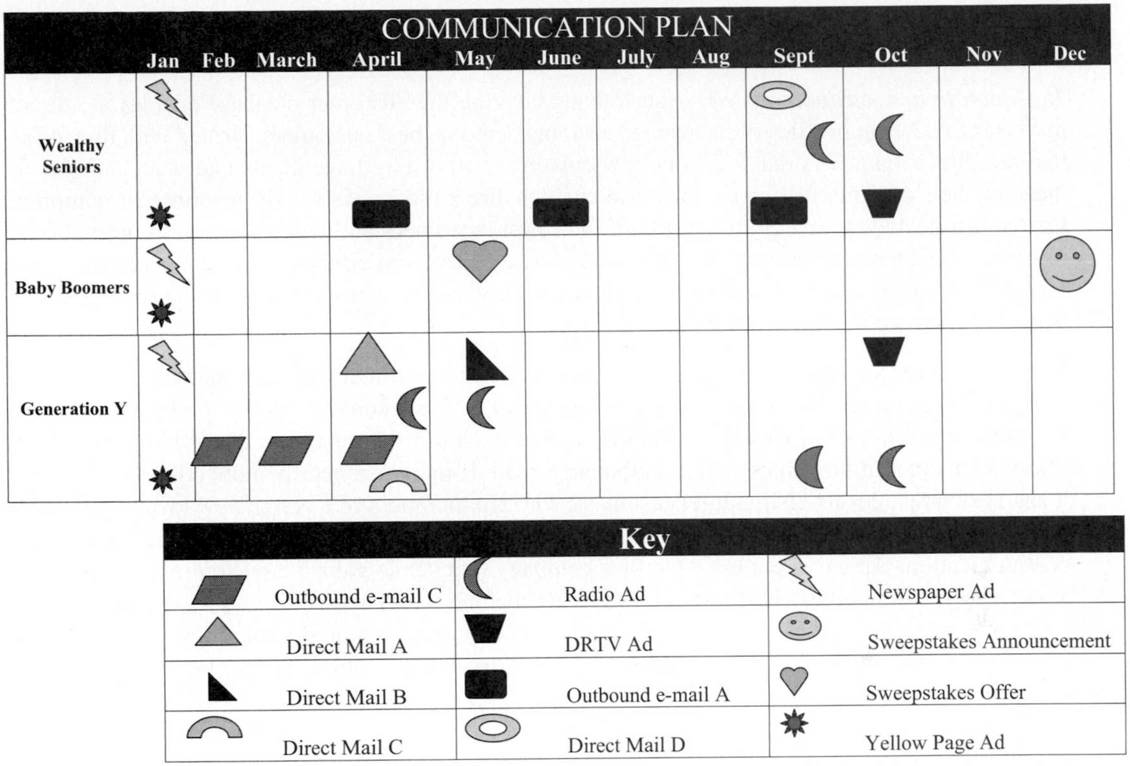

FIGURE 2-9   Communications Plan.

Hotels, airlines, grocery stores, nonprofit organizations, magazines, and just about every direct marketer creates and uses one to guide its customer and prospect communications. If you purchase a new car, chances are likely that you will receive a variety of follow-up communications from the automobile manufacturer. Say you purchased a Honda Prelude. The first message you receive should be a "thank you" for your purchase. Next might be a mini-survey to assess the quality of your Honda shopping experience. After that, you might receive a number of updates about what is new at Honda and regular reminder notices about when you should bring your Prelude back to the dealer for servicing. Of course, at some point in time, Honda will suggest that it is time to trade your Prelude in for a new one!

6. *Perform marketing research.* The database is a natural arena for direct marketers to conduct marketing research to better understand the current and future needs and wants of their customers. Marketing research gathers, classifies, and analyzes information about customers. This information is normally "problem-specific" or "purpose-specific." For example, if the direct marketer is thinking of bringing a new product or service to the market, investigating the potential response from current customers is a natural application of marketing research. Marketing research activities can include customer satisfaction surveys, new product research, customer needs assessments, brand preference studies, media preference research, and much more.

     An example is Carnival Cruise Lines periodically sending surveys to its past-guest database. The company uses the surveys to update information about passengers' current cruise interests, what they'd like to see in new itineraries and new products, their cruise planning lead times, and general travel and vacationing patterns. The marketing research results are used to update their services and send special offers and targeted mailings to prospective passengers.[7]

7. *Generate new customers.* We've seen that analyzing the customer database enables the direct marketer to develop profiles of its average customers and its best customers. Armed with this information, direct marketers can seek out new customers who may have needs and wants similar to those of their current customers. This also enables direct marketers to rent response or compiled lists of prospects who match the profile of their best customers and target them with promotional offers to attract new customers. This is a much more effective and efficient way to generate new customers than merely blanketing the mass audience with advertisements in the hope that someone with a need or want for the product/service will respond.

8. *Send customized offers.* We've seen that analyzing the customer database enables a direct marketer to develop a profile of consumer needs and wants. It also enables direct marketers to create customized offers to individuals or market segments within the customer database. Customized offers often are sent via direct mail or outbound e-mail. E-mail is generally more cost effective, and it enables companies to easily target customers who are members of a company's loyalty program. Of course, all companies provide the opportunity for customers to opt out of receiving such e-mail communication. An excellent example of a company that sends valuable customized offers to its loyalty program members is Barnes & Noble. Its members receive weekly communication about new book titles and special offers for extra discounts on these featured book titles. Various offers encourage the sale of DVDs or used books, and sometimes these offers are limited to online shopping. As Figure 2-10 shows, occasionally members receive free gift offers, like a free book light, when they spend a specified amount or special limited time offers to obtain an extra discount on their in-store or online purchases. These are examples of how a company communicates regularly with its customers by sending customized offers. Keep in mind that the more data a direct marketer has about its customers, the more specific and customized the offers can be. For that reason, most direct marketers regularly update customer records and, whenever possible, incorporate new information to their customer records. This process is called *database enhancement,* and it is discussed later in this chapter. However, every direct marketer will regularly analyze the data contained in its customer database to learn more about its customers to more effectively serve them. This process is called *database analytics,* and it is the key to effectively using a customer database for all purposes. Let's discuss database analytics in greater detail.

Performing Database Analytics

Database analytics is where the direct marketer analyzes customer information housed within the customer database to draw inferences about an individual customer's needs. This relies on customer profiling, modeling, and data mining. **Data mining** uses statistical and mathematical techniques to extract knowledge from data contained within a database. It is the process of using software tools to find relevant information from large amounts of data, typically an enterprise data warehouse, and using the results for strategic business decision making.

A variety of database tools permit assessment of single-variable information. However, the multivariable patterns can allow assessment of causes and effects in the business process. The true value of the integrated data warehouse can be found by leveraging decision support tools, such as online analytical processing (OLAP) to mine the data for hidden patterns. OLAP has long been the domain of business analysts and statisticians. Today, sophisticated new tools enable business analysis capabilities via the data warehouse throughout the entire organization. Previous tools provided

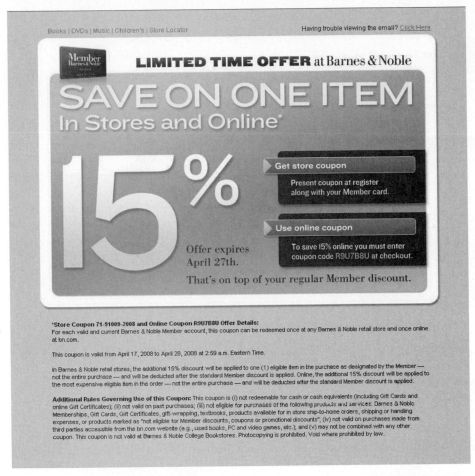

FIGURE 2-10   Barnes & Noble Offers.   *Source:* Used with permission of Barnes & Noble Inc.

only static reports, offering little flexibility in terms of what a user could glean or screen from the warehouse. With OLAP, users can slice and dice the data from a summary level down into the detail of the data record. Marketers can obtain information on customers by region or by revenue and do it all from their desktop. An example might be a direct mail transaction database in which responders are evaluated by different demographic characteristics. The analysis could allow the marketing team to select specific prospects from large compiled files that fit common customer profiles.

Let's take a look at another example. Teradata, a division of NCR, analyzed the sales data of a well-known retailer and found some interesting correlations. Based on the analysis, Teradata found a direct relationship between the purchases of beer and diapers in the evening hours.[8] On investigation, the retailer found that this was occurring because husbands were being sent out on Saturday night to buy diapers and subsequently purchased beer as an impulse item. Thus, retailers and merchandisers wanting to predict and model future consumer behavior use information like the beer and diapers relationship in their attempts to maximize the effectiveness of their marketing efforts. This example points to the fact that data analytics are only valuable if the new knowledge gained enables the users of the information to make *actionable decisions*. Yes, beer and diapers

FIGURE 2-10   (continued)

were found to be positively correlated, but most retailers would not rearrange their stores to stock these items side by side.

The secret to database analytics is for marketers to be able to identify their most and least valuable customers and clarify demographic and behavioral statistics that apply to each population. Then they must be able to clearly identify the differences between the two groups. Marketers use data analytics to make strategic business decisions to retain current customers and attract new ones. Think of it this way: if you can clearly identify specific differences between your "best" or most valuable customer and your least valuable customer, then you will know how to "mine" the most likely best customers from prospect lists and databases. Although this seems like common sense, many businesses do not take the time to analyze, evaluate, and act on this critical knowledge.

The drivers to using analytical data revolve around cost, value, and accuracy: cost of the analysis, long-term value (or lifetime value) of a current or prospective customer, and accuracy of the data to be used in strategic decision making. There is a plethora of data available to marketers, at a wide range of costs and detail. The key is in obtaining the most current, relevant, and accurate data to add to your existing customer database. The process of adding data to a customer database is the topic of the next section.

DATABASE ENHANCEMENT

Database enhancement is adding and overlaying information to customer records to better describe and understand the customer. Direct marketers also call it "appending" the database. It is a means to an end, not an end in and of itself. There are at least three specific reasons to enhance a customer database:

1. To learn more about the customer
2. To increase the effectiveness of future promotional activities targeted to current customers
3. To better prospect for new customers who are similar to current customers.

The kinds of information that enhance a database in this way include geographic, demographic, social, and psychological data. We can obtain the data either *internally* or *externally*.

Internal Data Enhancement

Direct marketers can obtain information *internally* when they conduct marketing research activities with their existing customers. Of course, each customer must be willing to furnish the given data. Examples of information that direct marketers, such as Carnival Cruise Lines, Gateway Computers, or Hallmark Cards, can collect internally from their customers include

- Age
- Gender
- Income
- Marital status
- Family composition
- Street address
- E-mail address
- Length of time at current residence
- Size of household
- Type of housing
- Telephone number
- Do not mail (preference)
- Lifestyle data

Direct marketers cannot gather all enhancement data internally; therefore, they must rely on some external sources as well. For example, when applying for a JC Penney credit card, the company must obtain some historical information about your credit rating prior to approving your application and establishing the limit of your line of credit.

External Data Enhancement

Direct marketers purchase external data from many different sources. They purchase data compiled by companies like Experian, Equifax, R. L. Polk, and Claritas and electronically overlay this information to their customer database. It is usually demographic, although some companies compile consumer lifestyle and leisure activity data. Claritas offers several products designed to assist direct marketers with customer database enhancement. Claritas MarketPlace File Enhancement helps direct marketers gain a better understanding of their customers and prospects. The behavioral profiles associated with this enhancement service include a variety of consumer buying behaviors, either from syndicated data or Claritas's own audits. Customer addresses can be standardized, geocoded, and appended with segmentation information in a matter of minutes. Claritas ConsumerPoint, customer targeting and strategic market planning software, connects a direct marketer's customer file with market data to expose hidden gaps in existing and untapped markets. ConsumerPoint's Internet-based data access provides insights into the most up-to-date segment distribution, behavioral profiles, and demographic/consumer demand data for targeting profitable customers and strategic market planning.

Examples of the data that direct marketers may obtain to enhance their customer database externally include

- Geographic address
- Telephone number
- Gender of head of household
- Length of time of residence
- Number of adults at residence
- Number of children at residence
- Income
- Occupation
- Marital status
- Make of automobiles owned

Companies like Equifax, Experian, R. L. Polk, and Claritas purchase census data from the government, sometimes for small geographic areas known as census tracts; direct marketers can purchase the data from these intermediary firms for a fee. Census data can help identify

- Specific age segments (i.e., adults aged 18 to 24)
- One-person households
- Households with children
- Households with specified income levels
- Households with homes greater than specified values
- Adults with some college education
- Adults in college
- Adults with specified occupations

Finally, firms can purchase external data about businesses, rather than final consumers. Companies such as Dun & Bradstreet and Experian collect data on businesses and make it available to direct marketers for a fee. Such data can include

- Company name/address/telephone number
- Industrial classification code

- Number of employees
- Gross sales
- Primary products produced
- Branch locations
- Name/title of key employees

In summary, direct marketers enhance their customer database in an effort to better serve the future needs and wants of their customers. This should result in a stronger relationship with each customer. While each customer is valuable to the direct marketer, all customers are not of equal value. Let's examine how direct marketers manage relationships with their customers.

CUSTOMER RELATIONSHIP MANAGEMENT

Customer relationship management (CRM) is a business strategy designed to identify and maximize customer value. This strategy requires a customer-centric business philosophy and culture to support effective marketing services processes. CRM is a collection of software tools that allows companies to understand customer needs and manage communications or service inquiries around all touch points for each media channel the company uses. Though there is no single definition of this important strategy, direct marketing experts Bob Stone and Ron Jacobs have defined it as "a business strategy that maximizes profitability, revenue and customer satisfaction by organizing around customer segments, fostering behavior that satisfies customers, and implementing customer-centric processes."[9] It is about developing and implementing business strategies and supporting technologies that close the gaps between an organization's current and potential performance in customer acquisition, growth, and retention.

CRM at its most granular level identifies the touch points between the business (company) and its customers and prospective customers. Once those touch points have been identified, the company can then target those points that allow it to optimize both the customer's experience and maximize (or increase) the value of the experience. For example, touch points can include something as simple as a customer query, by phone, on the Web, in person, or by mail. Or it may be as complicated as an order on the Web or by phone that is tied to inventory availability, shipping times, alternate choice products of a similar nature, and so on.

CRM provides a variety of sales, marketing, and service functions that allow interaction with prospects or customers across the organization and multiple media channels. The main benefit is that all information, from prospect communication to sales close to service history, are tracked and used for management of treatment for that customer and future prospects based on patterns that emerge with analytics.

Analytical CRM is a relatively new phenomenon that is designed to optimize marketing and sales effectiveness. Most CRM solutions have had gaps in this area, but many analytic providers, including RUF Strategic Solutions, have built modules that are CRM platform-independent and allow measured "what if" analyses of transaction history, acquisition scores, cross-selling scores, and loyalty. The end result is to allow strategic decisions to guide more predictive results that optimize the return on marketing or sales dollars spent. The goal of CRM is to allow the entire organization to be cohesive in how it communicates with each customer and manage that customer experience as if it has distinct knowledge of needs and prior support issues. This is a "closed-loop" process, as shown in Figure 2-11. To be effective with CRM strategies, companies must carry out the process of planning, researching, testing, and validating.

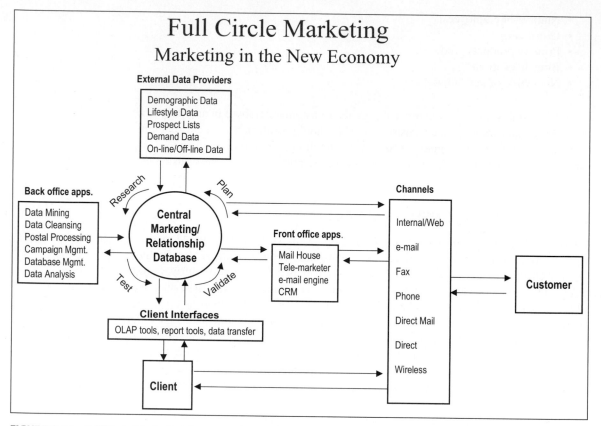

FIGURE 2-11   Full-Circle Marketing Process.   *Source:* Used with permission of RUF™ Strategies Solutions.

CRM has been evolving over the years and, with proper assessment of the organization process and readiness to adapt to a data and customer-centric strategy, can lead to significant business competitive advantage.

It's amazing when you consider that most residential and business consumers take the underpinnings of a highly sophisticated CRM system or platform for granted. Such systems include everything from point of contact to "is it available?" and "when will I receive it?" to a problem or complaint. By focusing on CRM at the initial point of contact, the company has a far better chance of nurturing a long-term relationship that generates satisfaction for the customer and revenue or value for the company. Understanding customer value is a necessary element in the development of effective marketing strategies.

Customer Value

All customers are not of equal value to a company or organization. We can categorize customers according to the strength of their relationship to our company or organization. As Figure 2-12 reveals, customers can be placed in a hierarchy with the least valuable at the bottom and the most valuable at the top. *Suspects* are those prospective consumers that you think may have a need or want for your company's product or service. *Prospects* are qualified "hand-raisers" who have identified themselves as having an interest in your company or organization. Prospects may have visited your Web site or dialed your toll-free number. Your *customers* have placed an order with your company. They could be

FIGURE 2-12 Customer Hierarchy.

called "single buyers" as you do not know if they will return for a repeat purchase. *Clients* are multi-buyers. These are repeat customers with whom you have an established relationship. At the top of the customer hierarchy are your *advocates*. These customers are your most valuable customers. They generate the most revenue for your company.

In direct marketing, the emphasis is on discerning between one-time buyers versus multi-buyers. A customer who has purchased twice is a proven repeat buyer and is far more likely to purchase again than a one-timer. Thus, marketing strategies are tailored to convert one-time buyers into multibuyers and expend fewer resources on them as they age, relative to multibuyers. Additionally, for companies that are multichannel (direct mail, Web, retail), those customers who purchase from more than one channel tend to be more valuable in the long run than those who purchase from a single channel. This has to be carefully evaluated to factor out the fact that a multichannel buyer is, ipso facto, a multibuyer. Thus, companies must determine what, if any, additional value for being a multichannel buyer comes above the multibuyer status.

Marketers must keep in mind that customers who buy once and never buy again have a one-time value. Prospective customers who never make a purchase usually cost the company in unrequited advertising and possibly service dollars. However, customers who buy frequently have a maximized or enhanced value to the company. Why? It's simple. As we mentioned earlier in this chapter, a company's best customers are loyal to the company, require less customer service and assistance, spend more per transaction, and generate valuable referrals. This combination adds up to greater value for the company. That is precisely why most companies have a customer-centric focus.

Therefore, a company's CRM strategies that focus on customers' wants and needs at the earliest possible touch point and make their experience long lasting and sustainable, prove their worth in value. As with all direct and interactive marketing, what is measurable is what translates into knowing what defines value. Although all facets of measurability are important to the direct model, a company that knows the economic worth or value of its customers is the most defining. The value of customers over their lifetime allows a company to claim these customers as assets on its balance sheet. Hence, the importance of LTV.

Lifetime Customer Value

The **lifetime value of a customer (LTV)** can be calculated as the discounted stream of net revenues that a customer will generate over the period of his or her lifetime of patronage with a company.[10] The information for calculating LTV is derived from transactions recorded in an organization's database. The term *LTV* is interchangeably called PAR, meaning it is an objective, as in the game of golf.

Whenever we gain or retain a customer as a result of good customer relations, we earn not only the revenue generated in one month or one year but also the *present value* of the *future profits* generated for as long as the customer remains active as a customer.[11] Just think . . . if a business were to be totally consumed in a fire, its tangible assets such as buildings, equipment, and inventory could be rebuilt in time, and each of these tangible assets is likely to be covered by insurance. The business would continue. However, if an organization lost its database of customers, an intangible but very valuable asset, the business likely could not continue. Without customers, there is no business! You might argue, well, the business would simply have to go out and get new customers. That may be true, but it would require much greater effort and cost than most companies could sustain.

Direct marketers spend a major portion of their time, effort, and money developing lists of customers and qualified prospects. In fact, many in direct marketing believe that such lists, along with descriptive databases, are in fact the key ingredients that differentiate *direct* marketing from general marketing. Therefore, direct marketers especially should view their customers as assets, as investments. They are the lifeblood of a direct marketing organization from which future sales accrue at a cost that is generally significantly lower than that attributed to the first sale.

It follows that if a marketing expenditure can result in the acquisition of *new* customers who will generate value over future time, that action is desirable even though the initial cost to obtain those customers might be greater than the short-term return on that investment. Some might call this long-term return on investment, LTV, the cost of goodwill. Savvy direct marketers call it "the value of a customer."

Naturally, when a new customer is acquired, the direct marketer does not know whether that customer will make only a single purchase or become an ongoing customer. The direct marketer cannot determine if that customer will purchase only low-margin products that have limited profitability or purchase without paying attention to price at all. However, direct marketers know that in most cases the cost of acquiring customers will yield a positive return on the investment. In Chapter 13 we explain how to calculate customer LTV and explore the implications of this important metric.

One-on-One Personalized Marketing

Segmentation analysis allows the company or organization to treat the customer with one-to-one personalization and customization. Just as the corner grocer of the past could anticipate his customers' exact needs, current modeled propensities can project likely results from variable treatment of millions of respondents. Everything from the offer, price, and graphic design can be changed, customized, and personalized for a single customer in a nanosecond with information on who is entering your Web site or responding at your fulfillment center. Many travel destinations use response scores to modify the fulfillment kit that will be delivered to the inquirer. For example, a senior with an affinity for art will be sent the museum tour piece, and the middle-aged household with highly active lifestyles will get the adventure kit. This type of customization and personalization is the result of detailed market segmentation made possible by customer and prospect database analysis.

The concept of micro-targeting has become a hot topic in marketing today. According to industry experts Penn, Schoen, and Berland, **micro-targeting** is creating customized winning messages, proof points and offers, accurately predicting their impact, and delivering them directly to individuals.[12] Micro-targeting is one-on-one personalized marketing based on advanced, precise psychographic and lifestyle data. One of the benefits of one-on-one marketing is that you are able to deliver your message to a select customer or prospect (or group of them) without others knowing about it. Earlier in this chapter we presented that concept of stealth marketing communications. This type of communication flies below the radar and can be thought of as the opposite of mass marketing. Micro-targeting abandons the concept of the big idea for an advertising campaign because those ideas included standardized offers and mass media communications. As more companies shift promotional budget allocations to more targeted media, such as e-mail, direct mail, special events, and trade shows, micro-targeting will continue to grow in both usage and applications.

Some key success factors to consider when planning a micro-targeting campaign include:[13]

- Conduct in-depth quantitative research: Quantitative research will serve to identify the right media, offer, and message for your micro-targeting campaign.
- Testing: Test messages, offers, creative design against competitors.
- Align the message: Be certain that the target customer who receives the message has been aligned.
- Don't tell your opponent what you are doing: Micro-targeting campaigns are most effective when nobody knows about them until after the campaign has been implemented.

In summary, as consumers' lives become more fragmented, and their interests become more specialized, micro-targeting and customized communications will continue to be a growing area for marketers.

Partner Relationship Management

Earlier in this chapter we discussed the important concept of CRM. Now we'll discuss **partner relationship management (PRM)**. PRM is where companies work closely with partners in other companies or departments to generate greater value to customers. In today's busy world, companies are networking with other companies and relying on partnerships to more effectively and efficiently serve the needs of their customers. Marketers cultivate relationships with prospective partners just as they cultivate relationships with their customers. According to Randy Jones of MindZoo, "Partner marketing represents one of the most effective ways to increase the visibility and open rate of your direct mail programs while decreasing your promotion costs and improving your return on investment."[14] In Chapter 14 we explore the various partner relationships that are forged between nonprofit organizations and private companies. Often, companies and organizations engage in relationships with multiple partners to support a cause. In this instance, the partners share a common goal or objective in that they want to promote and support a worthy cause. That is why these types of partnership strategies are often called "cause-related marketing." Selecting the right partner is one of the most important decisions in PRM. Critical to a successful PRM program is the identification of a partner or partners who can benefit from reaching your desired target audience.[15] Those PRM programs that are mutually beneficial to all partners will yield great success.

Let's explore an example of a mutually beneficial direct marketing partnership. The *Washington Post* and XM Radio teamed up to acquire new subscribers. As Figure 2-13 presents, these partners executed a direct mail campaign targeting urban young professionals with a contest that enabled responding new *Post* subscribers to automatically be entered to win an XM2go portable receiver and three months of XM Radio service. The *Washington Post* was responsible for this promotion and the majority of associated costs. XM Radio provided, at no charge to the *Washington Post*, products and services for contest winners, plus paid for 25 percent of total program costs. Basically, XM Radio was able to reach the target market for less than the cost of Standard A postage. This shows that partner relationships can provide cost-effective marketing venues.

FIGURE 2-13 *The Washington Post* and XM Radio Young Professionals Partnership.
Source: Used with permission of *The Washington Post* and MindZoo, LLC. Photo by Kim Kirby,
www.jimkirbyphoto.com.

Summary

A customer is the company's most important asset. Customer retention is more beneficial to most companies than is new customer acquisition. A customer database is a tool used to retain customers. It enables a company to establish and strengthen relationships with customers by allowing them to interact with each customer on a personalized basis. The information captured and stored in a database provides the company with knowledge about the particular needs, wants, and interests of each customer. Armed with this knowledge, marketers are better able to develop products and services that will satisfy each customer's needs and wants. In addition, the information housed in the customer database may assist the marketer in more effectively communicating with each customer. The end result is this: a highly satisfied customer, a loyal customer!

Database marketing employs a number of activities designed to acquire, store, and use customer information. Database marketing activities commonly include customer loyalty programs, such as the many airline, hotel, and grocery programs. In addition, direct marketers regularly assess the value of their customers. This may include applying the recency/frequency/monetary assessment and calculating the LTV over a period of time. Of course, direct marketers must keep their customer database current and accurate for it to be of value. Direct marketers perform common database maintenance activities, such as applying match codes and a merge-purge process to identify and delete duplicate customer records, identifying multibuyers, and performing status updates to keep each record current. Direct marketers also carry out a variety of activities designed to safeguard their database against improper use or theft. Some of these activities include salting or seeding their customer lists, applying access passwords, and ensuring information privacy protection for their customers. Each of these database marketing activities is critical in maintaining strong customer relationships, which, in turn, lead to the retention of customers. Database analytics, including data mining, are enabling marketers to better understand their current customers and target key prospects. CRM programs are highly valuable and are growing in popularity.

Key Terms

customer database *29*
customer loyalty programs *30*
source data *31*
transactional data *32*
recency/frequency/monetary
  (R/F/M) *32*
match code *34*
merge-purge process *35*

multibuyer *37*
nixie *37*
seeding *39*
salting *39*
stealth communications *39*
cross-selling *40*
continuity selling *40*
data mining *42*

database enhancement *45*
customer relationship
  management (CRM) *47*
lifetime value of a customer
  (LTV) *50*
micro-targeting *50*
partner relationship management
  (PRM) *51*

Review Questions

1. What is a *customer loyalty program?* Identify three customer loyalty programs with which you are familiar. What are the benefits to each of the organizations sponsoring these loyalty programs?

2. When building a customer database, what must an organization first determine? What must they first identify?

3. What is a *match code?* Explain its importance for database development and maintenance.

4. Describe the activities required to maintain a customer database? How often do you think database maintenance should be performed?

5. What is the purpose of the merge-purge process? How does it work?

6. If incorrect addresses or phone numbers result in misdirected advertising promotions, what is the cost to the organization? How can this be avoided?

7. Explain the value of applying the recency/frequency/monetary assessment to an organization's customer database. Is it possible to determine when an organization should place more weight on one of the three variables over the other? If so, explain why. If not, explain why not.

8. Describe the value of database analytics. Provide examples of what can be learned via data mining.

9. Explain what is meant by the term *lifetime value of a customer.* Why is it important?

10. Imagine that you have recently started a new business venture and that you already have a database of 10,000 customers. You are going to a financial institution to obtain a loan to expand your business. The financial officer asks you, "What is the biggest asset of your business?" How will you respond? Provide support for your answer using the information presented in this chapter.

Exercise

Congratulations! You have just been hired as the marketing director for a local grocery store chain. They have just launched a customer loyalty program, and one of your main responsibilities will be to oversee this program. What strategies and tactics will you employ in promoting the program to entice customers to become members? Also, how do you plan on generating real value for program members? Finally, what source data will you gather, and how do you intend to use the source data contained in the database?

CASE
Smithfield Foods

Overview

As lifestyles change, so do consumer needs and wants. Marketers must be keenly aware of consumers' changing needs and wants and constantly strive to produce products and services that meet their desires. All consumers are not alike—which is why database marketing is so effective. Armed with detailed customer information, marketers are able to profile their customer base, segment their customers, and provide more customer-specific information, products, services, and promotional appeals. Database marketing is highly effective in generating transactions, building customer relationships, and enhancing customer satisfaction. This case examines the uses of database marketing in building customer relationships, with diverse market segments. It demonstrates how various types of information can be collected to profile customers, select the media, and create more effective promotional offers.

Case

Smithfield Foods, headquartered in Smithfield, Virginia, is the largest hog producer and pork processor in the world. This $12+ billion corporation supplies food service customers and retailers and owns some of the most popular retail and food service protein brands in the world. Publicly owned and traded on the New York Stock Exchange under the symbol of SFD, it specializes in the vertical integration, processing, and marketing of pork products. Smithfield Foods is known through the corporate branding activities associated with its Smithfield brand. Smithfield is the only food brand that has been endorsed by the nationally recognized expert cook Paula Deen, who has become the company's spokesperson.

The company operates through subsidiaries in the United States, Poland, France, Romania, and Mexico, which produce value-added fresh pork and processed meats under scores of strong regional brands including Smithfield, John Morrell, Patrick Cudahy, Farmland, Krakus, Armour-Eckrich, and Gwaltney. Each operating company is responsible for aggressively pursuing marketing opportunities for its own products and brands.

Prospective customers of Smithfield Foods include supermarkets, food service operators, or organizational consumers, club/warehouse stores, and final consumers. This case focuses only on the final consumer segment. The typical final consumer target is a woman between 25 and 64 years with a median income level between $60,000 and $70,000. When considering these final consumers, Smithfield pays particular attention to lifestyle changes and the effect those changes have on purchasing behavior. Contrary to past purchasing behavior, today's U.S. families are always on the go, and their cooking habits reflect that. The typical consumer now spends less than 30 minutes preparing and cooking meals. He or she has less time to shop and cook, and families typically have at least two incomes that result in more disposable income to spend on prepared foods. The busy household needs food products that meet consumers' needs. What do these lifestyle changes mean to Smithfield Foods? They mean new business opportunities if the company can continue to bring products to market that meet these needs.

To take advantage of this new business opportunity, the company must know its customer. Smithfield must be aware of purchasing behavior, such as recency, frequency, and the monetary value of customer purchases. This type of data must be gathered, measured, and stored in a database that is capable of qualifying and quantifying the data into useful information. Smithfield Foods is aware of the significance of an effective customer database and the powerful results of going one-on-one with the customer. This type of direct marketing can only be achieved through database management.

**FIGURE 2-14   Smithfield Foods e-Newsletter.   *Source:* Used with permission of Smithfield Foods.

Database marketing clearly identifies known targeted users and prospective users of Smithfield products. It is a tool that is used in conjunction with the overall marketing mix. Smithfield first incorporated database marketing into their company's marketing mix by obtaining customer purchasing data from various supermarket chains and sending these customers specialized and valuable offers to opt in to the company's loyalty program by visiting its Web site. Smithfield worked in cooperation with its retail partners to gather and organize data based on customer purchases. Prospect information is obtained through grocers' incorporation of customer loyalty card programs. Smithfield currently works with many major grocers such as Kroger, Harris Teeter, Food Lion, Giant Landover, Publix, Pathmark, selected Albertson's divisions, Safeway, and many others. These grocery chains organize their data according to customer transactions—the product category and the amount and frequency of purchases. Smithfield evaluates the customer purchase data and searches for buying patterns and behaviors, such as whether they ever purchase, how often they purchase, and what other products besides Smithfield products they purchase. For example, Smithfield closely examines consumer purchases of other competing protein products, such as chicken breasts, as well as related items such as marinades, breads, and salads.

The objectives of the customer loyalty program include increasing product usage with average to frequent Smithfield customers, encouraging repeat purchases by low-frequency buyers, and developing users among nonusers who buy related items. The Smithfield.com Loyalty Program supports the card program with data gathering. Customers visit the site to receive information, coupons, recipes, and special offers, which correspond directly to their needs. This program increases the potential for long-term relationship building, while enabling Smithfield to gather customer-specific information about a person's preferences.

Needless to say, given all of the valuable need-satisfying information and offers Smithfield provides to each customer via its Loyalty Program, the company's customer database has quickly grown. It currently consists of more than 90,000 customer records. These customers now receive regular communication from the company in the form of e-newsletters, recipes, special offers, and seasonal greetings. Figure 2-14 presents a Smithfield e-newsletter that was distributed to its customers during the fall season.

An example of one of Smithfield's special offers is the Consumer Loyalty Program On-Pack/On-Line Sweepstakes—"Trip to Savannah to Meet Paula Sweepstakes." This special sweepstakes offer is promoted to members of the company's Loyalty Card Program. The sweepstakes winner will receive an all-inclusive trip for four to meet famous celebrity cook Paula Deen. As shown in Figure 2-15, every customer will be asked to enter (online) the unique code printed on the sticker found on specially marked packages of Smithfield Bacon, Reclosable Tub Lunchmeat, and Marinated Pork. In addition to the grand prize, 460 winners (5 selected daily throughout the duration of the contest) will receive their choice of either a Paula Deen Collection Gift Basket or a Smithfield Gift Book full of Paula's favorite recipes and $40 worth of free Smithfield products. This is a valuable and unique sweepstakes offer combining product purchase with online visitation.

Of course, as shown in Figure 2-16, Smithfield Foods's Web site features a sweepstakes link along with many other valuable tips and suggestions, such as new recipes, meal planning ideas, tips for entertaining, gifts for graduates, what to look for when purchasing a grill, and more!

Smithfield Foods has successfully integrated database marketing into its overall marketing mix. The objectives of its customer database are to identify prospects, decide which consumer receives which offer, deepen customer loyalty, and reactivate consumer purchases. Smithfield has had and will continue to have tremendous success with their database marketing programs. For example, the following response rates are a result of a typical mass-market consumer incentive program: 1 to 2 percent for Sunday consumer coupons and 1.5 percent for Wednesday through

FIGURE 2-15   Smithfield Foods Online Sweepstakes.   *Source:* Used with permission of Smithfield Foods.

**FIGURE 2-16
Smithfield Foods
Web Site.**
Source: Used with
permission of
Smithfield Foods.

Saturday. Compare these figures with the almost 40 percent redemption rates that Smithfield has experienced via its customer database marketing activities. The figures speak for themselves. Database marketing allows Smithfield access to information about how many offers are being accepted, the value of those offers, and which promotion produced the best value for the investment. No form of marketing is as effective at measuring results as database marketing.

Case Discussion Questions

1. Think about the objectives of Smithfield Foods's customer Loyalty Card Program. What other objectives could they try to achieve with their database marketing program?
2. How does Smithfield Foods currently obtain customer information? Identify some additional mechanisms by which they could gather customer data.
3. If you were the vice president of marketing for Smithfield Foods, how might you allocate your future promotional budget?
4. What role should the company's Web site play in future marketing programs and activities for Smithfield Foods?

Notes

1. "Love Those Loyalty Programs: But Who Reaps the Real Rewards?" *Knowledge @ Wharton,* April 4, 2007; "Marketing," retrieved January 28, 2008, knowledge.wharton.upenn.edu/article.cfm?articleid= 1700. Ron Shevlin, "The Cost of Acquisition versus the Cost of Retention," August 1, 2007, retrieved January 28, 2008, marketingroi.wordpress.com/ 2007/08/01/debunking-marketing-myths-the-cost-of-acquisition-versus-the-cost-of-retention.
2. Arthur Midleton Hughes, "How to Retain Customers" (n.d.) retrieved February 8, 2008, www.crm2day. com/editorial/EEEZpkplyyYXurvQw1.php.
3. Frederick F. Reichheld (1996), *The Loyalty Effect: The Hidden Force behind Growth, Profits and Lasting Value* (Cambridge, MA: Harvard Business School Press).
4. "Award Plans Earn Cash for Airlines," retrieved May 22, 2008, boardingarea.com/blogs/pointswizard/ category/american-airlines-aadvantage®-miles.
5. Pat Overton, Marketing Director, McDonald Garden Center, 2002.
6. *Colloquy* 5(3) (1996).
7. Ibid.
8. "Taking Data Mining beyond Beer and Diapers," (August, 2002) iStart: *New Zealand's e-Business*

Portal; retrieved from www.istart.co.nz/index/ HM20/PCO/PV21906/EX224/CS22580.
9. Bob Stone and Ron Jacobs (2008), *Successful Direct Marketing Methods,* 8th ed. (New York: McGraw-Hill), p. 121.
10. Martin Baier, Kurtis M. Ruf, and Goutam Chakraborty (2002), *Contemporary Database Marketing: Concepts and Applications* (Evanston, IL: Racom), p. 151.
11. Adapted from Jon Anton and Natalie L. Petouhoff (2002), *Customer Relationship Management: The Bottom Line to Optimizing Your ROI* (Upper Saddle River, NJ: Prentice Hall), p. 138.
12. Tom Agan (2007), "Silent Marketing: Micro-Targeting," Penn, Schoen and Berland Associates White Paper. Retrieved on April 29, 2008, from http://www.wpp.com/NR/rdonlyres/4D3A7EB2-9340-4A8D-A435-FDA01DD134DO/O/PSB_Silent Marketing_Mar07.pdf.
13. Ibid.
14. Randy Jones, *Partner Marketing,* whitepaper (Leesburg, VA: MindZoo).
15. Ibid.

3

...

Developing Lists and Discovering Markets

Opening Vignette: NextMark

Finding new customers is an important activity for all businesses and organizations. Therefore, effective customer prospecting is considered a highly valuable task in enabling a company or organization to grow. But how do direct marketers identify and locate the "right" prospects? The answer: they rent lists. A list is a specifically defined group of organizations or individuals who possess common characteristics. There are lists available for almost anything and everything. Just name it, and there's a list for it! Unfortunately, many marketing professionals don't realize how many highly targeted prospect lists are available to them because they do not have the right tools.

The challenge for most direct marketers is to locate appropriate lists that will enable them to communicate with prospects that are likely to have a need or want for their products or services. Fortunately, this task has become much easier due to the advances in technology, the availability of lists, and companies like NextMark. NextMark, headquartered in Hanover, New Hampshire, is a leading provider of list commerce technology. Joe Pych founded NextMark in 1999 with the vision of streamlining the direct marketing process, particularly the mailing list procurement process. The company has quickly risen to the top of its industry, serving marketing professionals, list brokers, and list managers. NextMark's innovations include being the first to apply modern search technologies to the problem of finding mailing lists; the first to syndicate access to mailing list information through Web sites such as Direct Magazine, Multichannel Merchant, and the Direct Marketing Association; and the first to build the biggest and most up-to-date index of mailing lists in the world. More than 3,000 users from 700 companies can attest to the value of NextMark's services.

In 2005, NextMark unveiled a free list finder service to provide access to insider information on virtually every list on the market—which totals more than 50,000 lists! As revealed in Figure 3-1, a simple click on the Find Lists tab on NextMark's Web site will take you to the list finder. Simply type in the keyword for the kind of list that you wish to locate and voilà! An entire page of lists pertaining to your keyword is likely to appear! What happened? The NextMark's list finder search engine identified the most relevant and popular lists based on your keyword. Each of these lists will have an associated rank—which indicates the "responsiveness" or fit of the data card to the specific set of search criteria used. In addition, the type of

FIGURE 3-1   NextMark Online List Finder Service and Example of NextMark List Search Results Page.   *Source:* Used with permission of Joe Pych, NextMark.

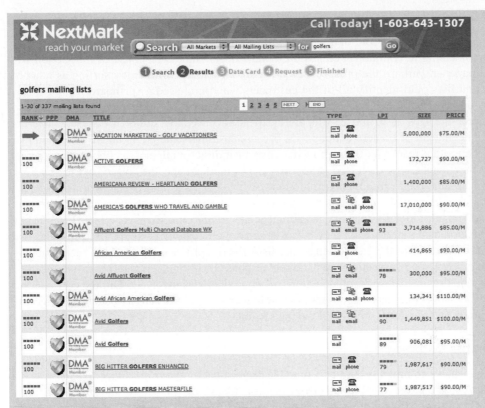

FIGURE 3-1   (continued)

channel for which the list is available, such as postal mail, e-mail, telephone, insert, or stuffer. Next, click on the list that you want to further explore and in seconds, a data card appears for that particular list. Each data card includes detailed information about the list along with buttons to request additional information and to place orders.

NextMark does not own or manage any of the lists found on its Web site. Instead, it works with more than 650 suppliers—the list managers—to promote their lists through the list finder. According to Joe Pych, "The main purpose of NextMark's new list finder service is to raise awareness of the excellent specialized lists that are available and to make them more accessible." Many companies are partnering with NextMark to make this service even more valuable. In some ways, NextMark is building the technology to help eliminate the administrative headaches associated with developing lists and discovering markets. So if you want to effectively prospect for new customers, visit NextMark at www.nextmark.com and explore its list finder—you will be pleasantly surprised at how easy prospecting can be with highly targeted lists.

Developing lists and discovering markets is the topic of this chapter. We explore the different types of lists, identify the key players in the list industry, and explain how to evaluate lists. Then we'll discuss how to use lists and market segmentation to effectively develop new markets and prospect for new customers.

LISTS AS MARKET SEGMENTS

Lists and data are at the very core of direct marketing. Lists identify prospects as well as customers who have something in common. Perhaps these individuals made a response or transaction with the direct marketer. Perhaps the prospects on a list are all females who enjoy surfing as a hobby. Or a different list could identify all of the customers who purchased a surfboard from a certain sporting goods store within a given year. Yet another list could possess the names and addresses of males between the ages of 20 and 25 who are independently wealthy and own a horse! Therefore, lists cannot be thought of as mere mailing lists, because customers and potential customers on marketing lists are often reachable through media other than direct mail such as phone, the Internet, magazines, newspaper, television, and radio. Lists are the marketplace, the "place" of the four P's of marketing (product, place, price, and promotion). A list denotes a market segment. Therefore, it follows that the direct marketer needs to accumulate data about the customers and prospects on them. Marketers must identify relevant geographic, demographic, social, psychological, and behavioral information using information they discover about their customers to identify prospects with similar characteristics. In the case of customer lists, the direct marketer needs to record activity in terms of responses or transactions. What direct response medium triggered the activity? Did the person buy, inquire, or take some other action? What product was involved? Did the customer pay by credit card? Direct marketers also want to know how frequently the activity occurs, how recently it last occurred, and the dollar amount of the transaction.

A Perishable Commodity

A list is a perishable commodity. Not only does the degree of activity (or inactivity) fluctuate, which means a list could be less valuable tomorrow than it is today, but the people and organizations on lists are far from static. They move. They marry. They die. Their attitudes change. In 12 months, for example, as many as 25 percent of the addresses on an average customer list could change.

The direct marketer must not only be aware of the condition of lists acquired from others but also be assured that the maintenance of the house list is current and adequate. Otherwise, part of the communication with an out-of-date list will be undeliverable and result in cost without potential benefit. List maintenance involves not only name and address correction but also continual updating of the data within the customer's record.

Data about a list are also perishable. No direct marketer wants to distribute messages indiscriminately. He wants to make sure not only that the message is delivered, it is also delivered to the right prospect. Direct marketers are particularly sensitive to the downside of indiscriminate mass communication, not only in terms of the waste of resources but also in terms of the possible antagonism sparked among nonprospects.

Types of Lists

There are three basic types of lists. In descending order of importance to the direct marketer, these are:

1. House lists
2. Response lists
3. Compiled lists

HOUSE LISTS   **House lists** are lists of an organization's own customers, active as well as inactive. Because of the very special relationship that an organization enjoys with its own customers, sometimes called goodwill, house lists are the most productive mailing lists available in terms of future response. Of lower potential (in terms of future response), but probably still more productive than lists from sources outside the organization, are the names of customers who have become inactive, who have inquired but not purchased, and who have been referred or recommended by present customers of the firm.

These four segments of a house list may be among an organization's most valuable assets, inasmuch as they generate future business at a cost much less than that of acquiring responses from outside lists. It is not uncommon for a house list to be four times or even ten times as productive as an outside list with which there is no existing customer relationship.

The kind and degree of customer activity is also relevant in terms of products purchased as well as the recency, frequency, and dollar value of such purchases. The source of the customer as well as the promotional strategy the marketer used to acquire that customer is information that can also help determine future response. The original list source and whether this source was direct mail, space advertising, broadcast media, the Internet, or even a salesperson have a bearing on future productivity. With inquiries, there is only an expression of interest rather than an actual purchase. Although this information is important, inquiries do not have equal value compared with customer purchase information. With referrals, the recommendation by a customer of the organization could offer an advantage, especially when the name of the present customer can be used in the promotional effort sent to the referred prospect.

RESPONSE LISTS   **Response lists** are the house lists of other organizations. In terms of future productivity, these lists rate right behind house lists. Obviously, the lists of those direct marketers offering similar products and services will yield the greater potential for response to a similar or even directly competitive offer. A customer who has subscribed to a news magazine by mail, *USA Today,* for example, could be an ideal prospect for a competitive news magazine, such as *Newsweek.* Similarly, a consumer who has purchased fitness equipment by mail could be an ideal prospect for a sporting goods store such as the Sports Authority. The first important qualification is that the name on a list from an outside source has a history of response to direct marketed offers. The second and possibly equally important characteristic would be an indication of response to a similar direct marketed offer. Beyond this could be a history of purchase of related items. Those who have purchased gourmet meat products, for example, might be good prospects for gourmet fruit products. They might even be good prospects for classical records or a book on interior decorating.

Lists of directly competitive firms, if available, are obvious choices. On the other hand, one of the real challenges to direct marketers is to determine *why* the purchaser of a home study course by mail, for example, might be a particularly good prospect for a book club.

Like an organization's house lists, other response lists should be looked at in terms of geographics, demographics, and social and psychological factors. They should also be segmented by type of response and/or ultimate transaction or purchase. Direct marketers should consider response lists in terms of source as well as the promotional strategy that caused them to be responsive in the first place.

COMPILED LISTS   Usually falling behind both house lists and response lists in expectations are compiled lists. **Compiled lists** are lists generated by a third party or market research firm. Individuals on compiled lists do *not* have a response history. Examples of such lists include phone directory listings; automobile and driver's license registrations; the newly married and the newly born; high school and college student rosters; public records such as property tax rolls and voter lists; rating services, such as Dun & Bradstreet; and a multitude of rosters such as those for service and civic organizations. Other potential sources of compiled lists include manufacturer warranty cards and coupon redemptions.

Although compiled lists typically do not have a response qualification built into them, market segmentation techniques coupled with sophisticated computer systems for duplication identification make possible selection of the best prospects (those most likely to effect a response or transaction) from very large compiled lists. Modern technology can also cross-identify characteristics of compiled lists, such as phone or automobile registration lists, with known response and thus further improve response potential. Combining a response list with an automobile registration list and further identifying those on the response lists who own a minivan, for example, is a way of identifying responsive households with children. Direct marketers use compiled lists in market segmentation and in further qualifying response and house lists. Let's take a look at an example of how direct marketers can effectively use compiled lists. The *Wall Street Journal* wanted to promote to one of its most challenging segments—college students. With their limited financial resources, college students have historically been a very difficult sale. The *Wall Street Journal* used a customized student segmentation strategy based on a profile of its current college student subscribers to determine high-probability prospect student responders for its nationwide direct mail campaign, shown in Figure 3-2. This profile data—major, class year, and most responsive geographical school locations—served as select criteria for obtaining student prospect data from a variety of compiled lists and data sources.

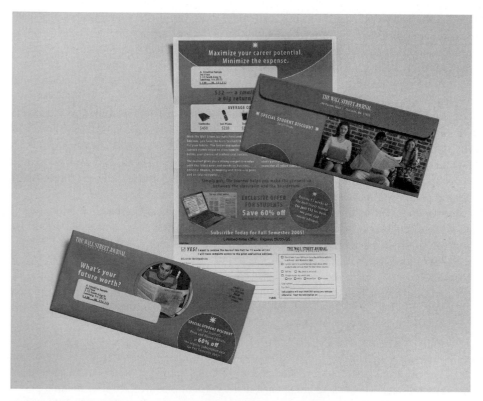

FIGURE 3-2   The *Wall Street Journal* Direct Mail Program for College Students.
Source: Used with permission of *The Wall Street Journal* and MindZoo, LLC. Photo by Kim Kirby, www.jimkirbyphoto.com.

The campaign was highly effective, with overall response rates three times greater than that of previous direct mail campaigns that targeted the college student market segment.

Development of House Lists

The discussion of house lists earlier anticipates that direct marketers must compile and develop the list along with relevant data through some appropriate mechanical means. Computerized systems hold a great deal of flexibility as well as long-range economy.

The marketer must first determine just what useful data, other than accurate names and addresses, it needs to qualify individual members of the list, how to collect and record it, and in what form. Consider, too, just what purpose the data will serve in the future. Keep in mind that collection of information costs money and must therefore produce benefits commensurate with its cost. How will the data be used, and can they be analyzed and evaluated properly?

THE LIST INDUSTRY

List owners and list users often come together through the efforts of list brokers, list managers, list compilers, and even service bureaus. Typically, marketers rent response lists under an arrangement allowing them to make a specific use of the data. Sometimes they buy compiled lists outright; there is no limit on the number of times these names can be mailed. List owners usually maintain rented response lists, so these lists often have better deliverability than compiled lists that have not been updated regularly. Figure 3-3 shows the relationship between the various members in the list industry. Service bureaus interact with all members of the list industry, providing expertise in the areas of data processing and analysis. Check out www.fastlist.com and www.alistnow.com. for more information on list building.

List Users

Virtually every direct marketer uses lists. For example, Victoria's Secret, L. L. Bean, Lands' End, Eddie Bauer, American Eagle, and Abercrombie & Fitch all use lists. There are literally thousands of response and compiled lists available from which to choose, and the starting point is usually the direct marketer's own list.

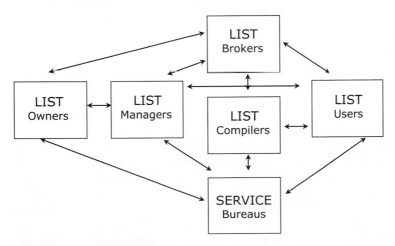

FIGURE 3-3 **The List Industry.**

A direct marketer using lists must obviously know its own customer profile to match it against available lists. Sometimes the marketer will use only segments of these lists, selecting them according to geographic, demographic, social, psychological, or behavioral characteristics. Matching one's house list against potential response and compiled lists is in itself a stimulating exercise. It often provides the direct marketer with basic knowledge of the marketplace the marketer can use to develop new products and determine successful promotional strategies.

List Owners

List owners are those who describe and acquire prospects who show potential of becoming customers of the list user. A key attribute of direct marketing, aside from its measurability and accountability, is the acquisition of lists and data about the individuals or organizations on these lists. Every direct marketer is a list owner. The lists that the marketer compiles during new business acquisition activities are described as house lists.

Although the primary reason for acquiring house lists is to build and perpetuate an organization through contact with its customers, many direct marketers view their house lists as profit centers in their own right. Firms rent their house lists to other direct marketers, under specified conditions, and this activity becomes an important source of added revenue. Nearly all credit card companies participate in list rental activities. Also, if you subscribe to any major magazines, your name appears on the magazine's house list.

All respondents to a renter's offer become additions to the renter's own house list. Under the usual rental arrangement, the rented list may be mailed only one time, and the list owner must approve the offer in advance. Directly competitive offers may not be approved except in an exchange that occurs when two competitive list owners provide each other with comparable numbers of their respective house lists or lists of active or inactive buyers.

An obvious advantage of renting a list rather than purchasing it outright (as is sometimes done with compiled lists) is that the list owner maintains the list, keeping it current and accurate. Another obvious advantage is that the names on such lists have a history of responding to direct marketing activity; thus they are termed "response" lists. A history of prior response, whether by mail, phone, or the Internet, is another important advantage to direct marketers.

Owners of response lists or compiled lists provide descriptions of them in a standard format, such as the example shown in Figure 3-4. The information on a list card normally includes list quantities, pricing, and general descriptions of the lists, including available selections (such as age, gender, ZIP code, state, marital status), as well as mechanical considerations, such as the type of labels desired, the label format, or the output medium in which the file is to be delivered. The type of label is normally pressure-sensitive, which is peel and stick, or Cheshire, which is cut and paste. Label format decisions address the number of labels to be placed horizontally across a page—normally referred to as one-, four-, or five-up. List files are normally delivered via CD-ROM, e-mail, magnetic tape/cartridge, file transfer protocol (FTP), or thumb drive. Other output mediums exist but are not commonly used given today's technology.

The costs of lists can range from less than $10 per thousand names for large quantities of broad-based compiled lists to more than $100 per thousand for highly selected up-scale response lists. The average list rental charge of approximately $40 to $50 per thousand for one-time use usually includes provision of these names on either labels or disks for computer processing. List selections (also called "selects") normally carry a fee of $5 to $25 per thousand depending on the list, with the majority priced at $10 per thousand. These list selections enable direct marketers to narrow the list and properly choose specific narrowed segments of prospects contained within each list population. The process of choosing list selects from a given list is a form of precise market segmentation,

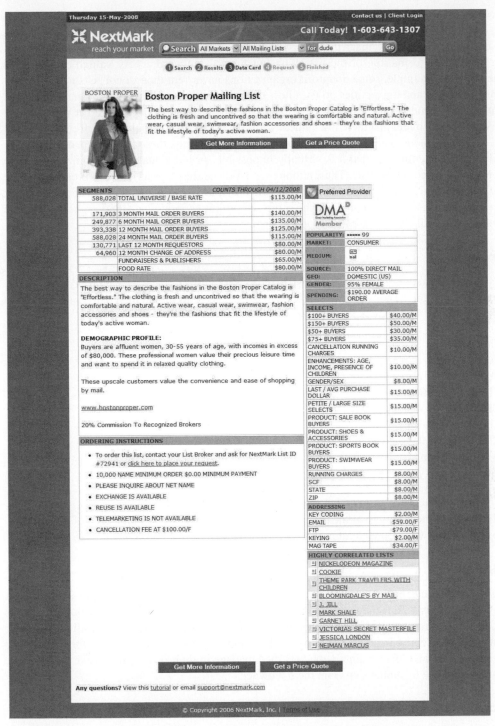

FIGURE 3-4 NextMark List Card. *Source:* Used with permission of Joe Pych, NextMark.

which we discuss in detail later in this chapter. Each list is a segment and by applying list selections to a list, direct marketers can pinpoint certain prospects with a high degree of selectivity and accuracy.

Not all direct marketers make their house lists available for use by others. Perhaps the list contains proprietary information, or the list owner wishes to safeguard a very valuable asset from improper use. For example, some nonprofit organizations never rent their donor lists to ensure privacy. Most colleges and universities do not allow their student lists to be used by other businesses. Can you think of some businesses that would like to rent the list of students enrolled at your school? Some list owners also feel that there is a tendency for a list to wear itself out. Even offers that do not directly compete can vie with each other for discretionary spending, these list owners contend.

The counterargument is that it is virtually impossible for individuals and organizations to be left off response or compiled lists. Thus, although a list owner has a proprietary interest in a house list, individuals and organizations on the list will inevitably appear on lists owned by others. Another counterargument contends that the more opportunities individuals and organizations are provided, the more likely they are to respond.

List Brokers

Like real estate brokers or stock brokers, **list brokers** serve as intermediaries who bring list users and list owners together. They do not actually own lists but serve as middlemen in the industry. In so doing, they perform the following functions:

- Find new lists
- Verify information
- Report on performance
- Check instructions
- Clear offer
- Check mechanics
- Clear mailing date
- Work out timing
- Ensure delivery date

List brokers are specialists in the process of bringing list owners and list users together. They should have a very clear picture of the products of the list owner as well as the needs of the list user. List brokers usually work on a commission basis, which is paid by the list owner.

List Managers

Although list rental can be an attractive profit center, direct marketers usually run it as a by-product of their basic business. Thus they often try to maximize returns from this activity through list managers. **List managers** represent the interests of list owners and assume the responsibility, on behalf of list owners, of keeping in contact with list brokers and lists users. They perform the advertising and sales functions and often maintain the lists they manage in their own facility. Like list brokers, list managers receive a commission from the list owner.

List Compilers

Organizations that develop lists and data about them, often serving as their own list managers and list brokers, are called **list compilers.** The form of list compilation they do is different from what direct marketers do in developing their own house lists through generation of responses and/or transactions.

List compilers usually develop their lists from public records (such as driver's licenses or motor vehicle registrations), newspaper clippings, directories, warranty cards, and trade show registrations. In fact, the compiler owns such lists and then resells them, rather than renting them for one-time use. Instead of regularly maintaining such lists, compilers usually recompile periodically. Names and addresses in phone directories, for example, are compiled regularly, at least annually, on issuance of newly published volumes.

Service Bureaus

Service bureaus provide data processing, data mining, outsourcing, online analytical processing (OLAP), and other services to support the interchange of lists and database information within the direct marketing industry. (These items are discussed in the next chapter.) Some of the larger direct marketing companies have their own service departments that perform this function on a regular basis.

EVALUATION OF LISTS

Recordkeeping is essential to properly evaluate the profitability of response lists as well as compiled lists. Marketers also rely on recordkeeping to predict future response from lists or segments of lists. Recordkeeping includes accurate measurement of results and evaluation of response differences attributable to timing.

Measurement of Results

Evaluating a list begins with selecting a **key code,** a unique identifier placed on the response device or order form prior to mailing a promotional piece. Key codes can be simple preprinted numbers identifying the source of the mailing list, or they can be so complex as to incorporate not just the source but the category of list, type of product offered by the list owner, or even the degree of prior direct marketing activity.

Direct marketers structure key codes so that they can accumulate information across several individual lists by different categories. Thus, the direct marketer can tabulate response not only by individual lists but also by sources of list, product lines, geographic location (ZIP code), and a variety of other broad qualifiers. The marketer then groups individual lists into such categories and makes assumptions about the overall efficiency of certain list sources, particular ZIP codes, or specific product lines.

Marketers should keep ongoing records of lists and monitor them even if they frequently contact the names on the list. The character and nature of lists change over time, just as the character and nature of the list owner's business may change. Many direct marketers have achieved the highest response rate when they have used so-called hotline names. **Hotline names** (also called "hotline buyers") are those most recently acquired, but there is no consensus in the industry about what chronological period "recent" describes. Many lists specify "three-month hotline" or "six-month hotline" to detail the name categories by recency.

Response Differences Attributable to Timing

Response differences can occur as a result of timing alone. Certain exogenous factors over which the direct marketer can exert no control (beyond the quality of the list itself), such as economic conditions or climate variations, can have a profound effect on results when lists are developed over a period of time. Other uncontrollable factors include major events or even catastrophes that divert public attention from the everyday.

Certain offers, such as a catalog of Christmas gifts, are timely and target seasonal differences in consumer buying habits. Some offers can be affected by the income tax season or by the vacation season. Some direct marketers try to time their promotional efforts so as to avoid arrival during any type of holiday event, especially those that take people outdoors. For example, if Lands' End were to send consumers a catalog offering winter sweaters in the early portion of summer, when most consumers are enjoying wearing light summer clothing, the response to their offer may be affected by the season. In addition, offers with expiration dates may need to be lengthened during the summer months due to the fact that many consumers take summer vacations and are not at home to receive their mail.

Even for nonseasonal offers, however, an apparent month-to-month cycle affects direct response advertising. All other factors being equal, many direct marketers have noted these ebbs and flows. For example, Bally's and other fitness centers probably receive a greater response to their direct marketing efforts during the months of January and February, although they are open for business 12 months a year. Each direct marketer should develop an index of monthly responses and determine which month generates the highest relative response. Noting monthly variances is useful to the direct marketer who is testing lists on an ongoing basis. It makes it possible to consider the variable of timing in comparing one list with another when these are released during different months of the year.

Many companies experience peaks and valleys in response rates based on the products and services they offer. In addition, an organization's customer database is also likely to be segmented, because not all customers have the same needs, wants, or interests. Thus, direct marketers must apply the principles of market segmentation prior to interacting with customers on a personalized basis.

Customers can be served best by organizations that know their characteristics. Because all buyers are not alike, marketing managers have developed ways to place them into groups or market segments, according to geographic, demographic, social, psychological, or behavioral factors. These market segments are the focal points of product differentiation and positioning.

Direct marketers have been using market segmentation strategies in their efforts to effectively promote and distribute products and services to consumers for many years. Think of a sports magazine. Its readers are probably interested in many different sports. It could easily identify its golf enthusiast consumers and offer them golf products and services. Likewise, it could offer its tennis-playing readers tennis equipment and clothing. The concept and theory of market segmentation and its special relevance in both consumer and business direct marketing are the subjects of the next section.

THE NATURE OF MARKET SEGMENTATION

Market segmentation is a strategy devised to attract and meet the needs of a specific submarket. These subgroups are referred to as **market segments.** A company may direct marketing strategies at several market segments. Each segment should be homogeneous (that is, its members should be similar to one another), heterogeneous (meaning its members should all be different from the members of other segments), and substantial in size (so as to be profitable).

Product Differentiation

Marketers target products and services to select market segments, rather than the total market, unless the product or service is unique and appeals equally to everyone. Many times it is necessary to *differentiate* products for particular market segments and *position* these products so that they will have special appeal to the intended market. **Product differentiation** is a strategy that uses innovative design, packaging, and positioning to make a clear distinction between products and services serving the same market segment. Product differentiation, like market segmentation, is an alternative to price competition. The difference might be real or simply an advertised difference. For example, a brand of toothpaste that contains fluoride is intrinsically different from one that does not. An airline may call its Boeing 727 aircraft a Star-Stream Jet without making it any different from the planes of its competitors. Product differentiation can distinguish a product from that of its competitors.

Product Positioning

Product positioning is the way the product is defined by consumers on important attributes. It enables consumers to rank products or services according to perceived differences between competing products or brands within a single product category.

Marketers can position products based on quality, size, color, distribution method, time of day the product is used, time of year, and price. Examples include Nike: "Just do it"; M&M's: "Melts in your mouth, not in your hands"; Taco Bell: "Think outside the bun"; Avis" "We Try Harder." Most big-ticket marketers, such as the manufacturers of Rolex watches and Mercedes-Benz automobiles, thrive by positioning their products as exclusive, high-quality items. So do the well-known direct marketers of specialty products like Harry and David, Brookstone, and Victoria's Secret.

Segmenting Business Markets

Like consumer markets, business markets break down into smaller, more homogeneous segments of the heterogeneous total industrial market.

STANDARD INDUSTRIAL CLASSIFICATION   The **Standard Industrial Classification (SIC)** coding system developed by the federal government serves as a basis for classifying statistical data and has been widely used by government, trade associations, and business enterprises. SIC codes classify business customers by the main economic activity in which they engage. All major activities are assigned a two-digit code number. Some of the major industry divisions include (but are not limited to) agriculture, mining, construction, manufacturing, transportation, wholesale trade, retail trade, financial services, and public administration.

As a company's business activity becomes more specialized, up to six digits can be added to the SIC code to identify subgroups. SIC codes can also designate the primary and secondary lines of a business as well as additional segmentation information based on the following statistical data: sales volume, credit rating, age of business, number of employees, net financial worth, and subsidiary and geographic location. Most direct marketers have used SIC codes in conjunction with proprietary information as the primary tool for segmenting business and industrial consumers. However, SIC codes posses certain limitations and are no longer in such wide use.

NORTH AMERICAN CLASSIFICATION SYSTEM (NAICS)   The **North American Industry Classification System (NAICS,** pronounced "nakes") has replaced the SIC coding system. Many business people felt that the SIC system failed to recognize the growth of information technology, the service industry, high technology, and international trade. The NAICS system offers several improvements over the SIC system. Figure 3-5 overviews the main differences between them.

The first improvement is relevance. NAICS identifies over 350 new industries, including high-tech areas, and 9 new service industry sectors that now contribute to the economy. The second improvement is comparability. NAICS was developed by the United States, Canada, and Mexico to produce comparable data for all three nations. Industries are identified by a six-digit code to accommodate a larger number of sectors and allow greater flexibility in designating subsectors. The first

SIC Codes	NAICS Codes
SIC codes classify establishments by the type of activity in which the business is primarily engaged.	NAICS is based on a production-oriented, or a supply-based, conceptual framework.
SIC is a 4-digit code.	NAICS is a 6-digit code.
SIC system lacked current information.	NAICS will be reviewed every five years so classifications will change with the economy.
SIC have 10 classifying sectors: • Agriculture, Forestry, and Fishing • Mining • Construction • Manufacturing • Transportation, Communications, and Public Utilities • Wholesale Trade • Retail Trade • Finance, Insurance, and Real Estate • Services • Public Administration	NAICS have 20 classifying divisions: • Agriculture, Forestry, Fishing, and Hunting • Mining • Construction • Manufacturing • Utilities • Transportation and Warehousing • Wholesale Trade • Retail Trade • Accommodation and Food Services • Finance and Insurance • Real Estate and Rental and Leasing • Information • Professional, Scientific, and Technical Services • Administrative Support; Waste Management and Remediation Services • Educational Services • Health Care and Social Assistance • Arts, Entertainment, and Recreation • Other Services (except Public Administration) • Public Administration • Management of Companies and Enterprises

FIGURE 3-5   Comparison of SIC Codes and NAICS Codes.   *Source:* Based on NAICS Association Web Site, accessed online at http://www.naics.com/info.htm, February 2003.

five digits denote the NAICS levels common to all three NAFTA (North American Free Trade Agreement) countries, whereas the sixth digit accommodates user needs in individual countries. NAICS is a two- through six-digit hierarchical classification code system. A complete and valid NAICS code contains six digits. Figure 3-6 shows the hierarchical structure of NAICS.

The third improvement is consistency. NAICS uses a consistent principle: businesses that use similar production processes are grouped together. This is entirely different from the SIC system, which focused on the industries served. The fourth improvement is adaptability. NAICS will be reviewed every five years, so classifications and information keep up with the changing economy. Finally, quality has been improved with key measures of U.S. economic activity such as retail services, manufacturers' shipments, and service industry receipts.[1]

xx	Industry Sector
xxx	Industry Subsector
xxxx	Industry Group
xxxxx	Industry
xxxxxx	U.S., Canadian, or Mexican national Specific

FIGURE 3-6   NAICS Hierarchical Structure.

THE BASES FOR MARKET SEGMENTATION

The needs, wants, or interests of the consumers belonging to various segments are different. However, it would be almost impossible to conduct marketing research for every product and service that could determine which market segment each consumer would best fit into; therefore marketers use other, more general indicators for segmenting markets. These indicators include geographic, demographic, social, psychological, and behavioral factors. A brief overview is provided here.

Geographic Segmentation

Potential geographic subdivisions range in size from the country as a whole down through census divisions and federal reserve districts to states, counties, trading areas, cities, towns, census tracts, neighborhoods, and even individual city blocks. In addition, there are numerical codes such as ZIP codes, geocodes, telephone area codes, computer "match" codes, and territory and route numbers. Once upon a time, census tract numbers were the best means of geographical segmentation. Do you know which census tract you live in? Most people probably do not. However, our ZIP code number *is* meaningful, and everyone knows that number.

An important form of geographic market segmentation is that which recognizes inherent differences among those buyers who reside in central cities, suburban, urban fringe, and rural areas. The last may be further divided into farm and nonfarm households. Geographic location can also affect the future purchase activity of consumers. For example, the level of consumer interest in purchasing nursery plants or snow blowers is often related to the climate of the geographic area in which the consumer lives.

Population changes within geographic areas, such as the decreasing population of a specific geographic area or the high mobility of the population in another, have significance to the marketer. Census data is invaluable for research regarding the changing geographic and demographic profile of the American population. The recent Census CD Neighborhood Change Database (NCDB) is a very powerful product that presents four decades (1970, 1980, 1990, and 2000) of census tract series data. Additional information about this product is available at www.uscensus.net.

Another geographic segmentation tool, the **Global Positioning System (GPS),** associates latitude and longitude coordinates with street addresses. Direct marketers use this system to identify geographic locations, establish business sites, locate competition, measure distance, and generate data about the demographics of a business location. Given this information, combined with the technological mapping capabilities of most businesses, a direct marketer can better determine the business penetration and market potential in certain geographical areas.

Today, computer systems are capable of analyzing **geographic information systems (GIS)** to help better understand data related to geographic areas. A GIS is a computer system capable of capturing, storing, analyzing, and displaying geographically referenced information identified according to location.[2] A GIS can help you answer questions and solve problems by looking at your data in a way that is quickly understood and easily shared.[3] The GIS software leader is ERSI, which provides a full spectrum of ready-to-use geospatial data products delivered either as a Web service or as packaged media.[4]

Demographic Segmentation

Demographics are identifiable and measurable statistics that describe the consumer population. The primary unit of observation in demography is the individual; the family unit and household are secondary concerns. Common demographic variables include age, gender, education level, income level, occupation, and type of housing.

There are three main sources for such data: (1) population enumeration, as in a census; (2) registration on the occurrence of some event, such as birth, marriage, or death; and (3) sample surveys or tabulation of special groups. The data obtained in these ways are generally available for marketing and other uses from governmental sources, especially the Census Bureau.

It is often wise to tabulate the effect of the interaction of many demographic variables at the same time. For example, it is highly valuable for a direct marketer to know the marital status of a certain 25-year-old male consumer. Just think of two male consumers, both aged 25; one might be married with two children and the other single with no children. These two consumers probably belong in totally different market segments based on their market needs. In this case, the more demographic data you can collect, the better. Often, a single demographic statistic can be misleading.

Marketers know that currency is the key to accuracy and validity of demographic data. *Changes* in demography, such as when someone marries or has a baby, have significant marketing implications.

Social Factor Segmentation

Social factors include a person's culture, subculture, social class rank, peer group references, and reference individual(s). Social factors demonstrate the impact that other people in our society have on our decision-making process and consumption activities.

Society may well have an impact on our behavior beyond our control. For example, **reference groups** (also called "peer groups") are the people a consumer turns to for reinforcement. This reinforcement normally comes *after* the consumer makes a purchase decision. Reference groups may have a direct and powerful influence on the consumption behavior of adolescents and teenagers. A **reference individual** is a person a consumer turns to for advice. This person or persons will influence the consumer *before* he or she makes a purchase decision. Therefore, reference individuals normally have a stronger impact on consumer decision making than do reference groups.

Psychographic Segmentation

Psychographics is the study of lifestyles, habits, attitudes, beliefs, and value systems of individuals. Even though buyers may have common geographic, demographic, and social characteristics, they often have different buying characteristics. Psychographic segmentation divides consumers into different groups based on lifestyle and personality variables. Individual buyer behavior is influenced not only by geographic, demographic, and social factors but also by variables that are more difficult to define, such as environment, self-perception, and lifestyles. When marketers can identify and measure these influences, they can use them effectively in segmenting mailing lists.

Direct marketers have the ability to identify psychographic market segments and thus predict potential consumer response by recognizing and evaluating the simultaneous appearance of a prospect's name on a variety of lists. For example, a registered owner of a particular type of automobile might also appear on the subscriber lists of the *Wall Street Journal* and *Better Homes and Gardens* as well as the customer lists of up-scale catalogs such as Neiman Marcus and Gump's. This same prospect might even be a contributor to Planned Parenthood and a member of the National Geographic Society. When merged, such multiple list identifiers can describe the psychographics of consumers (activities, interests, and opinions) more specifically than consumer surveys. Another means of psychographic identification of specific prospects is a comprehensive data file developed by Equifax under the trade name "Lifestyle Selector." The Lifestyle Selector is the direct marketing industry's largest and most comprehensive database of self-reported consumer information. More than 500 response segments cover all aspects of how consumers live, what they spend their money on, and what interests they possess. This file is primarily derived from two sources: responses to consumer surveys and product registration cards filled out voluntarily by consumers after they have completed a product purchase. Included for each of the 47 million consumer names and addresses are a variety of demographic characteristics and activities or hobbies. It is possible for a consumer direct marketer to develop a psychographic and demographic profile of his or her company's house lists by matching the lists with the Lifestyle Selector and extend his or her prospect base by adding other names from the data file.

Thus, measurement of environmental influences within geographic units combined with demographic and psychographic indicators derived from list cross-referencing and other expressions of activities, interests, and opinions all interact to enable the direct marketer to reach individual consumers within market segments. Such list selection is obviously more efficient and can be more effective than directing pinpointed messages to the total marketplace.

Behavioral Market Segmentation

The actions taken by consumers are certainly a viable base for market segmentation. The specific types of products and services consumers have purchased, the time the transactions took place, the method or location of their purchases, and the method of payment they choose can all reveal similarities among consumers. Each behavioral factor can indicate a consumer preference that may be shared by other consumers, consequently identifying a market segment.

"Cookies" provide marketers with the ability to segment consumers according to their online activity. A **cookie** is an electronic tag or identifier that is placed on a personal computer. Cookies are a tool for recognizing Web users again after they have interacted with a marketer's Web site in some capacity. The process is quite simple: whenever a Web site visitor makes a request to a Web server, that server has the opportunity to set a cookie on the personal computer that made the request. The Web site host can then use the cookie for tracking beyond the initial click to determine how often that visitor returns to the Web site, the length of time of each visit, and the particular Web pages visited, which can often detail the specific products or services in which the visitor is interested. Cookies provide valuable insight into consumer behavior.

Using Multiple Segmentation Bases

Relying on a single base for segmenting markets and selecting customers is rarely effective. Most direct marketers use multiple segmentation bases—such as combining geographic data with behavioral data. Thus, within a single ZIP code area, several smaller segments may exist on the basis of behavioral differences, like products purchased. A good example of multivariable segmentation is "geodemographic" segmentation. Several companies, including Claritas, Experian, Acxiom, and MapInfo, combine U.S. census data with consumer lifestyle patterns to profile customers by geographic areas. These services enable marketers to choose segments wisely based on multivariable segmentation data.

Claritas, featured in Figure 3-7, began geodemographic segmentation in 1976 by analyzing data, isolating key factors, and developing a clustering system. This clustering system began with two key drivers, age and income. But as Claritas quickly discovered, there was more than just age and income that needed to be evaluated. The statisticians who created PRIZM realized the importance of creating segments based on the demographics that correlate directly with consumer *behavior*. A new version of the PRIZM system was created in 2003 using the 2000 census to replace the earlier system, which used the 1990 census. Beyond having nearly a third more new segments, and 66 in total, the key enhancement to the system was to allow marketers to shift from a

FIGURE 3-7 **Claritas PRIZM Advertisement.**   *Source:* Used with permission of Claritas, a Nielsen Company.

five-digit ZIP code to Census Tract to Block Group to ZIP+4, all the way down to household level—all within a set of 14 social groups. Each social group contains creatively named segments that tend to cluster together. For example, the "Urban Uptown" group contains the nation's wealthiest urban consumers and has the following five segments: "Young Digerati," "Money and Brains," "Bohemian Mix," "The Cosmopolitans," and "American Dreams." Although this group is diverse in terms of housing styles and family sizes, residents share an upscale perspective that is reflected in their marketplace selections. Figure 3-8 shows some examples of the unique segments from a variety of social groups that Claritas created based on geodemographic analysis.

- **Close-In Couples:** Predominantly African-American couples, 55-year-old plus, who live in older homes in urban neighborhoods, high-school educated, empty nesting, enjoying secure, and comfortable retirements.
- **Winners Circle:** A collection of mostly 35- to 54-year-old couples with large families in new-money subdivisions. Surrounding their homes are the signs of upscale living: recreational parks, golf courses, and upscale malls. With a median income of over $100,000, these residents are big spenders who like to travel, ski, go out to eat, and shop at clothing boutiques.
- **Home Sweet Home:** Mostly under 55, these residents tend to be upper-middle-class married couples living in mid-size homes with few children, they have attended college and hold professional and white-collar jobs, and they have fashioned comfortable lifestyles, filling their homes with toys, TVs, and pets.
- **Up-and-Comers:** Mostly in their twenties, single, many are recent college graduates who are into athletic activities, the latest technology, and nightlife entertainment.
- **Shotguns & Pickups:** These Americans tend to be young, working-class couples with large families, most have two or more kids, they live in small homes and manufactured housing, nearly a third of the residents live in mobile homes, and many own hunting rifles and pickup trucks.

FIGURE 3-8 Examples of Unique Claritas PRIZM Segments. *Source:* Used with permission of Claritas, a Nielsen Company.

Claritas also provides an online service, MyBestSegments.com, which can help guide marketing campaigns and media strategies for specific market segments. Customer segmentation profiling information included in MyBestSegments encompasses PRIZM and a variety of categories about consumer markets, including travel, eating out, shopping, auto purchases, and more. Demographic data are also available. Plus, these data are continually updated to be in sync with Claritas's MarketPlace suite of products for additional consumer behavior data. Visit MyBestSegments (www.claritas.com/MyBestSegments/Default.jsp) to explore the "ZIP Code Look-Up" feature of this system, which allows you to plug in your ZIP code to obtain a profile of your neighborhood's top five segments, along with some descriptive detail about each segment's lifestyle traits. While visiting the MyBestSegment site, you may also want to investigate the "Segment Look-Up" feature, which provides detailed descriptions of each of its 66 unique market segments. As Figure 3-9 shows, direct marketers that subscribe to Claritas can quickly and easily obtain details about the best segments to target for a specific offer and additional customer profiling information.

ZIP CODE AREAS AS MARKET SEGMENTS

ZIP code areas, although originally conceived and developed by the U.S. Postal Service for the purpose of sorting and distributing mail, have become a convenient and logical method of geographic segmentation, especially in direct marketing. ZIP code areas have become a key basis for market segmentation in direct marketing, combining the characteristics of geographic, demographic, social, psychological, and behavioral factors. The value of ZIP codes for marketers is based on the simple fact that the codes tend to enclose homogeneous neighborhoods and geographical boundaries.

The old saying "birds of a feather flock together," explains why ZIP code areas constitute market segments. Because people with like interests tend to cluster and because their purchase decisions are frequently influenced by their desire to emulate their friends, neighbors, and community innovators, ZIP code areas provide the means to *identify* clusters of households that have a high degree of *homogeneity*. This homogeneity is inherent in the manner in which ZIP code areas have

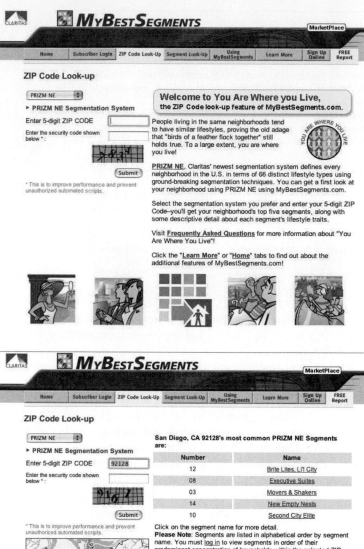

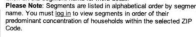

FIGURE 3-9   MyBestSegments.com Web Pages.   *Source:* Used with permission of Claritas, a Nielsen Company.

- Establish and define market segments, including sales potentials based on environmental data about the unit.
- Evaluate direct marketing results performance, based on a measurement of actual penetration against the projected potential, and realign market segments as such analysis warrants.
- Process inquiries and orders more efficiently and effectively without need for reference to a map, since the address immediately identifies the sales territory.
- Forecast more accurately based on objective analysis of the marketplace rather than on a collection of individual opinions about it.
- Pinpoint market segments in relation to profits.
- Increase regional and national advertising effectiveness when direct mail, magazines, or newspapers are used.
- Determine optimum distribution centers.
- Set up a territorial rating system for credit evaluation and perform continuing analysis of accounts receivable.
- Conduct market research, especially if demographic cross sections or probability sampling is called for.
- Develop differentiated products that have special interest to specific market segments that can be defined by ZIP code areas, certain educational levels, or target occupation groups, for example.
- Analyze penetration of present customers according to specific ZIP code area characteristics to more effectively direct and control marketing efforts.
- Identify growth areas, with updated demographics.
- Direct new product sampling more effectively.
- Control inventories according to historical territorial patterns.
- Coordinate data processing and information systems through use of the ZIP code as part of the computerized "match code."
- Distribute seasonal and climate-oriented products and information on a chronological schedule by ZIP code area.

FIGURE 3-10   **Uses of ZIP Code Area Data.**

been constructed and relies on accepted principles of reference group theory as well as the concept of environmental influences on buyer behavior.

Marketers can use ZIP code areas in many specific ways; we outline some of them in Figure 3-10.

Geographic Structure

The socioeconomic usefulness of these units, especially from a direct marketing perspective, results from the three criteria the U.S. Postal Service used in establishing each ZIP code:

1. A hub city is at the center of each cluster of ZIP code areas (termed a sectional center) that is the natural center of local transportation.
2. An average of 40 to 75 individual post offices lie within each sectional center, resulting in units with fairly consistent population density.
3. Each natural transportation hub is about 2 to 3 hours' driving time away from the farthest post office in the sectional center.

An obvious convenience of these geographic units which sets them apart from commonly used divisions such as counties is that each household and business within the unit is readily identifiable by a five-digit number assigned to it as a part of its street address. In dissecting the ZIP code, you will find that the first digit of the five-digit codes identifies one of ten (0 through 9) geographic areas of the nation, with the digit ascending from east to west. These regions are identified in Figure 3-11.

FIGURE 3-11   ZIP Code National Area Designations.

The next two digits of the five-digit number identify a major city or major distribution point (sectional center) within a state. The last two digits of the five-digit ZIP code fall into two geographic categories: (1) key post offices in each area, which normally have stations and branches in the city's neighborhoods; and (2) a series of associated small town or rural post offices served by the sectional center transportation hub or a specific neighborhood or delivery unity within a city.

ZIP+4

Figure 3-12 summarizes what the five-digit ZIP code designations represent. The U.S. Postal Service has added a four-digit extension to the original five-digit code. The sixth and seventh digits denote a *sector* and the last two denote a *segment* within a sector. These additional four digits permit mail to be sorted to carrier delivery routes. An example of the meaning of the additional four-digits is as follows:

- Digits 6 and 7—could denote the location of a specific organization, like a university.
- Digits 8 and 9—could represent a specific segment or department within the university, perhaps the office of admissions.

Clustering Areas to Segments

A key advantage of ZIP code areas is that they can be combined like building blocks to suit the individual need of the direct marketer relative to product differentiation or promotional strategy. A ZIP code–based marketing information system enables direct marketers to know more about their markets and organize them according to local transportation patterns. Many major coupon distributors segment their markets on the basis of ZIP code areas. These companies also know which ZIP code areas possess a heavy concentration of residential households and coupon users.

ZIP CODE DIGIT DESIGNATIONS

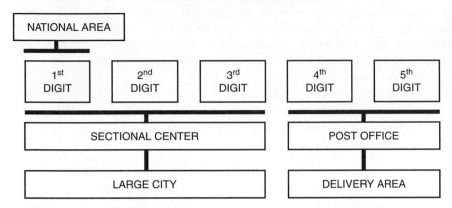

FIGURE 3-12   ZIP Code Digit Designations.

Availability of Statistical Data

During the past few decades, increasing amounts of data for ZIP code areas have become available. Some of these include organizations' own records along with consumer survey data compiled by the Census Bureau, Market Research Institute (MRI), and Simmons Market Research Bureau.

ZIP Code Business Patterns is a service published by Economic Information Systems. It identifies the top 10,000 five-digit ZIP code areas in terms of business activity measured by number of employees. This service identifies the number of business establishments within ten major economic sectors (based on the first digit of the SIC code) for each ZIP code area. The following information is provided for each ZIP code area and for each SIC category:

- Number of employees
- Number of business establishments (by employment class)
- Identification of the city and state in which located
- Total payroll levels in the ZIP code

ZIP Code Business Patterns provides segmentation information that is invaluable for direct marketers.

Summary

Most direct marketers conduct market segmentation to better serve consumer needs and wants. Lists are important market segmentation tools. There are three basic types of lists: house, response, and compiled. Each list is of value for direct marketers, although house lists are considered the most valuable. The list industry is comprised of list owners, list users, list brokers, list managers, list compilers, and service bureaus. Each member plays an important role in the list rental activities of direct marketers. Direct marketers strive to keep lists current and accurate. House lists normally hold a customer's name, address, and pertinent contact information. In addition, most direct marketers rent lists in an attempt to prospect for new customers. List rental strategies are made simple today due to computerized databases services with search techniques, such as NextMark's list services. List selections afford direct marketers the opportunity to further segment a list using a variety of segmentation variables. Direct marketers segment final consumers according to geographic, demographic, social, psychological, and behavioral characteristics. Often times, multiple variables are used to segment markets, such as geodemographic segmentation. Direct marketers also segment businesses or industrial consumers according to SIC codes or the NAICS. Direct marketers consider ZIP code areas to be geographic market segments that provide important customer information.

Key Terms

house lists *62*
response lists *63*
compiled lists *63*
list owners *66*
list brokers *68*
list managers *68*
list compilers *68*
service bureaus *69*

key code *69*
hotline names *69*
market segmentation *70*
market segments *70*
product differentiation *70*
product positioning *71*
Global Positioning System
 (GPS) *73*

geographic information systems
 (GIS) *73*
demographics *73*
reference groups *74*
reference individual *74*
psychographics *74*
cookie *75*

Review Questions

1. What is *market segmentation* and how do direct marketers use it?
2. How is segmenting industrial markets different from segmenting final consumer markets?
3. Overview the differences between SIC codes and NAICS. Name some companies who might use industrial classifications in segmenting their industrial or business consumer market.
4. What are *psychographics?* In what way are they useful to direct marketers?
5. In the four-digit extension of an original five-digit ZIP code, what does each of the numbers stand for?

6. How can ZIP codes help achieve product differentiation or promotional strategy?
7. What type of list is most important to an organization? Why?
8. Identify a few products or services that probably incur response differences attributable to timing.
9. Explain the difference between a *list user* and a *list owner.*
10. What are list brokers, list managers, and list compilers each responsible for?

Exercise

As a Nike employee, it is your responsibility to create a house list for the company. Create a list and include all the important characteristics about customers that would be beneficial to making the company most profitable. Keep in mind, Nike sells many different types of products, so you would want the organization of your house list to be segmented accordingly.

CASE

Lillian Vernon

Overview

This case study demonstrates the importance of a company's house list. It examines the processes used in prospecting to acquire new customers, the segmentation strategies used for retaining current ones, and the use of list rental in prospecting for new ones.

Technology has dramatically improved the manner by which direct marketers create, store, rent or acquire, and use lists. Today, the lists of almost all direct marketers are computerized and sophisticated. However, most direct marketing lists originated long before the computer age—and were housed on simple index cards. With computerization came the ability to research, rent, and test various lists and conduct precise market segmentation of house lists. Your objective in completing this case is to better understand how lists are developed, tested, and segmented by one of America's best known direct marketing companies—Lillian Vernon.

Case

On a little yellow kitchen table, one of America's largest specialty catalog companies, Lillian Vernon, was founded in 1951. Lillian Vernon started the firm when she placed a $495 advertisement for a personalized pocket book and belt in *Seventeen* magazine. With her initial investment of $2,000 in wedding gift money and the success of that first ad (shown in Figure 3-13), which resulted in $32,000 in orders, Vernon's business was off and running.

From the very beginning, entrepreneur Vernon knew that her customer list was the most valuable asset of her business (even though her bankers mistakenly thought the company's physical plant and computer systems were its main assets). Vernon exerted great care in maintaining her customer list. She would sit at her yellow kitchen table laboriously noting customer names and orders on index cards. Every two months she would pore over her cards—adding, deleting, and revising the information on each. Why? Because people relocate, stop ordering, marry, and die, and the customer list must be constantly updated.

FIGURE 3-13 Example of the Use of Personalization in the Offer.

Her efforts really paid off. When the Lillian Vernon catalog was first published in 1960, the customer list had 125,000 names on it. By the early 1980s, it had more than 10 million names, and by 1995, more than 18 million.[5] Today, Lillian Vernon's mailing list identifies more than 20 million households throughout the United States, and the number of *recent buyers* (defined as those customers who have made a purchase from the company within the past 12 months) totaled 1.8 million in 2007.[6] Today, the 56-year-old firm has become a leading national catalog and online retailer that markets gifts, housewares, gardening, seasonal, and children's products.

How Does Lillian Vernon Acquire Customers?

Back in the 1950s, Vernon simply added customer names to her list as new customers placed orders. This process continued for about a decade and the firm built its house list slowly. In fact, some of Lillian's very first customers—who were teenagers when they bought her bags and belts—are now grandmothers who still buy from the company. Thus, retaining satisfied customers is the foundation on which the customer list is built. However, every direct marketer must prospect for *new* customers as well. Lillian Vernon loses about 40 percent of its recent customers annually, which means that expanding the list requires prospecting to secure new customers on an ongoing basis.[7]

At first, most of the prospect names were found via ads in select magazines that target the same customer type (*House Beautiful, Better Homes and Gardens, Woman's Day*) or through word-of-mouth referrals. Ever since the first Lillian Vernon catalog was mailed, each catalog has included space on the order form that asks customers for the names of other people who might also like to receive a catalog.

In the 1970s, Lillian Vernon began participating in the list rental industry. The firm rented out its customer names and also rented names from other direct marketers. Frequently the company would also trade names with different direct marketers—essentially a noncash swapping of lists. Lillian Vernon focused primarily on renting *response lists,* because consumers who possessed some history of purchasing via direct marketing proved to be better prospects than someone who had no such history. The primary criteria used by Lillian Vernon when renting lists include the following.[8]

- **Merchandise compatibility**—select companies that have similar products (do not rent a list from a company whose merchandise is incompatible, has inferior quality, or is in poor taste).
- **Customer compatibility**—select companies that target similar customers (you wouldn't want to rent a list from a men's clothing company or a catalog specializing in power tools when the target customer is women).
- **Price compatibility**—select companies with similar price ranges (you generally shouldn't rent a list from a company which markets upscale products to high-income customers when your catalog specializes in moderately priced merchandise for middle-income consumers).

In 2002, Lillian Vernon hired the list managing services of ALC New York to be responsible for all list rental activities. ALC New York continues to manage the list and is responsible for screening all list rental requests the company receives, reporting on activity, and performing the necessary collection of revenue. The types of companies that have recently requested to rent Lillian Vernon's customer list include other catalogers offering complementary products to what Lillian Vernon offers, book and magazine publishers, membership clubs, and retailers of collectibles. Lillian Vernon does not rent its list for offers the company knows would be inappropriate for its customers.

Lillian Vernon also uses the services of several list brokers to order lists from list owners where there has been success in the past. These are considered "continuation" orders. The brokers also recommend tests of potential lists prior to making a major commitment to rent the entire list.

This is called "testing a new list." Most direct marketers permit other direct marketers to test a cross-section sample of 10,000 or 15,000 names from the list or from a specific segment of the list. Once the response to the test has been analyzed, the renter may require additional tests (of larger sample sizes) before deciding whether to rent the larger quantity available in the list or list segment. Through testing, Lillian Vernon can project the responsiveness and profitability of a particular list.

Lillian Vernon's online business also generates new customers. Most of these customers are generated by search (organic and paid) and affiliates. If a browser searches for a product through Google or Yahoo! and chooses to buy that product from Lillian Vernon, they become a new buyer. Similarly, Lillian Vernon allows affiliated companies' "affiliates" to drive their visitors and customers to Lillian Vernon's Web site. When these visitors buy merchandise, they are added to the Lillian Vernon's marketing database and are subsequently marketed to.

Who Are Lillian Vernon's Customer Segments?

Approximately 90 percent of Lillian Vernon customers are women, with an average age of 47 and an average household income of $75,000. About half have children living at home. Most live in suburban areas and own their single-family home.[9] However, all these customers are not alike. They have different lifestyles and different needs, wants, and interests, so the corporation segments its customer list accordingly. Through analysis, four distinct groups of customers are present:

1. Young moms with young children—average age mid- to late thirties, high income, heavy Internet users.
2. Mothers with older children—average age mid-forties, highest income, heaviest Internet users.
3. Women under 65 with no children ("aunts")—average age mid-forties, middle income, moderate Internet use.
4. Grandmothers—average age 65+, low household income, lowest Internet use.

The company also uses the marketing database to segment the buyer file based on recency of purchase, frequency of purchase, channel of purchase, and a proprietary score (which includes other variables such as dollars spent, seasonality, etc.).

The company combines these two elements: type of customer (young mom, grandmother, etc.), and quality of the customer (defined in behavioral terms such as recency of purchase, preferred channel, etc.) when developing their marketing and merchandising plans.

The corporation publishes two catalog titles, *Lillian Vernon,* which averages 92 pages per edition, and *Lilly's Kids,* which averages 72 pages per edition. Occasionally sale pages are inserted into the core Lillian Vernon catalog as a way to clear excess inventory. Target markets are kept in mind when selecting the products to be presented in each catalog. See Figure 3-14 for these catalogs.

Over the years, Lillian Vernon had tested and had mailed other catalog titles, such as *Lillian Vernon Gardening,* and found that the market segment did not meet its segmentation standards of size and/or responsiveness. Also, the company learned that some of these titles took business away from the core *Lillian Vernon* title. For these reasons the company has stopped producing many of these spin-off titles.

Summary and Conclusion

According to an Opinion Research poll, more than 39 million Americans are familiar with the Lillian Vernon name. Since 1951, the Lillian Vernon logo has appeared on 3 billion catalogs, 172 million shipping boxes, and 485 million products.[10] The corporation has been a successful direct marketer.

FIGURE 3-14 Lillian Vernon Catalogs.
Source: Used with permission of Current USA, Inc., dba Lillian Vernon.

Why? Because Lillian Vernon meticulously created, updated, refined, and segmented her house list, always believing that it was the corporation's greatest asset. She built her business by segmenting her customers and satisfying the individual needs and wants of each market segment. Customer satisfaction is also a company tradition at Lillian Vernon. Through precise market segmentation, the company has tailored its catalogs and product assortments to different customer segments. Through direct marketing, each customer has been marketed to on a personal basis.

Case Discussion Questions

1. Discuss the various methods used by Lillian Vernon to acquire names of prospective customers. Which methods have been most productive?
2. Given the three criteria used by Lillian Vernon when renting a response list; name some response lists that the company should pursue.
3. Identify some direct marketing companies that might have an interest in renting Lillian Vernon's customer list. Explain why each company would possess such an interest and whether Lillian Vernon should permit such a list rental transaction.

Notes

1. From the North American Industry Classification System (NAICS) Web site, http://www.census.gov/naics, February 2008.
2. http://erg.usgs.gov/isb/pubs/gis_poster, March 17, 2008.
3. http://www.gis.com/whatisgis/index.html, March 17, 2008.
4. http://www.ersi.com/index.html, March 17, 2008.
5. Lillian Vernon (1996), *An Eye for Winners: How I Built One of America's Greatest Direct-Mail Businesses* (New York: HarperCollins), pp. 131–132.
6. 2008 Lillian Vernon Data Card/company database.
7. Vernon, *An Eye for Winners,* p.131.
8. Ibid., pp. 135–136.
9. 2008 Lillian Vernon Data Card/company database.
10. Lillian Vernon Web site.

Planning and Creating a Value Proposition: The Offer

Opening Vignette: Smart Spacing Hangers

Do you love fashion? Were you born to shop? Do you have a closet full of clothes and accessories but can't seem to find the right outfit because your clothes are cluttered? Do you wish you could keep your closet organized? Is it a constant battle to keep your clothes from getting wrinkled or hangers from getting tangled? These are the needs and desires of many consumers—and retail clothing stores—that led to the invention of the need-satisfying offering called Smart Spacing Hangers. This new product innovation was the brainchild of Texas entrepreneur Lisa Box, who is referred to by many as the Martha Stewart of closet space. Lisa first realized that there was a need for such a product while working in a retail store in Houston,

FIGURE 4-1 Smart Spacing Hangers.
Source: Used with permission of Lisa Box,
Smart Spacing Hangers.

SMART SPACERS for hangers!

Triple Closet Space with attachable Spacers that not only space your
hangers but allows up to 5 cascading hangers that mix and match your
well planned outfits and accessories. Call or visit today!

FREE SHIPPING!

11152 Westheimer #127

713-468-3038 | www.SmartSpacingHangers.com

FIGURE 4-2 **Smart Spacing Hangers Magazine Advertisement.**   *Source:* Used with permission of Lisa
Box, Smart Spacing Hangers.

where she spent hours separating clothing hangers on the racks, only to have the hangers moved every time a consumer came browsing through the racks. As Figure 4-1 presents, the Smart Spacing Hanger is a product that separates hangers an equal distance apart to create a neat and orderly appearance.

Smart Spacing Hangers come in almost every color, shape, and material and are sold individually as detachable Smart Spacers or with a hanger. It's a basic concept, yet it makes so much sense, which is why it is such a success. The product offer itself satisfies a real consumer desire, although it certainly is not the desire of all consumers. A major part of any successful direct marketing campaign lies in making sure the right offer reaches the right target customers. That's where the marketing challenge comes in!

Smart Spacing Hangers are targeted to upscale consumers and clothing stores across the country. Lisa realizes that her market includes only those people who take pride in their clothes and value being organized. Smart Spacing Hangers are not sold in retail stores but are directly marketed via direct response communication and a Web site. Lisa places advertisements in upscale magazines to boost her Web-based business. Figure 4-2 provides an example of one of her magazine advertisements. Notice how each direct response ad encourages prospective customers to place an order via telephone or online and the ad offers free shipping to customers to make the offer more attractive.

Lisa utilizes search engine optimization strategies to make sure Smart Spacing Hangers appears on the first page of Google and Yahoo! when consumers search for closet-related products. In addition, Lisa partners with cleaners and tailors to promote Smart Spacing Hangers to their customers. Plus, she quickly follows up on all leads she generates when participating in various trade shows targeting retail clothing stores. She is constantly prospecting for new clients who may have a need or want for what Smart Spacing Hangers has to offer. For Lisa Box, planning and creating the value proposition for Smart Spacing Hangers entails constantly researching the needs and wants of her target market consumers, creating new products to satisfy those desires, and determining the best methods to reach her target market.

In summary, planning and creating a value proposition or offer takes creative and strategic thinking. It must satisfy a need or want and entice consumers to take action. That is the topic of this chapter. We define the offer, discuss the elements of an effective offer, the steps in planning the offer, the components of an offer, and how to create, target, and test the offer. In addition, this chapter examines a variety of different types of offers that have been successfully used by direct marketers through the years. Because creating the offer is both a science and an art, we can learn much from examining offers that have worked *as well as* those that have not worked.

WHAT IS THE OFFER?

The **offer** is the value proposition to the prospect or customer stating what you will give the customer in return for taking the action your marketing communication asks him or her to take. In essence, it is the terms under which a direct marketer promotes a product or service. The offer encompasses both the manner of presentation by a direct marketer and the all-important request for a response.

Creating need-satisfying offers is a part of ongoing customer relationship management (CRM) that drives the direct marketing process. Without an attractive offer, consumers would not initially respond to an organization, and thus the customer relationship would never originate. Without continuous monitoring of customer needs and wants, direct marketers could not create appropriate offers to keep their customers satisfied and encourage them to return and purchase again and again. The offer is the all-important "front-end" activity in the CRM process.

The Offer as a Component of Direct Marketing Strategy

According to Edward Nash, author of *Direct Marketing: Strategy, Planning, Execution,* there are five essential elements of direct marketing strategy: product, offer, medium, distribution method, and creative.[1] The offer must be created with these other five elements in mind. However, Nash claims that the offer is the element most quickly and easily revised for an improved result in the direct marketing effort. Nash claims, "even the slightest change in the price—whether it's in bold or buried in body copy or a coupon—can have dramatic effects on front-end performance."[2] Just think about all of the products that are priced at odd numbers, such as $19.99 or $199.97. These figures are pennies away from the even dollar amounts; however, consumers often perceive them to be far less. Research has proven that odd prices are very effective in generating consumer response; therefore, many direct marketers use odd prices in their offers.

Other direct marketers believe in the "40-40-20 rule," which states that the success of any direct marketing effort is 40 percent reliant on using the right lists, 40 percent reliant on having an effective offer, and 20 percent reliant on creating the right creative mix (copywriting, photographs, illustrations, etc.) in your direct marketing effort. However we may try to quantify its importance, the offer is clearly a major contributor to the success or failure of any direct marketing campaign.

Elements of an Effective Offer

To create an effective offer, the direct marketer must research and really know the target audience and the customers' likes, dislikes, "hot buttons," and, most of all, needs and wants. Without this information, it is difficult, at best, to create an effective offer. In addition, marketers must research how consumer needs and wants change. Direct marketers must constantly revise their offers, including the creative materials used to convey each offer. This normally requires printing a number of different catalogs or changing a company's Web site throughout the year to provide timely offers that appeal to consumers during a particular season or holiday. Figure 4-3 features a few of the various catalog covers used by well-known specialty food and gift direct marketer Harry and David when marketing to their customers. Note that the creative appeal used and the products offered are appropriate for each season or holiday.

According to Lois Geller, author of *Response: The Complete Guide to Profitable Direct Marketing,* effective offers have three characteristics: believability, involvement, and creativity.[3]

1. *Believability.* Using common sense when creating the offer can go a long way toward making it believable. An offer has to make sense to the consumer. It cannot give so much in the form of gifts or "freebies" that it makes the consumer wonder "what's wrong with the product or service?" For example, a sale offering 80 percent off at the end of a season makes sense to the consumer, because we all know that marketers need to make room for new inventory, but 80 percent off at any other time makes the consumer wonder "what's wrong with this product that it didn't sell?" Therefore, the offer should be believable.

2. *Involvement.* Geller believes that most shoppers suffer from what she calls the "glaze-over effect." She claims that some offers are so common that consumers' eyes simply glaze over when we see one.[4] For example, an offer of 10 or 15 percent discount is very common. It usually gets passed over. However, the offer that promises "buy one, get one at half price" is more exciting and appealing and may motivate the consumer to calculate his or her potential savings. The offer must attempt to get the consumer involved.

3. *Creativity.* The most creative offers usually get the highest response. Creativity can set your offer apart from all the other offers bombarding consumers. Geller believes that "exclusive

FIGURE 4-3 Examples of Seasonal Offers from Harry and David. *Source:* Used with permission of Harry and David.

offers" are very appealing and should be featured prominently if the product or service is really exclusive to the market. "Exclusive" means that the product is in limited supply or not available in stores and is special to your company.[5] An example of an exclusive offer is:

The recipe for these peanut butter balls has been in the Stafford family for 50 years. For decades, friends and neighbors have been savoring these tasty sweet treats. Buy one box of these peanut butter balls, and we'll throw in Grandma Stafford's special recipe for oatmeal cookies with a cinnamon swirl. You can't find this recipe in any cookbook or baker's magazine. We keep it so we can give it to our special customers. Enjoy!

PLANNING THE OFFER

The right offer can sell almost anything, but it must be carefully planned. Let's walk through a four-step process to heeding the details that can make or break an offer.

Step 1: Establish Objectives of the Offer

What is the offer designed to do? Get orders? Generate sales leads? Sell subscriptions? Encourage repeat purchases or renewals? Introduce and sell new products? Increase the amount that the customer is presently purchasing? Raise funds? Without clearly established objectives, you won't be able to measure the success or failure of the offer—and remember that measurement is imperative in direct marketing.

The underlying objective of any offer is to maximize profitability for a company or organization. Two of the most common methods of achieving increased profitability are (1) encouraging repeat purchases from existing customers, and (2) encouraging a company's current customers to purchase additional related or unrelated products beyond what they normally buy. The three direct marketing strategies that achieve this profit-maximization objective are continuity selling, cross-selling, and up-selling. Let's take a look at each of these strategies.

Continuity selling describes offers that are continued on a regular basis, whether weekly, monthly, quarterly, or annual. These offers are also called "club offers" and are a hallmark of direct marketers, who want to acquire customers who will remain active for an extended period of time. In continuity selling, customers buy related products or services as a series of small purchases, rather than all at a single time. Books, magazine subscriptions, insurance policies, and many other products are sold by means of club offers, as are periodic shipments of fruit, cheese, or other food items. An example of continuity selling is provided in Figure 4-4. Harry and David's Fruit-of-the-Month Club offers consumers an opportunity to receive select fruit throughout the year. The customer can choose to give or receive or giving as a gift the 3-Box Club, 5-Box Club, 8-Box Club, or the 12-Box Club.

The continuity selling offer includes a **positive option,** where the customer must specifically request shipment for each offer in a series, or a **negative option,** where the shipment is sent automatically unless the customer specifically requests that it not be. The negative option is a controversial marketing technique because some consumers don't realize that they must request the shipments be stopped or else they are responsible for paying for the products delivered. Most consumers normally expect to pay for what they order, but with negative option, they pay unless they request the shipment to be stopped. It is different from the norm. An example of a negative option club offer is a continuity mail-order marketer called Around-the-World-Shoppers Club. They shipped a variety of unusual gift items monthly to subscribers, each month from a different foreign country. Of course, if the consumer received an undesired shipment, it can be returned at any time for credit.

Another example of a negative option offer is a till-forbid. A **till-forbid (TF)** is an offer that prearranges continuing shipments on a specified basis and is renewed automatically until the customer instructs otherwise. TF offers are commonly used with insurance policies or magazine subscriptions. Other examples include some clubs, such as senior citizen groups or automobile clubs, which may include specific services with an annual membership fee.

Cross-selling offers new products to existing customers. The products may be related or unrelated to those the customers are already buying. For example, a purchaser of books and software might be offered other books and software or possibly an insurance policy, a home power tool, or a vacation package to a tropical resort. The most important element of successful cross-selling is the manner in which the customer views the direct marketer's reputation, reliability, and overall image.

Up-selling is the promotion of more expensive products or services over the product or service originally discussed or purchased. You might think of up-selling as suggestive selling, since the marketer is suggesting the more expensive product or service as opposed to the consumer requesting it.

FIGURE 4-4   Harry and David's Fruit-of-the-Month Club Newsletter.
Source: Used with permission of Harry and David.

In summary, continuity selling, cross-selling, and up-selling are important direct marketing strategies used to achieve different objectives when planning the offer. Each strategy has been used by direct marketers and has met with great success. It is important that the direct marketer decides which strategy he or she will employ when planning an offer.

Step 2: Decide on the Attractiveness of the Offer

Generally, the more attractive you can afford to make the offer, the better the response will be. How do you make an offer attractive? You dress it up with lots of freebies. However, direct marketers must be careful that the cost of the incentives like free gifts does not outweigh the added profit of the additional orders. This step entails close examination of both the objectives and the budget constraints within which the direct marketer must operate. An example of an attractive offer by Barnes & Noble appears in Figure 4-5. Note that this online offer is for two free gifts valued at $32.99.

FIGURE 4-5   **Barnes & Noble Valuable "Free Gift" Offer.**   *Source:* Used with permission of Barnes & Noble Inc.

† After you use your new Barnes & Noble MasterCard ® Credit Card to make a purchase for the first time, you will receive via mail a twenty-five-dollar ($25) Barnes & Noble Gift Card and a Hydration Bottle premium (while supplies last). Your purchase must be made by July 31, 2008 to qualify for the premium. Such purchase must not be invalidated for any reason. Please allow up to 4-8 weeks for delivery. The delivery of the Gift Card and premium will be made independently and under separate cover to the billing address associated with your Barnes & Noble MasterCard. This offer is subject to change or discontinuation without notice.

** When you use your Barnes & Noble MasterCard to make any purchase (other than the purchase of any Barnes & Noble Gift Card offered at a discount to face value) online at bn.com or in any Barnes & Noble Store nationwide, a credit in the value of five percent (5%) of such eligible net purchases will be posted to your Barnes & Noble MasterCard account. The five percent (5%) credit will appear on the same billing statement as the charge for the related eligible purchase.

†† See Terms and Conditions for details on the Barnes & Noble Reward Program.

Please note that product prices and availability are subject to change. Prices on bn.com may vary from those in Barnes & Noble retail stores.

How to unsubscribe:
This message was sent to lspiller@cnu.edu on May 3, 2008. If you no longer wish to receive promotional email from Barnes & Noble, please click here. If you have a Barnes&Noble.com account, you can also log in to your account and follow the instructions under Change Your Communications Preferences.

© 2008 Barnes & Noble. All Rights Reserved.
Barnes & Noble, Inc., 76 Ninth Avenue New York, NY 10011, Attn: Marketing Preferences

mhtmlmain: Page 2 of 2

FIGURE 4-5   (continued)

Step 3: Reduce Risk of the Offer

The direct marketing consumer bears risk, usually greater than in traditional retail buying, whenever he or she purchases a product without the added benefit of actually seeing, touching, feeling, and personally examining it. Therefore, the goal of the direct marketer is to reduce the perceived risk associated with purchasing the product unseen and unfelt.

Two basic components of the offer are designed to reduce the risk, a *free trial* or *examination period,* and a *money-back guarantee*. We talk about these in greater detail later in this chapter. For now, understand that their importance is magnified by their role in reducing the risk associated with any offer.

Step 4: Select a Creative Appeal

The appeal of an offer can be either rational or emotional. The rational appeal targets a consumer's logical buying motives. It presents facts in a logical, rational manner and targets basic needs such as the need for food, shelter, clothing, and safety. An example of a rational appeal is the National Association of Letter Carriers' Food Drive. This organization distributes a direct mail postcard to residents asking them to help "stamp out hunger" by placing a food donation at their mailbox on a certain day before their letter carrier arrives. The carrier will pick up the food donation and deliver it to a local food bank or pantry. The offer is clear, logical, and does not attempt to invoke great emotion on the part of the local resident who is being asked for a food donation.

The emotional appeal focuses on a consumer's desires and feelings. It targets the consumer's wants, such as social status, prestige, power, recognition, and acceptance, as opposed to physical needs. An example of an emotional appeal is the offer extended by Emode, a leading self-assessment company. Their offer is for a free IQ test to see how smart you are. This assessment test can determine how your IQ score affects your ability to compete and provide a comparison to other people. Although the offer may pique the consumer's curiosity and may provide some nice-to-know information, it is appealing to a person's wants. Nobody *needs* to have this information. The type of appeal selected must be appropriate to the media used to distribute the offer. For example, if a direct marketer is making an online offer to regular or prospective customers, the offer must be direct and to the point because most people only spend a few seconds on Web sites. In addition, the offer must enable the consumer to respond via a quick click of the mouse or keyboard. The offer must include messages that encourage the consumer to "click here" or "forward to a friend," as in the online offer shown in Figure 4-6.

Regardless of the creative appeal used, each offer must have the same basic parts or components. Let's investigate the components that encompass the offer.

FIGURE 4-6 Lillian Vernon Online Offer. *Source:* Used with permission of Current USA, Inc., dba Lillian Vernon.

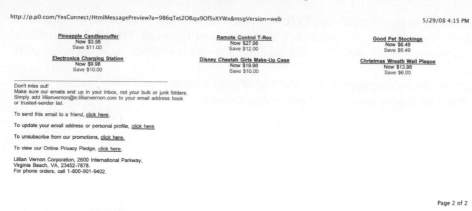

FIGURE 4-6   (continued)

COMPONENTS OF THE OFFER

The components of the direct marketing offer fall into two categories: those that are required and must be present in all offers, and those that are optional and may be included depending on strategy and costs.[6] The *required* elements are product, price, payment terms, length of commitment, and risk-reduction mechanisms. The *optional* elements are incentives, multiple offers, and customer obligations.

Product or Service

The actual tangible product or intangible service is critical to the success of any offer of course. It must satisfy the needs or wants of the target consumer to whom it is being presented. Physical features such as weight, dimensions, color, model, accessories, and any extended properties such as gift wrapping, alterations, delivery, and service are very important, as is the basic benefit the product will provide. Services have unique properties such as type of service, length of time or duration of the service, location, and frequency or schedule of the service. Appropriate timing of the offer can also affect the consumer's response, particularly if the product or service is seasonal, as we've discussed.

   Marketers must understand these product or service features well to create an effective offer that garners a response from the target consumer. If the product/service itself does not satisfy the needs or wants of the consumer, then no matter how attractive you make the rest of the offer, it will be to no avail. Simply stated, consumers are not interested in purchasing products and services for which they have no need or want.

Pricing and Payment Terms

Direct marketers must decide whether their price objective is to maximize profit or maximize sales. If the price is meant to generate the largest possible return on investment (ROI), that is, the objective is to maximize profit, then the direct marketer must use a **price skimming** strategy. This strategy establishes the price at the highest possible level to "skim the cream" off the top of the market and target only a select number of consumers who can *afford* to buy the product/service. Of course, a high price will result in fewer sales transactions but greater profitability per sale.

   A **price penetration** strategy will help the direct marketer maximize sales volume. This strategy sets the price at a very low level so that almost any consumer who wants to buy the product can afford to do so.

   The price elasticity of a product is another factor to take into account when establishing the price of the product. **Price elasticity** is the relative change in demand for a product given a change

Basic price statement	"One year supply for only $12.99"
Price stated as a fraction	"One-half off when ordered by May 1st"
Price stated by unit	"Now only $2.49 an issue"
Price savings stated by percentage	"Save 30% when ordered by May 1st"
Price savings stated by unit	"First two issues are free"
Price savings stated by dollar amount	"Save $25"
Price savings based on introduction	"Save $15 on your initial subscription"
Price savings based on multiple purchases	"Save $2.98 one two"
Price based on promotional offer	"Buy one, get one free"

Figure 4-7   Examples of Ways to Express Price in an Offer.

in its price. It measures the consumer's responsiveness or sensitivity to price changes. For example, let's pretend the Gap decreased the price of its jeans from $35 to $25. Would consumers buy two pairs of jeans instead of one? Let's also pretend Starbucks Coffee increased the price of their coffee by $2. Would consumers continue purchasing Starbucks, or would they switch to either a different brand of coffee or substitute product, such as hot cocoa or tea, instead of coffee? The direct marketer, in initially estimating the demand for products, first determines whether there is a price the market expects and then develops an estimate of the sales volume he or she expects at different price levels. If the consumer's demand for a product doesn't change substantially regardless of price increases, the product has an inelastic market demand. If, however, the consumer is very sensitive to price changes and market demand for the product decreases greatly as price increases, then the product has an elastic market demand. A product with an *elastic* market demand should usually be priced lower than an item with an *inelastic* market demand.

It is not just price level that is important. Equally important is the manner in which we state the price. Is it a buy-one-get-one-free offering? Is it a sale? Figure 4-7 shows various ways to present price in an offer.

Finally, payment method is a vital part of the offer. The payment methods direct marketers have offered in the past, cash with the order and collect on delivery, lacked convenience and often were a deterrent to ordering. On the other hand, an offer to absorb shipping costs if cash payment is sent with the order can be a distinct incentive.

A bill me later (BML) payment offer that includes credit card options, either the direct marketer's own, a bank card, or a travel and entertainment card, not only provides convenience but also spurs the customer not to procrastinate when placing an order. In certain cases, such as a free trial offer with full return privileges, the BML offer isn't just nice to have, it's a necessity.

Delayed payment is sometimes extended to provide installment terms. This option is usually confined to higher priced products and can be with or without an interest charge. Payment in installments is an attractive incentive to many consumers and such an offer can be a strong one. However, marketers must weigh the advantages of this incentive against the cost of financing the resulting accounts receivable, the potential for bad debts, and the ultimate return on the direct marketer's investment.

Trial or Examination Period

Typically, the buyer does not have the opportunity to see or feel the product before ordering. The free trial or free examination offer helps overcome this distinct disadvantage of ordering by mail or telephone.

The trial offer might be an introductory one requiring payment of a nominal amount, such as 25 cents for the first 30 days of coverage under an insurance policy or $1.97 for the first three months of subscription to a magazine. If the buyer's examination reveals that the insurance policy or magazine does not meet expectations, even the small introductory payment might be refunded.

Full return privileges are, of course, a vital part of any offer.

Guarantees

Direct marketers have been using guarantees for many years. In fact, the 1744 catalog of colonial America's first important printer, Benjamin Franklin, guaranteed customer satisfaction with the following statement on its front cover: "Those persons who live remote, by sending their orders and money to said B. Franklin, may depend on the same justice as if present."

A guarantee of "complete satisfaction or your money back" is an inherent necessity of direct marketing. This assurance, and the manner in which it is presented, is a vital part of the offer. L. L. Bean offered this "100 percent guarantee" in one of their recent catalogs:

> Our products are guaranteed to give 100% satisfaction in every way. Return anything purchased from us at any time if it proves otherwise. We will replace it, refund your purchase price or credit your credit card. We do not want you to have anything from L.L. Bean that is not completely satisfactory.

Certain direct marketers of collectible items even guarantee to buy back some products at a later time and certain direct marketers of insurance guarantee to accept all applicants for some types of policies. Guarantees have been developed for extended time periods. Some even offer "double your money back" if the buyer is less than completely satisfied.

Sweepstakes and Contests

Direct marketers have used sweepstakes and contests as an ordering stimulus. To avoid being considered a lottery, which requires a purchase as a condition for entry and is illegal in many states, a contest or sweepstakes must guarantee a winner, and making a purchase must not be a requirement, though it can be an option for entering. In addition, the law requires that the odds of winning the sweepstakes or contest be published on promotional materials. You should readily see that attractive prize offerings, such as trips to lavish resorts or big-ticket electronic devices such as flat-screen televisions, yield a large response in terms of contest or sweepstakes participation.

Winners selected by random drawing sometimes are made in advance of the mailing, so that the contest will not be construed as a lottery. How can a direct marketer choose a winner before people enter the contest? That may seem odd; however, based on the mailing list that will be used to distribute the contest or sweepstakes offer, the direct marketer can actually select a name or multiple names and then if that person does not enter the contest, they will not be awarded the prize. Remember, lotteries require a prior purchase, whereas contests and sweepstakes only require an entry form to be submitted. A key to the success of sweepstakes and other forms of contests is getting the respondents involved in some way, such as by returning perforated tear-offs, die-cuts, tokens, and stamps, as well as by giving answers to questions, problems, or puzzles. Direct marketers should be creative when designing contest or sweepstakes entry forms.

Gifts and Premiums

An effective device for stimulating response to a direct marketing promotion is the offer of a free gift or premium either for purchasing or for simply examining or trying the product. Although such incentives increase response, as do sweepstakes and contests, they may also attract less qualified respondents in terms of credit-worthiness or final product acceptance.

Some gifts are termed "keepers," meaning that the customer can keep the premium whether or not they keep the product. To be most effective, the premium should be related to the product or the specific audience. Sometimes, direct marketers offer customers a choice between multiple gifts. In other situations, direct marketers keep the gift "a mystery" and consumers do not know what particular gift they will receive until it is delivered. It can have tangible and apparent value or the value can be intrinsic, such as a booklet containing advice. Sometimes the free gift offer can be as nominal as information or a price estimate.

Time Limits

A limited time offer typically specifies a deadline, an enrollment period, a charter membership, a limited edition, or a prepublication offer. An example of a limited time offer can be seen in Figure 4-8. Lillian Vernon sent this online offer to its regular customer base. Note that the offer uses phrases such as "pre-order now!" and "hurry!" to encourage consumers to act quickly because it is an initial limited shipment of the product. The offer can even quote "while supplies last."

FIGURE 4-8 Lillian Vernon Online American Idol Exclusive! *Source:* Used with permission of the Lillian Vernon Corporation.

Do all offers possess all the components we've discussed? Probably not. However, these are the essential parts of most basic offers. Now you know the pieces of the puzzle, what do you do with them? You begin creating an offer for your consumers.

CREATING AN OFFER

The offer is not independent of the entire direct marketing strategy. While creating it, marketers must keep the other strategic elements of direct marketing in mind, especially the needs and wants of the customer. Let's discuss the five steps direct marketers should follow when creating an offer.

Step 1: Perform Market Research

When direct marketers attempt to predict and determine consumer needs and wants, they often rely on certain indicators, such as geographic, demographic, social, psychological, and behavioral characteristics of the consumer. (These were overviewed in Chapter 3.) Direct marketers strive to understand consumer needs and wants, not merely predict them. Thus, they often conduct consumer research to determine what *motivates* the consumer to purchase a given product/service. After all, consumer motivations drive the purchase process. **Motivations** are needs that compel a person to take action or behave in a certain way, such as purchase a product/service. Consumers have both internal and external motivations for their behavior. Internal motivators can stem from basic physiological needs, such as hunger or thirst, or other needs, such as the need for acceptance. However, external motivators can take the form of advertisements, free samples, a sales pitch, or even a persuasive offer.

In any event, direct marketers must understand what needs the consumer is attempting to satisfy to effectively create offers that will meet these needs and wants. Direct marketers are concerned with creating, caring for, and keeping customers. They want to create a customer, not just make a sale! The difference between the two is that a sale means a one-time purchase, whereas a customer is someone who will come back and make repeat purchases from an organization throughout his or her lifetime. Thus, long-term CRM is a constant focus of direct marketers.

Therefore, the underlying theme in creating any offer is the consumer. The development of an offer cannot occur without an understanding of the consumer's needs and wants. Think of it in this way: creating an offer without careful analysis of consumer needs and wants is like driving off in a car without making sure there is gasoline in the tank! Not a good idea, right? It is only by carefully researching the consumer and the competitive situation that the direct marketer will have the needed information on which to create an offer. The market research data collected by the direct marketer also provides specific details pertaining to the terms of the offer.

Windstream Communications launched a direct marketing campaign called Windstream Movers Program, featuring customized offers based on consumer analysis. Intuitively, Windstream knew that movers into single-family dwelling units (SFDUs) were more likely to be new homeowners, and therefore more likely to need a landline, broadband, and television services. Movers into multifamily dwelling units (MFDUs) were more likely to be younger renters, and therefore, they may eschew a traditional landline in favor of cell phones. As a result, Windstream employed duplex laser printing to customize the offer and text to the three different moving consumer segments. As Figure 4-9 reveals, this was achieved by preprinting a single self-mailer format that allowed for individualized and customized messaging to premovers, new homeowners, and movers/renters. In addition, these unique offers were mailed on a weekly basis to be in-home as close to the move date as possible so that the timing of the offers would correspond to consumer needs.

FIGURE 4-9   Windstream Communications Movers Program Customized Offers.
Source: Used by permission of Windstream Communications and MindZoo, LLC. Photo
by Kim Kirby, www.jimkirbyphoto.com.

Step 2: Determine the Terms of the Offer

Although brand names, packages, and labels along with advertising and other promotional strategies create product and supplier preferences, it is the quality of the product itself that must ultimately lead to repurchases. The quality (and this includes any warranty and service) must be consistent with customer expectations, and it is the terms of the offer that creates those expectations. Therefore, it is critical to meet (and even exceed) what is set forth by the terms of the offer.

Direct marketers must consider five specific product details when determining the terms of the offer. These product details include the following.

1. *A Choice of Sizes.* Whether the direct marketer will make the product available in a wide array of sizes, including extra-small, extra-large, and half-sizes are specific details that must be determined. Another term of the offer pertaining to product sizes is whether the direct marketer will allow consumers to place a special order for an unusual size if desired. Direct marketers must spell out these specific product terms.

2. *A Choice of Colors.* Whether the direct marketer will make the product available in a wide variety of popular colors is an important product detail. In addition, can the consumer select certain colors to be mixed and matched with other colors when ordering products with more than one component or piece? For example, when placing an order with Victoria's Secret, can a consumer select a bathing suit top in one color or design and a bathing suit bottom in a different but

coordinating color or design? Will the direct marketer allow consumers to place special orders for a unique color if desired? Direct marketers make these and similar determinations when creating the terms of an offer.

3. *Product Specifications.* Direct marketers must disclose the dimensions of the product including such elements as the weight, height, length, texture, and scent of the product in the offer. Direct marketers often use photographs or illustrations to depict the product; however, they must also be careful to spell out the exact specifications in words as well as photographs.

4. *Product Accessories.* Direct marketers must specifically state what product accessories are available. It is also important to specify which accessories are included with the purchase of the product and which can be purchased separately if so desired. Once again, the more specific the product details are identified in the offer, the smaller the chance of unmet consumer expectations.

5. *Personalization.* Personalization enhances the sale of a direct-marketed product, and thus should, if possible, be made available to the customer. The cornerstone of some very successful direct marketing companies has been offering personalized products. As presented earlier in the case for Chapter 3, Lillian Vernon founded a mail-order business by offering a leather bag and belt that could be personalized. The response to that personalized offer was beyond her wildest dreams! She sold $32,000 worth of merchandise.

Step 3: Target the Offer

In creating an offer and developing the copy or jargon that will position it, Donna Baier Stein and Floyd Kemske in their book, *Write on Target,* insist that every direct marketer or copywriter must ask themselves four essential questions.[7]

1. What am I selling?
2. Whom am I selling to?
3. Why am I selling this now?
4. What do I want my prospect to do?

They believe the key to effective direct marketing is unlocking the selling power that comes from knowing to whom you are targeting your offer. Knowing the target consumer requires market research on that target profile of consumers. It is only by knowing and understanding the target consumer that the offer can be "right on target" to generate the maximum response rate. Of course, not all consumers are the same. There are differences (and similarities) between them. That is the basis of market segmentation and is also the starting point of effectively targeting an offer.

The process of targeting the offer is directly related to the important concepts of market segmentation and product positioning we reviewed in Chapter 3. Market segmentation enables a marketer to view consumers as belonging to certain select groups based on shared characteristics and/or needs and wants. Thus, instead of trying to target a product or service to the total market, most marketers select certain groups of customers called market segments to whom they will target their promotional efforts.

Positioning is a marketing strategy that enables marketers to understand how each consumer perceives a company's product or service. This perception is based in part on the strengths and weaknesses of the product or service compared to other competing products or services. By knowing what that perception is, we can more effectively create an offer and target it toward a particular consumer segment. Of course, offers may or may not generate a positive reaction or consumer response. This is why direct marketers normally test different offers to determine which one is most effective with a particular consumer market segment.

Step 4: Test the Offer

We'll discuss research and testing in greater detail in a later chapter, but let's look at it briefly here because it is of such great importance to the success of the offer.

We might consider testing to be the ultimate consumer opinion poll. The research question we are asking each consumer is, of course, "does the offer make you want to buy the product or service?" If the offer is not attempting to sell something but trying to obtain a specific outcome, such as a vote for a politician or attendance at an upcoming meeting, does it make the target individual want to take the action for which the offer is requesting? The test determines the effectiveness of the offer and provides an answer to the critical question—does the offer *work?*

How do direct marketers conduct the tests? The answer is simple. They first determine what they want to test or investigate. For example, direct marketers may want to determine the free gift or premium they will offer consumers who make a purchase during some specified time period. Let's say a local restaurant wants to distribute direct mail offers to local residents in a particular ZIP code area to encourage consumers to patronize the restaurant. Prior to creating the offer, the restaurant wants to determine whether consumers will respond more readily to an offer for a free appetizer or a free dessert. Next, the direct marketer creates two direct mail cards, one containing the offer for the free appetizer and the other the offer for a free dessert, and mails these cards to a sample of consumers in the ZIP code area of interest. When consumers present these cards to the restaurant waiter or waitress, the cards are kept. At the end of the time period specified for the test, the direct marketer counts how many responses each free gift offer generated. The offer that generates the largest response wins the test. Direct marketers then use the test results to determine which free gift to include when creating the offer. Of course, direct marketers may perform multiple tests if they want to investigate other terms or components of the offer.

Lois Geller has offered a simple, four-step approach to testing the offer.[8]

1. *Test only one feature at a time.* When you are testing an offer, be sure to change only one variable at a time. If you change more than one variable, whether it is creative, product or service, or price, you will not know what variable change caused the change in consumer response.
2. *Code your tests so you can measure results.* Each version of a promotion must have its own specific/individual code so that you will know which offer has generated the best response. For example, if you are testing the same offer in two different magazines, the only difference between them should be the code printed on the response device so that when consumers respond to the offer, you will know which magazine was responsible for generating that consumer's order.
3. *Keep accurate records.* Record all coded tests so that you can measure and analyze the test results. Recording test results can be as simple as writing them in a ledger book, or as sophisticated as computing an ongoing summation in a computerized database.
4. *Analyze test results and take action.* Whenever a test for an offer is complete, you will want to know which offer polled best, in other words generated the largest consumer response rate, so that you repeat the most effective offer.

Marketers should test their offers on an ongoing basis. In fact, early testing of an offer on a small market segment, rather than waiting until the offer is complete and ready to be rolled out to the entire consumer market, saves time and money. Remember that given time and preparation, *all* components of an offer can be tested—one at a time. Keep in mind that the ultimate goal of testing is to determine what will work the best in generating a response from the consumer.

Step 5: Execute the Offer

Once the direct marketer performs marketing research, decides on the terms of the offer, appropriately targets the offer to the right consumer market segment, and employs tests on various components of the offer, it is time to execute the offer. The first part of offer implementation is where the direct marketer uses the results of each test to revise the offer and make it more attractive to consumers. Once the direct marketer makes the necessary revisions, he or she is now prepared to put the offer into action.

What does executing the offer mean? It means that the direct marketer must be ready to implement the decisions made thus far. The direct marketer must be poised and prepared to fulfill the terms of the offer at the time of implementation. This means that if a free gift is offered with a purchase, the direct marketer must have an adequate supply of the free gifts to distribute to those consumers making a purchase. If the direct marketer is offering a new innovative color of a given product, that new color of product is ready to be packaged and shipped as soon as an order is received from a consumer.

In summary, creating the offer is a step-by-step process that culminates when a consumer accepts the offer and carries out the action that the direct marketer has asked him or her to take. Direct marketers who follow the steps described in this section should find greater success in both the execution of the offer and consumer acceptance of that offer. Creating the offer is a bit of science and art. The science is the logical sequence of steps that direct marketers should follow when creating the offer and the art is the many different kinds of offers that direct marketers can create. Let's take a look at some popular offers that are used in direct marketing.

POPULAR OFFERS

Although some offers may be unique and no offer is "right" for all situations, most are extensions of common offers that have stood the test of time. With that said, the following is an overview of nine popular offers.

1. *Free gift offers.* Providing a gift for inquiring, trying the product, purchasing the product, or for spending a certain dollar amount can be very effective, given the right situation.
2. *Other free offers.* Offering a free catalog, information booklet, estimate, demonstration, tour, delivery, and more is generally effective.
3. *Discount offers.* Everybody loves a bargain! Discounts can come in many different forms: cash discounts, quantity discounts, seasonal discounts, early bird discounts, and trade discounts to name a few. Discounts are most effective when the product or service has a well-established value. However, discounting the price can also generate a negative image. If a watch is priced at $15, consumers may perceive either that it is a bargain or it is simply "cheap." Therefore, direct marketers must use discount offers in conjunction with the promotional message that the offer is trying to convey.
4. *Sale offers.* Sale offers are similar to discount offers; there has to be a reason for the sale such as preseason sales, postseason sales, and holiday sales. Direct marketers often repeat seasonal sale offers on an annual basis if they are successful. Examples of sale offers include the

99 PROVEN DIRECT RESPONSE OFFERS

Basic Offers
1. Right Price
2. Free Trial
3. Money-Back Guarantee
4. Cash with Order
5. Bill Me Later
6. Installment Terms
7. Charge Card Privileges
8. C.O.D.

Free Gift Offers
9. Free Gift for an Inquiry
10. Free Gift for a Trial Order
11. Free Gift for Buying
12. Multiple Free Gifts with a Single Order
13. Your Choice of Free Gifts
14. Free Gifts Based on Size of Order
15. Two-Step Gift Offer
16. Continuing Incentive Gifts
17. Mystery Gift Offer

Other Free Offers
18. Free Information
19. Free Catalog
20. Free Booklet
21. Free Fact Kit
22. Send Me a Salesman
23. Free Demonstration
24. Free "Survey of Your Needs"
25. Free Cost Estimate
26. Free Dinner
27. Free Film Offer
28. Free House Organ Subscription
29. Free Talent Test
30. Gift Shipment Service

Discount Offers
31. Cash Discount
32. Short-Term Introductory Offer
33. Refund Certificate
34. Introductory Order Discount
35. Trade Discount
36. Early Bird Discount
37. Quantity Discount
38. Sliding Scale Discount
39. Selected Discounts

Sale Offers
40. Seasonal Sales
41. Reason-Why Sales
42. Price Increase Notice
43. Auction-By-Mail

Sample Orders
44. Free Sample
45. Nominal Charge Samples
46. Sample Offer with Tentative Commitment
47. Quantity Sample Offer
48. Free Sample Lesson

Time Limit Offers
49. Limited Time Offers
50. Enrollment Periods

51. Pre-Publication Offer
52. Charter Membership (or Subscription) Offer
53. Limited Edition Offer

Guarantee Offers
54. Extended Guarantee
55. Double-Your-Money-Back Guarantee
56. Guaranteed Buy-Back Agreement
57. Guaranteed Acceptance Offer

Build-Up-The-Sale Offers
58. Multi-Product Offers
59. Piggyback Offers
60. The Deluxe Offer
61. Good-Better-Best Offer
62. Add-On Offer
63. Write-Your-Own-Ticket Offer
64. Bounce-Back Offer
65. Increase and Extension Offers

Sweepstakes Offers
66. Drawing Type Sweepstakes
67. Lucky Number Sweepstakes
68. "Everybody Wins" Sweepstakes
69. Involvement Sweepstakes
70. Talent Contests

Club & Continuity Offers
71. Positive Option
72. Negative Option
73. Automatic Shipments
74. Continuity Load-Up Offer
75. Front-End Load-Ups
76. Open-Ended Commitment
77. "No Strings Attached" Commitment
78. Lifetime Membership Fee
79. Annual Membership Fee

Specialized Offers
80. The Philanthropic Privilege
81. Blank Check Offer
82. Executive Preview Charge
83. Yes/No Offers
84. Self-Qualification Offer
85. Exclusive Rights for Your Trading Area
86. The Super Dramatic Offer
87. Trade-In Offer
88. Third party Referral Offer
89. Member-Get-A-Member Offer
90. Name-Getter Offers
91. Purchase-With-Purchase
92. Delayed Billing Offer
93. Reduced Down Payment
94. Stripped-Down Products
95. Secret Bonus Gift
96. Rush Shipping Service
97. The Competitive Offer
98. The Nominal Reimbursement Offer
99. Establish-the-Value Offer

FIGURE 4-10 Kobs's 99 Proven Direct Response Offers. *Source:* Jim Kobs, Kobs & Brady Inc., "Profitable Direct Marketing," NTC Business Books, Linconwood, IL, 1993.

Mother's Day sale or Presidents' Day sale. Sale offers, such as inventory reduction or clearance sales, provide an explanation for the sale and thus make it more believable to the prospect. Unlike discount offers, sale offers tend to be held at certain times of the year and usually provide explanatory terms for their existence.

5. *Sample offers.* Sample offers are designed to get the product into the hands of a prospective buyer. Usually, they are offered in conjunction with continuity selling. An example is a free sample issue of a magazine offered along with a trial year subscription.

6. *Time-limit offers.* Time-limit offers work because they force the consumer to make a decision by a certain time. It is normally more effective to use an exact date, opposed to a time period (ten days), when implementing a time-limit offer. Examples of time-limit offers include magazine publishers who offer consumers a special price on a subscription if the consumer places their order by a specified date and amusement parks that offer consumers a free gift for purchasing a season pass by a specified date. In addition, book publishers commonly extend prepublication offers to consumers who place an order for a new book prior to the official publication date of the book. In this case, the publisher uses the prepublication orders to help in determining the printing quantity.

7. *Guarantee offers.* We've seen that guarantees are very common in direct marketing. Direct marketers commonly use money-back or extended guarantees. However, it is important to use common sense when offering time limits with the guarantee. For example, when selling fishing lures, be sure to allow enough time for the consumer to use the lures for a fishing season, prior to returning them if not satisfied.

8. *Build-up-the-sale offer.* The objective of a build-up-the-sale offer is to increase the dollar amount of the average order. An example is offering a volume of books for $19.95, and then offering the same volume of books, leather bound, for $24.95.

9. *Sweepstakes offers.* Contests or sweepstake offers add the element of excitement to an ordinary direct marketing appeal. There are, however, certain rules that must be followed in executing a sweepstakes offer. In addition, they may not be used in some states due to local restrictions.

These nine sample offers are only a few of the many creative types of offers that direct marketers have effectively used throughout the years. Jim Kobs, a leading authority in direct marketing, developed an extensive listing of tested, successful propositions. See Figure 4-10 for Kobs's 99 proven direct response offers.

Summary

In summary, planning the offer is a critical part of the success of any direct marketing campaign. It is reliant on a solid understanding of consumer needs and wants. All direct marketing offers are response-driven. Direct marketers must plan each offer. This planning includes establishing objectives, deciding on offer attractiveness, reducing offer risk, and selecting a creative appeal. Every offer consists of basic components and decisions that must be made by the direct marketer. These components include the product or service, pricing or payment terms, trial or examination period, guarantees, sweepstakes or contests, gifts or premiums, and time limits. Direct marketers must carefully create the offer to ensure success. The step-by-step process to follow when creating the offer involves performing marketing research, determining the terms of the offer, targeting the offer, testing the offer, and finally, revising and executing the offer. Direct marketers can create many different types of offers. Many direct marketers vary the offer based on the season. Some popular offers include free gift offers, discount offers, sale offers, sample offers, time-limit offers, guarantee offers, build-up-the-sale offers, and sweepstakes offers. These different types of offers have been presented in this chapter. In the next chapter you will learn how the creative strategy is used to position the offer to the target market.

Key Terms

offer *90*	till-forbid (TF) *93*	price penetration *98*
continuity selling *93*	cross-selling *93*	price elasticity *98*
positive option *93*	up-selling *93*	motivations *102*
negative option *93*	price skimming *98*	positioning *104*

Review Questions

1. Why is it important for direct marketers to understand consumer motivations when creating an offer? What can drive these motivations?
2. What is an *offer?* What are the elements of an effective offer?
3. What are the main differences between continuity selling, cross-selling, and up-selling?
4. What are the basic components to include in planning an offer?
5. Describe the four-step process to planning an offer. Is the order of this process important? Why or why not?
6. There are several popular offers. Name a few of the popular offers described in this chapter. How can you determine which offer will work best in a particular situation?
7. What are the four questions Donna Baier Stein and Floyd Kemske in their book *Write on Target* suggest every direct marketer or copywriter ask? What do they believe to be the key to effective direct marketing?
8. How do market segmentation and positioning strategies play a role in planning an offer?
9. Review Lois Geller's four-step approach to testing the offer. Apply these steps in the creation of a test to determine the best price for a new set of golf clubs.
10. Name the five specific product details direct marketers must consider when planning the offer. Select any direct marketing catalog and determine whether it provides each of these important product details.

Exercise

You are a part of the marketing team of a new brand of cola just introduced to the market. Your job is to plan the offer to promote the new product to the 21 to 35 age group via an online and direct mail campaign. As you already know, you have several variables to consider. To start with, examine the basic components to planning the offer. Next, follow the four steps to planning the offer. Of all the common popular offers presented in the chapter, which type of offer would you choose, or what combination would you use? Why do you think they would be effective?

CASE

Old American Insurance Company

Overview

There is nothing new about offers—in fact, direct marketers have been creating and using them for centuries. What you are about to read is a success story from long ago. It is a great example of how a direct marketer can use different offers to target different markets and achieve different objectives. This case focuses on planning and creating effective offers. It demonstrates how a direct marketer can use a variety of different offers to achieve numerous marketing objectives. It provides examples of how creatively the offer must be worded to maximize the rate of customer response. Finally, it illustrates how planning the offer is critical when attempting to maximize customer value by creating, cultivating, and retaining customers.

Case

In 1939, when Old American Insurance Company began to offer personal insurance to older Americans who were largely bypassed by traditional insurance agents, senior citizens were a widely dispersed minority group and difficult to reach. The best strategy for reaching this market segment seemed to be mail order—at the time, a completely new, untried strategy for selling insurance.

At that time, no one had compiled a list of senior citizens—no one, that is, except the departments of motor vehicles of the various states issuing driver's licenses. These early public records contained a wealth of customer identity factors, including color of eyes and hair, weight, and date of birth. Now, here was more than a list—here was a *database*. It was now up to Old American Insurance to compile this market segment from driver's licenses records. And it did.

Let's look at how Old American Insurance used a series of offers emphasizing continuity selling and cross-selling strategies to pioneer its Building-a-Customer program. Initially, Old American engaged in mail-order direct sales without involving an agent. Later, it applied its expertise in direct marketing to lead-generation programs for agent sales.

An older age prospect, identified from a databased mailing list, might first become a policyholder of Old American Insurance through purchase of an introductory term of a low-cost senior accident policy, from an initial short-term introductory offer such as this: "You are invited to spend 25 cents and receive 30 days of coverage under Old American Insurance Company's $25,000 Senior Accident Policy."

On conversion from the 30 days' introductory term, that is, when the prospect became a buyer or made a subsequent renewal, he or she might receive a thank-you letter like this one, along with another offer—an application form to pass along to another member of the family, which is a member-get-a-member offer.

Dear Policyholder:

Thank you for renewing your Senior Accident Policy. Your payment has been received and we have extended your coverage for the full period you requested.

You made the right decision to continue your Senior Accident protection. Now you can face the future more confidently, knowing that in case you have a covered accident, you'll be able to claim important cash benefits right when you need the money most.

Since you're a satisfied policyholder, I'm asking you to share this protection with others. That's why I've enclosed a Senior Accident Policy application for you to give to another member of your family. You'll see it makes the same offer that you took advantage of.

There is also enclosed with this letter a reply card on which can be listed names and addresses of friends and other relatives to whom you would like us to mail information on the insurance policies we offer.

The Senior Accident policyholder may also need supplemental life insurance. A cross-selling strategy follows, inviting the customer to buy *another product*—Guaranteed Acceptance Life Insurance—with the offer stating "the plain facts about our revolutionary plan of life insurance that guarantees to accept you if you are between the ages of 50 and 80."

To express appreciation and strive for continuity, a month or so in advance of the life insurance policy's renewal date, the company sent each customer a reproduction of a Norman Rockwell illustration suitable for framing. Of course, the objective of this incentive is to boost the response rate to the foregoing offer.

From its increasingly sophisticated database, Old American observed that its customer is approaching the age of eligibility for Medicare and quite likely will need private coverage to supplement Medicare benefits to reimburse health insurance deductible and co-pay amounts.

So Old American used another cross-selling strategy and provided the following "bill-me-later" offer:

HOW CAN YOU SAY "NO"
TO OUR INVITATION
TO TAKE A FREE LOOK AT
OUR MEDICARE-PLUS POLICY?

Dear Customer:

You can't possibly say "no"—it would be imprudent to pass up this offer to apply for this Medicare supplemental plan . . . for people 65 and over . . . for a full 30 days.

I believe you can only say "yes" once you see all the benefits this plan provides. And you do not have to send any money to apply.

Still another product cross-selling opportunity was used to present a related product—the Cancer Indemnity Protection Policy. This new product was offered to specific customers about whom Old American has information in its database. That offer used a free gift for inquiring and it read:

THere's some of the best news you'll ever hear about coping with cancer!
Get this book free—*CANCER . . . There's Hope*—
just for reviewing our CANCER INDEMNITY PROTECTION POLICY.

The gift book by H&R Block co-founder Richard Bloch tells how he used his positive mental attitude, prayer, and a will to fight to beat his cancer diagnosed as terminal.

Here's a final cross-selling offer that Old American used to create, care for, retain, and cultivate customers, whose lifetime value turned out to be the company's greatest asset. Old American wanted its customers to examine and be protected temporarily by a new product: coverage for surgical procedures. It sent each customer another BML offer with an actual policy labeled

> OFFICIAL POLICYHOLDER NOTIFICATION
> Valuable Insurance Policy
> Enclosed for Old American Policyholder:
> (Customer's Name/Address)
> In force, right now
> *at no cost to you!*

The envelope containing this document was stamped "Handle with Care," which applied to both the policy *and* the customer! Through inserts with premium billing as well as direct mail, Old American Insurance customers received a variety of offers designed to increase their existing coverage. They were also provided the opportunity to request information about other Old American Insurance products. Using the right offer, targeting the right customers, and executing effective attention-getting and direct response–driven creative appeals (the 40-40-20 rule) can spell great success for any direct marketer. Consumer response to the offers described in this case was outstanding. Old American Insurance was highly successful in using the variety of offers to increase both the number of new policyholders and renewals. The objective of each offer was met and exceeded, which is the real measure by which direct marketers gauge success.

Case Discussion Questions

1. What variety of offers did Old American Insurance use in marketing its Building-a-Customer program? What was the objective of each offer?
2. How were the strategies of cross-selling and continuity selling applied by the company?
3. What other offers could the company have used in marketing to the senior citizen market segment?

Why do you think these offers would have been successful?
4. Provide a specific example from the case of how the direct marketing 40-40-20 rule is being followed by Old American Insurance.

Notes

1. Adapted from Edward L. Nash (2000), *Direct Marketing: Strategy, Planning, Execution,* 4th ed. (New York: McGraw-Hill).
2. Ibid., p. 25.
3. Adapted from Lois K. Geller (1996), *Response: The Complete Guide to Profitable Direct Marketing* (New York: Free Press).
4. Ibid., p. 26.
5. Ibid., p. 27.
6. Adapted from Mary Lou Roberts and Paul D. Berger (1999), *Direct Marketing Management,* 2nd ed. (Upper Saddle River, NJ: Prentice Hall).
7. Adapted from ibid.
8. Adapted from ibid.

5

Planning and Creating Compelling Message Strategies

Opening Vignette: UPS Whiteboard Campaign

There is a copywriting principle that has been around for decades, maybe centuries, and it goes like this: "Keep it simple, stupid" or KISS. It's an easy formula to follow—keep the promotional message simple, easy for the audience to understand and remember, and it will be effective. But this is no small feat!

Effective ad copy, especially for a medium like television, where there is a good deal of "noise" or distractions for the average viewer, must break through the clutter and reach its audience. Of course, if the advertisement is a direct response ad, the copy must do even more. The creative message must not only seize the audience's attention, it must evoke the desired measurable response or transaction from its audience. Generate awareness and interest. Motivate the audience. Stimulate action.

That is just what The Martin Agency in Richmond, Virginia, did for its client, United Parcel Service (UPS), when it created the UPS Whiteboard campaign series. The UPS Whiteboard campaign breaks through and grabs the viewer's attention because it is different. It is less, which is more effective! With its series of simple and direct messages, it communicates real value to the prospective customer in a direct and straightforward manner.

FIGURE 5-1   UPS Whiteboard Small Business Advertisement.   *Source:* Used with permission of United Parcel Service.

FIGURE 5-2   UPS Whiteboard Morning Delivery Advertisement.   *Source:* Used with permission of United Parcel Service.

The UPS Whiteboard campaign features a handsome man with long dark hair and a bit of a smile on his face, standing at a whiteboard with a brown marker in hand, scribbling images and words about what differentiates UPS from its competitors in the package shipping business (see Figure 5-1). The man in these commercials is Andy Azula, creative director for The Martin Agency. In each ad it appears that Andy is having a conversation with his audience.

The campaign targets small business owners, shipping managers, and C-level audiences, but its message is compelling for all viewers: UPS offers a surprising array of services that help you manage your shipments. UPS provides services that help businesses succeed—beyond efficiently delivering packages. UPS will help eliminate normal business operation hassles and will give business owners more free time to spend on the really important and desirable things (see Figure 5-2).

Each 30-second TV spot presents basic images and clear and concise messages that end with an invitation to the viewing audience to visit its Web site and learn more about UPS's capabilities. In other words, it's a continuation of the well-known UPS campaign, "What Can Brown Do for You?" The Whiteboard campaign objectives were to get people to understand that UPS offers surprising solutions to business problems, showcase different products and services, and drive traffic to its Web site to learn more. The key to the success of this campaign is the sheer simplicity of the creative design and copy. Indeed, the UPS Whiteboard campaign is a prime example of where less is more!

Planning and creating compelling copy is what this chapter is about. In direct marketing terms, creativity encompasses the *content* of the direct mail package, direct response advertisement, Web site, or whatever media format is being used to convey the direct marketing offer. Creative strategies include decisions about the words, terms, symbols, designs, pictures, image, and media format that will be used in direct marketing activities. The old cliché "it's not creative unless it sells" implies that the creative strategies must attain the objectives set forth by the direct marketer. These objectives may be to generate a response, transaction, political vote, or charitable donation. Regardless of the objectives, direct marketers make many decisions in planning and developing creative strategies. These decisions include research, objectives, brand and image, design and format, copywriting and graphics, and message creation and execution based on media selection. These are the key topics of this chapter.

Creating promotions in direct marketing requires the special kind of creativity with which this chapter is concerned. With emphasis on the "message" aspect of promotion, we discuss the need for conducting research and setting creative objectives. Then we explore copywriting and graphics techniques and strategies. Finally, we look at creating messages for specific media. The "media" themselves—printed media (direct mail, magazines, newspapers), broadcast media (television, radio, telephone), and high-tech digital media (Internet, blogging, social networking, mobile)—will be dealt with in turn in later chapters, as will the adaptation of messages to these.

CREATIVE RESEARCH

The creative process to develop compelling messages for any direct response promotion, in any format or in any medium, begins with research and leads to idea generation and finally copywriting. Direct marketers must really understand their target audiences. This includes customer preferences, buying patterns, offer and media preferences, contact preferences, and more. In the perspective of traditional economics, the demand by individual consumers is often viewed as a function of their money income or their accumulated wealth. In the real world, money income is not the *only* determinant of demand; in fact, it might not even be the major one. In addition to recognizing the real complexity of demand, the direct marketer also needs to study and understand buyer behavior.

What motivates buyers to take action? A buyer's ability to buy can be evaluated by well-understood demographic indicators such as income, wealth, age, gender, and marital status. However, buyer behavior is also influenced by environmental factors and psychographic indicators of lifestyle that are not readily identifiable or easily measurable. Marketers want to measure these environmental factors to determine the proneness to spend and the willingness to buy. To do this, they use such measurements as income in relation to what others are earning in a particular ZIP code, they study purchase actions of record, as well as the educational level and the social class of the area. These can be important customer qualifications. As social economist Thorstein Veblen observed,[1] so can the "conspicuous consumption" of a neighborhood.

The basic concept of human ecology that behavior is a response to environmental influences tells us that a household with a $20,000 annual income located in a ZIP code area in which the median household income is $30,000 is likely to emulate that median level. The reverse is also true, with a $50,000 household tending to behave like its $30,000 ZIP code area neighbors. This tendency contributes to homogeneity of behavior within such areas, even though there is a variance of characteristics among and between individual households.

Discretionary household purchases under such circumstances are dependent not just on the *ability to buy* but also on the *proneness to spend*. Because this is such a potentially powerful economic force, direct marketers are well advised to understand it as they study the qualifications available within customer databases, the readership of magazines and newspapers, or the characteristics of television viewers and Internet browsers.

It is imperative for direct marketers to understand the economic and social differences among an infinite variety of consumers in the marketplace. They must also be aware of a vast number of factors motivating these individuals. The challenge to those responsible for creating compelling message strategies is to get inside the head of a buyer and to know what the benefits to the customer will be and what will motivate the customer to take action to gain them.

To plan effective messages, marketers must also understand how the consumer thinks and what he or she perceives. What are the key benefits each consumer is trying to obtain? In addition, direct marketers must research the competition to determine what other alternatives consumers have to fulfill their needs, wants, and desires. Armed with detailed knowledge about consumers, direct marketers can begin to plan and create effective messages that will not only get the attention and interest of consumers but hopefully stimulate action—if action is the objective.

MESSAGE OBJECTIVES

Planning and creating compelling messages also relies on the objective of the message. Is it intended to sell a product, generate a Web site visit, obtain a donation, evoke an inquiry, or secure a vote? Does the message have some other measurable intention? Is there more than one objective that must be taken into consideration? If so, there may be a need for more than one message strategy based on differing consumer needs. In Chapter 3 we explored the need for segmenting consumers into homogeneous groups with similar needs, wants, desires, and so on. Customer research can also determine which segments of consumers are more prone to respond based on the objectives of the message. Often, customized messaging is required to effectively communicate with different market segments of consumers. Therefore, long before you can create compelling messages, you must know all about your customers as well as the intention of your promotional message.

Direct marketers relate the costs of promotion to the results achieved from it. Managers need to see costs such as advertising and selling as adding value. Organizations work continually to improve efficiency of direct marketing by measuring its costs and its results accurately. It has been said that "if it weren't for advertising, you would pay more for most things you buy." The informational value of promotion makes this so through creation of demand resulting from product awareness by customers. Thus a key objective of creative copy is to generate a return on investment for the direct marketer. Of course, it is up to each individual direct marketer and creative campaign to determine exactly what the desired return should be.

Mindful that a major goal of marketing is to convey product benefits to present and potential customers, advertising professionals have vacillated in recent times between creative messages that create brand awareness, or are image building, and those more directed to immediate sales or response.

Many direct marketers do indeed feel that it's not creative unless it sells something! Though this is likely an exaggeration, we need to distinguish between advertising that promotes brand and builds long-term image and advertising that seeks an immediate response or transaction. Those creating direct marketing campaigns are more attuned to the latter objectives, but that is not to say they are oblivious to the former. Direct response copywriters must not only possess skill as a wordsmith but also create copy to achieve message objectives. This entails many different copywriting and graphics techniques. Let's delve into that topic.

COPYWRITING AND GRAPHICS TECHNIQUES

Every successful promotion has at its heart a concept and an offer . . . and blends product, price, and place in a way that provides benefits to a target market. As we presented in the previous chapter, customers will respond to offers if they provide benefits that appeal to them. Such benefits can be the physical attributes of a product, translated into terms that meet customer needs. Customers don't buy quarter-inch drill bits; they buy the ability to make quarter-inch holes! They don't buy power steering; they buy ease in parking a car parallel to a curb. Direct marketers therefore use promotion that is benefit oriented. They sell benefits in a manner that matches a customer's motivation.

Features versus Advantages versus Benefits

Charles B. Mills, a direct response copywriter at O. M. Scott's Lawn Products, when asked why he was so adept at writing copy for Scott's grass seed, replied, "Because I like to talk about your lawn, not about my seed." Airlines sell a vacation in some exotic place, not the trip to get there. Designers sell fashion and acceptance more than the practicality of clothing. Insurance companies sell security and peace of mind, not a paper contract. Elmer Wheeler, sales motivator, summed it up, saying, "Sell the sizzle, not the steak." Direct response advertisers rely on copy that emphasizes such benefits to motivate responders.

Vic Schwab, a successful advertising copywriter with such ability, described the copywriting art as "learning to think like a horse." As an illustration, he told the story of a farmer who had lost his horse. "How'd you find him so quickly?" asked a neighbor. To which the farmer replied: "Well, I just asked myself, if I were a horse, where would I go? I went there and there he was!" Schwab used this story to drive home his copywriter's maxim that you have to "show people an advantage." This meant, to Schwab, that *you had to know them!*

Today, a database can provide the knowledge that enables the trained copywriter to "think like a horse," to relate the benefits of offers to customers. Direct response copywriting is an art. Those who have the talent and have achieved a track record of success are much in demand. They have the ability to translate product features into advantages, these into benefits, and benefits into words, design, and graphics.

Phrases such as these typify compelling promotional copy:

- "An important message for persons over age 65."
- "Are you tired of the back-breaking work caring for your lawn?"
- "At last . . . a simple, effective way to rid your house of bugs."
- "Do you need more room in your house . . . or a new roof?"
- "Here's good news for taxpayers!"

Offers incorporating customer benefits are structured to incite action and overcome human inertia. An analytical technique for identifying benefits, FAB (features-advantages-benefits), appears in Figure 5-3.

As demonstrated in Figure 5-3, a washing machine might be of compact size, feature high spin speed, provide a variety of wash temperature choices, accommodate a range of colors, and might include a tumble dryer. These are *features* of the washing machine included in its manufacture—features often promoted in consumer advertising.

The direct response advertising copywriter seeks to translate these product features into advantages and, then, from these into benefits. Compact size, for example, provides the advantage

---

Translating Features of a Washing Machine into Advantages and Then into Benefits

Features (what the product has):
- compact size
- high spin speed
- wash temperature choice
- range of colors
- integrated tumble drier

Advantages (what the features do):
- fits into a smaller space
- clothes dry faster
- accommodates a full range of fabrics
- offers choice to consumer
- moves from wash to dry automatically

Benefits (why customers buy):
- space saving
- time saving
- does a good job
- flexibility
- convenience
- economy
- no more hand washing
- choices

How to get from features to benefits:
. . . imagination
. . . technology
. . . product design
. . . common sense

FIGURE 5-3 Features/Benefits.

of the machine fitting into a smaller space, the benefit being space saving. High spin, as another example, provides the advantage of clothes drying faster and the resulting benefit is the customer saving time. Figure 5-3 provides the direct response copywriter with a useful procedure for identifying benefits as a necessary prelude to actual copywriting.

Writing the Copy

Effective copywriting begins by determining the **big idea** and then creatively weaving that big idea into all aspects and elements of the creative campaign. Think of the big idea as a highlighted unique selling point or creative phrase that becomes the star or focal point of an entire promotional campaign. The big idea should become the company's tagline, logo, symbol, or slogan and should be consistently used throughout all creative strategies and materials. The big idea should be branded to create a synergy with real identity and meaning for the company or organization. How does a company create the big idea? Many different ways. The big idea is often the result of individual or group brainstorming sessions. However, some of the best big ideas are created by simply honing a wild off-the-wall idea. Creative experts say that many off-the-wall or potential big ideas usually come to mind when they least expect them. Some of these different moments may include when a copywriter is out jogging, socializing, or taking a shower! Regardless of how the big idea is developed, it should be catchy, a real attention getter, and brief—not too many words, easy to recognize and remember. Of course, the big idea usually ties in with the company's overall copy appeal.

The **copy appeal** is the basic underlying theme of the promotion or campaign. Most copy appeals are timeless because they stem from basic human needs—what people want to gain, save, avoid, or become. Some examples include the following:

People want to gain self-confidence, improved appearance, time, professional advancement, increased enjoyment, personal prestige, popularity, praise from others, financial wealth.
People want to save time, money, memories.
People want to avoid criticism, physical pain, trouble, discomfort, embarrassment, work, worry, effort, emotional suffering.
People want to become good citizens, creative, efficient, knowledgeable, good parents, physically fit, influential over others, popular, successful, recognized authorities, respected.

Copywriters must determine and use the appropriate copy appeal based on the desired response. There are three basic types of appeals: rational, emotional, and moral. *Rational* appeals emphasize logic and reasoning. They usually present facts and figures. *Emotional* appeals are irrational and may focus on love, pride, joy, and humor. *Moral* appeals emphasize ethics and target consumers' feelings of what is "right" or "proper" from an ethical perspective. In some cases, copywriters may use a combination of the three basic appeals.

Figure 5-4 provides several creative examples of effective copy appeals used in direct response advertisements. Each of these advertisements for Hauser's Jewelers, a family-owned upscale jewelry store located in Newport News, Virginia, presents a simple message laced with subtle humor.

Each of these advertisements has an attractive and effective layout featuring a creative headline, a picture of the featured jewelry, Hauser's Jewelers name, and its address and Web site to encourage action. Moreover, each headline offers a message appeal that stems from the basic human desire of most men—to give a truly special and memorable gift. The copy in each advertisement stems from basic human desires, and it is presented in a humorous tone. This combination is what makes copy appeals highly effective.

FIGURE 5-4 Hauser's Jewelers Copy Advertisements.

Successful copywriting often follows a formula to keep copy flowing in a logical sequence. Several of these formulas, which have been used extensively for many years, are presented here.

BOB STONE'S SEVEN-STEP FORMULA

1. Promise a benefit in your headline or first paragraph, your most important benefit.[2]
2. Immediately enlarge on your most important benefit.
3. Tell the reader exactly what he or she is going to get.
4. Back up your statements with proofs and endorsements.
5. Tell the reader what will be lost by not acting.
6. Rephrase your prominent benefits in the closing offer.
7. Incite action now.

A-I-D-A Of unknown origin, this formula has been used a great deal by direct response copywriters for many years:

1. Attract *A*ttention
2. Arouse *I*nterest
3. Stimulate *D*esire
4. Call for *A*ction

P-P-P-P Created by Henry Hoke, Sr., and popularized by Edward N. Mayer Jr., two pioneer direct marketers, is this tried-and-true formula for direct response copywriting:

1. *Picture*—get attention early in copy to create desire.
2. *Promise*—tell what the product or service will do, describe its benefits to the reader.
3. *Prove*—show value, backed up with personal testimonials or endorsements.
4. *Push*—ask for the order.

STAR-CHAIN-HOOK L. E. "Cy" Frailey, who authored many books on letter writing, described "the star, the chain, and the hook" invented by another professional letter writer, Frank Dignan, as follows.[3]

1. Get the reader's favorable attention. Do it with an opening paragraph which is bright and brisk—*the star.*
2. Follow quickly with a flow of facts, reasons, and benefits, all selected and placed in the best order to transform attention to interest and finally to desire—*the chain.*
3. Suggest action and make it easy as possible—*the hook.*

KISS PRINCIPLE   Of unknown origin, this creative copywriting formula stands for "keep it simple stupid." We presented the KISS principle earlier in this chapter's opening vignette. The KISS copywriting formula has been effectively used by creative geniuses for centuries. The basic premise is to keep the message simple and easy to understand and remember.

Figure 5-5 presents an excellent example of the KISS copywriting formula in creative design. The creative design on this oversized self-mailer postcard for Calico Corners, a high-end retailer of custom draperies, furniture, and home accessories, is divided into three portions. Each portion features a photograph and a simple message shown in a shadow box for prospective consumers. The message is bold and punchy. "Dream It." "Design It." "Done." It conveys the ease and simplicity involved in the thinking, buying, and implementing processes when new homeowners shop at Calico Corners.

FIGURE 5-5   CalicoCorners Creative Design.
Source: Used with permission of CalicoCorners and MindZoo, LLC. Photo by Kim Kirby, www.jimkirbyphoto.com.

Using Design and Graphics

Hand in hand with copy—the words, the expressions, the ideas, the meanings—go design and graphics—the art, the layout, the symbols, the effects. Here are included the impact of photographs, illustrations, type styles, paper, inks, size, and a variety of other attention-getting devices. Through design and graphics, the designer, like the copywriter, creates mood and feeling while getting and holding attention. In direct marketing the ultimate goal of the designer, like that of the copywriter, is to stimulate action, to generate measurable response. Thus, design (like copy) becomes a means and not an end—another element of the total promotion process.

The designer of direct marketing promotion has available a great many graphic techniques for use in a variety of media: direct mail, print, broadcast, and interactive electronic display as well as posters and billboards. These include the following.

LAYOUTS   A **layout** positions copy and illustrations not only to gain attention but also to direct the reader through the message in the sequence intended by the copywriter. Compelling layouts make optimal use of type as well as white space, photographs along with illustrations, and other graphic techniques, including shapes, sizes, folds, die-cuts, and pop-ups. Figure 5-6 shows the effective use of a die-cut shape, as well as effective layout with multiple headlines, body copy, art, company logo, and response information.

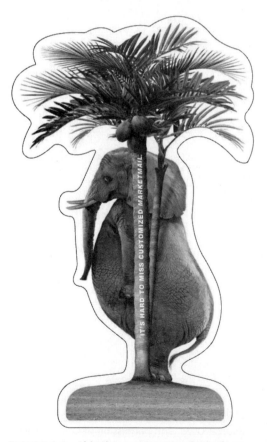

FIGURE 5-6   ShipShapes Direct Mail, Elephant.

ILLUSTRATIONS AND PHOTOGRAPHS   A compelling illustration can create attention. Photographs of products in use, especially showing people, can dramatize benefits. The designer, using graphic illustrations, can even extend to designed borders, highlighting copy elements for prominence, tint blocks, and emphasis of elements such as product features and response forms.

INVOLVEMENT DEVICES   Many direct response advertising devices spur action by **involvement devices** that engage the reader in some way. These include tokens, stamps, punch-outs, puzzles, premiums, and gadgets that the reader returns to the seller. Links and click buttons are natural involvement devices of Web sites.

TYPE   Designers use typefaces to suggest boldness or dignity, Old English or Asian, antiquity or space age, movement or emphasis, masculinity or femininity. They know that typefaces need to be relevant to the message, and they also need to be easily and instantly readable. Sizes of typefaces are a factor to consider as are the thickness and complexity of the type's structure. When the designer uses more than one typeface or type size, these should blend, and the variety should not become complicated. Sometimes, to create emphasis, typefaces can be overprinted on one another and sometimes they are reversed, that is, white on color. Certain special designs become recognizable logotypes for organizations, such as the typefaces used in advertising for Sears, Swiss Colony, *Time,* and IBM.

PAPER   Here the designer is concerned with substance, texture, and finish as well as color, weight, size, and shape of paper. A linen or laid finish can denote elegance. A parchment stock can denote permanence. Paper can have a high-gloss finish for use in a catalog of upscale merchandise, or it can simulate the look of a newspaper to convey timeliness. Paper can convey the impression of the Yellow Pages of a phone book or the urgency of a telegram. Paper not only helps set the tone of a direct response advertisement but its texture, weight, and size can have substantial impact on cost.

INK   Like paper, ink can convey impressions through color, gloss, intensity, and placement. Ink selection must consider the paper and the printing process as well as design. Some inks are even available with fragrances, such as the smell of lavender or pine trees. Some can be embossed to simulate gold and silver coins. Some can be scraped off to reveal a printed message underneath. Some can be printed on unusual paper stock, such as cellophane, waxed paper, or foil.

COLOR   Much information has been developed about the physical and psychological effects of color since Sir Isaac Newton first associated basic colors with sunlight. We know that light, heat, and color have much in common. The darker the color, the more light and heat are absorbed. Certain colors, notably yellow, can be seen farther than others; black printed on yellow provides maximum readability. Some colors convey associations: Purple implies royalty, red is associated with danger, green denotes safety, and blue is a "health" color (i.e., health insurance provided by Blue Cross). Psychologically, the "warm" colors (yellow, orange, red) stimulate, and the "cool" colors (blue, green, violet) sedate. Thus, the former might more likely encourage action if used in a direct response advertisement. Colors have different meanings to various cultures, to various ages, in various geographic locations; the direct response advertising designer needs to be aware of these.

     The JCPenney Dorm Living direct mail piece featured in Figure 5-7 is an excellent example of effective layout. This direct mailer was designed to promote merchandise to rising freshmen entering college for the first time and to motivate these students to shop from its online Dorm Shop at www.JCPenney.com. The creative design matched the branding established for the Dorm Shop so that online and direct mail branding strategies complemented each other.

FIGURE 5-7 **JCPenney Dorm Living Promotion.** *Source:* Photo by Jim Kirby, www.jimkirbyphoto.com.

The format presents products with compartmentalized product messages, such as "Must-Haves" and "Nice-To-Haves," where photographs and bullet points provide detailed lists for each category. A handy dorm shopping checklist is provided with product items listed under various categories, such as eat, sleep, decorate, shower, clean, and travel. It uses a variety of type styles and colors along with enough white space to allow for easy reading. Notice how the photographs show the variety of different product colors available and how the front panel appears to be written on note-book paper. The offer of free shipping is circled to gain attention, and the Web site is clearly displayed repeatedly throughout the direct mail piece. Finally, the direct mail piece contains action words such as "Order Today" with multiple options for doing so, along with a promotional code to take advantage of the free shipping offer. Careful layout and design planning will boost the rate of response for any direct marketing creative format. Joining compelling messages with effective layout and design is indeed a formidable combination!

CREATING MESSAGES FOR SPECIFIC MEDIA

The copywriting and graphics techniques discussed in the preceding sections apply to all the media used by direct response advertisers: direct mail, print, broadcast, and electronic. This section is concerned with special considerations when creating messages for each of these media. The characteristics of the media themselves are discussed in subsequent chapters.

Direct Mail

Compared with other media, direct mail provides considerably more space and opportunity to tell a complete story. It can gain attention and develop an orderly and logical flow of information leading to action by the reader. Direct mail, too, has a unique capability to involve the recipient and faces less competition for attention at the time it is received than other advertising media. It is the most scientifically testable of all media because marketers can control experimentation with variables such as format, copy, and graphics.

With adequate marketing research, direct mail affords the opportunity for positioning products to specific market segments and can, through computer and printing technology, individualize each piece to each recipient. The following example illustrates how companies effectively use market research to create a direct marketing campaign and target different consumer groups. Family-owned Lacks Home Furnishings, headquartered in Victoria, Texas, performed a customer database analysis to determine the need for two different creative versions in a recent direct marketing campaign. Research showed that 33 percent of the new homeowner prospect population qualified as "affluent" shoppers, and the remaining 67 percent were classified as "careful" shoppers. As Figure 5-8 shows, the company targeted each shopper category with unique direct mail pieces—each one featuring different creative images. Both direct mail pieces contain the same two coupon

FIGURE 5-8   Lacks Unique Homeowner Program Direct Mail Pieces.   *Source:* Used with permission of Lacks Home Furnishings and MindZoo, LCC. Photo by Jim Kirby, www.jimkirbyphoto.com.

offers to promote multiple shopping trips; however, photographs of both the home elevation and interior design are different in an effort to target the two unique market segments.

The advantages of direct mail also give it the highest cost per reader, so that marketers must always seek the highest response rate, when compared with other lower-cost media. There are three basic formats of direct mail: the self-mailer, the classic format, and the catalog.

SELF-MAILERS   A **self-mailer** is any direct mail piece mailed without an envelope. Figure 5-9 presents an innovative format of a self-mailer. This distinctive (ten-panel, small, odd-sized) creative design was used by The *Spokesman-Review* to target new subscribers in the Spokane, Washington, area. This piece was quite different from all other pieces used by The *Spokesman-Review,* which helped it stand out in the mailbox. Additionally, the creative copy featured The *Spokesman-Review*'s 125th anniversary, a once-in-a-lifetime event, enabling a unique subscription sales message to be crafted to prospective consumers. The *Spokesman-Review* is an example of how special events can sometimes motivate unique direct mail formats.

Self-mailers can range from simple postcards to tubes to a variety of different sizes and shapes of direct mail. Self-mailers can promote a single product/service or many products/services at one time. Mailing pieces promoting a single product or a limited group of related products are often called **solo mailers.** Figure 5-10 presents some examples of ShipShapes, a company specializing in

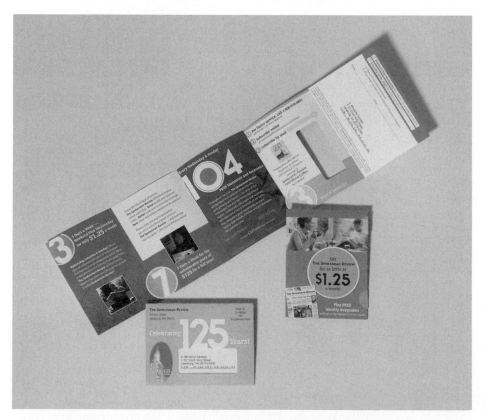

FIGURE 5-9   The *Spokesman-Review* 125th Anniversary Innovative Self-Mailer Format.
Source: Reproduced with permission of The *Spokesman-Review.* Permission is granted in the interest of public discussion and does not imply endorsement of any product, service, or organization otherwise mentioned herein. Used with permission of MindZoo, LLC. Photo by Jim Kirby, www.jimkirbyphoto.com.

FIGURE 5-10   ShipShapes Self-Mailers, Frog and Car.   *Source:* Used with permission of ShipShapes™.

the creation of unique self-mailers. ShipShapes provides customized self-mailers that really grab attention. Nearly any shape goes, a car, frog, elephant, cartoon character, floral bouquet—if you can imagine it, ShipShapes will create it! So think out-of-the-box and out-of-the-envelope and explore the many creative, colorful, and eye-catching designs associated with self-mailers.

CLASSIC FORMAT   The **classic format** consists of these components: a mailing envelope, a letter, a brochure, and a return device. Some direct marketers include an extra enclosure or separate slip of paper that highlights a free gift or some other information, which is often printed on a different color and size of paper to make it stand out from the rest of the mailing package. If there is lack of experience about the promotion format to be used, this is usually the starting point.

    Mailing Envelope.   The envelope is a vital component to the success of a direct mail package, for unless the envelope receives attention and is opened, the contents will never be revealed. For this reason, direct response advertisers often use teaser copy on the outside of a mailing envelope in order to lead the recipient inside to entice but not reveal. Figure 5-11 shows examples of how Valpak effectively uses teaser copy on its famous blue outer envelopes. In addition to teaser copy, the size, color, shape, and paper texture of the outer envelope can provide feelings of importance, urgency, prestige, or bargain to the recipient.

    Letter.   The principal element of the direct mail package, the **letter**, provides the primary means for communication and personalization. Databases enable personalization of letters. Marketers frequently ask, "How long should a letter be?" The answer is obvious: as long as it needs to be; or, as Abraham Lincoln responded when he was asked how long a man's legs should be,

FIGURE 5-11   Valpak Teaser Copy.

"Long enough to touch the ground." Letters can be narrative and intriguing, such as those setting the scene for books or magazines, or they can be factual and staccato, such as those used for merchandise or insurance.

The P.S. (postscript) at the end of a letter has high visual value. The recipient will frequently read this part of the letter first. For that reason, the copywriter often uses the P.S. to restate the offer, highlight benefits, and direct the reader to another part of the package.

Brochure   The **brochure** (often called a flyer, folder, or circular) is an optional piece that augments the letter (if needed) to provide product specifications, cover technical points such as pricing, provide scene-setting narrative and photographs, and dramatize and illustrate while incorporating benefits to the reader. A brochure is sometimes a physical part of the letter itself—pages two and three of a four-page letter/brochure format, for example. It can be as simple as a single sheet printed on one side only or as complicated as multifolded brochures, giant broadsides, or multipage booklets. Headlines and illustrations are vital parts of brochures, along with adequate subheads and body copy to provide full description and entice action. Sometimes testimonials or endorsements can lend credence to product claims or report satisfied users.

Response Device.   Once the mailing envelope, letter, and brochure have performed their particular function, the **response device** provides the means for action. This device can be as simple as a postage-paid return card with a mere "check off" of instructions, or it can be an order form providing for remittance or credit instructions along with specific product selections, or it can be as complex as an application for insurance, a credit card, or an investment. In any event, it should be a selling piece. It should have a name to identify it, it should be well designed, and it should contain compelling and clear-cut copy. It should be easy to complete. Figure 5-12 shows an order form used

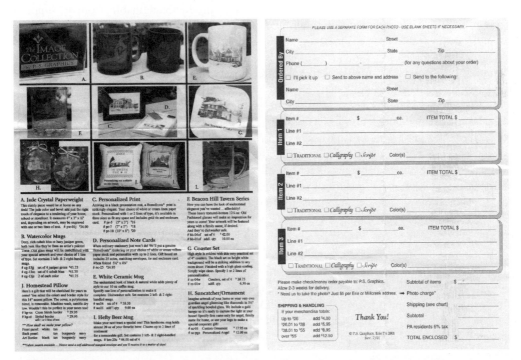

FIGURE 5-12   **Example of an Order Form as a Response Device.**   *Source:* Used with permission of P.S. Graphics.

by P. S. Graphics when marketing Homefronts personalized stationery. The order form is the response device for the company. Note the adequate amount of space and special instructions to guide the consumer in completing the order form.

The real challenge to the direct response advertiser in developing response devices is to provide, in a condensed format, all the necessary elements of the response/transaction while at the same time keeping the form logical, orderly, and simple. Involvement devices should be constructed to lure the reader into action. A signature is often required, such as with a charged merchandise order, an insurance application, a credit authorization, or an investment instruction.

Reply Envelope. Unless a card is used as a response device, a separate reply envelope is usually provided as an incentive and as a convenience and to ensure privacy, especially if remittance is requested. Often, depending on the mathematics of the offer and whether curiosity seekers are to be discouraged, reply postage is prepaid. Sometimes wallet-flap envelopes incorporate an order form on the seal flap. Specialty envelopes provide an order blank combined with a reply envelope. Examples of such order forms can be found bound, as a convenience, into many mail-order catalogs. Like other elements of the classic direct mail package, the reply envelope should be designed to encourage action.

Catalogs

Certainly one of the most challenging and popular formats for direct marketers is the catalog. A **catalog** is a multipage format or booklet that displays photographs and/or descriptive details of products/services along with prices and order details. A catalog can have just a few pages or hundreds of pages. Direct marketers may produce their catalogs in house or by contract with an outside agency or organization. Catalog shopping offers almost every product imaginable, from art supplies to gourmet food and drink, children's clothing, games, toys, home furnishings, perfumes, gear for camping and sporting, automotive supplies, gardening tools, jewelry, and books. You can also find the latest, greatest fashions.

Figure 5-13 presents an excellent example of creativity in catalog design. Hauser's Jewelers created its holiday catalog with a unique twist.

This 12-page booklet was designed to feature extraordinary jewelry collections as well as be a keepsake holiday recipe booklet for its customers. Each page contained a jewelry collection along with a corresponding page with a recipe and a picture of the baked good that coordinated with the colors of the jewelry. For example, the ruby collection was presented with a picture and recipe of red velvet cake and the brown Fabergé collection was shown with a picture and recipe of pecan pie. The catalog itself was a holiday greeting from Hauser's Jewelers family to each of its customers. Each recipe, shared by an associate of Hauser's Jewelers, featured a hand-written note about the recipe and how it brought back holiday memories. Let this example serve to inspire creativity in catalog design.

COPY, DESIGN, AND GRAPHICS A notable attribute of catalog copy is succinctness, brevity, and conciseness—few words and to the point. Catalog copy goes hand in hand with design, illustration, and graphics. Pictures show it, words describe it. Descriptive words often found in catalog copy include these: *quality, genuine, fine, full, comfortable, heavy, natural,* and *best.* Like all direct marketing promotional copy, the words are arranged to spell out benefits. The words *inform* at the same time they *sell.*

The beauty that is ruby: 18k, ruby & diamond clip/post earrings, $3,925. Art Deco inspired platinum,
ruby & diamond ring, $7,195. Platinum, ruby & diamond bracelet, $11,750.

Red Velvet Cake

Ingredients: 1 cup margarine (2 sticks) ~
1 1/2 cups sugar ~ 2 eggs ~ 1 oz. red food
coloring ~ 1 tsp. baking soda ~ 1 tsp. vinegar ~ 2 tsp. cocoa ~ 1/4 tsp. cinnamon ~
1/2 tsp. salt ~ 2 1/2 cups flour ~ 1 tsp.
vanilla ~ 1 cup plus 2 Tbs. buttermilk.

Recipe: Cream the margarine, sugar, and
eggs on medium speed. Mix the food coloring, cinnamon, and cocoa in a separate
bowl, then add to creamed mixture and
mix well. Add salt and vanilla. Then alternate with the buttermilk and flour. Beat
well. Add baking soda and vinegar. Mix
well. Bake in 3 round cake pans at 350
degrees for 25 - 30 min. Cool well, then
frost.

Frosting: Mix 2 Tbs. cornstarch with 1 cup
water. Cook until thick and cool. Mix 2
sticks of softened butter and 1 cup of
granulated sugar. Add 1 tsp. vanilla and a
few drops of lemon extract. Cream 10
min. well, then add cornstarch mixture.
Blend until all lumps are gone. Frost.

*when you eat into this cake, the smile on your
face will reach all the way down to your tummy!
Jamie*

Fabulous Faberge®: The rich beauty of chocolate brown enhanced by 18k gold & diamonds.
Earrings, $7,730. Egg pendant, $6,150. Matching chain, $1,750. Cufflinks, $3,520.

Pecan Pie

3 eggs ~ 1/4 lb. of butter, melted (1 stick) ~
3/4 cup brown sugar ~ 3/4 cup dark Karo syrup ~
3/4 cup pecans, chopped ~ 1 tsp. vanilla ~
1 9-inch pie shell ~ pecan halves

Beat eggs thoroughly. Add melted butter, brown
sugar, and dark Karo syrup. Beat mixture. Add
chopped pecans and mix. Add vanilla and mix.
Pour into unbaked pie shell. Cover top with pecan
halves. Bake at 350 degrees for about 40 minutes
or until firm.

*a dollop of vanilla ice cream is
the perfect topping for this wonderful
combination of meaty pecan crunch
and delightful robust sweetness — Lee*

FIGURE 5-13   Hauser's Jewelers Holiday Catalog and Recipe Book.

Platinum & pave' diamond ring with 1.50 ct diamond, $21,250. Diamond fleur-de-lis lavalier, 18k, $1,995. Fancy brown 2.09 ct marquise diamond surrounded by micro pave' diamonds, platinum, $12,925. Platinum, 2.62 ct diamond ring, price upon request.

FIGURE 5-13 (continued)

Layout, including space allocation, is important. Like the store retailer who allocates shelf space and position according to the potential profitability of products displayed, a catalog retailer allocates space and position in print. Successful catalogers allocate space, including preferred positioning, such as covers, according to a product's potential profitability.

The copywriter must anticipate objections and overcome them in advance, at the same time holding the number of words used to a minimum. The catalog copy must be concise, yet it must be complete and clear. Notice the effective use of copy, design, and images in the Cheryl&Co. catalog shown in Figure 5-14. The free shipping offer is clearly presented, as is the company's Web site and

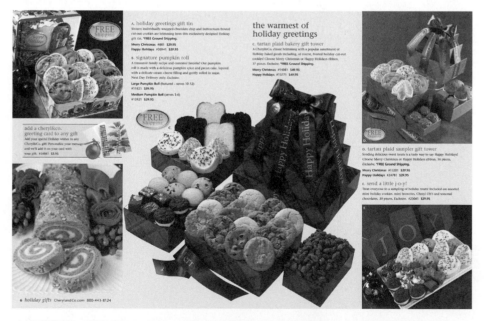

FIGURE 5-14 Cheryl&Co. Catalog Page. *Source:* Used with permission of Cheryl&Co®.

toll-free number for easy ordering. The pictures feature the products in an appetizing and appealing fashion. This catalog page inspires gift giving.

Print Advertising (Magazines and Newspapers)

A key consideration for direct marketers, in the development of direct response advertisements for use in print media, magazines, and newspapers, is space limitation, when compared to direct mail. Because print advertisements must compete with other advertisements as well as the editorial content of the print media, the headline is the most important element. Like catalog copy, the headlines of print ads must gain attention quickly and the body copy must tell the story completely yet concisely. Copy must be benefit oriented and the graphic design should lead the reader through the advertisement's elements in intended sequence. Illustrations augment copy.

ELEMENTS OF PRINT ADS   Direct response print advertisements must contain an attention-getting headline, compelling body copy to stimulate interest and desire, and a strong call-to-action response device that can be traced, tracked, and measured. Let's explore each of these elements in greater detail.

   Headlines   Possibly the most important element of a direct response print advertisement is the headline, and possibly the most famous direct response headline of all times is this one created long ago by John Caples for the U.S. School of Music:

> They Laughed When I Sat Down
> at the Piano . . .
> but When I Started to Play!

Many years after the first appearance of this headline, the following appeared in a business magazine advertisement sponsored by a regional telephone company:

> They Laughed When I Sat Down
> at the Telephone . . .
> but When I Started to Dial!

More recently, this headline appeared in a trade publication advertisement for a high-tech manufacturer; in fact, it won an advertising industry award for its creator:

> They Laughed When You Sat Down at the Computer . . .
> but Then You Started to Type!

Productive headline ideas are often repeated, as the previous examples demonstrate. Here are some other effective headlines:

> How to Subscribe to *The Wall Street Journal*. (*The Wall Street Journal*)
> Suddenly I Lost My Memory! (Career Institute)
> The Lazy Man's Way to Riches. (Joe Karbo)
> Instant Heat Wherever You Want It. (Better Ideas)

How to Save Your Life. (Henniker)
Now . . . $25,000 Term Life Insurance for Only $1.00 a Month. (Allstate Insurance)
What Everyone Ought to Know . . . About This Stock and Bond Business. (Merrill Lynch)

Attention-getting words often found in headlines include:

How	You	Save
New	Free	At Last
Why	Today	Limited Offer

Body Copy. Direct response copy starts with benefits and ends with a request for action. Typical sentences are short and active, including phrases such as these:

Today more than ever . . .	Authorities have proved . . .
Fortunately for you . . .	Try it for ten days . . .
There's a new way . . .	Judge for yourself . . .

Response Devices. When all is said and done, the time comes to ask for the order. A good way to determine whether the advertisement can be categorized as direct response is to see whether it asks for action and how effectively it does so. Remember that a key characteristic of direct marketing is that it is measurable and accountable. Marketers measure transactions, that is, orders, inquiries, contributions, or votes. A direct response can be mailing a coupon or order form, phoning an inquiry or order, browsing and responding to a Web site, a visit to the seller's location, or a request for the seller to come to the buyer's location. Many otherwise good advertisements with effective headlines and compelling body copy fall down when they do not specifically ask the reader to order the product, fill out the coupon, click on the shopping cart, or call.

If the designer includes a coupon in the direct response print advertisement, he or she must be careful to provide enough room for the requested fill-in and select paper to take handwriting with ink. This may sound overly basic, but a good designer will, as a test, fill out the coupon to see whether it is adequate.

The terms of the offer, including price, need to be clearly stated. The response mechanism must provide a sense of *action now*. Although layout is not always easy to control, it is desirable to have right-hand coupons on advertisements that run on right-hand pages of print media (especially magazines) and vice versa for left-hand pages. The reason is obvious: it's easier to clip such a coupon if it adjoins an outside edge of the page.

Inserts. A popular form of print advertisement in a magazine or newspaper is an **insert**. Printing technology has made possible a great many variations for such inserts, including folding, gumming, consecutive numbering, die-cutting, and personalization on a printing press. The insert might be a multipage piece, or it can be a simple reply card bound next to a full-page advertisement and serving as the response device.

Newspaper inserts abound and appear in a variety of formats, especially on Sundays and midweek, on Wednesdays and Thursdays, which are typically grocery shopping days for many newspaper advertisers. Coupons are a major response format used in such inserts. Direct response advertisers using newspaper inserts include insurance companies, land developers, record clubs,

FIGURE 5-15 Hauser's Direct Response Print Advertisement.

trade schools, retail stores, book clubs, magazine publishers, and film processors. A key advantage of newspaper inserts is controlled timing. In many markets, demographic selection, often by ZIP code definition, makes possible pinpointing messages to market segments.

Copy and format are important considerations for inserts in newspapers and magazines. Single-page or multipage formats are available along with special features, such as perforated coupons and gummed reply envelopes, incorporated right into the format. Inserts offer a chance for unbounded creativity for the writer and designer of direct response print.

The direct response print advertisement from Hauser's Jewelers shown in Figure 5-15 demonstrates many of the necessary elements of an effective print ad. This print ad was a newspaper insert, so it contained two sides of colorful copy. Direct response advertisements often incorporate photographs to convey visually what the words describe. The call to action "Drop everything! Head to Hauser's Jewelers" is very strong, and it is creatively pictured on a clothes line to get the prospective customer to think about Mother's Day. The Hauser's Jewelers print ad presents a compelling picture of "Splendor in the Grass" followed by the announcement of Hauser's annual pearl event. The direct response advertisement is measurable in that customers must present the ad to receive the 15 percent discount incentive on all pearl jewelry purchases. The advertised offer contains a time limit, May 7–12, which is clearly presented on both sides of the advertisement. Location and contact information is also provided on both sides.

Broadcast Advertising (Television and Radio)

Television's limitations for direct response are its high cost and, with the exceptions of programmed infomercials and continuous home shopping, short duration of an individual commercial in which to present a message. The advent of cable and emerging interactive features make possible specifically directed messages and even market segmentation, thus increasing the effectiveness (results versus costs) of the medium.

Radio has practical limitations, too. Most radio messages reach listeners while they are driving a car or otherwise occupied, when telephones or pencil and paper are out of reach. Furthermore, radio does not provide the opportunity to visualize; thus, it is most effective with known products or those that do not require visualization.

CREATING TV COMMERCIALS   Television is especially suited to visualization of action as well as demonstration. Products appropriate for direct response include these, which are often bought on impulse: recordings, housewares, specialty items such as jewelry, and a variety of services.

A major limitation in creating direct response TV commercials is *time*. Commercial time is usually available in multiples of 10, 20, 30, 60, 90, and up to a usual maximum of 120 seconds. A maximum air time of 2 minutes allows for approximately 200 spoken words. Because audio and visual can be used simultaneously in TV, the old adage that "one picture is worth a thousand words" applies *if* the product is one that can be demonstrated, such as the "handy, dandy, utterly amazing kitchen slicer-dicer."

Marketers generally feel they need 20 seconds for attention getting, up to 75 seconds for demonstration, and the remaining 25 seconds of a typical 120-second spot announcement for action such as providing a mailing, Web site address, or telephone number. Because 120 seconds on prime-time television is usually too expensive for a direct response advertiser, most of these commercials appear during low-cost fringe time (early morning, late night, and weekend hours). Often, markets can be segmented through specific programs, such as movies or wrestling, usually aired at such other than prime times.

Many direct marketers have experienced profitable response rates using infomercials, program-style narrated commercials that may run as long as 30 minutes in other than prime time, usually on special-interest cable channels. Featured are products, such as exercisers or nutrition supplements, which can benefit from extensive demonstration and enjoy audience involvement.

Concept. The logical starting point in creating direct response TV commercials is determining just what the advertising is about and what it is to do—its concept. It might be used as support, to call attention to a newspaper insert or a forthcoming direct mail package. Or to get leads for sales follow-up. Or to generate orders or create store traffic. Unlike the case for direct mail or print media, there is no written record of the product's features and benefits for the audience to refer to at a later time. The TV viewer can't be expected to remember too much, so logic and clarity are important.

Storyboards. The visual portion of a television commercial is shown through a series of illustrations called **storyboards**, which demonstrate the continuity, the graphics and photographs, and the video action. Most of these storyboards are now computerized, which makes commercial design much faster and easier.

Script. Although a script for a TV commercial containing no more than 200 words cannot verbally "explain" as thoroughly as a direct mail package or print advertisement, the combination of words with pictures and graphics, audio with video, can exert considerable impact. That is why one of the most effective uses of direct response TV is to support other direct response advertising media through copy, such as "Watch your mailbox for . . ." or "Watch for this offer in next Sunday's Chicago Tribune." A visualization of the insert to which attention is being drawn often accompanies this copy. An effective TV script needs to be tightly woven and fully coordinated with the visual and graphic elements involved. Like good letter copy or well-written print ads, the script needs to first get attention, through audio coupled with video and graphics, and then do its job in presenting product features and benefits as it gets the viewer involved and geared to action.

Graphics. Direct response TV graphics begin with the words or script coordinated with the other elements that bring the message to life in both audio and video: images, actions, effects, and direction. Actors who deliver the words must be credible, professional, and appropriate to the product. Filming and editing are important so that words are synchronized with pictures. Written words are often superimposed on video to present localized response addresses or phone numbers. Television graphics are concerned with the interaction of audio and video so that the ultimate effect of the message on the viewer will be maximized.

Production   The production team for a direct response TV commercial consists of a variety of highly specialized technicians, coordinated by a producer. Typical concerns at this juncture are whether to use motion picture film or videotape and live actors, animation, or still illustrations. Directors, actors, and graphic designers become involved, as do camera people and film editors. Decisions as to which to employ must relate costs to response.

CREATING RADIO COMMERCIALS   The process of developing radio commercials is less complex than for television. Radio offers the additional advantage of flexibility in that live commercials, often read by a station announcer or known local personality, can be scheduled quickly. If need be, these can be revised right up to air time. Radio commercials are far less expensive than TV, too, in air time costs as well as production costs. Through use of particular radio station formats—easy listening, rock and roll, or news/talk programs—the direct response advertiser can develop a substantial degree of market segmentation. Positioning adjacent to particular programs, such as early morning farm programs or a popular disc jockey, can further segment markets. Positioning during morning and evening drive times, when office or factory workers are driving to and from their jobs, is another means of market segmentation.

Like other media, radio advertising must first get attention. Sometimes a radio personality reading a script, even in an ad-lib manner, can attract attention. If the product being sold involves music, a few bars or a few headline words can make an effective headline for a radio commercial.

The close and request for action are of special concern in using radio for direct response. Many times, radio listeners are performing another activity simultaneously, such as driving, reading a book, taking a shower, or doing household chores. Pencil and paper for writing down addresses and phone numbers are not readily available nor is it feasible for a listener to stop everything and get them. As a result, the most effective response instruction is one that is easy to remember such as use of a telephone number that spells out a word: "Dial 'Dickens' for your tickets to see *A Christmas Carol.*" Or the use of a post office box with a significant number can be more easily recalled, such as "Write P.O. Box 1776, Philadelphia, Pennsylvania, to subscribe to *Colonial America.*" Repeating the address or number helps, too.

Telephone Promotion

The telephone is used by direct marketers as a promotional medium, outbound as well as inbound. Here, the promotion is actually presented via phone by a sales representative, a fundraiser, or a politician. The intricacies of telephone marketing will be dealt with in a later chapter. Our consideration at this point is concerned with creative strategies applicable to these.

Well-prepared scripts and well-structured offers can cause phone promotion to prospective customers to be highly effective, but the medium is usually most efficient if calls are directed to currently active customers or else to prospects that have been prequalified in some way. The reason for this is that the cost of an individual telephone call can be as much as four times the cost of an individual direct mail letter, so it must be four times as productive to be comparable cost-wise.

Prequalified outbound calls might include inquiry response, upgrade of a new order, new product offering to an existing customer, reactivation of a dormant account, or generation of responses/transactions from a carefully selected list.

SCRIPTS   The development of scripts for outbound phone calls offer the dual challenge of maximizing the words to gain a favorable response and, at the same time, minimizing the length and cost of a call. In some cases, a live operator might introduce a call and request permission to play a taped message, often from a celebrity or a personality. At the end of the taped message, the live operator comes back on for close and action.

Internet

In developing Web sites and creating Internet promotions, the direct marketer first of all must recognize a key distinction of this medium. Direct mail and phones are proactive in that after a customer or prospect is identified via a database, these media allow the market to send *messages* directly. Print and broadcast media also take the initiative in delivering themselves to readers/viewers/listeners and then providing content or programming attracting them. Whereas outbound e-mail can be proactive, the majority of Internet marketing is not.

Therefore, the first step in creating Internet promotions must be the dissemination of incentives for the prospect to visit a company's Web site in the first place. This is in contrast to the entrepreneur targeting the prospect, as is the case with direct mail or the telephone, as well as print and broadcast media. This is now typically being done through print, broadcast, and Internet search engines, all of which can let a prospect know the location of the Web site, as well as benefits to accrue from browsing. We discuss the Internet and other high-tech digital mediums in greater detail in Chapter 8; for now, let's concentrate on the creation of compelling copy for Internet platforms.

The copywriter and the graphic designer must design a Web site, starting with its home page, so that the browser is motivated to becoming a customer. At this stage, everything we've said about creating promotions for all media—direct mail, print, and broadcast—apply as well to the Internet. Especially important, however, is the *sequencing* of each visit with clicks and links. *Information,* as needed, becomes a literal goldmine. The logic and convenience of ordering online is readily apparent. Of course, once a relationship has been established with a customer, then the Internet becomes an effective and efficient way of doing business.

Let's explore the message strategies used by Lillian Vernon in its online promotion by reviewing both its Web site and outbound e-mails.

HOME PAGE   The Lillian Vernon Web site in Figure 5-16 uses the four basic design principles: alignment, proximity, repetition, and contrast. There is horizontal alignment across the main navigation bar on the top of the page. The use of proximity and repetition in the banner like advertisements below the central image on the page tie the various product lines together. Finally, the eye is drawn to the page through the use of contrast with the addition of larger and bolder fonts and a variety of colors in the central image. This site also contains several key elements that prospective customers would expect to find on a B2C Web site. The search box is located adjacent to the company

FIGURE 5-16 **Lillian Vernon Web Site Home Page.** *Source:* Used with permission of Current USA, Inc., dba Lillian Vernon.

name within the upper left-hand quadrant of the site. A toll-free phone number is provided for the convenience of current and prospective customers. There is also a text link regarding the company's policy on privacy and security within the simple text links found at the bottom of the page. The copyright notice is up to date.

ONLINE STORE   As shown in Figure 5-17, there is repetition between the Lillian Vernon home page and the holiday and celebrations page within its online store. For example, the highly visible search box appears in the same place on the two pages, as does the main navigation bar across the

FIGURE 5-17 Lillian Vernon Holidays and Celebrations Web Page. *Source:* Used with permission of Current USA, Inc., dba Lillian Vernon.

top of the site and the contact information along the bottom of the site. The online store is divided into a reasonable number of subcategories (seven). A standard rule of thumb is that a site should contain five to ten subcategory pages.

OUTBOUND E-MAIL Figure 5-18 provides two separate examples of Lillian Vernon outbound e-mail promotions. There are several elements that make these two campaigns successful and eye-catching. First, the look and feel of each of the e-mails (Lillian Vernon and Lilly's Kids) complements the two Web sites. The e-mails open with the corresponding logo and navigation bar that are found on each of the home pages for these Web sites. As marketers invest in more multichannel marketing, they must ensure that the brand is consistent across the multiple channels,

FIGURE 5-18   Lillian Vernon Outbound E-mails.   *Source:* Used with permission of Current USA, Inc., dba Lillian Vernon.

whether that be on the Web site, through direct mail, or in the actual store. Second, both of the e-mails encourage subscribers to act now by including offers at the top of the e-mail. The offer utilized in the Lilly's Kids promotion also takes advantage of the principles of design with contrast between the red type and aqua background in the image and the call to action words in the ad "Go Wild!" Additional good features in the Lillian Vernon e-mail promotion include the use of testimonials below the featured products as well as an enticing photo of a son embracing his mother.

Summary

Direct response copywriting is both art and science, and those who have mastered it are very much in demand. FAB (features-advantages-benefits) analysis is often used by direct response copywriters to position products so that these provide benefits to users. There is a variety of copywriting formulas available to guide creative development and many of these are set forth in this chapter. Design and graphics are important adjuncts to copywriting, used to create attention and guide the reader through copy.

These include the art, layout, symbols, and effects. Consideration should be given also to such factors as photographs, illustrations, type styles, paper, inks, size, and a variety of attention-getting techniques.

Development of direct response advertising must be concerned with the special characteristics of the medium to be used: direct mail, catalogs, print (magazines and newspapers), broadcast (television and radio), telephone, and the Internet.

Key Terms

big idea *119*

copy appeal *119*

layout *122*

involvement devices *123*

self-mailer *126*

solo mailers *126*

classic format *128*

letter *128*

brochure *129*

response device *129*

catalog *130*

insert *134*

storyboards *136*

Review Questions

1. How do measurability and accountability, characteristics key to direct marketing, apply to advertising?
2. What, specifically, is *direct response advertising?*
3. Why is an understanding of buyer motivations important in the creation of direct marketing promotions?
4. What is meant by "writing by formula?" Give an example.
5. Why are design and graphics important in the creation of direct response advertising?
6. What are the elements of design?
7. Why is direct mail considered the primary medium for use by direct response advertisers?
8. Of what elements does a "classic" direct mail package consist?
9. What distinguishes direct response advertising in newspapers and magazines?
10. What are some important considerations when creating message content for Internet and e-mail marketing?

Exercise

Busch Gardens, a well-known amusement park located in Virginia, is holding a contest for college students. The first-place prize is a season passport for two people to enjoy the park for a lifetime for each member of the winning team! The challenge is to identify as many features of the park as possible and their associated advantages. Then, you must convert each advantage into a benefit that the amusement park may use in marketing their park to consumers. You may select your target market customer, either (1) families or (2) young adults. Have fun and good luck!

CASE

Barely There

Overview

How does a creative idea for a direct and interactive marketing campaign originate? Is it a product of sheer genius? Or is it hatched when a bunch of brilliant minds get together and spit out off-the-wall ideas in a brainstorming session? Could it be the result of extensive research? Maybe it is based on a thorough understanding of the target customers' deepest desires? Or could it be just a stroke of good luck?

Whatever it takes, The Martin Agency in Richmond, Virginia, surely has it and has demonstrated sheer ingenuity when it created the Barely There campaign for its client, Hanesbrands. This case is a success story of creativity that really worked. It demonstrates the exceptional things that can happen when you combine commonsense thinking with clever ideas.

In direct and interactive marketing terms, creativity encompasses the content of whatever media format is being used to convey the offer. Creative strategies include decisions about the words, terms, symbols, designs, pictures, images, and media format. The old cliché "it's not creative unless it sells" implies that the creative strategies must attain the objectives set forth for the campaign. These objectives may be to generate a response, transaction, political vote, charitable donation, and so on. Regardless of the objectives, direct marketers must make many decisions about the creative elements included in a campaign. These decisions include brand and image building, copywriting and graphics, and message creation based on media selection. This case lets you explore how Hanesbrands and The Martin Agency made these decisions when they developed the direct and interactive marketing campaign for the Barely There Invisible Look collection of bras.

Case

With a fraction of the advertising budget in comparison with category leaders, the company was intent on creating a more meaningful and intimate connection with women with the Barely There Invisible Look collection of bras. Hanesbrands challenged The Martin Agency to achieve this objective, and the company and agency worked together and did just that and more! After months of market research, positioning, and creative development, the end result was great success. Let's take a look at how this creative campaign was developed.

Research

The campaign was driven by innovative consumer research and then by the realization that the ultimate goal of bras for women was not to look sexy with their clothes off but to help them look and feel great with their clothes on. This realization was further developed when Hanesbrands began to gain consumer insights via research across the country.

The team flipped through a variety of fashion magazines, and all they saw were pretty women in pretty bras. In fact, the ads of the largest competitor in the lingerie industry, Victoria's Secret, featured beautiful models with perfect shapes and bras that fit perfectly. These models are often shown with slinky body parts, naked torsos, and stiletto heels. Where's the humanity? It seems that the intimate apparel category has been missing the mark for years, overlooking the underlying reason women wear bras in the first place—to help them look good in their clothes.

So the team got busy, and they uncovered that women try to avoid the dreaded "bad bra day" when bras don't fit right or don't look right. The team created a dictionary of "bad bra moments" and began to completely understand the consumer's perspective (the mono-boob, the quadra-boob, the puffed-up chicken chest). These bad bra moments were extremely annoying for most women. Research also found that millions of women are wearing ill-fitting bras. What many consumers really need is a friend to help them avoid bad bra moments. The solution? A new positioning strategy for Barely There intimates to be the bra brand to own solutions to the most common universal bra problems and allow women never to have a bad bra day. The Invisible Look bra collection addresses the practical concerns women have about shape and fit.

Positioning

Positioning Barely There intimates as the brand that can help women look and feel better in their clothes was a new direction for the lingerie industry. The new campaign is viewed as part sales pitch and part public service announcement. It doesn't focus on the supermodels but illustrates the problems women often encounter with the wrong bra and provides practical solutions to correct the problem. The new positioning strategy fills a niche that is currently unfulfilled. Victoria's Secret may command the market segment of women desiring a sexier bra, but that still leaves a large portion of the consumer lingerie market to capture. The Martin Agency team, armed with its new dictionary of bad bra moments, seized the opportunity and history was made with a totally unique and entertaining creative campaign for the Barely There Invisible Look bra collection.

Creative Development

Due to the strategic direction and the desire to significantly drive brand awareness, the creative team found a simple way to convey the message using three words—two of which were the brand name. The result is a problem solution campaign, your bra is either "there" or "barely there." On the left is a bra that is bumpy or misshapen (labeled "There"). On the right is a smoothly shaped bra (labeled "Barely There"). The value proposition of the campaign was that other bras are painfully "there." Figure 5-19 shows a few of these creative executions.

FIGURE 5-19 Barely There Print Advertisements.

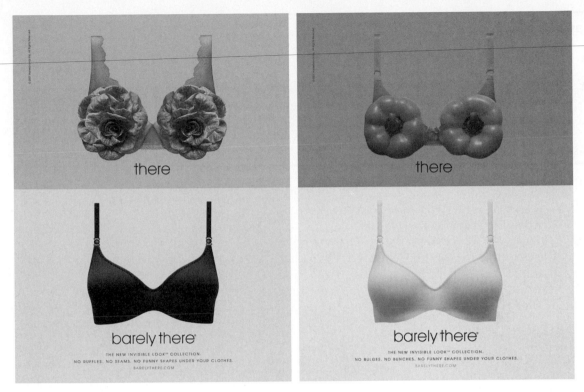

FIGURE 5-19   (continued)

The creative team at The Martin Agency had fun imagining all of the crazy shaped items that could be used to portray an ill-fitting bra. Of course, most women wouldn't intentionally stuff their shirts with cocktail umbrellas, red bell peppers, pine cones, or decorative bows, but many would be quick to admit that some bras do create the odd appearance of some of those items.

Color was also an important aspect to the creative development of the campaign. The creative team knew that the campaign needed to be both sophisticated and fashion-y as well as funny. The creative team decided to photograph the items attached to the garments rather than composite the images of the items and bras in postproduction. The art director strongly felt that it would be more "real," and this method would ensure the color and reflections would work with each other. Therefore, the campaign entailed a photo shoot with each bra presenting its own set of different challenges for the creative team and the photographers.

The result? A company and agency partnership that produced a brilliant campaign that clearly passes everyone's giggle test. The campaign is nationally acclaimed as it has won numerous creative awards. Finally, and most important, it effectively conveys a message along with a Web site, barelythere.com, where consumers can purchase a bra that will really make them feel and look good in their clothes.

Case Discussion Questions

1. What role did marketing research play in the development of the Barely There campaign?
2. Provide some examples of how this campaign converted the features of the Invisible Look bra collection into benefits.

3. What basic human needs did the copy appeal of the Barely There campaign address?
4. Would you categorize the copy appeal used in this campaign to be rational, emotional, or moral? Explain why.

Notes

1. Thorstein Veblen (1917), *The Theory of the Leisure Class* (London: Macmillan), p. 110.
2. Bob Stone (2001), *Successful Direct Marketing Methods,* 7th ed. (New York: McGraw-Hill), pp. 294–395.
3. Ibid.

6

■■■■

Designing and
Employing Print

Opening Vignette: Zoo's News

With rising costs for postage and materials, coupled with declining response rates for the newspaper industry in general, it had become increasingly difficult for regional newspapers, with limited distribution potential, to achieve direct mail response rates that would result in acceptable profit margins. However, with limitations on telemarketing, newspapers have few cost-effective outlets remaining to target potential new subscribers. Plus, research shows direct mail subscribers tend to retain at a higher rate. Given this situation, individual newspaper companies needed to find innovative ways to cost-effectively achieve new subscriber acquisition goals. The answer? Zoo's News!

Zoo's News is an innovative direct mail product, developed by MindZoo, a direct marketing firm in Leesburg, Virginia. Zoo's News is a comprehensive subscription acquisition program that enables individual newspapers to pool their collective resources to gain significant economies of scale on creative development, printing, and production. As Figure 6-1 shows, this program was launched in January 2008 with seven regional newspapers featuring the seasonal theme of Happy New(s) Year. This award-winning creative concept enabled newspapers to link their content to popular New Year's resolutions.

FIGURE 6-1 Zoo's News *Happy New(s) Year* Direct Mail Promotion. *Source:* Used with permission of MindZoo, LLC. Photo by Kim Kirby, www.jimkirbyphoto.com.

The seven launch participants included the *Chicago Tribune, Atlanta Journal-Constitution, Newsday, Orlando Sentinel, South Florida Sun-Sentinel, Orange County Register,* and *Milwaukee Journal-Sentinel.* All seven newspapers selected their own prospect data from their in-house databases based on MindZoo's recommendation to mail to a mix of geodemographically selected nonsubscribers and former subscribers. The result was a series of seven different Happy New(s) Year direct mail solicitations hitting mailboxes from coast to coast with a total of 535,000 pieces in total distribution. By producing multiple versions of Zoo's News simultaneously, all participating newspapers enjoyed significant cost savings while taking advantage of the support of an award-winning agency supplier of direct mail services to the newspaper industry. Depending on the quantity chosen for mailing, participants saved 35–45 percent on the total cost of print and production for their Happy New(s) Year promotion, which greatly reduced the subsequent cost per order for all participants regardless of individual response rate. This seasonal approach has proven to be very effective for other solo mail programs developed on behalf of newspaper clients. Zoo's News is an example of the advantages that can be obtained by partner marketing and innovative direct mail concepts.

In this chapter we look at print media as direct marketers use them for direct response advertising.

Direct mail, in its various formats, is a print medium. Publications, magazines, and newspapers represent another form of printed communication. In contrast with direct mail ads, which are delivered individually, magazines and newspapers convey direct response advertising to groups of readers in a package along with other advertisements as well as editorial matter. The total content of these print media largely preselects the individual publication's readers. In most cases, too, the reader subscribes to and pays for the publication's content.

We talked about the promotion *formats* of direct marketing and their creation, categorized by media, in Chapter 5. In this chapter we are concerned with the print media themselves—direct mail (including self-mailers, classic packages, and catalogs), newspapers, magazines, and collateral printed materials—and their characteristics and advantages and disadvantages. We discuss the potential for market segmentation through readership of specific parts of a particular print medium at a particular time—sports or obituaries in today's newspaper, as examples.

Direct mail has long been the basic promotion format for direct marketers. It relies on mailing lists and data about the individuals or organizations on such lists to most effectively reach market segments.

DIRECT MAIL AS A PRINT MEDIUM

Direct marketers use virtually all forms of advertising media to generate measurable responses, but **direct mail** continues to be the dominant medium they use for direct response advertising. Not all direct mail is carried by the U.S. Postal Service, however; some go by private carriers, such as UPS, or other door-to-door distributors, such as newspaper carriers on their circulation rounds. Some are enclosed within newspapers and magazines. Sometimes marketers also combine several offers into a single package, such as coupons or other inserts into newspapers, or enclose offers with other mail or parcels, such as statement stuffers or package inserts.

Of all the media available for direct response advertising, direct mail can be the most selective and offers the most potential for personalization. It is the most flexible (mainly because of the many different formats available) and also the most suitable for test. Because of these pinpoint attributes of its distribution, it has the potential for the highest rate of response. Figure 6-2 provides a sample direct mail package for a graphic and stationery company. Note how the various elements of design are used (layout, illustration, type, etc.) to lead up to the all-important request for a response.

Its inherent advantages, however, cause direct mail to be the most expensive medium per prospect reached. Even with a volume of 100,000 pieces, it may be difficult to distribute a traditional direct mail package (mailing envelope, computer-processed four-page letter, circular, order form, and business reply envelope) for less than $1 per piece. This would include creative, art and preparation, printing production, mailing lists, computer processing, lettershop production, allocated fees, and postage.[1] This is true even though preferential postage rates apply to nonprofit organizations and to those large volume mailers who presort their direct mail by ZIP code or by postal carrier route. Volume mailers can benefit, too, from lower average printing and production costs.

Market Segmentation

Databases are most often the distribution vehicles for direct mail. Sophisticated techniques for compiling, warehousing, and mining such databases—coupled with computer technology for most effectively using transaction, demographic, psychographic, and other data inherent to them—can pinpoint prospects and identify market segments in a highly efficient manner.[2] With such data, the direct marketer can efficiently segment house lists (active and inactive customers as well as inquirers)

FIGURE 6-2 **HomeFronts Direct Mail Package.** *Source:* Used with permission of P.S. Graphics.

and compiled databases of other organizations. Figure 6-3 shows a direct mail piece that was mailed to the "best customers" segment of McDonald Garden Center's three retail locations. The offer states that those customers presenting the mailer along with their loyalty card by a specified date will receive a free gift. This encourages a timely response and the response device (which is the mailer itself) is both accountable and measurable.

Computer match coding and merge-purge techniques can eliminate duplicate mailings within and between lists, addresses can be standardized to maximize deliverability, and data about buying patterns can help determine customer potential. Databases are at the heart of direct mail as a print medium.

Catalogs

Catalogs have become a vital and productive format of direct mail. Although there is evidence of trade catalogs in mid-fifteenth-century Europe and even in pre-Revolution America, the pioneering general merchandise mail-order catalogs were those of Montgomery Ward and Sears Roebuck,

McDonald Garden Center
attn: Marketing Department
1139 West Pembroke Ave.
Hampton, VA 23661

Ms. Anne Stafford
6 Arlington Road
Hampton, VA 23666

FIGURE 6-3 McDonald Garden Best Customer Mailing Piece.
Source: Used with permission of McDonald Garden Center.

which were first issued after the Civil War. The specialty product catalogs of Joseph Spiegel and L. L. Bean first appeared in the early twentieth century.

While the original Ward and Sears catalogs endeavored to provide all things to all people—and ultimately became too big and prohibitively expensive to circulate—today's successful catalogs rely on databases to target specialized product lines to most likely interested market segments. Their fit with the marketplace has made catalogs such as Lands' End and Peruvian Connection successful.

Today's catalogs are not confined to consumer products; they also play an important role in business-to-business distribution. Interestingly enough, the office product catalogs of Staples, Office Depot, and others, augmented by extensive in-store distribution, were preceded long ago by similar catalogs that were circulated to offices by salespeople, who then took orders by telephone. John H. Patterson, who founded the National Cash Register Company (today's NCR), used direct mail catalogs as early as the 1920s to get qualified leads for follow-up by salespeople calling on industrial organizations.

A recent study by the Direct Marketing Association reveals that 49 percent of consumers buy from catalogs. "Sales from paper catalogs and sales from websites are projected to become roughly equal by year 2009."[3]

Syndication Mailings

Syndication mailings, usually arranged by an intermediary between the producer and the seller called a syndicate, offers a product to an established (and usually credit-approved) customer list. The most common users of syndication are publishers, oil companies, bank credit cards, department stores, catalog merchandisers, and other organizations that have an existing customer relationship. These direct marketers supply the databases of their customers and the goodwill inherent within customer relationships, and assume the accounts receivable after the sale. The producer (of a pair of binoculars, for example) benefits from an efficient and effective distribution system for its products. The syndicate bears promotion costs, supplies and ships merchandise, handles customer service, and pays the direct marketer a sales commission for the use of its databases of customers and their goodwill.

Syndication mailing had its roots in the 1950s when large lists of mail-order buyers and respondents began to proliferate, notably among publishers of encyclopedias and other books, as well as mail-order merchants and those with accounts receivables such as oil companies and credit card organizations. Most of these early syndications moved goods with relatively high unit prices, such as a home movie setup or a power tool, for example.

Whereas the early users of syndication mailings were as much interested in activating their credit customers as they were in earning a profit from the merchandise sale itself, today's direct marketers look on syndication as a profit center and another indication of the inherent value of a customer relationship. Syndication can provide an unusually high rate of return for a nominal investment.

Coupons

As a promotional medium—primarily for grocery, health, and beauty care products—a **coupon** is an offer by a manufacturer or retailer that includes an incentive for purchase of a product or service in the form of a specified price reduction. A major objective of coupons is to motivate buyers to try a new product or to convert occasional users into regular customers. A further objective is to increase sales so the retailer will give the product greater display space.

Coupons distributed by direct mail can be self-mailers for a single brand or enclosed in an envelope with descriptive literature; or there may be several brands cooperating in a single distribution sponsored by either the manufacturer or a mailing organization. Even cooperative coupon mailings can be directed to specific market segments, such as teenagers, senior citizens, professionals, or business organizations. Marketers also place coupons in their company newsletters. Figure 6-4 provides an example of how McDonald Garden Center offers dollar-savings coupons to those regular customers who receive its newsletter.

Of the 323 billion coupons distributed during 2005, only 3.0 billion were redeemed. Redemption rates have been declining since 1993 when 2.00 percent (6.2 billion) of 309.7 billion coupons distributed were redeemed. Most coupons, 58.4 percent, were distributed through newspapers

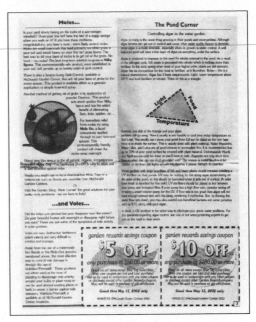

FIGURE 6-4   **Greenleaves Newsletter.**   *Source:* Used with permission of McDonald Garden Center.

in 2005, and just 4.2 percent were distributed through direct mail. However, in recent research, direct mail was named by 27.7 percent of respondents as a preferred method to receive coupons, and newspapers and magazines are favored by 27.4 percent of respondents.[4]

Fraudulent redemption of coupons, without purchase as intended, is a major problem for manufacturers as well as retailers. Because in direct mail the coupon is enclosed in a sealed envelope addressed to a particular person, making the coupons unavailable in volume for fraudulent redemption, direct mail is probably the safest way to distribute coupons.

Cooperative Mailings

Cooperative mailings provide participants, usually direct response advertisers, with opportunities to reduce mailing cost in reaching common prospects. The circulation of cooperative mailings ranges from consumer distribution, which reaches half of all U.S. households periodically, to highly pinpointed market segments, such as Doctor's Marketplace. In another form called a ride-along, a direct marketer might include one or more noncompeting offers with a catalog or individual mailing.

Mass cooperative mailings frequently combine coupon offers with other direct response offers, thus amortizing the total mailing cost among several advertising participants. Participation in a cooperative mailing can cost $10 or less per thousand; this cost rises according to the degree of selectivity in the mailing.

Some cooperative mailings provide opportunities to reach market segments such as new homeowners, new families, Spanish-speaking households, or consumers in particular ZIP code clusters. As many as a dozen or more offers might be contained in a cooperative mailed to a specific market segment. Such mass cooperatives are sometimes distributed through other print media: newspapers and magazines.

Valpak, the leader in cooperative mailings nationwide, allows its clients to select from a variety of format options including coupons, flyers, and postcards to fit each client's product or service, message, and budget. Valpak is the most recognized direct mail program there is, with more than nine in ten adults claiming that they are aware of and open that familiar blue Valpak envelope and look through the offers.[5] Based on research, the top six coupon categories most appealing to consumers include grocery stores, sit-down restaurants, fast food restaurants, mass retail stores, pizza, and video rentals/movie theaters.[6] As Figure 6-5 presents, a wide variety of businesses and industries use Valpak to distribute their direct mail offers.

Statement/Invoice Stuffers

Periodic bills and reminder statements mailed to customers of department stores, utilities, oil companies, publications, and bank credit cards provide an opportunity for merchandising complementary (but not competing) offers of products and services with **stuffers** inserted in the envelope with the invoice or statement. Distribution can be wide and cost is relatively low, ranging from $50 to $100 per thousand. Deliverability is ensured, because most bills travel via first-class mail, and virtually everyone opens their bills. The billing company implies an endorsement of the offer and, in some cases, also offers credit to make the purchase. Marketers can segment these mailings by selecting the organization sending out the bills.

Valpak Top 20 U.S. Categories

1. Pizza	11. Car Washes
2. Dry Cleaning & Laundry	12. Oil Change/Lube Shops
3. Auto Repair	13. Nail Salons
4. Dentists	14. Mexican Restaurants
5. Fitness Centers	15. Real Estate
6. Hair Salons	16. Amusement & recreation
7. Carpet & Upholstery Cleaning	17. Sub Shops
8. Chinese Restaurants	18. Tire Dealers
9. Home Improvement	19. Tanning Salons
10. Full Service Restaurants	20. Maid Service

FIGURE 6-5   **Valpak Outer Envelope with a List of Valpak Users.**   *Source:* Valpak® Category Census, 2004.

Package Inserts

Package inserts are related to stuffers but offer the additional advantage of arriving when the recipient has just made a purchase. Certain direct marketers offer the opportunity for one or more direct response advertisers to include inserts with customer shipments. Gourmet meat purveyor Omaha Steaks, for example, might enclose an offer of gourmet coffee from Gevalia in its shipments. Some package shippers may even offer specific selection by product line or geographic location. Inserts might be loose or contained within a separate folder in the package. Cost is about the same as that for billing inserts.

Take-One Racks

Another method of print distribution is the use of **take-one racks** in supermarkets, restaurants, hotels, drug stores, transportation terminals, buses and trains, or other high-traffic locations. These might be placed in a cardboard display container adjacent to a cash register, or could be placed in a wire rack strategically hung on a wall in a supermarket and containing many offers. An advantage of such distribution is that those who voluntarily take a promotion piece from the rack are usually more than casually interested. Thus, the response rate from take-one rack inserts is relatively high when lower cost is considered. Even though distribution within a single rack might be quite low—say, fewer than 100 pieces per month—the number of potential outlets for racks is quite large and distribution could total into the millions.

Other print media include magazines and newspapers, with which the following sections are concerned.

MAGAZINES AS A PRINT MEDIUM

A major restructuring of the magazine industry in the 1970s changed the way marketers use magazines for direct response advertising. The demise of three mass-circulation magazines—*Life, Look,* and the *Saturday Evening Post*—was followed by the proliferation of smaller-circulation special-interest magazines appealing to well-defined market segments.

Market Segmentation

Special-interest magazines, through their selection of content and resulting readership, serve to define market segments and even psychographic lifestyles for direct response advertisers. Categories of special-interest magazines are today virtually unlimited: class (the *New Yorker, Smithsonian,* and *Museum*), literary (*Atlantic, Harpers,* and the *New York Times Book Review*); sports (*Sports Illustrated, Ski,* and *Golf*), how-to (*Popular Mechanics, Popular Science,* and *Woodworking*), news (*Time, Newsweek,* and *U.S. News*), religious (*Christian Herald* and *Catholic Digest*), and many other diverse titles, such as *Entertainment Weekly, Self, Vanity Fair,* and *Playboy*). Figure 6-6 presents an example of a special-interest magazine, McDonald Garden Centers *Inspirations* magazine, "Four Season Solutions for Home and Garden." This high-quality publication focuses on interior and exterior lifestyle trends and designs. Each seasonal issue provides "down-to-earth" advice and information on garden-related issues written by experts and garden writers exclusively for the Hampton Roads and Eastern Virginia regional areas. It also contains advertisements related to home and garden improvement. This magazine is available for a fee in retail stores throughout the region and is mailed as a courtesy to McDonald Garden Center's best customers.

FIGURE 6-6 McDonald Garden Centers *Inspirations* Magazine Cover.

Certain national magazines—including, among many others, *New Yorker, Business Week,* and *Newsweek*—are available in demographic editions describing market segments, such as women, college students, and business executives. Some publications, including *TV Guide,* offer geographic editions that are described by ZIP code areas. Some, such as *Time,* combine both demographic and geographic market segmentation, offering selected advertisers access to these selected groupings. Occasionally, using laser printing technology, individual ads are personalized to individual subscribers.

Categories of Magazines

Magazines can be grouped by editorial content into five major categories:

1. *General Mass:* Characterized by high circulation and relatively low cost per thousand readers, general mass circulation magazines include *Reader's Digest, TV Guide, People,* and *National Geographic.*
2. *Women's Service:* Like the first category, women's service magazines are characterized by heavy circulation and reasonably low cost per thousand readers. Included are magazines such as *McCall's, Good Housekeeping, Family Circle, Seventeen,* and *Ladies Home Journal.*
3. *Shelter:* With selected demographics and increased cost, shelter magazines (those that focus on homes, decorating, and gardening) include *Architectural Digest, Better Homes and Gardens, House & Garden,* and *House Beautiful.*
4. *Business:* This category includes *Fortune, Forbes, American Banker, Business Week, Nation's Business, Fast Company,* and *Black Enterprise.*
5. *Special Interest:* With highly selected demographics and even lifestyle definition, this category would include magazines such as *Travel & Leisure, Cosmopolitan, Gourmet, Boys Life, Ski, Golf Digest,* and *Jogging.* Figure 6-7 provides a list of some special-interest magazines.

SPECIALTY MAGAZINES

Touring Times—The Travel Magazine of Rural Route Tours
International and American Group Travel

Baker's Digest

Personals—A Magazine for Meeting People

Diversion—The Magazine for Physicians At Leisure

WindRider—The Nations Leading Windsurfing Magazine

The Plate Collector

American Bicyclist and Motorcyclist

The Italians

OffHours—The Physicians' Guide to Leisure and Finance

Chain Saw Industry & Power Equipment Dealer

Physician's Assets

Hobby Merchandiser

The Logger and *Lumberman Magazine*

The Internal Auditor

Twins—The Magazine for Parents of Multiples

Cheerleader Today

Modern Bride

FIGURE 6-7 Unique Special-Interest Magazines.

Advantages and Disadvantages

Magazines can be selected to reach defined market segments: mass or class; rural, urban, or suburban; females or males; senior citizens or teenagers. Modern printing technology permits excellent reproduction at a relatively low cost per thousand circulation. Because magazines usually come out periodically—weekly, monthly, quarterly—they enjoy relatively long life and often many readers will read a single copy. Through split-run techniques in which alternative advertisements are placed in every other copy, magazines can be tested relatively inexpensively for ways to maximize direct response.

On the negative side, however, magazines offer direct marketers less space in which to tell their story than direct mail does. Additionally, closing dates for magazines (the date by which the magazine must receive the ad) are often considerably in advance of the issue dates and, because of staggered distribution, over a long period of time, response is usually spread out over time and thus slower.

RELATIVE COST   Although there are literally thousands of magazines published, the circulation of only a few hundred is audited and authenticated by the Audit Bureau of Circulations. These titles, however, have a combined circulation of hundreds of millions. The cost of one black-and-white advertising page could be in the range of $15 per thousand for large circulation publications and four or five times that for trade or business publications. This is, of course, considerably less than the cost of direct mail at $1,000 per thousand pieces, especially when we can obtain a degree of market segmentation by using specific magazines.

These factors influence the cost of magazine advertising: the amount of space purchased; whether the ad is in color or black and white; whether the ink bleeds off the edges of the page; and the use of regional, demographic, or test market selections. Certain magazines offer discounted rates for direct response advertisers as well as special rates for categories such as publishers or schools. Sometimes, standby or "remnant" space is available at publication deadline and at substantial discounts.

Position and Timing

Although the front and back covers usually get maximum readership in a magazine, many publications do not permit direct response coupons in these preferred positions. The front portion of the magazine, assuming a full page, is preferable. A right-hand page is usually better for direct response than a left-hand page, but there are exceptions, such as the last left-hand page in the publication. Whether on a right-hand or left-hand page, the response coupon, if there is one, should always appear on the outside margin and never in the gutter (center fold) of the magazine. Inserts and bind-in response devices, reply cards or envelopes, serve to call attention to the advertisement.

Many magazines offer advertisers an opportunity, along with a special cooperative advertising rate, to have their advertisement listed and highlighted on a bingo card. A **bingo card** (also called an information card) is an insert or page of a magazine that is created by the publisher to provide a numeric listing of advertisers. Bingo cards can be bound into the magazine or loosely inserted and serve as a response mechanism for consumers to request additional information by simply circling or checking the number corresponding to each advertiser. Advertisers will often reference the bingo card in their ad with statements such as "for further information circle item 27." Consumers send completed cards directly to the publisher who, in turn, sends compiled lists of inquiries to the appropriate participating advertiser. Figure 6-8 provides an example of a bingo card.

Aside from seasonal offers, response from magazine advertisements usually follows the normal direct marketing cycle. The strongest response occurs in January–February and September–October,

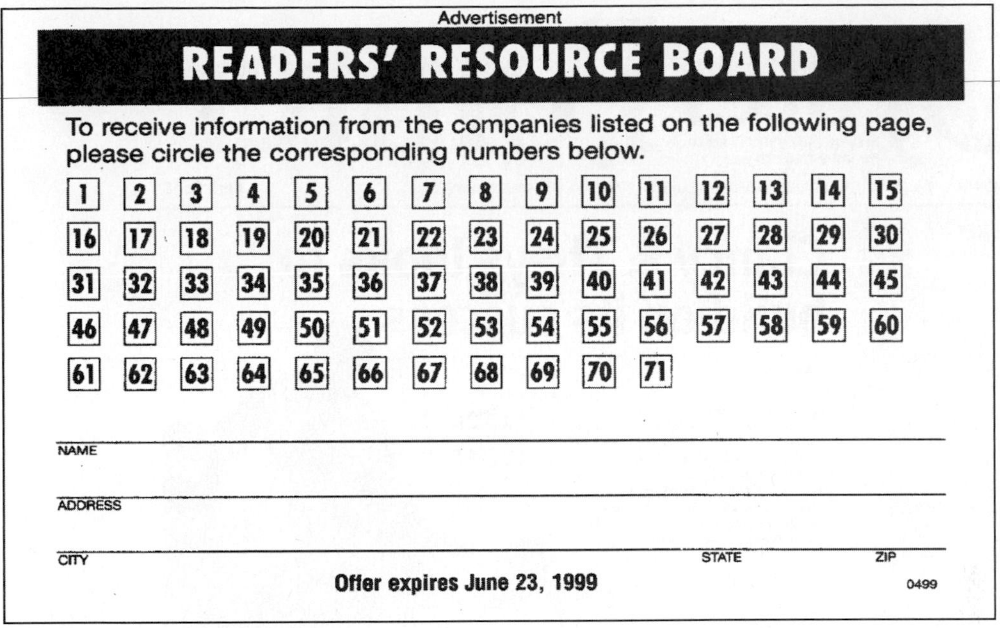
Advertisement

READERS' RESOURCE BOARD

To receive information from the companies listed on the following page, please circle the corresponding numbers below.

1	2	3	4	5	6	7	8	9	10	11	12	13	14	15
16	17	18	19	20	21	22	23	24	25	26	27	28	29	30
31	32	33	34	35	36	37	38	39	40	41	42	43	44	45
46	47	48	49	50	51	52	53	54	55	56	57	58	59	60
61	62	63	64	65	66	67	68	69	70	71				

NAME

ADDRESS

CITY STATE ZIP

Offer expires June 23, 1999

0499

FIGURE 6-8 Bingo Card Sample.

with the poorest response during June–July. (These are *circulation* dates and not always the dates appearing on the cover of the magazine.)

NEWSPAPERS AS A PRINT MEDIUM

Along with magazines, newspapers represent a major medium for distribution of printed direct response advertising. There are an estimated 1,500 daily newspapers in the United States. A sizable number of weekly and farm newspapers are also available for use by direct marketers. Figure 6-9 presents an example of a free monthly newspaper, the *Oyster Pointer,* which provides direct marketers with excellent opportunities to promote to local consumers. The *Oyster Pointer* is a business publication that features stories about businesses and people who work within the Oyster Point Business Park. The publication is distributed throughout the local area in governmental buildings, banks, office reception areas, local restaurants, and the local airport. The *Oyster Pointer* started as an 8-page newspaper, and today it spreads news about the business park area in 32 pages. Its circulation has grown to 10,000 with a readership of more than 37,000. Direct response advertisements are highly effective in this publication.

Market Segmentation

Like magazines, newspapers help segment the market for direct response advertising although not as finely as magazines. National newspapers, such as the *Wall Street Journal, USA Today, Christian Science Monitor, Capper's Weekly,* and *National Enquirer,* are directed to well-defined market segments. Some national newspapers are produced via franchises in local geographic regions. For example, *Kidsville News,* a newspaper created to promote literacy among children, is published in local editions to feature stories and artwork of children in the local area. This newspaper is distributed free of charge via local schools and is an excellent medium for direct marketers

Clancy & Theys looks to build on its success

BY KELLI CAPLAN

All cooks know that it is never a good idea to mess with the perfect recipe. Bill Goggins is certainly not a chef. But as the new leader at Clancy & Theys Construction Company in Oyster Point, he knows not to drastically alter the key ingredients, so to speak, that have made his firm so successful over the years: honesty, teamwork, incredibly good work and a pristine reputation.

Jamie Tollenaere, Dean Conklin and Bill Goggins (back to front) review plans for an upcoming project.

Continued on page 2

The Sandler Center for the Performing Arts in Virginia Beach   STEVE BUDMAN PHOTOGRAPHY

PHOTO COURTESY OF CLANCY & THEYS

PRSRT STD
U.S. POSTAGE
PAID
Hampton, VA
Permit #148

SEE INSIDE:

See how things
are developing.   **page 7**

Wear outer representations
of your inner beauty.   **page 10**

New York has come
to Newport News.   **page 18**

FIGURE 6-9 *Oyster Pointer* Magazine.   *Source:* Used with permission of Sylvia Weinstein, Publisher, the Oyster Pointer.

to reach families with school-age children in specific geographic areas. An edition of this highly targeted newspaper appears in Figure 6-10.

Additional opportunities for market segmentation through newspapers include urban versus rural, dailies versus weeklies, commuter editions versus those home-delivered, morning versus evening editions, tabloids, comic sections, and Sunday supplements. Marketers can also select specific types of readers by choosing the placement of direct response advertisements within the newspaper, such as in the sports, television, comic, or business sections, for example.

Categories of Newspaper Advertising

Aside from type and location of a newspaper's circulation, there are three distinct ways to reach a newspaper's readers: (1) run-of-paper, (2) preprinted inserts, or (3) syndicated Sunday supplements.

FIGURE 6-10   Newport News *Kidsville News!* **Cover.**   *Source:* Used with permission of Sylvia Weinstein, Publisher, Newport News Kidsville News!

RUN-OF-PAPER ADVERTISEMENTS   Although position in a newspaper can many times be specified and paid for, **run-of-paper (ROP) advertisements**—positioning the ad at the will of the newspaper—do not normally have the visual impact or dominance required for direct response advertisers. Most ROP direct response advertisements are small or appear in specific "mail-order" sections of newspapers. (Full-page direct response advertising in newspapers will, of course, increase dominance wherever placed.)

PREPRINTED INSERTS   **Preprinted inserts** run typically in Sunday editions or on Wednesday or Thursday mornings. The direct response advertiser usually prints them ahead of time and provides them to the newspaper according to the publication's specifications.

SUNDAY SUPPLEMENTS   Mass circulation **Sunday supplements,** such as *Parade* and *Family Weekly,* are edited nationally but appear locally in the Sunday editions of many newspapers. They offer large circulation and a great deal of flexibility at a relatively low cost. One variation of the Sunday supplement is the comics section, which reaches as many as 50 million households. Sunday supplements, both magazine and comic sections, have proven successful for many direct response advertisers.

Advantages and Disadvantages

Key advantages of newspapers for direct response advertisers include short closing dates and relatively fast response. A wide variety of formats is available, as well as broad coverage of geographic or demographic areas. A disadvantage is that response from newspaper advertisements is usually short-lived because tomorrow brings another edition.

Newspapers are well known for providing strong market penetration in a local geographical area. Figure 6-11 provides an example of a direct response space ad from a local newspaper. Note the offer being presented is designed to appeal to the consumers residing in a specific geographical area (Virginia Beach).

Although this is not necessarily true of preprinted inserts, the print quality of newspapers is generally not as good as that of the other print media, direct mail, and magazines, and there is limited color availability. At times, the timeliness of the editorial content of newspapers and the abundance of their advertising content detract from the readership of direct response advertising. Newspapers do not have the degree of selectivity or market segmentation that direct mail has. Therefore, most direct response ads in newspapers keep the message more generic. As shown in the newspaper ads in Figure 6-12, McDonald Garden Center knows its ad will reach both customers and prospective customers in the local geographical area.

FIGURE 6-11   McDonald Green Centers: English Rose Event.
Source: Used with permission of McDonald Garden Center.

FIGURE 6-12   McDonald Green Centers: Reward Yourself . . . Show Your Card and Take Advantage. . . .   *Source:* Used with permission of McDonald Garden Center.

Position and Timing

There are many opportunities for **positioning** in newspapers. An obvious one is placement of a funeral service inquiry ad adjacent to the obituaries. Another is placement of automobile tire and hunting gear ads in the sports section. Most newspapers have food sections—usually on Wednesday or Thursday—and relevant ads are obvious candidates for placement there. Financial advisors and stockbrokers are appropriate advertisers in business sections. Coupons, if used, should be positioned on the outside of the page for easy clipping.

Timing can be important, too. Seasonal interests are obvious. Sunday editions typically are read at a more leisurely pace and in a family setting. Morning editions may be more appropriate for retailers than evening editions. As already noted, Wednesday and/or Thursday may be more favorable to grocery shopping ads and weekend sport sections carry a lot of scores and other references for sports fans. Tuesdays may be relatively light days for advertising, so ads can be showcased. Friday editions may emphasize weekend activities. Of course, major news happenings (often unforeseen) can grab attention away from all the other contents.

Summary

Of all the media used by direct marketers, direct mail remains the primary one, relying on databases to most effectively reach market segments. Direct mail is the most selective, the most flexible medium, and it offers the greatest potential for the highest rate of response although it is the most expensive medium per prospect mailed. Variations of direct mail include self-mailers, classic formats, catalogs, syndication mailings, coupons, cooperative mailings, and miscellaneous distribution, such as statement/invoice stuffers, package inserts, and take-one racks.

Printed media, other than direct mail, include magazines and newspapers. Magazines, as they have moved away from mass circulation to special-interest circulation, offer increased opportunities for market segmentation through definition of content and readership. We generally categorize magazines as general mass, women's service, shelter, business, and special interest. Thus, magazine readership can help describe markets. Although they offer high-quality printing reproduction, magazines provide direct marketers less space for their messages than does direct mail.

The cost of circulation of magazines is substantially lower than that of direct mail, but response rates of individual advertisements are also much lower.

Daily newspapers in the United States reach about two-thirds of all households. There are also a good many weekly and farm newspapers, which are also used extensively by direct marketers. Like magazines, newspapers can be segmented for direct response advertisers by geographic location, special positioning within the paper, and other factors such as morning or evening editions, and commuter or home delivery circulation. Response advertisers can use ROP (run-of-paper), preprinted inserts, or Sunday supplements.

Key Terms

direct mail *149*
syndication mailings *152*
coupon *152*
cooperative mailings *153*
stuffers *154*

package inserts *155*
take-one racks *155*
bingo card *158*
run-of-paper (ROP)
    advertisements *161*

preprinted inserts *161*
Sunday supplements *162*
positioning *163*

Review Questions

1. What is the major advantage of direct mail over other media for direct response?
2. Discuss the attributes of a database that could be helpful for targeting direct mail to the most likely prospects. How can these be used in developing promotion copy?
3. In what ways do contemporary mailed catalogs differ from those pioneered by Ward, Sears, and Spiegel?
4. What is meant by syndication of direct mail?
5. Why is a coupon considered to be direct response advertising?
6. Evaluation of media for direct response advertising must relate results to costs. How might this be done?

7. Describe and show examples of these alternatives to traditional direct mail: cooperative mailings, statement/invoice stuffers, package inserts, and take-one racks.
8. Discuss the relative advantages and disadvantages of direct response advertising placed in magazines and/or newspapers.
9. Of what importance are position and timing of direct response advertising placed in magazines or newspapers?
10. How are print media being used in conjunction with high-tech digital media? Provide an example.

Exercise

Congratulations! You have just been hired as a marketing director for a specialty magazine. Your primary responsibility is to increase the number of subscribers to your magazine. Your assignment is to (1) describe the magazine and its target market; (2) create a media plan comprised of only print media; and (3) develop the rough creative materials you plan to use in the execution of the media plan. Your new boss didn't give you a budget, so be creative!

CASE

Newport News

Overview

This case investigates a multipage format of direct mail—the catalog. It stimulates thinking about the research and preparation involved in producing and distributing a catalog and, naturally, the costs incurred throughout the process. It also provides an overview of the critical roles that testing and product selection play in the successful execution of a catalog.

In the catalog business, direct marketers are constantly creating new offers to generate consumer purchases at some future time. Catalog development is a detailed process—one requiring much research and testing. Savvy direct marketers use their database as a tool to aid in numerous catalog production decisions, such as the product variety to be offered and the teaser copy to be placed on the front page of the catalog. Given the increasing popularity of online ordering, direct marketers are now strategically evaluating their catalog development and distribution decisions.

Case

A model example of a retail and catalog business is Spiegel (Spiegel Brands). Spiegel Brands is comprised of two separate and distinct brands, each uniquely designed to target and sell to different groups of consumers. They are Spiegel (women's apparel and home furnishings) and Newport News (moderately priced, trendy women's fashion). Each of these brands has a separate yet effective way of using database marketing in their respective catalog businesses. This case examines Newport News, which has developed a niche by offering versatile, on-trend, women's fashion at easily affordable prices through direct mail catalogs and the Internet.

Newport News has been in the direct marketing arena for 30 years. In this time it has learned many valuable lessons about the industry, the strategies of direct mail, and, most important, the ever-changing consumer.

The company started as a division of the popular cosmetics brand Avon. On November 6, 1987, the company, then called New Hampton, broke free and declared its independence from Avon, where the catalog was called Avon Fashions. However the company soon faced an uncertain future when in August 1993, it declared bankruptcy (Chapter 11). The Spiegel Group stepped in at the same time and purchased substantially all its assets, and the company was officially renamed Newport News in 1995. Through 2000 the company continued to grow; however, difficult economic conditions since then have presented challenging times. In March 2003 Spiegel, along with its principal operating subsidiaries, filed for bankruptcy protection under Chapter 11. The Newport News and Spiegel catalog operations were sold to a private equity group and became Spiegel Brands. This situation has pushed Newport News to focus even more attention on serving its existing customers and identifying prospective customers.

Improved technology has allowed Newport News to store important customer data in its data warehouse. Of its roughly 5 million customers, about 2.5 million are considered *active buyers*. An active buyer is defined by Newport News as "a customer who has ordered something from the company within the past 24 months." Active buyers are treated differently from inactive buyers. For example, people on the active buyer list receive more catalogs from Newport News, because these customers have recently shown an interest in its product(s) and are more likely to make a purchase.

Being in the direct mail business is very costly, so effective target marketing is extremely important. Newport News had 65 separate catalog mailings in 2007, an average of more than one per week, for a total of approximately 120 million pieces.

Companies such as Newport News recognize that customers develop certain perceptions about the product quality based solely on the quality of the catalog. A company with high-quality goods should have a high-quality catalog to project that same image to the consumer. The company must determine the most effective cover that will inspire the prospective customer to open the catalog and look inside. Research has determined that the model on the cover also can make the difference between whether a catalog edition makes a sale or not. Therefore, great care is taken when selecting models for each catalog cover. In addition, the company conducts market tests not only for the models but for the many product offerings in each catalog. Each catalog must be considered an asset and treated as such by targeting mailings as efficiently as possible.

Newport News has introduced an approach that utilizes a new direct mail format called a *magalog,* a cross between a catalog and a magazine. With this innovative approach, Newport News is positioning itself as the only fashion catalog that sells on-trend merchandise at great value *and* that shows its customers how to make informed shopping decisions to look their best. The innovative magazine-style format combines fashionable merchandise with authoritative editorial content and a fresh, new layout. The magalog is a larger booklet than a traditional Newport News catalog and has a magazine binding and feel to it. It provides the customer with more copy and fashion tips than would normally be found in a magazine, while still trying to sell products.

Figure 6-13 shows some of the different types of page layouts found in a recent Newport News magalog. So far, the magalog has shown signs of success by generating a response rate that is higher than that of the typical Newport News catalog.

The goal of every direct marketing company is to know exactly who its best customers are, but as of yet no one has determined an exact method of accomplishing this task. Newport News is always looking for ways to maintain and increase its response rate. As shown in Figure 6-14 (see page 168), the company is constantly testing a variety of different teaser copies on the front cover of its catalogs, product offerings, catalog layout, models, props, and photographs to determine which are the most effective.

Only through testing can the company determine what products and features of each catalog it should continue. The more information the company has, the better it can target customers who are more likely to make a purchase and avoid the extra cost of sending catalogs to those who are not. Newport News rents lists from other companies besides using in-house lists within Spiegel Brands. The process doesn't end with getting the name, however. That is only the beginning.

Newport News conducts extensive research to determine what other products its customers are purchasing and from what competitors. The company takes that data and compares trends to determine where potential customers may be found. It develops customer profiles through market research, and then it finds prospective companies that have current, qualifying customers that fit its desired customer profiles. It rents lists from those companies to target potential customers. This strategy enables the company to attract potential customers who may be interested in the products offered by Newport News but have had no previous exposure to the company.

Newport News can actually determine how certain segments or certain catalogs are performing simply by looking up the current information in the database. This is especially important because this is how the company determines the response rate that each segment and each catalog is generating. To provide information for the database, each Newport News catalog has a "campaign" number, which identifies the catalog mailing and a "mailkey" number to identify the customer segment. The sales associates ask for these numbers at the start of each order. Some of the metrics

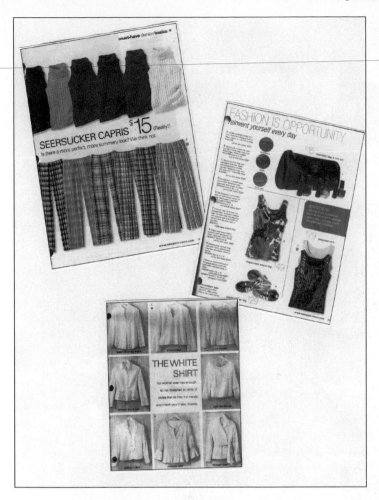

FIGURE 6-13   Page Layouts from a Newport News Magalog. *Source:* Used with permission of Newport News, Inc.

Newport News uses include orders generated, gross demand (in dollars) generated, and units generated. Each piece of information is collected for each catalog mailing. Newport News can then begin adjusting its marketing strategy directly toward certain customer segments, which may contain devoted customers who have been historically proven to be a company's best customers.

Newport News does something very interesting with its best customers: It refers to them as "trendsetters" and uses these customers and their preferences to forecast buying trends. These trend-setters may receive catalogs well before other customers, and Newport News will track their pur-chases, using this information to forecast demand for certain products offered in its catalogs. For example, if the trendsetter group has a high response to a particular leather coat, Newport News may increase the quantity of this coat in its inventory in anticipation of higher sales in the near future. The company also takes items with high trendsetter demand and places them in multiple catalog mailings. Newport News uses its trendsetter forecasts to increase overall productivity as well, by dropping items with low trendsetter demand. These strategies demonstrate the firm's confidence in applying its marketing research to creating successful catalogs.

The creation of a catalog begins with market research and database analysis. It is a continuous process that uses the company's database to track and compare the performance of each catalog

FIGURE 6.14   Examples of Teaser Copy on Newport News Catalog Cover.   *Source:* Used with permission of Newport News, Inc.

mailed to the customer. This is increasingly challenging given the fact that its Internet business has grown to represent a significant portion of all orders placed. Catalog-only customers represent 40 percent, with the remaining 60 percent equally divided between Internet-only and those classified as "multichannel"—having placed orders via both the telephone and the Internet. This has presented the company with the following three challenges.

1. *How to acquire new customers?* Database analysis shows that approximately 60 percent of new customers acquired are driven by the catalog.
2. *How do I tell what inspired a customer to shop via the Internet?* The Internet does not provide direct marketers with the typical key code information that is normally used to match back a customer to a particular catalog mailing. Spiegel Brands currently contracts with a third party to conduct a match-back of new customer names against direct mailings to determine how many were inspired by a direct mail piece to shop online.
3. *How often and with what type of direct mail should I contact an Internet customer?* The Internet customer buys less often and spends approximately 50 percent fewer dollars when compared to catalog-only or multichannel customers. In 2008, the company began testing four-page, eight-page, and "slim Jim" mailings in an effort to determine if the contact is the needed motivation and not the entire catalog—since Internet customers generally go online to experience the company's full store. Early test results show that this strategy may prove to be an effective one with lower costs and only minimal declines in response rates.

Overall, Newport News has been successful by understanding its consumers and their buying behavior, creating offers and producing catalogs and mailings that appeal to these consumers, and by never losing sight of the most important asset the company has—its customers.

Case Discussion Questions

1. Come up with a list of companies you think Newport News should consider for list rental. Why did you choose these companies? Would you consider these firms like or unlike Newport News?
2. Newport News uses trendsetters in an attempt to forecast demand. What factors would you look for when considering someone to be a trendsetter? What factors would make someone not suitable for being a trendsetter?
3. Describe how customer perceptions can be influenced by the *quality* of a direct mail catalog.
4. Why do you think Newport News implemented the campaign and mailkey numbers into their business model? What kind of information can these tools provide that is useful to marketers?
5. Describe the new brand positioning for Newport News and its innovative direct mail format. Why do you think this format might be more productive for the company than the typical catalog?

Notes

1. *Statistical Fact Book 2006* (New York: Direct Marketing Association), p. 55.
2. See Chapter 2, which deals with market segmentation strategies, and Chapter 3, which deals with database development.
3. *Statistical Fact Book 2006,* p. 58.
4. Ibid., p. 95.
5. Valpak Readership Study, *Directions in Research,* 2008.
6. Valpak Category Census, 2004.

Developing and Utilizing Electronic Media

Opening Vignette: Smithfield Foods

Today's wide variety and sheer number of cable television stations available make it easy for companies to target specific types of consumers with advertisements featuring their products or services. Television advertisements have always been an effective form of "mass advertising" because they generate excellent brand awareness and enhance brand recognition. However, television advertising is also an effective form of direct and interactive marketing when the advertisement requests consumers to take some specific action or response, such as the purchase of a certain product at a store, a phone call using a specific toll-free number, or a visit to the company's Web site using the Web address presented in the ad. This is the beauty of the medium—it is most effective when used in conjunction with other media. It is also most effective when tied into the company's overall branding strategy—thus contributing to the synergy being created by the use of several media vehicles to drive home the message. The use of television to generate a consumer response, commonly referred to as direct response television (DRTV) advertising, is especially effective when the product or service being marketed has mass appeal and is not limited to the desires of a specific consumer group or audience. This is the case of Smithfield Foods. Let's explore how this company effectively used national cable television to market its variety of delicious meat products.

In an effort to increase brand recognition and encourage brand loyalty, Smithfield Foods established a partnership with the "queen of Southern cuisine," Paula Deen. Paula Deen has endorsed the Smithfield brand. In fact, Smithfield is the only food brand endorsed by this world-famous cooking guru. With its new celebrity spokesperson on board, Smithfield created a series of 30-second TV spots promoting a wide range of its products. As Figure 7-1 presents, each advertisement begins with the opener of "Smithfield Cooks with Paula Deen" and then proceeds into the kitchen showing Paula cooking with a Smithfield brand product. Some of the newer spots being developed will take Paula out of the kitchen and put her on the road promoting Smithfield.

The objective of these DRTV spots is to entice and interest the consumer to purchase and use Smithfield products when making the excellent recipes being shared by Paula Deen. Of course, each advertisement directs the consumer to its Web site to learn more about Smithfield products. Have these direct response advertisements been effective for Smithfield? You bet! Unique visitors at its Web site increased 252 percent! In fact, because this DRTV campaign was such a success, Smithfield Foods plans to continue and expand the use of national cable television in its upcoming marketing campaign. The television channels to be included in its 2008–2009 marketing campaign include the following cable networks: Fine Living, the Food Network, the Learning Channel, Great American Country, TBS, USA Network, and Lifetime. A total of 1,928 television spots are planned for the 2008–2009 marketing campaign. Smithfield has successfully woven DRTV into its media mix. The company uses electronic media to create a synergistic effect in its overall marketing campaign.

FIGURE 7-1 Smithfield Foods DRTV Advertisement. *Source:* Used with permission of Smithfield Foods.

Electronic media is the topic of this chapter. We explore how direct marketers use the mediums of television, radio, and telephone to generate a response from customers and prospective customers. We also discuss the various formats available for each medium and the advantages and disadvantages associated with using each electronic medium for direct and interactive marketing.

Electronic media encompasses television, radio, and telephone. Television and radio are commonly referred to as broadcast media. **Broadcast** is the most universal of communications media. Unlike telephone and print media, broadcast reaches virtually everyone and every location. There are more radios than people in the United States, and most people listen to the radio during some part of each day. Virtually every one of the 111,617,402 households in the United States has at least one television set, and many households have more.[1] Nearly 84 percent of U.S. households are cable subscribers.[2] The average television set is used as much as 6 hours per day, and television long ago replaced the newspaper as the primary source of news.

With its universality, broadcast reaches the full range of geographic, demographic, and psychographic market segments, which are not always easily separated. Relatively high costs associated with relatively low response rates result from reaching (and paying for) nonqualified prospects. Measurability and accountability, hallmarks of direct marketing, are difficult, if not impossible, with broadcast media. Still, the potential reach is there, if it can be harnessed.

In spite of their universality, however, broadcast media—television and radio—account for only a small percentage of total expenditures for direct response advertising. As Figure 7-2 reveals, direct marketing advertising expenditures for DRTV and direct response radio (DR radio) accounted for only 16 percent of total advertising expenditures in 2007.[3] Most TV advertising creatively emphasizes product brand and image rather than asking for an immediate response, the preferred advertising mode of direct marketers. However, this is changing as direct marketers experiment with and learn about the broadcast media of television and radio.

DM Advertising Expenditures by Medium	2002	2006	2007	2008 (EST)	2012 (EST)	Compound Annual Growth 2002–07	2007–12
Direct Mail (Non-Catalog)	$24.6	$33.0	$34.5	$36.4	$44.5	7.0%	5.2%
Direct Mail (Catalog)	15.7	20.1	20.8	22.0	27.2	5.7%	5.5%
Telephone Marketing	45.3	45.3	46.1	47.0	52.1	0.4%	2.5%
Internet Marketing (Non-E-Mail)	5.8	16.1	19.2	23.0	39.7	27.2%	15.6%
Commercial E-Mail	0.2	0.4	0.5	0.6	1.2	14.5%	20.2%
DR Newspaper	14.3	12.0	11.9	12.0	13.2	−3.7%	2.1%
DR Television	17.0	22.0	22.8	24.2	29.5	6.1%	5.3%
DR Magazine	6.8	8.4	8.7	8.9	10.0	5.0%	2.8%
DR Radio	4.5	4.9	5.0	5.2	5.9	2.3%	3.4%
Insert Media	0.7	0.9	0.9	1.0	1.2	6.5%	5.3%
Other	2.4	2.8	2.8	2.9	3.4	3.3%	3.3%

FIGURE 7-2   Summary of DM Advertising Expenditures. *Source: The Power of Direct Marketing, 2007–2008* (New York: Direct Marketing Association, Inc., 2007), p. 58. Used with permission of the Direct Marketing Association.

In this chapter, we look at the ramifications of television, such as network, cable, and satellite transmission; then we discuss radio, and finally, we explore telephone as a direct and interactive medium.

TELEVISION

When it began, transmitted via established networks or local channels, television was not an important medium for direct response advertising. But its value has increased as direct marketers have learned how to use it. Cable and satellite transmission now provide an almost endless variety of programming and special-interest channels, defining the potential for market segmentation. Interactive modes of television provide the immediate response—along with measurability and accountability—on which direct marketers thrive.

Direct response advertisers use television in the following three ways, as we detail in this chapter:

1. To sell products or services, or a political candidate.
2. To get inquiries: expressions of interest or sales leads for personal follow-up.
3. To support other media: newspaper inserts or heavy penetration direct mail.

To accomplish these alternatives, direct response advertisers need to be mindful that television viewers have one of two objectives: *entertainment* or *information*. It also is important that advertisers know how to direct their messages to defined market segments so as to minimize the high cost of reaching television audiences.

Market Segmentation

When a farmer "broadcasts" seed, much of that seed lodges in moist, fertile ground and, under ideal growing conditions, it is nurtured into a living plant. Another portion of the seed is borne away by the wind or fails to achieve the proper conditions for germination for other reasons. Direct marketers using television are like the farmer sowing seed. Although television has the potential for reaching virtually everyone, it can achieve the objectives of the direct response advertiser only if it is seen in the right place at the right time under the right conditions. Market segmentation, in television as in other media, is one way to maximize direct response.

Television programming plays an important role in defining specific audience segments; sports, news, comedies, westerns, mysteries, variety, documentaries, wrestling, and opera or drama can describe market segments of viewers and thus provide a showcase for a particular direct response offer. Other factors that can help segment markets include time of day or day of the week. Viewers of one of television's most-watched audience events each year, the Super Bowl, are large in number and broad in characteristics. On the other hand, viewers of an Alfred Hitchcock movie are a more narrowly defined group, and whether they watch late at night or mid-afternoon also can make a difference in the demographic and psychographic characteristics of the audience. The "reach" of a local TV station can itself describe geographic markets differentiated by ZIP code characteristics.

Offering direct response advertisers even greater opportunities for market segmentation is cable television, with hundreds of specialized channels. Cable households have grown both more numerous and more affluent over the past 18 years. From 1985 to 2004, the average cable household income rose 112 percent from $32,182 to $63,381. The income gap between cable and noncable homes is $12,333. That represents a 92 percent increase over the $6,409 gap that existed in 1985.[4]

Highly specialized programming, "live" news, sporting events, and a variety of movie fare can help define desirable segments of cable TV audiences as can special-interest channels, such as CNN, ESPN, the History Channel, or the Golf Channel.

Characteristics of Television Time

Like empty seats on a departing airplane, television time is perishable. Furthermore, once 24 hours per day have been used within a market, coverage cannot be extended, nor can more time be manufactured or imported. Only actual viewing can be increased. This penetration of the potential market, the number of viewers, is what determines the price of commercial television time.

This price usually peaks during prime time, the early evening hours, and drops to a minimum during the wee hours of the morning. The cost of TV time is highest when the viewing audience is the largest, although the cost is often set without regard to audience composition. Prime time may not be the best time for direct response advertising unless an offer appeals to a large and diversified audience. Furthermore, large audiences attracted to a suspense-filled event like the Super Bowl are not inclined to break off watching to "call this toll-free number *now!*"

The cost of a 120-second selling commercial, as typically used for direct response advertising on television, is not an adequate indication of success unless it is related to anticipated (actual) response to the advertising. The key to maximizing such response lies in market segmentation: Just who are the viewers at a particular time and how receptive are they to a direct offer?

Because television costs as well as audience segments vary, the most valid measurement for the direct marketer is **cost per response (CPR)**, not **cost per viewer (CPV)**. Nielsen audience ratings, **gross rating points (GRPs)**, and areas of dominant influence (ADI)—the glossary of TV time buying for the general advertiser—have little or no relevance for the direct marketer who wants somewhat more from direct response advertising than simply "recall." For example, GRPs are a combination of **reach** and **frequency** measures. GRPs are determined by multiplying *reach* (the number of people exposed to vehicles carrying the ad) by *frequency* (the number of insertions purchased in a specific communication vehicle within a specified time period). GRPs may be able to measure the number of people exposed to an ad; however, they cannot determine whether that ad stimulated any subsequent action (response or order). As an example, the CPV of reaching one of television's largest audiences, those watching the Super Bowl, might be quite low, but because of the diversity of this audience, the CPR could be prohibitively high.

The acronym that counts is CPR, the total cost of a direct marketing campaign divided by the number of responses that campaign generated:

$$CPR = \frac{\text{Total Promotion Budget}}{\text{Total Number of Orders/Inquiries Received}}$$

Direct marketers must always relate advertising results to its costs.

Direct Marketing Uses of Television

We've said that there are three basic ways in which direct marketers use television. Let's now look at each in turn.

The first of these ways is to *sell something:* a recording, a subscription, a kitchen utensil. Consumers are ordering a broad assortment of products/services via DRTV. Direct marketers usually require a 2-minute (120-second) commercial to achieve a direct sale. Customers respond by mail or, more likely, by phone or through a Web site.

The second purpose of television for direct marketers is to *generate leads* for products or for political candidates seeking votes. These responses require a two-step process in which the commercial stimulates the original inquiry and the customer follows up by mail, phone, Web site, or personal visit to a store or a voting booth. Sixty-second television commercials are adequate to generate such leads.

The third direct marketing use of television is as *support* of direct response advertising in another medium, such as a newspaper. *Reader's Digest,* Publishers Clearing House, Time-Life, and others have used television successfully in this way. Usually 10- or 30-second commercials are adequate as reminders, with extensive repetition over a period of several days being the key to success. Support television, often purchased locally, creates interest in the offer and directs the viewer to the printed medium, which in turn provides detailed explanations as well as means for response.

Television Home Shopping and Infomercials

Home Shopping Network (HSN) and Quality/Value/Convenience (QVC) are notable examples of TV channels devoted to the continuous sale of merchandise. Though such programming does not yet provide random access for product selection—as would a printed catalog or a Web site—technology for such interactivity is emerging. For now, these networks primarily offer products such as jewelry, cosmetics, and electronics, which are frequently purchased on impulse. These products are extensively

Top 20 Infomercials on National Cable for 2007			
Based Solely on Frequency of Programs Aired on Networks Monitored			
Rank	**Show Title**	**Marketing Company**	**Category**
1	Free & Clear	Amazing Profits LLC	Business Opportunity
2	bareMinerals	Bare Escentuals Beauty	Beauty
3	Nutrisystem	Nutrisystem, Inc.	Health & Fitness
4	Hip Hop Abs	BeachBody.com	Health & Fitness
5	The Bean	GreenHouse International	Health & Fitness
6	Body Makeover	Provida Life Sciences	Health & Fitness
7	Dual Action Cleanse	Health Breakthroughs Magazine	Health & Fitness
8	P90X	BeachBody.com	Health & Fitness
9	Tempur-Pedic	Tempur-Pedic, Inc.	Household
10	Cash Flow Business	America's Note Network	Business Opportunity
11	Red Exerciser	Red Fitness	Health & Fitness
12	Fluidity Bar	Fluidity Fitness LLC	Health & Fitness
13	Leg Magic	Allstar/Kingstar	Health & Fitness
14	Auctions For Income	Auction Profits LLC	Business Opportunity
15	Girls gone Wild	Mantra Entertainment	Entertainment
16	Magic Bullet	Homeland Housewares	Kitchen
17	Shapely Secrets	Savvier	Health & Fitness
18	Total Gym	Total Gym Fitness LLC	Health & Fitness
19	Sheer Cover	Guthy-RenkerCorp.	Beauty
20	LIFE	Life Outreach International	Not for Profit

FIGURE 7-3   Top 20 Infomercials on National Cable for 2007.   *Source:* 2007 IMS/Infomercial Monitoring Service, Inc. in *Statistical Fact Book,* 30th ed. (New York: Direct Marketing Association, Inc., 2008), p. 88. Used with permission of the Direct Marketing Association.

demonstrated, priced for quick sale, and sometimes rely on well-known personalities for credibility. Television home shoppers claim that product demonstrations were the prime motivating factor for their purchasing from television.[5] So-called **infomercials** have become an important means of demonstrating and selling certain categories of products through television. These ads appear primarily on cable channels and often during early morning and late-night time slots. They usually last for 30 minutes. Featured products include exercisers, cookware, weight-loss offers, and sundry cleaning products. Figure 7-3 provides a list of the top infomercials on national cable in 2005.

Infomercial production costs generally start around $75,000 and go up from there with infomercial media tests costing around $10,000 to $15,000. If the test is successful, media expenditures will increase, which can translate into a larger ROI. For example, let's say you spend $10,000 per week on your infomercial campaign and it generates $20,000 in revenue. If you can maintain that same 2:1 **media efficiency ratio (MER)** and you spend $100,000 per week, then your informercial campaign will generate $200,000 in revenue per week.[6] It is also important to remember

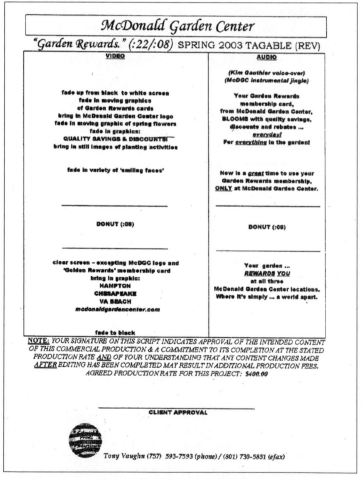

FIGURE 7-4   Script for a McDonald Garden Center Television Advertisement. *Source:* Used with permission of McDonald Garden Center.

that there are additional costs associated with an infomercial campaign, such as card processing, telemarketing, fulfillment, and other miscellaneous ones.

Advantages and Disadvantages

Television, when used for direct response advertising, can provide a wide choice of cost alternatives and achieve quick (but short-lived) responses. It reaches an extremely large audience and uses the combination of video and audio, simultaneously providing a sales message along with a product demonstration to deliver a lot of impact in a short time. Figure 7-4 provides a script for a TV advertisement prior to ad production. Note the coordination necessary between the video and audio components.

Television's major disadvantage is the high cost to prepare and place the ads. For example, to place a 30-second advertisement during prime time on *Grey's Anatomy* will cost roughly $419,000. The average price for 30-second ads on all prime-time programs is $127,990.[7] Limited time is also one of the medium's disadvantages when product descriptions are complex or not subject to simple demonstration. Another major drawback is lack of a response device that the viewer can reference at a later time.

RADIO

When radio broadcasting was still in its infancy in the 1920s, it became a major medium for direct response advertising. It was productive for books and records, as it is today, and also, in that early period, for proprietary medicines and health cures. A powerful radio station in Del Rio, Texas, with the call letters XERA, built its transmitter across the border in Mexico to circumvent curtailment of its power as well as regulation of its direct response advertisements. These advertisements were often "exaggerations of the truth" at best. XERA (and other stations) solicited orders for "genuine synthetic diamonds" as well as inquiries for Dr. Brinkley's "goat gland transplants" for those seeking perpetual youth. Mail-order nurseries, pioneers in direct marketing, offered their plants and trees, and religious groups raised funds for their evangelists through the medium of radio. Radio is still probably as strong a direct response medium as it was then, although it is minimally used today.

Market Segmentation

Even more than TV channels, individual radio stations tend to develop strong images of programming, attracting particular types of listeners. Such program formats can segment markets into an array of specific subgroups that is virtually unlimited: all music, all news, and all talk. Program format doesn't stop with just "music," however. Music can be rock, classical, easy listening, country/western, show tunes, or nostalgic music-of-your-life programming. Figure 7-5 reveals the number of different types of radio stations in a Southeastern metropolitan area of the United States. Notice that there are many different formats or programs available to satisfy the listening desires of all consumers.

Listeners are loyal to certain stations, so direct response advertising, presented within an established program format by a well-known personality, derives an air of credibility or even an implied endorsement from the station announcer. (For many years, syndicated radio news commentator Paul Harvey has provided a notable example, with his personally presented commercials for insurance and health products.) Unlike the case in television, in which viewers are constantly surfing among as many as a dozen or more favorite channels, according to the Radio Advertising

Radio Stations in Virginia (Licensed by the Federal Communication Commission)	
Programming Formats	**Number of Stations**
Active Rock	12
Adult Album Alternative	6
Adult Contemporary	12
Adult Hits	3
Adult Standards	8
Album Oriented Rock	1
All News	2
Bluegrass	3
Brokered Spanish	2
Children's	2
Classic Hits	1
Classic Rock	5
Classical	1
Classical/Jazz	2
Contemporary Christian	22
Contemporary Hit Radio	11
Country	45
Country/Bluegrass	6
Full Service	9
Hot Adult Contemporary	6
Korean Religious	1
Light Adult Contemporary	7
Mainstream Urban	3
Modern Rock	5
News/Talk/Sports	10
Oldies	5
Oldies/Classic Rock	8
Public Radio	16
Religious	19
Rhythmic Contemporary	1
Silent	3
Smooth Jazz	1
Southern Gospel	21
Spanish	6
Sports	23
Talk	16
Urban Contemporary	12
Urban Gospel	20
Variety	10

FIGURE 7-5 Radio Stations in Virginia. *Source*: Adapted from Wikipedia, "List of Radio Stations in Virginia," April 2008, http://en.wikipedia.org/wiki/Wikipedia:Copyrights#Reusers.27_rights_and_obligations.

Bureau, the average radio listener "tunes in regularly to less than three stations—no matter how many he can receive." Several thousand radio stations (AM as well as FM stations) provide a lot of choices, and there appears to be relatively little switching!

In addition to program format and station loyalty, another means of market segmentation through radio is by its use during particular times of the day or even days of the week. Unlike most

TV viewers, radio listeners can be involved in another activity while listening to the radio, so direct marketers can reach them in an automobile, on arising, or in front of a mirror while shaving. Of course, the listener's attention is not always undivided at these times, and the real challenge to the direct marketer is to deliver a direct response instruction that the listener will recall later.

Rate Structure

A major boost for radio in direct response advertising is its relatively low cost. Whereas the economics of television dictate a maximum commercial length of 2 minutes, commercial messages on the radio can be melded with DJ chatter. Entire 15-minute information radio programs have been built around the content of a magazine, such as *Kiplinger,* for which subscriptions are being simultaneously solicited. The same format has also been applied to advice for household repairs at the same time as orders are solicited for a *Home Handyman's Guide*.

Some radio stations accept per inquiry (PI) arrangements under which the station runs commercial messages, at its own discretion, in return for remuneration from a direct response advertiser for each sale or inquiry produced in this manner.

Advantages and Disadvantages

Radio is the most flexible of all response media in that it requires relatively little in the way of preparation, and it can be scheduled or the copy can be changed right up to the time the message is aired. In contrast with the cost of direct mail or other print media and the high preparatory cost of television video, radio has minimal production costs. In fact, the direct response advertiser accrues virtually no production cost if the message can be typed for reading by a local station announcer. Because the various program formats of radio are conducive to testing, the direct response advertiser can readily test alternative copy and formats at relatively low cost.

A major disadvantage of radio, like that of television, is absence of a response device that can be referenced at some later time. Radio also lacks the visual impact afforded by direct mail and the other print media as well as by television. Also, the recent introduction of radio through satellite services is significantly decreasing commercial air times. Here, customers pay a monthly subscription fee to receive satellite services and over 200 different radio channels from coast to coast. Among these are Sirius Satellite Radio and XM Satellite Radio, which offer commercial-free channels and channels with only about 6 minutes of advertising per hour compared with 15 to 20 minutes heard on "free" channels.[8]

TELEPHONE

The telephone occupies a dual position in direct marketing. Like print or broadcast media, it is a conduit for direct response advertising, and like mail or the Internet, it can carry the response itself. Thus, telephone marketing is both a marketing medium *and* a response mechanism. **Telemarketing** has been defined as the use of the telephone as an interactive medium for promotion or promotion response.[9] The contemporary term is teleservices or telephone marketing, which perhaps better define its role in direct and interactive marketing. Refer back to Figure 7-2 and you will notice that $46.1 billion was spent on telephone marketing advertising in 2007, representing 26.4 percent of all advertising expenditures for that year.[10] Therefore, much more advertising dollars are spent on telephone marketing than on television and radio advertising *combined*.

The objective of telemarketing is to reach customers in a personalized interaction that meets customer needs and improves cost-effectiveness for the organization. Its scope is limited only by the imagination of the direct marketer, who can use it both for profit and nonprofit organizations as well as for individuals (such as political candidates), alone or with other marketing media, and targeted to both businesses (B2B) and final consumers (B2C).

The telephone is an interactive medium, which provides the flexibility and immediate response of a personal conversation. It can be especially effective when used in concert with other direct response media, such as direct mail or a Web site. Experienced direct marketers report that, used correctly and often in tandem with other media, the phone can generate three to seven times the response achieved by mail alone. The cost of a telemarketing call averages $4 and the average cost of a direct mailing piece is $1; this difference means that to be cost-effective, a telemarketing call must be at least four times as effective as a mailing piece.

When calculating telemarketing costs, the direct marketer needs to consider not only the line and hardware but also the program design, creative development, and labor costs. The latter should include supervisory as well as clerical support costs. If the telephone is used as an alternative to a personal visit by a salesperson, as is often the case, it can be tremendously efficient.

Telemarketing has been woven into the planning of most direct marketers. To those who know how to use them, the interactive features of the telephone are, in many cases, replacing the face-to-face contact of a salesperson's visit to a prospect or a buyer's visit to a retail location. The phone obviates the need for travel and makes it possible to talk *with* and not just *to* customers and prospects.

The application of the telephone to direct marketing efforts is a most powerful combination. No other direct marketing medium can match its effectiveness. Telemarketing is actually a form of personal selling, because it occurs on a person-to-person basis but without the face-to-face aspect. Businesses use telemarketing with the sole purpose of receiving results. According to the DMA, telemarketing was the top direct marketing tool in 2006 in terms of average response rates and investments returned, and telemarketing response rates were highest among all direct marketing mediums with an average response of 5.78 percent for the third year in a row![11] Let's take a closer look at the two basic ways direct marketers use the telephone.

Inbound versus Outbound Calls

Telemarketing applications may be categorized as **inbound calls,** where customers are calling to place an order, to request more information, or for customer service. DRTV, radio, customer service centers, advertising responses, catalog call centers, after-hours sales, dealer locator services, and emergency call center responses are examples of typical inbound calls. The second category encompasses **outbound calls.** Here, organizations place calls to customers to make a sale or to offer information hoping for a later sale. These calls often deal with lead generation, appointment setting, market research fund raising, political calling, database verification, database appending, and of course sales. Outbound calls have become extremely regulated due to National Do Not Call Registry and regulations. Research indicates that already 76 percent of U.S. adults have signed up for the registry as of 2006.[12] More will be discussed about this topic in Chapter 11. Let's discuss each application of telemarketing in greater detail.

INBOUND CALLS   Inbound calls are also referred to as **reactive telemarketing** in that the initiator of the marketing communications is the customer. The customer places that call at his or her convenience to obtain information or to place an order, often using a toll-free number provided by the organization. The Federal Communications Commission has designated not only 800 numbers as *toll-free* but also the area codes 888, 877, and 866.

Customers are increasingly using the phone to place orders today. Catalog direct marketers report an increasing percentage of orders reaching them by phone, especially during holiday seasons. The recent surge of the Web and Internet marketing strategies has also increased the number of inbound calls to marketers. Consumers have used the Internet to search for product or service information, and then have turned to the telephone to place orders for products and services that were presented in a company's Web site.

Toll-free telephone service has itself been a tremendous incentive to the use of inbound phone calls to respond to offers or transact an order. The marketer's direct response advertising in other media must provide incentives as well by appealing to the emotions, pointing out the advantages of personal service, or highlighting the convenience of having a telephone order taker on hand 24 hours a day to answer questions and ensure faster deliveries or services.

The applications of inbound telemarketing generally include the following:

- Ordering or inquiring
- Clarifying or requesting assistance
- Responding immediately to an advertisement
- Expediting processing
- Locating a dealer or a product servicing location
- Making reservations for travel accommodations, hotel rooms, conferences
- Obtaining financial data, stock prices, yields, and so on
- Making pledges or contributions
- Obtaining warranty information

OUTBOUND CALLS   Outbound calls are also referred to as **proactive telemarketing** because the company is the initiator of the marketing communications. Outbound calls are generally longer in duration and require more experienced and higher-paid personnel.

The large outbound telemarketers are now using T1 service. A **T1** is a giant pipeline or conduit through which a user may send multiple voice, data, and even video signals. It supports simultaneous voice/Internet connectivity, enabling telephone sales reps (or telereps) to speak to customers while also participating in their Internet session. Instead of simply carrying one voice conversation at a time, a T1 can carry almost 100 conversations or data connections simultaneously.

Although well-prepared scripts and well-structured offers can make telephone promotion highly effective, the medium is usually most efficient if calls are directed to persons who have been prequalified in some way. The reason is that the cost of an individual phone call can be as much as four times the cost of an individual direct-mail letter, and thus it must be four times as productive to justify the expense of the call. Therefore, when telemarketers properly segment the market (according to a wide variety of segmentation variables) and prequalify prospects, the length of the call may be reduced and the number of positive consumer responses may be increased.

Prequalified outbound calls might include response to an inquiry, a new product offer to an existing customer, or generation of responses/transactions from a carefully selected list. **Cold calls** (which are calls made when there is no existing relationship with, or recognition of, the direct marketer) must be carefully structured in content because, by their very nature, they usually interrupt some other activity of the person being called and can create a negative response.

Direct marketers use the telephone for a great variety of outbound call applications, including the following:

- Generating new sales, including reorders and new product introductions
- Generating leads and qualifying inquiries for personal sales follow-up
- Serving present accounts
- Reactivating old customers
- Upgrading and increasing incoming orders
- Validating the legitimacy of orders before shipping
- Responding to customer service needs, including complaints
- Surveying customers, members, donors, voters
- Substituting for a personal sales call
- Expressing thanks to a customer, donor, or voter
- Credit screening and checking as well as collection
- Performing research and gathering or disseminating information

In summary, outbound calls have the ability to generate great profit when executed properly. Let's explore the advantages and disadvantages associated with telephone marketing.

Advantages and Disadvantages of Telephone Marketing

Some of the specific advantages of using the telephone as a marketing medium include the following.

- It provides *two-way communication* and *immediate feedback.* This quick feedback, often in response to a test campaign, can be of great assistance to the direct marketer in making any needed changes before the entire marketing campaign is executed.
- It is a *very flexible medium.* Although a telerep may use a prepared script, this doesn't limit the number of changes you can make to that script as needed. You may also change the message for each caller.
- It is a *most productive medium.* The telephone is actually more productive than traditional personal selling when you consider the sheer number of sales calls that a rep can make by phone on a daily or weekly basis. According to Bob Stone, a member in the Direct Marketing Hall of Fame, a traditional field salesperson can make 5 or 6 sales calls per day, which would compute to 25 to 30 sales calls per week, whereas a telemarketer can make 25 to 30 sales calls per day, which translates into 125 to 150 sales calls per week.[13] Therefore, the phone as a marketing medium is considered to be five times more productive in reaching prospects or customers than traditional personal selling. For example, during the time a field salesperson wines and dines a client over a 3-hour lunch, a telemarketing representative can contact about ten customers—and the company won't have to pay for an expensive meal.
- Telemarketing is a *cost-effective medium.* Although the exact costs vary depending on the type of call being placed, the average cost per call is far lower for telephone selling than for traditional personal selling. For example, outbound telemarketing as opposed to personal visits to current and prospective customers offers substantial cost savings. The average cost of a single field sales call on a customer typically runs around $350. This figure accounts for the salesperson's compensation, the travel and entertainments expenses, as well as the connected benefits. However, the telemarketing approach offers a much lower cost per sales call, ranging from $20 to $25 with little or no field expense included. These figures support the mass appeal for businesses to utilize

telemarketing services. It is estimated that over 100 million outbound telemarketing calls are made to home and businesses each year in the United States.[14]

Some of the distinct disadvantages of telemarketing include the following.

- It is by far the most *intrusive marketing medium* used by direct marketers. Telemarketing has a poor image among people who dislike the intrusion of marketers' outbound calling.
- Telemarketing *lacks visual enhancement.* It is not a visual medium, and thus its power is often related to being integrated with other media.
- Telemarketing *does not provide a permanent tangible response device.* Once again, it must be coupled with other media to provide a physical form for the customer to sign or a brochure to keep on hand to be reviewed at a later time.
- Its effectiveness depends on *retaining highly trained telephone operators.* It can be difficult to hire, train, and keep telephone operators because they must be able to handle intense personal interaction and frequent rejection.

Most direct marketers have concluded that although telemarketing has its share of disadvantages, it is a highly effective medium. Today, telemarketing is utilized by virtually every industry in the United States. The dramatic increase in the use of the telephone for marketing purposes is partially due to the driving force of technology. New sophistication in call handling technologies is partly behind the industry's explosion. Over the past two decades, there have been tremendous changes in telephone technology. Let's look at some of the technological breakthroughs in the telecommunications industry.

Telemarketing Technology

Major telecommunications technologies have been developed to support the call handling industry made possible by toll-free and 900 numbers. Telecommunications network suppliers including MCI, AT&T, Sprint Telemedia, and Telesphere now support two critical systems that permit more efficient and effective call handling. These are Dialed Number Identification System (DNIS) and Automated Numbering Identification (ANI).

DIALED NUMBER IDENTIFICATION SYSTEM (DNIS)   The **DNIS** allows any organization that has multiple toll-free or 900 numbers to differentiate incoming calls based on the number dialed by the caller. Marketers can also track media performance by placing different toll-free or 900 numbers in ads run in different media and then analyzing the DNIS records to trace which callers responded to which ads. This accountability allows marketing managers to better allocate their media resources. The main difference between toll-free and 900 numbers is the small fee associated with dialing a 900 number. The 900 number provides marketers with the ability to generate qualified responses. Although the initial charge associated with dialing the number may reduce the total volume of calls, the calls that do come are from customers who have a true interest in the product.[15]

AUTOMATED NUMBERING IDENTIFICATION (ANI)   **ANI** identifies the phone number of the person calling. Marketers can match the phone number against a name and address database, and the caller's name, address, and account history will be displayed on the screen of the telephone operator receiving the call. This enables the company to shorten the length of each call by eliminating repetitive information gathering. Marketers can also use ANI to place callbacks on abandoned calls and give priority handling to preferred customers.

In addition, there are types of voice technology to handle incoming calls. These have either replaced or complemented live telephone operators in reducing costs and improving customer service.

Predictive dialers are becoming the standard in B2C telemarketing. **Predictive dialers** are advanced hardware systems that use machines to dial and connect the call only when the computer detects a live human voice on the other end of the line. These devices increase the amount of time that sales representatives spend talking with live prospects (as opposed to fruitlessly calling answering machines or untended phones) from 20 minutes per hour to nearly 50 minutes.[16] The way predictive dialers work is simple. Using a specified database, the predictive dialer automatically enters phone numbers on the extra phone lines. When someone picks up the phone, the server automatically routes the call to an unoccupied telerep. A well-designed system is staffed and timed so that the gap between the prospect's hello and a friendly response from the agent is minimal, as is the rate of abandoned calls.

Short messaging service (SMS) is a service that provides alerts by delivering a text message to cell phones of users who have signed up for the service. The retailer logs on to a secure Web site and enters a message, specifying the band of users he or she wishes to reach. Users are segmented by gender and age—information they provided when they first subscribed to the service. However, the challenge is the large universe of prepaid cellular telephone users about whom marketers know very little. One of the greatest challenges in communication technology is just to keep up with the rate of change. Regardless of the type of communication technology used, all direct marketers must carefully create telemarketing programs if they want to use this medium to interact with their consumers. Let's examine what is involved in planning a telemarketing program.

Planning a Telemarketing Program

To be successful in telemarketing, telephone operators must convey a trustworthy, reliable image to the customer. Companies must train their operators to develop these skills and provide them with well-conceived scripts.

Preparing the Telephone Scripts

A **telephone script** is a call guide to assist the operator in communicating effectively with the prospect or customer. Most do not have to be read word for word; in fact, the most effective scripts are more like a detailed outline that provides structure to the conversation. Each outbound telemarketing call aims to deliver a sales presentation to the potential customer or client. The purpose of each inbound call is to deliver information to the customer or receive the customer's order information. Thus, different types of scripts are needed for different types of telemarketing calls. In either case, developing scripts offers the dual challenge of determining the right words to gain a favorable customer response or impression and, at the same time, minimizing the length and the cost of a call.

Writing a telephone script is both an art and a science. One valuable asset of a telemarketing script is the flexibility it provides, allowing the telemarketer to change or experiment. While most marketing media call for copy to be finalized by a certain date, telemarketing scripts can be revised after a few or a few dozen calls.

Many copywriters have developed strategies for successful script writing. Jim Kobs has offered the following seven principles for successful telephone script writing.[17]

1. *Know the target audience.* You must know who you are trying to reach and for what purpose.
2. *Get off on the right foot or you might as well get off the phone.* Everyone has heard of the old cliché "the first impression is a lasting one" or "you never get a second chance to make a

first impression." However worn out these phrases may be, they are true, especially when it comes to telemarketing scripts.

3. *Develop the basic copy story in a natural style.* In other words, write the telemarketing script for the ear, not the eye. Select the tone and words of the message to reflect how a person would speak, not write. Most people speak in a more friendly, low-key, and less professional manner than they write. They don't use long sentences; in fact, they often use sentence fragments. A good script must include good dialog for a telephone call.

4. *Encourage dialog.* A good script should talk *with* someone, not *at* them. The script should have areas where natural pauses would take place, giving the prospect or customer a chance to respond.

5. *Anticipate questions and objections.* *Objections* are reasons why the customer or prospect thinks he or she cannot complete the action that your offer is requesting. Another familiar saying is appropriate here: "The best defense is a strong offense." Anticipate those various objections and be prepared with answers that will capitalize on those objections.

6. *Close, close, close.* The chief objective of the personal selling process is to close the sale and create a customer. This principle applies to telephone selling as well. Though you can use many tactics to close a sale, the key thing to remember is that it often takes a minimum of three attempts, so you often have to help the customer agree to purchase a product or place an order.

7. *Don't wear out your welcome.* This is especially true of outbound calling, because the operator might be calling a customer at a less than convenient moment.

In creating persuasive telephone scripts, Aldyn McKean, telephone consultant, has suggested that a good script is composed of at least the following 11 parts.[18]

1. *Opening:* Greet the person being called; identify caller.
2. *Empathy/involvement:* Establish rapport, emphasize common concerns, and create involvement.
3. *Product information:* Describe the product/service and its benefits.
4. *Offer:* Explain and clarify terms.
5. *Close:* Request action(s).
6. *Reconfirmation:* Repeat the terms agreed to.
7. *Probe:* Inject a query designed to prompt negative or undecided prospects into asking questions or offering objections.
8. *Answers to questions:* These answers should lead back to the close.
9. *Responses to objections:* Commonly raised objections should have prescripted responses, also leading back to the close.
10. *Second effort:* An additional short presentation should be made whenever a prospect is undecided or is negative without offering specific objections.
11. *Farewell:* No matter what, the call should always end on a reassuring, friendly, and polite note.

Training Telephone Operators

Many people might think that the best way to develop an effective telephone operator is to take someone with field sales experience and transfer that sales knowledge to the phone. However, in reality, this rarely works. One of the reasons field salespeople often do not make good operators is that they are accustomed to face-to-face interaction with their customers and dislike working behind a desk. These work qualities are the exact opposite of the requirements of a telemarketing representative.

When hiring a telephone operator, companies normally look for the following six qualities:[19]

1. *Experience*—primarily in a call center or customer service situation. Prior experience may aid the telerep in being persistent and able to handle rejection and continue.
2. *Interpersonal skills*—an outgoing personality, good communication skills, articulate speech, and good voice quality—one that is clear and pleasant.
3. *Computer literacy*—including typing and word processing skills and being able to navigate through various computer menus and screens.
4. *Basic reliability*—because telephone operator turnover is so high, reliability and stability are important qualities. Employee turnover is high within call centers. In 2006 LeapFrog! Response Design Corporation's metric database reported that the average annual negative turnover for front-line agents was 26 percent. Negative turnover refers to agents leaving the company for good, whether through voluntary or involuntary termination.[20]
5. *Problem-solving skills*—ability to deal with complaints, handle irate customers, and field difficult questions. Telephone reps need the ability to remain calm and polite under fire and to interpret company policies to provide customers with quick and accurate answers. They must be flexible and adapt to different clients and different situations.
6. *Good organizational skills*—including time-management skills.

Finding and retaining good telephone operators is a constant challenge for telemarketers. In addition to high turnover rates, there has been a shrinking employment pool for this industry. Compensation for operators varies depending on such variables as industry sector, product prices, and the complexity of the sale. Most companies believe developing a mixture of base salary, commissions, and bonuses is most effective for retaining telephone operators.

Media Measurement

According to the DMA, annual telemarketing sales exceeded $402.6 billion in 2005.[21] Inbound calls are generally less expensive than outbound calls. This is due in part to the fact that inbound calls are generally shorter in duration than outbound calls. Inbound calls generally cost $1.50 to $7 per call depending on the type of call, duration, and complexity of the call. Outbound calls placed to final consumers (B2C) range between $1.15 and $4 per call. Outbound calls placed to businesses (B2B) typically range between $6 and $16.[22] The average costs for inbound and outbound calls are just some of the many costs involved in telemarketing. The DMA estimates that it costs close to $865,000 per year to operate a ten-person B2B call center.[23] These costs are itemized in Figure 7-6.

As Figure 7-6 details, the primary components that make up the cost of a telemarketing call are (1) personnel, (2) telephone service, (3) automation, (4) rent, (5) workstations (including office equipment and furnishings), and (6) mail, catalog, faxes, e-mail, and samples.[24] Personnel accounts for the majority of the costs, regardless of whether the call is outbound or inbound. Direct marketers incur substantial costs in the hiring, training, and maintaining of personnel needed to staff an in-house call center. Also, companies that extensively use interactive voice response instead of live agents have reduced personnel costs but raised equipment and overhead costs. The costs vary due to the fact that many organizations do not operate their own call center but outsource these duties to an external agency. We discuss more about call center costs and operations in Chapter 9.

Outbound & Inbound Business to Business and Consumer Annual Telephone Operation Costs

The following is a breakdown of costs for operating a B-to-B telemarketing center.

8 Representatives @ 230 days and 1,610 hours per rep.

STAFF
- (1) Manager/Supervisor @ $48,000 base plus commissions, incentives, and 30% tax and fringe.
- (8) Representatives @ $32,000 base plus commissions, incentives, and 30% tax and fringe.
- (1) Admin/Asst. @ $24,000 base plus 30% tax and fringe.

Commissions: at 100% of target
- Manager/Supervisor $15,000
- Reps $17,000 each

Incentives:
- Manager/Supervisor $5,000
- Reps $2,000 each

TELEPHONE
Network @ .05/minute of connect time for 28 connect minutes per hour.
Equipment: $13,000 (from capital expense statement).

AUTOMATION
H/W: $11,333 (from capital expense statement)
S/W: $22,000 (from capital expense statement)

RENT
$22,800 (from capital expense statement)

WORKSTATIONS & OTHER FURNISHINGS & OFFICE EQUIPMENT
(from capital expense statement)
Workstations: $4,650
Furnishings: 1,300
Office equipment: 4,375

MAIL, CATALOG, FAXES, E-MAIL, SAMPLES
Sent as a direct result of phone activity, estimated @ 3.00 per rep phone hour.

FIGURE 7-6 Outbound and Inbound Business to Business and Consumer Annual Telephone Operation Costs. *Source:* Oetting & Company, Inc. 2006 in *Statistical Fact Book, 2007* (New York: Direct Marketing Association, Inc., 2007), p. 85. Used with permission of the Direct Marketing Association.

Summary

In summary, electronic media encompasses television, radio, and telephone. Television and radio are commonly referred to as broadcast media. Broadcast media are the most universal of communications media because broadcast reaches virtually everyone and every location. There are a number of different advantages and disadvantages associated with both television and radio, as well as a number of different formats from which direct response advertisers may choose. Both mediums can be segmented according to different viewers and listeners. Direct response advertising on television and radio can be highly productive for direct marketers. These mediums are often used in conjunction with the telephone. Telephone marketing is frequently used by direct marketers for both inbound and outbound calls. It also has a variety of advantages and disadvantages. Technological changes have fueled the growth of telephone as a marketing medium; however, telephone marketers must be aware of the regulations on the use of this medium for marketing purposes. Planning a telemarketing program involves many steps. Training telephone operators is one of the most critical aspects in determining the effectiveness of telephone marketing. In conclusion, all forms of electronic media support one another. They create a synergistic effect in serving customers needs.

Key Terms

broadcast *172*
cost per response (CPR) *174*
cost per viewer (CPV) *174*
gross rating points (GRPs) *174*
reach *174*
frequency *174*
infomercials *176*
media efficiency ratio
   (MER) *176*

telemarketing *179*
inbound calls *180*
outbound calls *180*
reactive telemarketing *180*
proactive telemarketing *181*
T1 *181*
cold calls *181*
dialed number identification
   system (DNIS) *183*

automated numbering
   identification (ANI) *183*
predictive dialers *184*
short messaging service
   (SMS) *184*
telephone script *184*

Review Questions

1. Broadcast media (television and radio) are the most universal of all media, but what limits their effectiveness for direct response advertising?
2. Suggest ways to segment markets through broadcast media.
3. In what ways do direct marketers use television as a medium?
4. What is an *infomercial* on television? Describe some of the advantages and disadvantages in using infomercials for direct response advertising. What are some of the products or services featured in infomercials?
5. What are some of the most common products or services featured in infomercials?

6. Explain the difference between inbound and outbound calls as they are related to telemarketing.
7. Describe a few advantages and disadvantages of telemarketing.
8. How has technology changed telemarketing?
9. Why is it necessary for telemarketers to have a script to follow when communicating with customers or prospects?
10. Explain the role of telephone marketing for companies in today's highly technical world.

Exercise

Have you ever wanted to be a "couch potato"—even for a little while? Go ahead. Sit down this evening or weekend and watch television for a couple of hours. While you're watching, write down all of the TV commercials you view. How many of them are direct response ads? What makes each advertisement a direct response ad? For those ads that are not, identify how you could convert three into direct response ads that are measurable and accountable.

CASE

GEICO

Overview

This case explains the various types of message appeals available to marketers. It also explores the benefits associated with innovative media buys for DRTV campaigns. This case enables the student to appreciate the risk and value associated with the unique positioning strategies implemented by a direct marketer.

What you are about to read is a success story about a company that effectively uses DRTV campaigns with humorous ad appeals and innovative media buys to sell a commodity—automobile insurance. The DRTV campaigns are the products of the creative minds at The Martin Agency, located in Richmond, Virginia. These campaigns and case study are a testament to the great things that can occur when a client and an agency have a collaborative relationship. It also affirms the fact that being different and trying new things with an established medium can really pay off. Are you ready to read, learn, and think out of the box? If so, we'd like to introduce you to the client, GEICO.

Case

GEICO (which stands for Government Employees Insurance Company) was founded in 1936. Today the GEICO companies insure more than 13 million vehicles and have assets of more than $24.4 billion. GEICO is ranked the fourth largest in the auto insurance market behind State Farm, Allstate, and Progressive. It is one of the fastest-growing auto insurers and has more than 8 million policyholders.

GEICO's success has been largely attributed to its widespread television and radio direct-response advertising campaigns. However, before we present these DRTV campaigns, some background information about television advertising and advertising appeals in general is warranted.

Advertising on television presents strengths and weaknesses. As a marketing medium, it is often seen as an intrusion or an unwanted interruption. The ability of advertisements to attract attention and engage the viewer's senses is unique.

Creating and producing direct response ads for television is a laborious and expensive process, however. The objective of DRTV commercials is to break through the high degree of clutter associated with television and evoke action from the audience. Of course, before any DRTV ad can ever hope to generate a response, it must grab the viewer's attention and maintain it. This is no small task because most people do not view TV ads while sitting idle without distraction. In an attempt to obtain the viewer's attention and subsequent action, direct marketers such as GEICO may use any number of different advertising appeals in developing the message strategy. There are two broad categories of message appeals—rational appeals and emotional appeals.

Rational appeals present facts or information to the consumer in a logical manner. These appeals focus on the consumer's practical need for the product or service. Rational appeals aim at the logical buying motives of a consumer. Though rational appeals can be very effective, they can also be viewed as boring or dull. In contrast, emotional appeals are seen as more exciting and are more effective in attracting the attention of most consumers. Emotional appeals focus on the wants or desires of consumers as opposed to their basic needs. Emotional appeals target consumer feelings or social and psychological needs. Humorous messages are one form of emotional appeal. Humorous ads have

FIGURE 7-7   GEICO "Coffee Cups" TV Spot. *Source*: Used with permission of GEICO Direct and The Martin Agency.

strong message permanence (the amount of time the ad remains in the consumer's memory). Humor is most effectively used with the media formats of television and radio. When used appropriately (tastefully) and in the right circumstances, humor has been found to be an extremely effective advertising technique. Indeed, this is the case with GEICO and its series of innovative and award-winning direct-response advertising campaigns. Let's take a closer look at a few GEICO DRTV campaigns (Figure 7-7).

Campaign: "15 minutes could save you 15 percent or more on car insurance"

The initial GEICO "15 minutes could save you 15 percent" campaign took the idea of buying automobile insurance (which doesn't seem very exciting, and the insurance product itself is probably considered an unsought good by most consumers) and turned it into a personalized, quick process with a worry-free consequence. The Martin Agency's work with this campaign was among the more innovative campaigns of the 1990s. At the time, 60- and 120-second spots were the standard TV media buys in direct marketing. Instead, GEICO ran back-to-back 15-second spots in a 30-second media buy. This media strategy of pairing two 15-second DRTV spots did a number of smart things for GEICO, including the following.

- First, it allowed smaller, customized messages to be tailored to individual market needs, creating a cafeteria menu of creative options. For example, a new market might get a spot with a message about how many new drivers sign up with GEICO every day paired with a spot focusing on price. In Washington, DC, GEICO's hometown, a different pair of service and savings messages was teamed to address specific needs in that market. Thus, segmented messages were relatively easy to execute with this new media format.
- Second, it provided two opportunities for the toll-free phone number and Web site to appear in the 30-second media buy. This longer exposure allowed the number to make a better impression, while still leaving room for the creative work to stress the brand. Most important,

it contributed to the ability of each DRTV spot to generate a consumer response—the ultimate goal of a DRTV campaign.

• Third, it enabled the message to break through. Different was good, especially when battling against giants who had worked for years to build their brands. Most insurance companies' ads were similar, many incorporating "scare tactics" in their messages. However, there was no confusing a GEICO ad with another insurance company's. GEICO's unique positioning strategy effectively generated consumer awareness and placed GEICO in the minds of millions of consumers as an exciting and easy-to-deal-with insurance company. The catchy tagline "15 minutes could save you 15% or more" became extremely well known by consumers and it branded GEICO as the most affordable choice for consumers making auto insurance purchase decisions.

Campaign: "Gecko"

GEICO's Gecko trademark character—that cute little green lizard with a British accent—emerged to help people properly pronounce and remember the company's name, GEICO. Many people weren't sure how to pronounce it—was it pronounced "geeko" or "gecko" or what? So the company created the Gecko to teach the world that you pronounce the company's name as "GUY-co" and history began for GEICO's Gecko. The continued use of the Gecko in GEICO advertisements was also due in part to an actors' strike at the time, which made it difficult to find humans to star in advertisements. So the little Gecko was fate for GEICO (Figure 7-8).

FIGURE 7-8 GEICO's Gecko. *Source:* Used with permission of GEICO.

The Gecko was used to deliver GEICO's message with humor. It uniquely positioned GEICO as an inexpensive and fun insurance company. This was opposite of the perceptions of GEICO's competitors, which were thought of as more expensive and serious. This unique positioning strategy, combined with the cuteness and liveliness of the Gecko's personality, worked. In each ad the Gecko makes a claim in a sassy manner. For example: "I am a gecko, not to be confused with GEICO, which could save you hundreds on car insurance. So stop calling me!" Each commercial attracts the attention of the audience and generates a smile or laugh. More important, consumers remember the little Gecko, his messages, and along with it, GEICO.

The animated lizard quickly became both effective and popular for GEICO. In fact, the Gecko has been named one of America's top two favorite icons by the public who voted in *Advertising Week*'s annual contest in 2005. The Gecko's charismatic personality and popularity made it a natural choice to become a symbol to promote wildlife conservation for the Association of Zoos and Aquariums (AZA). As a form of cause-related marketing, GEICO's Gecko has joined the AZA with a traveling live gecko exhibit and is featured in a series of TV commercials on behalf of the AZA.

Campaign: "Caveman"

To continue the humorous appeal and drive home the fact that not only would GEICO save consumers money on car insurance, but consumers will find it easy to work with the company, GEICO introduced its Caveman campaign. The campaign objective was to convince tech-savvy 25- to 49-year-olds that shopping for car insurance was easy with the company's Web site. The Martin Agency created a series of TV commercials, each playing on the theme of a fictitious slogan: "GEICO.com. So easy, a caveman can do it" to drive the message home. Each advertisement shows modern-day cavemen in various scenarios complaining about how offensive the slogan is. The cavemen are hairy, hostile, and dressed in designer clothes. They play tennis, they visit therapists, and order fancy meals like roast duck with mango salsa. They are much more sophisticated than one would have thought—and thus the simple message The Martin Agency was trying to get across (GEICO's Web site is really easy) was wildly effective in a humorous and fun-loving way (Figure 7-9).

GEICO's cavemen have quickly become a pop-culture phenomenon. Their popularity in TV commercials is now being extended to the Web. Launched in January 2007, the Flash site www.cavemanscrib.com allows visitors to get to know these cavemen—their personalities, preferences, and possessions. The primary purpose of the Web site is to entertain visitors. Selling auto insurance is considered secondary. GEICO receives fan mail for the cavemen, and kids dress up like them for Halloween. The cavemen ads have been so effective that the cavemen have had to fend off groupies!

Campaign: "Testimonials"

Another mini-DRTV campaign created for GEICO by The Martin Agency was the Testimonials campaign, a series of TV ads featured real customers providing testimonials to correct a misperception that lower price meant lower-quality service. To continue with GEICO's humorous appeals, each consumer was paired with a celebrity, such as Little Richard or Burt Bacharach, who helped "interpret" the testimonials.

Each advertisement contained the tag line: "Real Service. Real Savings." Also, each advertisement ended with the GEICO Web site clearly displayed—causing people to process what they had just heard from a fellow consumer and encouraging them to visit the Web site to learn more about how their needs might be better served. Because these ads used real consumers, the messages were highly believable, yet fun. They were also quite effective.

FIGURE 7-9   GEICO's Caveman.   *Source:* Used with permission of GEICO.

Summary

Because most of GEICO's customers work with the company through direct channels, the DRTV spots themselves needed to have personality. They were in fact the human voice for the company until the call was made and a real voice could answer. The fact that the GEICO marketing group understood this and was brave enough to be different from their competitors and embrace a humorous tone in each of its DRTV campaigns are additional reasons this brand has made its mark so effectively. Consumers were pleasantly surprised that an insurance company could make them smile. Humor can be a fine line to walk, and consumers' perceptions of humor can vary. The humor in GEICO ads pokes fun or makes light of the human condition but does not belittle the serious nature of the product. The campaigns include everything from snappy one-liners to buttons at the end and over-the-top visual exaggeration.

These GEICO campaigns have proven you should never underestimate the value of a strong call to action and never change it if it's working. The modular media and messaging needed glue to hold it all together and keep the phones ringing and the Web visits coming. The glue for most of these campaigns was a strong call to action that remained constant in every spot—"15 minutes could save you 15 percent or more on car insurance."

Have these innovative and humorous DRTV campaigns been effective in selling car insurance? You bet! While GEICO may be the number 4 company in the insurance business based on market share, it ranks number 1 in new customer acquisition and in recent polls, 91 percent of shoppers say they have seen or heard at least one GEICO message in the past 12 months. Finally, in 2007, GEICO achieved an 8.8 percent increase over the previous year in voluntary auto insurance business.

In conclusion, GEICO now owns its look, tone, and feel. No other name in the business can be substituted for GEICO. That has been the goal for the GEICO marketing group from the very first spot produced with The Martin Agency to the present. Indeed, the GEICO story is an impressive one—and one that most direct response advertisers would like to emulate. So, the next time you are faced with the task of creating a DRTV campaign—think about doing something different. Think about GEICO.

Source: This case is based on information provided by The Martin Agency, Richmond, Virginia and GEICO, Washington, D.C.

Case Discussion Questions

1. GEICO's marketing team took a great risk in agreeing to a new approach to direct response advertising. How did their approach set them apart from other insurance companies?
2. With its heavy emphasis on humor, GEICO has managed to gain the attention of many prospective customers. Was this risky? Why or why not? Could GEICO have achieved the same success without the use of humor?
3. How did GEICO differ from the norm of TV advertising and was it effective?
4. Has the use of emotional appeals been successful for GEICO? In your opinion, would the use of rational appeals be as successful based on what you know about this company and the industry? Why?
5. In your opinion, what could GEICO do to maintain such a spectacular marketing performance in the future?

Notes

1. U.S. Census Bureau American Fact Finder, *2006 American Community Survey*; retrieved from http://factfinder.census.gov/servlet/ADPTable?_bm=y&-geo_id=01000US&-qr_name=ACS_2006_EST_G00_DP4&-ds_name=&-_lang=en&-redoLog=false&-format=).
2. *Statistical Fact Book 2006* (New York: Direct Marketing Association), p. 99.
3. *The Power of Direct Marketing,* 2006–2007 edition (New York: Direct Marketing Association), p. 58.
4. *Statistical Fact Book 2006,* p. 99.
5. *Statistical Fact Book 2002* (New York: Direct Marketing Association), p. 116.
6. *Infomercial DRTV,* retrieved from http://www.infomercialdrtv.com/infomercial-faq.htm.
7. Brian Steinberg, "McPricey ABC Leads Way with 'Grey' This Fall," *Advertising Age* (October 1, 2007), 1, 41.
8. Adapted from Cara Beardi, Advertising Age, *Radio's Big Bounce* (August 27, 2001), 52; and from Roger Kerin, Steven Hartley, and William Rudelius (2009), *Marketing,* 9th ed. (New York: McGraw-Hill/Irwin), p. 526.
9. Bob Stone and Ron Jacobs (2008), *Successful Direct Marketing Methods,* 8th ed. (New York: McGraw-Hill), p. 642.
10. *The Power of Direct Marketing,* 2006–2007 edition, p. 58.
11. Telemarketing Consultant.com, *TCs' Telemarketing Outsourcing Tips,* retrieved on May 8, 2008, from http://www.telemarketingconsultant.com/Telemarketing%20Tips.html.
12. Deborah Vence, "Majority Rules," *Marketing News* (February 15, 2006), 4.
13. Bob Stone (1997), *Successful Direct Marketing Methods,* 6th ed. (Lincolnwood, IL: NTC Business Books).
14. Adapted from Kerin, Hartley, and Rudelius, *Marketing,* p. 526; and from *Stop Calling Us* (April 29, 2003), 56–58.
15. Charles Lamb, Joseph Hair, and Carl McDaniel (2008), *MKTG2* (Mason, OH: South-Western), p. 203.
16. Kelly J. Andrews, "Predictive Dialers: Better Dialing through Technology," *Target Marketing* 21, no. 11 (1998): 30.

17. Jim Kobs (1993), *Profitable Direct Marketing,* 2nd ed. (Lincolnwood, IL: NTC Business Books), pp. 171–174.

18. Adapted from Aldyn McKean (1983), "Promotional Techniques in Telephone Advertising," in *Statistical Fact Book* (New York: Direct Marketing Association), pp. 127–131.

19. Adapted from Steve Jarvis, "Call Centers Raise Bar on Hiring Criteria," *Marketing News* 34, no. 19 (September 11, 2000); adapted from Stone, *Successful Direct Marketing Methods,* p. 147.

20. Kathryn E. Jackson, "Multi Channel Merchant," *Overturn the High Cost of Employee Turnover,* June 27, 2006, retrieved May 2, 2008, from http://multichannelmerchant.com/opsandfulfillment/contact_center_advisor/overturn_turnover.

21. *Statistical Fact Book 2006,* p. 220.

22. Stone and Jacobs, *Successful Direct Marketing Methods,* p. 323.

23. *Statistical Fact Book 2006,* p. 82.

24. Adapted from Oetting & Company, 2005, in *Statistical Fact Book 2006,* pp. 85–86.

8

...

Crafting and Applying
High-Tech Digital Media

Opening Vignette: MyFishStory.com

Imagine a place where you could congregate with others who enjoy the same sport or activity you do. This is a place where you could exchange stories or views with others who have similar interests. Are you curious? If so, let us introduce you to MyFishStory.com (Figure 8-1)!

    This is a Web site, also referred to as a Web community, for people who like to catch fish or simply eat fish. It's an online social networking community where you can post pictures, tell stories, and find friends.

    MyFishStory.com was founded in 2007 by two fishing buddy brothers, Mike and Doug Downs. They saw the need for a community whereby fishermen and -women could share their experiences with others and decided to launch a new business called the Clearwater Group. This company currently operates this Web site and is in the process of developing another for a different Web community.

    When you visit MyFishStory.com, you are invited to create your own tacklebox space and invite your family and friends to see your "catch of the day." The Web site allows people to register, which is free, to

FIGURE 8-1   MyFishStory.com Logo.   *Source:* Used with permission of The Cleawater Group Inc.

view blogs, recipes, advertisements, and events all related to fishing. You can submit recipes, post your favorite fishing pictures or stories, check out upcoming fishing-related events, and search for other anglers with whom you can fish. As Figure 8-2 reveals, this Web site has a number of links that provide for subcategories for those members who prefer a certain kind of fishing, such as fresh water, salt water, or fly fishing. In addition, with a quick click on the Classifieds link, you can submit advertisements to sell or trade items. The Monthly Creel link will allow you to read fishing tips from registered guides. The Fish Talk link invites you to have conversations with other fishermen and -women by reading and submitting a blog.

The best part about this Web community is that you get to create your own tacklebox where you can upload your pictures and stories and select which of these will be shared "globally" with everyone and anyone—and which pictures and stories you reserve for only those friends you invite to your tacklebox to view. The tacklebox is designed to serve as an excellent source for fishing guides who want to post tips and send monthly newsletters to registered users. These guides will be required to pay a small fee per year to be able to use the Web community for marketing purposes—but it will alleviate the need for these guides to create and maintain their own Web sites.

Has this new Web community taken off? You bet! Within less than a year from its launch, MyFishStory. com is visited approximately 2,000 times per week—and that is despite any active promotion of this Web community. So if you enjoy the sport of fishing or enjoy feasting on fish dishes, check out MyFishStory.com. But look out, you might just get hooked!

FIGURE 8-2   MyFishStory.com Web Site.   *Source:* Used with permission of The Cleawater Group Inc.

In this chapter we explore high-tech digital media. We examine how they evolved and how direct marketers use them today. In addition, we review the advantages and disadvantages of digital media and their many applications and formats. The Internet has permeated virtually all marketing strategies and tactics today. Perhaps nothing has had a greater impact on the conduct of business today.

THE INTERNET

The Internet is an interactive marketing medium for direct marketers offering information access and two-way communication with customers in real time via the computer. Interactivity is what makes marketing on the Internet different from other forms of direct marketing media. According to the Direct Marketing Association (DMA), to be considered "interactive," a new medium must meet the following three criteria.[1]

1. Consumers must be able to control when they view the products and which types of products they are viewing.
2. Consumers must be able to control the pace at which they review products. They must be able to review the product content at their leisure, reading the product literature at a pace that is convenient to them, rather than being forced to progress to the next product.
3. Consumers must be able to place an order or request additional information directly via the medium rather than having to order through another method.

If one or more of these characteristics is missing, then the medium cannot be considered interactive. Thus, infomercials and television home shopping are not considered interactive media at the present time because they present product information in a predetermined order and according to a set time frame. We cannot predict how technology will change in the future to enable more media to meet the interactive criteria. However, at present, the Internet (which includes the World Wide Web and e-mail) is the only medium that is considered to be truly interactive according to the DMA.

There has been a great deal of hype about interactive media, and many new buzzwords have emerged. Keep in mind as you read this chapter that interactive media simply provide another means for reaching consumers directly in their homes and offices. "Technology and marketing have coexisted—generally to the benefit of each—for hundreds of years. In this sense, the Internet is merely one of the more recent formats for the delivery of marketing."[2] Let's take a look at the growth of this interactive medium.

Growth of Internet Marketing

Research shows that $19.2 billion was forecasted for Internet marketing (non-e-mail) expenditures in 2007. This figure, combined with an expected annual growth rate of 15.6 percent, is expected to rise to $39.7 billion in 2012.[3]

The Internet also has the fastest growth and acceptance rates of all other technological media. Consider the time it has taken these technologies to reach 50 million users: telephone—40 years; radio—38 years; cable television—10 years; the Internet—5 years.[4] As of November 2007, there were more than 237 million Internet users in North America, which is nearly a 71 percent population penetration rate.[5] (To obtain an update of these statistics, visit Internet World Statistics at www.internetworldstatistics.com.) However, several factors affect the rate of growth of this new medium for global interactions. These include computer access or ownership; computer literacy, an understanding of both hardware and software; network availability, especially in developing nations; language differences; cultural differences; and governmental regulations. Finally, although it is a global medium, most of what has been written about the Internet is based on experiences of companies and consumers in the United States and other highly developed nations.

Other statistics documenting the explosion of interactive media include the following.

- Sales revenue from Internet marketing (non-e-mail) expenditures reached $397.4 billion in 2007 and is projected to grow annually by 15.1 percent to reach $801.7 billion in 2012.[6]
- Nearly 1,491,000 workers were employed in Internet marketing (non-e-mail) in 2007. In 2012, with growth expected to be at 11.5 percent per year, 2,586,800 are forecasted.[7]

These statistics underscore the importance of the Internet to marketers. Marketers must clearly understand all aspects of the Internet if they are going to be successful in taking full advantage of this new enabling technology and integrating it into their promotional mix. Let's examine some of the applications of Internet marketing along with its advantages and disadvantages.

Internet Retailing

Online or **Internet retailing** is a type of shopping that is conducted via the Internet. In 2006, 44 percent of consumers shopped online, and that number is expected to grow.[8] Average annual Internet retailing spending per household is projected to increase to $1,396 by 2009.[9] Approximately 94 percent of Internet households will be shopping online by 2009.[10] Online retailing is very convenient to consumers and saves time during the day. Did you know that 42 percent of New Yorkers would rather clean their bathroom than stand in a checkout line?[11] Time is a very valuable thing to waste! Just how popular is Internet retailing? Just consider the following statistics associated with Cyber Monday.

Most Americans are familiar with Black Friday. This is the first Friday after Thanksgiving, where in-store retailers experience their highest sales figures of the year. Cyber Monday has now taken form for Internet retailers. Cyber Monday refers to the first Monday after Thanksgiving, when Internet retailers experience their highest sales figures of the year. In 2006, Black Friday earned in-store retailers $434 million, and Cyber Monday earned Internet retailers $608 million. Cyber Monday in 2006 earned the status of the biggest online spending day on record.[12]

In 2007, Internet sales exceeded the 2006 mark. Cyber Monday in 2007 grossed $733 million in online spending. Internet retail sites saw a remarkable increase in visitors in online traffic in 2007. Best Buy Web sites saw a 110 percent increase, Wal-Mart reported a rise of 103 percent, and MSN Shopping Online saw visitors increase 261 percent on Cyber Monday.[13] Online retailing is a huge industry that is likely to continue to grow in the future.

As presented in this section, Internet marketing targeting final consumers is a highly profitable activity and has received a great deal of publicity. However, using interactive media for business consumers is a common and profitable strategy as well. The next section will provide details about the growth of the Internet for business consumers.

Business-to-Business Internet Transactions

The use of interactive media for business-to-business (B2B) interactions is on the rise. B2B online sales revenues are expected to grow at 14.6 percent annually.[14] In 2007, B2B driven sales revenue attributed to Internet marketing (non-e-mail) was $210.6 billion and is expected to grow to $352.5 billion in 2011.[15]

Most B2B Web sites should contain the following information:

- Company name
- Company logo
- Company history
- Listing of sales offices
- Listing of corporate offices
- New products
- Product ordering information
- Catalogs
- Product specifications
- Listing of distributors
- Listing of repair facilities
- Listing of clients/customers
- Frequently asked questions page
- Privacy policy

In addition, many companies include a company catalog on their Web site.

Like B2C interactions, B2B interactions aim to produce a measurable transaction. Business consumers select which Web sites they want to visit, just as final consumers do. However, unlike final consumers, business consumers normally have a specific task—locating information or purchasing products/services—to complete in a specified period of time. Thus, B2B interactions may be subject to greater time constraints than B2C interactions. Another difference is that B2B interactions often lead to a repeat purchase; thus, the possibility of establishing an ongoing customer relationship is greater than with B2C interactions. Regardless of the type of customer to be served by a company's interactive media campaign, both marketers and consumers must first understand the differences between the Internet and the World Wide Web. The next section allows you to check your understanding of these terms.

Differences between the Internet and the World Wide Web

THE INTERNET ("NET") The term *Internet* is actually a combination of the words *international* and *network*. The **Internet** is a worldwide network of computers connected to one another to enable rapid transmission of data from one point to another. For direct marketers, the Internet is a means of communication between consumers and millions of other organizations. The Internet is more than computers and their contents. The Internet is a social space where users communicate with each other via e-mail, Usenet (consisting of over 50,000 discussion groups arranged hierarchically by topic), and the Web. This global network includes millions of corporate, government, organizational, and private networks, as well as e-mail, newsgroups, and the Web.[16] It is similar to the telephone in that just as phone calls can be made anywhere in the world, a computer can link up to anywhere in the world, provided it is connected to the Internet. In 2007, there were 155 million sites on the Web.[17] Additionally, there were 237 million Internet users surfing these sites in North America alone.[18]

The Internet began as a high-tech tool for facilitating communication between scientists developed under the sponsorship of the U.S. Defense Department's Advanced Research Projects Agency (DARPA). In 1969, the network, then called DARPAnet, became a reality when two nodes were linked together. By 1989, the National Science Foundation had replaced the Defense

Department as the chief source of support for the network of networks, renamed NSFnet. Originally intended to facilitate research and communication within the scientific community, the Internet has grown to include networks and users across a wide variety of backgrounds and interests. The first widespread interest in the Internet as a vehicle for commerce occurred in 1993.

THE WORLD WIDE WEB   The Web began as a very small part of the Internet. However, because the Web has had such strong appeal, it is now the dominant part and is what most people think about when they think of the Internet. The **World Wide Web** is the portion of the Internet that has color, sound, graphics, animation, video, interactivity, and ways to move from one Web page to another.[19] It is made up of millions of individual pages that are linked to other pages.

Given the differences between the Internet and the Web, can you explain how the concept of e-commerce fits in? Many business strategies that involve the Internet are commonly referred to as "electronic commerce." **Electronic commerce** is the completion of buying and selling transactions online.[20] E-commerce is a label that encompasses a wide variety of business activities, including those most typically associated with marketing. Electronic commerce had its start in corporations and banks, primarily as a means of facilitating business transactions electronically. Two of these early applications of electronic commerce were electronic data interchange (EDI) and electronic funds transfer (EFT). Now that you have reviewed the key concepts associated with the Internet, let's examine some of the advantages and disadvantages associated with this new marketing medium.

Advantages and Disadvantages

As a medium, the Internet offers the following advantages.

- **Wide reach.** The Internet reaches a worldwide audience of millions of consumers and enables small companies and entrepreneurs to be transformed into global entities instantaneously.
- **Convenience.** The Internet is almost like a global trade show that is open 24 hours a day, 7 days a week. Consumers can shop from their homes at any time of the day or night.
- **Selective communication.** The Internet enables marketers to target and personally communicate with customers and interested prospects, both locally and globally, and offers instant worldwide access with 24 hours per day, 7 days per week, 365 days per year.
- **Low cost.** Direct marketers pay for the Internet based on local phone access, not on how widely they distribute their message. Thus, the Internet offers a near zero incremental contact cost and worldwide access without long-distance charges.
- **Creative variety.** Direct marketers can select from an endless array of creative formats and options, including, animation, sound, text, graphics, and video. Just check out the Web sites of 1-800-FLOWERS (www.1800flowers.com) or the Gap (www.gap.com) and see for yourself.
- **Inbound transmission ease.** The Internet enables quick and easy inbound transmissions and replies, since systems now exist that will automatically fulfill information requests from visitors to the direct marketer's homepage. Just check out any of the airline Web sites, such as Delta (www.delta.com), and you can obtain flight schedule information and availability along with airfares with just a few clicks of your mouse.
- **Flexibility.** The Internet offers great flexibility and permits changes in offers and direct response communications instantly, instead of waiting until the next printed catalog is published to change prices or other features.

The Internet also possesses several disadvantages.

- **Unregulated.** The Internet is still evolving and is unregulated at the present time. Many uncontrollable variables, such as legal aspects, must be constantly monitored.
- **Lack of control.** The Internet is difficult to control—anyone can click on a Web site and obtain information. In addition, it is driven by the end user—because the end user must seek out what he or she wants and when he or she wants it. Thus, direct marketers cannot control who visits their Web site or when.
- **Limited reach.** The Internet can only reach certain consumer types—omitting anyone who does not have computer access, and failing to reach those who have computer access but opt not to spend time online.
- **Lack of privacy.** Privacy concerns are on the rise—once again, marketers must keep abreast of changing policies. Chapter 11 explores this topic in greater detail.
- **Lack of technical support.** Internet users often need technical support for their online activities. This is a deterrent for some prospective Internet users, especially those in other countries where technology and technological support lags behind that of the United States.

Regardless of its disadvantages, the Internet is an important direct marketing channel and can provide support to and be supported by other channels. In fact, cross-channel influence has become so important that direct marketers are beginning to measure the percentage of customers that looked for or purchased something previously seen in another channel. Research has shown that 73.7 percent of Internet purchasers say they sometimes or often browse in retail locations and then buy online.[21] In 2005, the average online buyer made 34.6 purchases online during the course of the year.[22] The next section explains the many applications of the Internet—beyond purchases.

APPLICATIONS OF INTERACTIVE MEDIA

Some companies use the Internet to provide customer service, whereas others use it to sell goods and services. However, most companies have established a Web site with the primary purpose of disseminating product/service information. Three primary marketing activities are well suited to the Web. They include:[23]

- making information available to prospective customers,
- providing customer support and service, and
- enabling transactions to occur.

Direct marketers have been performing these activities for decades without the Internet, but now due to technological advances, they are able to transfer their knowledge and experience to this new, interactive marketing medium. It is also clear to many companies that merely having a Web presence is not enough. What it takes to succeed in this electronic marketplace is a clear plan for the organization to follow and execute, along with a strong commitment of both human resources and capital for the technological infrastructure to support the various online marketing activities.

The popularity of personal computers combined with the development of the Web has spawned the growth of electronic technology. Most companies have followed a natural pattern of evolution in their e-business initiatives. As shown in Figure 8-3, this evolution can be summarized in the following six stages: Brochureware, Customer Interactivity, Transaction Enabler, One-to-One Relationships, Real-Time Organizations, and Communities of Interests.[24]

EVOLUTION OF e-business Initiatives

Stage 1:	Stage 2:	Stage 3:	Stage 4:	Stage 5:	Stage 6:
Brochureware	**Customer Interactivity**	**Transaction Enabler**	**One-to-One Relationships**	**Real-Time Organizations**	**Communities of Interests (COINS)**
In this stage organizations began o use the Internet as a bulleting board for brochures, employee telephone directories, and, over time, for more critical documents such as catalogs and price lists.	This next phase is when companies created an interactive dialogue with their customers, encouraging them to inquire, request, register, etc. on-line.	In this stage companies began using the Internet to expand transactions (selling products, procuring supplies, enabling internal processes such as human resources activities).	This is when the Internet began to be used to create customized silos of interactivity. Because Web technology allows companies to deal with customers on a one-to-one basis, product pricing became fluid, dictated by individual customers, often in an auction process.	Zero latency organizations are able to plan, execute, and aggregate buyers and sellers in a virtual arena. These companies understand customer needs and deliver value in real-time.	The Internet helps companies create communities of common interests (by content, by community, and/or by type of commerce) that closely link various partners in a value chain. Examples of this stage of involvement include marketing companies such as eBay where consumers who possess common needs or interests can competitively bid on a given product.

FIGURE 8-3 Evolution of E-Business Initiatives. *Source:* Adapted from Amir Hartman and John Sifonis, with John Kador, *Net Ready: Strategies for Success in the E-Conomy* (New York: McGraw-Hill, 2000), xviii-xix.

Although marketing on the Web is the primary use of interactive media for direct marketers, e-mail marketing, online market research, Web advertising, and e-branding are other tasks effectively conducted on the Internet. Let's look briefly at each.

E-Mail Marketing

E-mail is a part of the Internet that is separate from the Web. It is electronic communication that travels all over the world via the Internet. There are three types of e-mail of interest to marketers.[25]

1. *E-mail from companies targeting promotions to specific customers.* This method is most effective when it is database-driven and customized to match the needs of specific market segments of customers. This includes both B2B and B2C e-mail.
2. *E-mail from the consumer to the company.* This is often used for placing an inquiry or a request for additional information.
3. *E-mail from the consumer to another consumer.* This is the electronic version of word of mouth. This form of e-mail has also been referred to as **viral marketing** where e-mail messages are forwarded to other consumers by a consumer. In fact, the term *viralocity* has been coined to measure both the number of messages and the rate of speed by which e-mail messages are forwarded by a consumer to other consumers. According to Go Viral and

London's *Financial Times,* Cadbury's gorilla drummer ad, with more than 5 million views for the original video on YouTube, was the top viral video ad in 2007, followed by Smirnoff's Green Tea Partay, with 3.4 million views.[26]

E-mail is similar to traditional direct mail in that it is conducted on a one-to-one, personal basis. However, e-mail costs a lot less than traditional mail and therefore enables companies to communicate on a more frequent basis. E-mail marketing spending reached $885 million in 2005 and is expected to reach $1.1 billion by 2010.[27]

In addition, consumers respond more quickly to e-mail than to direct mail, with replies normally coming from consumers within 36 hours from the time they received the message. Consumer response for an average direct mail campaign will take weeks. The DMA projects that the return on investment (ROI) for commercial e-mail will more than double the ROI of other direct marketing media in 2008. According to the DMA, for every dollar spent, commercial e-mail will return $47.65, with non-e-mail online marketing a distant second at $20.19.[28]

E-mail direct marketing is most productive when companies use their own customer lists instead of lists generated by third parties. Did you know that in 2005, more than 50 percent of companies used their Web sites for e-mail marketing?[29] Many companies have developed an e-mail list of their customers and send newsletters and other communication on a regular basis. For example, Figure 8-4 shows an e-newsletter that is distributed to business executives to provide them with regular updates about employment trends.

E-mail is also an effective means of distributing special promotional information to customers. An example of effective e-mail marketing is a well-known hotel that sent an e-mail message offering discounted hotel rooms to about 8,000 customers who agreed to be put on its mailing list; the offer received a 45 percent response and resulted in the sale of 2,000 rooms.[30]

While most direct marketers offer multiple channels from which customers may place orders, many companies are finding that its customers prefer to order products online. For example, Lillian Vernon's Web site garners 63 percent of its direct orders, with telephone representing 30 percent and

FIGURE 8-4   Express Employment Professionals E-Newsletter.   *Source:* Used with permission of Randy Yocum, Express Employment Professionals.

mail-in orders accounting for only 7 percent. Indeed, the online revolution has dramatically changed the way consumers shop for products. As a result of the number of customers who prefer to order via Lillian Vernon's Web site, the company has become more proactive with its e-mail marketing efforts. There are approximately 4 million customers on the database with an opt-in e-mail address. The company is excited about the opportunity that e-mail provides to target specific customer segments with versioned merchandise and promotional offers in a timely manner. As presented in Figure 8-5, various types of outbound e-mails are created—some announce sale or clearance events on the Web site. Others are targeted to those customers who will be receiving a printed catalog in their mailbox

FIGURE 8-5 Lillian Vernon Outbound E-Mail Examples.
Source: Used with permission of Current USA, Inc., dba Lillian Vernon.

with a "watch your box" message and a link to the digital catalog. Other e-mails to customers are based on past purchase behavior and suggest replenishment items for something that they have already purchased (an example is suggesting napkins with seasonal designs to buyers who have purchased napkin holders). E-mail allows companies to send tailored messages to specific customers based on needs. This is both highly effective and efficient for direct and interactive marketers.

Because sending e-mail messages is easy, cheap, and fast, some companies have misused this medium. **Spam** is the term for unsolicited e-mail messages. Spam is considered the junk mail of the Internet. Direct marketers can avoid sending spam by handling customer information carefully and adhering to ethical e-mail marketing practices. Providing a way for consumers to opt in to a mailing list is a starting point for practicing ethical e-mail marketing. Direct marketers must follow the established rules for using e-mail. One commandment with which direct marketers must comply is "Thou shalt *not* send e-mails to consumers without obtaining their permission." According to Hans Peter Brondmo, founder of Post Communications, a company that creates customized e-mail marketing programs, there are many rules that marketers should follow when conducting e-mail marketing. However, when done right, an e-mail campaign can build profitable customer relationships at a fraction of the cost of other direct marketing methods. E-mail marketing programs are most effective when combined with other digital media.

Let's take a look at an excellent direct and interactive marketing campaign that combined e-mail with banner ads and a customized Web site to produce impressive results. The U.S. Department of Navy recently used a 100 percent digital direct marketing campaign to change perceptions of the role of women in the U.S. Navy. An outbound e-mail campaign targeting women aged 18 to 24 who were not attending a four-year college explained the benefits of joining the navy, including training and money for college. Banner ads showed women in this age group in common jobs, and then showed them in a navy uniform doing exciting and important jobs like diving or fixing planes. As shown in Figure 8-6, on its Web site, Navy.com, a customized "just for women" community showcased opportunities for women in the navy. The combined digital campaign was extremely successful with leads exceeding goals by 400 percent in 90 days, and the digital campaign increasing overall recruitment leads by 15.25 percent.

Online Market Research

Technology has made marketing information readily available, easy to access, current, and affordable. It has transformed secondary data collection into a highly effective and relevant marketing activity. Much of the information available online, such as government reports, is free of charge, which enables marketers of any size to access and obtain this valuable market data. The main cost involved in conducting online market research is the human resource costs, because it requires manpower to surf the Web and identify and download relevant information.

Primary data collection has also been enhanced by technological progress. Consumers seem to be more receptive to participating in surveys conducted via the Internet as opposed to mail and phone surveys. Thus, the Internet offers an alternative medium for executing marketing research studies on a one-to-one basis with customers. Some of the more common primary data collection techniques being implemented online include online surveys and online panels.

ONLINE SURVEYS   Online survey research is carried out by either sending electronic questionnaires to customers via individual e-mails or by posting a survey on a company's Web site. Sending questions via e-mail allows for personalization and control over the timing and distribution of the survey. E-mail surveys are also the preferred method of data collection in countries where users

FIGURE 8-6   U.S. Navy Web Page Targeting Women.   *Source:* Used with permission of the U.S. Navy in accordance with their Limited Release of Rights letter and the Attachment.

must pay by the hour for Internet connection because e-mail may be answered offline, whereas a respondent must be online to complete a survey on the Web.

However, Web surveys can be written in a more user-friendly fashion than e-mail, with radio buttons, drop-down menus, and blank spaces for each customer to record responses. Although Web surveys are not as easy to create as most other types of Web pages, Web surveys are converted to hypertext markup language (HTML) files and do not need lengthy printing, collating, and mailing time. **HTML** is a simple coding system used to format documents for viewing by Web clients. Web pages are usually written in this standard specification. Among its other advantages, online survey research is still relatively fast and inexpensive and can be conducted nearly instantaneously on a worldwide basis.

ONLINE PANELS   Online panels overcome the sampling and response problems associated with online surveys. **Online panels**, which are similar to focus group interviews, are discussions marketers conduct with people who have agreed to talk about a selected topic over a period of time. For example, a fitness magazine might conduct an online panel to discuss the latest available fitness equipment and obtain feedback as to the ease and effectiveness of the equipment. Normally, panelists receive a fee or gifts for their participation. Each person must complete a comprehensive survey after being accepted to participate as a panelist so that researchers have data about their characteristics and behavior. Online panels provide marketers with a supply of willing respondents about whom they already have extensive data. Thus, there is no need to ask demographic questions each time. Marketers contact panelists on a regular basis with high expectations for a positive response to their request for information. Many publishers have online panels to assist in the development of magazine content. For example, *Working Mother* magazine has an online reader advisory panel. Digital Marketing Services (DMS) has exclusive rights to millions of America Online (AOL) members for marketing research purposes. DMS provides survey opportunities to AOL members and gives respondents credits on their monthly AOL bill for participating in market research activities.[31]

Web Advertising

Web advertising is highly versatile. It can be as simple as text (a few paragraphs or literally pages of text), or highly detailed to include graphics, sound, animation, and hyperlinks. Check out the Web sites of Starbucks (www.starbucks.com) and Ben & Jerry's (www.benjerrys.com) to enjoy the colors, animation, and sound they provide. The most common form of Web advertising is banner ads.

BANNER ADVERTISING   Banners and buttons basically occupy designated space that is available for rent on Web pages. **Banner advertising** is the digital analog to print ads, targeting a broad audience with the goal of creating awareness about the product or service being promoted. Banner ads are similar to space ads used in print media; however, they have video and audio capabilities because they are designed for interactive media. There are a variety of sizes that have been standardized per the Interactive Advertising Bureau. Those primary sizes include rectangles, pop-ups, banners, buttons, and skyscrapers. There are also standards for digital video ad formats. Visit www.iab.net to learn more about the latest standards in banner advertising.

Because banner ads request an immediate action from the viewer, they are a direct response ad. The goal of banner ads is twofold: first, to increase brand awareness by exposing consumers to the banner ad, and second, to maximize the "click-through" rates or "ad clicks." **Click-through rates,** also called **ad clicks,** are defined as the number of times a user clicks on an online ad, often measured as a function of time (ad clicks per day). Typically, click-through rates are relatively low, less than 1 percent in most cases.[32] Direct marketers must be creative to increase these rates.

There are many strategies to maximize click-through rates; these include the following.

- **Ask for the click-through action.** The easiest way to increase click-through is to simply ask for it.

- **Animate a banner advertisement.** Animation increases the likelihood that the ad will draw the user's attention and also generates more clicks than static banners, all else being equal.
- **Involve the audience.** The third generation of banner ads is interactive. Engage the viewers to allow them to personalize ads to their needs. Involving the viewer allows the advertiser to get to know them better, one of the primary goals of direct marketing!
- **Change creative messages frequently.** The nature of the Internet means that responses occur quickly, on the first few impressions. Therefore, creative wears out more quickly than with traditional media.

As shown in Figure 8-7, banner ads have changed dramatically over the years. The first banner ad appeared on Hot Wired in 1994. Since that time, banner advertising has rapidly progressed through four stages.[33]

Banner advertising is not the only advertising tool available on the Web, although it is the dominant form. Embedded ads are gaining attention, too. **Embedded ads** allow the viewer to receive more information without having to link to other Web sites. These ads are designed to overcome the space limitations of banners. Other forms of Web advertising are being investigated and will likely change the nature of Web advertising in the near future as this dynamic medium evolves. Savvy marketers are incorporating Web advertising in their promotional mix, but not replacing traditional media. The effectiveness of combining Web ads with other promotional strategies is illustrated in the following example.

In an effort to attract younger customers, Oldsmobile launched a Web campaign. It placed banner ads on Web sites, sponsored contests on partner Web sites such as Launch.com and ETRADE.com, and used print and television advertising. During a Super Bowl game, Oldsmobile gave away thousands of autographed footballs to fans who visited and registered on the Oldsmobile

Stage 1: Call-to-action Ads	Stage 2: Animation Ads	Stage 3: Interactive Ads	Stage 4: Truly Interactive and Integrated Ads
This early stage of banner advertising utilized action oriented words such as "click here," "free," and "download" in an attempt to get the user to view a company's products and services.	As the banner ad evolved, businesses began to incorporate some of the same features as those found on popular Web sites with flash animation.	Ads started to become interactive incorporating activities designed to engage the user in addition to getting them to click such as drop-down menus, built-in games, check boxes, and search boxes.	New rich media ads are "truly interactive and integrated" meaning the user interacts with the ad, but the ads are used in combination with various technologies including sound, video, flash animation, Java, and Javascript. The ads may also include special forms such as floating ads, page take overs, and tearbacks further designed to get the attention of the user. The rise in popularity of these ads parallels the growth of high-speed broadband in the United States.

FIGURE 8-7 Banner Advertising Evolution. *Source:* Created by Michelle Carpenter; based (in part) on Judy Strauss and Raymond Frost, *E-Marketing* (Upper Saddle River, NJ: Prentice Hall, 2009), pp. 288–291 and the Interactive Advertising Bureau (IAB) Ad Standards and Creative Guidelines (www.iab.net).

Web site. Additionally, Oldsmobile partnered with Blockbuster Video where those individuals who registered online and test-drove a Silhouette would earn a $50 gift certificate to Blockbuster. How well did the promotional mix work? Quite well. In 18 months, the age of the average Oldsmobile buyer dropped from 60 to 48, while at the same time the average income and educational level of its customers increased.[34]

E-Branding

Using the Web to provide customer service and support while maintaining customer awareness of a company's brand is an important marketing strategy. **Branding** refers to the use of a name, term, symbol, or design (or a combination of these) to identify a company's goods and services and to distinguish them from their competitors. **E-branding** refers to carrying out branding strategies electronically. The benefits of branding include the customer's recognition of the brand and the ultimate trust the customer places in the brand name (and parent company). Remember that on the Internet the customer is in the driver's seat and can select which Web sites to visit. Without name-brand familiarity, the customer will likely fail to click on a Web site that could contain needed information or need-satisfying products and services. Using one of the company's brand names in the Web address will help the consumer quickly find the site and reinforce the brand name.

When consumers go to a company's Web site, they are looking primarily for product and business information. Thus, marketers should use the Web for more than traditional advertising and entertainment; they should use it as a forum to communicate a company's brand and its benefits to consumers. The Web is one of the places where one can effectively combine branding and direct marketing.

General Mills provides a good example of how branding on the Web may be executed. The Web site for its Betty Crocker brand (www.bettycrocker.com) is extremely service- and relationship-oriented, offering recipes, menus, and more. The Web site, shown in Figure 8-8, attracts approximately 400,000 visitors a month, for 9 million page impressions. Consumers have downloaded over 5 million Betty Crocker recipes from the site.[35]

FIGURE 8-8   Betty Crocker Web Site.   *Source:* Used with permission of General Mills, Inc.

INCREASING AND MEASURING SITE TRAFFIC

In the foregoing section you reviewed the many applications of the Internet. Now let's discuss how direct marketers make these applications work effectively to meet marketing goals and objectives. One of the primary goals of using interactive media is to communicate and interact with consumers and prospects on a one-to-one basis. But unlike most traditional media, which flows from the company to the customer or prospect, interactive media relies on consumers to locate the Web site and click on it to receive the message. This dynamic is an example of the **pull strategy** in which consumers must seek out and demand information and/or products and services from the producer. The opposite is a **push strategy,** where information and marketing activities follow the normal path of distribution of a product (from the producer to the consumer). Therefore, promoting a Web site is a critical part of successfully marketing via interactive media.

Web Site Promotion

For decades, the advertising community has argued that if consumers are not aware of a company's products or services, they cannot purchase them. The same is true for a company's Web site. The theory that if you "build a better mousetrap," consumers will beat a path to your door doesn't work. Investing thousands of dollars into developing the most creative Web site means nothing if potential customers don't know it exists.

Here are some strategies designed to promote a Web site to increase site traffic.[36]

- Put the **URL** (universal resource locator, otherwise known as the Internet address) *everywhere*. All promotional literature should contain the URL, including business cards, letterhead, print and other advertisements, direct mail packages, and so on.
- Ask and you shall receive. Ask visitors to bookmark the Web site.
- Give customers a *reason* to bookmark the Web site. Give away free stuff such as advice, contests, premiums, and so on. Be creative and be sure to promote the fact that the Web site offers free stuff. By providing value to the customer you give them a reason to click, stick, and come back.
- Develop a blog to create buzz, and in turn get customers to talk about your new products and services. Don't be afraid to get creative by including photos, videos, and anything else that will create interest and make the blog easily accessible from your home page.
- Offer a chat room or provide a bulletin board to open communication among consumers and give them a reason to come back.
- Develop an e-newsletter to make the Web site more dynamic. The more dynamic the site, the more often your customers will come back. Be sure to give customers a choice; offer both text and HTML versions of the newsletter, and let the customer determine the frequency of the newsletter as well.
- Create an e-business card that accompanies each e-mail message. Be sure to include the URL in hyperlink format.
- Establish a reciprocal Web linking program. Most people find Web sites by following links from other sites. Be selective in whom you swap links with. Only link to those sites that meet one of the two following criteria. They should either be local links from other businesses or topical links from your line of business, that is, other related but not competing companies.

For example, go to Apartments.com and not only can you view apartments for rent throughout the United States, you can link to many services commonly related to apartment rental. The Web site provides links to moving companies, truck rental companies, banks, insurance companies, storage facilities, utility connections, furniture for rent, and much more. A good way to add links to a Web site is to explore competitors' URLs and develop a list of sites from which you should be linked. One final tip, quality should outweigh quantity of the links.

- Use search engines and register the site at directories and other Web sites. A **search engine** is similar to a library card catalog. It is an index of key words that enables Web browsers to find what they are looking for. Some search engines such as Yahoo! will search the entire Web, making them more powerful than those that only search by category type and a site description. We discuss more details about search engine optimization in the next section.
- Promote the site in mailings and newsgroups. Be sure to offer useful advice in a newsgroup related to the business and discretely add your short e-business card at the end of the message.
- Create a banner ad. In return for showing banners on your Web site, Bannerexchange.com will place your banner on the Banner Exchange Network of Web pages.
- Promote the site using good old word-of-mouth advertising. Tell everyone about your Web site.

Search Engine Marketing

Search Engine Marketing (SEM) is the entire set of techniques and strategies used to direct more visitors from search engines to marketing Web sites. **Optimization** is the *process* of improving Web site traffic by using search engines. In general, when the link to a Web site is listed in a higher position on the search engine results page, the user is more likely to view it. Thus, search engine optimization aims at moving the link to one of the top links on the results page. The four most common purposes for SEM use include increasing or enhancing brand awareness of products or services; selling products, services, or content directly online; generating leads; and driving traffic to a Web site.[37] Research shows more than 85 percent of companies are listed on at least one search engine.[38]

Let's explore the three different types of SEM that could be used by companies wanting to improve their Web site traffic.

1. *Paid placement.* Sometimes referred to as "pay-per-click" (PPC) or "cost-per-click" (CPC) paid placement advertising uses text ads targeted to keyword search results on search engines through programs such as Google AdWords and Yahoo! Overture Precision Match. Paid search advertising spending has remained the major portion of online spending since 2003. In 2006, paid search advertising accounted for 42.5 percent of total online advertising spending. In that same year, paid search advertising spending reached $7 billion.[39]
2. *Paid inclusion.* Paid inclusion entails the practice of paying a fee to search engines and similar types of sites such as directories or shopping comparison sites, so that a given Web site or Web pages may be included in the service's directory, although not necessarily in exchange for a particular position in search engine listings. The fee structures will vary.
3. *Organic search engine optimization.* This form of optimization includes the use of a variety of techniques to improve how well a site or page gets listed in search engines for particular search topics. Some of these optimization techniques include augmenting HTML code, Web page copy editing, site navigation, linking campaigns and more.

Yahoo! and Google are by far the biggest players in SEM. In 2007, Google and Yahoo! accounted for 91.9 percent of paid search advertising in the United States, with 75.6 percent attributed to Google alone. Yahoo! cites four key ways to rank high on the search results page: key word density, site structure, backlinks, and aging. Key word density is the number of times that the key word in the search appears on that Web site. The more times the word appears, the higher the site will rank. Site structure mostly includes the content of the Web site. Backlinks involve the quality of links, number of broken links, the anchor text, and the positioning of the link. Another important factor is how often a site is updated—the more often the better. Last, aging refers to the recency of the site and is based on the date by which it was established on the Web. The newer the site, the less weight it will be given compared to already established Web sites. Google uses all of the same methods as Yahoo! with a slight difference. Google named their aging criteria for the improved search results Google's Sandbox.[40]

Today, many consumers take the approach of typing in what they are searching for using key word search engines such as Yahoo! or Google. Before that, consumers often browsed through catalogs prior to visiting Internet retailers. Some consumers still do; however, that is certainly not the trend. Today, technological advances such as Like.com makes it even easier to search for items online. Like.com uses visual search engine technology that allows a consumer to search for a product with only a photo. For example, when consumers see a photograph of a sweater they really like that is worn by a celebrity online, they can search for that same sweater online by using Like.com.[41] Just imagine what other technologies lie ahead to help consumers save time and shop online.

Creating Web Site Stickiness

Once consumers click on a company's site, they want them to stick or, at the very least, bookmark the site for easy navigation when returning. It is well known that when surfing the Web, consumers may click on many Web sites, but only stay or stick for 15 seconds to 1 minute, depending on the visitor's objectives.[42] Furthermore, direct and interactive marketers want the Web site to achieve whatever objectives it is intended to achieve. That takes both strategic and creative thinking.

Some strategies to get consumers to "stick" on a particular Web site include:

- Make the Web site easy to navigate—consumers should not and will not work to make sense of the Web site.
- Offer free giveaways.
- Provide relevant, timely news and information.
- Create dynamic Web pages—ones that change every time the customer revisits.
- Offer chat rooms.
- Personalize the Web page.
- Develop specific landing pages that pertain to the marketing offer so the customer doesn't have to spend extra time searching for an item of interest. **Landing pages** are those Web pages where people "land" when they click on an ad banner, search engine result, or e-mail link or when they visit a special promotional URL that they heard about on television, radio, or other offline media.[43] For example, if a customer searches for a Sony Cybershot DSC-T300 Digital Camera, create a landing page featuring that product or take them to the Web page in which the camera appears in the online store.
- Be sure to establish necessary links for the consumer to pull in relevant data from other sites to create a one-stop shopping effect; thus, there will be no need to go to other Web sites. For example, if you go to www.hotels.com, you can make reservations from 6,500 hotels in over 300 cities. In addition, the Web site enables you to link to rental car companies, such as Alamo, and reserve an automobile for your trip or vacation. You can even plan a vacation package complete with hotel, airline, and automobile reservations directly from the Web site. That's one-stop shopping!

An example of an exciting Web site that was highly effective in achieving its objective is that of the 2007 Silver ECHO Award–winning campaign created by OgilvyOne Worldwide called "Metamorphosis." Spain's Telefonica wanted to drive traffic to its booth at a local trade show. An e-mail invited prospective clients to visit a microsite where they could reserve tickets online. Once on the site, visitors were met with an intriguing video with images from nature depicted in ones and zeros. With every click visitors saw images transform unpredictably, with a jaguar morphing into birds, which then became frolicking dolphins. A short video displayed the unpredictable nature of technology, hinting at the unexpected and exciting things Telefonica had to share at its trade fair booth. This interactive marketing campaign was highly effective, with 2,000 tickets being requested in less than 8 hours![44]

Media Measurement: E-Metrics

The foregoing section described a variety of ways direct marketers can make Internet applications effective. This section explains how direct marketers measure that effectiveness. All direct marketing activities must be accountable and measurable, and those carried out on interactive media are no different. They provide direct response advertising opportunities whose effectiveness we can measure. However, because consumers (not the marketer) initiate most of the interactions on the Internet, the measurement tactics are different from those used for traditional media.

The most common interactive measurement technique is based on a clickstream model. A **clickstream** is "the database created by the date-stamped and time-stamped, coded/interpreted, button-pushing events enacted by users of interactive media."[45] The following five elements make up the clickstream and provide direct marketers with the measurement needed to determine the effectiveness of Internet applications.[46]

- **Hits** are basically the equivalent of an advertising impression, that is, given that a person is viewing a particular page at a particular time. A hit is Web terminology for any request for data from a Web page or file. It is often used to compare popularity/traffic of a site in the context of getting so many hits during a given period. Regardless of how long or short the visit to a Web page, each link on the page counts as a hit. For this reason, hits are easily measured, but may provide little real information to the direct marketer.
- **Pages** are a measure of the number of pages downloaded from a specific site at a particular time. One link may allow the viewer access to many pages, but too often the viewer may not scroll through all of them and therefore may not see all the material contained in the Web site. Thus, a count of pages also may not provide meaningful measurement.
- **Visits** count the total number of times a user accessed a particular site during a given period of time. This measure is similar to frequency in mass media advertising. Visits are different from hits. A single visit is usually recorded as several hits and, depending on the browser, the page size, and other factors, the number of hits per page can vary widely.
- **Users** measure the number of different people, that is, unique visitors, who visit a particular site during a given period of time. This measure is similar to reach in mass media advertising.
- **Identified users** is the demographic profile of either visits or users of a site during a specified period of time. It is similar to the demographic profiles of readers, listeners, or viewers that mass media provides to their advertisers.

Other forms of measurement include tracking or measuring capabilities that enable companies to follow and document the Web surfing habits of consumers. The process is simple. When a consumer visits a Web site, the site plants a **cookie** (an electronic tag) on the consumer's computer.

The cookie enables the Web site to follow consumers as they shop and recognize them on return visits. Cookies can reveal how long the consumer stays at a page, which products the consumer likes, and which other sites the consumer visits. Although it is possible to program a computer to reject cookies, cookies allow personalized information to be stored at the consumer's favorite Web sites, making shopping and other online transactions more convenient.

Marketers can also track how many people have received the company's e-mails, how many have opened them, how many have responded by clicking on the link in the e-mail, and how many have taken the action the e-mail requested. Direct and interactive marketers demand measurability and accountability, and interactive media delivers it in real time. This section reviewed how direct marketers evaluate the effectiveness of online activities. The online phenomenon is clearly here to stay. In fact, there are new online strategies and high-tech formats being created every day. Some of those new formats are quite popular and have become yet another online avenue for direct and interactive marketing activities. Let's explore some of these high-tech formats.

NEW HIGH-TECH FORMATS AND STRATEGIES

Blogging

The word *blog* is short for the phrase "Web log." **Blogs** refer to Web sites that contain up-to-date, continuous information that is posted for all viewers to read.[47] The primary goals of blogs include creating public awareness, increasing viral marketing activity, and generating Web site traffic. The following statistics show the increasing popularity of blogs.[48]

- Over 12 million American adults currently maintain a blog.
- Over 120,000 new blogs are created every day.
- Over 1.4 million new blogs are posted every day.
- Approximately 22 out of the 100 most popular Web sites in the world are blogs.
- Blog readers average 23 hours online every week.

Check out General Motor Company's Fastlane Blog featuring GM Vice Chairman, Bob Lutz at http://fastland.gmblogs.com/about.html. This blog effectively uses video images of new vehicles and new features. Other auto manufacturers are using blogging strategies as well.

Online Social Networking

The Internet is coming under the grips of a rapidly developing new avenue for online advertising: **online social networking.** This marketing strategy occurs when a person or company publishes its information on an online social community, such as Facebook, YouTube, MySpace, or Friendster. Posting information on these sites allows the user to update current news, features, or interesting statistics. Viewers of the site can add comments on the page that the user created. The end result of online social networking is to increase traffic to the social community site, create inbound links, and increase traffic to the users own Web site by creating a Web page in the social community.[49]

Social networking spending was expected to increase in 2008. Marketers plan to spend roughly $1.6 billion on social Web sites. This is a 69 percent increase from 2007 spending.[50] Social networking spending on advertisements may even reach $4 billion in 2011.[51] The growth of social networks has prompted popular social networking sites Facebook and MySpace to team up with agencies to use and deploy these social network communities for advertising purposes.[52] Major advertisers that have adopted this new marketing tool include Procter & Gamble, Microsoft, PepsiCo., and Ford Motors.[53]

A recent report by the Pew Internet and American Life Project on social networking sites found that more than half of all online American youths between the ages of 12 and 17 use online social networking sites. The sites are the most popular with girls between the ages of 15 and 17, with the largest social networking site being MySpace. In the Pew report, 85 percent of teens said they used MySpace compared to the second most widely used site, Facebook, which garnered only 7 percent.[54]

An example of the effective use of blogging and online social networking is the 2007 ECHO Award–winning direct marketing campaign created for Transport for London by Chemistry Communications Group. To reduce high-speed accidents on London's roads, Transport for London needed to reach males aged 18 to 25, who happen to be the most common culprits of speeding. This target market is not the ideal group to reach via public announcements, so a direct marketing campaign using blogs, online social networks, and YouTube was created. The viral campaign used short films that were made to look like typical online clips and showed guys who had to get their driving thrills from "air driving" contests, having lost their licenses due to reckless driving violations. The outbound e-mail campaign promoting the clips achieved open rates of 15 and 2 percent click-through rates. In addition, the YouTube clips earned five-star ratings from viewers.[55] This is an excellent example of how these new high-tech digital formats are effective in targeting select consumer groups.

Online social networking, combined with the proliferation of entertainment and information, might be the drivers of high-tech digital marketing. Online social networking not only generates large quantities of Web traffic, but the information and entertainment value motivates consumers to stay online longer and to return more often. Therefore, online social networking is certainly a valuable high-tech digital format for marketers.

Mobile Marketing

Mobile marketing refers to marketing on mobile phones. This ranges from anything including advertising to text messaging voting campaigns. How do most people view mobile marketing? Harris Interactive research shows that 90 percent of people said that they were not interested in receiving ads on their mobile phones.[56] However, keep in mind that when the Internet first started in the 1990s, there was much debate as to whether companies should be able to advertise online. Now, almost everyone partakes in online advertising activities. With this in mind, mobile marketing is a form of advertising that may be the norm tomorrow. It is estimated that mobile advertising spending will reach $4.76 billion by 2011.[57] AirG, a company that develops mobile communities for Sprint and other services, generated more than 20 billion mobile advertising impressions (basically slots for advertisers) in 2006, but sold less than 2 percent of that inventory.[58] To encourage consumer adoption of mobile marketing, Virgin Mobile USA announced a product to consumers promoting the opportunity to earn extra airtime minutes in exchange for allowing third parties to advertise to their mobile phones.[59] Research shows that over a third of adult mobile phone users say they are willing to accept incentive-based advertisements, with 78 percent indicting a preference for cash incentives.[60]

Even though there are a large number of people who currently do not prefer mobile marketing, there are others who are interested in receiving advertisements and promotions via their mobile phones. These consumers vary in their preferred contact methods for receiving mobile marketing promotions. Research shows 56 percent of consumers prefer receiving text messages, 40 percent prefer picture messages, 24 percent opt for videos, 23 percent prefer ads transferred automatically to e-mail,

22 percent prefer voicemail messages, while the remaining 7 percent prefer "other" methods.[61] Research also shows that approximately 35 percent of children aged 8 to 12 years own a mobile phone, with 20 percent having used text messaging and 21 percent having used ring tones.[62] This demonstrates the potential impact mobile marketing can have targeting the consumers of tomorrow.

Summary

High-tech digital media are hot and growing rapidly for direct and interactive marketers. The Internet has surely changed the way most consumers make purchases today. The Internet is considered interactive because it meets the three criteria established by the DMA where consumers must be able to have control over the information being presented, the pace at which the products are reviewed, and the ability to place an order or request additional information directly from the medium itself. Direct marketers use the Internet to communicate with both final consumers as well as business consumers. This chapter details the importance of B2B Internet transactions. The chapter also explains the differences between the Internet and the Web.

The Internet offers direct marketers a number of advantages over other media channels, yet it also has distinct disadvantages. Some of the advantages include cost, speed and ease of communications, great flexibility in creative formats, and effective targeting of messages to consumers. Some of the disadvantages include limited reach, lack of control, and lack of regulation. There are many applications of interactive media—e-mail marketing, online market research, Web advertising, and e-branding are some of the chief applications. Each of these applications along with strategies to maximize their effectiveness is explained in this chapter. As with any direct marketing medium, accountability and measurability are important characteristics. Strategies for increasing Web site traffic and stickiness are presented in the chapter, along with how to measure the effectiveness of this direct marketing medium. There are new high-tech digital formats and strategies emerging daily. Some of the latest formats and strategies are presented. Who knows what new digital formats and strategies new future technological changes will bring? To keep abreast of the exciting changes in the high-tech digital world, we suggest you visit the following Web site resources:

- Brandchannel.com, www.brandchannel.com
- ClickZ, www.clickz.com
- eMarketer, www.emarketer.com
- MarketingProfs, www.marketingprofs.com
- MarketingSherpa, www.marketingsherpa.com

Key Terms

Internet retailing *199*
Internet *200*
World Wide Web *201*
electronic commerce *201*
e-mail *203*
viral marketing *203*
spam *206*
HTML *208*
online panels *208*
banner advertising *208*
click-through rates *208*

ad clicks *208*
embedded ads *209*
branding *210*
e-branding *210*
pull strategy *211*
push strategy *211*
URL *211*
search engine *212*
Search Engine Marketing (SEM) *212*
optimization *212*

landing pages *213*
clickstream *214*
hits *214*
pages *214*
visits *214*
users *214*
identified users *214*
cookie *214*
blogs *215*
online social networking *215*
mobile marketing *216*

Review Questions

1. What makes marketing on the Internet different from other forms of direct marketing media?
2. What are some advantages of interactive media?
3. Explain the evolution of e-business.
4. What are the requirements of interactive media?
5. How has technology changed marketing research?
6. What are four of the many strategies to maximize click-through rates?
7. Discuss some of the strategies companies use to increase Web site traffic.
8. Identify and explain the three different types of search engine marketing.
9. Name some of the characteristics that make a blog an effective tool for marketers. Provide an example of a blog that you think is especially creative.
10. What are some positive and negative characteristics of mobile marketing?

Exercise

You have recently been assigned to head up a special high-tech digital marketing team for a small upscale women's retailer that you work for. The owner of the company wants you to evaluate and propose at least two high-tech digital marketing strategies that would complement the company's current offline marketing efforts. As you begin the evaluation process, be sure to address the challenges of the strategies you have selected as well as tips for success. Finally, be creative! For example, if you believe the retailer should adopt an e-mail newsletter, provide a mock newsletter they might send out to prospective and current customers.

CASE

TreadMoves

Overview

This case is an example of how direct marketing methods provide a cost-effective alternative and improvement over traditional marketing methods. It demonstrates how a new entrepreneurial venture was successfully launched on a very small budget by concentrating on direct response communication channels, customer relationship management, and measurement. The case specifically details how the Internet can be used as both a promotional medium and a selling method. It is proof that direct marketing can work for any company, organization, or entrepreneur—regardless of size.

As a learning experience, the student should focus on the basic elements of direct marketing, including marketing research, database development, customer relationship management, measurability and accountability, and multichannel distribution. We show how this case demonstrates the application of the newest direct marketing medium—the Internet. Then, we examine how direct marketing strategies and techniques play an integral role in the development and execution of a twenty-first-century business.

Case

Out of the fitness craze of American consumers, one piece of home exercise equipment has emerged as the most popular and the fastest growing: the treadmill. Research has shown that there are approximately 14 million treadmills in U.S. consumers' homes today. Interestingly, however, approximately half are *not* being used for exercise—but as a place to hang clothes! Why? It has been suggested that the consumer got bored with his or her walking or running routine on the treadmill.

In response to this dynamic, TreadMoves was developed to provide a much-needed rejuvenation for treadmills. TreadMoves is a series of four exercise videos for treadmill users. Gone are the days of jumping on a treadmill only to stare at the timer and wait for the workout to end. TreadMoves provides many new moves and combinations from which to choose—treadmill exercisers never have to do the same workout twice.

The TreadMoves video series, as shown in Figure 8-9, consists of many different workouts to meet the needs of different target market segments. For example, some videos include moves and combinations such as shuffling, boxing, knee lifts, and kicks to appeal to exercisers who enjoy choreographed classes like step aerobics. Conversely, other videos consist of strictly walking, running, hill climbing, sprinting, and weight training to appeal to sports enthusiasts. Additionally, each video also includes moves that can be performed while the treadmill is turned off, such as push-ups, abdominal exercises, and stretching; however, all components of the workouts are performed on a treadmill.

In 2001, Meredith Hines, pictured in Figure 8-10 (see page 221), a 24-year-old graduate student with an intense passion for health and fitness, founded TreadMoves. Meredith lacked the financial backing needed to mass market her exercise videos through traditional retail channels or advertise via traditional mass media—fitness magazines, newspapers, and television. Her challenge was to create the look of a professional and credible business on a very limited budget. Given this considerable financial constraint, certain decisions were critical to the viability of the business. Some of these key decisions included determining how to conduct marketing research, how to promote the videos to target consumer segments, how to select marketing channels through which to distribute the products, and how to measure the effectiveness of the marketing techniques she used.

FIGURE 8-9 **TreadMoves Video Covers.**
Source: Used with permission of TreadMoves.

Direct marketing techniques provided the solution to each of her needs. We'll look at how she used direct marketing methods for each of the following five phases in marketing TreadMoves.

- Phase I: Marketing Research
- Phase II: Promotion
- Phase III: Database Development and Customer Relationship Management
- Phase IV: Channel Selection
- Phase V: Measurement

Phase I: Marketing Research

The Internet provides a wealth of general market data such as industry trends. However, gathering very specific information about customer segments and demographics is very expensive to purchase and was not an option for TreadMoves. So the TreadMoves team utilized chat rooms to gather this specific type of information. To find these types of chat rooms, the TreadMoves team searched the Internet for sites that hosted chat rooms related to fitness, weight loss, and exercise videos. One of the Web sites the team discovered was VideoFitness.com—dedicated to people who work out at home with exercise videos.

FIGURE 8-10   Meredith Hines, TreadMoves Founder.

This site has a very robust chat room with thousands of members who participate in discussions on a wide range of topics. The TreadMoves team read through many discussion threads (which are groups of posted comments that are responding to one original question or posted comment) to gather information about demographics and consumer behavior. This information heavily influenced the exercise content of the initial set of videos.

Once the first two TreadMoves videos were available for sale, the TreadMoves team visited the VideoFitness.com Web site and was able to read discussion threads about their own videos. The information gathered from these threads allowed the team to tailor new videos and products to the needs of their targeted customer segments and ultimately, create even better products.

Phase II: Promotion

Promotion objectives for TreadMoves were twofold—first, generate awareness of the videos, and second, stimulate product purchase. To generate awareness for the new product, the TreadMoves team created a direct response brochure. Since these brochures were quite expensive and the entrepreneur was operating on a small budget, their use was somewhat limited. Thus, the brochures were primarily used in an attempt to gain publicity for TreadMoves.

Figure 8-11 demonstrates other promotional activities including the development of a Web site to be used for both promotion and selling. The TreadMoves team mailed complimentary copies of the new videos to the Webmasters of the chat rooms for them to review. Once the Webmasters posted their reviews of the workouts, the reviews intrigued the members of the chat rooms enough for them to visit the TreadMoves Web site and buy their own copies. Once the members of the chat rooms tried and loved the workouts, they posted their own discussion threads about TreadMoves

FIGURE 8-11   TreadMoves Web Site: Home Page.
Source: Used with permission of TreadMoves.

and generated additional traffic to the TreadMoves Web site, which further sold the videos to other chat room members.

Once the initial market introduction was made via the Internet, the team researched several other promotional methods, such as acquiring lists of e-mail addresses, placing banners on related Web pages, buying magazine advertising space, and so on; however, the costs of each of these methods was prohibitive. Therefore, the TreadMoves team decided to focus their promotional efforts on database marketing activities.

Phase III: Database Development and Customer Relationship Management

Once the initial two videos were successfully introduced to the market, the TreadMoves team took advantage of its most valuable resource: its customer database. Information about each customer who purchased products from the Web site or inquired about information was captured in the database. When the second set of videos was ready for market introduction, all current customers and inquirers were sent an introductory e-mail offer to be the first to try out the new workouts. The response to this offer was very good—it garnered a 20 percent return within two days!

The company also developed customer profiles and used these to enable the identification of prospective buyers who possessed characteristics similar to those of the TreadMoves customers. The TreadMoves team then surfed the Internet in an attempt to compile lists of prospective buyers. For example, Gold's Gym posts e-mail addresses for the managers of each of its gyms. It took quite some time, but the TreadMoves team was able to gather their e-mail addresses and add them to their database. They then sent information about product offerings to all of the new e-mail addresses in the database.

Each customer and prospect also received information or news related to TreadMoves. For example, when TreadMoves was ranked in the top 10 videos in 2002 by *Fitness* magazine, the e-mail message shown in Figure 8-12 was sent to each customer and prospect in the TreadMoves database.

The TreadMoves team constantly used their database to interact with their customers and prospects. In addition to promoting new products or sharing newsworthy information, the TreadMoves site encouraged feedback from its customers and provided answers to customer questions about

FIGURE 8-12 TreadMoves
E-Mail Advertisement.
Source: Used with permission
of TreadMoves.

fitness. Such interaction strengthened customer relationships and enhanced the value of the TreadMoves brand.

Phase IV: Channel Selection

The TreadMoves team initially chose the Web site to be their primary channel. Through the site, customers could obtain information and purchase products. Minus the initial cost of designing the site, this channel enabled TreadMoves to conduct business for just the cost of Web site hosting, credit card processing, and domain name registration, which totaled about $100 per month. Additionally, the Internet store was easy to update with new products and information, so the content of the site could be quickly and inexpensively changed to grow with the business.

As a result of being able to demonstrate significant Web site traffic as well as a 30 percent repeat purchase rate, the TreadMoves team investigated other channels of distribution. Within two years, TreadMoves began selling via multichannel direct marketing. In addition to the TreadMoves Web site, customers could purchase the videos from multiple catalogs (such as Collage Video), through online retailers (such as Amazon.com), and via bricks-and-mortar retailers (such as Barnes & Noble retail stores). This enabled TreadMoves to reach even more customers. With the exception of consumers who purchase the videos from retail stores, all video orders were fulfilled by mail.

Phase V: Measurement

The company that was selected to host the TreadMoves Web site on its server provides statistics such as number of visitors per day and click-through patterns. These data provide infinite amounts of information and allow small companies, like TreadMoves, to have an inexpensive way to test and measure the effectiveness of its creative appeals. For example, each customer who visits the TreadMoves Web site has a unique digital fingerprint that can be tracked and monitored. So the TreadMoves team has experimented with two different copy appeals and has compared the percentage of people who make an immediate purchase with each.

The team has also cross-tested this data with another variable—the buying season—to provide additional information. The test results showed that more people made an immediate purchase on their first visit to the TreadMoves Web site during the holiday season than during the New Year's resolution month of January, when shoppers seemed to take longer to make their purchase decision. Based on this information, the TreadMoves team was able to tailor their marketing efforts toward these different types of buying patterns.

The measurability and accountability aspects of direct marketing provide a great advantage over traditional marketing methods. For example, the TreadMoves team sent animated e-mail advertisements to each customer in its database. Since the actions of each customer can be tracked, TreadMoves was able to measure the effectiveness of each advertisement. TreadMoves could also measure how the advertisement was effective, whether it simply built traffic or actually increased sales. Finally, the TreadMoves team also was able to use the Web site statistics, specifically site traffic statistics, to influence other distributors to carry their products. By demonstrating that thousands of unique visitors explored the TreadMoves site monthly, the TreadMoves team was able to prove that there is significant demand and interest for TreadMoves' products that would in turn build traffic to the distributors' Web sites. Thus, direct marketing measurement, by itself, has proven to be a very profitable marketing tool for TreadMoves.

Summary and Conclusion

As of May 2008, TreadMoves has sold more than 20,000 videos worldwide and continues to get recognition from top fitness publications, such as *Fitness* magazine. Given the success of the video series in the residential market, the TreadMoves team has since expanded its product offerings to include DVDs as well as an audio series for treadmill users who want to take their workouts to the gym, on vacation, or any other location without TV accommodations. Additionally, TreadMoves has ventured into the commercial markets, offering instructor certifications and license packages so that the exercise techniques can be taught in commercial gyms and fitness centers. This means that TreadMoves will be using additional methods to communicate to its business customers, such as trade shows and conventions. However, regardless of the media, the TreadMoves team will apply the same basic tenants of direct marketing wherever they go. At each trade show, there will be a clipboard that collects e-mail addresses of customers who want more information. Then the direct marketing process of creating and cultivating a customer one at a time will begin again.

So if you're tired of your same old exercise routine, go and check out your school fitness center or local gym. You might be able to enjoy a taste of twenty-first-century fitness called TreadMoves. Or you can find out more information about TreadMoves videos by giving your fingers a little exercise and visiting www.TreadMoves.com today.

Case Discussion Questions

1. What was the single most important direct marketing technique that the TreadMoves team employed early on?
2. What other ways could the TreadMoves team use the Web site statistics to make their e-mail marketing even more effective?
3. Given TreadMoves' recent entry into the commercial market, in what other ways could the TreadMoves team use their customer database to promote to the commercial market?
4. Taking into consideration the limited budget of the entrepreneur, what else could be done to increase the size of the TreadMoves database?
5. Overview the various direct marketing methods that have led to the success of this new business venture. Could traditional marketing methods have achieved the same level of success? Why or why not?

Notes

1. *Interactive Direct Marketing: A DMA Guide to New Media Opportunities,* Introduction Section (New York: Direct Marketing Association, 2000), p. 5.
2. Eloise Coupey (2001), *Marketing and the Internet* (Upper Saddle River, NJ: Prentice Hall), p. 7.
3. *The Power of Direct Marketing, 2007–2008* ed. (New York: Direct Marketing Association, 2008), p. 58.
4. Coupey, *Marketing and the Internet,* p. 5.
5. Internet World States, *Internet Usage and Population in North America,* retrieved March 7, 2008, http://www.internetworldstats.com/stats14.htm.
6. *The Power of Direct Marketing, 2007–2008* ed., p. 68.
7. Ibid., p. 94.
8. *The Statistical Fact Book 2006* (New York: Direct Marketing Association, 2006), p. 108.
9. Ibid., p. 111.
10. Ibid.
11. Charles W. Lamb, Joseph F. Hair Jr., and Carl McDaniel (2008), *Marketing,* 9th ed. (Mason, Ohio: Southwestern), p. 203.
12. Dianna Dilworth, *Cyber Monday Generates $608 Million in Online Sales: Comscore,* November 2006, retrieved March 23, 2008, http://www.dmnews.com/Cyber-Monday-generates-608-million-in-online-sales-comScore/article/93655.
13. ComScore, *Cyber Monday Online Retail Spending Hits Record $733 Million, Up 21 Percent Versus Last Year,* November 2007, retrieved March 23, 2008, http://www.comscore.com/press/release.asp?press=1921.
14. *The Power of Direct Marketing, 2006–2007* ed. (New York: Direct Marketing Association, 2007), p. 69.
15. Ibid.
16. Judy Strauss and Raymond Frost (2001), *E-Marketing,* 2nd ed. (Upper Saddle River, NJ: Prentice Hall), p. 9.
17. Netcraft, *January 2008 Web Server Survey,* January 2008, retrieved March 7, 2008, http://news.netcraft.com.
18. Internet World States, *Internet Usage and Population in North America.*
19. Robin Williams and John Tollett (2000), *The Non-Designer's Web Book,* 2nd ed. (Berkeley, CA: Peachpit Press), p. 21.
20. Coupey, *Marketing and the Internet,* p. 17.
21. *Statistical Fact Book 2006,* p. 114.
22. Ibid., 112.
23. Mary Lou Roberts and Paul D. Berger (1999), *Direct Marketing Management,* 2nd ed. (Upper Saddle River, NJ: Prentice Hall), p. 414.
24. Adapted from Amir Hartman and John Sifonis, with John Kador (2000), *Net Ready: Strategies for Success in the E-Conomy* (New York: McGraw-Hill), pp. xviii–xix.
25. Strauss and Frost, *E-Marketing,* p. 21.
26. See http://www.marketingcharts.com/television/top-5-viral-video-ads-of-2007-ranked-2722.
27. Metrics 2.0, *Email Marketing Stats, Facts and Metrics—Metrics 2.0 Quick Pack,* retrieved on March 8, 2008, http://www.metrics2.com.
28. Grant Johnson, "Direct Marketing ROI Projected for 2008," *Marketing Direct* (November 5, 2007), 1.
29. *Statistical Fact Book 2006,* p. 115.
30. BoldFish, "Top Ten Strategies for Direct Email Success," BoldFish, Santa Clara, CA, retrieved in August 2002, www.boldfish.com.
31. Maryann Jones Thompson, "When Market Research Turns into Marketing," *Industry Standard* (August 30, 1999), 68–76.
32. See http://www.businessweek.com/magazine/content/07_46/64058053.htm, retrieved in April 2008.
33. Strauss and Frost, *E-Marketing,* p. 227.
34. Adapted from Mark McMaster, "Reinventing an Old Brand Online," *Sales & Marketing Management,* 152, no. 11 (November 2000), 25–26.
35. David Klein, "Advertisers Should Invest in Sites, Not Just Banner Ads," *Advertising Age* 68, no. 43 (October 27, 1997), 52.
36. Adapted from Michelle Carpenter (2001), Electronic Commerce Education and Training Services Manager, "The Virginia Electronic Commerce Technology Center" (unpublished presentation presented at Christopher Newport University, Newport News, Virginia June 13), updated May 2008.
37. *Statistical Fact Book 2006,* p. 118.
38. Ibid., p. 113.
39. EMarketer (2007), *The Unstoppable Surge of Search Advertising.*
40. Dave Davies (2006), ISEBD, *Search Engine Optimization for Yahoo,* retrieved on March 10, 2008.
41. Lamb, Hair, and McDaniel, *Marketing,* p. 204.
42. Marketing Sherpa, Landing Page Handbook 2007, see http://www.sherpastore.com.
43. Ibid.

44. *The DMA ECHO Winners Program 2007* (New York: Direct Marketing Association), p. 55.

45. Roberts and Berger, *Direct Marketing Management,* p. 426.

46. Ibid., pp. 426–427.

47. Word Press, "What Is a 'Blog'?" retrieved on March 3, 2008, http://codex.wordpress.org/Introduction_to_Blogging.

48. Blog World, Important Blogging Statistics, retrieved March 10, 2008, http://www.blogworldexpo.com/general-information/general-information/important-blogging-statistics.html.

49. Web Duck Designs, *Online Social Marketing Guide,* retrieved March 10, 2008, http://www.web-duckdesigns.com.

50. Kristina Knight, "eMarketer: Social Spending to Increase in '08," *BizReport,* January 2008, retrieved on March 23, 2008, http://www.bizreport.com.

51. Mashable, *eMarketer: Social Networking Ad Spend to Hit $4 Billion by 2011,* retrieved March 23, 2008, http://mashable.com/2007/12/14/social-networking-ad-spending.

52. Debra Aho Williamson, "Hooking up with Social Networks," *eMarketer,* July 25, 2006.

53. Merissa Marr, "Video's New Friends," *Wall Street Journal,* February 28, 2008.

54. Pew Internet & American Life Project, Social Networking Websites & Teens, retrieved from http://www.pewinternet.org/pdfs/PIP_SNS_Data_Memo_Jan_2007.pdf.

55. *DMA ECHO Winners Program 2007,* p. 25.

56. EMarketer, "Incentives Key to Mobile Marketing," March 2007.

57. Ibid.

58. Stephanie Mehta, "How Marketers Plan to Invade Your Phone," CNN Money, February 2007, retrieved on March 10, 2008, http://money.cnn.com/2007/02/14/magazines/fortune/mehta_pluggedin_mobilemarketing.fortune/index.htm.

59. EMarketer, *Incentives Key to Mobile Marketing.*

60. Ibid.

61. Ibid.

62. Nielsen Mobile, *One Third of US Tweens Own a Mobile Phone,* December 2007, retrieved on March 10, 2008, http://www.marketingcharts.com.

9

∎∎∎

Fulfilling the Offer and Serving the Customer

Opening Vignette: DuPont Building Innovations, DuPont Corian

Fulfillment entails anything and everything that happens *after* the customer or prospective customer responds to some form of direct response communication from a company or organization. If a customer places an order, he or she expects delivery of the ordered item. If a prospective customer places an inquiry, he or she expects to receive the requested information. In some cases, consumers need additional information to make appropriate product or service selections. In those cases, the task of fulfillment is to provide information and assistance to empower consumers to make informed decisions. Of course, fulfillment of these requests should be handled in a timely manner. Direct marketers strive to fulfill customer and prospect desires both efficiently and effectively. The more specific a customer or prospect is with his or her request, the more accurately and effectively the company or organization is able to fulfill that request.

What you are about to read is an example of a well-known company that provides real-time customer fulfillment online. DuPont Building Innovations, a division of the DuPont Company, had customer service in mind when it created its extremely customer-friendly Web site. Here's what this savvy company did to better serve its prospects. DuPont wanted to boost sales of its Corian solid surface, a popular material used for countertops, sinks, and showers, while satisfying each prospective customer's individual and unique need for information. The solution was to create a robust Web site that enables prospective customers to move through their buying decision-making process step by step. It also offers interactive decision tools for each prospective customer to best select the materials that fit his or her lifestyle and budget. The Web site offers a surface selector feature that can help narrow surface choices for those customers who are uncertain of their needs and wants. This interactive site permits potential customers to explore numerous color combinations and different types of surfaces—including some that are not manufactured by DuPont. This is true customer service!

The Web site is helpful and user-friendly. As Figure 9-1 reveals, with a couple of quick clicks on the Room Designer feature, prospective customers can choose the room to be designed and select the type and color of the countertops for that room. There are a series of drop-down menus to assist prospective customers in making design decisions. The Web site also allows customers to calculate an estimated price based on their selections, request a free color design guide, and locate a retail store in their area to visit a showroom.

An e-mail response is sent immediately after the visit to thank the prospect and confirm the request for the Color Design Guide. Additionally, within seven days of the prospective customer's online visit, DuPont

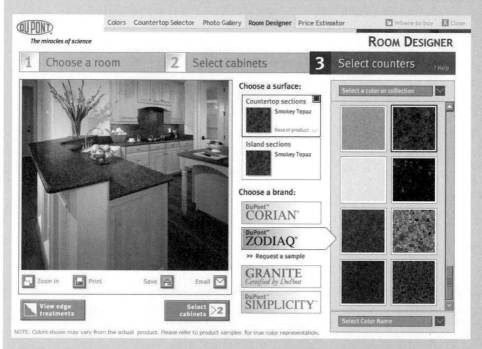

FIGURE 9-1 DuPont Surface Web Site and DuPont Room Designer Web Page. *Source:* Used with permission of DuPont.

FIGURE 9-1   (continued)

generates a personalized e-mail for each prospect. This follow-up e-mail serves to determine how DuPont can further serve the prospective customer's needs. This customized fulfillment is online and excellently timed to contribute to the buying decision-making process of each prospective customer. DuPont has increased its Web presence over the past two years and its interactive Surfaces Web site certainly has prospective customers talking. DuPont provides an excellent example of how to serve the needs of prospective customers. Serving customers and prospective customers is what we discuss in detail throughout this chapter. This is the most important aspect of every business.

This chapter discusses what many professionals refer to as the "back end" of the direct marketing process—the fulfillment, call center, and customer service operations. Many experts contend that back-end functions alone cannot make a sale but certainly can break one. More important, the lack of efficient fulfillment operations and good customer service can injure the relationship the direct marketer has with the customer and ultimately lead to the loss of that customer. As we see later in the chapter with a simple order from Lillian Vernon online, business does not end when the firm receives an order. We also discuss the components of fulfillment, call centers, and customer service along with strategies to help direct marketers maximize their customer's satisfaction level.

FULFILLMENT

What Is Fulfillment?

Fulfillment is the act of carrying out a customer's expectations. Strictly defined, fulfillment means sending the product to the customer or delivering the service agreed on. Loosely defined, it includes the entire dialogue (all interactions with the customer) and delivery functions. Marketers also see fulfillment as a part of the "extended product," or the intangible part of the product. For example, think in terms of the dialogue that a customer has with an organization. A customer or potential customer may communicate with the direct marketer by making an inquiry or placing an order and then expects to receive a response in a timely fashion. Likewise, customers expect their orders to be filled and delivered in a timely fashion. These dialogue and delivery activities are fulfillment.

Adequate fulfillment, by minimizing the time between ordering and receiving, can alleviate two distinct handicaps inherent in direct marketing: (1) a time lag between placing an order and receiving it, and (2) a lack of familiarity with the actual product, which has been purchased remotely by mail, telephone, or online. Ultimate success in direct marketing depends on adequate fulfillment. It has been said, "The best copy, the best graphics, and the wisest choice of lists are all a sheer waste of money, time, and talent if they are not followed through with really outstanding fulfillment."[1] Let's investigate the standards direct marketers must meet to provide really outstanding fulfillment.

Traditional Fulfillment Standards

Fulfillment standards have changed over the past couple of decades. The consumer is increasingly desiring, demanding, and expecting faster turnaround times on orders and all forms of communication with companies. This is especially true of those orders and inquiries that come to the organization via the high-tech media. Consumers are busier today, they are more astute, and they procrastinate. With overnight delivery, toll-free numbers, fax machines, and the Internet, direct marketers have inadvertently encouraged customers to wait longer before placing an order because the consumer expects an immediate delivery service from the direct marketer.[2] Though not every direct marketer can provide immediate delivery services, all direct marketers must uphold certain delivery standards. The following are some basic fulfillment standards that direct marketing organizations should follow to ensure excellent customer service.[3]

1. Orders should be shipped between 48 and 72 hours of placement.
2. Organizations should strive for an 85 to 90 percent rate on shipment, where 85 to 90 percent of the products are available in the warehouse to be shipped upon receipt of the order. If the product is not available, the customer should be informed of that at the time of order, and given the option either to wait for the back order or to select a different item.
3. Customer refunds should be processed within 72 hours, or at least acknowledged, so that an already dissatisfied customer is not further inconvenienced.
4. Ninety percent of all telephone calls placed to the organization should be answered without a holding delay. This requires good operational planning on behalf of the organization.
5. Customers should receive a response to any inquiry they place to the organization within one calendar week from the time of receipt of the inquiry.[4]

THE FULFILLMENT PROCESS

The fulfillment process consists of the following six basic elements: offer, response, processing, shipping, billing, and customer service. Figure 9-2 shows a model of the elements involved in the fulfillment process. Let us now take a closer look at each element.

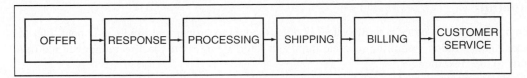

FIGURE 9-2   **The Fulfillment Process.**

The Offer

We saw in Chapter 4 that the **offer** is the terms under which a direct marketer promotes a specific product or service to the customer. To create an offer, the direct marketer first undertakes a number of activities, such as a close examination of the target customer, market segmentation, product or service research, database analysis, price determination, packaging requirements, and others. Direct marketers should properly address and direct the product/service offer and ensure that it is relevant to the needs of the addressee. This description should be adequate and fair and communicate the offer's relevance to the prospect's needs. Direct marketers should clearly state all disclosures and all options, such as sizes and colors. Direct marketers must specify credit terms. They should leave nothing to the imagination of the consumer during this initial stage.

A relevant product offering is timely and clear. Because an order form is an essential contractual document, it should be legally correct as well as distinct, simply stated, and easy to follow. When creating the order form, the direct marketer may use check-off boxes, or something equally easy to identify, for allowing customers to select size, color, or style variations and any other specialized information, such as personalization.

The Response

Direct marketers generally receive consumer responses (inquiries) or transactions (orders) via mail, phone, fax, or the Internet. If an order or inquiry is placed through the mail, fax, or Internet, it is critical that the consumer completes the order form in a full and accurate manner. The consumer must provide all information necessary for the direct marketer to fill the order. If the order or inquiry is placed via telephone, then operators need to be especially diligent in collecting order information. The way an organization handles the receipt of an order or inquiry is critical in the fulfillment process.

Processing

After receiving an order, the marketer undertakes editing and coding as well as credit checking and capturing of vital data for updating the database. The seller also prepares a series of documents such as shipping labels, billing notifications, and inventory instructions. At this stage, if there might be a delay in shipping an order, the marketer lets the customer know and anticipates any possible complaints.

Inventory control is another critical part of fulfillment operations. Direct marketers must examine inventory for quality checks prior to packaging and, if possible, after packaging as well. Computer technology can be of great assistance in processing orders. For example, at Lillian Vernon, computers are programmed to catch errors such as an invalid address or an invalid credit card. Furthermore, if an item can be personalized and the order information provided by the customer does not include personalization information, the computer flags the order and alerts the employee of the situation.[5]

Shipping

A computerized inventory control system is often the key to proper and timely shipment. Out-of-stock and back orders, requiring separate shipments later, are costly to the direct marketer and frustrating to the customer.

Back orders may even result in corrective action by governmental agencies. The Federal Trade Commission (FTC) trade regulations require all direct marketers to comply with strict guidelines in out-of-stock situations by notifying the customer if an item cannot be shipped within 30 days of the time it was placed. In addition, the customer must have the opportunity to cancel the order because of the out-of-stock condition. Direct marketers should not substitute a similar item to try to fulfill the sale, nor send a different color or size, without explicit authorization from the customer. If these FTC guidelines are not followed, the FTC may take punitive actions, including fining the company.

Billing

Once an order is on its way, the organization should receive payment as expeditiously as possible. If the customer did not use a credit or debit card and payment did not accompany the order, then clear billing instructions, with appropriate follow-up, are vital to ensure not only payment but also customer goodwill.

This need for clarity and accuracy also extends to proper receipt and posting of the payment, especially with extended-pay options. We often hear of computer errors, such as incorrect billings and incorrect postings, but more than likely these are human instruction errors.

Customer Service

The customer service function of the fulfillment process specifically refers to the handling of complaints, inquiries, replacements, and special problems. The high costs associated with this kind of customer service should be one of the incentives to getting it right the first time. Another more important incentive is, of course, that only a satisfied customer comes back. Therefore, because direct marketers place great importance on repeat business, they should pay great attention to detail in all aspects of the fulfillment process so as to eliminate the need to handle complaints and special problems. This care will also eliminate the risk of losing a valued customer.

However, because 100 percent quality control is often unattainable, shipping and billing errors inevitably occur, and only prompt handling and adjustment can overcome these. A customer might receive an incorrect shipment, be erroneously double-billed for a product, or be billed incessantly for a product that was returned. Though such occurrences can become extremely complicated, all should be meticulously adjusted as soon as possible.

Not all communications from customers relevant to fulfillment are complaints—many are inquiries. Many seek further information and some request additional orders. These, too, are a proper concern of the fulfillment operation and fall under the heading of customer service. Good customer service is simply good business. Some tips for providing excellent customer service are presented in Figure 9-3.

FULFILLMENT OPTIONS

Options for fulfilling a customer's order include handling all of the processing within the company (in-house), outsourcing the fulfillment activities to an outside fulfillment service, and handling the fulfillment activities online, either in-house or with an outside agency. Let's see what each of these entails and how marketers choose among them.

TIPS FOR PROVIDING EXCELLENT CUSTOMER SERVICE

1. *Conduct Customer Satisfaction Research*. A simple survey asking customers to indicate how well the company and its competitors are performing should be conducted on a regular basis.

2. *Simplify Your Guarantee*. Omit the confusing legal jargon and explain the refund and replacement policy in simple everyday language.

3. *Acknowledge Orders*. If merchandise cannot be shipped immediately, send a postcard acknowledgment. Many customers probably won't mind waiting a short time period for their order if they know that their order has been received and is getting careful attention by the direct marketer.

4. *Ship Merchandise More Promptly*. Most professionals believe that order turnaround time should be one week. Thus, the product should be in the customer's hands the week following the one in which the order was placed.

5. *Don't Bill Before You Ship*. Customers should be told that payment is not necessary until after the order has been received—just in case they receive an invoice prior to the merchandise they order.

6. *Acknowledge Returns and Cancellations*. When customers return merchandise, they want to be assured that the direct marketer has received it. Send a simple acknowledgment card telling the customer you received the returned goods or cancellation request, explain that it may take a couple of weeks to process it, and to disregard any invoice for the product(s) that they may receive in the interim.

7. *Answer Correspondence Promptly*. Nothing is more bothersome to the customer than having to write multiple letters or make multiple calls to get a problem straightened out with the direct marketer. Direct marketers can use a form with check-off boxes, if necessary, to make it easier for the customer to reply. Most importantly, follow through to get the problem straightened out to minimize the inconvenience of the customer.

8. *Make Complaint Resolution a Priority*. Recent research points to the fact that customers who have a complaint or problem satisfactorily resolved become *better* long-term customers than those who never had a problem. In addition, it is well documented that an unhappy customer tells many more people about their dissatisfaction than does a happy customer.

9. *Appoint Your Own Consumer Affairs Manager*. This person might be called the "customer service manager." Their job is to keep customers happy, seeing that orders go out promptly and that complaints are handled properly. This person should be empowered by the organization to make changes in policy and procedures.

10. *Make Customers Your Top Priority*. Everyone within an organization should understand the value of keeping customers satisfied and happy. Train and reward employees for good customer service.

FIGURE 9-3   Tips for Providing Excellent Customer Service.

In-House Fulfillment

Many traditional direct marketing organizations (L. L. Bean, Lands' End, Lillian Vernon, Speigel, Williams-Sonoma, Orvis, Avon, etc.) operate their own fulfillment centers. Most of these direct marketers have invested heavily in automation and bar code systems to make their fulfillment centers more efficient and improve customer service. However, as many professionals agree, automation in a fulfillment operation warehouse must benefit the customer as well as the company. Some direct marketers believe that the ability of an organization to deliver good customer service is *not* dependent on automation alone. They believe that new technology, coupled with a well-trained staff, can create good customer service.

THE IN-HOUSE WAREHOUSE PROCESS   Although some in-house fulfillment centers may differ, most traditional fulfillment warehouses operate in a similar manner. The fulfillment warehouse process normally follows the steps presented in Figure 9-4. Let's walk through the process step by step.

1. The direct marketer receives the customer's order via mail, phone, fax, or the Internet.
2. The marketer processes the order and checks inventory levels (if they have not already been checked while receiving the order).
3. The direct marketer sends several documents per order to the warehouse, including the packing slip and the picking list. The **packing slip** identifies the products to be included with the order, and the **picking list** normally provides routing information regarding the most efficient way to physically move through the warehouse and assemble the items ordered by the customer.
4. Fulfillment center personnel, often called *pickers,* physically move through the warehouse and as items are picked, the items are merged with the packing slip. The pickers check the items against the packing slip and indicate a correct match with his or her initials. The picker is responsible for order accuracy. Figure 9-5 shows employees picking merchandise from the warehouse of Lillian Vernon's National Distribution Center.
5. The order then moves to a packing area, where the *packer* rechecks the products picked against the order and initials the packing slip before boxing the order. This is a second quality control checkpoint.
6. The packer packs the items into an appropriately sized carton enclosing a variety of materials, including a catalog, gift boxes, dunnage material (like foam or bubble wrap to protect products during shipment), and promotional inserts. These materials are within an arm's reach of the packer to ensure high productivity levels. As shown in Figure 9-6, warehouse employees must inspect, weigh, and scan each package before it is shipped to the customer.
7. Finally, as shown in Figure 9-7, (see page 236) the package moves via conveyor belt to the appropriate truck for transportation to its destination. Often, prior to the package leaving the warehouse, a warehouse supervisor randomly opens packages to check for order accuracy. This is the third quality control checkpoint.

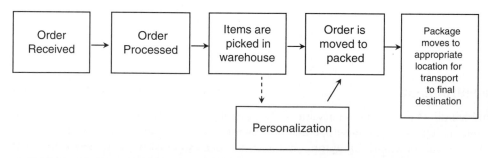

FIGURE 9-4   Flow Chart of Warehouse Process.

FIGURE 9-5 Lillian Vernon National Distribution Center Employees Pick Merchandise from the Warehouse Shelves.

FIGURE 9-6 Lillian Vernon National Distribution Center Employee Inspects a Package.

FIGURE 9-7   Conveyer Belts Move Packages through the Lillian Vernon National Distribution Process.

Other warehouse activities occur simultaneously. For example, the direct marketer is collecting customer database information and updating customer records. Additionally, the warehouse is receiving shipments of products and warehouse employees are responsible for restocking the inventory as well as replenishing the packaging stations with packing materials, such as tissue paper, inserts, and bulk packing material called peanuts. Often a portion of a customer's order is sent to be personalized. This may involve a wide array of sophisticated machinery and trained operators to fulfill the customer's request for personalization. Let's briefly explore what is involved in personalization processes.

PERSONALIZATION   Free personalization is popular with many customers. Approximately 65 percent of the packages that leave the Lillian Vernon Distribution Center include personalized items. Personalization operators must carefully read the packing slip to ensure accuracy in the personalization process. For example, Lillian Vernon offers many personalization processes. Figure 9-8 overviews these processes and shows a personalization operator applying heat press. It takes skill and two weeks of training to learn to operate the high-tech computerized machines used to personalize the company's items. Though computers run many of the personalization machines, operators are responsible for ensuring accuracy and preventing malfunction. Once the operators personalize the product, the fulfillment process continues to order processors in the picking department, where it is placed with the rest of the customer's order.

Inventory availability drives the efficiency and success of the entire fulfillment process. Occasionally a customer will not be shipped their complete order due to the inventory not being in

LILLIAN VERNON CORPORATION PERSONALIZATION PROCESSES

Engraving – A mechanical diamond chip used on steel, silver, gold, Lucite, and plastic.

Gold Stamp – A heat transfer of pressure sensitive gold foil on leather.

Sandblast – An etching system using silica carbide pressure to personalize on glass, metal, ceramic, resin, stone and plastic.

Heat Press – A heat transfer of pressure sensitive vinyl or felt letters used on textiles.

YAG-based Lasers – Light lasers that burn into ceramic, plastic, resin, and metal.

Epilog, LMI and Meistergram Lasers – Lasers that burn on wood, plastic, leather and resins.

Embroidery – A computerized sewing machine that embroiders or sews names, initials, monograms and graphics primarily on textiles.

Multi-Head Embroidery – A computerized sewing machine with multiple embroidery heads that embroiders several products at once.

Linotype – A linotype machine that makes dies and imprints foil onto pencils and greeting cards.

Sublimation – A thermal transfer which can be applied to textiles, metals, ceramics and plastics.

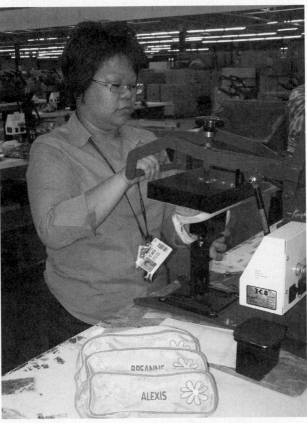

FIGURE 9-8 Lillian Vernon Personalization Processes.

stock. In this situation, the customer is informed that the product is on back order and will be shipped by a specified date. Most in-house warehouses, such as that of Lillian Vernon, store huge quantities of inventory, stocked so high that special equipment is needed to obtain the merchandise cartons as needed. Figure 9-9 reveals the large quantity of inventory and the turret truck used to retrieve merchandise at Lillian Vernon's National Distribution Center.

FIGURE 9-9   Lillian Vernon National Distribution Center Warehouse.

The warehouse processes of most in-house fulfillment operations are highly sophisticated and automated. Most distribution center operations use computer-originated bar codes to enable orders to be tracked and packages to be physically moved throughout the center and routed to appropriate distribution areas for timely delivery. Figure 9-10 shows Lillian Vernon's National Distribution Center operations. However, some direct marketers do not believe in this traditional in-house fulfillment process. They do not support the storage of products and having inventories sitting in a warehouse waiting for an order to be placed by the customer. They support the concept referred to as "integrated order fulfillment."

INTEGRATED ORDER FULFILLMENT   **Integrated order fulfillment** is an emerging business concept based on the idea that the process of building and delivering products should not begin until after the firm receives an order for them. This is in sharp contrast to the traditional fulfillment model, in which assorted products are collected and stored in the distribution center warehouse until an order arrives.

The following eight steps describe the process of integrated order fulfillment.[6]

Step 1   The direct marketer receives a customer's order via mail, phone, fax, or the Internet.

Step 2   The direct marketer processes the order. This includes logging the order into the computer system and determining whether any special promotions or discounts should be noted on the customer's invoice.

FIGURE 9-10   Lillian Vernon National Distribution Center Operations.

Step 3 Next, sourcing occurs. This is where the direct marketer determines where the individual products or components needed to fill the order will come from. The primary choices are the company's own production lines or an outside, contract manufacturer.

Step 4 Now it is time for the direct marketer to store the product. This is the brief holding of products or components in a warehouse until their scheduled delivery or manufacture times.

Step 5 The direct marketer assembles the product. Product assembly includes the gathering of parts in a central place where they are put together to form the finished product.

Step 6 Next, the direct marketer ships the product to the customer.

Step 7 The direct marketer tracks the distribution of the product and fulfills any after-sale service needs.

Step 8 Finally, the customer grades the company on how well it performs the entire process on each individual order.

Integrated order fulfillment will not work for every organization. It is primarily designed for those direct marketers who manufacture custom-made products on a customer-by-customer basis. According to Stig Durlow, chairman and CEO of the Swedish software company Industrial Matematik International, who manufactures a popular fulfillment software system called System ESS, "Integrated order fulfillment helps companies make the jump from the industrial age to the information age by forcing everyone within the enterprise—including outside contractors—to think first about exactly what the customer has asked for before taking any action toward fulfilling a particular order."[7]

Integrated order fulfillment is carried out at the fulfillment center of well-known direct marketer and personal computer manufacturer Gateway. Gateway's customers decide what computer they want and what features they want on it. They then visit Gateway's Web site or call the company, and the customer custom-designs their computer online or over the phone with a representative. In about five days, the computer is built and shipped to the customer in Gateway's trademark white boxes with black cow spots. When a consumer places an order, Gateway builds the computer to the customer's specification. Gateway often changes product configurations every three days. Probably the most valuable thing they offer their customers is a customer-oriented approach to product customization that carries over to a comprehensive approach to customer service. Ted Waitt, Gateway's founder, calls this the "value equation." Companies like Gateway, who primarily base their business on a direct marketing model—blending marketing and manufacturing—are far ahead of most other companies in meeting the needs of individual customers.[8]

Outside Fulfillment Centers

Once upon a time, most traditional direct marketers had their own fulfillment or distribution center to warehouse products until picked and packed for shipment to customers. However, this traditional fulfillment model is changing. Today, many direct marketers are extending their businesses to the Web and are realizing their need to quickly convert their operating models from shipping in bulk to processing thousands of daily online orders consisting of just a few items.[9] So they are outsourcing their fulfillment operations to third-party fulfillment centers or online fulfillment providers to obtain the customer service expertise they need. Many direct marketers are moving toward the business model that management experts have dubbed the **virtual enterprise.** According to this model, the company whose name appears on any given product is primarily a marketing and customer service entity, with actual product development and distribution being handled by a broad—and sometimes far flung—network of subcontractors.[10]

ADVANTAGES OF AN OUTSIDE FULFILLMENT SERVICE   There are certain distinct advantages of hiring an outside contractor to provide back-end support versus handling fulfillment in-house. Some of those advantages include the ability of the company to focus more specifically on marketing and sales activities, as opposed to warehousing and distributing tasks. Another advantage is that outside fulfillment companies are likely to have state-of-the-art fulfillment software that most direct marketers would otherwise find too expensive to acquire. A third advantage concerns financial risk. By contracting outside fulfillment services, direct marketers can treat fulfillment costs as variable costs. Thus, there will be less financial risk because fulfillment costs will be more predictable. A final advantage is that the direct marketer may receive equivalent fulfillment services at a lower cost per order than the in-house cost per order.

Some traditional retailers just getting started in direct marketing activities, especially those planning to use electronic media, have also decided to outsource their fulfillment operations to a third party. Some quickly realize that fulfillment capabilities are outside their general core competencies. Many other direct marketers are outsourcing fulfillment operations so that they may concentrate on multichannel marketing activities, especially those tasks associated with the Web.

AN EXAMPLE OF AN OUTSIDE FULFILLMENT COMPANY   The executives of Limited Too, a fashion leader in preteen clothing and accessories, decided to outsource fulfillment to SubmitOrder.com, a firm based in Dublin, Ohio. What attracted Limited Too executives to contract SubmitOrder.com was the broad range of services they offered beyond online order fulfillment. Dennis Spina, CEO of SubmitOrder.com, believes that what separates them from many outside fulfillment companies are their comprehensive services. SubmitOrder.com can do everything from setting up the information technology system to integrating the front-end sales and marketing activities with the back-end order processing and order fulfillment activities.[11] In addition, SubmitOrder.com has an IT system that can be easily linked with retailers' systems and its distribution facilities are designed to quickly move products—more than 99 percent of orders are shipped the same day they are received.[12] It was that quick order turnaround time that attracted Limited Too executives to partner with SubmitOrder.com, because in the trendy fashion business, you can never deliver too quickly. In addition, the customer base of Limited Too is primarily preteens who both demand and are accustomed to receiving instant gratification.

Online Fulfillment

Of all the changes that computers and information technology have brought to our modern society, few are more visible than the change in the way products and services are bought and sold. High-tech media raise new managerial and customer service challenges for direct marketing organizations. Many organizations have learned the hard way that there is more to e-commerce than just opening a Web site and inviting consumers to come and shop. It is well established that the primary problem with e-commerce customer satisfaction is *fulfillment*.

Fulfillment guru Bill Kuipers sees little change in fulfillment as a result of electronic media. "You still have to warehouse, pack, and ship."[13] Kuipers believes that companies need to plan for the fulfillment process when they use the Internet. Customers shopping online have higher expectations and service standards than do their offline counterparts.

Customers are looking for a quicker response to their order or inquiry. They often expect to receive a response to their online communication the same day—and no later than the next day, and they like to be able to investigate the shipping status of their orders online. These high consumer expectations can be a real fulfillment nightmare for the online direct marketer who isn't able to meet them.

E-FULFILLMENT   **E-fulfillment** refers to the integration of people, processes, and technology to ensure customer satisfaction before, during, and after the online buying experience.[14] It is another way of referring to fulfillment strategies for online orders. The term was developed by Dennis Spina, CEO of SubmitOrder.com. Online retailers have what may be the unique ability to extend the interaction with their customers by creating a memorable and distinct fulfillment experience. Unlike passive traditional media, interactive media put the consumer in control, with both positive and negative consequences. The positive include the great opportunity for building brand awareness and enhancing the relationship with the customer. The organization's Web site might earn that all-important bookmark status on the consumer's computer. However, just one poor online experience can have disturbing effects. Not only will the consumer not purchase from your organization again, they are likely to tell many friends about their bad experience . . . leading to brand image deterioration.

The major problem with many e-commerce organizations is that they lack the needed focus and emphasis on e-fulfillment. According to Kuipers, e-commerce organizations treat fulfillment and customer service as incidental rather than fundamental. They're interested in technical capabilities—instant messages, e-mail, click to talk, and so on—and they don't realize that what they need most to satisfy the customer and keep the customer coming back is a polished customer fulfillment infrastructure.[15] However, that may be in part due to the fact that most organizations wanting to attract and obtain customer orders electronically don't have the fulfillment systems or infrastructures and don't want to be in the warehousing business. Therefore, these organizations normally outsource or hire third-party service bureaus to sort, pick, pack, and ship the product.

DELIVERY OPTIONS

Because the delivery of products is such a vital part of the fulfillment operations of direct marketers, we should look at the alternative delivery options that are available, especially those that provide individual delivery to households and businesses rather than those that handle bulk shipments. Direct marketers are concerned with product delivery, but also with the delivery of advertising and other promotion materials.

U.S. Postal Service

The volume and scope of operations of the U.S. Postal Service (USPS) is mind-boggling.[16] The USPS handles over 212 billion pieces of mail annually. In 2005, the growth rate of domestic mail volume was 2.7 percent, slightly higher than the growth rate for 2004 (1.9 percent). Much of the recent growth in mail volume is attributable to direct marketing. The total number of pieces of mail attributable to direct mail in 2005 was 104.3 billion. First class and standard mail represented almost the same percent of total mail volume, 46.3 and 47.8 percent, respectively.

FIRST-CLASS MAIL   This category includes business reply envelopes and cards. The postage rate is higher than for the other classes but so is the cost of priority handling and individual sorting. This category of mail is the largest source of mail revenue for the USPS, although that percentage has been steadily shrinking over the past few decades. It generated 70 percent of USPS revenue in 1977, 64.6 percent in 1987, and 54.1 percent in 2005.

PERIODICALS   The periodicals category consists of publications. It includes magazines, newspapers, and miscellaneous periodicals, such as classroom publications. It accounted for 4.3 percent of total mail volume in 2005. This category of mail generated 3.6 percent of USPS revenue in 1977, 4.4 percent in 1987, and 3.2 percent in 2005.

STANDARD MAIL   Standard mail is the category mainly used for the distribution of direct response advertising. Although postage rates are lower per piece, mailers of this class must ZIP code their mail, sort and bundle, tie, bag, and personally deliver the sacks of mail to the post office. Thus, the direct mailer performs up to half the basic tasks normally performed by the postal service for first-class mail. Delivery is also deferred. This class accounted for 28.4 percent of total mail revenue in 2005, which is an increase from 15.2 percent in 1977 and 21.1 percent in 1987. This class represents the second largest source of revenue for the USPS. Standard mail accounted for 47.8 percent of the total mail delivered in 2005, an increase from the 39.3 percent share of the total mail delivered in 1987.

SPECIAL MAIL SERVICES   There are certain alternatives for expedited mail service of special interest to direct marketers. These include services such as Express Mail, which is guaranteed overnight service to designated destinations for items mailed prior to 5 P.M. In addition, the USPS continues to offer more online services (att www.usps.com) such as Mailing Online, Card Store, Certified Mail, and Postecs. Using NetPost, for instance, you can send professionally printed letters, postcards, and booklets that have been created on a personal computer. NetPost also offers CardStore, an ideal way to customize your business or personal message.

Alternative Delivery Systems

Although the Private Express Statutes grant the USPS a form of monopoly over first-class mail delivery, they have been in transition and now make private delivery services possible under certain conditions. Alternatives to first-class mail, permitted under the Private Express Statutes provided they meet certain criteria, include FedEx and major airlines. (Other alternatives of course are the telephone and the Internet, as well as additional emerging forms of electronic message transmission.)

Certain publications, including *Better Homes and Gardens* and the *Wall Street Journal*, among others, have been experimenting with delivery alternatives to the periodicals category of mail. These alternatives have been increasing as have the number of private firms distributing direct mail advertising, including samples, in selected markets.

FULFILLMENT PROBLEMS

Everybody makes mistakes—and fulfillment centers are no exception. The crucial point for the direct marketer is becoming aware of the mistake and fixing it promptly—making it right for the customer so that the final impression is a positive one. Keep in mind that the fulfillment experience often determines whether the customer will respond to the next sales offer.

What are some common sources of fulfillment problems and how can direct marketers attempt to avoid these mistakes? Let's examine these two important issues.

Sources of Fulfillment Problems

Many of the most common fulfillment problems originate in the warehouse. These problems can occur in many ways. Let's look at some of the potential sources of fulfillment problems.

- **Accuracy of the order**—Delivering the wrong product to the customer is a costly mistake. It may result in losing the customer's future business as the customer has lost a certain degree of confidence in the direct marketer.
- **Package presentation**—Packaging is an extension of the company's image, and sloppy packaging communicates a poor image. Small details like the correct position of the label on the mailing carton and the neatness of the outer carton seal are important. Even more important is the product placement within the package—making sure that the product is upright or positioned the best way to ensure it reaches the customer in good condition.
- **Speed of delivery**—In today's electronic age, customers demand faster delivery than ever before. However, accuracy cannot be sacrificed for speed. Therefore, the fulfillment challenge is to process and fill orders as efficiently as possible.
- **Stock availability**—Delivering what you offer is the ultimate role of fulfillment. Maintaining an accurate inventory system and an adequate amount of inventory is crucial to fulfillment success. Back orders commonly result not only in the loss of a sale but also loss of a customer.
- **Return processing**—It would be wonderful if every product a customer ordered was received and kept. The fact is that many products get returned for many different reasons and direct marketers must process these returns in a timely and professional manner.

Other common fulfillment problems come from areas outside the warehouse and are commonly related to customer database files. Included in this category of fulfillment mistakes are not thanking the customer for the order, sending the customer an invoice *after* payment has already been sent, misspelling the customer's name, and using the incorrect prefix (for example, using Mr. or Ms. instead of Dr.). Mistakes like these can make the customer skeptical and could result in the loss of future business.

Ways to Avoid Fulfillment Problems

Fortunately, direct marketers can take simple steps to avoid fulfillment problems and actually assist the organization in exceeding consumer expectations. Although many of these may seem like commonsense marketing, not all direct marketers exercise these steps. The ways to avoid fulfillment problems include the following.

- Pay careful attention to the packing slips and picking lists to ensure that orders get filled accurately and expediently. The packing slip identifies the items ordered by each customer. The picking list also identifies each item on the order and serves as a routing guide to move the picker efficiently through the warehouse.
- Include a toll-free number for customer service in a prominent place on the catalog, direct-mail piece, Internet site, or packing slip with the order. If your toll-free phone line is too expensive because too many calls are coming in, then maybe you've got too many service problems. So fix them.[17] However, you should encourage your customers to call you even if the problem is small.
- Hire a professional, well-trained customer service staff. If your customers are important to you, make sure their interaction with your organization is a positive experience. Nothing is more frustrating for a consumer than dealing with an inept customer service representative. The more positive you can make the customer experience the greater the probability the customer will return and purchase from your organization again. Smart direct marketers ensure repeat business by establishing customer service standards and monitoring customer service representatives (often via tape-recorded phone calls) to measure and control the service level.

- Establish quality control measures for each phase of the fulfillment process. From order receiving to warehousing, from order processing to shipping and delivery, from picking and packing to handling customer complaints, each part of the fulfillment process is important and you should establish and monitor quality control standards that focus on the customer. Service levels are shaped by the needs of the target audience, the desired image of the company, and management's ability to define and implement the necessary programs and systems in the operation.[18] Setting up these quality control standards, communicating them to all employees, and monitoring their performance and ultimate effect on customer satisfaction is a proactive approach to delivering quality service and to avoiding fulfillment problems before they begin.

CALL CENTERS

A **call center** is a dedicated team supported by various telephone technological resources to provide responses to customer inquiries.[19] Some marketers think of call centers as the "telephonic front door" to the company or the main access point for obtaining information or placing an order. In essence, the call center is the formal entity of an organization, or representing an organization, that handles communication with any type of stakeholder. Regardless of whether a customer is placing an order, calling to check on the status of an order, inquiring about new products or services, seeking technical support, or placing a complaint, the call center should provide a seamless communication process and quality service.

In addition to receiving phone orders, the call center provides answers for customers who call with questions or problems they may have concerning a product or an order. For example, Lillian Vernon customer service associates receive many hours of training and are taught that the call they answer is *their* call and they are responsible for assisting that customer. This is the Lillian Vernon concept of "One Call, One Person," which means customer service associates are given tiered authority and can resolve most problems without supervisor intervention or assistance. Another example of an organization effectively carrying out this communication and service is Pittsburgh-based PNC Bank. It has devised a customer rating program that automatically activates when customers contact its National Financial Services Center. It uses software that requires customers to enter their PIN or Social Security number. The bank determines the customer's identity and analyzes that person's past transactions with the bank and places the customer into one of several preset "needs-based segments." Callers with basic transactions are transferred to an entry-level representative. Callers with complex financial histories are given to handlers with a specific expertise. A "most valuable customer" is routed to a relationship consultant—one of 30 or 40 service representatives deemed the bank's very best.[20]

Call centers can operate (1) within the company or in-house; (2) outside the company, when calls are made or taken by a teleservice outsourcing firm; or (3) a combination of both. Each type of call center organization has similar functions, yet all have unique features and challenges. The decision about how to carry out telemarketing activities ultimately is a function of the company's financial situation and the nature of its telemarketing program. A major factor in determining whether to establish the call center in-house or outsource it is the expected pattern of calls. When customer orders are expected to come into the company all at once (or within a relatively short time interval), it becomes difficult to staff the call center to receive and process each order on a timely basis. This is when outsourcing begins to look attractive because nothing is worse than putting your customers "on hold." Only outsourcers with thousands of positions can handle such call volume effectively. According to Peppers and Rogers, "Customers today are accustomed to having their needs met immediately, completely, conveniently, and inexpensively."[21]

Organizations measure the level of customer dissatisfaction by calculating the rate of **call abandonment,** the number of callers who hang up before being served by a sales representative. Many companies strive to keep this rate below 2 to 3 percent.[22] However, during peak calling times, consumers may abandon 20 to 30 percent of the calls. To reduce customer frustration, many companies route incoming calls through interactive voice response equipment to capture preliminary information and balance the workload among teleservice agents. Nonetheless, even one missed call can lead to the loss of a sale and, more important, the loss of a customer. At these times outside service centers should handle customer orders. Let's examine both in-house and outsourced call centers.

In-House Call Center

In-house call centers require substantial investment in facilities and equipment. Direct marketers can place outbound calls or receive inbound calls from the same call center due to advances in telephone and computer technology. The process of setting up an in-house call center and managing an ongoing program entails many activities. These include (but are not limited to) obtaining support from top management, setting goals and objectives, developing scripts and guides, recruiting and training personnel, designing a productive work environment, developing measurement systems, testing systems and procedures, and reporting and controlling the operation. Personnel issues comprise a sizable portion of this process—from obtaining support of top management to reporting and controlling the operation.

The biggest advantage of establishing an in-house call center is the degree of control the company has over the telemarketing operations. The biggest disadvantages of an in-house call center are the time it takes to properly train representatives and the large financial burden. Many in-house call centers, especially those B2C organizations that offer seasonal products, rely on a large number of seasonal, part-time, or flex-time employees. For example, Lillian Vernon hires approximately 2,200 seasonal employees each year to assist in handling the 2.5 million inbound calls from customers. Though many of these employees may return for a second, third, fourth, or fifth year, the expenses of retraining them are enormous. Thus, farming out a company's telemarketing activities can cut costs and eliminate a large portion of the company's personnel load.

Outside (Outsourcing) Call Centers

Outsourcing formally refers to the process of having all call center activities handled by an outside organization or a teleservice outsourcer. The primary advantage of outsourcing for the marketer is a reduction in expenses and capital outlays. Most call center outsourcers are larger than in-house call centers and can more easily accommodate a large volume of seasonal orders. Additionally, because of their size, they offer lower costs and provide better formal training for telephone operators than in-house call centers. In addition, most call center outsourcers tend to use the most advanced technology available to stay efficient.

There are five main advantages to using an outside service bureau to conduct a company's telemarketing program.

1. *Low initial investment*—marketers pay for the telemarketing program on a short-term basis only.
2. *Elimination of hiring needs*—marketers eliminate the day-to-day managerial tasks associated with hiring employees.
3. *Fixed operating costs*—with a defined rate schedule provided by the call center outsourcer.

4. *Quick start-up*—shorter lead times for implementing the telemarketing program.
5. *Time flexibility*—24-hour, 7-day-a-week service for inbound calling and, as required by the FTC, restricted hours for outbound calling.

There are also disadvantages associated with call center outsourcers.[23]

1. *Lack of direct control*—the company does not have the same degree of control over an external organization.
2. *Lack of direct security*—because of the remote location of the call center outsourcer, the company cannot keep its customer information in its exclusive possession. However, most call center outsourcers take great security measures.
3. *Lack of employee loyalty*—employees possess greater loyalty to the call center outsourcer than to the company that they are representing on the telephone.
4. *Mass-market approach*—service bureaus are high-volume businesses, thus the quality of the sales pitch for any single company could suffer.
5. *Caliber of personnel*—often call center outsourcers pay less than in-house call centers, thus the quality of personnel is affected.

Regardless of the aforementioned disadvantages, many telemarketing companies successfully outsource their call center activities to service bureaus. In fact many outsource their call center operations to call centers in international locations as the geographic location has an impact on its operating costs. For example, as shown in Figure 9-11, the annual operating costs of call center operations in Mexico, Dominican Republic, India, Philippines, and other off-shore locations are much less than those for domestically located call centers.[24]

Call Center Location	Total Annual Operating Costs
San Jose, California	$22,629,532
Boston, Massachusetts	$21,648,707
Philadelphia, Pennsylvania	$21,260,060
Los Angeles, California	$21,083,491
Seattle/Belleview, Washington	$20,682,774
Providence, Rhode Island	$19,636,960
Salt Lake City, Utah	$19,267,458
Tucson, Arizona	$18,995,850
Jacksonville, Florida	$18,153,083
Portland, Maine	$17,758,710
Wichita, Kansas	$17,301,385
Toronto, Ontario	$17,125,096
Augusta, Georgia	$16,629,906
Bangalore, India	$ 5,276,544
Manila, Philippines	$ 5,186,330

FIGURE 9-11   A Comparative Analysis of Call Center Costs.
Source: BizCosts.com, "A Comparative Operating Cost Analysis for U.S. and Off-Shore Call Centers, 2007." BizCosts is a registered trademark of the Boyd Company, Inc., Location Consultants, Princeton, NJ. In the *DMA Statistical Fact Book*, 30th ed. (New York: Direct Marketing Association, Inc., 2008), p. 182.

THE IMPORTANCE OF CUSTOMER SERVICE

Each customer wants to be satisfied. **Customer satisfaction** has been defined as the extent to which a firm fulfills a consumer's needs, desires, and expectations.[25] Contrary to what many believe, the customer doesn't care about what has to happen behind the scenes to get the product or service delivered on time. The customer is primarily interested in what the marketer can do to satisfy his or her needs.

Direct marketers know that simply providing a quality product or service is not enough. So they have begun to create strategies designed to move goods from factories and warehouses directly to the customer in the shortest possible time and at the lowest possible cost, using the level of service to differentiate their organization from others. Customer service also enables the organization to exceed rather than simply meet the customer's expectations. Delivering high-quality customer service can enable the direct marketer to develop a long-term relationship with each customer, which is, after all, the ultimate goal of direct marketing. In essence, the task of **customer relationship management (CRM)** as discussed earlier in Chapter 2, is a big-picture approach that integrates sales, order fulfillment, call center operations, and customer service and coordinates and unifies all points of interaction with the customer, throughout the customer life cycle and across multiple channels.

Business doesn't end when an order is received. In fact, most direct marketers believe that is when it begins. Let's take a look at the customer service strategies direct marketers implement before and after a customer places an order. What does a customer experience when shopping online?

Imagine you are sitting at your computer in the comforts of your home. You have just connected to Lillian Vernon online (www.lillianvernon.com). Stop there for a moment. How did you get to this point? This is also a part of customer service—because serving the customer begins with researching and analyzing the customer's needs and wants. A great deal of business planning, consumer research, and historical sales analysis has gone into determining which products are displayed on the homepage. In addition, great care has been put forth to organize and design the Web site so you, the customer, can easily navigate and shop from it.

Once you make a product selection (such as a leather handbag, as shown in Figure 9-12) the Web site automatically offers additional related products or services (e.g., matching leather organizers). This is an example of up-selling, cross-selling, and suggestive selling. Any of these suggested items may be added to your shopping cart with a simple click. Then the Web site visually displays your updated shopping cart, as shown in Figure 9-13 (see page 250). This point provides another cross-selling opportunity with an offer to purchase some inexpensive unrelated items (e.g., a small box of candy). Think of this as offering impulse items—similar to those that are located near the checkout counters in traditional retail stores. Once you make your final selections, you proceed to a checkout stage where the Web site totals the order, adds shipping and handling fees, and verifies personalization (if applicable). Figure 9-14 (see page 251) shows a sample customer checkout form for a customer purchasing three personalized leather bags. The shipping and billing addresses are determined as is the method of payment. Most direct marketers offer several payment methods to enable each customer to select the preferred method. Next, Lillian Vernon sends you an order confirmation.

Figure 9-15 (see page 252) shows that this is an opportunity for the company to thank the customer and to provide the order number in case the customer has an inquiry about that particular order. In this example, Lillian Vernon also confirms the customer's gift message.

What happens next? A few days later, Lillian Vernon may send you an e-mail providing details about the status of your online order. This is an additional opportunity for the direct marketer to thank you for your order and to provide an update. In addition, it allows the company to remind you about their customer service priority and how their products carry a 100 percent money-back guarantee. In sum, it enables the direct marketer to strengthen the relationship it has with the customer.

Lillian Vernon enters the information collected about you and your transaction data into their customer database. The company will use this information to target future direct response communications to you. From this point on, the direct marketer will communicate with you on a regular basis. Each time Lillian Vernon contacts you via some direct response media (e.g., an outbound e-mail, phone call, or catalog), the contact and response (if applicable) will help further the customer relationship. Although we've used an online example here, all customer service activities are similar whether online or through a catalog or a telephone contact. The main purpose of all back-end functions is to more effectively serve the customer. When carried out effectively, such back-end functions can strengthen customer relationships and encourage customers to continue to purchase from the organization.

Beyond waiting for the customer to repeat purchase, how do direct marketers determine the strength of their relationship with the customer? How does a direct marketer assess the level of

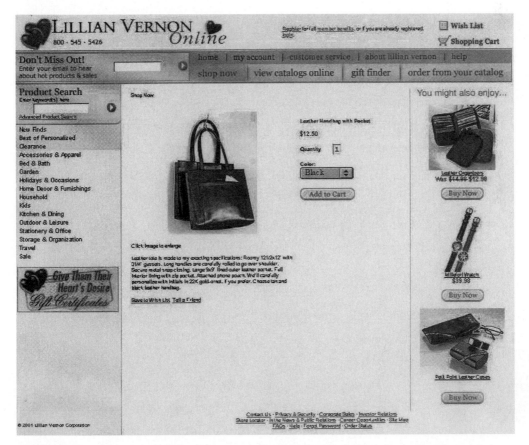

FIGURE 9-12   Lillian Vernon Online Shopping (Leather Handbag).   *Source:* Used with permission of the Lillian Vernon Corporation.

service the customer is receiving from their organization? How will direct marketers determine whether their relationship with each customer can be improved? How can they know what is best for the customer? The next section details how direct marketers can evaluate customer satisfaction levels.

Evaluating Customer Satisfaction Level

Direct marketers can evaluate the level of customer satisfaction in a number of ways. First, they might begin by pretending they are the customer. Every organization likes to think they are doing a good job of serving their customers. But savvy direct marketers investigate this from both sides of the relationship. Are inquiries processed in a timely manner? Are customer complaints addressed as quickly and as professionally as they should be? Is delivery time as expedient as you promised the customer it would be? Direct marketers determine the answers to these questions in two ways:

1. Place an inquiry, order, or a complaint with the organization under a fictitious name and experience firsthand the level of customer service your organization really delivers.

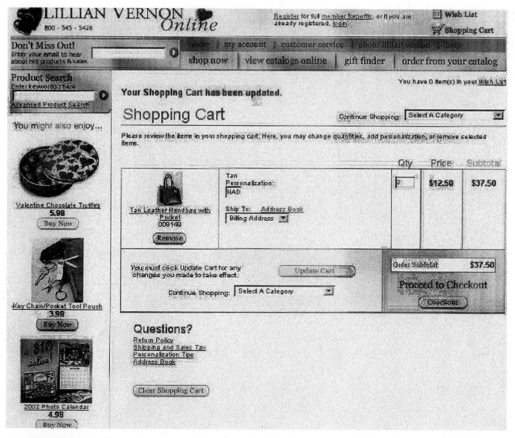

FIGURE 9-13 Lillian Vernon Online Shopping Cart. *Source:* Used with permission of the Lillian Vernon Corporation.

2. Send periodic follow-up surveys consisting of only a few questions designed to address the customer's fulfillment experience. Questions might address the speed, accuracy, and degree of staff friendliness the customer experienced when interacting with the organization. An example of a brief customer survey designed for assessing the fulfillment experience is shown in Figure 9-16 (see page 253).

Regardless of how you obtain this information, it is critical to perceive the fulfillment experience from the customer's point of view. This experience and any subsequent action you take should lead to an improved relationship with the customer.

A strong focus on CRM is crucial to the success and profitability of every direct marketing organization. Many professionals believe that it may be necessary to make CRM part of the broader

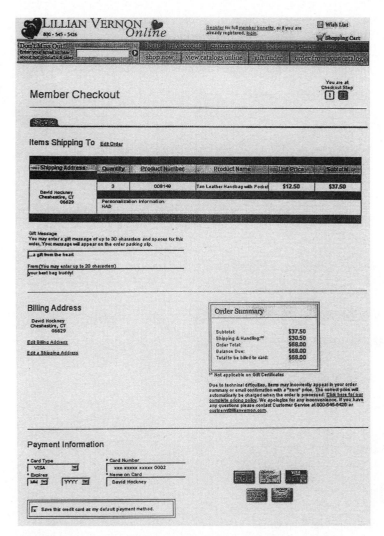

FIGURE 9-14   Lillian Vernon Online Shopping: Member CheckOut.
Source: Used with permission of the Lillian Vernon Corporation.

concept of customer management because the whole organization must support and participate in customer relationship maintenance. These words from Robert McKim, CEO of MS Database Marketing, sum up the value of customer relationship marketing:

> Gone are the days of empty 'customer is king' lip service. The key to the new rules of success is the ability to address each customer's idiosyncrasies and needs, balanced with their current and future value to the company. Firms that do this can differentiate themselves from the competition, forge long-term customer relationships, engender customer loyalty, stop attrition and enjoy success in the 21st century.[26]

The next section provides suggestions and examples of how to keep customers happy.

Keeping Customers Happy

At the foundation of customer service is the simple notion of *keeping the customer happy*. Only a satisfied customer is a happy customer. Only a satisfied customer will come back and purchase from your organization again and again. However, keeping customers happy does not happen by accident. Direct marketers need to constantly keep abreast of the customer's changing needs and wants

FIGURE 9-15   **Lillian Vernon Online Shopping: Your Order Confirmation.**   *Source:* Used with permission of the Lillian Vernon Corporation.

and must always strive to satisfy these. Some classic suggestions for keeping customers happy are shown here.

- Remember that the customer is always right.
- Don't promise something you cannot deliver.
- Inform your customers about how to return products.
- Inform your customers about how to complain.
- Test your own service.
- Date and record all customer correspondence.
- Investigate your competitor's offerings on a regular basis.
- Exercise care in billing and collection.[27]

Many companies go out of their way to exceed customer expectations and delight the customer. Let's look at some examples of great customer service.

SubmitOrder.com, an outside fulfillment center, recently handled a customer service incident for Limited Too. The dimensions of a toy were missing in the catalog, and the customer called to get assistance prior to placing an order. The SubmitOrder.com representative checked both the Limited Too Web site and the store catalog but was unable to locate the needed information. Eventually, the employee put the customer on hold and went and measured the toy himself. After taking the customer's order, the employee notified Limited Too executives that the toy dimensions should be added to the catalog along with the product description.[28] That's good customer service.

Here is another example. One holiday season a customer ordered two Towers of Treats from the Harry and David Specialty Foods and Gifts catalog to have delivered to two neighbors. The customer had placed the order in time to have the packages arrive the day or two prior to seeing the neighbors at a dinner party. The packages didn't arrive before the date of the dinner, nor did they arrive before the holiday. When the customer found this out, she phoned the company. The customer service department was very professional and apologetic and offered to resend the ordered items that had not arrived. Within a week, the packages were received by each of the neighbors and the customer received a note of thanks for both her order and her patience, another apology for the inconvenience, *and* a free gift. Mistakes happen, but how they are handled can either contribute to a positive customer experience or reinforce a negative one.

Providing good customer service can sometimes be just a simple response to a customer's suggestion. For example, Lillian Vernon once received a letter from a customer who explained that while she purchased a lot of presents from their catalog for her nieces and nephews, she sometimes had trouble figuring out what present was suitable for which age group. Since the time of that letter, Lillian Vernon catalog copy includes age guidelines to assist customers with making those purchase decisions.[29] Good customer service is an important part of fulfilling the customer's expectations.

Please tell us how we rated:	Excellent	Good	Fair	Poor
Knowledgeable Phone Operators	❏	❏	❏	❏
Promptness of Delivery	❏	❏	❏	❏
Overall Impression of Service	❏	❏	❏	❏
Other Comments:	_____			

FIGURE 9-16 **Sample Customer Survey.**

Summary

In summary, fulfillment is the final impression left with the customer. It is also a chance to communicate with the customer by enclosing additional promotional materials and/or new catalogs. Being attentive to detail in the fulfillment process should generate satisfied customers and future business for the organization. This chapter discussed how customer service and fulfillment activities are vital to the success of any direct marketing organization. They may not be glamorous, but they are the guts of direct marketing. There are six steps in fulfillment process—offer, response, processing, shipping, billing, and customer service. Direct marketers may select from various fulfillment options, including in-house fulfillment, outside fulfillment centers, and online fulfillment, to serve its customers. In addition, direct marketers must select from the various delivery options, available for shipping products to consumers. These delivery options include multichannel distribution, USPS, and alternative delivery systems.

The chapter provided an overview of some of the most common fulfillment problems along with ways to avoid these problems. The chapter also explored call center operations as an important component to fulfilling customer's needs and expectations. Call centers can operate within the company, outside the company, or a combination of both. Regardless of where the call center is located, qualified personnel is the key to effectively serving the customer. The importance of customer service begins with an understanding of customer satisfaction and CRM. Direct marketers follow a step-by-step process to ensure customer relationships are managed properly. Direct marketers use personal experience and surveys to determine whether the organization is providing good customer service and keeping customers happy. Good customer service, correct order entry, and prompt order delivery generates satisfied customers and repeat buyers.

Key Terms

fulfillment *230*
offer *231*
packing slip *234*
picking list *234*
integrated order fulfillment *239*

virtual enterprise *240*
e-fulfillment *242*
call center *245*
call abandonment *246*
outsourcing *246*

customer satisfaction *248*
customer relationship
    management (CRM) *248*

Review Questions

1. List and describe the six steps of the fulfillment process.
2. Discuss some common fulfillment problems along with actions direct marketers may take to avoid future fulfillment problems. Why don't all direct marketers exercise these preventive measures?
3. What are some of the ways a firm can keep their customers happy? Describe from your own personal experience the actions direct marketers have taken to keep you happy.
4. Describe the relationship between fulfillment and customer service.
5. Describe how the traditional fulfillment model is changing.
6. Compare the advantages and disadvantages between in-house fulfillment and outside fulfillment services. Name some companies that are using the different types of fulfillment services.
7. List and explain the eight steps of the integrated order fulfillment concept.

8. What is the function of a call center? How is telemarketing carried out via call centers?

9. Explain some of the primary challenges associated with operating a call center?

10. Describe the ways a company can interact with its customers to strengthen those relationships and maximize customer satisfaction.

Exercise

You are an employee of a small clothing boutique that also distributes a catalog. You work in the fulfillment department. Currently the company uses in-house fulfillment, but you learn that your boss is considering using an outside fulfillment service to meet demand. Business has grown rapidly since the company has gone online and is now receiving online orders. He is also suggesting that the boutique may save money by using an outside fulfillment service. Voice your opinion on the matter. Should the company keep fulfilling orders in-house or should they use an outside fulfillment source? What variables would impact your decision? Be sure to give specific reasons to support your position on the matter.

CASE

1-800-FLOWERS.Com

Overview

This case provides real stories of how 1-800-FLOWERS.com has made its customers the top priority and how it has been able to motivate its employees to embrace this customer orientation. The roles of changing technology and changing consumer needs have led the company to become a successful multichannel direct marketer. This case illustrates the important role that high-quality customer service and employee motivation play in building a successful enterprise. Jim McCann, CEO of 1-800-FLOWERS.com, demonstrates how his company combines recognition of people with technology to build a highly profitable direct marketing business.

Case

The original 1-800-FLOWERS was started by a group of successful businessmen from Dallas, Texas. The founders spent $30 million during their first year of business and built the world's largest telemarketing center. This call center consisted of million-dollar telephone switches, state-of-the-art computer systems, 700 workstations, and a detailed bridge command to oversee the entire operation. The operation was housed in 55,000 square feet of office space. A network of 6,800 "fulfilling florists" were paid on a commission basis to create, package, and deliver the orders received by the 1-800-FLOWERS telecommunications call center.

Sounds great? You bet! Was it profitable? No way! With that kind of killer overhead and nobody with a burning desire to manage the business on a daily basis, the company lost money right from the start. What was missing in the business start-up was a focus on the customer. The original owners failed to establish relationships with their customers.

One day, in walks Jim McCann, then owner of Flora Plenty, a successful 14-store retail chain of florists in New York. Flora Plenty was doing extensive telemarketing for its retail chain, plus it was one of the fulfilling florists for 1-800-FLOWERS. McCann had a passion for serving the customer, and he sincerely believed in the 1-800-FLOWERS concept. He thought the company could be highly successful if managed properly. Thus, on November 6, 1984, after a few years of negotiation, McCann bought 1-800-FLOWERS for $7 million, and managed it first as a partnership, then later as sole proprietorship. The acquisition gave McCann the right to use the 1-800-FLOWERS phone number but left him buried in debt and scrambling to create a makeshift operation for the new company with very little overhead. In the beginning McCann himself went back to answering the phone: "Thank you for calling 1-800-FLOWERS, how can we help you today?"

McCann knew the three big challenges that were ahead for this troubled business:

1. At that time, toll-free numbers were still new to most consumers, and it was going to take time to build consumer confidence in purchasing via toll-free technology.
2. Most consumers were not aware of 1-800-FLOWERS yet often had a need to purchase flowers. Thus, brand awareness would need to be developed such that consumers thought about 1-800-FLOWERS whenever they had the urge to buy flowers.
3. Most important, there was the challenge of building relationships with customers—one at a time—to gain their loyalty for a lifetime. McCann realized that if he were going to make a business out of something impersonal like buying flowers over the telephone, he would have to create a personal relationship with *every* caller. The sale would be almost secondary.

When McCann first bought the business, it was a lousy deal: several million dollars of debt and a telephone number with a not very good track record. One of the keys in turning 1-800-FLOWERS into a success story in the world of telemarketing has been getting people to want to buy flowers over the phone for someone they really care about. In 1992, as 1-800-FLOWERS entered online commerce (www.1800flowers.com), the company had to give people a reason to want to be in its virtual store. See Figure 9-17 for the company's Web site.

The company added personal contact and entertainment to the value equation to make people want to visit its site. McCann credits the fact that 1-800-FLOWERS was named the single most successful business operation on the Web in 1996 to the lessons he learned ten years earlier in telemarketing. He believes the Internet fulfills the same functions as any other retail system, so the jump from telemarketing to modem marketing was a natural one for 1-800-FLOWERS. On the Internet, as with telemarketing, a company must have strong infrastructure to keep track of inventory, process orders, secure billing, and deliver the product. Above all, the business must focus on people.

Today, the company is called 1-800-FLOWERS.com and people are still its top priority. Training and motivating customer service representatives to provide top-notch customer service is critical to ensure long-term customer relationships. How does 1-800-FLOWERS.com motivate its customer service representatives? Here are a few examples:

- It is not uncommon for managers to place smiley face stickers on a customer service representative's computer whenever the customer service representative has been seen smiling while on the phone with a customer. Customers can tell a smiling, happy person over the phone, and it makes the customer experience more enjoyable. Thus, the customer service representative is rewarded simply for smiling.
- Like many companies, 1-800-FLOWERS.com monitors customer service representative phone calls. However, the primary reason for the monitoring is to reveal strengths to be shared with others. This ensures the quality control of customer service representatives and provides clues on how to sharpen the script and improve customer service.
- Public praise of the customer service representative is also common at 1-800-FLOWERS.com. In fact, the company purchased a refrigerator door and mounted it on the wall at the entrance to the customer service area. Whenever a customer service representative was found doing something noteworthy, the manager wrote it up and stuck it to the door with a magnet.
- There is a legends book at 1-800-FLOWERS.com. This book is filled with stories of associates going the extra mile to please a customer. This book is given to new customer service representatives as a part of their training—it provides the rules for working in customer service. The new employees are told that if what they are doing to serve a customer is not worthy of being included in the Legends book, then they are probably not doing enough.

In summary, old-fashioned rules have been the guiding light to McCann in building 1-800-FLOWERS.com into a successful business. McCann believes in putting a premium on people and making an emotional contact—by planting emotional seeds that will yield sales and build customer relationships far in excess of a simple sale. The company tries to please each and every customer. If a customer isn't happy, company policy is to "find out what it will take to make the unsatisfied customer happy, then do it." The 1-800-FLOWERS.com "Absolute Guarantee" policy is unique to the floral industry: "If at any time, you are not satisfied with the product you ordered, we will replace it. Or refund your money. Or do whatever it takes to ensure that you, the customer, are happy and will continue to be a customer of ours in the future."

FIGURE 9-17   1-800-FLOWERS.com Web Site Home Page.

Technology also plays a key role in the success of 1-800-FLOWERS.com. The company uses technology to

1. process orders more quickly,
2. confirm product delivery more accurately,
3. remind customers of birthdays and anniversaries more faithfully, and
4. free employees to devote themselves to creating customer relationships.

Figure 9-18 shows an example of how 1-800-FLOWERS.com electronically communicates with its customers. Once a customer places an order, she instantly receives an order confirmation and thank-you e-mail. Follow-up e-mails are sent to update that customer on the status of her order and ultimately confirm delivery.

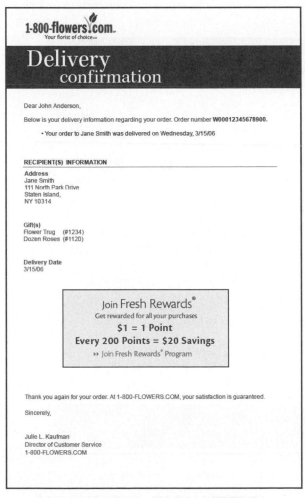

FIGURE 9-18   An Example of 1-800-FLOWERS.com Delivery Confirmation.

In addition, 1-800-FLOWERS.com sends out regular e-mail offers to its customers featuring weekly specials or holiday reminders. Figure 9-19 presents examples of these special offers. Notice how the company effectively promotes its free reminder service.

As McCann puts it, "Computers aren't friendly, people are." Technology is very effective at improving a business, but too much technology can depersonalize a business—which is a bad thing. Over the years, 1-800-FLOWERS.com has investigated new telephone technology and has experienced both positive and negative outcomes. Technology allowed the company to adjust the length of the phone ring. During the busiest times (Mother's Day, Valentine's Day, and Christmas), customer service representatives had the alternatives of putting people on hold with canned music or letting the phone ring. Since it was already established that people like to have their telephone call answered by the third ring, 1-800-FLOWERS.com simply extended each ring from 6 seconds to 9 seconds. The company found that there was no perception of a longer wait, so with the same number of rings, it was able to serve customers during peak seasons without turning them off with too many rings or too much "elevator music." This same technology enabled the company to pick up the

FIGURE 9-19   (A-B) 1-800-FLOWERS.com Outbound E-Mail Offers.

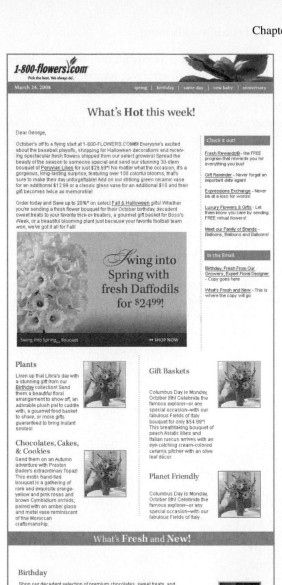

FIGURE 9-19   (continued)

phone before the caller even heard a ring—but callers thought it was downright creepy, as if the company knew what the customer was doing before they did it. Therefore, although technology would allow the company to eliminate phone rings, 1-800-FLOWERS.com chose to stay with the old-fashioned ring cycle because people felt comfortable with it.

What began as a simple, toll-free number is now a well-established brand. 1-800-FLOWERS.com has blossomed into a successful direct marketer with a database of loyal customers and a nationwide network of BloomNet florists who have been handpicked to fulfill. The company has become a multichannel direct marketer. It now sells its products via phone, Internet, on-site retail stores, and even catalogs. Figure 9-20 shows a couple of 1-800-FLOWERS.COM catalogs.

The 1-800-FLOWERS.com call center, once a bunch of crates and boards and telephones down in the basement of a Queens, New York, floral shop, now has the capability to handle millions of calls and Internet orders per week. With unparalleled attention to customers, motivated employees, and modern technology, 1-800-FLOWERS.com, the world's largest florist, is poised to continue its direct marketing success story well into the future.

In conclusion, according to McCann, "Today 740,000 people are celebrating their birthdays, tomorrow another 740,000 will be celebrating theirs. If you'd like to make one or two of them feel terrific on their special day . . . I know a 1-800 number you can call!" Of course, if you prefer, you may place your order by visiting its Web site instead at 1-800-flowers.com.[30]

FIGURE 9-20   1-800-FLOWERS.com Catalog Covers.

Case Discussion Questions

1. Discuss how 1-800-FLOWERS.com became a direct marketing success story. What were the main ingredients in its success?

2. Why did 1-800-FLOWERS.com become a multichannel direct marketer, instead of specializing solely in telemarketing? How should the company use these channels to support one another?

3. What role did technology play in assisting the company in achieving its goals? Has improved technology always lead to success for 1-800-FLOWERS.cp,? Support your answer with specific details and examples.

Notes

1. Robert D. Downey, "Proper Fulfillment—Image with the Proper Stuff," *Direct Marketing* (July 1985), 28.

2. Jack Schmid, "How the Back End Drives the Bottom Line," *Target Marketing* 13, no. 5 (May 1990).

3. Heather Thiermann, "Fulfillment: Do It Right," *Target Marketing* 9, no. 11 (November 1986).

4. Adapted from Thiermann, "Fulfillment: Do It Right."

5. Lillian Vernon (1996). *An Eye for Winners* (New York: HarperCollins).

6. Sidney Hill, "Integrated Order Fulfillment for the Virtual Enterprise," dmnews.com, February 1998, retrieved on May 10, 2000, http://www.manufacturingsystems.com.

7. Ibid., p. 3A.

8. Michael Warshaw, "Guts and Glory: From Farm Boy to Billionaire," *Success* (March 28, 1997); Denise Duclaux, "Gateway Casually Builds Booming Business in Direct Sales," *DM News* (February 17, 1997).

9. Susan Reda, "Customer Service, Brand Management Seen as Key Aspects of On-Line Fulfillment," *Stores* (October 2000), 44.

10. Hill, "Integrated Order Fulfillment for the Virtual Enterprise."

11. Ibid., p. 42.

12. Ibid.

13. Jonathan Boorstein, "Customer Service: Fulfillment 101," *Direct,* May 2, 2000, retrieved May 2000, http://www.directmag.com/Content/monthly/200/2000050119.htm.

14. Reda, "Customer Service, Brand Management," pp. 40–44.

15. Boorstein, "Customer Service: Fulfillment 101."

16. All statistics are based on *The Statistical Fact Book 2006,* 28th ed. (New York: Direct Marketing Association), pp. 200–215.

17. John M. Chilson, "The Top 10 Fulfillment Mistakes," *Folio: Magazine for Magazine Management* 27, no. 7 (May 1998), 61–62.

18. Jeffrey A. Coopersmith, "Customer Service: The Final Link," *Catalog Age* 5, no. 7 (July 1988), 76.

19. Bobette M. Gustafson, "A Well-Staffed PFS Call Center Can Improve Patient Satisfaction," *Healthcare Financial Management* 53, no. 7 (July 1999), 64.

20. *Sales & Marketing Management* 151, no. 9 (September 1999), 26.

21. Ibid.

22. Gustafson, "A Well-Staffed PFS Call Center," p. 64.

23. Ibid., pp. 39–40.

24. BizCosts.com, "A Comparative Operating Cost Analysis for U.S. and Off-Shore Call Centers, 2006," in *Statistical Fact Book 2006*.

25. William D. Perreault Jr. and E. Jerome McCarthy (1999), *Basic Marketing: A Global Managerial Approach,* 13th ed. (New York: Irwin McGraw-Hill), p. 5.

26. Robert McKim, "Is CRM Part of Customer Management?" dmnews.com, March 13, 2000, retrieved on May 10, 2000, http://www.dmnews.com/ archive/2000-03/7058.html.

27. Adapted from Stanley J. Fenvessy (1979), "Introduction to Fulfillment," in *Direct Marketing Manual* (New York: Direct Marketing Association), p. 500:1.

28. Reda, "Customer Service, Brand Management," p. 44.

29. Vernon, *An Eye for Winners*.

30. Case adapted from Jim McCann and Peter Kaminsky (1998), *Stop and Sell the Roses: Lessons from Business & Life* (New York: Ballantine Books). Updated based on information provided by 1-800-FLOWERS.com, 2008.

10

....

Conducting Research and Utilizing Tests to Measure Performance

Opening Vignette: Omaha Steaks International

Experimentation, or testing, as it is usually called by direct marketers, is second nature to them. All too often, however, such experimentation is conducted under the guise of scientific procedure, but the sample selected is not representative, the test structure is faulty, and the sample size is inadequate. The resultant measurement of differences between the test and control reveals differences that are not significant.

True experimentation, if it is to be accomplished properly, should be structured in a valid manner. The results, when measured statistically, should be at an acceptable level of significance so as to provide a prediction with which the researcher can be comfortable. This case provides a means for evaluating a typical direct marketing test structure, one intended to measure the response differences among five advertisements run in a national newspaper.

FIGURE 10-1 Omaha Steaks Ad.   *Source:* Used with permission of Omaha Steaks International.

Advertising Copy	Circulation	Ad Cost	Results Index
(A) "Try a Little Tenderness" (Control)	367,000	$ 578	100%
(B) "Perfect Steaks" (Experiment 1)	634,000	$ 824	28%
(C) "Journal" (Experiment 2)	652,000	$ 863	29%
(D) "Love at First Bite" (Experiment 3)	458,000	$ 721	74%
(E) "Attention Steak Lovers" (Experiment 4)	652,000	$1,027	76%

FIGURE 10-2 Experiment Results.

Omaha Steaks International has long offered six 6-ounce filet mignons, 1.25 inch thick, for $29.95 (plus $2 shipping/handling) through space advertising in print media. In an October issue of the *Wall Street Journal,* the direct marketer scheduled an experiment of a control advertisement (A) against four test advertisements (B), (C), (D), and (E), all of which are illustrated in Figure 10-1. In testing the existing control advertisement against the four alternatives, each of which had a particular promotional theme, the management wanted to find out which ad, the existing control or any of the four new advertisements, would produce better response and generate more sales. After experimentation, the management determined that the control advertisement did in fact produce orders at a lower cost per sale than did any of the alternatives tested. This determination was based on the results shown in Figure 10-2.

Many marketers, citing their "years of experience," use what has been aptly termed "seat-of-the-pants" judgment, relying on their own intuition for making decisions. They are inclined to feeling "my mind is made up, don't confuse me with the facts." Direct marketers, however, are more inclined to make their decisions scientifically, turning to objective research as well as statistical tools and techniques to guide them.

Research in direct marketing serves direct marketers in both fact finding and information gathering. They also use it for problem solving and decision making. In fact, given the huge amount of market information available and the need to make decisions quickly, marketing managers rely on both basic and advanced research techniques utilizing *surveys* as well as *experiments*.

THE NATURE OF RESEARCH

Shown in Figure 10-3 is a listing of definitions of commonly used statistical terms, presented here as a refresher for students as well as a reference for the technical discussions that appear throughout this chapter.

The result of research is often **quantitative,** that is, it is expressed in terms of numbers: population sizes, income levels, housing values, and the like. Beyond the rigor of numbers, though, we often need **qualitative** information about consumer behavior and the reasons people buy, not just data about who or how many buy. We need to know, for example, about their lifestyles and how these motivate their buying decisions.

Research, using both surveys and experiments, enables direct marketers to obtain both quantitative and qualitative data. The most valid research, moreover, measures *results* and not *opinions,* because what survey respondents say and what they do are frequently quite dissimilar. In one study by a life insurance direct marketer, for example, in which the company remained anonymous during interviewing, the majority of the respondents said they would not purchase life insurance by mail. Yet every one of them had purchased life insurance by mail from the company conducting the survey!

A better alternative is to experimentally offer the product or service for sale and count those who actually buy; not, as in a survey, those who say they would buy if given the opportunity. Experimentation is a key characteristic of direct marketing.

Surveys and Experiments

Direct marketing research is comprised of *research* and *experiments*. Determining the response rates to various offerings involves survey research; determining which advertising strategy resulted in more responses involves experimentation research.

Accuracy—The difference between the sample statistic and the actual population parameter.

Alternative Hypothesis—Determined when a null hypothesis is proven wrong (i.e.,the hypothesis is shown to be true).

A Priori—In statistical analysis,before the fact.

A Posteriori—In statistical analysis,after the fact.

Bias—A methodical error that occurs in selection of respondents or measurement (i.e.,the difference between the expected value of a statistic and the population parameter estimated by the statistic).

Breakeven—The point at which the gross profit on a unit of sale equates to the cost of making that unit sale.

Central Limit Theorem—Assures us that,in a number of random samples taken from a population,the sample means tend to be normally distributed. The shape of such a normal distribution—the so-called "bell-shaped curve"–is completely determined by its two parameters:mean and standard deviation.

Central Tendency—Adherence to the Central Limit Theorem.

Chi-Square Test—One technique for determining whether an observed difference between the test and the control in an experiment is (or is not) *statistically significant*.

Confidence Level—Is the area of the estimated values of the sample within which the true value lies within a predetermined probability, as measured by the number of standard deviations from the mean in a normal distribution.

Control Group—A group on which the experiment is not conducted but that is otherwise identical to the test group.

Dependent Variable—A variable which is influenced by independent variables.

Degree of Freedom—The number of observations that are allowed to vary in a numerical system without changing associated constraints or assumptions.

Dry Testing—An experimental technique used to test a new product not yet available in the marketplace.

Experimentation—A testing process in which events occur randomly in a setting at the discretion of the experimenter and controls are used to identify sources of variation in subjects' response.

Focus Group Interview—Unstructured small group,representative of an appropriate market segment,under skilled leadership, converses in a relaxed environment about the subject of the research.

Hypothesis—An assertion about the value of a variable.

Independent Variable—A variable that exerts influence on various events or outcomes called dependent variables.

Key Code—A unique number or other identifier placed on the order form or other response device so as to identify source of the response.

Law of Large Numbers—Assures us that,as sample size increases,the distribution of sample means concentrates closer to the true mean of the total population.

Limit of Error—Describes the number of percentage points by which the researcher is allowed to comfortably miscalculate the actual value.

Mean—Arithmetic average;a measure of central tendency in a normal distribution.

Median—An average,the mid-point of values;also a measure of central tendency.

FIGURE 10-3 **Definitions of Statistical Terms.**

Mode—An average, the value that occurs most frequently; also a measure of central tendency.

Normal Distribution—The so-called "bell-shaped curve,"whose shape is completely determined by its two parameters: mean and standard deviation.

Null Hypothesis—The statistical hypothesis that the result of an experiment is due only to chance.

Parameter—A characteristic of a population.

Population—The total domain or group of items being considered.

Primary Data—Those data collected specifically for the current research need.

Response Rate—The percentage of those who respond to an offer.

Qualitative Research—That which deals with behavior.

Quantitative Research—That which deals with numbers.

Random Event—An occurrence which has several possible values and occurs with some definable frequency if many repetitions are undertaken.

Random Assignment—Random assignment of subjects to both test and control groups so that differences between groups occur by chance alone.

Random Sample—A sample in which every element of a population has an equal chance of being selected and differences occur by chance only.

Reliability—Standard error of a statistic;its precision.

Sample—Subsets of the total population,for which data are available.

Sample Size—The number of observations in a sample,determined by first looking at two major considerations: (1) the cost of reaching the sample and (2) the amount of information we need to make an efficient decision.

Sampling—A method of choosing observations from which we can predict estimations.

Sampling Error—The difference between sample result and the population parameter (which most often is unknown). Sampling error declines as the sample size increases, assuming an unbiased sampling procedure.

Sampling Method—The means of obtaining a sample from a population.

Secondary Data—Those data originally collected for another purpose,that have relevance to,and are available for, the research needs of others.

Simple Random Sample—A sample drawn from a population in a manner in which every possible sample of equal size has the same probability of selection.

Standard Deviation—A measure of dispersion;square root of the variance about a mean.

Statistic—A characteristic of a sample.

Survey—A research method in which hypotheses are tested using questionnaires.

Test—What direct marketers call an experiment.

Type I Error—Occurs when the decision maker rejects the null hypothesis even though it is,in fact,true.

Type II Error—Occurs when the decision maker accepts the null hypothesis when it is,in fact,not true.

Valid—A valid statistic is one without bias.

Variance—A measure of variability from the mean.

FIGURE 10-3 (continued)

A **survey** looks at things the way they are; for example, a mailed questionnaire tries to profile respondents to an offer, measure product preferences, or determine future buying intentions. An **experiment,** often called a **test** by direct marketers, is designed to measure the effect of change. What happens, for example, when we raise or lower a price level? What is the result of selective promotion to specific market segments? What is the influence on response of one particular promotional strategy versus another? Direct marketers, like traditional marketers, have many ways to conduct surveys. When it comes to experimentation, however, they have become adept with the statistical tools and techniques of such testing and they are thus inclined to use experiments more often than they use surveys.

Apart from knowing the mechanics of conducting surveys and experiments, direct marketers also need to know how to define people, things, and events in quantitative as well as qualitative terms. Where do they obtain what kinds of information and what do they do with it? How do they design research and how do they structure problems? How do they conduct valid experiments, through proper sampling and estimation techniques? How do they present findings, evaluate them, and then benefit from them? The tools and techniques of research enable them to do all these things.

Problem Structure

How do direct marketing researchers define and structure problems? First, let's consider typical problem areas, such as the following.

- *How much advertising is needed?* How is an answer determined in dollars and cents? Is the amount of advertising going to be a *result* (of, say, past sales) or a *cause* (of, say, expected future sales)? Do expected results warrant estimated costs? Do anticipated rewards outweigh potential risks?
- *How will the direct marketing mix be selected?* Once determined, how will the budget be allocated? What products will be offered and at what prices? What market segments will be solicited? And, certainly a major area for testing, what is the most productive promotional strategy: offer, copy, graphics? What media should be used? Will the Internet be used?
- *How will our resources be utilized?* Should promotional efforts be concentrated in one geographic area, considering its climate and the logistics of distribution? Should resources be allocated over time, taking into account potential seasonal or cyclical variations or the stage of the product's life cycle?

There is an art as well as a science to defining marketing challenges such as these, and not all the solutions are derived from challenges, of course. Sometimes direct marketing researchers are trying to fulfill specific objectives. Research is simply the way direct marketing managers seek solutions to problems or become knowledgeable about objectives so that they can find solutions or new opportunities.

Marketers must remember, of course, that they can influence their definition of the research goal by researcher/experimenter bias, especially when trying to justify their actions. The findings are also subject to **sampling errors** when the respondents are nonrepresentative, or there is error either in the randomness of the sample or in the sampling process. Asking an apartment dweller what type of lawnmower he or she intends to purchase is an obvious example of a sampling error. Furthermore, people are human, and their behavior as consumers cannot always be measured precisely.

What to Research and Test

There is virtually no limit to the possibilities for conducting surveys or experiments. So it is exceedingly important to research and test only the *important* things and to do this *adequately*. Important things include the following six big areas: products/services, media selections (lists, print, broadcast, Internet, etc.), offers or propositions, copy platforms, formats, and timing. Direct marketers of an earlier era tested a host of relatively insignificant things, such as the manner of addressing (typing versus handwriting versus computer labels), the manner of paying postage (postage stamps versus meter imprints versus printed indicia), the covering of the window in a mailing envelope (glassine versus cellophane versus an open window), or the color of ink used for the signature reproduction on a letter. None of these had much impact on the results of the direct marketing effort. Today, the rule of thumb to "test the big things"—those that may have an impact on the rate of response or level of profitability of a direct marketing campaign or program—is crucial given the strategic decisions made on the basis of test results. "Adequately" refers not only to the size of the research sample but also to the nature of the sample.

Today's direct marketers test in a manner that will provide statistically valid results that they can project to a larger sample. To ensure control, they test one variable at a time or else test everything, such as a complete package or a new product. Even though the tools are there, they try not to become "test happy." Later in this chapter, we cover in detail the tools and techniques of testing. First, let's examine how and why direct marketers collect data.

DATA: TYPES, SOURCES, AND COLLECTION

The goal of research is the acquisition of data from which we derive information. After determining what information is needed, the direct marketer must determine where and how to obtain it and what to do with it. Information is all around us, if we would but recognize it, collect it, catalog it, and refer to it.

Data can be characterized as either primary or secondary. **Secondary data** are those originally collected for another purpose that have relevance to and are available for the research needs of others. **Primary data** are those collected specifically for the current research need. Direct marketers try to collect primary data only when secondary data are not readily available from outside sources or the organization's own internal records, including its own prior experimentation.

Primary data can be collected through survey research as well as experimental research. Surveys are usually conducted by personal interview, by mail, by e-mail, by telephone, via a Web site, or by on-site observation. Experiments are conducted in either a field or a laboratory environment.

Secondary Data

Figure 10-4 lists a variety of sources of secondary data. Digging for and obtaining information that is already available, as contrasted to survey or experimental testing, doesn't appear to be a very exciting activity. Still, one of the most costly mistakes researchers make is reinventing the wheel. It is quite likely that someone has already traveled your road, *including yourself*. The use of secondary data, when available, can save valuable time and is usually less costly. (Secondary data might well have been primary data for the organization originally gathering them.) The volume of secondary data is virtually limitless. The problem, actually, is how to manage the derived information. Where is it? How do you find it? How do you get it? What do you do with it? How do you analyze and evaluate it? How reliable and relevant is it?

A. The Organization's Own Internal Records

B. Government Sources: Federal, State, Local

    1. U.S. Department of Commerce
        -- Bureau of the Census

    2. U.S. Department of Labor
        -- Bureau of Labor Statistics

    3. U.S. Department of Agriculture

    4. Other U.S. Government Sources
        -- President's Office
        -- Congress
        -- Treasury Department
        -- Interior Department
        -- Health & Human Services Department

    5. State and Local Governments
        -- Economic Surveys
        -- License Registrations
        -- Tax Records

C. Trade, Technical, Professional & Business Associations

D. Private Research Organizations

E. Foundations, Universities and Other Nonprofits

F. Libraries, Public and Private

G. Advertising Media

H. Financial Institutions, Utilities, Service Organizations

FIGURE 10-4 Secondary Data Sources.

The first source to consider for secondary data, although not always realized, is the internal records of your business or organization itself. For example, there is no need for a life insurance company to conduct survey research to determine the average age of its policyholders; a quicker and easier way is to look at its own policy records already on file.

Traditionally, organizations have collected and used little internal marketing information. Although costs of advertising, for example, are duly recorded on a typical accounting statement, there is little or no allocation of advertising costs to media or results on that statement. Typically, accounting approaches and operating statements are not adequate nor have they been designed to provide the information needed by marketing decision makers.

Decision makers go to great lengths to measure and predict direct marketing results, but they expend only a fraction of their effort on the matter of costs. Usually, such costs appear on accounting statements according to the objective of the expenditure; that is, advertising, printing, postage, mailing list rental, and Web site development. From a manager's standpoint, it would be more appropriate to look at these by products, price level, type/size of customer, market segment, and/or promotion effort.

As Figure 10-4 shows, there is also a great variety of potential sources of secondary data outside the organization's own records. In addition to the government and other public sources listed, there are many private organizations, including research firms, as well as communications media that provide syndicated or custom-designed data on a periodic or one-time basis. The A. C. Nielsen Company, for example, provides an ongoing stream of information about food and drug purchasing and the automobile aftermarket. Daniel Starch monitors magazine readership and advertising recall. Other organizations, such as the Yankelovich Group, George Gallup, the Harris Poll, and the Roper Poll, monitor social, economic, and political changes. Other types of information come from consumer panels, diary groups, store audits, and field enumerations.

Primary Data

Marketers gather primary data specifically for current needs, usually from respondents. The data include:

- *Behavior:* what respondents have done or are doing
- *Intentions:* anticipated or expected future behavior
- *Knowledge:* how respondents perceive specific offerings
- *Socioeconomic status:* age, income, education, occupation, gender, marital status
- *Attitudes and opinions:* respondents' views or feelings
- *Motivations:* reasons for respondents' behavior
- *Psychological traits:* respondents' state of mind; that is, personality

There are six major survey methods for collecting primary data.

PERSONAL INTERVIEW   The personal interview is the most costly method of survey but it has several advantages: It provides the opportunity for a more complete and accurate sample; it provides the opportunity for more complete information; it offers greater flexibility in structuring questions to the situation; and it ensures a high response rate. Its major disadvantage, besides cost, is the possibility of bias created by the interviewer along with the need for extensive interviewer supervision and control to standardize the interview and avoid cheating.

TELEPHONE INTERVIEW   The advantages of telephone interviews are economy, speed, representative sampling, minimal nonresponse, simple callbacks, and the ability to make the interview coincide with other activities, such as television viewing. The disadvantages include limited availability of information at the time of contact, and the fact that those without telephone service are not included. Certain types of questions, such as those that require demonstration or visualization, cannot be used. The public also is becoming increasingly resistant to intrusive phone calls and those with unlisted numbers can be reached only through random-digit dialing.

E-MAIL SURVEYS   E-mail surveys are an excellent method for reaching hard-to-reach consumer segments. Advantages include the speed, economy, and the ease for respondents to reply at the time of their choosing. However, e-mail surveys lack the dynamics of more personalized methods, like telephone or personal interviews. Other disadvantages associated with e-mail surveys include the degree of difficulty in obtaining a representative sample due to restricted Internet access and privacy regulations and higher degrees of nonresponse bias caused by differences between those who do and do not respond to the e-mail survey.

MAIL QUESTIONNAIRE   Mail questionnaires provide great versatility at low cost. There is no interviewer bias, no field staff is needed, and some respondents are easier to approach by mail and therefore more likely to respond. The respondent may reply at leisure and without interruption; replies may remain confidential as well. Disadvantages include the relatively high rate of nonresponse, the need for follow-up, response bias introduced by the fact that those with strong feeling (either way) tend to respond in greater numbers, the time required to develop the questionnaire, and the lack of assurance that respondents clearly understand the questions.

ONLINE SURVEYS   Web-based research, using online survey techniques, offers the major advantage of reaching potential respondents at the most opportune time. Many Web sites have incorporated surveys into the process of registering to visit and/or conduct transactions at the site, thus targeting their questionnaires to those who have already expressed some degree of interest in them. Potential respondents can also be directed to Web sites to retrieve survey questionnaires and respond to them while online. Speed and convenience help increase the response rate.

OBSERVATION   The key advantage of observation is that it removes respondent bias. Johnson Wax found that reported usage of its products by respondents differed as much as 50 percent from reality when compared with the actual brand the consumer had at the time of an in-home interview. The major observation methods include in-store and in-home audits, recording devices, and direct observations at the point of purchase, such as a shopping mall. An automobile dealer wanting to know what radio stations prospects for service listen to didn't ask them; its employees observed the dial settings on radios in cars brought in by customers.

Another survey research tool is the **focus group interview,** wherein unstructured small groups, representative of appropriate market segments, under skilled leadership, converse in a relaxed environment about the subject of the research, which is often not specifically identified. Although marketers can use such groups for creative stimulation or evaluation, they cannot scientifically control them, so it is not really possible to make scientific projections from the results of a focus group.

EXPERIMENTATION AS TESTING

Many equate marketing research with survey research, but they are not the same. Survey research attempts to observe and record various activities as they naturally arise in the environment. Experimentation, on the other hand, manipulates one or more controllable factors called **independent variables,** to determine their influence on various events or outcomes called **dependent variables.** Experimentation, often called **testing,** is especially prevalent in direct marketing. In experimentation, the experimenter creates an environment in which controls serve to pinpoint the causes of behavior differences among respondents. This method of gathering data requires close adherence to statistical techniques to ensure validity. Because direct marketing researchers rely heavily on experimentation, we look closely at certain relevant tools and techniques of statistics in this chapter. Some examples of direct marketing questions that call for experimentation are the following.

- How does frequency of mailing to a particular record on a database affect total response?
- How can direct marketers benefit from the World Wide Web?
- Is it possible to increase profits by servicing small industrial accounts totally by mail, telephone, or online, rather than using personal salespeople?
- How productive are various segments of a total market?

- Is a newspaper advertisement more effective in color than in black and white?
- What is the best season to offer spring-blooming bulbs to be planted in the fall?
- What is the most profitable pricing strategy?

Independent variables could be the product or service offered, its price structure, or some attribute of the promotional strategy used in the offer. They can also describe the demography or geography of a market. Independent variables should reflect the situation in the real world, for example, the age, gender, marital status, or ZIP code of residence of a respondent. Marketers should generally evaluate only one independent variable at a time. Certain advanced statistical techniques, however, such as multivariate correlation and regression analysis, offer the opportunity to measure the interaction of many independent variables simultaneously. Although direct marketers may investigate many different independent variables, they commonly use the following four types of tests.

List tests: Investigating whether certain lists will generate a higher response rate than other lists is an ongoing task for most direct marketers. Direct marketers constantly test the lists they use—for both prospective customers and current customers. Most will test a small sample of a prospect list prior to renting the entire list for new customer acquisition purposes. Most list brokers permit small samples of prospect lists to be rented for list testing.

Offer tests: Investigating whether incentives, such as free shipping or discounted shipping, percentage discount or dollar discount, have an impact on the rate of response to the offer. In other words, do the incremental sales generated by the promotional offer offset the forgone shipping revenue or discounts given?

Creative tests: Most direct marketers have a printed catalog. One common creative test has to do with the design of the catalog cover. Thus, a test would be conducted to determine whether a test cover creative beat a control cover. This would require testing either a unique design or an alternative style of the control cover design. It could also include variations in images or copy compared to the control design or norm.

Contact strategy tests: This common type of test is related to a direct marketer's customer database. Contact strategy tests investigate whether altering the number of catalogs sent to a group of customers over a specific period can have an impact on sales or profit. Direct marketers often include additional variables, such as using e-mail or other types of direct mail contacts, in the contact strategy tests. In essence, what combination of contacts will maximize the sales or profits associated with each particular customer or select market segment?

In direct marketing, the number of responses or transactions is often the dependent variable. In other research situations the dependent variable could be favorable or unfavorable reactions to a product or overall rating of a brand preference. At least three levels of observation are normally needed for measurement.

Experiments usually take place in a field setting, but marketers do sometimes conduct them under laboratory conditions. In a laboratory, marketers must be sure that the setting is realistic and that the subjects are representative. It would not be appropriate for example, to use college students in a laboratory setting to test a product geared to the senior citizen market. Laboratory experiments can also measure the impact of particular advertisements through such devices as eye motion cameras and mechanical devices that gauge emotional reactions by measuring dilation of the pupil of the eye.

Designing the Experiment or Test

Valid experiments are characterized by (1) the presence of a **control group** on which the experiment is not conducted but that is otherwise identical to the test group and (2) **random assignment** of subjects to both test and control groups so that differences between groups occur by chance alone.

It is naive to compare responses from two groups that are not randomly selected but may not be similar in their composition. Consider, for example, the often repeated statement that those who receive a college education earn more in their lifetimes than those who do not. The two groups are not comparable, and thus it would be foolish to draw a conclusion that college education in and of itself causes higher lifetime income. It is conceivable that the drive that caused the student to enter college in the first place also affects lifetime income.

Common forms of experimental design measure the effect of an experiment as the difference between what is observed about the dependent variable of the test group and what is observed about the dependent variable of the control group. But even with control and randomization, there is still no guarantee that the two groups are identical. Differences between them that arise by chance alone may be substantial.

Adequate scheduling of experiments, their timely release, and key coding are vital. Marketers should devise a comprehensive schedule to describe the purpose of the experiment and also its various components, costs, and expected results for the test segment as well as the control.

Tracking Responses and Measuring Test Results

Obviously, response differences to a product offering—between tests and control—cannot be measured unless there is a complete record of results for all segments of the experiment. There must be a means to identify the sources of these results. This is accomplished through **key codes** placed on each response device, such as an order form, to make it easy to record results. In direct mail, the key code can be a unique number or other identifier placed on the order form. When the phone is used for response, the key code can be a unique telephone number, a departmental number, or an individual's name. Many direct marketers using the phone or a Web site ask respondents for the key code printed in the advertisement or on the label of a catalog to which they are responding. As Figure 10-5 shows, often an outbound e-mail from a direct marketer will contain a specific code for customers to use when placing their order. This is an excellent tracking device where the code will vary based on the element being tested. In this case, Lillian Vernon may be testing its discount offer where customers can obtain 10 percent discount on orders of $65, 15 percent discount on orders of $80, and 20 percent discount on orders of $100.

Another offer, such as free gifts based on size of the order, would have a different corresponding code.

However, today most direct marketers are multichannel merchants where customer orders are often placed via the company's Web site or at a retail location without a key code. Tracking these responses and correctly linking the results of tests back to a customer database is crucial. The objective is to find ways to match the orders placed on the Web site or in the retail stores that were driven or caused by the specific catalog, offer, or direct mailing that is being tested. Typically, direct marketers use "matchback" rules to most accurately track the results of these tests when key codes are not used. **Matchback** simply refers to the process by which an order response is tracked back to the original source (catalog or offer) from which it was generated. For example, suppose a customer places an online order for a pair of shoes. The direct marketer's task is to determine what specific offer or catalog was responsible for motivating that customer to place the order.

Measuring results involves comparing the response rate generated by the control format versus that of the test format. In direct marketing, the control is normally that direct mail format, package, offer, creative, and so on that has proven time and time again to generate the highest rate of response. When the results of a test shows that a test format or package "beats" or surpasses that of a control format or package, the direct marketer faces a strategic decision point. At this point many direct

Lillian Vernon

| Personalized Gifts | Holidays & Celebrations | Home & Office | Garden & Outdoor | Store & Organize | Bags, Jewelry & Accessories | Shop for kids at **LILLY'S KIDS** |

CHECK OUT OUR BESTSELLERS!
Use Media Code **968830900*** And Get....

| **10% OFF** Any **$65** Order | **15% OFF** Any **$85** Order | **20% OFF** Any **$100** Order |

Embroidered Grandmother Throw
"This is the perfect gift for one perfect Grandmother to receive from another."

Teacher's Canvas Tote
"Great gift for my son's teacher. A quick and concise way to say thanks for all you do."

Wood "Welcome" Sign
"I ordered these as Christmas gifts for several families. I hoped they would be cute. They far exceeded my expectations."

Backseat Car Organizer
"I am impressed with how many toys, books etc. I could fit into it. Easy to install: my 3-year-old can do it by himself."

95-Piece Steel Tool Set
"I love it! My husband uses some of the items as well! I love that the everything inside is pink! It gives it a nice girly touch!"

Silver-Plated Whimsical Key Rings
"Such a great idea and it gives me a chance to talk about my boys when someone compliments my keychain."

FIGURE 10-5   **Lillian Vernon E-mail Offers.**   *Source:* Used with permission of Current USA, Inc., dba Lillian Vernon.

marketers decide to perform additional testing to validate that the new test format is repeatedly more successful in generating a higher response rate than that of the control format prior to determining which format to use for its rollout. Therefore, the validity in measuring test results is crucial to direct marketers.

Let's look at how a direct marketer conducts a creative test. Calico Corners, a high-end retailer of custom draperies, furniture and home accessories, recently conducted a **split test** on a direct mailer. A split test is where two or more samples are taken from the same list, each considered to be representative of the entire list and used for package tests or to test the homogeneity of the list. An A/B split was performed on the prospect database with the A group receiving the control piece presented in Figure 10-6, and the B group receiving the same postcard and offer but an alternative creative design. Both the control and the alternative piece contained a key code to track which piece was responsible for the response and order. The control creative design won, with a response rate that was 11 percent higher than the alternate creative design. This sizable difference in response rate qualified the control creative piece for rollout.

In summary, direct marketers must track responses and measure results carefully to ensure the validity of a test. Direct marketers are also concerned with making sure the samples selected for the control and test groups are selected carefully. This is the topic of the next section.

FIGURE 10-6   Calico Corners "Control" Direct Mail Piece.   *Source:* Used with permission of Calico Corners and MindZoo, LLC. Photo by Kim Kirby, www.jimkirbyphoto.com.

SAMPLES AND ESTIMATIONS

Sampling is a method of choosing observations from which one can predict estimations. In experimentation, without properly selected samples, the resultant estimations and predictions will be invalid. Direct marketers must know the major means of selecting samples from a population, and they need insight into sampling problems and opportunities.

Note that statistical methods, no matter how sophisticated, are not useful for inferring any traits of a larger population if the sample itself is bad. Direct marketing researchers should be able at least to obtain adequate samples from a population, compute sample sizes and confidence intervals, and know what is there and why. They should also understand the key terms presented at the start of this chapter in Figure 10-3.

Random Samples

To ensure that experimental or test and control groups are as nearly alike as possible, direct marketers work to make any differences between the two attributable only to chance. There are a variety of ways to obtain **random samples** from a total population.

- *Simple random samples:* To construct a simple random sample, select each subject randomly from a population from which the preceding selection has been removed. Preprinted tables or computer-generated lists of random numbers help ensure that all members of the population are equally likely to be chosen.
- *Systematic random samples:* Systematic random samples are technically not purely random samples, but, since they require only one pass through a large mailing list, they are the type direct marketers most frequently use. Starting with a random number *n,* the marketer selects every *n*th name until the sample is the size desired as a percentage of the entire population.
- *Stratified random samples:* In stratified random samples, names are drawn in proportion to a particular parameter of a population. For example, the distribution of the sample can be set by age to be proportional to the known age distribution of the population.
- *Cluster samples:* Marketers can select an entire cluster at random to create a cluster sample, such as the entire ZIP code in an *n*th selection of all ZIP codes.
- *Replicated samples:* Replicated samples can be created by taking several independent random samples in turn. For example, a direct marketing researcher might first choose a stratum from among all 50 of the United States, then a stratum of counties within these states, then a stratum of census tracts within the selected counties. The researcher would vary the choices over a period of time.
- *Sequential samples:* For a sequential sample the selection of names is based on progressive data, that is, on prior predictions of an outcome, in much the same way television networks predict election outcomes.

In their quest for randomness, marketers should remember that the arrangement of the list from which they draw their sample could itself bias the selection. Alphabetic arrangement of a list, for example, could result in ethnic concentrations within certain letters that would not be present if names were not alphabetized. A similar problem could occur when a list is geographically arranged so that location differences are concentrated. Most large lists today are arranged in ZIP code sequence, numerically from East Coast to West Coast, and this form of arrangement is probably as conducive as any to *n*th name selection without bias.

Sampling error (that is, lack of randomness) can also arise when not everyone in the population of interest is included, such as when selections are made from a telephone directory that includes neither households without telephones nor those with unlisted numbers. Another instance of sampling error is the inclusion of nonprospects; for instance, a direct marketing researcher would not use a list that includes apartment dwellers to test an offering of lawn furniture. Another form of error, *nonresponse error,* occurs when an individual is included in the sample but for one reason or another is not reached or refuses to respond.

Determining the Sample Size

The proper **sample size** is determined by first looking at two major considerations: (1) the cost of reaching the sample, and (2) the amount of information needed to make an efficient decision, that is, the number of responses that will enable a direct marketer to predict a future response rate within a comfortable limit of certainty. A judgment call can be made about the sample size, such as "test 5,000" or "test 10 percent," or a calculation can be used. The basis for the formula for sample size calculation lies in a determination of probabilities. In the paragraphs that follow, we show all the individual elements in the formula for calculating sample size and then we will put these together into the formula. This formula tells us how many pieces need to be mailed (or calls need to be made, or Web site visits are required, or whatever) to get back a certain number of responses and have a certain degree of confidence in those responses.

The **law of large numbers** ensures that as sample size increases, the distribution of sample means (in this case, response rates) concentrates closer to the true mean of the total population. In other words, the more names in a sample, generally, the closer the response is to the response of the total population. Further, the **central limit theorem** ensures that in a number of random samples taken from a population, the sample means (response rates) tend to be normally distributed. The shape of such a **normal distribution**—the so-called bell-shaped curve—is completely determined by its two parameters: **mean** (average response rate) and **standard deviation** (variance from the mean).

Statistical evaluation helps the direct marketing researcher arrive at conclusions that are reassuring. Having determined a *confidence level* that is satisfactory, as well as an acceptable *limit of error,* the researcher can estimate the *response rate* to calculate an appropriate *sample size.* Or, after the fact, knowing the actual response rate, he or she can calculate the limit of error. All four elements—confidence level, limit of error, expected (or actual) response rate, and sample size—enter into this calculation. We define these terms here.

- *Confidence level:* The **confidence level,** as expressed in our formula, is the number of standard deviations from the mean in a normal distribution; for example, 1.96 standard deviations from the mean contain 95 percent of the area under a normal curve. (Published statistical tables provide standard deviations for confidence levels, i.e., 99 percent, 90 percent, 85 percent.) The expressed level denotes the number of times in 100 attempts that the resultant predictions must be correct. At a confidence level of 95 percent, for example, it can be concluded that 95 times out of 100 attempts, the prediction will be correct.
- *Limit of error:* **Limit of error** describes the number of percentage points by which the researcher is allowed to comfortably miscalculate the actual response rate. In other words, if a 1 percent response is expected, by how much can it be miscalculated and still be in an acceptable (or at least a safe) position? A 20 percent limit of error, for example, assuming a

1 percent response rate, could result in a range of actual response as low as 8/10th of 1 percent to as high as 1.2 percent; that is, 1 percent ± 20 percent of 1 percent.

- ***Expected (actual) response rate:*** The response rate (*expected,* before conduct of an experiment; *actual,* after conduct of an experiment) represents the number of positive responses expressed as a percentage of the total. In terms of the toss of a coin, how often will heads appear? In terms of a direct mailing, how many positive responses will be received? The difference between this positive response and the total quantity mailed describes the percentage of nonresponse, or negative response. If there is 1 percent response, then R (for "response") would equal 0.01 (expressed as a decimal) and 1 minus R (the negative responses) would equal 0.99.
- ***Sample size:*** The determined sample size is the number of observations in our experiment. This is, as example, the number of individual pieces of direct mail sent out in a test from which will be determined, ultimately, the percentage of response and the percentage of nonresponse. The formula for determining sample size is

$$N = \frac{(R)(1 - R)(C)^2}{E^2}$$

where (R) is the frequency of response, a percentage expressed as a decimal; $(1 - R)$ is the frequency of nonresponse, also a percentage expressed as a decimal; (C) is the confidence level, expressed as a number of standard deviations; (E) is the limit of error expressed as a decimal; and (N) is the sample size, the number of pieces to be mailed.

To illustrate the use of the aforementioned formula, one determines the sample size required in terms of mailing pieces when the expected response is 1 percent and the desired limit of error is ±0.2 percent at a confidence level of 95 percent. Thus,

$$R = 1\% \ldots \text{or } 0.01, \text{ expressed as a decimal}$$
$$1 - R = 99\% \ldots \text{or } 0.99, \text{ expressed as a decimal}$$
$$C = 1.96 \text{ standard deviations, if a } 95\% \text{ confidence level is accepted}$$
$$E = 0.2\% \ldots \text{or } 0.002, \text{ expressed as a decimal}$$
$$N = \text{to be determined}$$

Substituting the above values into the formula,

$$N = \frac{(0.01)(0.99)(1.96)^2}{(0.002)^2}$$
$$= \frac{(0.01)(0.99)(3.8416)}{(0.000004)}$$
$$= \frac{0.03803184}{0.000004}$$
$$N = 9{,}508 \text{ pieces to be mailed}$$

Suppose that in the above experiment, 9,508 pieces had been mailed, and the actual response rate turned out to be 1.5 percent, rather than 1 percent. Still, at a 95 percent confidence level, what would be the limit of error if, on the basis of the 1.5 percent response rate predicted from this mailing, further mailings were sent out? The formula for determining limit of error is

$$E = \sqrt{(R)(1 - R)/N} \times C$$

Substituting the new values (with the same notation as before) into this formula and solving for limit of error, there is

$$E = \sqrt{(0.015)(0.985)/9580} \times 1.96$$
$$E = \sqrt{0.000001554} \times 1.96$$
$$E = 0.00124 \times 1.96$$
$$E = 0.00243 \ldots \text{ or, } 0.243\% \text{ limit of error}$$

These two examples illustrate, first, the statistical importance of setting up direct mail experiments in such a manner as to ensure a sample size adequate for meaningful projection of response within acceptable tolerances. Second, they demonstrate the need for accurate determination of the limit of error, the variation that could occur by chance alone and not as a result of significant differences in particular direct marketing efforts. When comparing the response from two diverse market segments, for example, such "error by chance" difference during the evaluation process must be recognized.

In this example, in which the actual response was 1.5 percent and the error limit was calculated to be 0.243 percent, any response from continuation mailings or comparative tests within the range of 1.257 and 1.743 percent would be statistically the same as 1.5 percent, and such variation could have occurred by statistical chance alone at a 95 percent level of confidence.

MEASUREMENT OF DIFFERENCE

Assuming that the direct marketer has properly selected a sample of adequate size and designed and conducted the experiment itself in a valid manner, he or she must also know how to validate the difference between the results of the experiment group and its control group. Only by understanding this can direct marketers decide to change from one promotional strategy to another, from one market segment to another, or to adopt a new product in place of an old one.

Typically, in direct marketing experimentation the mean response to a direct mail solicitation is expressed as the average number of responses for each 1,000 pieces of mail sent out, and attributable to the test (in which a single variable has been injected) in relationship to the control. That variable could be the mailing list used. Or it could be a pricing variance or a product difference. When we compare the test and the control, we must determine whether, in fact, the difference is real, in a statistical sense, or whether it might have occurred through chance alone. The difference in results must be further related to difference in cost, if there is any. In effect, one tests the hypothesis that there is no difference between the test and the control.

Hypothesis Testing

In testing a **hypothesis**—an assertion about the value of the parameter of a variable—the researcher decides, on the basis of observed facts such as the relative response to a test of variation in advertising copy, for example, whether an assumption seems to be valid. The assumption is called the **null hypothesis** and the researcher must state it in such a way that it can be proved wrong. Assuming that the null hypothesis is in fact true, we can determine the probability to assign to an **alternative hypothesis.** Hypotheses are typically stated in negative terms; that is, a null hypothesis (H_0) versus an alternative hypothesis (H_a) in a form such as the following:

H_0: Direct mail response from the test promotion is at or below direct mail response from the control promotion.

H_a: Direct mail response from the test promotion is above direct mail response from the control promotion.

The null hypothesis then states that direct mail response *will not* be better than the control. Measurement sets out to *disprove* this null hypothesis. The probability of this happening might be very small, considering that the experiment involves new and untried copy intended to outperform the control, which presumably is the best copy now available.

In the event the direct marketer decides to *reject the null hypothesis,* it is rejected in favor of the alternative hypothesis. In this instance, if the null hypothesis is rejected, it is because that test response is at or below the control response, it is done in favor of the alternative hypothesis because that test response is significantly better than the control response.

Some results, obviously, are more significant than others. A statistician puts a special interpretation on the word *significant,* associating it with a specific probability, often denoted by the Greek letter alpha (α), which is decided on prior to testing the hypothesis. The researcher might state that the null hypothesis will be rejected only if the result is significant at a level of, say, 0.05 (5 percent). That is, the test result must diverge enough from the control result so that such a result would occur with the probability of 0.05 or less if the hypothesis were true. The statement of a level of significance should be made *prior* to testing the hypothesis to avoid vacillation on the part of the researcher when the actual response is observed.

Types of Errors in Hypothesis Testing

Two types of error can occur in tests of hypotheses. A **Type I error** results when the decision maker rejects the null hypothesis even though it is, in fact, true. In this instance the "wrong" decision allows an action when it should not. The probability of doing this is fixed and equal to α. Note that α determines a critical result so rare that it is preferred to reject the null hypothesis rather than believe that an event that rare actually occurred. Thus, α measures the probability of committing a Type I error.

A **Type II error** occurs when the decision maker accepts the null hypothesis when it is in fact not true. In this instance, the wrong decision is to not do something when something should be done. The probability associated with a Type II error is called beta (β) and it is more difficult to measure than α, prior to conducting an experiment, because it requires a fixed value, other than the one assumed within the null hypothesis, around which confidence intervals associated with an alternative hypothesis can be based.

Although researchers are not as concerned with Type II errors in evaluating the results of an experiment, these can be every bit as expensive in opportunity costs as Type I errors. We usually think of wrong decisions in terms of doing something when we should not, but there is a lost opportunity cost associated with *not* doing something when we should!

This examination of risks should have even the die-hard nonbeliever convinced that probability theory is a way of *measuring risk and assessing uncertainty, not a way of eliminating either!* To make an adequate decision, the direct marketing researcher must sample a population, measure relevant variables (one at a time), compute statistics using these variables, infer something about the probability distributions that exist in the population, and, finally, make a decision based on the chance of incurring either a Type I or Type II error.

Statistical Evaluation of Differences

Frequently, when evaluating the results of an experiment and comparing the response from a test with the response from a control, we need to know whether a difference is (or is not) *statistically significant.* The **chi-square (χ^2) test** is one way to determine such a difference.[1] The null hypothesis offered in making the determination is that there is, in fact, no difference between the response from the test and the response from the control. A statistic χ^2 is computed from the observed samples and compared with a chi-square distribution table that lists probabilities for a theoretical sampling distribution.

The shape of a χ^2 distribution varies according to the number of **degrees of freedom,** defined as the number of observations that are allowed to vary. The number of degrees of freedom is determined by multiplying the number of observations in a row (minus 1) times the number of observations in a column (minus 1), thus, $(r-1)(c-1)$, where r is the number of rows and c is the number of columns. For example, the contingency table in Figure 10-7, expressed as "2 × 2" (and read "2 by 2") would involve just one degree of freedom, $(2-1) \times (2-1) = 1$. A table of this form can be used for evaluating the significance of the difference between a test and its control in an experiment.

The typical chi-square table, found in most statistical textbooks, will show critical values for 30 (or more) degrees of freedom for reference when as many as 30 observations are measured *against one another*. Because direct marketers are urged to test just one variable at a time (i.e., a single test against a single control, only the top row of the table)—that for one degree of freedom—needs to be referenced. Here, then, are the critical values of a chi-square distribution for one degree of freedom along with associated probabilities:

Chi-square critical value of $0.00016 = 0.99$ *probability*; $0.00063 = 0.98$; $0.0039 = 0.95$; $0.16 = 0.90$; $0.064 = 0.80$; $0.15 = 0.70$; $0.46 = 0.50$; $1.64 = 0.20$; $2.71 = 0.10$; $3.84 = 0.05$; $5.41 = 0.02$; $6.64 = 0.01$; $10.83 = 0.001$.

	Test	Control	Totals
Response	A	C	$A + C$
Nonresponse	B	D	$B + D$
Total mailed	$A + B$	$C + D$	$A + B + C + D = N$

The statistic χ^2 is computed as follows:

$$\chi^2 = \frac{N[/(A \times D) - (C \times B)/ -N/2]^2}{(A + B) \times (C + D) \times (A + C) \times (B + D)}$$

Here is a sample calculation:

	Test	Control	Totals
Response	200	100	300
Nonresponse	800	900	1700
Total mailed	1000	1000	2000

$$\chi^2 = \frac{2,000 \times [|180,000 - 80,000| - 1,000]^2}{1,000 \times 1,000 \times 300 \times 1,700}$$

$\chi^2 = 38.4 \ldots$ *which is significant at the* 99 ++ % *level since it exceeds the critical value in the* χ^2 *table for one degree of freedom for a significance level of 0.001, given as 10.83*

FIGURE 10-7 Example of Chi-Square Measurement of Difference in an Experiment between a Test and a Control.

A Priori versus a Posteriori Analysis

A differentiation should be made between the statistical analysis used in setting up an experiment, particularly the choice of sample size, *before the fact,* **a priori,** and the statistical analysis used in evaluating a test for significant differences *after the fact,* **a posteriori.**

In our discussion of sampling earlier, a priori analysis assumes (1) a response level, (2) a confidence level, and (3) an acceptable variation for limit of error to be deemed significant. Based on these three assumptions, sample size can be determined by formula. A posteriori analysis, performed after the test versus control experiment has been conducted, uses the *known* sample size and *known* response level as inputs to a calculation of confidence intervals; that is, the degree of variation or limit of error associated with varying levels of significance. For an $\alpha = 0.05$, there is one set of very broad limits; for an $\alpha = 0.10$, there is a set of different, more narrowly defined limits; for an $\alpha = 0.25$, there is a set of even more narrowly defined limits.

In a priori analysis, the decision maker is asked to use his or her best judgment in arriving at three assumptions: expected response, confidence level, and acceptable limit of error. In a posteriori analysis, having established a confidence level in the a priori setting and having the willingness to live with the choice after the fact, together with known sample size and response level, the limit of error around the known response level becomes a simple mechanical calculation.

Note that a posteriori analysis is possible regardless of the level of response; the analysis can be made even if the actual level achieved differs widely from the level assumed in the a priori analysis. The important point is test results must be read and calculations must be made in relation to what actually occurred, irrespective of what was assumed would occur at the time the test was initiated.

Direct marketers do not, however, enjoy a completely pure laboratory environment; rather, it is a marketplace environment. These two environments differ widely in the degree of control that can be exercised over the exogenous factors affecting the realities of the marketplace environment. A few examples will accentuate this point.

- Does seasonality affect results?
- Is the list used in the continuation mailing to the total population derived from the same group as the test sample?
- How does the environment in which the experiment was conducted compare with that of the continuation, that is, current economic conditions, consumer optimism, and world events? All can be significantly different.
- At what stage is the product in its life cycle; that is, have new models been developed and is there increasing competition?

Put simply, the actual level of response of even a meticulously controlled experiment may not always be projected into the future. Conditions might be different. Thus, whereas the relationship between a test and its control may be the same, that is, one is still better than the other, the entire level of response for both might be either higher or lower than that originally experienced.

STRUCTURING AND EVALUATING AN EXPERIMENT

We conduct an experiment to make an adequate decision. To do this, the direct marketing researcher must

- sample a population,
- measure relevant variables, ideally one at a time,
- compute statistics using these measurements,

- infer something about the probability distributions that exist in the population,
- make a decision mindful of the chance of incurring a Type I error (when the decision maker rejects the null hypothesis even though it is true) or a Type II error (when the decision maker accepts the null hypothesis when it is *not* true).

Let's say that a direct marketing researcher wants to test a new promotion strategy against his or her present strategy, to be offered to the control group in the experiment. Past experience indicates that he or she can expect a 2 percent response rate from the present promotion.

Here is a framework for implementation of the experiment:

1. State the hypothesis.
2. Develop, by a priori analysis, the assumptions required and compute the appropriate sample size.
3. Structure and perform the experiment.
4. Develop, by a posteriori analysis, statistics for judging hypothesis validity.
5. Make the decision.

This procedure sounds simple and appears to be reasonable. Let's follow it step by step.

Step 1 State the Hypothesis. The null hypothesis is

- H_0: Direct mail response from the test promotion is at or below direct mail response from the control promotion.

Although it is not necessary to state an alternative hypothesis at this stage, doing so could imply that he or she is hoping to reject the null hypothesis in favor of the alternative, that is, the test promotion would be better than the control, so that

- H_a: Direct mail response from the test promotion is above direct mail response from the control promotion.

Step 2 A Priori Analysis. The response level of 2 percent is the first of three assumptions. The second assumption is the significance level, which, when $\alpha = 0.05$, describes a confidence level of 95 percent. (The confidence level is equal to 1.0 minus α, thus $1.0 - 0.05 = 0.95$, or 95 percent.) The final assumption relates to limit of error or variation around the mean or, more descriptively, the error limit we wish to maintain around the assumed level of response. In this example, we will assume 15 percent. Having established figures for our three assumptions, 2 percent response, 95 percent confidence level, and 15 percent limit of error, we can use the formula given earlier in this chapter to establish the sample size. The three assumptions and resultant sample size are summarized in Figure 10-8, which shows the effect of the 15-percent error limit. At a 95 percent confidence level, any response below 2.3 percent would not be better than a control response (as assumed) of 2.0 percent.

Step 3 Structure of the Test. Having determined (in the manner demonstrated earlier in this chapter) an objective sample size of 8,365 pieces to be mailed for the control and a comparable volume for the test promotion and having obtained the sample in a valid manner, he or she conducts the experiment through release of the test mailing versus the control mailing.

Step 4 A Posteriori Analysis. When all results are in, the direct marketing research examines the response from both the test and the control promotions. One evaluation procedure for determining whether an observed difference is (or is not) statistically significant is the chi-square (χ^2) test, as demonstrated earlier in this chapter.

Step 5 Make the Decision. The decision to accept or reject the promotion tested in the experiment should be clear-cut, based on the a posteriori analysis.

Expected (Assumed) Response Rate: 2%, 20/M pieces mailed.

Significance Level (α): .05

Confidence Level ($1.0 - \alpha$): 95%

Limits of Error:

Percent Response/M Pieces Mailed

+15% 20/M + 3/M = 23/M (2.3%)

−15% 20/M − 3/M = 17/M (1.7%)

Sample Size: 8,365 mailing pieces (determined separately)

FIGURE 10-8   A Priori Assumptions and Sample-Size Determination.

OPPORTUNITIES FOR EXPERIMENTATION

Under rigidly controlled conditions, direct marketing offers a great deal of opportunity for experimentation. This opportunity provides an environment susceptible to measurement and accountability. The availability of lists and data about these lists also provide populations from which scientifically determined samples can be drawn to properly conduct experiments: within lists or within segments of them. The profiling of these lists also makes it possible to further describe market segments for prospecting whether the medium is direct mail, magazines, or newspapers; TV or radio; or phone or Web. Within such list refinements, described as market segments, one can test product and price variations and the multitude of variables that compose promotional strategies: copy, art, graphics, color, format, and the offer itself. Individual components of ads or the effort itself, such as a completely new direct mail package, can also be tested. With this limitless array of possibilities, however, it is exceedingly important, as noted earlier, to *test only the important things and test them adequately.*

Direct marketers favor testing over survey research because they can translate many of the techniques used to ask prospects whether they *intend to buy* into direct marketing offers actually *asking them to buy.* One happy compromise of survey research with experimental research, used to test a new product not yet available in the marketplace, is called **dry testing.** Those who use the dry-testing technique must be meticulously careful not to misrepresent the offering. Payment in advance should not be requested and remittances, if received, should be returned promptly; those who respond should receive first priority if and when the product ordered becomes a reality.

Research, utilizing the tools and techniques of both survey and experimentation as highlighted in this chapter, is a key requirement of the science of direct marketing. While those steeped in the creativity of the arts, who put their emphasis on promotion, often shy away from the rigors of numbers, a healthy respect for statistics is essential to the professional direct marketer. That is why a course in basic statistics must be a prerequisite to a basic course in direct marketing.

Summary

Direct marketing is research-oriented and is especially susceptible to the tools and techniques of experimentation. Such experimentation is called testing by practitioners and usually measures the impact of changing a variable within product, price, place, or promotion. Although research is concerned with fact finding and information gathering, it has as its objective problem solving or action recommending. Research enables the collection of data, from which information can be derived. Data are categorized as *secondary,* collected originally for another purpose, and *primary,* collected specifically for the research need. Collection of primary data involves either survey or experimentation, the latter most often being used in testing by direct marketers. Survey research observes various activities as they naturally arise in the environment whereas experimentation involves the manipulation of one or more independent variables to determine their influence on an outcome, which is the dependent variable.

Valid experiments require controls and randomized samples. In designing experiments it is important to understand the methods for obtaining samples and determining sample sizes. Otherwise, resultant estimations and predictions will not be helpful. Samples may be obtained in many ways. Determination of sample size is concerned with confidence level, error limit, and expected (or actual) percent of response. Sample size and error limit can be calculated statistically, with tables readily available for such determination. Direct marketers must evaluate statistically significant differences in observed responses between test and control. The chi-square distribution describes one statistical tool for analyzing the significance of such differences.

Experiments must be designed and sampling must be controlled so that results are measurable and accountable. Hypothesis testing enables such measurement. It is important to schedule experiments carefully and record results utilizing key codes to identify sources of response for accurate evaluation.

Key Terms

quantitative *266*
qualitative *266*
survey *269*
experiment *269*
test *269*
sampling errors *269*
secondary data *270*
primary data *270*
focus group interview *273*
independent variables *273*
dependent variables *273*
testing *273*
control group *274*

random assignment *274*
key codes *275*
matchback *275*
split test *277*
sampling *278*
random samples *278*
sample size *279*
law of large numbers *279*
central limit theorem *279*
normal distribution *279*
mean *279*
standard deviation *279*
confidence level *279*

limit of error *279*
hypothesis *281*
null hypothesis *281*
alternative hypothesis *281*
Type I error *282*
Type II error *282*
chi-square (χ^2) test *282*
degrees of freedom *283*
a priori *284*
a posteriori *284*
dry testing *286*

Review Questions

1. Why might a survey of buying expectations not be a valid indication of actual behavior in the marketplace?
2. Distinguish between surveys and experiments. Which is more used by direct marketers and why?
3. Where might a direct marketer obtain secondary data about
   a. age distribution of a population?
   b. number of corrugated carton manufacturers in a city?
   c. number of households in a ZIP code area?
   d. retail sales of shopping goods in a county?
4. What are the advantages and disadvantages of seeking primary data by each of these survey methods?
   a. personal interview
   b. telephone interview
   c. mail questionnaire
   d. Web site registration
   e. observation
5. Give examples of some questions to which a direct marketer might seek answers through experimentation.

6. What is the ideal way for a direct marketer to structure an experiment?
7. Why is the determination of a proper sample size important in an experiment? What factors must marketers consider in setting sample size?
8. In testing a hypothesis, is a Type I or Type II error more serious? That is, are there greater consequences in (I) "doing something when you shouldn't," or (II) "not doing something when you should?"
9. Why is it important in measuring an experiment that the researcher determine the statistical significance level of observed differences?
10. Does the direct marketing researcher have absolute and complete control over an experiment? Discuss possible situations in which the researcher may not.
11. Why should direct marketers confine experimentation to only those tests that have high consequences?

Exercise

Congratulations! You have just been hired as an associate for a well-known advertising agency. Your first task is to assist a client in determining which of the four direct mail packages they have been using is the most productive.

Structure a test to investigate the two different offers the firm has been using along with the four different direct mail formats.

CASE

The American Heart Association

Overview

Particularly in the sale of intangible services and especially in fundraising, the direct marketer needs a keen awareness of what motivates response. Donors to worthy causes often contribute for reasons of their own, and these reasons may have nothing to do with the cause itself. The potential benefits received by such donors are not always readily apparent, which poses a particular challenge to the direct marketer engaged in fundraising.

This case study presents a variety of different copy approaches featured on several mailing envelopes, with each experimentally control-tested against the others. Certain of these copy approaches describe benefits whereas others use persuasion. All are designed to get attention. Discussion should develop the rationale for each copy approach and why it was featured before considering the relative response results. Evaluating the results reported in the case history suggests why the "best" package provided the highest response and why others were "good" or "poor."

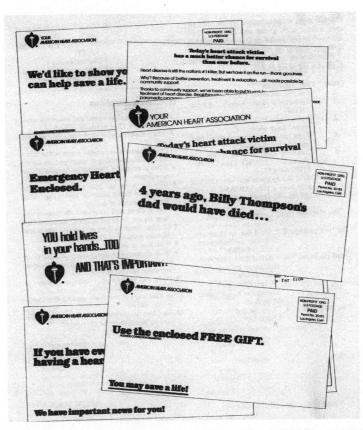

FIGURE 10-9   Copy Approaches Tested by the American Heart Association.   *Source:* Freeman G. Gosden Jr., President of Smith-Hemmings-Gosden, Direct Response Advertising, El Monte, California.

Case

The American Heart Association needed to raise more funds for its health improvement activities at a lower cost. Direct mail had historically been the most important medium for the organization's fundraising and an effort was to be made to improve on current response.[2]

Several new copy approaches were developed. Through scientific experimentation involving test mailings in excess of 200,000 pieces and confirmation with another 200,000 pieces, these copy approaches were tested against each other and against the "control" currently being used. With experimentation, of course, it is necessary to have all aspects of the mailing remain the same except for one variable within each test segment. In this way the change in response can be attributed to change in that variable.

The American Heart Association decided to test six copy approaches in the form of teasers displayed on the outside of the mailing envelope. These six envelope teasers would be tested against each other and also against the control, the envelope that the fundraiser had been using successfully in the past, but which had no teaser at all.

These seven envelope panels (six tests and one control, visualized in Figure 10-9), included a letter, contribution form, and reply envelope enclosed in each mailing envelope. These forms were essentially the same for all seven packages except for the beginning of the letter, which emphasized the teaser copy approach that was featured on the outside mailing envelope.

The American Heart Association sent solicitation mailings to their current donors as well as "cold" prospects, those who had not given a contribution before. The response from each group and for each copy approach was tabulated separately through key coding appearing on the contribution form.

These copy approaches were tested:

Effort	Copy Approach
1	Use the enclosed FREE GIFT.
2	Emergency Heart Attack Card Enclosed.
3	4 years ago Billy Thompson's dad would have died . . .
4	If you have ever worried about having a heart attack . . .
5	You hold lives in your hands . . . TODAY . . . AND THAT'S IMPORTANT!
6	We'd like to show you how you can help save a life. YOURS.
7	(Control) No teaser copy.

The response results were these:

The best package:	6	We'd like to show you how you can help save a life. YOURS.
Good packages:	4	If you have ever worried about having a heart attack . . .
	3	4 years ago Billy Thompson's dad would have died . . .
Poor packages:	1	Use the enclosed FREE GIFT.
	5	You hold lives in your hands . . . TODAY . . . AND THAT'S IMPORTANT!
	7	No teaser copy.
	2	Emergency Heart Attack Card Enclosed.

Source: This case was originally developed by Freeman F. Gosden, Jr., President of Smith-Hemmings-Gosden, Direct Response Advertising, El Monte, California, who conducted the test from which it was derived.

Case Discussion Questions

1. Review the envelope teaser copy shown in Figure 10-9 and explain the rationale for each approach. Keep in mind, each envelope teaser was created to get attention.

2. Based on the test results, the best package was no. 6, "We'd like to show you how you can help save a life. YOURS." Do you personally agree with the test results? Why or why not?

3. Create three additional envelope copy teasers that could be tested against the best package. What is the rationale behind each of your newly created teasers? Why do you think each would be effective?

Notes

1. Other statistical techniques used for measuring significant differences include ANOVA (analysis of variance, the F-test), the t-test (for sample sizes through 30), and the Z-test (for sample sizes larger than 30).

2. This case was originally developed by Freeman F. Gosden Jr., President of Smith-Hemmings-Gosden, Direct Response Advertising, El Monte, California, who conducted the test from which it was derived.

11

...

Understanding the Industry's Environmental, Ethical, and Legal Issues

Opening Vignette: Snow and Associates

Have you ever wondered about the drug your doctor prescribed to you or a loved one? Do you ever wish you could talk to someone who has a similar condition? Have you ever done research on a condition you or a loved one has in advance of a doctor's visit so you can be better prepared to ask the right questions? If you've answered "yes" to any of these questions, you are among the hundreds of millions of people across the nation who have helped to make direct-to-patient and direct-to-consumer (DTP/DTC) pharmaceutical and biotechnology marketing a burgeoning endeavor. While most consumers desire more information on the products they take or have been prescribed, the U.S. Food and Drug Administration (FDA) closely regulates this type of communication.

DTP/DTC pharmaceutical advertising is considered to be any marketing communication for prescription drugs that directly target the final consumer or individual patient, as opposed to promotions that target the physicians who write prescriptions. DTP/DTC marketing is currently allowed only in the United States and New Zealand. As a result, the pharmaceutical industry is one of the most highly regulated of all industries. The FDA Center for Drug Evaluation and Research has a division dedicated to establishing and policing guidelines for all pharmaceutical marketing communications. The mission of the Division of Drug Marketing, Advertising, and Communications (DDMAC) is to protect the public health by assuring prescription drug information is truthful, balanced, and accurately communicated.[1] DDMAC has a team of reviewers who are responsible for reviewing prescription drug advertising and promotional drug labeling to ensure that the information contained in those promotional materials is not false or misleading. DDMAC goes beyond the monitoring of DTP/DTC pharmaceutical print and broadcast advertisements; they also travel to major medical meetings and pharmaceutical conventions to monitor promotional exhibits and activities.

Given the stringent federal regulations and scrutiny imposed on the direct marketing of pharmaceutical products, innovation is a prerequisite for success in this space. One company that has found a way to innovate and create value for clients is Snow and Associates, a DTP and word-of-mouth health care marketing agency. Brenda Snow, pictured in Figure 11-1, founded Snow and Associates in 2001 and developed its proprietary Patient Ambassador program after being diagnosed with multiple sclerosis and becoming frustrated at how little was being done to help educate, empower, and engage people like herself. The company identifies, develops, trains, and manages Patient Ambassadors, or people with a medical condition who have undergone legal, regulatory, and storytelling training and help provide a human face to the brands they represent. Patient Ambassadors help raise awareness of treatment options and educate others about therapy

FIGURE 11-1   Brenda Snow, Snow and Associates Founder.

choices by sharing their personal stories, thereby becoming a resource for other patients with the same condition under the guidelines established by the FDA. This powerful and persuasive personal communication has proven to be a success and has helped Snow and Associates and its sister agencies become one of the largest independently owned health care marketing agencies in the world in less than three years.

Snow and Associates employ a variety of direct marketing strategies in the execution of tactics to support clients including outbound and inbound telephone marketing, e-mail marketing, Internet marketing, and direct mail to reach target audiences. Because of the highly regulated nature of the industry, all of the company's activities come under tough scrutiny from regulatory, legal, and medical reviewers who closely monitor all of these activities to ensure compliance. Snow and Associates uses direct marketing tactics to interact with its prospective Patient Ambassadors, as well as to promote its Local Patient Outreach Programs (LPOP). LPOPs are targeted educational symposia for patients, caregivers, family members, and friends to learn about a specific condition and possible treatments for that condition. At these events, a Patient Ambassador shares his or her personal story of their trials and tribulations of living with a chronic medical condition with the event attendees. As you would expect, marketing strategies for an LPOP must be highly targeted; thus direct and interactive marketing is highly effective. Snow & Associates is a great example of a company that has found a way to be highly successful by effectively employing myriad direct and interactive marketing strategies and tactics within the constraints of a strict regulatory environment, which is the topic of this chapter.

The regulatory environment of direct marketing includes the two very important areas of ethical and legal issues. **Ethics** are the moral principles of conduct governing the behavior of an individual or a group. **Morals** are often described in terms of good or bad. To be *ethical* in marketing means to conform to the accepted professional standards of conduct. However, you might ask, what exactly are the "accepted professional standards of conduct"?

This chapter discusses ethics and the ethical behavior expected of direct marketers as set forth by the Direct Marketing Association (DMA) along with the law as it pertains to direct marketing activities. The legal regulations affecting direct marketing activities on the federal, state, and local levels primarily deal with three broad legal issues: intellectual property, security, and privacy. We detail the legal issues in each of these three areas in this chapter, after an overview of the ethical aspects of direct marketing.

ENVIRONMENTAL ISSUES

Protecting the environment is an important issue for direct marketers. The DMAs around the world are taking a lead role in shaping the industry by partnering with other organizations to create environmental standards. The UK DMA, for instance, has developed an alliance of like-minded member companies to partner with BSI British Standards to create the first standard for environmental performance in the field of direct marketing.[2] The U.S. DMA has taken a lead on this issue, starting in 2005 with the formation of a Committee on Environment & Social Responsibility (CESR) comprised of DMA member organizations. In January 2007, DMA launched an Environmental Planning Tool & Policy Generator (www.the-dma.org/envgen). In May 2007, DMA board of directors passed an Environmental Resolution. That same month, the DMA also announced a nationwide "Recycle Please" campaign. For more information on these major milestones, please visit DMA's Environmental Resource Center at www.the-dam.org/environment. The following section provides an overview of the key environmental issues.

The DMA's Environmental Resolution and "Green 15" Program

The U.S. DMA has taken a stance on protecting the environment by promulgating greener marketing practices with its May 2007 Environmental Resolution. The main objectives of this new initiative include the following:

1. Offering notice and choice to mail recipients, and implementing effective list hygiene and targeting strategies into marketing practices.
2. Questioning paper suppliers where the paper comes from, to protect forests and to ensure the wood was harvested legally.
3. Reviewing direct mail and direct marketing pieces, testing and downsizing where appropriate.
4. Encouraging packaging suppliers to submit alternate solutions for environmentally preferable packaging.
5. Purchasing office papers, packaging, and packaging materials made from recycled materials with postconsumer content.

The DMA has also created a nationwide public education campaign called "Recycle Please" that asks all DMA members to display prominently the "Recycle Please" logo, shown in Figure 11-2, in their catalogs and direct mail pieces to encourage consumers to recycle them after reading. The DMA coordinated with the Envelope Manufacturers Association and the Magazine Publishers of America, and launched this campaign in 2007.[3] The DMA hopes this campaign will overcome the lack of public awareness that catalogs and mixed paper can be recycled. The other objective of this campaign is to improve the overall recycling/recovery rate of used catalogs and direct mail in the United States. Increasing recycling and recover activity benefits our envirnoment by

- making efficient use of raw material,
- reducing the amount of new fiber that must be obtained from wood to make new paper products,
- conserving valuable global resources,
- decreasing landfill waste, and
- reducing greenhouse gas emissions from incinerators and landfills.[4]

FIGURE 11-2 The DMA "Recycle Please" Logo. *Source:* Used with permission of the Direct Marketing Association.

Paper Procurement & Use

1. Encourage your paper suppliers to increase wood purchases from recognized forest certification programs.
2. Require your paper suppliers to commit to implementing sustainable forestry practices that protect forest ecosystems and biodiversity as well as provide the wood and paper products that meet industry needs.
3. Ask your paper suppliers where your paper comes from before buying it with the intent of not sourcing paper from unsustainable or illegally managed forests.
4. Require your paper suppliers to document that they do not produce or sell paper from illegally harvested or stolen wood.
5. Evaluate the paper you use for marketing pieces, product packaging and internal consumption to identify opportunities for increased environmental attributes.

List Hygiene & Data Management

6. Comply with DMA Guidelines for list management, including: Maintaining in-house do-not-market lists for prospects and customers who do not wish to receive future solicitations from you. Using the Mail Preference Service (MPS) monthly for consumer prospect mail. Providing existing and prospective customers with notice of an opportunity to modify or eliminate direct mail solicitations from your organization in every commercial solicitation.
7. Maintain "clean" mailing lists by using USPS or commercial equivalent files where applicable for: ZIP Code correction; address standardization; change of address, address element correction, delivery sequence file and/or address correction requested.
8. Apply predictive models and/or Recency-Frequency-Monetary (RFM) segmentation where appropriate.

Mail Design & Production

9. Review your direct mail and printed marketing pieces, and test downsized pieces when and where appropriate.
10. Test and use production methods that reduce print order overruns, waste allowances and in-process waste.

Packaging

11. Encourage packaging suppliers to submit alternate solutions for environmentally preferable packaging, in addition to quoting prices on approved or existing specifications.

Recycling & Pollution Reduction

12. Purchase office papers, packing and packaging materials made from recycled materials with post-consumer content where appropriate.
13. Integrate use of electronic communications (email, Web and intranets) for external and internal communications.
14. Ensure that all environmental labeling is clear, honest and complete, so that consumers and business customers may know the exact nature of what your organization is doing.
15. Participate in DMA's "Recycle Please" campaign and/or in another recycling campaign and/or demonstrate that your company or organization has in place a program to encourage recycling in your workplace and/or your community.

FIGURE 11-3   The DMA Green 15: Benchmarking Environmental Progress Business Practices.
Source: Used with permission of the Direct Marketing Association.

The DMA enacted a resolution calling on members to implement and benchmark a set of 15 business practices called "The Green 15."[5] These practices address the areas of paper procurement and use; list hygiene and data management; mail design and production; packaging; and recycling and pollution reduction. Figure 11-3 provides an overview of the Green 15. In summary, the DMA is making a concerted effort to move its members along the continuum of ongoing environmental improvement. These new standards are a part of its commitment to corporate responsibility and its efforts to promote sustainable and ethical business practices, which is the topic of the next section.

ETHICS OF DIRECT MARKETING

A different kind of e-business is receiving an increasing amount of attention from the direct marketing community. In this case, the "e" doesn't stand for *electronic,* it stands for *ethics,* and direct marketers are paying close attention. Ethics is concerned with morality: the rightness and wrongness of individual actions or deeds. As former Supreme Court Justice Potter Stewart once said, "Ethics is knowing the difference between what you have a right to do and what is the right thing to do." A **code of ethics** is a set of guidelines for making ethical decisions.

The DMA's Guidelines for Ethical Business Practice

The DMA has established a detailed code of ethics for direct marketers. These guidelines are intended to provide individuals and organizations in direct marketing in all media with generally accepted principles of conduct. These are self-regulatory measures as opposed to governmental mandates. Visit www.dmaresponsibility.org/Guidelines to obtain updated versions of these guidelines. Figure 11-4 provides an overview of DMA's guidelines for ethical business practice.

The Terms of the Offer
Honesty and Clarity of Offer - Article #1
Accuracy and Consistency - Article #2
Clarity of Representations - Article #3
Actual Conditions - Article #4
Disparagement - Article #5
Decency - Article #6
Photographs and Artwork - Article #7
Disclosure of Sponsor and Intent - Article #8
Accessibility - Article #9
Solicitation in the Guise of an Invoice or Governmental Notification - Article #10
Postage, Shipping, or Handling - Article #11

Advance Consent Marketing
Article #12

Marketing to Children
Marketing to Children - Article #13
Parental Responsibility and Choice - Article #14
Information from or about Children - Article #15
Marketing Online to Children Under 13 Years of Age - Article #16

Special Offers and Claims
Use of the Word "Free" and Other Similar Representations - Article #17
Price Comparisons - Article #18
Guarantees - Article #19
Use of Test or Survey Data - Article #20
Testimonials and Endorsements - Article #21

FIGURE 11-4   Direct Marketing Association's Guidelines for Ethical Business Practice. *Source:* Used with permission of the Direct Marketing Association.

Note: The above is an overview of the articles that are addressed in each area; however, to receive a complete DMA *Ethical Business Practice* guide, contact the Direct Marketing Association at www.the-dma.org or call (212) 768-7277.

Sweepstakes
Use of the Term "Sweepstakes" - Article #22
No Purchase Option - Article #23
Chances of Winning - Article #24
Prizes - Article #25
Premiums - Article #26
Disclosure of Rules - Article #27

Fulfillment
Unordered Merchandise or Service - Article #28
Product Availability and Shipment - Article #29
Dry Testing - Article #30

Collection, Use, and Maintenance of Marketing Data
Collection, Use, and Transfer of Personally Identifiable Data - Article #31
Personal Data - Article #32
Collection, Use, and Transfer of Health Related Data - Article #33
Promotion of Marketing Lists - Article #34
Marketing List Usage - Article #35
Responsibilities of Database Compilers – Article #36
Information Security - Article #37

Online Marketing
Online Information - Article #38
Commercial Solicitations Online - Article #39
E-Mail Authentication – Article #40
Use of Software or Other Similar Technology Installed on a Computer or Similar Device – Article #41
Online Referral Marketing - Article #42
E-Mail Appending to Consumer Records - Article #43

Telephone Marketing
Reasonable Hours - Article #44
Taping of Conversations - Article #45
Restricted Contacts - Article #46
Caller-ID/Automatic Number Identification Requirements – Article #47
Use of Automated Dialing Equipment - Article #48
Use of Prerecorded Voice Messaging - Article #49
Use of Telephone Facsimile Machines - Article #50
Promotions for Response by Toll-Free and
Pay-Per-Call Numbers - Article #51
Disclosure and Tactics - Article #52

Fundraising
Article #53

Laws, Codes, and Regulations
Article #54

FIGURE 11-4   **(continued)**

The DMA Corporate Responsibility Department

In addition to providing guidelines for ethical business practices, the DMA sponsors several activities in its Corporate Responsibility Department. The Mail Preference Service (MPS) offers consumers assistance in decreasing the volume of national advertising mail they receive at home.

The Telephone Preference Service (TPS) offers consumers assistance in decreasing the number of national phone calls received at home. (TPS is now offered to consumers only in the states of Pennsylvania and Wyoming; most consumers are referred to the federal Do Not Call registry operated by the Federal Trade Commission.) The E-Mail Preference Service (EMPS) is designed to assist consumers in decreasing the number of unsolicited e-mail offers received. In essence, the DMA supports a consumer's right to choose the channel by which he or she would prefer to shop. The DMA's consumer page for registering with the Preference Services is www.DMAChoice.org. The DMA also publishes a variety of publications designed to assist direct marketers in complying with federal and state regulations. Visit the DMA Web site at www.the-dma.org to obtain a list of such publications and information sources. The DMA has established both the Guidelines for Ethical Business Practice and an office of corporate responsibility to assist direct marketers in developing and maintaining consumer relationships that are based on fair and ethical principles. With these ethical guidelines, the DMA is encouraging all direct marketers to act in a morally correct business manner and to safeguard basic consumer rights.

BASIC CONSUMER RIGHTS

Consumers possess the following basic human rights: (1) the right to safety, (2) the right to be informed, (3) the right to selection, (4) the right to confidentiality, and (5) the right to privacy.[6] Direct marketers should respect and safeguard these rights. Let's look at each.

The Right to Safety

The **right to safety** allows consumers to be safe from both physical and psychological harm. They cannot be harassed or made to feel bad if, for example, they declined a phone request to purchase a product or service. These circumstances may cause the consumer to experience undue stress.

The Right to Information

The **right to information** includes the consumer's right to receive any and all pertinent or requested information. This includes the right to be informed about all stages of the direct marketing process. It is an obligation of direct marketers to fully disclose what they intend to do with the consumer's name and address once it is put onto a mailing list. In addition, direct marketers should provide the consumer with an explanation of why they collect information about consumers and their lifestyles.

The Right to Selection

The **right to selection** includes a consumer's right to choose or make decisions about his or her buying behavior. In other words, the consumer can accept or reject any offer from a direct marketer or a telemarketer, be it a request to purchase a product or service, subscribe to a magazine, attend a meeting, donate to a charitable organization, or vote for a political candidate. Consumers cannot be made to feel forced into taking an action against their wishes.

The Right to Confidentiality

The **right to confidentiality** is a consumer's right to specify to a given company that information they freely provide should not be shared. Like information disclosed in a physician–patient or attorney–client relationship, information a consumer provides to a direct marketing organization with expressed confidentiality must not be shared. Savvy direct marketers know that to be successful, they must build long-term relationships with their customers based on trust. This trust must not be betrayed. Direct marketers can uphold the consumer's right to confidentiality by developing proper security measures (electronic watermarks, firewalls, digital signatures, authentication, data integrity, encryption, etc.) to protect the security of the proprietary data the direct marketer has promised to safeguard.

Suppose a nonprofit organization specifically stated in its printed materials that it will not share the names of donors with other charitable organizations, and then it turns around and rents its donor lists! This is unethical and constitutes a breach of confidentiality.

The Right to Privacy

The final basic consumer right, the right to privacy, is probably the most noteworthy consumer right affecting direct marketers. The **right to privacy** has been defined as the ability of an individual to control the access others have to personal information. Because of the heightened awareness and controversy over the matter, along with the legal ramifications of the consumer's right to privacy, we discuss privacy issues later in the chapter in more detail than the other four basic consumer rights.

LEGISLATIVE ISSUES

The three primary legislative areas designed to safeguard consumer rights are intellectual property, security, and privacy.

Intellectual Property

Intellectual property is defined as products of the mind or ideas.[7] Some examples include books, music, computer software, designs, and technological know-how. The protection of intellectual property afforded by copyrights, patents, trademarks, and databases is the province of several governmental agencies. Under copyright laws, a copyright owner has the exclusive right to distribute copies of the protected work. Thus, third parties are not permitted to sell, rent, transfer, or otherwise distribute copies of the work without the express permission of the copyright owner. Several channels currently exist for businesses to prevent unauthorized usage of protected material. The American Intellectual Property Law Association (AIPLA) is a 17,000-member, national bar association constituted primarily of intellectual property lawyers in private and corporate practice, government service, and the academic community.[8] The AIPLA is one of the organizations available to assist direct marketers in protecting intellectual property.

Given the freedom of the Internet, protection of trademarks has recently become even more difficult. The Internet's focus on visual advertisements will increase the likelihood of a conflict over trademark rights as more company logos, slogans, brand names, and trademarks are appearing in Web sites. Therefore, this area of intellectual property protection must also be one of the top concerns for direct marketers.

With the introduction of faster computer applications and hard drives with larger capacity for data storage, a new kind of intellectual property has emerged—a database. Data collection, both online and offline, has soared in the past decade. However, intellectual property protection of an organization's database is a volatile area. Businesses are being caught between the threats of unauthorized access by hackers (which we discuss with regard to security in the next section), requirements to disclose certain data collected to law enforcement agencies, and consumer privacy concerns about data collection (which we discuss later in the privacy section).

Security

In addition to creating and storing databases, companies must also secure their databases from unauthorized access and outside damage. Failure to do so may cause the direct marketer much embarrassment, pain, and potential liability for breaches in security. Although technology exists to provide security via password controls and firewalls, these are not completely dependable, and security breaches may still occur.

For example, Carmichael Lynch, a public relations and advertising firm, accidentally published its administration password on its Web site. The slip-up went undetected for six months. During that time, unauthorized visitors could have accessed e-mail addresses and passwords for almost 12,000 people who had just registered on the American Standard Web site, or the names, addresses, and vehicle information of 75,000 luxury car and SUV owners.[9]

In another recent mishap, publishing giant Ziff-Davis Media suffered a security lapse that exposed the personal data of thousands of magazine subscribers. In restitution, the company agreed to pay $100,000 to the New York State Department of Law and $500 each to the 50 customers whose credit card information had been disclosed.[10]

In response to these types of incidents, a California law known as SB 1386 became the first state law to address security breaches. This law requires government agencies, businesses, and anyone else who stores personal information to notify the California resident when the data have been accessed. The purpose of SB 1386 is to give California residents adequate time to check their credit ratings and protect themselves against identity theft.[11]

Privacy

Consumers are more concerned about privacy today than ever before. However, privacy legislation has existed for a long time. Let's review the history of this important legislation.

PRIVACY LEGISLATION

Privacy legislation actually began over a century ago in 1890 when Samuel Warren and Justice Brandeis wrote a law review article advocating that a person should be protected from having personal matters reported by the press for commercial reasons. That marked the beginning of what many know today as a consumer's right to privacy. In 1950, laws protected citizens from allowing public organizations to intrude on their private matters. However, these laws did not protect consumers against a private organization's use of personal information. Still, it wasn't until recent years that privacy issues became increasingly visible.

From the explosion of credit cards to the advent of personal computers to the new marketing realities in cyberspace today, the process of direct marketing has attained new heights of marketing success. With this phenomenal success, businesses have also faced scrutiny on numerous aspects of the privacy issue. Whatever the root, the concern over information privacy has been going on for decades. Back in the late 1970s, prior to most technological advances, the following appeared in a newspaper:[12]

> They know about you. They know how old you are.
> They know if you have children. They know about your job.
> They know how much money you make, what kind of car you drive,
> what sort of house you live in and whether you are likely to prefer paté
> de foie gras and champagne or hot dogs and a cold beer.

They know all this and much, much more.
And you know how?
They know your name.
What they have done with it is very simple:
they have added it to a mailing list.

Though it was an exaggeration (at the time), this excerpt is evidence of a widely held concern that a list is a conduit through which personal information is transferred from one direct marketer to another. Although this may be true, as you should realize from the material contained in Chapters 2 and 3, to a direct marketer, a list is an instrument for describing a market segment. Market segments enable direct marketers to target appropriate promotional offers to consumers, thus reducing the amount of irrelevant marketing communication each consumer receives. This is good for both direct marketers and consumers. Information technology has made it possible for marketers to design promotional campaigns directed at different segments of prospective and current customers. From a marketing and customer service perspective, the purpose of gathering consumer information is to achieve greater selectivity and to make direct response advertising more relevant to the recipient. The use of personal information enables marketers to develop closer relationships with customers that foster brand loyalty and better customer service. However, regardless of the noble purpose information serves for direct marketers, privacy issues have now become legal matters.

Marketers have always had an interest in knowing consumer information, dating back to the days of corner "mom and pop" stores when everyone knew everyone else and their families and their business. Today is no different. Marketers still want to know about their customers to serve them better. Technology makes it easier to do that. With the swipe of a customer loyalty card, consumers receive discounts on purchases or earn bonus points toward free gifts while retailers download information about customer purchasing preferences and habits. From there, with a few clicks of the mouse or strokes on the keyboard, the purchase information can be shared with any number of interested parties—for a fee. Technology has made direct marketing database activities easier and more efficient. However, before direct marketers start thinking beyond this, they have to realize that along with advances in technology come additional legislative regulations. Perhaps the best-known legislation regarding privacy has come from the Privacy Protection Study Commission.

Privacy Protection Study Commission

The concern of the U.S. consumer and Congress over the broad issue of privacy, including the subject of mailing lists and databases, culminated in the **Privacy Act of 1974.** This act established the Privacy Protection Study Commission to determine whether the various restrictions on what the federal government could do with personal information, as provided in the Privacy Act, should also be applied to the private sector. Significantly for direct marketers, Section V (c), B (i) of the act directed the commission to report to the president and Congress on whether an organization engaged in interstate commerce should be required to remove from its mailing list the name of an individual who does not want to be on it.

In July 1977, after months of hearing testimony and studying the issues, the commission issued its 618-page *Report from the Privacy Protection Study Commission*. Chapter 4 of this report was devoted entirely to the subject of mailing lists. The commission basically concluded that the appearance of an individual's name on a mailing list, so long as that individual has the prerogative to remove it from that list, was not in and of itself an invasion of privacy. In reaching this conclusion, the commission observed "that the balance that must be struck between the interests of individuals and the interests of direct marketers is an especially delicate one." The commission also noted the economic importance of direct mail "to nonprofit organizations, to the champions of unpopular causes, and to many of the organizations that create diversity in American society."

Agreeing that the *receipt* of direct mail is not really the issue but how the mailing list record of an individual is used, the commission further recommended that a private sector organization that rents, sells, exchanges, or otherwise makes the addresses or names and addresses of its customers, members, or donors available to any other person for use in direct mail marketing or solicitation should adopt a procedure whereby each customer, member, or donor is informed of the organization's list practice. In addition, each consumer should be given an opportunity to indicate to the organization that he or she does not wish to have his or her address or name and address made available for such purposes.[13]

These were the privacy issues of the past. Now direct marketers must prepare for handling the privacy issues of the future. Let's take a look at privacy today.

Privacy Today: Antispam Laws

Spam is unwanted, unsolicited bulk commercial e-mail messages. It has also been referred to as junk e-mail. Most people today complain about spam. Recipients find it annoying, Internet service providers say it clogs up and slows down the online systems, and many direct marketers claim it is ruining e-mail as a legitimate media channel. The minutes e-mail recipients spend clicking through unwanted e-mail messages add up quickly in a nation with millions of Internet users. However, spam is a worldwide issue. Spam accounts for 14.5 billion messages globally per day.[14] This world-wide phenomenon of spam had to start somewhere. There is some speculation of who actually sent out the first spam e-mail and when it happened. The first "tasteless" spam e-mail was most likely sent out in 1996 by Dave Rhodes. Rhodes was a college student who advertised a pyramid scheme in the e-mail messages. The message was relayed to all newsgroups on Usenet. Thousands of users were hit with a message that read, "MAKE MONEY FAST!" It's said that Rhodes made a substantial amount of money from several people chasing an elusive dream. The most interesting twist of the story is the great possibility that Rhodes never existed. The university that he supposedly attended had no records of him. Because chain letters began as early as the 1970s, it's very probable that someone else copied the format onto a computer and distributed it via Usenet under an alias.[15]

Internet providers have tools for blocking spam; however, these filtering programs are often time-consuming and ineffective. Senders of spam are finding ways to defeat the filtering software simply by misspelling key words that trigger the filters. To get consumers to open these e-mail messages, the senders of spam also use a variety of attention-getting subject lines and sender names in the "from" field of the e-mail message. Some examples include: "Claim Your Prize" or "Payment Past Due" or "You Have Won." This is where the law comes into play. When the subject line of an e-mail message misrepresents its point of origin or the nature of the message itself, it is considered deceptive.

The CAN-SPAM Act of 2003 sets requirements for everyone involved in sending commercial e-mails. This act also states various penalties for spammers and companies whose products are advertised as spam. The CAN-SPAM Act gives the power to the consumer to ask the e-mail sender to stop sending their address e-mails. The U.S. Federal Trade Commission (FTC) has the power to enforce the act, which came into effect on January 1, 2004. CAN-SPAM gave the Department of Justice (DOJ) the power to enforce criminal sanction for noncompliance. The main provisions of The CAN-SPAM Act are that it

- bans false or misleading header information,
- prohibits deceptive subject lines,

- requires that your e-mail give recipients an opt-out method,
- requires that commerial e-mail be identified as an advertisement and include the sender's valid physical postal address.[16]

Federal and state legislation covering the broad range of privacy issues today is rapidly changing. The legal environment concerning spam is also constantly changing. For updated legislative information contact the Internet Alliance at www.internetalliance.org or visit the spam laws Web site at www.spamlaws.com. Direct marketers must constantly monitor key information sources.

Annoyance and Violation

To get at the heart of privacy concerns, you have to understand two basic consumer perceptions: **annoyance** and **violation.**[17] People feel annoyed because they receive too much unsolicited marketing communications, and they feel violated because they believe too much information about their personal lives is being exchanged between marketers without their knowledge and/or consent. Many consumers want to place restrictions on the amount of information that may be collected, warehoused, and shared about them. However, not all consumers feel the same way. Some are willing to disclose personal information to marketers providing they receive something in return. This may include a targeted offer that meets the consumer's needs and wants, or informative updates on a certain topic of interest to them. In fact, it has been determined that a consumer's willingness to disclose personal data may actually depend on the type of information being disclosed.

Type of Information

The degree of control or the amount of restriction an individual wants to have over their personal information may depend on the *type* of information requested. We can divide personal information into four different categories: general descriptive information, ownership information, product purchase information, and sensitive/confidential information.[18] Let's discuss each of these types of information and look at some examples of each category.

GENERAL DESCRIPTIVE INFORMATION   General descriptive information is the easiest to obtain. Often considered demographic or classification information, it includes race, height, age, gender, level of education, and occupation. Consumers are the least restrictive with this category of information and usually provide marketers easy access to this data.

OWNERSHIP INFORMATION   Ownership information contains data about the various products the consumer owns. Consumers consider some belongings to be status symbols, like a home, an expensive automobile, or an American Express Platinum travel and entertainment credit card. Consumers generally place moderate restrictions on the release of these data, and it is believed that some may want to share this data to achieve greater self-esteem or status.

PRODUCT PURCHASE INFORMATION   The information contained in the product purchase information category includes a variety of purchase activity data, including magazine subscription information, credit record information, and lifestyle information obtained from such purchases as vitamins, cat food, hunting and fishing equipment, or certain medications. This category is similar to the ownership information category; however, these purchases are not necessarily considered to be status symbols. Consumers generally place moderate restrictions on this information category.

SENSITIVE/CONFIDENTIAL INFORMATION The final category of information contains facts about an individual that are considered to be most private: sensitive/confidential information, such as annual income, medical history, Social Security number, driving records (including any motor violations), and home value. Consumers are most restrictive with this category of information and usually exercise the strongest control over the release of these facts.

Consumer Privacy Segments

Not *all* consumers possess the same feelings and opinions about privacy issues, regardless of the type of information. Just as information can be grouped into categories, consumer opinions and behaviors toward information privacy can be categorized as well. In fact, research conducted by Alan Westin of Columbia University and Lou Harris Organization/Equifax has concluded that consumers may be grouped into three possible segments (the privacy unconcerned, privacy fundamentalists, and privacy pragmatists) when it comes to their feelings about privacy.[19] Let's take a closer look at these segments.

PRIVACY UNCONCERNED The **privacy unconcerned** group represents about 20 percent of the population and consists of those who literally do not care about the issue of privacy at all. They are aware of the benefits of giving information for marketing purposes and enjoy the information and opportunities they receive in exchange for it. These consumers say their lives are an open book. They feel they have nothing to hide. They welcome most contacts by businesses, nonprofits, and others and have little concern about information about them being transferred from one organization to another. This group is most likely to be receptive to the activities of direct marketers.

PRIVACY FUNDAMENTALISTS The **privacy fundamentalists** also make up approximately 20 percent of the population. These individuals are likely to take the point of view that they own their name, as well as all the information about themselves, and that no one else may use it without their permission. This group includes activists who will write letters to their congressional representatives or the editor of a local newspaper about privacy. They may call companies and file complaints on this issue. Direct marketers should be certain to purge these consumers from their lists because they are the least receptive to direct marketing activities.

PRIVACY PRAGMATISTS The **privacy pragmatists** represent approximately 60 percent of U.S. consumers. They look at the contact, the offer, and the methods of data collection and mentally apply a cost/benefit analysis to make a determination about a marketer's use of information.
    They ask themselves:

- What benefits can I get from this?
- Are there choices that I would not otherwise have?
- Is there an opportunity for me?
- Can I get a product or an offer that is valuable to me?
- What harm can come from this? For example:
  - Will I be inconvenienced in some way?
  - Will I be embarrassed or feel discomfort?
  - Will I be disadvantaged in some way?

Pragmatists will allow their buying patterns to be tracked by supermarkets, if they get valuable coupons or other deals in return. They have no problem with a catalog company providing its list to another organization or company so long as they appreciate the subsequent offers they receive. They will receive telemarketing calls from an organization they patronize and respond to an offer they consider valuable. The privacy pragmatists represent the majority of consumers in the United States. Developing relationships with these customers is an important strategy for the direct marketer to take. So what have companies done to respond to consumer's privacy concerns?

Corporate Response to Privacy

The **chief privacy officer (CPO)** is the newest arrival in corporate hierarchies, the new white knight of the twenty-first century. Like the CEO and the CIO, the CPO is overseeing something very important in the corporation: *privacy!* The CPO is responsible for protecting the sensitive information the corporation collects, from credit card accounts to health records.

Privacy executives have an open-ended job. They must guard against hackers and articulate uses for sensitive personal, financial, or medical information. They must not only set guidelines, they must figure out how to communicate those guidelines to customers and employees. Figure 11-5 shows the privacy policy booklet the J.C. Penney Company distributes to its customers. Hiring CPOs to oversee privacy matters may be the price of doing business in today's corporate world as consumers and government officials more aggressively sue companies over breach of privacy cases.

Many companies already have information privacy policies and actively communicate these to their customers. Take, for example, the following privacy notice provided to customers at Universal Bank:[20]

> Keeping customer information secure is a top priority for all of us at Universal Bank. We are sending you this privacy notice to help you understand how we handle the personal information about you that we collect and may disclose. This notice tells you how you can limit our disclosing personal information about you. The provisions of this notice will apply to former customers as well as current customers unless we state otherwise.

Universal Bank goes on to provide their customers with a "Privacy Choices Form," which allows them to select one of the following four choices and return the form to the bank:[21]

1. Limit the personal information about me that you disclose to nonaffiliated third parties.
2. Limit the personal information about me that you share with Citigroup affiliates.
3. Remove my name from your mailing lists used for promotional offers.
4. Remove my name from your telemarketing lists used for promotional offers.

Like Universal Bank, many direct marketers have become proactive in handling information privacy issues. Perhaps no organization is more proactive than the DMA. The DMA initiated a Privacy Promise in 1999 that provided public assurance that all members of the DMA follow certain specific practices to protect consumer privacy. The practices were designed to have a major impact on those consumers who wish to receive fewer advertising solicitations. DMA updated and expanded its Privacy Promise and now requires its members to adhere to the Commitment to Consumer Choice (see www.DMACCC.org).

The DMA Commitment to Consumer Choice

In 2008, the DMA initiated its new, redefined preference Web site, DMAchoice. This new site addresses consumers' need for choice across a multitude of channels, not just mail. The primary mission of DMAchoice is to give consumers the opportunity to make what they receive more relevant

Your Choices Regarding the Use of the Information We Collect

If you prefer that we NOT

- share information about you with any of the companies outside the JCPenney Family that we have authorized to send you promotional information about their products or services, or
- share your JCPenney credit card account history information with affiliated companies within the JCPenney Family, just write to us at J. C. Penney Company, Inc., P.O. Box 10001, Dallas, TX 75301-7311, Attention: Corporate Customer Relations, call us at 1-800-204-3334, or e-mail us at privacy@jcpenneyservices.com. We will make every effort to implement any choice you make as soon as possible.
- **E-mail Communications.** You will receive promotional e-mail communications only if you have asked to receive such material.

Safeguarding the Information We Collect

Within the JCPenney Family, we protect against unauthorized disclosures by limiting access only to those of our employees who need the information to do their jobs. We also inform all JCPenney employees about their responsibility to protect our customers' privacy and give them clear guidelines for adhering to our own business ethics standards and confidentiality policies.

We limit the information we provide to outside companies to only the information we believe is appropriate to enable them to carry out their responsibilities under our contracts or to offer you products and services we think might be of interest to you. We contractually require that the information provided be used only for the specifically authorized purpose and that its confidentiality be maintained.

Updating Your JCPenney Contact Information or Checking the Status of Your JCPenney Card Account

You can update or correct your name, address, telephone number, or e-mail address by writing to us at J. C. Penney Company, Inc., P.O. Box 10001, Dallas, TX 75301-7311, Attention: Corporate Customer Relations, calling us at 1-800-204-3334, or e-mailing us at privacy@jcpenneyservices.com.

You can update or correct your name, address, or telephone number for your JCPenney Card account, or check the status of your account, by writing to Monogram Credit Card Bank of Georgia at P.O. Box 27570, Albuquerque, NM 87125-7570, or calling 1-877-969-1233 (Puerto Rico 1-800-981-8400; U.S. Virgin Islands 1-800-474-5580). For account status, you can also log onto JCPenney.com and click on Customer Service and the indicated button under JCPenney Credit Services.

The Privacy of JCPenney.com Customers

For information on the measures we take to protect the privacy of our Internet shoppers, please visit our web site at JCPenney.com and click on Customer Service and Privacy Policy.

Further Information

If we change our privacy policy in the future, we will let you know. When considering any change, your privacy will remain a priority.

If you would like further information, or have any questions, about our privacy policy, please write to us at J. C. Penney Company, Inc., P.O. Box 10001, Dallas, TX 75301-7311, Attention: Corporate Customer Relations, call us at 1-800-204-3334, or e-mail us at privacy@jcpenneyservices.com.

it'sallinside:

JCPenney

stores catalog .com

Privacy Policy

J. C. Penney Company, Inc.

935H

J. C. Penney Company, Inc. Privacy Policy

At JCPenney your privacy is a priority.

At JCPenney we seek to provide products, services, and offers of value to you and your family. We use information from our interactions with you and other customers, and from other parties, to help us achieve that goal.

We also recognize and respect your privacy. Accordingly, we have procedures intended to ensure that your personal information is handled in a safe, secure, and responsible manner.

Note: If you have a JCPenney credit card, a separate privacy policy adopted by the Monogram Credit Card Bank of Georgia, the issuer of the JCPenney Card, describes Monogram's collection, use, and protection of information about you and your account. To obtain Monogram's privacy policy for the JCPenney Card Program, you may write to Monogram Credit Card Bank of Georgia at P.O. Box 27570, Albuquerque, NM 87125-7570, or call 1-877-969-1233 (Puerto Rico 1-800-981-8400; U.S. Virgin Islands 1-800-474-5580).

The Information We Collect

- Whenever you shop in our stores, through our catalogs, or at JCPenney.com, we obtain from you the information we need to complete your transaction. This information may include your name, address, telephone number, driver's license number, birth date, and e-mail address. If you use a credit or debit card or pay by check, it will include your account number.
- If you choose to use or participate in one of our various services, clubs, promotions, programs, or surveys, we may collect additional information. For example, if you sign up for our gift registry service, we will ask you for information concerning the event and your gift selections.
- From your transactions and other interactions with us, we also obtain information concerning the specific products or services you purchase or use.
- We also receive information from other companies. For example, if you have a JCPenney credit card, we receive application and account information from the Monogram Credit Card Bank of Georgia.

Using the Information We Collect

We use the information we collect for various purposes, including:

- to complete your purchase transactions;
- to provide the services you request;
- to send you our catalogs and other offerings through the mail;
- to contact you about the status of your store, catalog, or JCPenney.com orders;
- to identify your product and service preferences, so that you can be informed of new or additional products, services, and promotions that might be of interest to you;
- to notify you of product recalls or provide other information concerning products you have purchased; and
- to improve our merchandise selections, customer service, and overall customer shopping experience.

Information We Share with Others

- **JCPenney Family:** We share the information we collect with affiliated companies (like Eckerd and Genovese Drug Stores) and licensees (like the optical and photography departments in JCPenney stores) within the JCPenney family of businesses.
- **Service Providers:** We provide information to other companies, including those within the JCPenney Family, to help us bring you the products and services we offer.
- **Third-Party Offers:** We provide information to responsible outside companies we carefully select so they can let you know about those of their products or services we think might be of interest to you.
- **Others:** On rare occasions, we may be required to disclose customer information pursuant to lawful requests, such as subpoenas or court orders, or in compliance with applicable laws. Also, if the ownership of all or a part of a business within the JCPenney Family were to change, customer information pertinent to that business's operations would likely be transferred to, or licensed for use by, the new owner.

FIGURE 11-5   J.C. Penney Company Privacy Policy.   *Source:* Used with permission of J.C. Penney Company Inc.

to their needs and interests. This Web site will educate consumers and enable them to make more informed decisions about their preference choices. The Commitment to Consumer Choice includes the following four components:[22]

1. Provide customers, donors, and prospects with notice that they may eliminate or modify their future receipt of direct mail solicitations "in every marketing offer" (see Figure 11-6 for examples of notice language).

A. "We make our customer information available to other companies so they may contact you about products and services that may interest you. If you do not want your name passed on to other companies for the purpose of receiving marketing offers, just tell us by contacting us at _____, and we will be pleased to respect your wishes."

B. "We make portions of our customer list available to carefully screened companies that offer products and services we believe you may enjoy. If you do not want to receive those offers and/or information, please let us know by contacting us at _____."

FIGURE 11-6   Examples of Notice Language.   *Source: The DMA Privacy Promise Member Compliance Guide* (New York: The Direct Marketing Association, Inc., 1999), p. 6. Used with permission of the Direct Marketing Association.

2. Honor consumers' opt-out requests within 30 days, and for a period of at least three years, not to receive further mailings or have their contact information transferred to others for marketing purposes.
3. Disclose, on the consumer's request, the source from which the marketer obtained personally identifiable data about that consumer (see Figure 11-7 for examples of in-house suppress language).
4. Update mailing lists using DMA's MPS suppression file each month.

In addition, the DMA has developed privacy principles and guidelines for those direct marketers operating online sites. The next section explores these principles.

The DMA Online Privacy Principles

While millions of consumers have been quick to embrace technology, consumers have called for regulation. Some consumers view online data collection as an invasion of privacy that, at best, inundates them with spam and, at worst, risks putting their financial or personal information in the hands of potential employers, lenders, or insurance companies. Most consumers freely provide their e-mail address or shopping preferences in exchange for better customer service. However, they don't expect marketers to share the information without their consent and use it to target them for other offers (especially from other companies).

A. "If you decide you no longer wish to receive our catalog, send your mailing label with your request to _____."

B. "We would like to continue sending you information only on those subjects of interest to you. If you don't wish to continue to receive information on any of the following product lines, just let us know by _____."

C. "If you would like to receive our catalog less frequently, let us know by _____."

FIGURE 11-7   Examples of In-House Suppress Language.   *Source: The DMA Privacy Promise Member Compliance Guide* (New York: The Direct Marketing Association, Inc., 1999), p. 6. Used with permission of the Direct Marketing Association.

UNSUBSCRIBE: Please use this link to unsubscribe—Or please write UNSUBSCRIBE in the e-mail subject heading and reply to this e-mail.

FIGURE 11-8   Example of an Opt-Out Notice.

DMA Online Privacy Principles state that all marketers operating online sites should

1. make available their information practices to consumers in a *prominent place* on their Web site; and
2. furnish consumers with the opportunity to opt out of the disclosure of such information. An example of an opt-out notice is shown in Figure 11-8. In addition, the online notice should be easy to find, easy to read, and easy to understand.

The DMA privacy policy specifically expects the online notice to perform the following seven tasks:[23]

1. Identify the marketer.
2. Disclose their e-mail and postal addresses.
3. State whether the marketer collects personal information online from individuals.
4. Contain a disclosure statement regarding the *information collected.*
5. Contain a disclosure statement regarding the *uses of such information.*
6. State the nature and purpose of disclosures of such information and the types of persons to which disclosures may be made.
7. Explain the mechanism by which the individual may limit the disclosure of such information.

With these privacy principles for online marketing activities in place, it is up to direct marketers to ensure that their programs include responsive personal information protection practices.

Third-Party Privacy Intervention: Infomediaries

Infomediaries are companies that act as intermediaries or third parties by gathering personal information from a user and providing it to other sites with the user's approval. These companies vary in their methods; each attempts to provide consumers with a type of privacy assistance by enabling consumers to control and limit access to their personal information when shopping online.

Critics of infomediaries claim that these companies fail to provide enough protection and that they have the potential to exploit what they claim to protect. The World Wide Web Consortium, the Washington-based organization that sets standards for the Internet, has been working on the Platform for Privacy Preferences initiative (called P3P). The initiative calls for the development of a software program that enables Web browsers to read a site's privacy policy automatically and compare it with the user's privacy preferences. What is unclear, at present, is how the P3P will work with existing infomediary programs and whether browser companies and Web developers will incorporate it into their products. Most recently, Microsoft's director of corporate privacy said the company was working toward developing a P3P compliance program for businesses and consumers. This program would automatically compare a Web site operator's privacy practices to the consumer's preferences and inform the consumer of any nonconformance or mismatch. Direct marketers need to stay abreast of infomediaries and the role they may play in the future as gatekeepers to consumers. They certainly could become a third-party regulator of many online marketing activities.

Now that we have reviewed the main privacy issues affecting direct marketers and the various DMA and corporate responses to these issues, we explore the regulatory authorities that are charged with enforcing these rules.

REGULATORY AUTHORITIES OF DIRECT MARKETING

By their very nature, direct marketing promotional activities, as they inform and persuade, often in very large numbers, are highly visible. The volume of direct mail grew rapidly over the past few decades. As it did, some of it was branded as junk mail by those people who received it and did not find it relevant, by those individuals who resented its intrusion, and even by those businesses that represented competing advertising media. This, coupled with the development and advances in telephone equipment, fiber optic cables, satellite transmissions, and the Internet, enabled direct marketers to transfer consumer data from internal or external databases to user databases quickly and easily and at low costs. During this period of proliferation of direct marketing, abuses by individual organizations ultimately resulted in intervention by regulatory authorities.

The Federal Communications Commission (FCC) and the Federal Trade Commission (FTC) have issued several very important trade regulation rules and guides that affect direct marketing as well as advisory opinions about unfair competition in the form of misleading or deceptive acts or advertising. State and local governments also intervene in advertising and selling practices as do the U.S. Postal Service, Better Business Bureaus, trade associations, the advertising media, and ultimately consumers themselves. Let's look more closely at each.

Federal Communications Commission

The FCC is an independent U.S. government agency directly responsible to Congress. It was established by the Communications Act of 1934 and is charged with regulating interstate and international communications by radio, television, wire, satellite, and cable.[24] The FCC enforces the Telephone Consumer Protection Act (TCPA), originally passed in 1992, and its rules governing telephone marketing.[25] From a telephone marketer's point of view, the most significant part of the TCPA regulations concern commercial solicitation calls made to residences. Direct marketers making those calls are required to do the following:

- Limit the calls to the period between 8 A.M. and 9 P.M.
- Maintain a do-not-call list and honor any consumer request to not be called again. The FCC permits one error in a 12-month period. The FCC worked closely with the FTC in enforcing the National Do Not Call Registry, which we discuss a little later in this section.
- Have a clearly written policy, available to anyone on request.
- If you are a service bureau, forward all requests to be removed from a list to the company on whose behalf you are calling.

A call is exempt from the TCPA if the call

- is made on behalf of a tax-exempt nonprofit organization,
- is not made for a commercial purpose,
- does not include an unsolicited advertisement, even if it is made for a commercial purpose,
- is made to a consumer with whom the calling company has an "established business relationship."

The TCPA prohibits both for-profit and nonprofit marketers from using an automatic phone dialing system (including predictive dialers) to call any device when the called party is charged unless that called party has given prior express consent. Therefore, marketers using automatic dialing systems should not call consumers or businesses' cellular phones, pagers, or toll-free numbers unless they have given you permission to do so. The FCC also has created strict rules concerning the use of fax machines for marketing purposes. We discuss the TCPA in greater detail later in the case at the end of this chapter.

In addition, the FCC, in concert with the FTC, enforces the National Do-Not-Call (DNC) Registry. This registry permits consumers to sign up via the telephone by calling (888) 382-1222 or online at www.donotcall.gov to declare that they do not wish to receive telephone marketing calls. Section 310.2 of this new federal DNC legislation provides for an established business relationship exemption. Thus, direct marketers may still call customers who appear on the registry providing they are calling on them

- within 18 months of their last purchase, transaction, shipment, end of subscription/membership, or
- within three months of their last inquiry or application.

Exemptions to the DNC legislation have also been made for most business-to-business calls, common carriers, airlines, some financial institutions, and insurance companies to the extent regulated under state law; intrastate calls; nonprofit organizations and third-party marketers calling on their behalf are required to honor in-house suppress requests.[26] Visit the FCC Web site at www.fcc.gov/cgb/donotcall to obtain updates on the National DNC Registry.

Federal Trade Commission

The major federal legislation regulating the promotional activities of direct marketing is the FTC Act, together with its Wheeler-Lea Amendment. The FTC is charged with regulating content of promotional messages used in interstate commerce. In Section 5(A), intended to prevent unfair competition, the Wheeler-Lea Amendment to the FTC Act strengthened this provision by making it a violation of the law whenever such competition injured the public, regardless of its effect on a competitor. The amendment also prohibited false, misleading, or deceptive advertising by enumerating four types of products in which advertising abuses existed and in which the public health could be directly affected: foods, drugs, cosmetics, and therapeutic devices.[27]

In October 1995, the FTC and the DMA produced a check list for direct marketers. It was written for mail, telephone, fax, and computer order merchandisers to give them an overview of rules or statutes that the FTC enforces. Visit the FTC Web site to obtain complete details and updates of FTC rules and regulations at www.ftc.gov. Figure 11-9 provides a brief overview of these rules.

Those direct marketers using online mediums must be aware of and comply with the FTC regulations. The four elements in the FTC's privacy policy for online direct marketing are:[28]

1. *Notice:* Web sites should provide consumers clear and conspicuous notice of their information practices, including what information they collect, how they collect it, how they use it, whether they disclose the information to other entities, and whether other entities are collecting information through the site.
2. *Choice:* Consumers should be offered choices as to how their personal information will be used beyond completing a transaction.
3. *Access:* Consumers should be offered reasonable access to the information that a Web site gathers about them, including the opportunity to review such data and correct or delete data.
4. *Security:* Organizations that have Web sites should take reasonable steps to protect the security of information they gather from their consumers.

Advertisements: Product Offers and Claims All products and/or services advertised must be advertised truthfully. The FTC Act prohibits unfair or deceptive advertising.

Mail and Telephone Orders In order to comply with the Mail or Telephone Order Merchandise Rule ("MTOR"), you must have a reasonable basis for stating or implying that you can ship within a certain time when you advertise mail or telephone order merchandise.

Telemarketing If your business uses either inbound or outbound interstate telephone calls to sell goods or services, you must comply with the new Telemarketing Sales Rule (TSR) and Do-Not-Call laws.

900 Numbers All providers of 900 numbers must comply with the FTC 900-Number Rule requiring that they disclose the cost of the call.

Delayed Delivery Rule This rule provides that, if the marketer believes that goods will not be shipped within 30 days of receiving a properly completed order, an advertisement must include a clear and conspicuous notice of the time in which delivery is expected to be made.

Negative Option Rule This trade regulation rule, effective June 7, 1974, governs pre-notification negative option sales plans. Under negative option plans, sellers notify buyers of the periodic selection of merchandise to be shipped.

Guides Against Deceptive Guarantees The FTC promulgated seven guides on April 26, 1960, for the purpose of self-regulatory adoption by marketers in their advertising of guarantees. These guides are intended to ensure that the buyer is fully apprised of the conditions governing any guarantee.

Guides to Use of Endorsements and Testimonials These FTC guides, which became effective May 21, 1975, relate to the use of expert and organizational endorsements and testimonials in advertising.

Advisory Opinion on Dry Testing An advisory opinion issued by the FTC on March 27, 1975, allows such dry testing under very strict guidelines to ensure that the potential customer is in no way misled about the terms of the offer.

Mailing of Unordered Merchandise Coming under a category of fraud and deception is the mailing of unordered merchandise, sent without the prior expressed request or consent of the recipient, an unfair method of competition, and an unfair trade practice in violation of the FTC Act.

Guides Against Deceptive Pricing Made effective January 8, 1964, these guides cover offers stating reductions from a "former," "regular," "comparable," "list price," or "manufacturer's suggested retail price."

Guides Against Bait and Switch Advertising The four guides against bait and switch advertising that were issued by the FTC on December 4, 1959, define this type of advertising as that which is "alluring but insincere in offering to sell a product or service which the advertiser in truth does not intend or want to sell."

Guide Concerning Use of the Word "Free" This guide issued by the FTC on December 16, 1971, is intended to prevent deceptive or misleading offers of "free" merchandise or services if, in fact, such is available only with the purchase of some other merchandise or service.

Advisory Opinion on the Use of the Word "New" This advisory opinion, issued on January 4, 1969, is concerned with merchandise that has been used by purchasers on a trial basis, returned to the seller, refurbished, and resold as new.

Advisory Opinion on Disclosure of Foreign Origin Merchandise Direct marketers, when advertising or promoting goods of foreign origin, must clearly inform prospective purchasers that such goods are not made in the United States if, in fact, the goods originate elsewhere.

Warranties The FTC is empowered by the Magnuson-Moss Warranty Act, effective July 4, 1975, with enforcement. Although no organization is required to give a written warranty and state a minimum duration for a warranty, the National Retail Merchants Association, in summarizing the act and the FTC rules relative to it, describes the following responsibility of direct marketers under the act: Catalog or mail order solicitations must disclose for each warranty product either the full text of the warranty or notice that it may be obtained free upon written request.

Online Direct Marketing Due to the information explosion, online direct marketing activities have become one of the focal points of the FTC. In fact, the FTC has produced a four element "Privacy Policy" in an effort to assist companies in telling their customers what information they are collecting, how they will use it, what security is in place, and how consumers can opt out of providing information.

FIGURE 11-9   An Overview of the FTC Rules and Regulations for Direct Marketers.

Online marketing activities are not alone in receiving FTC attention. As the case at the end of this chapter explains, direct marketing activities using fax machines are being regulated as the FTC enforces the TCPA. Although in some cases their actions have been controversial, the FTC has become much more aggressive in its enforcement, especially when false or deceptive advertising is sent. All direct marketers should take note of the FTC rules and regulations prior to carrying out their marketing activities and utilizing various media.

U.S. Postal Service

Through its Inspection Service and in compliance with the Private Express Statutes, the U.S. Postal Service has established rules and regulations that impact the promotional activities of direct marketers. The Inspection Service is constantly on the lookout for fraud and deception through the mail; the Private Express Statutes, by granting the U.S. Postal Service a form of delivery monopoly, determine classification and cost of promotional matter that can be circulated outside the postal monopoly.

State and Local Regulation

Certain organizations using direct marketing strategies, including insurance companies, small lending associations, banks, and pharmaceutical companies, are closely regulated by state legislation, especially relative to promotion and pricing tactics. State legislators have become increasingly active in consumer issues and in privacy matters such as those that affect mailing lists and promotional use of the telephone. The matters of state sales and use taxes, as they relate to taxation of advertising and promotional services, are also of vital concern to direct marketers.

An example of state and local regulations that affect direct marketing activities is the Truth in Advertising legislation. Truth in Advertising was fashioned after a model statute first proposed in 1911. Most states have so-called truth in advertising legislation that govern the conduct of promotional activities in intrastate commerce.

Private Organizations

Better Business Bureaus, the history and influence of which go back more than half a century, are located in most major cities and are sponsored by private businesses and organizations to prevent promotional abuses though commonsense regulation. Likewise, trade groups, along with the DMA, have promulgated ethical guidelines for use by their members and others desiring to adhere to them.

THE FUTURE: SELF-REGULATION OR LEGISLATION

Self-Regulation

The preferred method to deal with the issues of the regulatory environment is through self-regulation by direct marketers. The DMA has attempted to assist member companies in complying with federal and state regulations, as well as industry self-regulatory responsibilities, attempting to lead the way for its members to meet their customer privacy expectations.

Years ago, Donn Rappaport, chairman of American List Counsel, presented an eight-step self-regulation plan for direct marketers to follow. The basic guidelines of that plan are still relevant today. Figure 11-10 provides an overview of Rappaport's plan.[29] For newer guidelines, please see DMA's Strategic Plan provided on its Corporate Responsibility Department's Web site.

1. *Allow the consumer some measure of control over what lists or types of lists his or her name is on.* Include a notice in every marketing communication stating your list rental practices and offering to remove the name of anyone who prefers that his or her name not be released to other mailers.
2. *Ensure that we know who's renting our lists and what they are planning to do with them.* Direct marketers must pay close attention to list renters that plan to combine your file with other files, abstracts, or overlays.
3. *Review all third-party cooperative arrangements with regard to list rights.* From time to time, a credit card processor will lay claim to the names of people who charge mail-order purchases to their credit cards. Remember, they are your customers regardless of how they paid. Be wary of any arrangement that dilutes your rights of ownership.
4. *Make sure that information is used for the purpose for which it was gathered.* In other words, if you sell women's clothes and happen to sell a significant volume in large sizes, use that information to develop more large-size business. Don't rent your large-size customer names to a weight-loss program.
5. *Stop scaring consumers unnecessarily over how much personal data on them is actually available.* For example, Pacific Bell Telephone Company once began promoting its customer file with the announcement: "Now a business list from the company that has everyone's number." Is this kind of claim really worth the scare it may instill in the consumer?
6. *Eliminate deceptive or misleading direct mail.* Does direct mail that looks like an official document from the IRS really work in the long run? Even if it did, it's deceptive and it raises suspicion about the direct marketing industry.
7. *Use personalization wisely.* There is a fine line between familiarity with the consumer and an invasion of their personal privacy. Keep in mind that certain types of personal data should not be included in personalization.
8. *Make sure that the consumer is not ripped off or compromised by the dissemination of personal data.* Since consumers are serious about the issue of personal privacy, direct marketers must safeguard against privacy abuses.

FIGURE 11-10   **Donn Rappaport's Eight-Step Self-Regulation Plan for Direct Marketers.**   Source: Adapted from Donn Rappaport, "What We Should Say (and Do) About Privacy," *Direct Marketing News,* October 11, 1993.

Legislation and Permission Marketing

Permission marketing obtains the consent of a customer before a company sends out a marketing communication to that customer via the Internet. In other words, permission marketing gives the consumer control over what online communications come to them. It is a parallel to opt-out procedures, whereby the consumer must opt in to receive marketing messages from select organizations seeking to communicate with the consumer. Permission marketing must start with consumers' explicit and active consent to receive online commercial messages and always give consumers the option to stop receiving messages at any time.

Summary

Upholding ethical guidelines in carrying out direct marketing activities is crucial to the present and future success of the direct marketing industry. The three primary areas of legislation include intellectual property rights, security, and privacy. Privacy is the area of greatest concern for direct marketers. Privacy issues encompass personal privacy, information privacy, and offline and online privacy—including spam. The opt-in and opt-out mechanisms along with permission-based marketing are some of the ways consumer privacy issues are being addressed. In addition, security concerns have arisen greatly over the past several years because of security breaches—companies are addressing these concerns as well. Direct marketers must be mindful of the consumer's right to safety, information, selection, confidentiality, and privacy.

The regulatory environment is both dynamic and uncontrollable. Direct marketing regulatory authorities include the FTC, U.S. Postal Service, state and local entities, and private organizations. The FTC rules govern advertisements, mail and telephone orders, telemarketing, 900 numbers, delivery, negative option rule, guarantees, endorsements and testimonials, testing, merchandise mailing, pricing, bait and switch advertising, use of the words *free* and *new,* disclosures of foreign origin merchandise, warranties, and online direct marketing. Direct marketers must maintain compliance with the many laws affecting direct marketing activities while not losing sight of the bottom-line objective: maximizing customer relationships and customer satisfaction while sustaining a profitable business.

Key Terms

ethics *294*
morals *294*
code of ethics *297*
right to safety *299*
right to information *299*
right to selection *299*
right to confidentiality *299*

right to privacy *300*
intellectual property *300*
Privacy Act of 1974 *302*
spam *303*
annoyance *304*
violation *304*
privacy unconcerned *305*

privacy fundamentalists *305*
privacy pragmatists *305*
chief privacy officer (CPO) *306*
infomediaires *309*
permission marketing *314*

Review Questions

1. What is the purpose of the DMA's guidelines for ethical business practice?
2. List and briefly explain the five consumer rights.
3. What is a chief privacy officer (CPO)? What is her or his primary role in an organization?
4. What are the four components of the DMA's Commitment to Consumer Choice?
5. Explain the "delayed delivery rule" and the "guides against deceptive pricing" set forth by the FTC.
6. What are the names and recommendations of some of the private organizations that provide ethical guidelines for direct marketing?
7. Explain the Privacy Act of 1974 and its impact on direct marketers.
8. What is spam? Why are there so many negative feelings toward spam? What is currently being done to eliminate spam?
9. What is the current status of the FCC/FTC Do Not Call Registry?
10. Using the online legal sources provided in the chapter, provide a legal update on permission marketing and spam as they affect direct marketing activities.

Exercise

Imagine you are the first CPO for a major credit card company. Your organization, like all credit card companies, unfortunately has the typical reputation of selling your customers' information to various firms. You want to change the reputation your company has regarding this matter so that you may gain a competitive edge over your competition. What do you think are some of the regulations and ethical codes you are subject to follow set forth by legislation, private organizations, and organizations such as the FTC? Also explain steps that your company can take to regulate itself that aren't currently being taken by other companies.

CASE

The Telephone Consumer Protection Act

Overview

The TCPA of 1991 provides a set of regulations for direct response advertising via the telephone and fax machine. Direct marketers must understand and comply with the TCPA to avoid costly lawsuits that can be filed against offenders of this law. This case explains the TCPA and provides an example of what may take place when there is a violation of the law. The objective of this case is to provide details on the TCPA that may be unclear to many direct marketers and marketing students. The law is still enforced today and encompasses direct marketing activities via phone and fax machines.

Case

Most direct marketers who use telemarketing as a medium for promoting their products and services are well aware of the FTC's Telemarketing Sales Rule. As discussed earlier in this chapter, this rule requires direct marketers to disclose certain kinds of information to the customer before the customer makes a purchase or places an order over the phone. However, what is less well known are the FCC's rules in implementing the TCPA. Telemarketers must be aware of and comply with both sets of regulations. The FTC and FCC rules are similar in many ways; however, the TCPA and FCC rules govern issues that are not encompassed in the FTC regulations.

One of the most common areas of concern for direct marketers is how fax machines can be used for direct response advertising purposes. Because the fax machine is a common business tool, direct marketers must be crystal clear in their understanding of what is permitted and what is not permitted when using a fax for marketing purposes. But even rules for conduct may be interpreted with unexpected results by courts in various state and federal jurisdictions.

History

In 1991, Congress amended the Communications Act of 1934 with the enactment of the TCPA. The TCPA was enacted to "protect the privacy interests of residential telephone subscribers by placing restrictions on unsolicited, automated telephone calls to the home and to facilitate interstate commerce by restricting certain uses of fax machines and automatic dialers." The TCPA states: "It shall be unlawful for any telephone facsimile [fax] machine, computer, or other device to send an unsolicited advertisement to a telephone facsimile machine."[30] The FCC's rules apply not only to stand-alone fax machines but also to computer fax boards or modems that can send a fax from a personal computer.

Effective August 25, 2003, there are some new FCC rules on sending faxes to both businesses and residents. The FCC announced that a portion of the new rules would not go into effect until January 1, 2005. This portion required companies to receive signed written permission from anyone (including their own customers) before sending any commercial faxes. In addition, you cannot send a fax to prospects, consumers, or even businesses unless the prospect has contacted you. Prior to January 1, 2005, direct marketers had a three-month window to fax to an inquirer.[31] For more information you can visit the following FCC site: ftp.fcc.gov/cgb/consumerfacts/unwantedfaxes.html. The TCPA is a federal law, so violations of the act are heard in federal court. However, the law allows jurisdiction in the various states to allow private citizens to sue in their own state courts if someone violates the TCPA. If the courts find the defendant liable, they could be subject to a $500 fine per fax or call as statutory damages. If the fax or call was a willful or intentional violation of the act, they could be fined $1,500 per fax or call, which is treble damages.

In summary of the legal jargon, the TCPA, and in turn the FCC regulations, impose a general ban on the use of fax machines to send an "unsolicited advertisement." This includes any advertising material promoting the "commercial availability" of any goods, property, or services that is transmitted without the recipient's prior express invitation or permission. However, there is an exemption for existing business relationships. The rule defines an established business relationship as "a prior or existing relationship formed by a voluntary two-way communication between a person or entity and a residential subscriber with or without an exchange of consideration on the basis of an inquiry, application, purchase, or transaction by the residential subscriber regarding products or services offered by such person or entity, which relationship has not been previously terminated by either party." The FCC has stated that an existing business relationship with the recipient can be deemed to reflect the recipient's permission to send a fax with a commercial message. However, even if a prior or existing relationship exists, each fax must identify, on each page or on the first page, the date and time the fax is being sent and the sender's identity and phone number of the fax machine sending the message. (This refers back to the regulations set forth by the FTC's Telemarketing Sales Rule.)

In summary, the basic premise behind these regulations is that sending unsolicited faxes to consumers is considered junk faxing. Some consumers believe that junk faxers steal the resources of the recipients—fax paper, ink, and personnel costs—and tie up the equipment, causing a busy signal to sound in place of receiving legitimate messages. In fact, some consumers felt so strongly about these issues that they developed a Web site (www.Junkfaxes.org) to disseminate information on various junk fax senders and assist the recipients in enforcing the above laws.

Examples of TCPA Violations

One recent enforcement of the TCPA in Georgia can be found in the case of *Nicholson et al. v. Hooters of Augusta, Inc.*[32] In June 1995, Sam Nicholson filed a class action against Bambi Clark Value-Fax of Augusta and Hooters of Augusta, alleging that Hooters used Clark, an independent contractor, to send unsolicited advertisements to fax machines in violation of the TCPA. The trial court ruled in favor of Nicholson and found Hooters of Augusta in violation of the TCPA. Hooters of Augusta then appealed the ruling to the Court of Appeals in Georgia. However, the court found that Georgia citizens had the right to seek the relief provided by the TCPA, even though Hooters of Augusta claimed that Clark was an independent contractor. Even if the court found that Clark was an independent contractor, the TCPA states "the entity or *entities on whose behalf* facsimiles are transmitted are ultimately liable for compliance with the TCPA's rule banning unsolicited facsimile advertisements."

On April 25, 2001, a jury determined that Hooters of Augusta willfully violated the TCPA by sending unsolicited advertising faxes and assessed full trebled damages of $1,500 per violation against Hooters. Hooters was ordered to pay each of the 1,321 class members who received six unsolicited faxed advertisements a sum of $9,000 per party, for a total of $11,889,000.[33]

Other examples of recent offenders of the TCPA include the Dallas-based firm American Blast Fax (ABF). On March 14, 2001, 23 individual plaintiffs received judgments totaling $83,000 against ABF and clients Cox Industrial Equipment, Advanced Digital Telemarketing, Breve Company, and Richard Townsend dba Financial Strategies Group. These companies had hired ABF to send fax advertisements on their behalf.[34]

In conclusion, the TCPA is an important law for direct marketers to be knowledgeable of and comply with when using the fax machine for direct response advertising and communications.

Case Discussion Questions

1. How are the FTC's Telemarketing Sales Rule and the FCC's TCPA similar? How are they different?
2. Can direct marketers comply with the TCPA and still distribute direct response advertising materials to consumers? If so, how?
3. Could Hooters of Augusta have avoided the lawsuit that was waged on them? Explain.
4. What is the position of your state in the interpretation of the TCPA?

Notes

1. U.S. Food and Drug Administration Center for Drug Evaluation & Research Division of Drug Marketing, Advertising, and Communications, http://www.fda.gov/cder/ddmac/lawsregs.htm, accessed May 24, 2008.
2. *New Environmental Standard on Direct Marketing,* September 21, 2007, http://www.bsi-global.com/en/About-BSI/News-Room/BSI-News-Content/Disciplines/Environmental-Management/DMA-PAS/ (May 7, 2008).
3. Melissa Campanelli, *EMA Unveils 'Please Recycle' Campaign,* July 2007, http://www.dmnews.com/EMA-unveils-Please-Recycle-campaign/article/html (April 16, 2008).
4. Direct Marketing Association, *Recycle Please,* http://www.the-dma.org/recycle (April 16, 2008).
5. Direct Marketing Association, *The Green 15: Benchmarking Environmental Progress,* http://www.the-dma.org/green15/overviewDMAgreen15.pdf (April 16, 2008).
6. Adapted from Carl McDaniel, Jr., and Roger Gates Contemporary Marketing Research, 2nd ed. (New York: West Publishing Co., 1993).
7. Charles W. L. Hill, Global Business Today (New York: McGraw-Hill/Inrwin, 2002), p. 50.
8. American Intellectual Property Law Association, www.aipla.org>.
9. Ibid.
10. "Help Wanted: Steal This Database," Wired News, January 6, 2003; Elaine M. LaFlamme, "Know the liabilities of Data Collection," New Jersey Law Journal (March 14, 2003), www.law.com>.
11. ZDNet.Co.Uk, California's S.B. 1386 Requires Notification of Customers When Unencrypted Data Are Stolen: Law Exempts Encrypted Data, November, 2005. http://whitepapers.zdnet.co.uk (April 11, 2008).
12. James Kindall, "Lists Help Build Dosier on You," Kansas City Star, September 5, 1978, p. 1.
13. Adapted from The Privacy Protection Study Commission, Report from the Privacy Protection Study Commission (Washington, DC: GPO, July 1977), p. 147.
14. Spam Laws, *Spam Statistics and Facts* http://www.spamlaws.com/spam-stats.html (April 16, 2008).
15. Spam Laws, *Spam Origin* http://www.spamlaws.com/spam-origin.html (April 16, 2008).
16. Federal Trade Commission, *The CAN-SPAM Act: Requirements for Commercial Emailers,* Washington, DC. http://www.ftc.gov/bcp/conline/pubs/buspus/canspam.shtm (April 16, 2008).
17. Saul Hansell, "Virginia Law Makes Spam, With Fraud, A Felony," New York Times, April 30, 2003, sec. C, p. 1, col. 5.
18. Karl Dentino, "Taking Privacy into Our Own Hands," Direct Marketing (September 1994).
19. Richard A. Hamilton and Lisa D. Spiller, "Opinions about Privacy: Does the Type of Informatin Used for Marketing Purposes Make a Difference?" International Journal of Voluntary Sector Marketing 4, no. 3 (September 1999): 251–264.
20. Page Boinest Melton, "Business Trends to Watch", Virginia Business (February 2001), 78–81.
21. Universal Bank, Important Information Regarding Your Privacy (2001), 1.
22. Ibid., 5.
23. The Direct Marketing Association, Inc., "Online Marketing Privacy Principles and Guidelines," July Direct Marketing Associations, New York, NY, July 1997, pp. 3–9.
24. http://www.fcc.gov/
25. Adapted from the Direct Marketing Association, *Telephone Consumer Protection Act (TCPA),* http://www.the-dma.org/guidelines/tcpa.shtml (September 17, 2003).
26. Direct Marketing Asociation, *10 Steps to Making a Sale Under the FTC's New Telemarketing Sales Rule,* DMA Telemarketing Resource Center,

http://www.the-dma.org/government/teleresource center.shtml (September 12, 2003).

27. The Federal Trade Commission, Privacy Online: Fair Information in The Electronic Marketplace (Washington, DC: GPO, May 2000).

28. Direct Marketing Association, "The FTC's New Telemarketing Sales Rule: Q & A's," http://www. the-dma.org (September 12, 2003).

29. Kristen Bremner, "CA Assembly Passes Amended Privacy Bill," Direct Marketing News, September 17, 2003.

30. Telephone Consumer Protection Act, The Direct Marketing Assoc. Telemarketing Resource Center, New York: NY Sept. 17, 2003.

31. The Direct Marketing Association, "A Matter of Fax: What Direct Marketers Need to Know About Sending Faxes," August 25, 2003, www.the-dma.org/guide lines/advertisingfaxes.shtml (September 12, 2003).

32. Case adapted from "Unsolicited Advertising Faxes are Illegal," September 24, 1998. The DMA Interactive Web site, http://www.the-dma.org/ library/guidelines/advertisingfaxes.shtml (August 8, 2002). Reprinted with permission.

33. Robert H. Braver, 2001, "Judge imposes maximum trebled damage of nearly $12 million against Hooters," http://www.junkfaxes.org/news/hooters-12.htm (April 2001).

34. Robert H. Braver, "American Blast Fax and Its Advertiser Clients Found Jointly Liable for Junk Faxes," "Blast Faxer and Clients Held Jointly Liable" access date 8/8/02. "Hooters Hit with $12 Million Damage Award," http://www.junkfaxes. org/news/abfmo.htm March 14, 2001.

12

...

Exploring and Adapting Direct and Interactive Marketing Strategies around the World

Opening Vignette: Body Parts Direct

If you are like most college students, you are often strapped for cash. What that small detail translated into was an opportunity for the Bank of New Zealand to target college students with a wildly creative direct marketing campaign called "Body Parts." The name of the campaign alone arouses curiosity, right? Well, allow us to satisfy your curiosity and reveal the details about this brilliant direct marketing campaign.

Most banks believe that the student market is a highly important one to target. Are you wondering why? It seems odd since most students do not have much money to be saved or invested. However, it is as a student that most customers begin a relationship with the bank that they are likely to stay with for many years. Therefore, establishing relationships with students is seen as investing in future profitability for banks. It makes good sense. Therefore, most banks offer lucrative incentives, such as MP3 players or cash sign-on bonuses, to get students to open an account. In New Zealand, many students are a bit cynical toward overt marketing, therefore banks have to be extra creative and strategic when developing and executing their marketing campaigns.

Bank of New Zealand sought out AIM Proximity to help it meet the challenges associated with marketing to students. The campaign objective was to open 6,500 new accounts, with a stretch target of 10,000 accounts—which was the same campaign objective as the previous year, but with the added challenge of a 10 percent reduction in the promotional budget over last year. With the student consumer culture in mind, AIM Proximity and Bank of New Zealand constructed a campaign to appeal to students' desire to *get something*. They wanted something different and unique—something that would really appeal to students. The answer was to develop a program where students could obtain discounts and get free stuff all year (as opposed to just once) to make their frugal life more enjoyable.

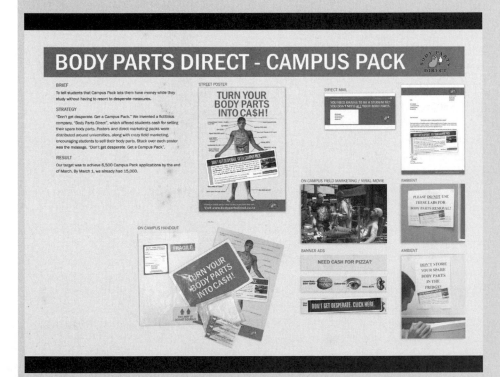

FIGURE 12-1   Body Parts Direct Campus Pack.   *Source:* Used with permission of Bank of New Zealand.

The offer featured Bank of New Zealand's Campus Pack, which is a student bank account with a free student discount card. The bank offered additional incentives to students to encourage them to open a Campus Pack account. The campaign was executed through a variety of traditional direct response media, such as print and direct mail, as well as some nontraditional media, such as mobile bank stands on campus, street posters plastered around campus, banner ads on student Web sites, inserts in new student orientation bags, and street theater–style stunts on campus. The campaign was creative, bold, and fun. As Figure 12-1 presents, all of the creative materials used in the campaign featured the same basic message—"You don't have to sell your body parts for cash—don't get desperate, get a Campus Pack instead."

The agency invented a fictitious company, Body Parts Direct, which offered students cash for selling their spare body parts. This was crazy marketing—but fun! Need extra cash for pizza? Consider selling an eyebrow! The call to action was to visit Bank of New Zealand's Web site, visit a branch office, or text message the company. The campaign was so effective that Bank of New Zealand opened 18,138 new accounts, far surpassing the stretch target of 10,000.[1]

This campaign is proof that highly creative and effective direct and interactive marketing campaigns are being used all over the world. That is the topic of this chapter. We explore international versus domestic direct marketing strategies, factors entering into the decision to market internationally, modes of market entry, and international direct marketing infrastructure needed to be successful in international direct and interactive marketing. In addition, this chapter enables you to explore how direct and interactive marketing strategies are being employed in geographical regions around the world. We hope you enjoy the international voyage!

The world is getting smaller. Facing saturated U.S. markets, many companies are looking overseas to achieve increased sales volume and greater profits. Over the past two decades, global trade has climbed from $200 billion a year to over $7 trillion.[2] Although those are the two reasons frequently named by businesses seeking international business, other reasons include the hope of expanding into new markets, diversification, achieving economies of scale, and business survival. The United States exports over $1 trillion in goods and services each year. The top trade partners according to the 2008 *World Almanac and Book of Facts* for the United States in 2006 were Canada at $533 billion, China at $343 billion, Mexico at $332 billion, Japan at $208 billion, and Germany at $130.5 billion.[3] Today, nearly half of the global brands are headquartered outside of U.S. borders. According to a recent study by Goldman Sachs, it is estimated that by 2050 the "BRIC" economies of Brazil, Russia, India, and China will in all likelihood surpass that of today's six largest economies, thus creating a new world order.[4] Revenue generated by international direct marketing activities has continued to increase over the years.

The Internet is one of the reasons many companies have entered international markets via direct exporting. Marketing on the Internet through a Web site is the same thing today as opening a global business with a worldwide audience. Unlike traditional exporting, which began with brokers and other intermediaries who assisted companies in generating international sales from preselected foreign countries, a Web site is immediate and inexpensive. However it does not permit much selectivity in choosing markets. Research has shown that more than 82 percent of Internet users are based in countries other than the United States and Canada.[5] This may often lead to fulfillment problems for direct marketers, who don't have the distribution network or capability of fulfilling international orders in some countries.

There are four compelling reasons for direct marketers to decide to go international in their marketing efforts. These are limited growth opportunities in the domestic market, shared global values, the high cost of new product development, and competitive forces.[6] The market potential of many international markets is extremely attractive for direct marketers and has been for a number of years. International direct marketing is not new. Let's take a short look at the use of direct marketing around the world.

DIRECT AND INTERACTIVE MARKETING AROUND THE WORLD

According to the Direct Marketing Association (DMA) *Fact Book,* the oldest known catalog was produced by Aldus Manutius of Venice in 1498 and listed the titles of 15 texts Manutius had published.[7] Next came seed and nursery catalogs, the earliest known mercantile gardening catalog being a printed price list issued by William Lucas, an English gardener. But it was in Germany that direct marketing truly has its roots. Germany had a parcel post system by 1874, and a collect on delivery (COD) system by 1878. The first known European consumer catalog was distributed in 1883, about the same time that Richard Sears was creating his first catalog in the United States.[8]

By 1912, a German businessman, August Stuchenbrok, produced a 238-page catalog—which was five years before Leon Bean (of L. L. Bean) sold his first pair of boots.[9] One of the largest catalog houses in the world is also owned by a German company, Otto Versand, who owns Spiegel, Eddie Bauer, and Newport News, among others.

DIFFERENCES BETWEEN DOMESTIC AND INTERNATIONAL DIRECT MARKETING

What makes international direct marketing different from domestic direct marketing? Market uncertainty is one of the biggest differences. The uncertainty of different foreign business environments is due to differences in infrastructure, technology, competitive dynamics, legal and governmental restrictions, customer preferences, culture, accepted payment methods (such as the use of credit cards), and many additional uncontrollable variables. These factors make many direct marketers hesitate to leap into international markets, regardless of their potential.

To ensure success in foreign markets direct marketers must first research the cultural differences of the prospective market. Primarily, the culture being examined needs to be recognized as being either a collectivist or individualistic society. In a **collectivist culture** emphasis is placed on the group as a whole. History, family ties, loyalty, and tradition are revered above individual accomplishments. Societies sharing strong attributes of collectivism include cultures like that of Latin America, Asia, and the Middle East. In **individualistic cultures,** the value lies on the achievements and successes of the individual person. Independence and a strong sense of self take priority over any group focus. Cultures such as the United States, Europe, Canada, and Australia maintain this individualistic quality. For example, Tang, the orange-flavored powdered drink, was marketed successfully in the United States as an orange juice substitute. However, in France, Tang had to be marketed as a refreshment beverage because the French do not normally drink orange juice at breakfast. Thus, customer preferences driven by cultural differences dictated the marketing strategy.[10]

Different country laws can also dictate marketing strategies. For example, in Europe there are many restrictions on advertisements for cigarette and tobacco products, alcoholic beverages, and pharmaceutical products. Ads for other products may also be regulated. Advertisements in the United Kingdom cannot show a person applying an underarm deodorant. Therefore, ads are modified to show an animated person applying the product.[11] In addition, many Western European countries allow partial nudity in late-night television advertisements. There may be tremendous opportunities in foreign markets, but direct marketers must conduct careful, calculated research before they venture abroad.

MAKING THE DECISION TO GO INTERNATIONAL

Various researchers have offered tips or processes to follow when deciding to begin international direct marketing activities. Today, it has become increasingly important to pursue **global market segmentation (GMS)** as a starting point for going global. GMS can be defined as the process of identifying specific segments, country groups, or individual consumer groups across countries of potential customers who exhibit similar buying behaviors.[12] The following five-step approach is a synthesis of the many processes suggested for screening, selecting, and marketing to an international country:[13]

Step 1: Assess Your International Potential

Direct marketers must analyze their domestic position in their industry to provide an indication of the strength of their foundation and resource base from which they can expand. A part of this assessment is determining whether there are adequate external resources to assist them in penetrating international markets. Some of these external resources may include *expert advice and counseling*. Many organizations exist in the private and public sector to assist firms in beginning an international marketing program. Some of these resources include the following:

- Bureau of the Census (www.census.gov)
- CIA—Country Fact Sheets (www.cia.gov)
- DMA Global Knowledge Network Services (www.the-dma.org)
- Forefront Corporation (www.forefrontinternational.com)
- GroupM (www.groupm.com)
- Market Development Cooperator Program—MDCP (www.ita.doc.gov/td/mdcp)
- Partners International (www.partnersinternational.com)
- U.S. Chambers of Commerce—AMCHAMS (www.uschamber.org/intl/amcham.la.htm)
- U.S. Department of Commerce—Foreign Trade Highlights (www.doc.gov)
- U.S. Department of State (www.state.gov)
- U.S. Market Development Group (www.usmarketgroup.com)
- U.S. Small Business Administration (www.sba.gov)
- U.S. Trade Information Center (1-800-USATRADE)

In addition, many industry trade associations and graduate business programs at universities provide assistance to companies beginning international marketing activities.

Step 2: Conduct Marketing Research

Conducting market research is critical to understanding the cultural differences and country market nuances that may exist. Identifying potential overseas markets involves a great deal of time, effort, and research. However, given the vast amount of data available about each foreign market, researching a single market is likely to provide information overload. Savvy direct marketers sort through all the data and determine the pertinent information they need to analyze the potential of a foreign market.

Direct marketers must determine whether consumers have a basic need for their products/ services and whether the resources necessary for them to carry out local business activities are available. International direct marketers must understand the local color of the destination country, including such information as what consumers buy, why they buy, how they pay for it, and what motivates them to make a purchase. At a minimum, direct marketers must understand local buying behavior, typical payment methods, advertising practices, and privacy laws. The customers in other countries are not Americans who simply live abroad. They have different cultures, different tastes, and different needs and wants and must be segmented accordingly. For example, Europe is highly diverse in terms of geography, language, economic development, spending habits, disposable income, and so on. Therefore, direct marketers aiming at one unified European Union will likely fail.

Direct marketers must also research the national business environment of the target country including its cultural, political, legal, and economic situation. Determine whether the language, attitudes, religious beliefs, traditions, work ethic, government regulation, government bureaucracy, political stability, fiscal and monetary policies, currency issues, cost of transporting goods, and the country image are clear and acceptable.

The state of a country's infrastructure must be factored into the potential for success in that country's market. Infrastructure is normally a leading indicator of economic development and must be in place to support the direct marketer. A country's **infrastructure** represents those capital goods and services that serve the activities of many industries. At a minimum, the infrastructure analysis should include the following essential services: transportation, communications, utilities, and banking. There are really three infrastructure pillars that support the international direct marketing industry—the publishing industry, the transportation industry, and advances in high technology.[14] Because of its importance, we discuss infrastructure in greater detail later in this chapter. Marketing research should also investigate the potential market or site to determine the suitability of the market for the particular product or service. Would the product succeed in this market? Certain locations may not be acceptable due to the lack of resources available for marketing a specific product or service. Therefore, direct marketers must conduct a detailed country-by-country analysis to properly select which markets to penetrate. Market research for each country under consideration can be boiled down to the following primary international market indicators. These include population, political stability, GDP/inflations, distribution of wealth, age distribution, currency, tariffs and taxes, and computer ownership. Let's look briefly at each.

POPULATION   Direct marketers should consider the size of the population segments that fit your targeted prospect profile. Direct marketers should take into consideration a country's population along with its overall wealth. For example, direct marketers should be cautious in entering a country with a large population but little monetary wealth. Direct marketers may prefer entering a market with a small population that has a high per capita gross domestic product (GDP), such as Singapore.

POLITICAL STABILITY   The political stability of a country becomes extremely important for those direct marketers planning to establish a physical presence there. In addition, political shifts in power and leadership may affect foreign exchange rates and tariffs.

GDP/INFLATION   The rate of inflation of a country affects the purchasing power of consumers within a country and is closely related to the country's GDP. GDP stands for **gross domestic product,** which is the total market value of all final goods and services produced within a nation's borders in a given year. When assessing a country's GDP and inflation rates, most direct marketers look for annual trends going back as far as five years.

DISTRIBUTION OF WEALTH   Direct marketers must assess the distribution of wealth in a country to determine whether there are a substantial number of consumers who are able to afford the product or service. As in the United States, some international countries, such as Mexico, have the situation where the top 10 percent of the population possesses more than 50 percent of the wealth. Thus, the size and viability of a market in any country depends on the target market customer's disposable income.

AGE DISTRIBUTION   A look at age distribution assesses both the average longevity of the citizens as well as the age breakdown of the population. The age structure of a population affects the nation's key socioeconomic issues. Countries with young populations (high percentage under age 15) need to invest more in schools, whereas countries with older populations (high percentage aged 65 and over) need to invest more in the health sector.[15] For example, a population comprised primarily of young adults is great if you are marketing soft drinks; however, if you are marketing automobiles, the likelihood of these young people having the income to purchase the product is considerably lessened.

CURRENCY   An assessment of the currency of a foreign country includes an evaluation of the convertibility and ease of exchange of currency, inflation rates, and credit card penetration. While currency and payment method may be separate issues, they may be related in some countries. For example, in 2005, 86 percent of Mexican consumer purchases were still made in cash. This lack of credit card usage was attributed to Mexican citizens' inability to afford the high interest rates accompanying credit cards, which at times exceeded annual interest rates of 39 percent![16]

TARIFFS AND TAXES   How difficult and expensive is it to bring goods across a country's international border? Do local regulations such as tariffs and taxes favor locally produced goods and services over imported ones? These are the types of questions with which direct marketers must be concerned when deciding to go international.

COMPUTER OWNERSHIP   How widely are computers used, and how many computer users have Internet access? In many countries, the majority of consumers do not have easy Internet access. This poses a problem for direct markers who seek to create a virtual business.

POSTAL/DELIVERY SERVICES   This category includes the postal system as well as private delivery alternatives. Some areas to address include the following:

(a) Adequacy of the change-of-address system available;
(b) The existence of parcel COD system;
(c) The existence of a track-and-trace system for parcels; and
(d) The level of sophistication and format of the postcode system.

If any of these researched items do not satisfy a business's requirements or justify the modifications necessary to carry out necessary marketing activities in that country, then perhaps that country should be eliminated from further business consideration.

Step 3: Select Your Trading Partners

Based on the research collected and analyzed in step two, careful analysis should provide an indication as to which markets would be receptive to the particular product and/or service. Direct marketers should select the market or site that holds the greatest potential for successful international marketing. Although many companies are anxious to get an international direct marketing campaign started, it can be extremely taxing on a company. Most experts suggest targeting only one country at a time. Multicountry rollouts are very difficult to execute successfully.

This is the step of the process that may require traveling to those countries or markets that have been selected. During these field trips, direct marketers should investigate the nuances of the market and perform a competitor analysis. Many countries select neighboring countries for trading partners or they select those countries that share a common language and culture.

Step 4: Develop an International Direct Marketing Plan

Direct marketers should create a detailed marketing plan itemizing their long-term goals along with the competitive niche the firm is attempting to fill. They should prepare the marketing plan to cover a two- to five-year period, along with a competitor analysis. This plan should detail communication and distribution strategies. For example, direct marketers must determine the media mix for communicating the promotional message. Keep in mind that internationally, postal reliability and postal rates may limit mail-order offerings, including many catalogs.

Regarding distribution strategies, direct marketers must determine whether they will have a physical presence in the country. Although many international consumers look for U.S. products on the basis of reputation and prestige, they also want the feel of a local presence. This translates into the need to have a local in-country return address along with customer addresses without country codes, response call centers handled in the native language, country- and language-specific Web sites, prices quoted in local currencies, and so on. However, given today's technological advances, it is possible for U.S. direct marketers to create a "virtual" local presence if the firm cannot attain a physical presence. (This is attained by making the intangible tangible.)

Step 5: Begin International Direct Marketing Activities

Implementing a direct marketing plan is expensive and time-consuming. However, for many direct marketers, it is very well worth it. As direct marketers begin to implement their strategies, revisions may be necessary. The international business environment is extremely unpredictable. It is a dynamic environment that must be constantly monitored. Therefore, as direct marketers begin international direct marketing activities, they will need to continue researching and analyzing the changing business environment.

With all the necessary research and preparation, of course, direct marketers entering foreign markets still do so with greater risk than they face when entering the domestic marketplace. Thus they should slowly, not hastily, penetrate one country's market at a time. International direct marketing is all about differences. It should be no surprise then that different foreign market entry strategies exist. We now turn to market entry modes.

MODES OF MARKET ENTRY

There are six basic modes of market entry for penetrating an international market: exporting, licensing, joint venture, contract manufacturing, direct investment, and management contracting.

Exporting

An **exporting** company sells its products from its home base without maintaining any of its own personnel overseas. IBM used direct exporting to expand its global distribution of products like the

OS/2 Warp operating system to businesses and consumers in Japan.[17] Many successful, well-known direct marketers, such as L. L. Bean, conduct their international marketing via direct exporting from their respective home bases. L. L. Bean is located in Freeport, Maine, yet fulfills orders from customers all over the world. However, sometimes the company must have a local mailing address because some customers are reluctant to place orders and send money overseas. For example, in Japan, L. L. Bean works with McCann Direct, the specialized direct marketing division of McCann-Erickson Hakuhodo, Japan's largest foreign advertising agency. When L. L. Bean places ads for its catalogs in Japanese media, those catalog orders are sent locally to McCann Direct. McCann Direct then forwards the orders to L. L. Bean's headquarters in Maine, where all the orders for catalogs or products are fulfilled.[18] L. L. Bean also has a distribution arrangement with FedEx for parcel fulfillment, enabling it to cut delivery time to Japan from two weeks (using air parcel) to three or four days, averaging deliveries of 9,000 parcels a day to Japanese customers.[19]

Licensing

Licensing occurs when a **licensor,** a company located in the host country, allows a foreign firm to manufacture or service a product or service for sale in the **licensee's** country. Licensing is similar to franchising in that a local business in an international country becomes authorized to manufacture or sell specific brand products for another company. Franchising is a form of licensing that has grown rapidly in recent years. More than 400 U.S. franchisors operate more than 40,000 outlets in foreign countries bringing in sales of over $9 billion. Over half of the international franchises are fast-food restaurants and business services.[20] The right to use a patent or trademark must be granted to a foreign company under the license agreement contract. The most common licensing agreements occur when a direct marketer allows a firm in a local country market to reproduce a direct marketing catalog in the local language. An example of a direct marketer using licensing agreements to market internationally is that of Orvis. It markets its outdoor clothing, accessories, and fishing equipment by mailing 50 million catalogs a year through four different titles, and operates about 50 retail stores in the United States, plus another 20 in the United Kingdom. Orvis sells through catalogs, a network of 400 independent dealers worldwide, and its Web site. It also partners with select licensees.[21] In fact, if you go to its Web site, www.orvis.com, you can obtain a listing of its worldwide dealer network along with a listing of international market opportunities Orvis wants to pursue in the future.

Joint Venture

A **joint venture** is created when two or more investors join forces to conduct a business by sharing ownership and control. It is similar to a partnership. Companies understand that marketing alliances with a foreign company can provide a number of benefits. These benefits include easy access to a foreign market, elimination of tariffs and quotas, faster growth and market coverage, and ability to penetrate markets that normally would have been closed to wholly owned enterprises. Joint ventures are normally a win-win situation for each of the partners. For example, Recreational Equipment Inc. (REI) and Austad's, a golf supply cataloger, worked out a cooperative venture with one another and mailed their catalogs together to names on both of their Japanese lists.[22] Another example of a joint venture is that of E*TRADE. E*TRADE, a U.S. Internet-based stockbroker, entered into a joint venture with Softbank Corporation of Japan to offer online investing services in Asia. E*TRADE also entered into a second joint venture with Electronic Share Information in Great Britain.[23]

Contract Manufacturing

Many times, a company will outsource or contract a local manufacturer to produce goods for the company. This strategy, known as **contract manufacturing,** enables companies to take advantage of lower labor costs and faster market entry, while avoiding local ownership problems, and satisfying legal requirements that the product must be manufactured locally for it to be sold in that country. For example, visit the Web site of Texas Instruments at www.ti.com and click on TI Worldwide and you will learn that TI has manufacturing sites and sales and support offices located in Europe, Asia, Japan, and the Americas.[24] While you're there, take note of the selection of TI Web sites featuring different languages designed to serve its international customers.

Direct Investment

Direct investment occurs when a company acquires an existing foreign company or forms a completely new company in the foreign country. For example, Wal-Mart currently has over 6,500 stores, with 2,000 being outside of U.S. borders and accounting for over 20 percent of company sales. In Brazil in 2004, Wal-Mart bought the Bompreco supermarket chain and boosted their company market share from sixth to third. Then the following year in 2005, Wal-Mart had 151 stores in Brazil and was opening 2 more each month. Today, the company reaches half of Brazil's 180 million consumers, and its total sales of $300 billion matches almost half of Brazil's GDP![25] The German company Otto Versand, for example, became the largest mail-order company in the world by buying existing companies or building new ones. Otto Versand owns mail-order companies or is part owner of direct marketing firms in Belgium, France, Italy, Japan, Spain, and the United States.

Management Contracting

In **management contracting** local business people or their government signs a contract to manage the foreign business in their country's market. An example of management contracting is Day-Timers, a U.S. firm located in East Texas, Pennsylvania. Day-Timers uses direct mail to market to millions of business people in the United States. However, it opened offices in Australia, Canada, and the United Kingdom and hired local employees to manage its foreign business locations because it needed to have people who were familiar with the culture and could handle incoming phone calls.[26]

Direct marketers must carefully weigh the advantages and disadvantages of each method and determine which is best for their company. The choice of mode of market entry depends in the end on many factors, one of which we address next.

INTERNATIONAL DIRECT MARKETING INFRASTRUCTURE

Direct marketers must assess the degree of sophistication of each country's direct marketing infrastructure with the goal of determining how well they can use it to implement direct marketing activities. Some questions and issues direct marketers might investigate include:

- Does the country have an active DMA?
- What is the degree to which the support services (printing and publishing services, transportation or package delivery services, postal services, and technological services) are present?
- How sophisticated is the credit card and banking system in the country?
- Is there an established pattern of purchasing via familiar direct channels?
- What legislative issues will affect direct marketing activities?

List Availability
Quality of Postal Service
Average Postage Costs
Percentage of Mail Friendly Households
Internal or External Database
Average Direct Mail Cost per Piece
Availability of In-Line Personalization
Standardized Addresses
Postal Codes
Inbound Telemarketing Availability
Outbound Telemarketing Availability
Availability of Credit Cards
Response Channel Opportunities

FIGURE 12-2   **Direct Marketing Infrastructure.**

Figure 12-2 provides an itemized list of the direct marketing infrastructure needed to support international direct marketing activities. Let's briefly look at some of the infrastructure supporting international direct marketing activities.

Lists and Databases

Lists of both consumer and business customers are normally available for most countries, although different kinds of lists are available in different countries. Mailing lists are one of the most important tools for a global direct marketer. However, the mailing list business (with the exception of Australia, the United Kingdom, Canada, and New Zealand) remains far less developed than that offered within the United States and list sharing among mail-order companies is nearly unheard of.[27] For example, in Europe, there are multinational lists and local lists. In China, lists of factories, ministries, professional societies, research institutes, and universities are available, though quite expensive.[28] A number of vendors in the United States offer international lists, but the quality will vary. It is good practice to test a small representative sample of any list before renting it. Because mailing lists in Russia are so unreliable, Hearst Corporation bypassed direct mail and opted for news-stand sales to distribute the first issues of *Cosmopolitan* to the consumer market.[29] However, Magnavox CATV, which markets cable television equipment, has increased its international mailings to support its many trade shows in developing regions.[30]

Also be aware that a number of laws pertain to information privacy—which normally affects direct marketing list and database activities. Canada's Personal Information Privacy and Electronic Documents Act has had significant impact for direct marketers on both sides of the border.[31] Lists and databases are certainly key areas of importance to international direct marketers.

Fulfillment

Distributing products to the customer is one of the prime difficulties associated with international direct marketing. Direct marketers have two main distribution options available to them—ship products from the home location, or establish a bulk distribution operation overseas. Those direct marketers using their home location have three basic options for distributing products: (1) the U.S. Postal Service (USPS) international mail; (2) non-USPS postal delivery via a foreign postal administration, such as the Royal Mail; or (3) consolidators within the United States (such as Worldpak, Global Mail, and FedEx) that act as a service agent for the international direct mailer.

Besides distribution issues, fulfillment concerns also include the determination of payment options. In the United States, most direct marketers offer consumers the option to pay by credit card, check, or money order. These are not necessarily the standards in foreign markets. Credit card penetration is considerably lower in other countries than it is throughout the United States. In addition and unlike the United States, many consumers in foreign countries primarily use their credit cards for vacation purposes only. Checks, direct debit, bank transfers (wire services), and invoicing are other payment options to be considered.

Another important fulfillment issue is customer service. Direct marketers must make their return policies simple and easy to understand, as well as have toll-free numbers available for consumers to place inquiries or complaints. Local fulfillment centers should be established to handle orders for foreign countries with language barriers. For example, U.S. inventory for Lands' End's U.K., German, and Japanese catalogs is shipped in bulk to local operations in the United Kingdom and Japan. The U.K. fulfillment center handles orders originating from its U.K. catalog and German-language catalog, and the Japanese fulfillment center handles orders for its Japanese-language catalog.[32]

Determining the locations for fulfillment centers and deciding whether to centralize fulfillment operations are among the other decisions international direct marketers must make. Garnet Hill and Paper Direct have centralized fulfillment. Garnet Hill is a consumer apparel cataloger that fulfills orders to customers in about 20 different countries from its centralized facility in Franconia, New Hampshire. Paper Direct is a leading direct marketer of preprinted papers and supplies for the laser and desktop publishing industry and offers more than 3,000 items through four separate catalogs to customers in 35 countries, fulfilling all orders from three distribution centers located in Lyndhurst, New Jersey; Hinckley, England; and Northmead, Australia.[33] Visit the Web site of Paper Direct (www.paperdirect.com) and you will learn that Vista Papers, based in Leicestershire in the United Kingdom, is the exclusive European supplier of Paper Direct products (www.paperdirect.com.uk).[34]

Media

Direct marketers must determine the most effective media mix based on consumer preferences in each foreign market. Media decisions are based on a number of market specific factors, such as media availability, legal restrictions, literacy rates, and cultural factors. A country's level of economic development may also enter into the media mix decision. For example, literacy rates, TV ownership, and computer ownership and technology tend to be lower in less developed countries. Figure 12-3 reveals that Internet advertising revenue is rising, typically at six times the rate of traditional media, although it significantly varies by country. This figure also shows that although country differences exist in Internet usage, there is no significant correlation between the Internet's share of advertising and either the number of connected homes or the number of regular Internet users. Mature countries with high broadband usages appear to be converging on a norm. However, Internet advertising revenue does not include all investments, like advertiser investment in building Web sites.[35]

Shipping products overnight and using telemarketing may also be difficult in less developed countries. In these countries, the establishment and maintenance of databases may prove difficult.

In some countries the price of postage is very low; in others, it is quite expensive. You might be wondering whether the recent increases in U.S. postal rates have affected international direct marketing. The answer is: not really. According to the DMA, 50 percent of direct marketers have increased international mail volume, while 40 percent remained the same.[36] The USPS is aware that it is competing with many foreign postal services. Savvy direct marketers investigate postal rates with six or seven competing postal administrations and then negotiate the best price.[37]

North America	2005	2006	2007	2008	2009 (EST)
Canada	77	82	86	88	89
USA	71	72	75	75	76
LATIN AMERICA					
Argentina	40	41	46	50	54
Brazil	0	0	19	23	27
Mexico	25	23	28	35	44
WESTERN EUROPE					
Austria	59	62	69	73	76
Belgium	53	57	60	62	65
France	49	65	80	80	80
Germany	53	56	62	65	67
Italy	32	33	40	42	44
Netherlands	73	76	78	79	80
Norway	55	60	66	70	74
Portugal	0	29	34	45	56
Spain	34	37	40	42	46
Sweden	66	70	75	77	81
Switzerland	57	68	75	76	78
UK	57	61	65	68	71
EMERGING EUROPE					
Czech Republic	39	46	51	58	65
Hungary	24	34	41	44	47
Poland	25	34	40	45	50
Romania	0	0	24	0	0
Russia	20	24	26	29	31
Slovak Republic	37	43	46	50	57
Turkey	11	20	28	35	46
ASIA-PACIFIC					
Australia	65	67	69	71	71
India	1	3	6	11	18
Japan	57	59	61	63	64
NORTH ASIA					
China	11	13	20	24	28
Hong Kong	59	63	64	64	64
Taiwan	51	51	55	60	65
ASEAN					
Malaysia	42	42	43	44	44
Singapore	66	71	75	77	80
Thailand	20	22	26	31	37
AFRICA					
South Africa	6	6	7	8	10

FIGURE 12-3   Adult Internet Users % of Population.   Source: Group M Interaction 2008. Used with permission.

In many developing countries the mail system is slow and not secure. For example, in Mexico, there is a dearth of mailboxes and the system is very slow, although improving. However, despite these poor conditions, Neiman Marcus Direct sent Mexico 100,000 copies of a Spanish version of its American catalog. Prices were listed in pesos and included all tariffs and duties. All orders were sent to a bilingual telemarketing center in Dallas. Because the response generated was positive, Neiman Marcus Direct now mails catalogs four to six times a year.[38]

In Argentina, mailboxes are considered a luxury and most residents do not have one. Therefore, mail is often delivered directly underneath the door. In an effort to increase delivery to residents, the Argentinean postal service charges lower rates for items that would fit underneath residents' doors. Telecom Argentina saved on postage and chose to capitalize on this cost-saving opportunity by creating innovative mail pieces targeting different market segments. A variety of designs were created, including flat items such as pencil cases which were mailed to students, along with flat sea waves which washed under doors promoting "a flood" of Internet savings through the company's Web site. This campaign won a Silver ECHO award for its creativity and achieved a response of 3.2 percent, which was more than double the goal set by Telecom Argentina.[39]

E-mail marketing can offer direct marketers lower development costs and excellent targeting. E-mail is an efficient and cost-effective alternative to direct mail. In addition, e-mail marketing can provide a faster response—just compare a direct mail campaign that typically takes months to roll out to an e-mail campaign that may take only weeks to execute. E-mail newsletters are a recommended first step into international e-mail marketing, because their circulation tends to be greater than that for solo campaigns. However, to successfully implement e-mail marketing, direct marketers must be aware of each country's local privacy laws.

International acceptance for direct response television (DRTV) has grown. Latin America has become one of the first regions outside the United States to be explored. To successfully use DRTV, direct marketers must be keenly aware of the media landscape, including the key TV stations, cable, and satellite opportunities; the role of third-party negotiators (representatives); federal regulations concerning advertising and infomercials; audience trends; media penetration; and viewing share.[40] Direct marketers normally have two options when launching a DRTV campaign—(1) set up local operations on their own, or (2) use an established DRTV international company.

General Motors used a DRTV campaign in Argentina supported with a series of follow-ups via direct mail, phone, and fax. The campaign, designed to increase test drives and sales of the Astra, offered consumers a free video by calling a toll-free number. The results were phenomenal. Astra's market share in Argentina increased from 5 to 11 percent.[41]

Telemarketing is another medium for direct marketing overseas; however, it is more limited than in the United States and varies greatly from country to country. In many countries, such as Japan, telemarketing is perceived to be too aggressive. As is the case with other types of media, the successful use of telemarketing depends on the level of sophistication of the telecommunications infrastructure.

Creative

In the process of developing the creative materials for any international direct marketing campaign, the four words of wisdom seem to be *research, test, translate,* and *adapt.* Visit the Web site of Nestlé in Peru (www.nestle.com.pe) and you will see how the company effectively translated its Web site for Peruvians. It is critical to present your promotional message in words and images to which your audience can relate. That is why direct marketers must properly research their audience, testing the offer and the copy, carefully translating the message into the proper language, and adapting to the local nuances of different cultures. Words that are entirely appropriate in one country's language are inappropriate and insulting in another. Certain colors, symbols, and designs may also be inappropriate to use in a marketing campaign.

One well-known example of a company adapting to local cultural differences is that of the Coca-Cola Company. In Japan, the word *diet* has a negative impression, because Japanese women do not like to admit they are drinking a product for weight loss. Therefore, the Coca-Cola Company revised the brand name of Diet Coke to "Coca-Cola Light" and successfully introduced and positioned the product in Japan as a soft drink for figure maintenance as opposed to weight loss.[42] Another example of the need to adapt to different cultures and consumer lifestyles is that of N.W. Ayer's Bahamas tourism campaigns designed for the European market. While the overall campaign focused on clean water, beaches, and air, it incorporated different appeals for select European markets. It emphasized sports activities to the German market, and it used humorous ads in the United Kingdom.[43]

To get maximum results, direct marketing campaigns must use promotional appeals that motivate prospects. However, consumer motives vary country by country, and what works in one market may not work in another. Direct marketers using the Web as a marketing medium must also be aware of the legal regulations that vary by country. For example, Germany sued Benetton for "exploiting feelings of pity" with one of its online campaigns.[44] Again, careful market research and cultural adaptation is the key to developing successful creative materials. For example, U.S. consumers are more receptive to advertisements that affect the emotional or even sensual aspects of their decision-making process, whereas the Japanese are more comfortable with logical and rational appeals. Then again, U.S. consumers are said to be far more conservative than are Canadians and Europeans. Regardless of whether the message appeal is emotional, rational, conservative, or liberal, it must be produced to maximize the response from the targeted customer. Cultural adaptation is crucial to the success of the direct marketing campaign when developing the creative appeal.

An excellent example of creativity that was effective was a direct mail campaign executed in India. Seagrams wanted to reinvigorate the image of its Chivas scotch whisky brand in India. Therefore the company invited the country's most famous figures to an elite art show and sale in which Chivas would be promoted. To convince famous guests to attend, a lavish invitation was created. The invitation was designed to look like an artist's portfolio and contained high-quality miniature prints as a preview of the works on sale at the show. The campaign was a great success. The invitation itself became a collectible item, and 90 percent of those invited attended the event. Furthermore, 60 percent of the art displayed was sold.[45]

One of the first measures a direct marketer can take to ensure cultural adaptation is to determine the country's receptiveness to direct marketing activities. Let's look briefly at the indicators used in this assessment.

GEOGRAPHICAL AREA ANALYSIS

Canada

Most Canadians are very familiar with products and services from the United States because the majority of Canadians reside within 100 miles of the U.S. border. In fact, Canada and the United States have many things in common—they even share a professional ice hockey league. However, there are some distinct differences that direct marketers should bear in mind when marketing to Canadians. For example, Canada is officially bilingual in English and French. However, in Quebec, local language laws require all advertising materials to be printed in French.

Taxes and duties assessed in Canada are another area of difference. Three taxes may come into effect when a U.S. company ships products to Canada. These are as follows.[46]

1. *The Goods and Services Tax (GST)*—A 7 percent tax on the total value of the parcel. This tax is applied to all goods imported into Canada with the exception of prescribed property such as magazines, books, or similar printed publications.
2. *The Harmonized Sales Tax (HST)*—A 13 percent tax on the parcel's total value, applicable to all imported goods destined for Nova Scotia, New Brunswick, and Newfoundland, with the exception of prescribed property.

3. *The Provincial Sales Tax (PST)*—An 8 percent tax on the parcel's total value applied to all noncommercial goods imported to Ontario. The provincial retail sales tax rates vary from province to province, as do the goods and services to which the tax is applied and the way the tax is applied.[47]

Duties, or charges imposed on shipments based on a country of origin and commodity, are also imposed by Canada. Under the North American Free Trade Agreement, products manufactured outside the United States or Mexico are subject to duty charges when shipped to Canada. Shipments of noncommercial goods at Can$20 or less are exempt from duties because they fall into an international category of low value shipment.

Canadians are experiencing the same societal pressures as their neighbors in the United States (single-parent families, two parents working outside the home, constant time pressures) that make the ability to shop from home appealing. Privacy issues are also on the rise. However, unlike the U.S. DMA, which has been a proponent of industry self-regulation with regard to privacy, the Canadian Marketing Association has been active in calling for federal privacy legislation.

Other differences between the United States and Canada include cultural ones. For example, Canadian direct marketing appeals don't normally include appeals to patriotism and vanity as U.S. appeals often do.

Europe

The European Union represents 490 million consumers and 10 million businesses at the time this text is being written. Total trade with the United States is over $545 billion.[48] The European Union is made up of 27 different countries with 23 official languages, cultures, and legal systems.[49] Direct marketers are advised to conduct an in-depth study of each country prior to conducting business in that country.

Differences between U.S. and European markets also exist. For example, European stores are not open seven days a week, as many are in the United States. In fact, many European stores maintain hours and service levels that most U.S. consumers would find unacceptable. For example when actual vacation time is calculated, workers average 7.9 weeks in Italy, 7.8 in Germany, and 7 weeks in France, whereas in the United States, the average is 3.9 weeks.[50] Is Europe still an attractive avenue for direct marketing? The answer is, you bet! There are many successful U.S. direct marketers in Europe including Lands' End, Viking, and Allstate Insurance, as well as successful European direct marketers.

An example of a successful direct mail and print campaign in Europe is that of Diageo Ireland's Guinness Relationship Marketing program. Diageo Ireland needed to regain lost market share from competing lagers and ciders that were strongly associated with sporting and music events through sponsorships. To accomplish this task, the company created its own event, "poker night," and chose to communicate with customers on a personal level by sharing stories about the history and heritage of the Guinness product and its bond with consumers. As shown in Figure 12-4, this campaign, "A Passion Shared," helped convert in-pub drinkers of Guinness to also become at-home Guinness drinkers, a vital change in the market, and generated an increase of 17 percent of Guinness consumption.[51]

French direct marketing for consumer products and services is one of the largest markets in the world and one of the fastest growing in Europe, with a 17 percent growth rate between 2005 and 2006. It was valued at $22.5 billion in 2006. The total number of Internet users in France and the total number of commercial Web sites has increased drastically. Currently, there are approximately 30 million Internet users and over 19 million online buyers in France. Among total direct marketing

FIGURE 12-4   Guinness "A Passion Shared" Direct Marketing Campaign.   *Source:* Used with permission of Guiness.

sales, France has the highest rate of Internet sales in Europe. France experienced an increase in online sales of products and services of 37 percent between 2005 and 2006. This attests to the significant role that the Internet will play in future direct marketing sales.[52] Despite the high level of spending on mail-order products, most Europeans are not bombarded with direct mail as are U.S. consumers. In 2005, approximately 5 million items were mailed in the United Kingdom, down 5.3 percent from the previous year.[53]

Some factors affecting direct marketing activities in Europe include:

- *Postal requirements*—formats, location of the window, teaser copy on the outer envelope— must comply with local postal authorities, which differ by European country. Euro Intermail, the leading full-service direct mail company in Italy, is finding great success by designing innovative direct mail pieces for its clients while still complying with the local postal regulations. Many of the direct mail packages it has created have used clear see-through outer envelopes, personalized messages, compelling copy, and small premiums, such as a free pencil or coin. Figure 12-5 provides an example of one of Euro Intermail's creative direct mail pieces.
- *Data protection* is far more stringent in Europe than it is in the United States. Throughout Europe, an opt-out provision is mandatory at the point where you collect data. Until recently, individual countries had their own privacy legislation—which varied from country to country. However, now a Europe-wide privacy directive is in place and must be adopted by every European Union country.[54]
- *Mailing restrictions and policies* may differ by European country. For example, in the United Kingdom, each direct mail package must be approved by the Advertising Standards Authority.

FIGURE 12-5   Euro Intermail Direct Mail Piece.   *Source:* Used with permission of Euro Intermail.

- *The list industry* is strong in Europe. Multinational lists include names and data about individuals who are usually responsive to direct mail offers, speak English, and are internationally minded. The list selections available, output formats, and guarantees equal U.S. standards. Multinational lists allow the direct marketer to test many countries at the same time without incurring additional fees. Local lists tend to be more numerous and offer greater selections.
- *The Benelux,* which includes the countries of Belgium, Netherlands, and Luxembourg, is ideal for direct marketing because of its well-developed direct marketing infrastructure. Lists, payment options, and call centers are all quite advanced in this region of Europe.[55]

Latin America

The population of Latin America is 552 million, and total trade with the U.S. approaches $500 billion—twice that of the European Union. Different dialects of Spanish are spoken across Latin America, and Portuguese is spoken in Brazil.[56] Overall, the direct marketing industry—commercial and business-to-business—is growing at a rate of about 40 to 50 percent per year in most of Latin America.[57] Latin America is a continent of countries made up of very different direct marketing infrastructures. It cannot be treated as a single market except on paper.

For direct marketers, Brazil is the most sophisticated market in Latin America. The lists and databases available there are of fairly high quality. However, fewer public sources of data are available in Latin America than in the United States. With the exception of Brazil, direct marketing is largely underdeveloped in terms of the number of agencies and telemarketing companies in Latin America. However, Latin America is not expected to follow the path the United States did in developing sophisticated direct marketing machinery. The Internet will likely enable Latin America to make revolutionary strides in direct marketing development. An example of a successful online direct marketing campaign in Spain is that of the 2007 Gold ECHO award–winning campaign "The Factory of Dreams" created by the ad agency Uncommon (Havas Group). This multimedia campaign conducted for ESIC, one of Spain's leading business schools, targeted teens contemplating business school. The campaign entailed the distribution of flyers for career events and invited students to play an online interactive game called the Dream Factory. The game led prospects through a series of various challenges faced by professionals in the world of public relations, marketing, and business. Daily text messages prompted players to return to the site to learn more about a prospective career with another game. The campaign was a huge success and generated nearly double the expected online visits, and 65 percent of those who registered for ESIC online played the game.[58]

Although the direct marketing industry is trailing behind in Latin America, the outlook is promising. One reason for this is that the amount of communication one Latin American consumer receives is much lower than that received by U.S. or European consumers. For example, the average household in Mexico receives only six or seven pieces of mail per month.[59] Therefore, the amount of communication clutter is significantly reduced. However, keep in mind that mail services in Mexico are considerably slower than in the United States.

Latin American consumers are very receptive to products made in the United States and have recently shown acceptance of DRTV media as well. Some successful DRTV marketing campaigns in Latin America include the following:[60]

- AB Flex, one of the fitness industry's top-performing products, generated more than $10 million of sales in a nine-month period.
- Murad International Skin Care generated more than $7 million in sales in Mexico alone. The brand awareness generated created an extremely successful continuity program and catalog.

A large part of Mexico's 108 million population subsists below the poverty line. It's the top 10 percent that commands 41.2 percent of the nation's wealth, as well as the next 10 percent, with 14 percent of the wealth. This may be of concern to direct marketers. With 39 percent of the Mexican market under the age of 15, the prospect for future success in direct marketing is great. Thus, Mexico is a very concentrated market—ideal for direct marketers.[61]

Building relationships is important in direct marketing, and this is especially so in Latin America, where consumers crave personal contact and *confianza* (trust). Many Americans find the Latin American perspective on human-space and physical interaction somewhat alarming. They are not nearly as conscious of body-space as Americans are; thus, physical contact is quite common. For example in most Latin American countries, it is expected for men conducting business from the second meeting onward to greet one other with an *abrazo* or hug or sometimes even with a kiss on the cheek. Most business deals will not develop until a friendship has been established. Unlike in the United States, time is not money in Latin America.

Asia

Asia has a population of over 4 billion consumers and millions of businesses.[62] Catalog marketers have struggled with the Asian market for over a decade. The major challenges include the lack of reliable mailing lists, a scarcity of local talent, inadequate phone systems, and the inability to fulfill orders through traditional retailers. Among the lessons many direct marketers have learned in Asia is that you must treat each country separately and understand the local laws and policies. All Asian markets are not equally attractive. Recent research shows that the more accessible Asian countries for direct marketers include South Korea, Taiwan, Hong Kong (China), and Japan.[63] However, one of the major challenges faced by Americans and other Western international companies is a propensity to lump together these markets and assume that all Asian consumers have similar tastes and preferences. This is not true and is an unwise assumption made by companies seeking to enter these markets. Each market demonstrates different preferences toward marketing and often differs in its consumer buying behavior. Let's take a closer look at each of these markets.

SOUTH KOREA   Direct buying in South Korea is growing at 30 percent per year, and South Koreans import $25 billion in U.S. goods annually, and import $359.5 billion total annually.[64] Furthermore, U.S. products are desirable to South Koreans because most of the population is concentrated in cities, especially near Seoul, which accounts for about 20 percent of the entire population.[65] These urban consumers tend to possess a stronger desire to keep up with the latest innovations in technology and trends in fashion. For example, Life's Good (LG), the world's top producer of air conditioners and one of the top three players in washing machines, refrigerators, and microwaves, introduced the Kimchi refrigerator in this market. Kimchi, a spicy cabbage concoction, is very popular in Southern Korea. However, the problem was the dish's odor is so strong that it penetrates all surrounding food items when it is stored in the refrigerator. Therefore, LG implemented their focus on in-depth localization to target the southern Korean community. This approach emphasizes understanding the idiosyncrasies of key local markets by opening in-country research, manufacturing, and marketing facilities. Their efforts paid off when the new Kimchi refrigerator became all the rage in South Korea.[66]

TAIWAN   The direct marketing infrastructure in Taiwan is not fully developed. List availability is very poor and telemarketing is available, but not yet popular. Although the postal service is of very good quality, there is no bulk discount rate for mailings. Direct marketing in Taiwan should expand as its infrastructure improves.

CHINA   Direct marketing in China is relatively new, but growing. With 1.3 billion people, China has great potential for direct marketers with heavy concentrations of wealth in mostly coastal cities.[67] However, like Taiwan, its direct marketing infrastructure is lacking. Although the middle class is growing, the vast majority of the Chinese population has little money, no credit cards, no telephones, and no direct way to receive merchandise. Surprisingly, information privacy is very strict in China, and there are privacy code laws in place. Anyone caught breaking the privacy code laws may be subject to a prison term.

JAPAN   Japan is one of the most advanced countries in the Pacific Rim. Its direct marketing infrastructure is superior to that of its Asian counterparts. Direct mail, telemarketing, home-shopping programs, and even infomercials continue to grow in popularity. The Internet was the most used ad medium by 86.5 percent in Japan in 2004.[68] Japanese consumers used the telephone (59.4 percent), mail (13.9 percent), and Internet (8.8 percent) when ordering products in 2004.[69] An example of a highly successful direct marketing campaign in Japan is that of DHL Japan. Faced with customers who increasingly regarded air express services as commodities, DHL Japan wanted to build loyalty among its customers via a campaign with an emotional appeal. The campaign included year-round greeting cards mailed to customers depicting a seasonal scene with a DHL vehicle or airplane in one of the major International cities of the world, such as Australia in the summer or New York at Christmas. Customers were captured by the beautifully illustrated cards and the campaign exceeded all targeted projections, garnering an ROI of 700 percent.[70]

Egypt

Direct marketing in Egypt is in the early stages of development. Lists of business organizations are available in a directory referred to as KOMPASS. This list contains information such as the nature of business, address, phone number, and key personnel. Also some key highlights about each company are offered, such as number of employees, annual revenues, date of establishment, and legal form of operations. Most direct marketing activities are based on out-bound telemarketing calls to customers. These databases are based on purchases of databases. There are no strict laws and regulations for information privacy in Egypt. Many companies share information with other companies maybe for a fee. Consumers in Egypt are not very concerned about sharing their private information for marketing purposes.

Africa

The African continent is home to more than 840 million individual consumers. The largest country in terms of population is Nigeria, with a population of over 113 million.[71] Over 47 percent of the population is between the ages of 5 and 24. With a large percentage of the population uneducated, the literacy rate varies from one country to another.[72] There is very limited computer access and also low Internet penetration. The North African countries are considered to be the most developed in Africa. Yet there are some counties that exhibit different characteristics. Africa has the fastest growing mobile market in the world. Seven out of ten telephones in Africa are mobile. Direct marketing is considered to be a new phenomenon for many African countries and does not exist in most African markets.

South Africa is considered to be one of the most developed nations in the African continent. There is a direct marketing association in South Africa. This association regulates direct marketing practices and ensures that the rights of consumers and the organizations are protected.

Direct marketing activities in South Africa are growing rapidly. Examples of effective campaigns are those of MWEB. Recently MWEB executed the following two unique direct marketing campaigns with totally different objectives and target markets. "The Voice Box" campaign, created by the Primaplus Agency, targeted a business community in South Africa that was paying extremely high telephone rates but was shy about adopting new technologies. MWEB introduced its ADSL

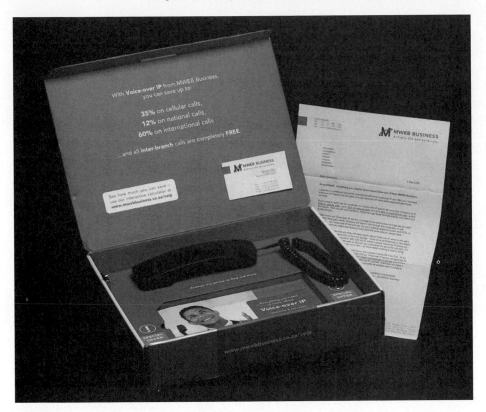

FIGURE 12-6   MWEB's "The Voice Box" Direct Mail Package.   *Source:* Used with permission of Primaplus.

VOIP product to selected CFOs and medical doctors of its high-value ADSL customers, sending them a substantial 3D pack that gave them a unique way to try the new phone service. As shown in Figure 12-6, the pack came with a telephone, which rang as soon as the box was opened and directed them to a designated account manager. The campaign was highly effective with this hard-to-convert audience and achieved an outstanding 60 percent response rate.[73]

The other successful direct mail campaign, called "Babushkalopes," was created for MWEB by Ogilvy One Cape Town. In the South African market, where broadband services are new, the objective of this campaign was to ensure that MWEB's dial-up customers converted to its new broadband service before the competition reached them. To achieve this, a direct mail campaign was built around the theme of the bigger world available through broadband. The mailing conveyed that message with a series of envelopes within envelopes, each of which unfolded to reveal a larger envelope, which resulted in a large poster promoting the product. The campaign was a success, with 9 percent of all consumers receiving the mailing opting to upgrade their service to broadband.[74]

Summary

International direct marketing is on the rise. Many U.S. businesses are seeking to expand by penetrating international markets. In doing so, direct marketers must keep in mind the many unique differences between domestic and foreign markets. Many researchers offer suggestions for how to enter a foreign market. These steps include assessing your international potential, conducting marketing research, selecting your country markets, developing an international marketing plan, and implementing your international marketing strategies. Careful market research, including an assessment of consumer needs, direct marketing infrastructure, and political, economic, and business environments, is necessary prior to commencing international direct marketing activities.

Direct marketers must make decisions involving the mode of market entry—direct exporting, licensing, joint venture, contract manufacturing, direct investment, or management contracting—that they will employ. Direct marketers must make a careful examination of the unique infrastructure needed to support direct marketing operations, including an analysis of lists and databases, fulfillment operations, media, and creative. The direct marketing infrastructure varies by country market and each market must be thoroughly researched and analyzed.

Key Terms

collectivist culture *323*
individualistic cultures *323*
global market segmentation
  (GMS) *324*
infrastructure *325*

gross domestic product
  (GDP) *325*
exporting *327*
licensing *328*
licensor *328*

licensee *328*
joint venture *328*
contract manufacturing *329*
direct investment *329*
management contracting *329*

Review Questions

1. What makes international direct marketing different from domestic direct marketing?
2. Why are companies looking outside the United States to do business?
3. Describe the different modes of market entry that can be used to enter a foreign market.
4. Discuss the primary infrastructure necessary for international direct marketing activities to be carried out with success.
5. Name some of the ways direct marketers have adapted to cultural differences when marketing internationally.
6. Identify and explain the five-step approach direct marketers should follow when marketing to an international country.

7. How do the media preferences vary by country markets? Which country is attractive for DRTV?
8. Compare and contrast direct mail and e-mail as international direct marketing mediums. Which one would be most appropriate to use when marketing in Canada? Europe? Latin America? Asia?
9. Discuss fulfillment operations. What advantages do both centralized and decentralized fulfillment operations offer international direct marketers?
10. Overview the history of direct marketing around the world. Be sure to explain when and where it began and how it grew.

Exercise

The U.S.-based motorcycle company that you are now employed with wants to expand its business overseas. Using the marketing research issues described in this chapter, describe how the company should go about doing this. Based on your analysis, which countries might be considered likely candidates for international expansion? Provide an explanation to support your selections.

CASE
Globalizing an American Catalog
Overview

Mail order's historical roots were in Europe, where catalogs first appeared in the mid-fifteenth century, soon after the invention of movable type and the advent of printing. Its popularity, however, emerged in the United States after the Civil War via the efforts of Aaron Montgomery Ward and Richard Sears. Its burgeoning growth occurred after World War II, spearheaded by a diverse proliferation of catalogs and, most recently, the World Wide Web coupled with electronic ordering. This case is a presentation of a niche catalog, one most likely to succeed in the direct marketing environment of segmented markets, benefit-oriented promotions, and scientific decision making. The purpose of this case study is to demonstrate the application of certain considerations in the globalization of direct marketing, as presented in this chapter, to actual practice. It illustrates how the tools and techniques of direct marketing, used by a successful American catalog, the Peruvian Connection, were applied as the catalog entered first Japan and then the United Kingdom and Germany.

CASE

The Peruvian Connection began when Annie Hurlbut, aged 19, packed a duffel bag and headed for South America.[75] It was the summer of her sophomore year at Yale and, drawn by an interest in archaeology, she volunteered to help an American archaeologist working at the pre-Inca site of Pachacamac outside Lima. She arrived in Peru knowing not a word of Spanish and unsure if anyone would understand her. Asked how she survived those three months in South America, Annie grinned and said, "Blind luck, I guess." But what started as a whimsy evolved into a fascinating business.

Midway through graduate school in anthropology, much of which was spent doing research on women who sell in markets in the Andes, Annie learned about the extraordinary properties of alpaca wool. It is light enough for year-round wear but warm due to unusually high lanolin content, and few fibers in the world equal its softness. She began to export alpaca wool sweaters, and within a few months the new company was christened the Peruvian Connection. Her mother, Biddy, a partner in the business, received the first orders while Annie was doing fieldwork for her thesis in Peru. Since the company's beginning, the business has been run from the family's farm in Tonganoxie, Kansas.

Annie, who had virtually no background in clothing design, began by working with beautiful and unusual sweaters of local artisans. A sense of style enabled her to adapt the sweaters to North American tastes. Now the Peruvian Connection does its own designing, but the same artisans knit for the company on the same antique looms.

Annie insists on using the finest. She keeps prices low by selecting and buying raw materials directly from the producers, and maintains control over quality by checking each product before it is exported from Peru. Annie now augments alpaca wool products with products made of pima cotton.

The Peruvian Connection uses mail order as its primary distribution system, along with three stores in the United States and one in England. Its luxury fiber clothing, blankets, rugs, and hangings are available only from the company. Customers range from enthusiasts of cheap chic to collectors of colonial (from Pizarro's conquest to the Republican era, 1825) native crosses. Contemporary clothing is complemented by wearable art from Peru's rich past. Authenticity and complete satisfaction are guaranteed.

FIGURE 12-7   Comparative Item Presentations from American and German Versions of the Same Peruvian Connection Catalog.   *Source:* Used with permission of the Peruvian Connection.

In the process of building her retail mail-order business, Annie learned early on the value of a customer. After a first sale, her promotional strategy is to send periodic mailings to customers. Annie seeks new customers via market segmentation techniques, matching the profile of her present customers and calculating a present value of new acquisitions to justify their cost. About 260,000 customers purchase from the Peruvian Connection in the United States; another 70,000 customers are in the United Kingdom; and 38,000 are in Germany. These customers generate sales revenues in the range of $40 million, and about half of this amount is from repeat orderers.

Annie herself produces the catalogs, sales copy and photo shoots included. About 6 million catalogs are mailed domestically; another 4 million are mailed internationally.

The Peruvian Connection's global direct marketing began in the late 1980s, first to the United Kingdom, where a retail store was also opened. Even though product selection and page positioning are the same in the U.S. and U.K. versions of the catalog, descriptive copy and pricing differ. The U.K. catalog version contains Anglican spellings and local sizes, and pricing is in pounds sterling. Pricing must incorporate value-added tax and often must anticipate currency fluctuation. The German catalog version, with pricing in deutschemarks, has standard copy translated into German so as to reflect cultural differences. Even though copy is basically the same, review by a native consultant is very important. Figure 12-7 shows similar catalog presentations from the American and German versions of the same catalog.

A real challenge is finding prospects to whom to mail. Annie recognized this early on as she engaged local direct marketing experts and consultants for guidance in list refinement. (It is interesting to note that demographic profiles of her customers are similar in all countries.)

However, the Peruvian Connection must accommodate various cultural differences. It considers cultural differences in payment preferences when fulfilling orders. For example, German customers do not share the U.S. propensity to use credit cards, preferring open-account billing. Foreign funds need to be managed. In addition, the Peruvian Connection considers cultural differences regarding local distribution as well as local use of the telephone and the Internet.

Case Discussion Questions

1. What economic, social, and cultural differences does the Peruvian Connection need to consider as it applies the tools and techniques of direct marketing to diverse international markets?

2. What are the main factors that led to the international success of the Peruvian Connection?

3. If you were hired by the Peruvian Connection to expand its international direct marketing efforts, what additional information would you need to provide suggestions for market expansion? What are some of the avenues you might investigate and recommend for international market expansion?

Notes

1. Adapted from the *Direct Marketing Association International ECHO Awards 2006.*

2. Charles W. Lamb, Joseph F. Hair Jr., and Carl McDaniel (2008), *Marketing,* 9th ed. (Mason, Ohio: Southwestern), p. 106.

3. *The World Almanac and Book of Facts,* 140th ed. (New York, 2008), p. 67.

4. Bob Stone and Ron Jacobs (2008), *Successful Direct Marketing Methods,* 8th ed. (New York: McGraw-Hill), p. 148.

5. Internet World Stats Web site, retrieved in February 2008, http://www.internetworldstats.com/stats.htm.

6. Richard N. Miller (1995), *Multinational Direct Marketing: The Methods and the Markets* (New York: McGraw-Hill), pp. 7–8.

7. Ibid., p. 2.

8. Ibid.

9. Ibid.

10. Michael R. Czinkota and Ilkka A. Ronkainen (2004), *International Marketing,* 7th ed. (Mason, Ohio: Southwestern), p. 539.

11. Ibid., p. 545.

12. V. Kumar and Anish Nagpal (2007), *Marketing,* 29th ed. (New York: Irwin/McGraw-Hill), p. 174.

13. Adapted from John J. Wild, Kenneth L. Wild, and Jerry C. Y. Han (2003), *International Business,* 2nd ed. (Upper Saddle River, NJ: Prentice Hall); adapted from William J. MacDonald, "Five Steps to International Success," *Direct Marketing* 61, no. 7 (November 1998), 32–35; Rainer Hengst, "Plotting Your Global Strategy," *Direct Marketing* 63, no. 4 (August 2000), 52–54; and Richard N. Miller, "Where in the World . . . How to Determine the Best Market for Your Product or Service," *Target Marketing* 24, no. 3 (March 2001), 57.

14. Miller, *Multinational Direct Marketing,* pp. 6–7.

15. Central Intelligence Agency (2007), *2008 World Factbook* (New York: Skyhorse Publishing), p. 346.

16. Stone and Jacobs, *Successful Direct Marketing Methods,* p. 58.

17. Lawrence J. Gitman and Carl McDaniel (2002), *The Future of Business* (Mason, Ohio: Southwestern), p. 81.

18. Czinkota and Ronkainen, *International Marketing,* p. 318.

19. William J. McDonald (1999), *Direct Marketing: An Integrated Approach* (New York: Irwin/McGraw-Hill), p. 349.

20. Lamb, Hair, and McDaniel, *Marketing,* p. 379.

21. Hoovers Web site, retrieved in February 2008, http://www.hoovers.com/orvis-company/—ID__89473—/free-co-profile.xhtml.

22. H. Katzenstein and W. S. Sachs (1986), *Direct Marketing,* 2nd ed. (New York: Macmillan), p. 417.

23. Gitman and McDaniel, *The Future of Business,* p. 83.

24. Texas Instruments Web site, retrieved in September 2003, http://www.ti.com.

25. Philip Kotler and Gary Armstrong (2008), *Principles of Marketing,* 12th ed. (Upper Saddle River, NJ: Pearson Prentice Hall), pp. 565–566.

26. Terry Brennan, "Day-Timers Makes Foray into U.D. with First 100,000-Piece Mail Test," *DM News,* November 15, 1989, p. 14.

27. Stone and Jacobs, *Successful Direct Marketing Methods,* p. 164.

28. Czinkota and Ronkainen, *International Marketing,* p. 318.

29. MacDonald, "Five Steps to International Success," p. 35.

30. Czinkota and Ronkainen, *International Marketing,* p. 318.

31. Beth Negus Viveiros, "As the World Turns," *Inside the DMA* (2002), D19.

32. Lawrence Chaido and Lisa A. Yorgey, "The Back-End of Global Delivery: How to Transport Your Products around the World," *Target Marketing* 21, no. 9 (September 1998), 64–66.

33. Paper Direct Web sites, retrieved in February 2008, http://www.paperdirect.com.

34. Ibid. and http://www.paperdirect.com.uk.

35. "All Change: Marketing in Addressable Media," *Interaction* (April 2007), 24.

36. "The DMA 2005 International Postal Usage Survey," *Statistical Fact Book 2006,* 28th ed. (New York: Direct Marketing Association, 2006), p. 189.

37. Amy Traverso, "A Global Perspective," *DMA Insider* (Fall 2002), 6.

38. MacDonald, "Five Steps to International Success," p. 34.

39. *The DMA ECHO Winners Program 2007* (New York: Direct Marketing Association), p. 39.

40. Priya Ghai, "Southward Bound," *Target Marketing* 24, no. 5 (May 2001), 64.

41. Stan Rapp, "Something New Under the Advertising Sun," *DMA Insider* (Fall 2002), 10–14.

42. Czinkota and Ronkainen, *International Marketing,* p. 257.

43. Ibid., p. 552.

44. Rose Lewis, "Before You Advertise on the Net—Check the International Marketing Laws," *Bank Marketing* (May 1996), 40–42.

45. *DMA ECHO Winners Program 2007,* p. 87.

46. Lisa A. Yorgey, "Navigating Taxes and Duties," *Target Marketing* 22, no. 10 (October 1999), 76.

47. Susan Munroe, About.com: Canada Online, *Provincial sales tax-PST,* retrieved in February 2008, http://canadaonline.about.com/od/personalfinance/g/pst.htm.

48. *The World Almanac and Book of Facts,* 140th ed. (New York, 2008), p. 67.

49. EUROPA Web site, "Education and Training," retrieved in March 2008, http://ec.europa.eu/education/policies/lang/languages/index_en.html.

50. Lamb, Hair, and McDaniel, *Marketing,* p. 112.

51. *DMA ECHO Winners Program 2007,* p. 81.

52. U.S. Commercial Service, "Direct Marketing and E-Commerce Business to Consumer - Best Prospect 2008," retrieved in February 2008, http://www.buyusa.gov/france/en/207.html.

53. *DMA Statistical Fact Book 2006,* 28th ed. (New York: Direct Marketing Association), p. 188.

54. Erika Rasmusson, "The Perils of International Direct Mail," *Sales & Marketing Management* 152, no. 4 (April 2000), 107.

55. Lisa A. Yorgey, "Direct Marketing in the Benelux," *Target Marketing* 22, no. 7 (July 1999), 40.

56. *World Almanac and Book of Facts,* p. 67.

57. Laura Loro, "Zeroing in on Latin America: Infrastructure Varies by Nation, But Marketers Say Opportunity Huge," *Business Marketing* 83, no. 1 (January 1998) 19.

58. *The DMA ECHO Winners Program 2007,* p. 23.

59. Traverso, "A Global Perspective," p. 8.

60. North American Publishing Company, "Southward Bound," *Target Marketing,* 24, no. 5 (May 2001), 64.

61. *World Almanac and Book of Facts,* p. 799.

62. Ibid., p. 845.

63. Rainer Hengst, "Plotting Your Global Strategy," *Direct Marketing* 63, no. 4 (August 2000), 52–57.

64. CIA Web site, "The World Fact Book," retrieved in March 2008, https://www.cia.gov/library/publications/the-world-factbook/geos/ks.html.

65. Hengst, "Plotting Your Global Strategy," p. 55.

66. Elizabeth Esfahani (2006), "Thinking Locally Succeeding Globally," *Annual Editions International Business,* 14th ed. (New York: McGraw-Hill), p. 86.

67. *World Almanac and Book of Facts,* p. 760.

68. *DMA Statistical Fact Book 2006,* p. 190.

69. Ibid.

70. *The DMA ECHO Winners Program 2007,* p. 27.

71. The Africa Guide Web site, retrieved in March 2008, http://www.africaguide.com.

72. Ibid.

73. *The DMA ECHO Winners Program 2007,* p. 42.

74. Ibid., p. 55.

75. The globalization experience presented here, with permission, was conceived and developed by Annie and Biddy Hurlbut. Although the Peruvian Connection's mail-order catalog sales were initially confined to the United States, the company was already international in that its product originated in Peru and other South American countries.

13

...

Applying Direct and Interactive Marketing Math and Metrics

Opening Vignette

Suppose you are the marketing vice-president for a company that has just produced a truly revolutionary running shoe. You have a marketing budget of $5.4 million for the coming year, and since you are introducing the product next year, you decide to spend half of your budget, or $2.7 million, on one 30-second direct response television ad during the Super Bowl in January. The ad provides a Web site address that will allow your company to know when a hit has resulted from people seeing this particular ad. You get 1 million hits on that Web site after the Super Bowl telecast. Is this good? How many shoes did you eventually sell as a result? Did the ad pay for itself or not? Could you have done better by spending your money in some other form of advertising? In this chapter, we'll give you the tools to find out! Remember: Every business is in business to make money for investors, and to do this, a company must create and keep customers. Marketing is a *cost* that leads to *benefits*. It's the ratio between the two that matters. That is why we have a chapter on Marketing Math.

In the next sections, you will learn about key terms and concepts, including response rates, conversion rates, and how to calculate them; customer lifetime value; the concept of a lift; fixed and variable costs; margins; net order contribution; break-even and how to calculate it; and return on investment/return on advertising investment. At the conclusion of the chapter, you will find a case that will allow you to apply what you have learned.

Direct marketing can be called successful, that is, creates *benefits,* when it gains new customers (or new orders from existing customers) for a company. We need to remember that direct marketing also has *costs,* e.g., conducting research, acquiring lists, creating advertising campaigns, and fulfilling orders. The goal is to create a marketing campaign that not only breaks even—that is, gains enough sales to pay for all costs—but results in a profit. To figure out how to be profitable and whether marketing activities are profitable, we need to understand a number of different concepts, terms, and formulas.

USING MATH AND METRICS TO DETERMINE THE "RIGHT" TARGET MARKET

As we have already established in earlier chapters, all consumers are not alike. They can be grouped into market segments on the basis of similar needs and wants. Most companies build profiles of their customers on the basis of the customer data they gather and store in their databases. We discussed the different types of data used for segmenting customers in Chapter 3. The actions taken by consumers are certainly a viable base for market segmentation. The most valuable customer information a company can collect is that which comes after the first sale or transaction. The specific types of products and services consumers have purchased, the time the transactions took place, the method or location of their purchases, and the method of payment they choose can all reveal similarities among consumers. Each behavioral factor can indicate a consumer preference that may be shared by other consumers, consequently identifying a market segment. The creation of a database enables direct marketers to analyze customer transaction data to determine the value of each customer. How does a database help you quantify customer value? How do you measure and calculate customer value? How do you use transaction data to determine customer value? Those are the questions we address in the next section.

Determining Customer Value

It is well established that some customers generate the majority of a company's transactions. We refer to that as the 80/20 principle—approximately 20 percent of a company's customers generate 80 percent of its profits. If that is true, then shouldn't marketers identify those top 20 percent and concentrate on keeping them happy and loyal to the company? Of course! But how do you identify which customers are in the top 20 percent? There are a number of different methods for calculating customer value, such as recency/frequency/monetary assessment, which was discussed in Chapter 2. Another method is to calculate quantitatively customer value via a value equation. Let's take a look at this method. To calculate average customer value, you should follow this four-step process:

1. Take a random sample of customers (active and inactive) who first bought from you about three years ago.

2. Add up the total dollar amount they have purchased in the three years since the date of their first purchase.

3. Divide by the number of customer records in your sample.

4. Multiply by the percentage that represents your average profit margin.

For example, let's pretend you now own a catalog operation selling household gifts. You are in your fourth year in business and want to calculate the average value of your customers. What do you do?

- You randomly select 1,000 customers who have been purchasing with your company for a minimum of three years and obtain a computer printout of their buying history. You see that these customers have placed 1,775 orders during this period with a total value of $89,300.
- You calculate your average profit margin on your household gift lines and determine it to be 20 percent.
- Now let's perform the math! Dividing total sales by customers ($89,300 by 1,000) results in average sales of $89.30 per customer. Then, by multiplying that figure by the average profit margin percent (20 percent), you determine that average customer value is $17.86.

That figure represents what the average customer you acquired three years ago was worth to you in terms of future profits.

What if you were able to motivate your customers to spend twice as much? How much do the 1,000 customers now account for in terms of total sales? The answer is $178,600. Therefore, what is the average value of these customers now? Going through the rest of the calculations, the average customer is now worth $35.72. That figure tells you that you'll now be able to spend twice to acquire a new customer—$35.72 instead of $17.86!

The real benefit of calculating customer value is that it can be calculated on a segment or cluster basis, or on an individual basis. The process for calculating individual or segment customer values is basically the same; however, you would not select a "random" sample of customers but concentrate on the segment or cluster of interest. On the basis of these customer value calculations, you can determine which customers or customer segments are generating the most profitability for your company and concentrate on retaining those customers.

Why calculate the value of customers? Because . . .

- It determines how much each customer is worth to your organization.
- It tells you how much money you can afford to spend to acquire a new customer like your current customers.
- You need to identify your best customers in order to seek out new prospective customers who match the customer profiles of your best customers.

Determining customer value is important, but as described, it is based on past purchasing behavior. Customer lifetime value takes on more of an investment view where you regard your customers as investments in future profitability. Let's explore how to calculate customer lifetime value.

Calculating Customer Lifetime Value

As we discussed in Chapter 2, **customer lifetime value (CLTV)** is the present value of profits to be realized over the life of a customer's relationship with an organization. Customer relationships translate into customer retention, which usually means repeat customer purchases or transactions over time. When a customer is retained, it is not only the revenue generated in a one-month or one-year

$$R = \frac{1 - \dfrac{1}{(1 + i)^N}}{i}$$

where
R = annual revenue from a loyal customer
i = annual relevant interest rate
N = no. of periods in which a customer makes purchases

FIGURE 13-1   Customer Lifetime Value Equation.
Source: Jon Anton and Natalie L. Petouhoff, *Customer Relationship Management: The Bottom Line to Optimizing Your ROI* (Upper Saddle River, NJ: Prentice Hall, 2002), p. 138. Electronically reproduced by permission of Pearson Education, Inc., Upper Saddle River, New Jersey.

period that constitutes the value of that customer, it is the present value of the future stream of revenue that must be taken into consideration. This is the basic premise behind CLTV. Let's see how CLTV can be calculated. Refer to the equation shown in Figure 13-1.

Now let's look at an example to apply the formula and calculate CLTV. Let's assume that you own a fitness business. Based on customer database analysis, you can determine the following about a given customer:

- The stream of revenues from a specific customer is level across time at $25 per month or $300 per year.
- The interest rate (opportunity cost) is the bank rate paid on the money for which no other specific use is made and will be assumed to be 9 percent.
- The amount of time a typical customer stays with a company is three years.

Based on these assumptions, you can calculate CLTV using the formula, where

R = $300; I = 0.09; and N = 3. Therefore, the CLTV of this customer is $759.39.

You might increase a customer's LTV by enticing the customer to spend more on each transaction, thus increasing his or her annual stream of revenues. In addition, you might increase the length of time a customer stays loyal to a firm which in turn would lengthen the investment period. In summary, calculating CLTV is critical for those direct marketers who view their customers as investments.

Determining the "Right" Customer to Target

Quantifying customer value and CLTV can help marketers determine which current customers or prospective customers to target for future direct marketing campaigns. However, it is important to note that customer retention strategies normally generate greater profitability for companies than do new customer acquisition strategies. This is partially due to the value of the established relationship that current customers have with a given company. You must keep in mind that strong customer relationships are directly correlated to strong customer loyalty, and loyal customers are less price-sensitive, spend more per transaction, cost less to serve, and generate positive word-of-mouth referrals! The bottom line: Loyal customers are more profitable!

Many marketers claim that it costs at least five times more to replace a customer than it does to retain a current customer. Mathematically, this can be easily calculated. For example, let's say it costs $5 to keep a customer happy and loyal to your firm (a customer retention strategy) and it costs $25 (five times $5) to replace a customer (a new customer acquisition strategy). Let's perform the math given a budget of $175. Figure 13-2 shows that if we allocate the majority of our budget on acquiring new customers, we net 11 customers. However, if we allocate the majority of our budget

Customer Acquisition Focus	Customer Retention Focus
$150 to acquire customers = 6 $25 to retain customers = 5	$75 to acquire customers = 3 $100 to retain customers = 20

FIGURE 13-2 Customer Acquisition versus Customer Retention.

on retaining current customers, we achieve 23 customers. Given the same budget, the mathematical difference is significant.

The calculations show that it is more cost-effective to concentrate your direct and interactive marketing efforts on customer retention and customer relationship building than it is to concentrate on new customer acquisition. Of course, you will want to first focus on your most valuable customers and then search for customers who possess similar characteristics to these highly valued customers.

It sounds simple, right? But where do you look? How do you begin? How do you know which markets, market segments, or clusters of customers will be more likely to respond to your offer? One method is by conducting market penetration analysis. Let's examine that concept in greater detail.

Analyzing Market Penetration

Modeling techniques can correlate market penetration with demographics, lifestyle research, transaction data, and buyer behavior to reveal those markets that contain the largest proportion of a company's customers. **Market penetration** is the expressed percentage relationship of customers to some benchmark universe. Thus, it tells what percentage of the total universe of potential buyers are customers. Market penetration analysis may be performed on any universe, including ZIP code areas, product lines, customer market segments, or specific demographic categories, such as gender, age, or education. Market penetration is calculated by dividing the number of customers in a specific category (such as a ZIP code area) by the total number of customers the company has in general. Let's take a look at the following example to better understand how market penetration is calculated and used.

Betty's Bakery is located in Erie, Pennsylvania, and is well known locally for offering delicious baked goods. Betty was able to create a customer list and collect information about her customers by offering weekly drawings for a free pie over the past year. She has determined that the 52 free pies were well worth the customer data she has now collected. Looking over the 5,000 customer cards, she noticed that her customers primarily reside in four ZIP code areas as shown in Figure 13-3.

Let's calculate the customer market penetration for each ZIP code area by dividing the number of Betty's customers in each area by the population for each respective ZIP code area. Figure 13-4 shows the market penetration for each ZIP code area.

Based on an analysis of these market penetrations, we can conclude that ZIP code area 16502 contains the largest proportion of Betty's customers, while area 16501 contains the smallest proportion.

Zip Code Area	Population	Betty's Customers
16501	17,050	1,384
16502	11,288	1,785
16503	10,035	876
16504	9,398	1,010

FIGURE 13-3 Betty's Bakery Customer Distribution by ZIP Code.

Zip Code Area	Population	Betty's Customers	Market Penetration %
16501	17,050	1,384	8.1
16502	11,288	1,785	15.8
16503	10,035	876	8.7
16504	9,398	1,010	10.7

FIGURE 13-4   Betty's Bakery ZIP Code Market Penetration.

Thus market penetration analysis can assist Betty in determining which ZIP code area should be targeted for future direct mail promotions. Because it is well known that prospective customers are similar to current customers, Betty should target ZIP code area 16502 for new customer acquisition efforts.

Often, companies make the mistake of targeting the market in which they have the least penetration in an attempt to increase the presence in that specific market segment (for example, ZIP code area 16501). This is not normally a wise strategy because there is usually a reason that the consumers in that market are not responding to company offers in the first place. Perhaps these customers do not have a need or want for the company's products or services. Therefore, a more effective strategy is to concentrate future marketing efforts on those market segments that contain larger customer penetrations.

MEASUREMENT IS THE KEY

The single most notable feature of direct and interactive marketing is that it always seeks a measurable response. Regardless of whether that response was in the form of a Web site or in-store visit, or a phone call to place an order or request additional information, all responses can be measured and evaluated. Thus, determining *what* to measure becomes the challenge. First and foremost, let's discuss how to calculate response rates to conduct response rate analysis.

Calculating Response Rates and Conducting Break-Even Analysis

Possibly the most frequently asked question in direct and interactive marketing is, "What response rate should I expect to my offer?" In reality, there is no universal or normal response rate. The rate can vary relative to such important considerations as the product itself as well as the demand for it, price competition, market preference, and the nature of the promotional offer. A preprinted insert in a Sunday newspaper will generate more response if there are no directly competitive offers in the same issue. A product in the early stages of its life cycle will create more attention and more interest than one that is generally available and displays little if any differentiation.

A more realistic question to be asked in evaluating the response to an offer is probably, "What response do I *need?*" What would it take to just **break even** on a particular offering? And, what response rate will give me a *profit?* We will discuss the concept of break-even in more detail in the next section, but let's look here at how knowing the number of sales it takes to break even allows us to calculate what we need to sell to earn a profit.

The formula for determining break-even point for a single sale to a new customer is shown in Figure 13-5.

$$\text{Break-even number of sales} = \frac{\text{Promotion cost}}{\text{Unit margin (or profit) per sale}}$$

FIGURE 13-5   Break-Even Formula.

Product/Offer: *Practical Mathematics* @$39.95, net 30 days

Assumptions:

# Promotions Mail'd	9,508
Shipments Return'd	8%
Sales Uncollectable	6%

Order Processing/Collection Costs:

Gross Orders	100@$1.80=$180.00
Less: Returns	8@8% of 100
Net Sales (A)	92@$0.50=$ 46.00
Total (B)	$226.00
Cost Per Net Sale (B/A) =	$2.46

Cost of Returns:

Return Servicing	$1.30
Shipping/Delivery	$2.20
Total (C)	$3.50
Returns Project'd(D)	8%
Cost Per Net Sale	$0.30
(C x D/1.00-D)	

Break-Even Calculation:

Line	Description		
1	Selling Price		$39.95
2	Cost-of-Goods Sold	$5.99	
3	G&A Allocation	$3.80	
4	Shipping/Delivery Costs	$2.20	
5	Processing/Collection Costs	$2.46	
6	Cost of Returns	$0.30	
7	Sales Uncollectable	$2.40	
8	Premium Gift Cost	$0.54	
9	Total Production Costs		$17.69
10	UNIT PROFIT (Line 1–Line 9)		$22.26
11	Total Promotion Costs per M Pieces Mailed (includes database, print, mail, postage, overhead)		$345.83
12	BreakevenNtSales/M PiecesMailed(Line11/Line10)		15.54

Total Profit at Alternative Levels of Net Sales:

13	Projected Net Sales per M Pieces Mailed	17	20	25	30	35	40	45
14	Less: Break-even Sales (Line 12)	15.54	15.54	15.54	15.54	15.54	15.54	15.54
15	Net Sales Earning Full Unit Pro (Line 13–Line 14)	1.46	4.46	9.46	14.46	19.46	24.46	29.46
16	Unit Profit (Line 10)	$22.26	$22.26	$22.26	$22.26	$22.26	$22.26	$22.26
17	Net Profit per M Pieces Mailed (Line 15 x Line 16)	32.61	99.39	210.69	322.00	433.30	544.61	655.91
18	M Pieces Mailed	9,508	9,508	9,508	9,508	9,508	9,508	9,508
19	Total Net Profit (Line17 x Line 18/1000)	$310.01	$944.98	$2,003.26	$3,061.55	$4,119.83	$5,178.11	$6,236.40
20	NtPr'fit %NtSales: Line19/Line1 x Line13 x Line18/1000	4.80%	12.44%	21.10%	26.87%	30.99%	34.08%	36.49%

FIGURE 13-6   Break-Even Worksheet.

That is, if the marketer recovers promotion cost from the gross profit (beyond cost of goods sold and overhead) of the total number of units sold, he or she breaks even *on those sales.*

Figure 13-6 provides a worksheet for calculating the break-even point and profit at various levels of unit sales per thousand pieces of direct mail promotion. A variation of this worksheet can be used for any medium.

Lines 2 through 8 of the break-even calculation in Figure 13-6 represent production costs, totaling $17.69 (line 9) per copy of a book, *Practical Mathematics.* Order processing/collection costs (line 5) and costs of returns (line 6) are amortized and allocated to net sales, in the manner shown at the top of Figure 13-6.

Unit margin (also known as unit profit or unit contribution), calculated by subtracting $17.69 (line 9) from the selling price of $39.95 (line 1), is $22.26 (line 10). Unit margin divided into total promotion costs of $345.83 per thousand pieces mailed (line 11) provides break-even net sales (line 12). This is 15.54 units per thousand (M), or 1.55 percent. That is the answer to our earlier question: "What advertising response is needed to just break even?" Having calculated a break-even response rate of 1.55 percent, lines 13 to 20 of Figure 13-6 present alternative profit amounts at assumed alternative levels of net sales.

The calculation assumes the offering of only a single item and anticipates a desirable net profit at various levels of response beyond the break-even point. However, a more likely and realistic calculation for direct marketers uses continuity, and is applicable to long-term recovery of future time periods, such as that experienced by magazine publishers, insurance companies, fundraisers, and catalog merchandisers who expect repeat orders from new customers.

Response rates will also vary widely according to prequalification of the mailing list or the narrowness and appropriateness of market segments targeted. Typically, all other factors being equal, current customers will respond to an offer for a new product at a much higher level than will prospective customers. In addition, a company's more valuable customers, with whom a stronger customer relationship has been cultivated, will likely respond at much higher rates to company offers than will all other customers. This phenomenon is called a *lift,* and it can be mathematically measured and evaluated. Let's learn more about this valuable concept.

Calculating the Impact of a Lift

A **lift** is an increase in the average response rate due to making an offer to only those market segments or clusters that are predicted to be most responsive. A lift can be applied to any direct response communication where selectivity is involved. For example, if you are creating a direct mail campaign, a lift can decrease the mailing quantity needed (via selectivity) and increase the overall response rate. Thus, a lift will produce a double cost advantage for a company in its direct and interactive marketing efforts.

How is a lift calculated? Figure 13-7 shows that a lift is basically the *new* response rate divided by the *old* response rate (achieved prior to selectivity).

For example, let's say we distributed a direct mail package to all of the 10,000 clients in our database and it garnered a 2.0 percent response rate. Not bad, right? But could it be improved? Maybe, via database analysis! Let's say we analyzed our database to identify those clients who purchased from our organization within the past month. Based on our analysis, we determine that 3,255 clients actively purchased from our company during that time period. For our next direct mail campaign, we decide to selectively mail to those 3,255 individuals instead of our entire client population. We have now decreased our costs (printing, production, postage) and achieve a response rate of 3.52 percent. What happened? That is what we call a lift. As Figure 13-8 shows, the lift for this example was 1.76 percent.

Most companies are striving to maximize response rates to their direct and interactive marketing campaigns. All else being equal, a lift can generally generate an increase in response rate due to greater selectivity and produce lower costs associated with the more precise, targeted niche promotional effort. However, beyond increasing response rates, most companies want to generate sales and maximize profitability.

Marketers evaluating the concept of a lift will normally seek to reduce any extraneous variables that may factor into the difference in response rates. Therefore, in an attempt to isolate and measure the impact of a lift, many marketers use a control group and an experimental group. These concepts were presented in Chapter 10, but apply here as well. Once a direct marketing effort has been made to two different groups at the same time, the lift in response rates can be calculated. Marketers will also create and impose rules to more accurately measure lift on the marketing effort.

Beyond using a control and test group, some marketers have created a panel group that is reserved for calculating the potential lift in response rates. This method may be used to determine

$$\text{Lift} = 100 \times \frac{\text{New response rate}}{\text{Old response rate}}$$

FIGURE 13-7 Lift Calculation Equation.

$$\text{Lift} = 100 \times \frac{3.52}{2.00}$$

FIGURE 13-8 Example Lift Calculation.

the impact that a catalog or mailing has had (if any) on customer response rates and transaction amounts. Thus, the concept of a lift can be applied to the measurement of almost any medium. For example, let's say we want to investigate the impact of catalog mailings on a company's Web site sales. We plan on mailing a million catalogs. So, we take a random sample of 100,000 customers and these customers will not receive the catalog in the mail. We then review the 21-day Web site sales at the household level and factor out sales for the group that did not receive the catalog mailer. The results show that those customers treated with receipt of a physical catalog generated sales of $1.10/online catalog, and those who did not actually receive the mailed catalog generated sales of $1/online catalog. Therefore, the implied Web lift due to catalog receipt is 10 percent. At the source code level, the measurement of a lift is complete. However, many marketers want to know additional details about responses at the customer or household level, which is a bit more sophisticated and entails more detailed database analysis.

Often consumer responses are in the form of an inquiry or request for additional information. These responses, called leads, afford the marketer the opportunity to convert those inquiries or leads into sales. This is called lead conversion and it is the topic of our next section.

Determining Conversion Rates

Conversion refers to the transfer of a prospective customer to an actual buying customer. Many consumers do not actually place an order or make a donation during their first interaction with a company or organization. In fact, the initial objective of a company's offer is often to entice the prospective customer to request additional information. This is the process of lead generation. These initial inquiries are then followed up with additional interaction between the company and the prospect, with the ultimate goal of new customer acquisition. The rate by which a company converts these leads into sales is called its **conversion rate.**

As Figure 13-9 reveals, a conversion rate is calculated by dividing the number of buyers by the number of inquiries, expressed as a percentage.

For example, let's say you have 1,000 inquiries and 300 of them have subsequently become buyers. You have a conversion rate of 30 percent. Achieving a high conversion rate is important because each direct marketing effort will likely cost the company additional dollars and will need to be allocated in a company's promotional budget. The concept of planning the direct marketing budget is the topic of our next section.

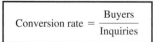

$$\text{Conversion rate} = \frac{\text{Buyers}}{\text{Inquiries}}$$

FIGURE 13-9   Conversion Rate Formula.

PLANNING THE DIRECT MARKETING BUDGET

To help us put together all the concepts we will be working with in this next section, let's create a mythical company: Permanent Wear (PW). This company produces all kinds of clothing from micro-fibers. Their director of marketing is Charlie Perry. This year, PW is introducing a new line of jeans for men and women. Their jeans will be more expensive than some other brands, but they can be washed and worn for a much longer time than regular cotton fabric jeans, and they look good! As part of their new line introduction, PW has to conduct research, evaluate its probable market, create a marketing campaign, prepare a budget, and decide how it will measure the success of its direct marketing campaign. Let's see how Charlie and PW do, using marketing math.

PW has conducted its research, segmented its market, bought and created lists, prioritized the media it wants to use for advertising, and generated some preliminary ideas for creative materials, so it's time for Charlie to develop his direct marketing budget. Many companies will use one of the following traditional approaches to establish how much money to allocate to marketing:

- Establish a percentage of probable sales revenue
- Take a percentage of last year's profit
- Use last year's marketing budget, plus a small percentage increase
- Make a good guess on how much is needed

In direct marketing, the budget is a function of:

- Net order contribution of the item(s) sold
- Media/sales costs
- Response rates
- Desired level of profitability

Another difference between traditional marketing budgets and direct marketing budgets is that in direct marketing, campaign results are constantly monitored, and changes can be made in strategy even while the campaign is in progress—or before the next one is executed. Remember: Direct marketing is *always* measurable and accountable.

How to Begin: Estimating Costs

Each advertising campaign needs to be treated as an individual cost/profit exercise. So, in the case of PW, if Charlie is planning to use the Internet for one major introductory campaign of the new jeans, he will need to work up a budget for that campaign.

Where does he start? One way is to list all the elements he would like to use in the campaign as if he had an unlimited amount of money. For example, maybe he would like to run banner ads for one month on three major Internet sites. Here are some of the elements he would have to include in his preliminary budget.

For the ad itself:

- Creative/production/cost of hiring a designer
- Cost of the banner ad for 30 days on 3 sites
- Cost of hiring someone to record and analyze the hits

For the campaign:

- Fixed costs
- Cost of goods sold
- Other variable costs
- Fulfillment costs
- Credits and returns

If Charlie wanted to create campaigns using other media, for example, direct mail, national television, magazine advertising, his advertising costs would involve different elements.

As Figure 13-10 shows, each medium has its own costs, but two constants are the costs of the *creative materials* (both the personnel to create them and the production and duplication) and the *media buy* (the cost of time or space to present the creative materials), except in direct mail and

Medium	Creative Cost Elements	Related Costs
Broadcast	Script writer(s)	Cost of air time
	Talent (announcers, actors)	Cost of distributing
	Studio time/rental to film/tape	or disseminating
	Recording equipment	finished product to
	Crew (camera people, engineers, etc.)	broadcast outlets,
	Duplication equipment	e.g., by mail, satellite
	Discs, film, tape for duplication	Time buyer (if used)
	Rights to use copyrighted material	
	Pre-produced sound effects, pictures	
Electronic (Internet)	Artists/writers who create ads	Cost of placements
	Computer design software	Cost of site maintenance
Catalogs	Writers, artists, photographers	List creation/rental
	Rights to use copyrighted pictures, photos	List maintenance
	Materials: computer software, drawing	Production/duplication
	boards, artists' supplies	costs of catalog
Direct Mail	Writers, artists, photographers	Duplication costs
	Production equipment, e.g., computers,	List creation/rental
	design software, printers	List maintenance
	Paper stock/photo stock	Lettershop
		"Nixies" and returns
Out-of-Home:**		
Billboards	Writers, artists, photographers	Billboard rental
	Production equipment	Billboard maintenance
	Paper stock (if not provided by	
	billboard co. as part of rental)	
Buses	Writers, artists who create copy	Bus side rental
	Production equipment	Duplication costs
	Paper stock	
Point of sale	Same as for buses	Duplication costs
Print	Writers, artists, photographers	Space buy, e.g., in
	Production equipment and costs	newspaper, yellow
	Rights to copyrighted material	pages, magazine
Telemarketing	Writers to create scripts	Telephone lines
		Salaries for staff
		making/taking calls
		Computers and programs
		for call makers/takers

* For several of these media, e.g., broadcast, out-of-home, and print, there may be additional costs of working with personnel at an ad agency, if one is used.

** Other "out-of-home" media may include posters in subways, airports, other public places; aerial banners or other mobile media displays; table-top ads at large events. Generally, all of these will share the common creative costs of artists, writers, and photographers, plus any special space/place rental costs.

FIGURE 13-10   Costs of Creative Elements by Media.[*]

telemarketing, where instead of media buy costs, Charlie would have mailing costs or personnel and telephone line rental costs.

The First Calculations: Margins, Fixed and Variable Costs

Let's say Charlie has added all his costs for his ideal Internet campaign, and they come to $3 million. Can PW afford this campaign? How many jeans can they sell and at what price to afford it and

Fixed Costs	Variable Costs
Rent/mortgage on facilities	Costs of goods sold, tied to production
Salaries of permanent staff	Commissions to sales people
Amortization of facilities	Order processing
Overhead of running company	Shipping, delivery, returns, restocking
Advertising	Costs of money (financing)
	Bad debt
	Fulfillment activities

FIGURE 13-11 **Types of General Fixed and Variable Costs.**

make money? Charlie has to look at some other factors. First, he needs to understand what the likely margins on sales of the new jeans are likely to be.

Let's start with total sales. If the new jeans retail for an average price of $88 a pair, and the company expects to sell 100,000 pairs in a year, then their **gross sales** or total sales would be: $88 × 100,000 = $8,800,000. But of course, it costs the company something to make and distribute the jeans. Therefore, we use the term **cost of goods sold** to include the **variable costs** that come into play when making and selling the jeans. PW knows that their cost of goods sold for this line of jeans will be $22 per pair. This includes the cost of manufacturing the fabric, sewing the jeans, shipping them out, processing orders, allowances for bad debt, and handling returns. Variable costs are those costs that vary with production. **Fixed costs** are those costs that do not vary with production. (See Figure 13-11 for examples.)

Another important concept here is the **unit margin** or trade margin (also called unit contribution or unit profit) that each sale provides. Remember, we talked about this in discussing response rates. This is like the concept of the gross margin except that the unit contribution is simply the amount that *each sale* provides to cover all other costs. In our example, the unit margin of each pair of jeans is $66.

$88	average selling price for one pair of jeans
−22	cost of goods sold/variable costs
$66	unit margin

This $66 is what is left over after a sale to cover all fixed costs, which, as we have seen, include the overhead necessary to run the entire business. Why do advertising costs count as fixed costs? Because the advertising dollars will be spent regardless of how many units are produced and sold. It is going to cost Charlie the same amount to advertise on the Internet whether the company gets 3 orders or 3 million. The same is true of his advertising budgets for all other media: if he plans to spend $2 million this year on network television, that is a fixed cost, regardless of how many orders he gets as a result of this particular advertising campaign.

Another important concept comes into play here: the **allowable margin.** Many companies will establish an allowable margin for each promotional campaign. Basically, it represents the amount of money you have left over to cover advertising/promotion and profit after *all* other expenses have been deducted. It can be the same as the unit contribution or less, depending on whether fixed costs have been allocated to the product sales before the unit contribution has been figured. In our example with PW, we will assume that the allowable margin is the same as the unit contribution, that is, $66 per pair of jeans.

Net Profit and Breaking Even

The next concept we encounter is **net profit** or net profit margin. This is the amount of money the company will have (before taxes) after the fixed costs are subtracted from the gross revenues. Often, a company will set a goal for its net profit margin and measure its success for a product line in terms of whether this goal was obtained or not.

To know how many jeans have to be sold to make a profit, Charlie first needs to know how many jeans PW has to sell to break even before he adds in the cost of his advertising campaign. The simple formula for calculating break-even is:

$$\text{Break-even in units sold} = \frac{\text{Fixed Costs in Dollars}}{\text{Net Unit Margin in Dollars}}$$

We don't know what PW's fixed costs are on a per unit basis, but let's say they are $6 million a year. Therefore, to break even on their new line of jeans:

$$\text{Break-even in units sold} = \frac{\$6,000,000}{\$66}$$
$$\text{Break-even} = 90,910 \text{ jeans}$$

However, PW wants to do better than just break even: they want to make a profit. So let's say that they want a 20 percent profit before taxes over and above recovery of their fixed costs. (They could establish their profit target in other ways, e.g., as a percentage of the sale of each pair of jeans, or as fixed dollar number for the year based on increasing the profit percentage from a pervious year.) Then we have to add 20 percent of the fixed costs *to* the fixed costs and recalculate the units to be sold:

$$
\begin{aligned}
\$6,000,000 &= \text{fixed costs} \\
\times\ .20 &\ \\
\hline
\$1,200,000 &= \text{profit} \\
+6,000,000 &= \text{fixed costs} \\
\hline
\$7,200,000 &= \text{new target to be achieved}
\end{aligned}
$$

$$\text{New target in units to be sold} = \frac{\$7,200,000}{\$66}$$

New target units: 109,091 jeans

Remember: Always add the desired profit margin (in dollars) to your other fixed costs to give yourself the new number to divide by the unit margin (in dollars).

This is the number of jeans PW would have to sell over one year to not only recover all fixed costs but to arrive at a 20 percent net profit before taxes. In our example of Charlie's Internet campaign, all he has to be concerned about is how many jeans *this particular campaign* will sell—and whether he can do better than break even. He has initially calculated his costs for the Internet advertising as $3 million. His boss has told him that he expects to see a 10 percent profit on this specific campaign. That means adding $300,000 to the fixed costs of $3 million, giving Charlie $3,300,000 to work into our formula. We need to know how many total pairs of jeans it will require PW to sell to meet this target. Again we can use our break-even formula, realizing that we have already added a profit amount:

$$\text{Target units to be sold} = \frac{\$3,300,000}{\$66}$$
$$\text{Target units to be sold} = 50,000 \text{ jeans}$$

At this point, Charlie needs to consult with others in the company. Is it reasonable to expect this one campaign to sell 50,000 jeans, which allows for covering fixed costs (before advertising), plus a profit, plus Charlie's Internet advertising campaign? If the company has no previous experience in the clothing field, it may be that they will want to test the market with a smaller campaign to start with. Or, Charlie's boss, the president, may feel that she has enough knowledge to predict that this is too ambitious a sales goal for the first campaign. We'll talk about how to compare a test with a roll-out later, but at this point, let's assume that Charlie's boss tells him to cut back on the costs of his Internet advertising campaign so that he can have a less ambitious sales target. He does this by cutting back to one Internet provider, AOL, which has quoted him $100,000 to run a banner ad on their home page for one month. He also has to pay a designer $15,000 to design the ad, and he has a contractor who will charge $5,000 for recording the hits. His new fixed-costs budget for the Internet campaign is $120,000. Because this is going to be a two-step campaign—in other words, PW will advertise on the Internet, then send samples to people who respond before actually getting any orders—Charlie is told that he can budget up to $1,200,000 for the second step of the campaign, the mail out of samples.

Since Charlie now has the advertising budget that he needs for this campaign, he recalculates the number of jeans he needs to sell to achieve his target of break-even:

$$\text{Units to be sold} = \frac{\$1,320,000 \text{ (fixed costs plus profit)}}{\$66 \text{ (unit margin in this campaign)}}$$

$$\text{Units to be sold} = 20,000 \text{ pairs of jeans}$$

As we can see, if the variable costs in this campaign had risen even more, so would Charlie's target for sales. Or, if he could reduce his fixed costs (or his profit margin), then the total number of jeans to be sold would be reduced.

Cost per Inquiry/Cost per Order

In direct marketing, it is important to know how much it costs us to obtain a new customer and a new order. We can have basically three kinds of possible prospective customer behavior:

- People who are exposed to the campaign but do nothing (nonresponse)
- People who are exposed and inquire (inquiry response)
- People who are exposed, inquire, and buy (buyer response)

Since there is a cost to doing any kind of marketing, we need to know how to calculate it for those who inquire and those who buy (those who do nothing don't figure into our calculation). We also need to understand that calculating costs and responses varies from medium to medium. Figure 13-12 shows the special calculations that need to be made in measuring the results in different media.

Let's look at an example in which PW uses Charlie's Internet campaign to target 12 million customers. The campaign has two steps: The first step is intended to get people to request a sample of the jeans fabric. When PW mails back the fabric sample, they also send an order form. Their next step is to sell jeans based on this inquiry/mail-out campaign. They will have a **cost per inquiry (CPI)** which is sometimes called a cost per lead (COL), and then a **cost per response (CPR)** or cost per order (CPO). Figures 13-13 and 13-14 detail the elements included and the process involved in the calculations of CPI and CPO.

Medium	Special Calculations
Broadcast (radio/TV)	Cost of the schedule is the marketing cost Measurement of viewers reached based on rating points, e.g., number of responses divided by gross rating points*
Electronic (Internet)	Cost of Web site and maintenance are the marketing costs
Catalogs (treat each item as its own campaign)	Divide the number of pages by cost to determine cost per page Divide the number of items per page by cost per page to determine the marketing cost of each product
Clubs/Continuity Programs	Higher advertising allowables used here because customers are expected to buy beyond their first purchase
Direct Mail	Use total number mailed as basis to determine net profit
Print Advertising	Use circulation figures to determine net profit, e.g., number of responses divided by circulation

*Gross Rating Points are calculated by the "reach" of a commercial—how many people watch or listen to the program in which it is inserted (as measured by commercial ratings services such as Arbitron and Nielsen) times the frequency (number of times) the commercial is presented in a given program vehicle.

FIGURE 13-12   Special Calculations for Different Media.

AOL subscribers:	12,000,000
Response rate:	5%
Total number of people responding:	600,000
Banner ad cost:	$120,000
Banner ad cost per thousand:	$10*
Cost per inquiry:	$.20**

*In marketing, costs are generally quoted in terms of how much it takes to reach 1,000 people via a given medium. In this example, PW knew that via AOL it could reach 12,000,000 people. If we divide 12,000,000 by 1,000, we get 12,000 "groups" of 1,000 people each. Therefore, we take the total banner ad cost of $120,000 and divide it by the 12,000 "groups" and say the "cost per thousand" is $10.
**To derive the "cost per inquiry," we take the total cost, $120,000, and divide it by the total number of people who inquired, 600,000, giving us a cost per inquiry of $.20. Note that this is a pure cost at this point—there is no profit associated with it.

FIGURE 13-13   Cost per Inquiry of a Banner Ad on AOL.

Mailings of fabric to AOL inquirers:	600,000
Response rate (% who ordered):	4%
Number of orders:	24,000
Average order price:	$ 88
Gross sales:	$2,112,000
Gross profit before advertising: @75% margin	1,584,000*
Cost of fabric mail-out campaign @$2.00 per mailing:	1,200,000
Advertising cost (inquiry campaign):	120,000
Promotional costs total:	1,320,000
Profit (or loss):	264,000
Cost per order:	55.00**
Profit (or loss) per new customer/order:	11.00***

*The company has a COGS of 25%, so they have a profit margin of 75% before advertising costs.
**The cost per order is derived by taking the total marketing costs ($1,200,000 + $120,000) and dividing their sum of $1,320,000 by the total orders of 24,000.
***Since there was a profit of $264,000 from the campaign, we divide that by the number of orders, 24,000, to get the "profit per order."

FIGURE 13-14   Cost per Order Based on the AOL Ad Campaign.

We don't know if Charlie was given targets for CPI or CPO in this campaign or a number of new customers to be obtained, but we do know that he achieved the following:

- His target for breaking even was 20,000 pairs of jeans sold, and they sold 24,000.
- In addition to making a profit on his campaign, the sales covered all the variable costs (at 25 percent of revenue) of the 24,000 pairs of jeans *before* the advertising costs were subtracted.

There is one more measure of success that we need to know about.

Return on Investment/Return on Advertising Investment

It is important to note that the goal of an advertising campaign may *not* be to make a profit if, for example, the campaign focuses on a product introduction, achieving penetration in a new market, or even gaining market share. In these cases, the number of new customers acquired, new orders acquired, or total market share gained may be the measures of success. However, what *is* important is that these goals be clearly stated when the budget is being planned. At some point, of course, the company has to make money on the products it sells, so understanding the basics of how to calculate profit and loss are important.

One popular measurement tool in the business world is **return on investment,** or **ROI.** This is a simple calculation: net profit divided by the average amount invested in the company in a year. When we look specifically at calculating ROI for an advertising campaign, we need to know what the gross profit is for that campaign; remember: gross profit or margin is total sales less cost of goods sold (COGS). Then we subtract from the gross profit all the promotional (advertising) costs, which gives us a net profit (but without consideration for other fixed costs that the company incurs). We then divide this number by the total promotional costs. To express the answer in percentage terms, which is how we talk about ROI, for example, "his ROI in that campaign was 20 percent," we multiply the answer by 100. We can do this for Charlie's Internet campaign for the jeans:

Gross Sales:	$2,112,000	
Less COGS:	−528,000	(25% of gross sales)
Gross Margin:	$1,584,000	
Less Promo:	−1,320,000	
Net Profit~normal~:	$264,000	
ROI =	$\dfrac{\$264,000}{\$1,320,000} = .2$	

$$\text{ROI} = .2 \times 100 = \mathbf{20\%}$$

Is this a good ROI for Charlie? Well, we don't know if his boss gave him an ROI target. Since the jeans are a new product, it's possible that one of the company's goals was to gain a minimum number of orders while not losing money. Of course, a higher ROI is always better. If, for example, Charlie's campaign had sold two pairs of jeans for each order (without any additional promotional expenses), the gross margin would have doubled, and we would have the following numbers:

Gross Sales:	$4,224,000	
Less COGS:	−1,056,000	(25% of gross sales)
Gross Margin:	$3,168,000	
Less Promo:	−1,320,000	
Net Profit:	$1,848,000	
ROI =	$\dfrac{\$1,848,000}{\$1,320,000} = 1.4$	

$$\text{ROI} = 1.4 \times 100 = \mathbf{140\%}$$

Also, if Charlie had been able to cut his advertising costs, the ROI would have improved. Overall, though, it looks like Charlie did a reasonable job with his first campaign for the new jeans!

One more note: In doing the math to arrive at the proper ROI for an advertising campaign, there is another way to calculate the ROI. We can take the total number of units sold and *subtract* the units we know it takes to break even on the cost of the campaign; in other words, the number of units it will take to pay for the entire advertising campaign. We then multiply the remaining number of units sold, which will be earning full profit by the net unit contribution. Then, we can divide that net profit number by the cost of the campaign and arrive at the same ROI answer as we did above. Let's see how Charlie would calculate this.

Charlie's break-even units:	20,000
Total units sold:	24,000
Units earning full profit:	(24,000 − 20,000) = 4000 units (pairs of jeans)
Net Profit:	(4000 units × $66 net unit contribution) = $264,000
ROI for the advertising campaign:	$\dfrac{\$264,000 \text{ profit}}{\$1,320,000 \text{ ad costs}} = .20$ **20% ROI**

Budgeting for Tests

Sometimes, a company will want to test a planned campaign on a small scale to see if the assumptions about costs and response levels are reasonable. In the case of PW and Charlie, he believes that direct mail might be a good way to market the new jeans, but he wants to run a test with a small sample. He has in mind a mailing that includes color pictures of people actively working and playing in the jeans, plus a small fabric sample—and of course an order form that can be returned, although he will provide the Web site address, a fax number, and a toll-free number for ordering also.

Charlie first has to determine his advertising allowable (sometimes called **allowable margin**), or the amount that can be spent to get an order while still allowing for media costs and the designated profit to be made. From previous experience and his budget projections, he believes that he can use an advertising allowable of $4.50 per unit (pair of jeans) ordered via direct mail. He has bought a mailing list from the magazine *Field and Stream,* and he plans to use just a portion of that list (people subscribing in four Northeastern states) for his test campaign. This portion of the list has 2,000 names. The cost per thousand is $300 for the test. We could also express this cost as $.30 per name:

CPM = $300 for the test

2,000 names on the mailing list

2,000 divided by 1,000 = 2 "groups" of 1,000 names

2 (groups of 1,000) × $300 (per group of 1,000) = $600 for the test

$600 divided by 2,000 = $.30 per name

What Charlie is looking for is a response rate that either comes in at a cost of $4.50 per response or less than that.

Charlie sends out the mailing in April, with an offer that expires by the end of May. He gets a 5 percent response, or 100 orders:

2,000 mail pieces × .05 response rate = 100 orders

It cost him $600 to run the test. Did he achieve his $4.50 CPO?

$600 divided by 100 orders = $6 per order

No! It cost him $6 per order—but he came close. So he decides to run a second test. This time, he eliminates the fabric sample from the mailing, which saves him the cost of the sample and also lowers his postage costs. He now has a CPM of $250. He picks 3,000 names from the *Field and Stream* list, this time people from four Southwestern states. This time, his budget looks like this:

CPM = $250 for the test

3,000 names on the mailing list

3,000 divided by 1,000 = 3 "groups" of 1,000 names

3 (groups of 1,000) × $250 (per group of 1,000) = $750 for the test

Charlie sends out the new test mailing in May and gets a 6 percent response, or 180 orders:

3,000 mail pieces × .06 response rates = 180 orders

It cost him $750 to run this test. Did he achieve his $4.50 CPO?

$$\$750 \text{ divided by } 180 \text{ orders} = \$4.166$$

Yes! It cost him $4.17 per order. You will note that he did several things that improved his CPO. He lowered his actual costs by not sending the sample. He used a different mailing list, perhaps with people more interested in the product. He ran the test later in the spring, perhaps a better buying time. He used more names.

Sometimes, of course, companies are willing to take a chance on rolling out a large campaign even if the test has not quite met their goals. Like Charlie, they may know of ways to cut costs, reach better prospects, or even pick a better time of year for the campaign. As we already know, varying the creative format, the message, and the price of products can make huge differences in how people react to advertising, but it's always a good idea to test first.

Summary

Remember at the beginning of this chapter we talked about how you would evaluate your Super Bowl ad if you were marketing vice-president for a company that has just produced a new running shoe. You spent $2.7 million on one 30-second direct response ad, which got 1 million hits. Now that we've been through the basic marketing math, you can evaluate whether your ad was successful once you know a few more things.

Let's say that of the one million visitors to your site, .035 percent ordered a pair of the shoes by visiting your Web site. You, of course, created a special Web address *just* for this commercial, so you could accurately evaluate how many responses and orders this one ad produced. Let's also say that a pair of the shoes at the price offered in this ad sold for $110, including shipping and handling. The variable costs come to $65. You had an advertising allowable of $8 per order. So, you can now make some calculations:

Selling Price:	$110.00
Variable Costs:	−65.00
Unit Margin:	$ 45.00

One million prospects (hits) × .035 response rate = 350,000 orders

Cost of your ad: $2,700,000

Break-even in units ordered: $\dfrac{\$2,700,00}{\$45}$

= 60,000 units to break even

Pairs of shoes sold:	350,000
Break even needed:	−60,000
Units at full profit:	290,000
Unit margin:	× $45
Net Profit:	$13,050,000

ROI: Profit divided by ad costs: $\dfrac{\$13,05000}{2,700,000}$
= 4.83 or 483% ROI

CPO: $2,700,000 divided by 350,000 = $7.71 versus an allowable of $8.

We now know you beat your advertising allowable and came in with a healthy profit, although we do not know if your boss gave you a higher ROI target. But 483 percent looks good! The point is not the numbers themselves, but that you now know how to make calculations that tell you how successful you have been—and very likely what you might want to consider doing (or not doing) in the future. In this case, it looks like the one-time Super Bowl ad worked well for your product introduction. Direct marketing math can also help you to determine which customers to target based on the calculation of customer value and CLTV. By calculating and analyzing response rates, lift, market penetration, and conversion rates, you may be able to create more effective future marketing strategies to grow the profitability of the organization. Indeed, quantitative analysis is important in direct and interactive marketing!

Key Terms

Customer lifetime value (CLTV)
  350
Market penetration *352*
Break even *353*
Lift *355*
Conversion *356*

Conversion rate *356*
Gross sales *359*
Cost of goods sold *359*
Variable costs *359*
Fixed costs *359*
Unit margin *359*

Allowable margin *359*
Net profit *360*
Cost per inquiry (CPI) *361*
Cost per response (CPR) *361*
Return on investment (ROI) *363*

Review Questions

1. Why do we bother to examine the costs of marketing? What should result from spending money on marketing?
2. Why calculate the value of customers?
3. What steps would you take to calculate average customer value?
4. How much more does it cost to replace a customer than to retain a current one?
5. How is a lift calculated? Why is it important to know about lifts?
6. Why is the concept of break-even important? Is this always a goal in a direct marketing campaign? What might be another goal of the campaign?

7. What are some examples of fixed costs and variable costs in a clothing manufacturing business like PW?
8. Why do advertising costs count as fixed costs?
9. In a specific direct marketing campaign, if we want to improve the ROI, what are some ways to do this?
10. Why would a marketing manager run a test of a direct marketing campaign before rolling it out? What would he or she be hoping to learn from the test?

Exercise

Let's see where Charlie at PW is with his direct marketing campaign for the new jeans. After two years, he has learned that using the Internet and direct mail are effective ways to attract new customers and retain current customers who make repeat buys. But he would like to gain market penetration. How could he plan to do this? How could he achieve a lift in response during the third year of the campaign? By now, his boss is looking at the increased costs of producing the jeans and tells Charlie to work toward a better ROI. What steps could Charlie take to do this?

CASE

SafeLife

Note: The company presented here, SafeLife, is fictional and bears no direct resemblance to other companies that may operate in this field. However, the data is taken from a variety of sources, and the breathalyzer industry is a real one.

Overview

Direct marketers use math and metrics to help them in developing effective marketing strategies and tactics. This case provides you with the opportunity to apply direct and interactive math and metrics by allocating a budget, calculating response rates, and determining break-even and profitability.

Case

Situation Analysis

Consumers are purchasing increasing levels of alcoholic beverages. One state in the Southeast found that its liquor stores rang up record gross sales of $607.4 million in fiscal year 2007, an increase of $35.4 million from the previous year. This same state has opened 14 new liquor stores in 2008.

With social organizations like Mothers Against Drunk Driving (MADD), Fathers Against Drunk Driving (FADD), and Students Against Destructive Decisions (SADD), the news of increased alcoholic beverage sales is not encouraging. In fact, according to the National Highway Traffic Safety Administration, statistics show that from 2001 to 2005, 40 percent of holiday traffic fatalities involved at least one driver who had been drinking.

Organizations like MADD, FADD, and SADD primarily concentrate on preventing drinking and driving. While these social organizations focus on prevention, the police focus on enforcing laws against drunk driving. Police in many jurisdictions have beefed up patrols and increased sobriety checkpoints to try and catch individuals who are driving while under the influence of alcohol. These checkpoints may prevent accidents from occurring, but they also may result in costly fines, tarnished driving records, and even the loss of employment for many individuals. Isn't prevention a better way?

One such preventive measure is to ensure that people who have consumed too much alcohol do not drive. This prevention comes in the form of breathalyzers. That is a product that SafeLife produces and markets. SafeLife's alcohol detection products help improve existing protective and safety measures in law enforcement agencies, the work environment, and communities. SafeLife's products exceed the current national standards and are custom-designed to meet its customers' needs.

Primary organizational customers might include:

- Restaurants/bars/clubs
- Institutions, university organizations/fraternities/sororities
- Bowling alleys/social clubs
- Federal government/branches of the military
- Correctional facilities
- Anywhere where alcoholic beverages are served
- Anywhere where alcoholic beverages are consumed or used (but not actually served)

Note: To date, the target customers for SafeLife have primarily been the government, mainly police and military.

Marketing Mix

Product   The product is a hand-held breathalyzer. It is small, lightweight, yet functional. To use the device, two small straws are required. These are packaged and sold separately.

Pricing   SafeLife charges a per unit price of $1,200. The COGS and other variable costs are $950 for the unit. The desired profit (in dollars) that the client hopes to obtain via its investment in this direct marketing campaign varies based on levels of response. These include:

(a) better than BEV at the 2 percent response level;
(b) better than BEV at the 5 percent response level;
(c) better than BEV at the 8 percent response level.

Distribution Channels   The desired distribution channel for this case is direct-to-organizational consumer or business-to-business (B2B) only.

Promotion: Image   The image of SafeLife's breathalyzer is that it will help promote greater safety in the community. It serves both police and citizen needs by providing greater safety in traffic control. It is a product that can assist in preventing drinking and driving.

The Decision Problem   SafeLife now wants to create a marketing campaign to promote its line of breathalyzers to organizational consumers (B2B market) and seeks to utilize direct marketing strategies. It wants to investigate whether such a B2B direct marketing campaign would be profitable for the company and if so, at what point?

The Budget Analysis

For the budget analysis, you will need the following profit measurement strategies:

- Determine the required break-even units before profit
- Determine the number of units to be sold at each response level to meet break-even plus profit requirements
- Determine whether profit margins were met at each response level
- Determine the ROI at each level

Assume the following:

Fixed marketing costs (print, direct mail, one cable ad) come in at:	$49,500.00
Average selling price per unit (given):	1,200.00
Variable cost per unit (given):	950.00
Total prospects identified by your research:	36,000

Conclusion

To plan the expanded direct marketing campaign for SafeLife's breathalyzer, the company needs to determine what level of sales, or break-even, it requires to achieve the specified profit goals, with a marketing budget of $49,500. The total prospects (businesses and organizations) identified as targets for this campaign is 36,000.

Case Discussion Questions

1. What value propositions or offers would you rec-ommend that the company use in targeting orga-nizational consumers? How do you plan on measuring the response to these offers?

2. How would you allocate a budget of $49,500? What media and message strategies would you recommend to the company for inclusion in its direct and interactive marketing campaign?

3. What rate of response is needed for SafeLife to break even on this campaign?

4. Are Safelife's desired profit and ROI realistic for this campaign? Why or why not?

14

■■■

Examining Direct and Interactive Marketing Applications in a Variety of Sectors

Opening Vignette: DuPont Personal Protection

The DuPont Personal Protection group helps protect workers with its safety consulting services and a variety of protective apparel made from Nomex, Kevlar, Tyvek, and Tychem materials. DuPont uses direct and interactive marketing to promote its protective apparel to two primary customer segments: emergency responders and industrial workers. Therefore, DuPont is a business-to-business (B2B) direct marketer. What you are about to read is an example of an effective B2B direct and interactive marketing campaign used by the DuPont Personal Protection group to increase end user awareness and stimulate demand for its new line of protective apparel.

The Tyvek line of personal protection garments (Figure 14-1) posed some unique marketing challenges. This product line has a lower price point and a broader range of applications than do DuPont's other personal protection products. In addition, end users were beginning to perceive all-white garments as Tyvek,

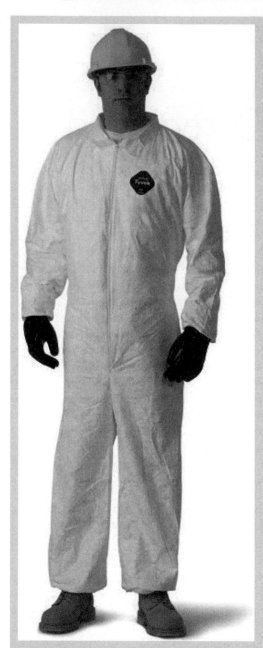

FIGURE 14-1 Tyvek Personal Protection Garments.

so it was difficult to differentiate Tyvek from other white, general protective apparel. Finally, industrial workers were complaining that general protective garments did not fit well—a tremendous drawback for people who need mobility while they are performing work-related tasks. To solve these product issues, DuPont Personal Protection introduced its new line of Tyvek comfort fit design apparel. The marketing challenge was to get these improved garments to potential consumers to experience firsthand the garment's comfort and durability (Figure 14-1).

Although the line is sold through distributors, DuPont realized it needed to increase end user awareness to increase demand. The marketing team decided to launch a comprehensive direct and interactive marketing campaign integrating offline and online marketing tactics to drive traffic to the DuPont Personal Protection Web site, where potential customers could request a free garment sample. DuPont's marketing team could then serve customer requests and convert these leads into sales. The budget for this multimedia campaign included the following allocations: approximately 30 percent was spent on Google AdWords, 30 percent on direct mail, and the remaining 40 percent on traditional print and online banner ads (Figure 14-2).

The entire campaign was effective in generating leads for DuPont Personal Protection group. Google AdWords proved to be the most successful tactic in driving traffic to the Web site. In fact, immediately after launching the Google portion of the campaign, the marketing team noted a 702 percent increase in page views. In addition, once visitors landed on the DuPont Personal Protection page, they spent 73 percent more time there than they did before the campaign began. DuPont Personal Protection's campaign is an example of the effective application of direct and interactive marketing strategies in the B2B sector.

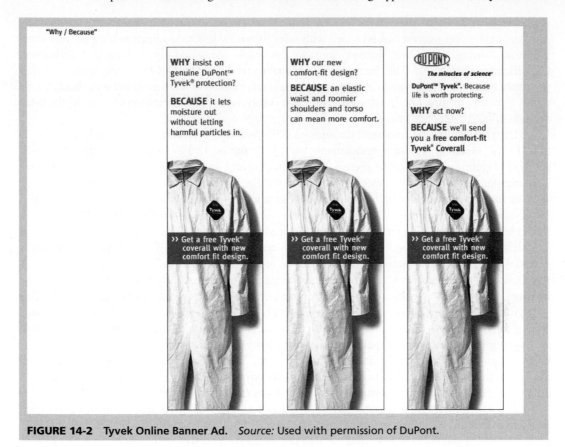

FIGURE 14-2   Tyvek Online Banner Ad.   *Source:* Used with permission of DuPont.

Direct and interactive marketing can be successfully applied in many different sectors—which is the topic of this chapter. Here we explore the applications of direct and interactive marketing in B2B, nonprofit, governmental, political, and sports sectors. However, keep in mind that these are just a handful of the many different applications of direct and interactive marketing—in reality, there are many more.

BUSINESS-TO-BUSINESS

B2B direct marketing is the process of providing goods and services to industrial market intermediaries, as opposed to ultimate final consumers. Although the distinction is not always easy to make, we differentiate industrial goods from consumer goods based on their ultimate use. **Industrial goods** are generally used as raw materials or in the fabrication of other goods. Whereas iron ore is almost always an industrial good, a personal computer can be either an industrial or a consumer good, depending on its ultimate use.

John H. Patterson, who founded the National Cash Register Company (today's NCR), was the first to use direct mail to get qualified leads for follow-up by salespeople. The firm's lead generation in the early 1900s was oriented to specific industries. The salesperson assigned to call on each prospect expressing interest was provided with sales literature directed to firms using cash registers: groceries, druggists, movie houses, and so on—each identified by a Standard Industrial Classification (SIC) code. This literature was often stored in the trunk of the salesperson's car for reference and delivery to a qualified prospect. Today, this method of sales prospect qualification utilizing a variety of direct response media (not just direct mail) plays an important role in the total scheme of B2B direct marketing.

Direct marketing is employed throughout B2B distribution channels. This is not so much in the "direct" sense of bypassing middlemen (via a Web site or a catalog) as it is in the "directed" sense of targeting prospects, thus increasing the effectiveness and the efficiency of the salesperson. The salesperson is, in fact, an important adjunct to the direct marketing process, now more than ever used as an interactive medium, face to face or electronically. In the case of consumer goods, the buyer usually visits the seller. The opposite is true of industrial goods—usually, the seller comes to the buyer. Direct marketing techniques are often used in lead generation among potential buyers of industrial goods. An IBM system, for example, is usually not shopped for in a retail store, but a well-designed direct mail letter can often entice an industrial prospect to invite an IBM representative to make a presentation. A further characteristic of industrial goods is that their purchase usually involves group decision making because a particular component represents only a part of the whole.

Integrating direct marketing into an existing organization is not an easy task. It takes a great deal of top-down, long-range commitment. Direct marketing is not a "sometimes thing" but requires an ongoing belief coupled with adequate funding. Fortunately, use of the tools and techniques can be tested and fine-tuned before they are implemented. The wise traditional organization absorbs direct marketing slowly, testing as it goes, without throwing out what it already does well (thus creating havoc). However, the opportunities for B2B direct marketing are nearly endless.

The Direct Marketing Association (DMA) reported that B2B sales generated through direct marketing was $821.4 billion in 2006, representing about 4.3 percent of total B2B U.S. sales. This compares to consumer sales generated through direct marketing, estimated to be almost $1.118 trillion, which is about 12.1 percent of total consumer U.S. sales.[1]

As much as 50 percent of manufactured output is sold to the industrial market and as much as 80 percent of farm produce is considered industrial. Wheat, for example, is an industrial good when it is sold for the production of flour; flour is an industrial good when it is sold for the baking of bread; and bread is an industrial good when sold to a restaurant. But bread is a consumer good when sold to a household.

Characteristics of Industrial Demand

Industrial demand differs from consumer demand by these four characteristics, which are worth noting and understanding:

Derived demand: Demand for industrial goods is derived ultimately from consumer demand. The industrial demand for automobile tires, steel, or glass, for example, depends in part on the consumer demand for automobiles.

Inelastic demand: Because a variety of industrial goods go into the manufacture of a single product, and thus each represents only a fraction of the product's total cost, there is not as much price sensitivity in industrial goods. The cost of tires for an automobile, for example, might double, but this increase would represent a relatively small part of the total cost of the car.

Widely fluctuating demand: The demand for industrial goods is subject to wide fluctuation, ultimately dependent on consumer demand but also dependent on rises and falls in inventories as well as in the optimism of entrepreneurs.

Knowledgeable demand: Industrial buyers are usually much better informed about their purchases than consumers are about theirs, have more specialized interests, and benefit from the process of joint decision making.

Although the number of industrial organizations is but a fraction of the number of consumers, the volume of purchasing is as great in the industrial market as it is in the consumer market. The buying power of industrial organizations is highly concentrated, however, within certain industries (i.e., manufacturing), and there are also heavy concentrations regionally and geographically. This buying power is often measured by various forms of activity, such as manufacturing, wholesaling, retailing, mining, agriculture, and construction.

In comparing B2B transactions with business-to-consumer (B2C) transactions, we should note that consumer purchases are often consummated at the seller's location (i.e., clothing bought at a retail store). In industrial buying, the seller normally comes to the buyer's location (i.e., a computer installation sold to a chain of retail stores). A major factor contributing to the increasing use of direct marketing by businesses and industries is the rising cost of these personal sales calls made to a buyer's location. According to ongoing McGraw-Hill research, the cost of the average B2B sales call, which was about $50 in 1969, has now risen to more than $300, a sixfold increase. Please note that this cost is per *call,* not per *sale;* it takes an average of three calls to make one sale.

In contrasting business buyers with consumer buyers, apparent differences between these are sometimes exaggerated. Individual buyers within business organizations are obviously also consumers in their own rights. Conversely, many consumers also wear different hats when they are at work as industrial buyers. Some B2B organizations, recognizing this comparison, have gone so far as to look at the demographics of buyers within organizations at the same time as they look at the demographics of organizations themselves. A comparison of database demographics, contrasting consumer and industrial markets, is shown in Figure 14-3. These characteristics are not all-inclusive, of course, but they do indicate some interesting differences and, at the same time, similarities.

All buyers—consumers as well as industrial organizations—have a name and address. Beyond that identification, a consumer's age can be important in product differentiation as can the years a company has been in business. The gender of an industrial buyer may very well have the same influence as it does on that buyer making a purchase as a consumer. A consumer's income can be looked at in the same light as an organization's revenue, just as a consumer's wealth can be looked at in the same light as an organization's net worth. Though many marketers see lists of business buyers being different from lists of consumers, we argue that there is as much sameness as there is difference!

B2B Applications

Lead generation for follow-up by salespersons, using the tools and techniques of direct marketing, is a major contributor to the rapid growth of B2B direct marketing. A major stimulus, too, has been the Internet. Even though the number of consumer households in the United States is at least 10-fold and the number of individual consumers is at least 25-fold that of the number of businesses, total B2B sales volume is more than double that of B2C sales.[2] Because the average revenue per industrial response is typically larger, it follows that response rates from B2B direct response advertising can be lower than that which is consumer directed and still be profitable for the direct marketer.

CONSUMER	*INDUSTRIAL*
Name/Address	Name/Address
Source code	Source code
Age	Year started
Gender	Gender of decision maker
Income	Revenue
Wealth	Net worth
Family size	Number of employees
Children	Parent firm or subsidiary
Occupation	Line of business
Credit evaluation	Credit evaluation
Education	Education of decision makers
Urban/rural resident	Headquarters/branch
Own or rent home	Private or public ownership
Ethnic group	Minority ownership
Interests	Interests of decision makers
Life-style of ZIP area	Socio-economics of location
Mail respondent	Mail respondent
Transactions & R/F/M	Transactions & R/F/M

FIGURE 14-3   Comparison of Demographic Items in Consumer and Industrial Direct Marketing.

The tools and techniques of direct marketing used by businesses are basically the same as those for consumer direct marketing, as presented throughout this textbook. These tools and techniques are used in industrial markets to

- generate qualified "leads" for salesperson follow-up,
- achieve direct sales remotely (i.e., via catalogs and Web sites),
- reinforce all sales efforts,
- introduce new products,
- develop new markets and applications,
- build industrial customer goodwill,
- conduct industrial market research.

Notable users of the tools and techniques of direct marketing have been makers of office products, industrial plant supplies, computers and their peripherals, building equipment, and even aircraft and the complex array of aircraft parts. Much has changed since John H. Patterson founded the National Cash Register Company and first used direct mail to get qualified leads for follow-up by salespeople. Today, the direct mail and online methods of sales prospect qualification as well as direct selling, when augmented by direct response advertising in a variety of print and broadcast media and the telephone, play an important role in the total scheme of B2B marketing.

As noted earlier in this chapter, an important feature of B2B distribution that makes it especially susceptible to the tools and techniques of direct marketing is this: producers and their middlemen are more likely to make sales calls on buyers of industrial goods, whereas buyers of consumer goods are more likely to make purchases at the locations of producers and middlemen. Direct marketing has been used effectively throughout industrial distribution channels—producer to agent to distributor to industrial user—to augment personal selling.

B2B marketers, like B2C marketers, combine relational databases to obtain information about their customers *as well as their customers' customers*. They perform statistical analyses to identify their own best customers and then seek prospects that look like these. Let's take a look at how FedEx used database information to conduct a successful B2B direct marketing campaign.

FedEx offers and prices its delivery services in a variety of categories including, several years ago, a category called Priority 1. To expand its market, increase its penetration, and hold its present customers for this premium service, FedEx conceived a B2B direct mail campaign to announce a new discount schedule. Based strictly on its potential value in the immediate future, the program was divided into three segments:

1. Frequent users of Priority 1: 29,126 individual customers
2. Infrequent users of Priority 1: 121,705 individual customers
3. Other FedEx customers who had never used Priority 1: 63,431 individual customers

The symbol to be used for dramatizing the Priority 1 service was the same for all three market segments: a five-pound reproduction of a 1913 exercise weight. Frequent users of Priority 1 received the exercise weight immediately as a goodwill gift; infrequent users had to request it; nonusers received it as a premium with the purchase of Priority 1 service for the first time. Frequent users were also asked to identify other prospects and decision makers within their own organizations. A total of 7,044 (24.1 percent) of the 29,126 frequent user recipients of the promotion did just that.

Of the 121,705 infrequent users contacted, a total of 25,985 (24.0 percent) responded by requesting the gift, and, in the process, they also supplied 14,723 names of new prospects within their own organizations.

Of the 63,431 nonusers of Priority 1 among FedEx customers, a total of 9,300 (15 percent) actually purchased the service and submitted a copy of the FedEx air bill as proof of purchase to receive the exercise weight.

In summary, the following total results were tabulated:

21,767 new prospects

40,000 responses from *old* customers

25,985 "market research" forms returned

9,300 proven direct sales to *new* customers

$500,000 in immediate traceable sales to these new customers alone

Because each user of Priority 1 service was known to average $4,000 in sales per year for an undetermined number of future years, the potential value of these new customers is impressive.

Changes in today's global economy are forcing B2B marketers to adapt to many challenges. To be successful, these marketers must be able to account for each nuance of change in their customers' organizations, as well as in their own organizations and in the overall economy. In addition, they must find new ways to cultivate their current customer database, locate qualified prospects, and reduce marketing costs.

The challenges facing industrial marketers include:

- Marketing costs that are increasing while the audience reached is decreasing. It costs more to generate awareness than ever before.
- Face-to-face selling, down in efficiency, is up in cost. Travel expenses are up, and the cost of a salesperson's call on a prospect/customer is a larger part of revenue than before.

- Communication clutter brings individuals up to 10,000 messages per day and many have tuned out nonrelevant marketing messages.
- Customer relationship managers often do not integrate an analytical approach to combining operations with marketing programs and campaigns. There is generally not nearly enough analysis of customer data.
- Industry classification of customers/prospects, most commonly used in the past, is not adequately predictive in the current business environment. Such market segmentation assumes that businesses within the same industry type are similar; however, a business in a rural area can be dramatically different from an inner-city business with the same industry classification.

How to Identify B2B Market Segments

Industrial markets are much smaller in number than consumer markets, but they are certainly not smaller in sales volume. Like consumer markets, industrial markets break down into smaller, more homogeneous segments of the heterogeneous total industrial market. Market segmentation may be even more important in industrial applications than in consumer ones, because of the diversity of activities in each segment.

B2B market segments can be identified by industry, financial strength or size, number of employees, or sales volume. Geographic selectivity includes urban/rural orientation, city size, and location. There can also be selection by form of ownership, by branch/headquarters, or even by extent of telephone directory advertising.

Within organizations, industrial markets also can be segmented by job functions. Demand within firms is not generated by purchasing agents alone but by engineers, chemists, architects, and a good many other specialists. Direct marketers must appeal not only to firms as such but to many relevant individuals within them.

Maintaining customer/prospect databases is a real challenge for B2B direct marketers. The most important database, of course, is that of their customers. Such a compilation should include, in addition to names and addresses, prior purchase behavior, as well as the organization's—and possibly even the individual buyer's—demographic profile. Let's discuss some of the more commonly used methods for segmenting B2B markets.

1. *Standard Industrial Classification.* The **Standard Industrial Classification (SIC)** coding system is a means of industrial market segmentation developed by the federal government many years ago. SIC codes, which identify businesses by industry and segment of industry and serve as a basis for statistical data about industries, are in broad use by government, trade associations, and business enterprises. Within the broad SIC classification system, these are the terms in frequent use:

> *Industry:* A grouping of establishments engaged in a common economic activity is identified by the four-digit primary SIC code. Approximately 950 industries make up the U.S. economy. These produce approximately 75,000 products and services that are further divided by five- and seven-digit SIC codes.

> *Establishment:* Within four-digit SIC codes describing their primary lines of business, these are economic units producing at a single physical location, such as a manufacturing plant, a farm warehouse, or a retail store.

> *Company:* An entity that owns one or more establishments. SIC codes are assigned to establishments (economic units) rather than to companies (legal entities). These, in turn, may be further designated as headquarters or branch offices. The SIC codes also identify their form of ownership: individual, partnership, or corporation.

Within SIC codes, which designate the primary and secondary lines of business, establishments can also be segmented on other bases: sales volume, credit rating, age of business, number of employees, net financial worth, subsidiary, and location.

The first two digits of the four-digit code indicate a major classification of industry, of which there are ten:

- 01–09 Agriculture, forestry, and fisheries
- 10–14 Mining
- 15–17 Construction
- 20–39 Manufacturing
- 40–49 Transportation, communications, public utilities
- 50–51 Wholesale trade
- 52–59 Retail trade
- 60–67 Finance, insurance, real estate
- 70–89 Services (medical, legal, schools, churches, etc.)
- 91–97 Public administration
- 99 Nonclassifiable establishments

The final two digits of the four-digit SIC code classify individual organizations by subgroup within industry. For example, SIC 2300 identifies manufacturers of wearing apparel. Within this classification, SIC 2311 identifies men's suit and coat manufacturers. An example of the primary four-digit coding system applied to manufacturers of apparel and other textile products is shown in Figure 14-4. This example breaks down the 2300 series SIC codes, assigned to such manufacturers, breaks these into subgroups, such as men's and women's categories, and then further divides these categories into specific types of apparel manufacturing concerns.

SIC #	DESCRIPTION
2300	Apparel and other finished product mfgrs.
2310/2320	Men's, youth's, and boy's clothing
2311	Suits and coats
2321	Shirts except work shirts
2322	Underwear and night wear
2323	Neckwear
2325	Separate trousers and slacks
2326	Work clothing
2329	Clothing not elsewhere classified
2330	Women's, misses, and junior's outerwear
2331	Blouses and shirts
2335	Dresses
2337	Suits, skirts, and coats
2339	Outerwear
2340	Women's, misses, and junior's undergarments
2341	Underwear and night wear
2342	Brassieres, girdles, and allied garments
2350	Hats, caps, and millinery
2353	Hats, caps and millinery
2360	Girl's, children's, and infant's outerwear
2361	Dresses, blouses, and shirts
2369	Outerwear, not elsewhere classified

FIGURE 14-4   Standard Industrial Classification (SIC) System.

2. *North American Industrial Classification System.* The SIC system has for some time done a good job of detailing the manufacturing industry, but many feel it fails to recognize the existence of today's information technology. With the rapid growth of the service industry, high technology, and international trade, a new system has arisen, in response to the North American Free Trade Agreement of 1994, to compare U.S. statistical information with that of Canada and Mexico and ensure future compatibility with an International Standard Industrial Classification System being developed by the United Nations.

All three countries have agreed on a system now called the **North American Industrial Classification System (NAICS).** This system has formulated a six-digit code, with the first five digits denoting the NAICS levels used by all three countries to produce compatible data. NAICS is an entirely different classification system than SIC, because it focuses on production activities rather than on those that the industries serve. A more detailed explanation of NAICS appears in Chapter 3.

Different agencies within governments are now converting to NAICS coding, but businesses have done relatively little to adopt the new coding system in marketing applications.

3. *Input–Output Analysis of Industrial Markets.* **Input–output analysis,** derived basically from Census Bureau data, traces the distribution of goods from their origins to their destinations. In matrix form, each industry (SIC) appears as both seller and buyer in row and column headings. At the point at which the rows and columns of any two industries intersect, the matrix records the transaction between them. Such analysis is the means by which our country's gross national product is calculated.

Input–output analysis determines the impact that specific industries have on the total economy, not just in terms of what they sell but also in terms of what they buy. A decrease in sales of new automobiles, for example, would result in reduced purchases from the steel industry. This in turn would result in reduced sales by the steel industry and would ultimately reduce the steel industry's purchases from the mining industry. Input–output matrices can be particularly useful to B2B marketers wanting to reach organizations producing industrial goods for further processing by other organizations. Such a table can systematically record how much of the organization's product is consumed by every other industry in the economy and describe market segments using that product.

An example (see Figure 14-5) relates to the demand for corrugated boxes (SIC 2653), which are used by at least 75 percent of all SIC manufacturing industries. A box manufacturer seeking a description of the national market for corrugated boxes can compile consumption data for each plant in each county (or ZIP code area) in each state in the nation. The seller would determine the total number of plants in the compilation by the number of consuming industries for the product (corrugated boxes) as well as, in each industry, the number of plants using corrugated boxes.

4. *The Census Bureau's TIGER System.* **The Global Positioning System (GPS)** and the Census Bureau's **Topologically Integrated Geographic Encoding Referencing (TIGER)** system both associate latitude and longitude coordinates with street addresses. Used to pinpoint geographic locations, they can establish business sites, locate competition, measure distance, and generate data about the demographics of a business location. With mapping capabilities and information in its database, a B2B direct marketer can visualize the reach and penetration of the geographic territories of its resellers.

5. *Business Clusters.* Industrial markets can be clustered and defined by ZIP code area, just like consumer markets.[3] Data by SIC classifications have been associated with ZIP code area data. Ruf Corporation (Olathe, Kansas) has identified ZIP code areas in terms of economic activity (number

STATE AND COUNTY NAME	SIC #	# OF PLANTS	ANNUAL PURCHASE OF CORRUGATED BOXES
ALABAMA			
Autauga County			
Botany Inds., Inc.	2256	1	$10.9M
Nappies, Inc.	2631	1	25.8M
Continental Gin Co.	3559	1	15.0M
County Total		3	$51.7M
Baldwin County			
Woodhaven Dairy	2024	1	$22.4M
Hale Mfg. Co.	2221	1	8.0M
Bay Slacks, Inc.	2253	1	20.4M
Std. Furn., Mfg. Co.	2511	1	82.0M
Kaiser Alumn. Co.	3643	1	31.9M
County Total		5	$164.7M
Barbour County			
Cowikee Mills	2211	1	$13.3M
Dixie Shoe Corp.	3141	1	9.2M
County Total		2	$22.5M

FIGURE 14-5   A Prospect List of Users of Corrugated Boxes Derived from Input–Output Analysis and Showing User's Name and SIC Arranged Within County (or ZIP Code) Within State.

of businesses, commerce input–output, bank savings, retail sales, etc.) as well as in terms of consumer demographics and lifestyles (number of households, home value, income, autos owned, etc.) Ruf's **business clusters** reveal the impact these variables have on the buying behavior of businesses located in these areas.

Marketing professionals know that customers are not equal in value. In fact, it is quite simple to distinguish between the repeat customer and the customer who has made a single, inexpensive purchase some time ago. Such cluster analysis is more descriptive than traditional segmentation methods because it can reveal hidden relationships. For example, cluster analysis may reveal that past purchasing patterns, economic growth, and interdependency factors are far better predictors of future purchases than size of the firm, its revenues, or industry classification.

By analyzing data from many firms across the spectrum of industries, a marketer can derive "business lifestyles." Using input–output matrices, the marketer can use statistical models to describe the *consumption* and *digestion* of products and services a company uses to produce its final products and services. Once indexes are attached to a business file, hidden relationships of the business environment are revealed. Clusters thus provide a detailed understanding of businesses by summarizing their lifestyles.

Business cluster analysis can also incorporate consumer factors to provide an additional dimension to the picture. A correlation exists between the location of a business and the consumer behavior in the same location. The final demand of consumers can define the commerce area's footprint. By incorporating the consumer component, business clusters can reveal the hidden relationships of the surrounding economy. Additional matches allow business owners and their employees who purchase to be linked to their home addresses. This results in a descriptive profile giving expanded information on consumption, media usage, and credit behavior.

Business clusters provide meaning to the thousands of variables and hidden relationships in the business ecosystem. They allow the zeroing in of target markets necessary to survive and thrive. B2B marketers can identify their best customers, increase market penetration, and boost advertising effectiveness. They can optimize location of markets (identified by ZIP code areas), target new customers more precisely, and more clearly visualize their markets for better strategic decision making.

6. *Other Industrial Market Segmentation Criteria.* We can also categorize industrial organizations by financial strength or size as well as in terms of number of employees or sales volume. Geographic data are also often used, including city size and location. Other criteria differentiate form of ownership and whether the enterprise is a headquarters or branch office, a parent, or a subsidiary. A proven predictor for many B2B direct marketers, too, is the extent of Yellow Pages advertising.

Direct marketers must appeal not only to organizations but to individuals within organizations. Purchasing agents alone do not generate demand. More likely, engineers, chemists, architects, production managers, and a host of other specialists make joint decisions. Personalities and the demographics of these decision makers and influencers are now also becoming a basis for market segmentation. With data on contacts within the business, further market segmentation based on titles and utility of the function can enhance response rates. Experimentation by IBM has justified the acquisition of such data, and direct response copy has been versioned to appeal to, as examples, "scientists" or "creatives" or "egocentrics."

When all is said and done, certainly the most important basis for B2B market segmentation is an industrial organization's own customer list, including prior purchase behavior, recency/frequency/monetary scoring, and each customer's demographic profile. Regardless of whether an organization is designated as for profit or not for profit, direct marketing strategies still apply. The next section examines direct marketing applications for nonprofit organizations.

NONPROFIT ORGANIZATIONS

Direct marketing is ideal for nonprofit organizations because it is measurable, accountable, targeted, cost-effective, and requires a direct response—qualities that are all of particular importance to organizations that exist to support and advance a cause. Nonprofit organizations serve as a forum for the creation and distribution of new ideas. These organizations, like hospitals and universities, may deliver services. The American Cancer Society and the March of Dimes actively support advancing medical research in an attempt to find a cure for diseases. Mothers Against Drunk Driving (MADD) focuses on safety issues. What they all have in common is that they want people to know about their cause and respond to their pleas for support. This response could be in the form of a donation to a charitable organization or help to achieve any number of an organization's communication objectives. Any nonprofit organization can effectively use direct marketing to achieve its communication objectives. This section is designed to present direct marketing strategies for nonprofit organizations. It addresses the important area of fundraising and also provides numerous examples of successful direct marketing campaigns that have worked for a variety of nonprofit organizations.

According to the DMA, fundraising activities generated $17.6 billion in 2006, and that figure is expected to increase to 21.7 billion by 2011.[4] Just think about that fact the next time a local Girl Scout asks you to buy a box of cookies or when a local Boy Scout asks you to purchase a tin of popcorn. Fundraising organizations employed about 235,100 people in the United States in 2006.[5] The next section discusses the different kinds of nonprofit organizations using direct marketing for enhancing relationships.

Nonprofit Applications

What nonprofit organizations employ direct marketing strategies to achieve their goals and objectives? The answer is probably *every* organization. Most health-concerned organizations, such as the American Cancer Society, the American Heart Association, the American Diabetes Association, and the American Lung Association, avidly practice direct marketing to obtain donations to support research for their worthy causes. Organizations concerned with protecting the environment, such as the World Wildlife Fund, the Nature Conservancy, and the Rails-to-Trails Conservancy, use direct marketing. Educational institutions have long relied on direct marketing to obtain student enrollments, offer continuing education courses, raise funds, garner political support, and communicate with alumni and the larger community. Other nonprofit organizations include those concerned with helping our youth, such as Big Brothers Big Sisters, Boys & Girls Club of America, and the Rappahannock River Rats Youth Hockey Association. Nonprofit organizations also exist to protect women, such as the Miles Foundation and Battered Women's Organization, whereas others exist to provide support to minorities, such as An Achievable Dream.

The goal of most nonprofits is to maximize their relationships with their many constituents, including clients, donors, volunteers, and customers. Let's explore the tasks associated with maximizing these important relationships for nonprofit organizations.

1. *Building New Customer Relationships.* Regardless of the direct marketing application, most nonprofit organizations look to individual volunteers and private organizations for support. Clients, patrons, donors, members, board members, students, volunteers, the public—they are all *customers;* even if most nonprofit organizations would not refer to them that way, we do so throughout this chapter. Though initiating customer relationships is challenging for many nonprofit organizations, *maintaining* them is the key to success. Building lifetime customer relationships is critical to successful nonprofit direct marketing. For the nonprofit organization, **customer relationship management (CRM)** simply means developing a relationship with donors, thus ensuring their future support.[6] Nonprofit organizations must cultivate relationships with donors by communicating regularly with them and making them feel valued.

Nonprofit organizations, especially charitable organizations must understand *each* donor, understand what motivates them to contribute their time, talents, and money to the organization's cause. Most people purchase or donate to support a cause and see it advance. People are normally driven in their donation choices by their personal/core values and donating to specific causes helps them act in accordance with these personal values. Thus, people do not normally give just to help an organization improve its revenue stream. To ensure a customer's long-term support, the nonprofit organization must focus on meeting its customer's needs, instead of its own. Therefore, maintaining loyalty is of paramount importance in maximizing the strength and duration of the donor's output.

2. *Maintaining Existing Customer Relationships.* Nonprofit organizations can effectively maintain and strengthen relationships with their customers by adding a feedback element to each communication form they make use of. Today's customers want to tell you their opinions and develop their own visions for your organization. Let them. The single most important way to enhance customer relationships is to *listen* to these customers and, while maintaining focus on the organization's mission, incorporate the ideas and suggestions they offer. Provide networking opportunities for them so that they feel a part of your organization. Keep them up to date on your activities. According to a recent survey, donors agreed that it was very important to be kept up to date on a nonprofit's activities. The following methods for providing this update were rated most desirable:[7]

- Videos sent every three or four months, showing some of the organization's recent work
- Online bulletin board services to give donors information and let them ask questions and receive answers electronically
- Recordings of the organization's board meetings
- Periodic phone calls, not asking for money but letting donors know what the organization is doing

- Copies of the organization's internal documents, such as financial reports and strategic plans
- Newsletters, e-newsletters, or e-mails sent regularly to notify donors about the work, needs, and impact of the organization. Figure 14-6 presents an example of an e-mail that was distributed to inform and thank the donors about the success of a special event.

PAWS FOR A CAUSE
DOG WALK & FESTIVAL

Final Event Update	May 20, 2008

We raised over $52,000!

The rain dance must have worked because it held off for our Second Annual Paws for a Cause Dog Walk & Festival, held at Riverview Farm Park in Newport News on Sunday, May 18, 2008.

Over $52,000 was raised to benefit the 10,000 animals that come through the Peninsula SPCA each year.

Hundreds of animal lovers and supporters came out throughout the day to take part in the festivities including on-going demonstrations by Sit Means Sit and Coastal Dog Training, Avenue of Heroes local rescue groups and browsed pet related exhibitors.

The nearly 500 registered walkers and their canine companions also enjoyed activities such as the Police K-9 and Fire Bomb Dog demonstrations, Busch Gardens "Get Wild!" exotic animal presentation, the Peninsula SPCA's Puppy Parade of adoptable pets, and contests which included a Kissing (Licking) Contest and Best Costume contest.

We want to hear from you!

The Peninsula SPCA wants to learn from you on how we can make next year's event even better!

Click here to take a quick survey.

Thanks for supporting our event and we will see you next year!

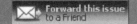
Forward this issue to a Friend

Congratulations to our top winners!

Top Teams & Vet Challenge Winner:
Salty Dawgs of Salty Paws Veterinary Hospital- $5,555

Top Individual Fundraiser:
Amy Dudeck- $2,897

Largest Teams:
Salty Dawgs of Salty Paws Vet Hospital with 36 members

2009 SpokesDog Winner:
Cathy McQuade

Register Today for Paws for a Cause 2009!

The registration fee is $10 per person. Click here to register. If you have any questions, please contact Vicki Rowland at 595.1392.

FIGURE 14-6   An Example of a "Thank You" E-mail Sent to Donors.

Though it may seem complicated, direct marketing in the service of CRM is the most effective way to satisfy the needs of a nonprofit organization's current customers.

As we saw in Chapter 2, focusing on customer retention is far less costly and much more productive than trying to obtain new customers. CRM is well suited for nonprofit organizations with limited budgets. It can initiate and cultivate relationships, encourage charitable giving, and foster partnerships with businesses in the local community to join in the support of the nonprofit organization's cause.

3. *Securing Corporate Partnerships.* For nonprofit organizations, CRM hasn't always meant CRM. In fact, for years it meant "cause-related marketing." **Cause-related marketing** is defined as a commercial activity by which businesses and charities or causes form a partnership with each other to market an image, product, or service for mutual benefit.[8] American companies spend nearly $1 billion on cause-related marketing campaigns.[9] These cause-related marketing partnerships may include more than one partner and multiple nonprofit organizations. For example, the mission of the Junior League of Hampton Roads (JLHR), a chapter of the Association of Junior Leagues International, is to improve the lives of women and children through the effective action and leadership of trained volunteers. The JLHR has been serving its local community for more than 50 years and has enjoyed long-standing relationships with many different corporate partners, such as Anheuser-Busch, Ferguson Enterprises, Hutchens Chevrolet, Goodman, and W. M. Jordan. Recently, it has partnered with another nonprofit organization, the Food Bank of the Virginia Peninsula, to become a sponsor of the Food 4 Kids Program. The JLHR provides volunteers, holds food drives, and generates funds for this program to send elementary-aged children of the working poor home from school on Fridays with their backpacks stuffed with nutritious, nonperishable food on a weekly basis. As Figure 14-7 shows, JLHR volunteers regularly assist in preparing the food bags for delivery to local schools throughout the year. This kind of collaboration is certainly a "win-win-win" situation for all partners involved in the program.

For decades, corporations and nonprofit organizations have been forming partnerships to create innovative cause marketing campaigns. However, in the past, many nonprofit organizations found themselves in uncharted waters, with considerable demands for information, strategic plans, and program details made on them in return for this private-sector funding. Thus, corporate partnerships required too much effort to attempt. Today these nonprofit organizations have become savvy marketers and understand the workings of the corporate community. Therefore, cause-related marketing is on the rise again. In fact, corporate executives are commonly knocking on the doors of nonprofit organizations to initiate business relationships.

Linking with a charity or cause can bring significant benefits for both the business and nonprofit organization. Greater awareness and support for both is one of the likely benefits. Examples of cause-related marketing are all around us. There are many companies sponsoring local marathons, 5K and 10K races, walkathons, and other events in support of national organizations such as the American Cancer Society, March of Dimes, or the Cystic Fibrosis Foundation. There are also many companies that sponsor special events to support local organizations, such as a local rehabilitation center, youth group, or a faith-based group. In addition, many manufacturers exercise cause-related marketing by donating a set amount to select charitable organizations for each product or service sold. For example, when consumers purchase Purina cat food, the company makes a donation to the American Association of Zoological Parks and Aquariums. When consumers rent automobiles from Dollar Rent A Car, they may also be supporting MADD. Even local grocery stores and discount stores support local schools. These programs are normally linked to customer loyalty card programs through which the retailer allows a percentage of the customer's store

FIGURE 14-7   JLHR Volunteers Assist with the *Food 4 Kids* Program.

purchases to be donated to the school of the customer's choice. Figure 14-8 provides some specific examples of business–nonprofit alliances.

Nonprofit organizations have long used direct marketing activities in building donor relationships, maintaining and strengthening these relationships, and establishing corporate partnerships to advance their respective causes. Nonprofits effectively use direct marketing methods in their fundraising efforts as well. These groups recognize the efficiency of direct marketing as a means of raising funds, driving memberships, and creating greater awareness for their cause. Let's explore direct marketing fundraising strategies for nonprofit organizations in greater detail.

Fundraising

The basic foundation of all good fundraising is marketing, and all fundraisers are involved in marketing campaigns. It has been said that "fundraisers are in the vanguard of direct marketing because theirs is one of the most competitive situations."[10] With so much competition out there, how does a person or an organization determine whom to support? What are the primary causes the public supports? Americans donated nearly $300 billion to charitable causes in 2006.[11] Statistics reveal that religious organizations received the overwhelming majority of donations, with educational

Business Partner	Nonprofit Partner	Description
Walt Disney Co. donated	Habitat for Humanity	Walt Disney $70,000 for construction of a townhouse in Burbank, California
Florida Department of Citrus	American Cancer Society	American Cancer Society's logo has been used to promote the role of orange products in preventing cancer.
Nabisco	American Zoo Aquarium Association	Nabisco produced a special edition of its Barnum's Animal Crackers. Five cents from the sale of each box up to $100,000 was donated.
SC Johnson Wax	15th Annual Night Out Against Crime	SC Johnson Wax agreed to pledge up to $200,000 based on consumers coupon redemption for various products (Glade, Ziplock, Shout).
Borders Bookstores	National Literacy Nonprofit Organization, Reading is Fundamental (RIF) and local libraries	At the checkout, Borders asks each customer to donate $1. On a quarterly basis, Borders Bookstores matches customer donations and gives money to targeted nonprofit organizations.

FIGURE 14-8   **Examples of Business—Nonprofit Alliances.**

institutions coming in a distant second place, followed by foundations.[12] Research shows that 67 percent of all households donated to charity, and the average total household donation was $1,872.[13] With that much money at stake, nonprofit organizations cannot afford not to practice savvy direct marketing fundraising techniques in an attempt to garner support for their cause.

Bob Stone, direct marketing guru and member of the Direct Marketing Hall of Fame, presented the classic way to raise funds for a worthy cause. His advice was to take the following three-step approach:[14]

Step 1 Form a committee of influentials to make contacts with potential contributors, establishing a targeted contribution amount for each potential donor.

Step 2 Mount a direct response campaign to a list of identified prospective contributors.

Step 3 Organize a follow-up campaign to support the initial direct response campaign or to reach those who have not responded to the direct mail campaign.

Stone noted some additional facts to keep in mind as nonprofit organizations develop their fundraising campaigns:[15]

- The highest percentage of response in a fundraising effort comes from previous contributors.
- Favorable response to telephone solicitations usually can be enhanced when calls are made by people of stature in a community or in an industry.
- People respond best to emotional appeals when they are backed by a rationale for giving. See Figure 14-9 for some examples of emotional appeals.
- People tend to respond more readily to appeals for specific projects rather than to appeals for general needs. For example, an elementary school's request for funds to help build a new playground for the children is a more effective appeal than a request to help reduce the school's debt.

> *"Every minute of every day there are 14 incidents of child abuse or domestic violence happening somewhere in this country."*
>
> *"In the few seconds it took you to open and read this letter, four children died from the effects of malnutrition or disease somewhere in the world."*

FIGURE 14-9 **Examples of Emotional Fundraising Appeals.**

- When pledges are made by telephone, 75 to 80 percent of the pledges will be collected, if they are properly followed up.
- The total amount pledged tends to be greater when a multipayment plan is offered.
- The average contribution tends to increase when specific contribution amounts are suggested. Example: "You contributed $15 last year. May we suggest you contribute $20 this year to help cover our expanded needs?"
- Setting a specific date for meeting a fundraising goal tends to increase response and total contributions.

Stone's three-step approach is still applicable today, as is the following eight-step fundraising plan for nonprofit organizations.[16]

Step 1 *Listen to your donors.* It is vital that your donors feel that you listen to them and that their input makes a difference in the operation of the nonprofit organization. Involving them as partners in solving your organization's problems often leads them to become longtime supporters, rather than one-time funders.

Step 2 *Keep your mission in mind.* Each nonprofit organization must communicate its mission clearly and implement its goals and objectives effectively. In addition, it must remember that the organizational mission will assist it in building long-term relationships with donors.

Step 3 *Tell your story vividly.* The best people to tell the story of a nonprofit organization are volunteers and clients. Include them. Their personal, heartfelt experiences make a unique impact on potential donors. Put these stories in brochures, videos, and Web pages. Making these stories both memorable and credible will yield more dollars from donors.

Step 4 *Go high-tech, but stay people-focused.* Using the Internet to communicate with a vast number of donors and volunteers is both fast and efficient. If the organization doesn't have a Web site, it should create one. A home page is a good way to stay in touch with donors and volunteers and strengthen relationships with them.

Step 5 *Let donors fund projects.* It is well known that when donors know exactly what their donations are being used for, they are much more generous. People like to feel they are helping to accomplish something good with the money they donate; it goes back to *why* they give in the first place. To that end, the nonprofit organization should keep its "wish list" updated, in case a donor inquires about the organization's current needs.

Step 6 *Target your audience.* Using technology and databases to target the best possible list of customers is the most efficient method of selecting who will receive a fundraising request. In fact, when database technology is used properly, the nonprofit organization can send out several different fundraising letters requesting different amounts from targeted donors—all at the same time.

Step 7 *Involve the CEO and board of directors.* Fundraising is part of the job description of the CEO as leader, facilitator, and communicator. In fact, many potential donors will not give unless the CEO makes the solicitation. Likewise, fundraising should be a part of every board member's job, and board members should be the first to make donations to the organization.

Step 8 *Launch a fundraising campaign.* A good fundraising campaign should go beyond raising money and focus on building the reputation of the nonprofit organization. Creating brochures and newsletters, hosting special events, and distributing press releases are some of the ways to reinforce the reputation of the organization and communicate with the organization's many different constituents as well as the general public.

Despite what many people think, nonprofit organizations are not always seeking money. Sometimes they want what is even harder to come by—a commitment. Nonprofits realize the great value of long-term commitments from donors. It is one thing to obtain a single monetary donation, but to secure a long-term commitment to help move a particular cause forward in the future is another thing. Additionally, nonprofit organizations recognize the great value of dedicated volunteers. According to the U.S. Department of Labor, about 60.8 million people volunteered through or for an organization at least once between September 2006 and September 2007, which represents 26.2 percent of the total U.S. population.[17] The average U.S. resident volunteers approximately 36.5 hours per year, although that number varies greatly by state.[18]

Thousands of nonprofit organizations use direct marketing methods to secure volunteers to assist in carrying out their mission. Just check out the Web site of the Make-A-Wish Foundation (www.wish.org), and you will see that volunteers serve as wish granters, fundraisers, special event assistants, and in numerous other capacities to help the organization grant the wishes of children with life-threatening medical conditions. Or visit the Web site of Operation Smile (www.operationsmile.org), and you will learn how that organization relies on physicians and other medical professionals who serve as volunteers to provide reconstructive surgery and related health care to indigent children worldwide. There is a nonprofit organization in need of volunteers for almost every cause—regardless of whether the cause is medical, environmental, social, educational, or political.

Regardless of what the nonprofit organization is seeking, the right appeal is of great importance for the organization when communicating with potential donors. The appeal must come from an individual (not the organization as a whole), and it should request action for a specific activity. The direct response fundraising message must accomplish the following three things.[19]

1. *Strike fast:* Gaining the attention of the potential donor is a challenge when there are so many other organizations clamoring for attention. A rule of thumb for attracting attention is to segment your message to your target audience. A couple of strategies to attract attention include telling stories and explaining how each person can make a difference in a campaign.

2. *Personally grab and shake:* The appeal must hit the donor or customer on a personal level. It must motivate them to take action. For example, a person who is an outdoor enthusiast is naturally more prone to make purchases of outdoor equipment and to support organizations that protect the outdoors. H. G. Lewis offers some tips for grabbing and shaking. He points out that examples are more personal and usually generate a greater response than do mere statistics; single causes have more personal impact than do multiple ones; and it is more effective to relate to the donor on the local and personal level, than on the national level.

3. *Make action easy:* The goal of any fundraising message or appeal is to inspire action from the target audience. A smart nonprofit organization will make responding to its request for

support as easy as possible. Some tips for doing so include supplying a reply card with any direct mail package; presenting a toll-free number and Web address often and in prominent places; specifying certain amounts or categories of donations; and suggesting realistic figures based on the purpose of the request.

Figure 14-10 presents a fundraising campaign that was used by the Peninsula Rescue Mission in Virginia to raise both awareness and funds for feeding homeless people at Thanksgiving. It was sent to select ZIP code areas as a newspaper insert and delivered to 25,000 residences throughout the Virginia Peninsula, a section of the greater Hampton Roads region located in southeastern Virginia.

The campaign was effective in generating $8,000 in funding and eliciting a response from 529 new donors. Its success came about because the campaign followed the fundraising principles we've discussed. Let's take a look at some of the details of the campaign and the fundraising appeal.

- The fundraising campaign targeted the local community to benefit a local cause—providing meals for the homeless.
- The message attracted attention because it played off the Desert Storm operation in which the U.S. military was involved at the time by naming the campaign Operation Drumstick.
- It injected guilt. The appeal was asking for funds to help feed those less fortunate at a time when people were to be giving thanks for their plentiful bounty. How could anyone be planning his or her own annual Thanksgiving celebration and not have feelings for those who could not afford a meal?
- It provided premiums that were designed to make the donor feel good about his or her decision to support the mission. One of these that worked particularly well was a table tent (which is a small tent-shaped sign designed to be placed on a table) that could be displayed on the donor's dinner table as a reminder of his or her generosity in helping the less fortunate and a reminder to give thanks at Thanksgiving.
- The funding request provided realistic figures (e.g., "$12.16 will provide 8 Thanksgiving meals; $23.85 will provide boxed goods for 5 Thanksgiving baskets; $53.28 will provide turkeys for 6 Thanksgiving baskets," etc.). By design, the Peninsula Rescue Mission did not round off the numbers. The Peninsula Rescue Mission could have stated "$12 will provide 8 Thanksgiving Dinners." These figures certainly would have made the accounting tasks of the organization much easier; however, the figures would not appear as realistic to the potential donor as the exact (dollars and cents) amounts.
- The campaign made it easy to take action. A reply envelope was included, as was a reply card where donors only needed to check a box indicating how many Thanksgiving meals they wanted to provide.

Any fundraising campaign can succeed when it follows the basic principles and strategies of direct marketing and especially direct response fundraising. We can learn a great deal from examining other successful direct marketing fundraising campaigns, although what worked for one organization at one time, may not work (1) at a different time and (2) for a different organization. Nonetheless, we can mine examples to generate ideas for future fundraising campaigns and to find models that allow us to analyze and evaluate the components of a good campaign. In fact, there is a blog that shares fundraising tips with nonprofit organizations. Visit www.donorpowerblog.com to obtain book reviews, recent articles, and more information on how to be successful in cultivating relationships with donors and executing fundraising activities.

Helping people help themselves... that's us!

For over two and one-half decades the ministries of the **Peninsula Rescue Mission** have assisted worthy individuals with the essentials of life, enabling them to survive while becoming self-supporting.

Without any tax money, we ministered last year to thousands of people, providing shelter, meals, groceries, clothing, furniture, and other necessities - all **at no charge!** We were able to do this with the prayers and financial help of many kind friends.

It is no small miracle that we could share nearly **44,000 meals** with the hungry, provide over **14,650 nights lodging** for the homeless; we took **120 needy children** to a free week of summer camp - an experience which changed some of them for life.

As we approach our 26th Thanksgiving, *Operation Drumstick* gives you an opportunity to share with some needy person or family with a Thanksgiving Day meal or other food help.

We look forward to hearing from you in this matter. Our success in Operation Drumstick depends entirely on the generous support that we receive from concerned and caring community members like yourself. **Help someone else to help themselves. Your kind gift can give someone a new chance in life. Will you help?**

Please support generously

OPERATION DRUMSTICK

and

Peninsula Rescue Mission Ministries

Rev. Lindsay Poteat, Executive Superintendent

"I command you to be openhanded toward your brothers and toward the poor & needy in your land."
Deuteronomy 15:11

FIGURE 14-10   Peninsula Rescue Mission Operation Drumstick Flyer.   *Source:* Used with permission of The Peninsula Rescue Mission.

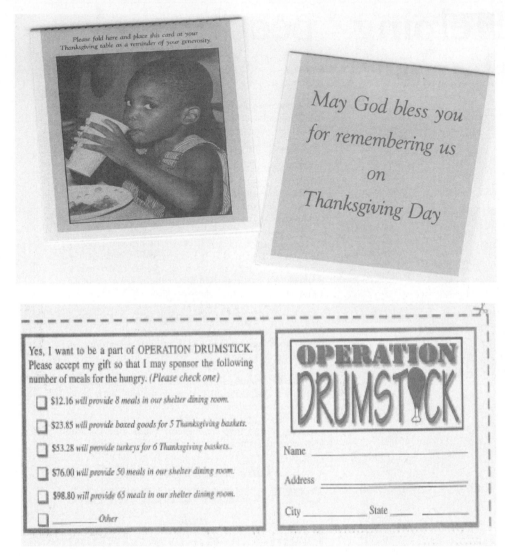

FIGURE 14-10   (Continued)

Media Strategies

Like any other organization, nonprofits can effectively use a variety of media in conducting direct marketing activities. In fact, many nonprofit organizations find great success in mixing the media and launching campaigns supported by several different media strategies. Understanding a donor's media habits and news consumption habits is very important when attempting to secure loyalty, enhance relationships, and cultivate new support. Let's take a look at a few examples of nonprofit organizations that have used different media in executing their direct marketing campaigns.

DIRECT MAIL   Direct mail is the stellar medium for nonprofit organizations. More personalized formats have been one way to build and sustain donor/member relationships. In fact, research has shown that direct mail contained in letter size envelopes (15 percent) were most likely to inspire a response to a request from a nonprofit organization in 2004, closely followed by larger than letter envelopes (14.7 percent) and catalogs not in envelopes (12.4 percent).[20] Nonprofit organizations use direct mail to solicit funds from membership, as well as keep members informed and engaged in supporting an organization's cause. Research has shown that donors recruited by mail on average tend to support the organization for the longest period of time.[21]

An example of an effective direct mail campaign for a nonprofit organization is the campaign titled "August Notebook Bounceback" created for World Vision.

World Vision needed to raise at least $800,000 to continue caring for unsponsored children in developing countries. The charity decided to target current sponsors to see if they would be willing to expand their gifts to sponsor additional children. The direct mail package included a letter from World Vision president, a sticker with the sponsored child's name on it, and a small notebook. World Vision explained in the letter that paper for schoolchildren is extremely scarce. It asked the potential donor to affix the sticker to the cover of the notebook, sign the inside cover, and mail the book back in an enclosed, postage-paid envelope. The organization would then deliver the notebook to the sponsored child, along with another rarity—a pencil. The letter was highly personal, mentioning both the sponsor and the sponsored child by name and made a compelling case for sending money to aid additional children. World Vision enclosed a tear-off coupon requesting a gift of $20, $50, or "other." The results were tremendous. With a total budget of $117,796, World Vision mailed 240,893 direct mail packages and received a response rate of 46.1 percent, beating their previous campaign by almost 26 percent. The cost per response was a low $1.06, and the total income generated exceeded their goal by $197,000 (23 percent). In addition, more than 80 percent of sponsors returned their notebooks for their children, thus bonding their relationship even further.[22]

TELEPHONE   Technological advances and increased list penetration can help phone-a-thons attain successful pledge rates. The new technology allows an organization to reduce staff while increasing the amount of time callers spend actually talking to potential donors. Let's examine an example of a successful telephone fundraising campaign conducted by the Ohio Special Olympics.

The objective of the Ohio Special Olympics campaign was to add the element of the telephone to its direct mail campaign in an effort to reactivate as many donors as possible to support their Summer Special Olympics games. An additional objective was to thank donors for their support, building goodwill, and cultivating a closer relationship. Because many of the donors had family or friends participating in the Special Olympic Games, it was important to train the phone operators to answer questions about the Summer Games and specific events. The organization employed two strategies to enhance the response rate. First, a focus was placed on an athlete in each of the 13 local regions of Ohio. The organization programmed each computer so that the athlete's name and area would appear on the computer screen for reference in the phone script. This enabled a more personal interaction, because many of the donors recognized the athlete's name in their area. Second, the organization timed the campaign so that the operators placed calls just prior to the time of the games—which reinforced the urgency of the campaign. The program was a success. It yielded an average contribution of almost $28 and the program's net income totaled over $28,000.[23]

TELEVISION   Television has earned its fame as a fundraising medium courtesy of the annual Jerry Lewis Labor Day Telethon for Muscular Dystrophy in the United States. Legendary actor Jerry Lewis is the national chairman of the Muscular Dystrophy Association. He has been hosting this 21-and-a-half-hour telethon every Labor Day weekend since 1966. For more information about the telethon, check out the Web site of the Muscular Dystrophy Association (www.mda.org/telethon).

Most fundraising appeals on television are in the form of infomercials. To be successful on TV, a nonprofit organization must know what it wants to accomplish, know what it wants the viewer to take away, and clearly present the benefits of donating. The goal of most infomercials is still to get the viewer to the telephone. Other nonprofits have effectively used direct response television (DRTV) advertisements and public service announcements (PSAs) to generate awareness of their organization and its worthy cause. The United States Golf Association (USGA) television campaign is a prime example.

The USGA aired TV spots during the week of the U.S. Open that were intended to drive in new memberships. Membership in the USGA is a contribution to the game of golf and a show of support for the projects for which the USGA provides funding. Because USGA is a nonprofit organization that hosts the U.S. Open, its network contract specifies that 80 percent of its broadcast communication must be run in the form of PSAs. That meant that fewer than one out of four TV spots could include membership drive messages. The solution was to use television PSAs as a "pure image" foundation on which to build a DRTV campaign.

To communicate the century-old mission of the USGA, the television spots used archival footage and still photography of golf heroes past and present. The USGA was able to connect on a nostalgic note with older golfers and establish themselves as the credible steward of the game among younger golfers. After the PSAs ran, a DRTV ad provided a phone number for golfers to call. The TV spots, combined with a traditional direct mail campaign, appealed to over 2 million golfers.

The results proved the effectiveness of both the TV campaign and the media mixing. The budget for the television campaign totaled $300,000, with an additional $30,000 spent on direct mail. The TV ads generated 21,503 calls, 67 percent of which were converted into memberships. Officials said results of the campaign far exceeded objectives, and membership in the USGA soared 60 percent over the previous year's figures.[24]

THE INTERNET   It was inevitable that as more companies enter the information highway, nonprofit organizations would head in that direction as well. Given the increases in postal rates and cost of paper along with increasing legislative restrictions on telephone marketing, the Internet may become an important media for nonprofit organizations. The first step nonprofit organizations should take before investing funds in support of the Internet is to determine what their customers/donors preferences are for receiving information. How often do they want to receive information about the organization? How accessible is the Internet for them?

Nonprofit organizations effectively use the Internet to solicit potential volunteers, communicate with regular volunteers, and cultivate stronger relationships with current donors/member. The Internet has not been overly successful as a fundraising medium for most nonprofit organizations. People do not normally use a search engine to find places where they can donate their hard-earned dollars. However, since the terrorist attacks of September 11, 2001, "donate here" buttons on charity Web sites are no longer idle. Experts claim that the Internet has accounted for as much as $150 million or 10 percent of an estimated $1.5 billion in individual relief donations during the six-month period after these attacks. Prior to the September 11 attacks, online donations accounted for less than 1 percent of U.S. charitable giving.[25]

Nonprofit organizations also have new opportunities to raise funds on the Internet thanks to numerous online marketing initiatives. To learn more about these opportunities, check out the Internet Nonprofit Center (www.nonprofits.org/fundraising.html) for an alphabetic listing of resources for online fundraising. Let's explore a couple of these avenues. One opportunity is sponsored by BarnesandNoble.com, a subsidiary of Barnes & Noble, headquartered in New York City. Nonprofit organizations joining the affiliate program may create links to BarnesandNoble.com bookstores (www.bn.com) on their Web sites. Whenever someone uses the link, the sender receives 5 percent—which they can donate to a charity or keep for themselves. In addition, 1 percent of such sales are donated to First Book, a group in Washington, DC, that gives books to poor children.[26] Another opportunity is Donor Trust. This is a full-service e-donations solution created by Merkel Direct Marketing to benefit nonprofit organizations seeking to offer potential donors a quick, secure, and cost-effective way for donating online. Donor Trust attaches a "Donate Now" link to a Web site to provide donors with an instant connection to the donation process.[27] This new service provides nonprofit organizations a way to make their Web site secure for credit card donations without having to invest their own time and money in the technology associated with building and maintaining a secure e-commerce Web site. Moreover, donors can sign in and make an online donation with a major credit card; on completion of the transaction, the Donor Trust system will automatically generate a customized e-mail confirmation and thank-you acknowledgment.

In summary, nonprofit organizations are using a variety of media and direct marketing tactics to generate awareness of their cause and obtain volunteers, donors, and friends. The next section explores how political organizations are using direct marketing to promote both their cause and their candidates.

POLITICAL ORGANIZATIONS

Most political organizations rely on direct marketing, too. Just take a look at the DMA membership roster and you'll see many political organizations listed from every part of the political spectrum. The National Women's Political Caucus, People for the American Way, Citizens for Free Enterprise, and the Physician's Committee for Quality Medical Care have been shaping public opinion with their direct marketing efforts. So if you want to be elected to city council, or become mayor of your town, governor of your state, or president of the United States, try direct marketing!

During an election year, most people receive at least one direct response ad or direct mail package promoting a political candidate. But political fundraising marketing takes place in nonelection years as well. The National Republican Congressional Committee (NRCC) currently has a house list of more than 10 million names and has been very successful in raising funds via direct mail. Small gifts (i.e., photograph, book) are used to generate a favorable response from the donor/prospect.

The Internet is a valuable tool used by both Republican and Democratic parties to raise funds to support their campaign candidates. For example, President George W. Bush disclosed a list of campaign contributors on his Web site.[28] However, political direct marketing activities are not always aimed at raising money. Often these parties are interested in gaining support for their cause and securing new members. The Internet also permits the parties to send customized messages to specific groups and individuals and to use online discussions and instant messaging in support of their candidates.

With restrictions placed on ad spending, political parties are trying to secure support via other means. Direct marketing offers several alternatives to mass advertising—such as distributing a newsletter to current and prospective members. The ultimate question is "just how successful are political direct marketing efforts?" Unlike most nonprofit organizations, political parties don't measure success by response rates or dollars. They measure it by votes. In today's sophisticated world, political organizations use unique analytical tools, such as micro-targeting, to create specific offers designed to woo voters. Let's discuss this innovative technique.

Political micro-targeting, also referred to as *narrowcasting,* is aggregating groups of voters based on data about them available in databases and on the Internet—to target them with tailor-made messages.[29] Political parties gather personal information about voters to deliver narrowly targeted messages calculated to influence their votes. Micro-targeting goes beyond traditional segmentation bases to gather data at the individual level. This information can include magazine subscriptions, real estate records, consumer transaction data, demographics, lifestyle data, geography, psychographics, voter history, and survey response data. Micro-targeting can add great value to political marketing activities.

Political micro-targeting is being used by both the Democratic and Republican political parties to determine which voters care about specific campaign issues. For example, research has shown that all people who regularly attend church are not alike. Political micro-targeting can be used to identify those churchgoers who would be more interested in hearing a Democratic message of social justice.[30] Given that direct and interactive marketing messages can be personalized and delivered to individuals on a one-to-one basis, micro-targeting is seen as a powerful tool for directing appropriate messages to voters. For example, in the Bloomberg mayoral campaign in New York City, African American homeowners in Queens were sent the same direct mail message as Staten Island Italian American homeowners, with the same impact on their respective voting behavior.[31] In conclusion, political micro-targeting helps campaigns deliver more effective messages to specific individuals and households by tracking and analyzing information on a person-by-person basis.

Political organizations are not the only public administrative bodies to narrowly target select groups of individuals. A wide variety of governmental organizations regularly apply direct and interactive marketing strategies as well. This is the topic of our next section.

GOVERNMENTAL ORGANIZATIONS

The government has relied on direct marketing for many of its public interactions. The U.S. Postal Service (USPS) distributes direct mail to both final and organizational consumers to promote its many products and services. Direct mailers encourage final consumers to purchase uniquely designed stamps, online postage services, as well as schedule convenient and time-saving pick-up and delivery services. In addition, the USPS distributes a free kit filled with creative ideas for using direct mail to marketing organizations and advertising agencies to promote the use of its wide array of business services.

For many years tax refund checks issued by the Internal Revenue Service have been accompanied by mail-order forms for liberty coins from the U.S. Mint. In fact, one of the busiest days for the USPS is April 15—the day tax returns are due. Just think about the response rate the Internal Revenue Service receives on its annual offer!

All branches of the military use direct and interactive marketing for targeted recruiting to high school juniors and seniors. Figure 14-11 presents some of the direct mail pieces being used by the U.S. Department of the Navy in its recruiting activities. Note the variety of motivational headlines it uses. "No sense hiding from the hero you were born to be." "How many people can put world traveler on their resume?" "Jump-start your life." The copy of each direct mail piece is compelling, promoting the benefits—world travel, exposure to cutting-edge technology, opportunity for college education, respect, and the ability to make a difference—associated with joining the military.

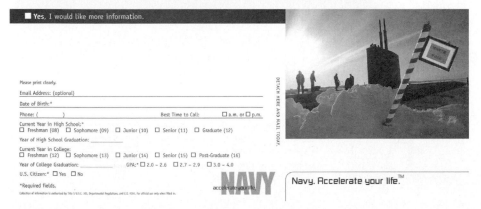

FIGURE 14-11   U.S. Navy Direct Mail Examples.   *Source:* Use of the Department of the Navy's Accelerate Your Life® marks is granted with permission of the Department of the Navy and does not constitute an endorsement of any author, publisher or product there of, by the Department of the Navy or the Department of Defense.

Now's the time for a wake-up call.

Alarm sounds. Another day. Another dollar. Then reality sinks in: There's got to be a better way.

There is. The prospect of a more **promising career.** A more **fulfilling life.** A more **exciting routine.**

In today's Navy, you can wake up to something new and meaningful every day. Pursue a line of work that's about **making the most of your skills.** For your benefit. And for that of those around you.

Take pride in what you do for a living.

Step into any of over 60 high-tech fields. Explore your interests and sense of adventure. Expand your job description. Protecting freedom. Supporting global relief missions.

All while **earning impressive benefits** along the way, including good pay. Comprehensive health care. **College credit** for on-the-job training. Plus **potentially over $70,000 to use toward school.**

Enjoying your work. Securing your future. Serving your country and humanity. Now that's something to get out of bed for.

Being defined by your work.
See how satisfying that can be.

Want to do great things in your world? Then spend some time in ours. Learn more about careers. Educational assistance. And the benefits waiting. In the Navy. Simply fill out and mail the attached reply card, call us at **(XXX) XXX-XXXX** or email **recruiter@localxxxxxxxxxxx.com** for more details. There's no pressure. No obligation. Just an exciting opportunity to do something extraordinary in life.

Department of the Navy
Navy Recruiting Command
P.O. Box 2981
Warminster, PA 18974

OFFICIAL BUSINESS

BUSINESS REPLY MAIL
FIRST-CLASS MAIL   PERMIT NO. 9280   MILLINGTON TN

POSTAGE WILL BE PAID BY ADDRESSEE

DEPARTMENT OF THE NAVY
PO BOX 2981
WARMINSTER PA 18974-9858

NO POSTAGE
NECESSARY
IF MAILED
IN THE
UNITED STATES

FIGURE 14-11   (Continued)

Beyond the U.S. military, many other governmental entities use direct and interactive marketing on a regular basis. Just think about the travel and tourism industry where most destination marketing organizations and convention and visitor bureaus fund their promotional efforts through local and state tax dollars.[32] Most state and local tourism organizations use direct and interactive marketing because it produces campaign results that are measurable and attributable to specific media, like media sourcing, response rates, conversion rates, and sales revenue generated from visiting tourists. Measuring advertising effectiveness is especially important for these entities since most state and local governments seek a $10 to $20 return on every dollar spent on marketing.[33]

The City of Virginia Beach concentrates its direct marketing efforts on prospective tourists in the northeast region of the United States. This geographic region is important because the city's convenient location makes it only a day's drive for two-thirds of the nation's population. Figure 14-12 presents an example of a direct mail piece used by the Convention and Visitors Bureau

FIGURE 14-12   City of Virginia Beach Direct Mail Piece.   *Source:* Used with permission of the City of Virginia Beach Convention & Visitors Bureau.

of the City of Virginia Beach to promote its beautiful beach resorts to prospective tourists. The bureau distributes its Vacation Planner to anyone who requests travel information about the City of Virginia Beach. Most requests are submitted online or via telephone.

Often hand-in-hand with travel and tourism marketing is sports marketing, because the direct response that both of these marketers are often seeking is in the form of visitation. Let's now explore how sports organizations utilize direct and interactive marketing activities.

SPORTS ORGANIZATIONS

A variety of direct marketing strategies and tactics are frequently used by sports organizations to help them achieve their objectives. Virtually all sports team marketers share the common objective of filling the seats of their stadium, arena, park, or rink with loyal fans cheering them on to victories. Of course, sports marketers would prefer if these fans purchased season tickets and supported the home team for the entire season and not just one game. Sports marketers may also be interested in obtaining corporate sponsors or hosting fundraising events. These are additional areas where direct marketing can be applied in an especially effective manner. However, before you begin to think about the glamor and fun associated with sports marketing, you should be aware of its unique challenges.

One uncontrollable variable that often presents a challenge to direct marketing to gain attendance for an upcoming game is the record and reputation of the visiting team. When the home team plays against a big contender or rival, or a team with an excellent winning record, securing attendance is much easier. When the contender doesn't have a good reputation or record, it is much more difficult to fill the seats. Similarly, the record of the home team is an important component of sports marketing. A winning team is easily marketed. Everyone wants to support a winning team! But when the team is not performing well, the task of selling season tickets becomes quite a challenge. Let's discuss some of the direct marketing activities associated with securing season ticket holders—regardless of how the team is performing.

Think about CRM and partner relationship management and apply it to sports teams. Yes, constant communication, in the form of a newsletter, e-newsletter, outbound e-mails, direct mail, or phone calls, to existing season ticket holders is a typical starting point. The regular communication is meant to strengthen the loyalty between the team and the fan. Promoting special events to regular season ticket holders is another common communication objective. Often sports organizations will partner with nonprofit organizations to hold special events to raise funds for a specific cause. For example, the Norfolk Admirals Hockey Team supported a breast cancer cause by creatively painting the ice pink! The Admirals donated a portion of ticket sales to the cause, auctioned off pink hockey sticks and autographed jerseys, held a pregame Women's Hockey 101 Clinic, and provided cause-related educational materials. Figure 14-13 presents the flyer it distributed via e-mail and postal mail to area businesses. People were directed to respond via phone or e-mail to purchase tickets for this special event. The event produced the second highest game attendance for the season and generated more than $13,000 for the charity.

Of course, sports marketers also use direct marketing activities to prospect for new fans by offering group discounts. It is also common for sports marketers to promote attendance at select games that might not naturally garner a high attendance.

So far we've discussed how sports marketers use direct marketing activities targeting final consumers (B2C). However, equally important is their efforts to market to business consumers (B2B). Most sports marketers actively promote to business consumers to obtain sponsorship support for their

FIGURE 14-13 **Norfolk Admirals: Pink in the Rink Flyer.** *Source:* Used with permission of Norfolk Admirals Hockey Club.

team. Many of these activities entail direct marketing strategies and tactics. As Figure 14-14 shows, the Norfolk Tides Baseball Club offers a variety of sponsorship packages to prospective sponsors. Prospective sponsors are asked to respond by placing a phone call to the number provided at the bottom of the brochure or by visiting the Norfolk Tides Web site. These brochures are distributed via postal mail to both current and prospective sponsors.

These savvy marketers place direct response advertisements on television and radio; in newspapers, magazines, and a variety of miscellaneous local programs; publications; and brochures. Unique to the field of sports marketing is the concept of trading or bartering. It is common for sports organizations to secure air time on television or radio, or obtain space in newspapers and magazines without directly paying for it. In fact, most sports organizations do not pay for the majority of the advertisements they place in various media. They simply exchange season tickets and offer cross-promotion opportunities to the various media vehicles.

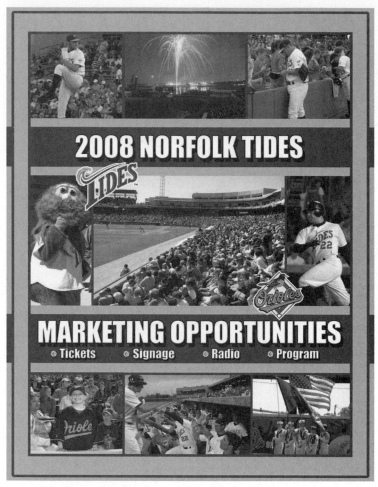

FIGURE 14-14   Cover of the Norfolk Tides Sponsorship Brochure.   *Source:* Used with permission of Norfolk Tides Baseball Club.

Summary

The applications of direct and interactive marketing are almost endless. This chapter has explored just a few of the many different sectors using direct and interactive marketing strategies and tactics. Direct and interactive marketing is effectively used by both B2C and B2B marketers. B2B direct marketing is the process of providing goods and services to industrial market intermediaries, as opposed to ultimate consumers. B2B direct marketers have become quite adept at using databases to generate leads for personal sales follow-up, to encourage browsing of their informative Web sites, and to consummate direct sales.

Nonprofit organizations have also embraced direct marketing methods because of their unique cost-effective and personalized format. Direct marketing is highly effective in enabling nonprofit organizations to establish stronger relationships with their donors. This, in turn, means greater support for the nonprofit cause. However, to be effective, a nonprofit organization must understand its donors' giving behavior. This requires an understanding of the donors' media preferences and knowledge of basic fundraising principles. Direct response fundraising appeals must be specific and follow certain guidelines as presented in this chapter. The fundraising appeal should be targeted, provide suggested donation amounts, carefully create and test the copy of the message, keep the format or presentation simple, and select the premium or free gift cautiously based on the results of tests. Similar to nonprofit direct marketing, understanding the dynamics of voter behavior prior to and during elections is critical for political organizations employing direct marketing methods. Many political organizations now employ political micro-targeting to effectively deliver specific messages to select voters. Political marketers use direct response advertising to generate both support for their political party to and votes for their candidates.

A wide variety of governmental organizations apply direct marketing methods to generate a specific response from targeted individuals or businesses for a number of different purposes. We examined the direct and interactive marketing applications of the USPS, Internal Revenue Service, U.S. Navy, and state and local convention and visitor bureaus.

Finally, we explored how sports organizations apply direct and interactive marketing to generate game attendance, obtain season ticket holders, secure sponsorships, or promote special events. Sports organizations face unique uncontrollable challenges in their marketing efforts based on the performance of the team. Direct and interactive marketing is effectively used to strengthen relationships with season ticket holders to promote team spirit and fan loyalty. In conclusion, direct marketing is regularly used by sports organizations in their marketing efforts.

Key Terms

business-to-business (B2B)
   direct marketing *373*
industrial goods *373*
Standard Industrial
   Classification (SIC) *378*
North American Industrial Classification System (NAICS) *380*

input–output analysis *380*
Global Positioning System
   (GPS) *380*
Topologically Integrated
   Geographic Encoding
   Referencing (TIGER) *380*
business clusters *381*

customer relationship
   management (CRM) *383*
cause-related marketing *385*

Review Questions

1. What are major factors contributing to the increasing use of the tools and techniques of direct marketing in B2B distribution?
2. Describe the U.S. Commerce Department's longtime system of Standard Industrial Classification (SIC). What is its key feature relative to the emerging North American Industrial Classification System (NAICS)?
3. How does direct and interactive marketing help nonprofit organizations reach their goals?
4. Fundraising is extremely competitive. How can nonprofit organizations convince donors that they should donate to their organization?

5. How can nonprofit organizations maximize their relationship with their customers?
6. What is cause-related marketing? Provide some examples of how direct marketers use cause-related marketing and why.
7. Why has direct marketing recently become more important to political parties? What are the objectives of political direct marketing methods?
8. Describe the use and benefits of micro-targeting for political parties.

9. What are some of the ways governmental organizations apply direct and interactive marketing strategies? Provide some examples not mentioned in the chapter.

10. Explain why sports organizations use direct and interactive marketing to target business and final consumers with their direct response advertisements? Provide some specific examples.

Exercise

Because of your knowledge of direct and interactive marketing, you've just been promoted to a sales representative position with a large pharmaceutical company. They want you to recommend different ways they can implement direct and interactive marketing techniques when marketing their prescription drugs to physicians. Outline the various B2B direct marketing strategies and tactics you would recommend to the company and explain what each activity will produce.

CASE

Peninsula Society for the Prevention of Cruelty to Animals

Overview

This case is an example of how numerous direct marketing methods have been employed by a chapter of the Society for the Prevention of Cruelty to Animals (SPCA) to enable donors and partners to be obtained and cultivated. It demonstrates how a nonprofit organization can effectively launch a fundraising campaign via basic direct and interactive marketing principles. It also details the creation and use of an organization's in-house database. Finally, it shows how multiple direct mail campaigns, combined with effective Web site and special event promotions, can make a difference in assisting the SPCA to fulfill its mission of finding a good home for every adoptable pet.

Case

In 1866, New York resident Henry Bergh decided that he could no longer sit idly by and watch a street merchant beat his defenseless horse. On that day, the first SPCA was born. Named the American Society for the Prevention of Cruelty to Animals, this organization became the first of its kind to exist for the sole purpose of helping make the world a better, safer place for tens of millions of companion pets.

Since that time, hundreds of SPCAs and Humane Societies have been formed across the United States to serve their community's needy and homeless animals. While the primary goal of these organizations is to find new homes for their community's homeless pets, these groups also provide humane education to their community's pet owners, provide low-cost medical services for pets of indigent families, and care for sick and injured stray animals. These SPCAs also have the difficult responsibility of euthanizing animals who are not adopted. In 2007, approximately 50 percent of sheltered animals, totaling more than 4 million animals, were euthanized because people opted to buy pets rather than adopt and because people allowed their pets to breed.

SPCAs generally have small staffs and largely rely on volunteers and private donations to operate. Given that these organizations must raise their own money, they often lack the funds necessary to employ skilled employees or to even engage in the most basic business practices. Modern-day tactics such as direct marketing are often overlooked or are not considered due to a lack of time or money. This was the case for the Peninsula SPCA (PSPCA) located in Newport News, Virginia.

PSPCA

Founded in 1967, the PSPCA became the only facility in a four-city region to provide sheltering and adoption services. For over 35 years, the PSPCA provided these services to the best of its ability; however, its adoption rate never exceeded 30 percent. As the nation's best shelters evolved and began attaining adoption rates of 50 percent or more, mounting community demands pressured the PSPCA to reorganize and begin integrating modern business practices.

In 2004, a new volunteer board of directors was elected to achieve this goal. At that time, there was no marketing plan, no marketing strategy, and no employees focused on marketing or fundraising. The only marketing activity that the PSPCA engaged in was direct mail, and even this activity was outsourced to a vendor that charged 35 percent for cookie-cutter solicitations. For an organization that relies on donations to exist, this required a prompt overhaul of massive proportions. But where to begin? The first item was to form a task force of a few board members with the sole job of focusing on

FIGURE 14-15   Vicki Rowland, PSPCA Marketing Coordinator.

marketing initiatives. This small group quickly focused on creating the PSPCA's first ever marketing plan. The next challenge was to create a marketing coordinator's position and fill that position with someone to handle the marketing duties. Meet Vicki Rowland, pictured in Figure 14-15, a 24-year-old college graduate with a love for animals and a keen understanding of direct and interactive marketing. With a new marketing coordinator, a solid team of employees, volunteers, and advisory board members in place, the next job was to create the foundation that would enable the execution of the new marketing plan: the database.

The PSPCA Database

Several database solutions were investigated and evaluated on several criteria: ability to synchronize with the PSPCA's sheltering software, importing/exporting functionality, reporting tools, and price. Ultimately, WiseGuys, by Database Marketing Solutions, was selected.

The next task was to import existing donor names and addresses from a spreadsheet into the new database. Source codes were established and assigned to each name to allow the PSPCA team to analyze which sources provide the most responsive and profitable donors.

To create a sound segmentation strategy, more than 15 of the top SPCAs across the country were surveyed by a team of volunteer market researchers. The results showed that most SPCAs were not segmenting their database—a result of a lack of time and inability to integrate current marketing practices. Of the few SPCAs that did segment their database, the following segments were identified: donors, potential donors, and volunteers.

The final step was to establish ways to generate leads and to train volunteers to handle entering new data. Processes were created to capture the names of people adopting, visiting the PSPCA, or participating in a fundraising event. With the database foundation established, it was time to begin executing the marketing plan.

The PSPCA Marketing Plan

The PSPCA marketing plan had two goals: increase animal adoptions and raise funds. The Increase Funds Raised goal was largely driven by direct marketing principles and is the focus of the rest of this case. This overall goal was broken down into multiple strategies, which included creating both a direct mail program and special fundraising events.

Direct Mail Program   Research revealed that the optimal frequency of direct mail solicitations is four to six times per year. Therefore, the direct mail plan was built around executing four fundraising campaigns per year.

As Figure 14-16 reveals, the first fundraising campaign focused on the transformational changes taking place at the PSPCA. It included a callout box that highlighted the work local vets were donating to the PSPCA, a fact that was not known in the community and that would inspire confidence in the PSPCA's operations. Another callout box was included that highlighted the story of a rescued dog—the purpose of this box was to test how many people would visit the PSPCA's Web site to read his rescue story.

This direct mail campaign was distributed to more than 7,000 past donors and cost $2,500. It yielded a 7.1 percent response rate and raised $19,415, which translates into a 677 percent return on investment. Because response rates of 1 to 2 percent are generally considered good, this was an excellent response that validated the profitability of the direct mail strategy.

The results of the subsequent direct mail campaigns can be seen in Figure 14-17. Notice the response rates on the campaigns varied greatly from 7.24 to 0.34 percent.

As Figure 14-17 illustrates, direct mail fundraising campaigns are not created equal, and there are many factors that determine their success. The dip in January 2007 could have been caused by seasonal fluctuations in donation activity. Or it could have been caused by a more complicated reason, such as lack of communication with donors other than solicitations, poor messaging, or a combination of political or market factors. Additional time will be needed to either confirm or rule out a timing or seasonal cause; however, conducting focus groups or small surveys might shed some light on why some solicitations performed better than others. Notice that the 2007 Holiday Appeal campaign garnered the most funds and generated the highest return on investment for the PSPCA. Thus, future seasonal appeals might be an effective strategy for the PSPCA to continue.

The dip in June 2007 is likely to be attributable to an attempt to cultivate new donors. In an effort to grow the database, the PSPCA team partnered with its veterinary community to solicit its clients. Because clients of vet clinics own pets, the PSPCA team speculated that they would be sympathetic toward the PSPCA's mission and be willing to support it financially. Prospective solicitations often lose money in the short run; however, the lifetime value of each donor far exceeds the initial gift, so effective prospecting can be a lucrative long-term investment. In this instance, 112 new donors were cultivated. Overall, the PSPCA direct mail campaigns were highly effective in both strengthening relationships with its donor base and generating funds for the shelter. However, Rowland and her team were not solely focusing on direct mail campaigns to generate both awareness and funds for the PSPCA; they were also busy planning special events.

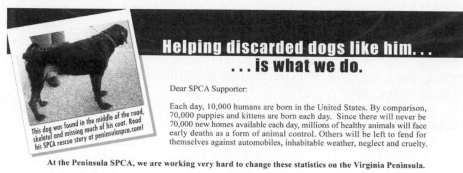

Helping discarded dogs like him. . .
. . . is what we do.

This dog was found in the middle of the road, skeletal and missing much of his coat. Read his SPCA rescue story at peninsulaspca.com!

Dear SPCA Supporter:

Each day, 10,000 humans are born in the United States. By comparison, 70,000 puppies and kittens are born each day. Since there will never be 70,000 new homes available each day, millions of healthy animals will face early deaths as a form of animal control. Others will be left to fend for themselves against automobiles, inhabitable weather, neglect and cruelty.

At the Peninsula SPCA, we are working very hard to change these statistics on the Virginia Peninsula.

Over the last few years, we have overhauled our management and Board of Directors, replaced outdated financial systems, scrutinized our expenses, improved our relationship with our municipal partners, and examined every aspect of our operations. The transformation continues, and we vow to leave no stone unturned! As a result of this tireless effort, we have proudly established an unshakable foundation for our future.

Now, we need your help!

We are creating an aggressive strategic plan to realize our mission of finding a good home for every adoptable pet. This will be impossible to achieve without your support! The suggested donations below illustrate how your money could be used TODAY to improve the quality of life for our animals. If you will donate to our animals today, we pledge to you that 100% of your contribution (yes, every penny!) will go towards helping the precious animals in our care.

On behalf of all of our animals, I thank you for your generosity and support.

Sincerely,

Doug

G. Douglas Bevelacqua
President, Peninsula SPCA Board of Directors

P.S. We are now on the web! Please visit us at *www.peninsulaspca.com!*

Through the Peninsula Veterinary Association, area vets volunteer their expertise on a rotating basis to treat our injured animals.

PENINSULA SPCA

Your donation will go directly toward improving the lives of the animals in our care. See what your donation could provide:

❏ $15 keeps one homeless animal free of fleas and ticks for one month.

❏ $25 provides antibiotics for one injured animal.

❏ $50 provides complete grooming for one severely neglected pet.

❏ $75 spays or neuters one underprivileged pet.

❏ $100 provides all vaccinations, flea & worm treatments, and a microchip for one homeless pet.

❏ _____ I want to help more!

Name: _____

Address: _____

City, St., Zip _____

Yes, I want to receive email updates from the SPCA!

email: _____

Visa   Master Card   Discover   (circle one)

Card # _____ Exp. Date: _____

Signature: _____

FIGURE 14-16   Paws for a Cause Dog Walk & Festival Direct Mail Piece.   *Source:* Used with permission of the Peninsula Society for the Prevention of Cruelty to Animals.

Special Fundraising Events   With the exception of a golf tournament, the PSPCA did not host fundraising events before the marketing coordinator was hired and the new marketing plan was put into effect. To determine what fundraising events were most profitable, many of the top SPCAs across the country were again surveyed. It was determined that the flagship fundraiser of most SPCAs was a pledge walk, with top SPCAs earning between $100,000 and $200,000 each year on that event alone.

Date	Mailing	Number Mailed	Number Responded	Response Rate	Income	Cost	Net Income	ROI
April 2006	Helping Discarded Pets Is What We Do	7,389	525	7.10%	$19,415	$2,500	$16,915	677%
Sept. 2006	Operation: On The Run & Having Fun!	7,390	535	7.24%	$21,089	$2,500	$18,589	744%
Jan. 2007	Together, We Changed Lives	8,794	437	4.97%	$14,759	$3,300	$11,459	347%
June 2007	PVA/SPCA Clinic Fund	46,000	369	0.80%	$22,885	$24,000	($1,115)	−5%
	(SPCA Donors)	*8,806*	*244*	*2.77%*	*$13,860*	*$4,594*	*$9,266*	*202%*
	(Pet Owner Prospects)	*37,194*	*125*	*0.34%*	*$9,025*	*$19,406*	*($10,381)*	*−53%*
Sept. 2007	Never Again (Disaster Planning)	9,548	397	4.16%	$16,985	$3,000	$13,985	466%
Dec. 2007	Holiday Appeal	9,548	573	6.00%	$27,500	$3,000	$24,500	817%

FIGURE 14-17   Paws for a Cause Dog Walk & Festival Direct Mail Rate Analysis.   *Source:* Used with permission of the Peninsula Society for the Prevention of Cruelty to Animals.

The premise of the pledge walk is simple: motivate individuals to register and raise money from their friends and family. Participants have many ways to raise money: ask in person, mail requests, hold their own mini-fundraisers at work/school/church, and so on. Participants can also create their own fundraising Web page that allows them to e-mail their plea, complete with a picture of their pet, with ease. Team formation is encouraged and prizes are awarded for top individual and team fundraisers.

So how could this basic idea yield hundreds of thousands of dollars? The answer is simple: It's a direct marketing extravaganza! Rather than using a mass request to ask thousands of people for money, a pledge walk provides a fun way for individuals to make requests on behalf of the PSPCA. The beauty of this approach is that each request is a highly targeted, one-on-one plea to the hottest leads of all—friends and family. In addition to requesting donations, registered individuals also ask for their friends and family to register themselves, thus exponentially expanding the PSPCA team's reach.

The marketing coordinator and the PSPCA team launched their first dog walk, named Paws for a Cause Dog Walk & Festival, with great anticipation. Following the advice of the Tampa Bay SPCA, the majority of the team's energy was focused on recruiting walkers to fundraise on its behalf. Additionally, however, local businesses were also solicited to sponsor the event so that 100 percent of pledges raised could benefit the animals. A massive festival was put together to draw nonparticipants to witness the walk, which included local rescue groups, pet-related vendors, canine games and contests, and canine demonstrations. Figure 14-18 presents the direct mail piece promoting this event.

The event was a resounding success and raised more than $77,000! Since only $15,000 was raised in company sponsorships, the remaining $62,000 came from the direct marketing engine comprised of hundreds of motivated individuals making targeted, individualized requests on piping hot leads.

Conclusion

As the successes and disappointments of the PSPCA's marketing efforts illustrate, direct marketing is not a success-only journey, and the PSPCA team learned several important lessons along the way.

Come join us for a fun-packed day to raise money for our animals!

Riverview Park,
Newport News

Sunday, May 20, 2007
12:00 - 4:00 pm

EVENTS WILL INCLUDE:

- Demonstrations including the Great American Disc Dog Show
- Police & bomb dog demonstration
- Dog trick workshop
- Tail wagging & dog costume contests
- Avenue of Heroes (local rescue groups)
- Woofstock stage featuring music & entertainment
- Raffle & prizes
- Food & exhibitors

PRE-REGISTER TO BEGIN COLLECTING PLEDGES NOW!

Benefits of pre-registration include:

- Exclusive event t-shirt
- Goody bags
- Prizes for top fundraisers in both individual & team categories
- Pledge packet
- Free personal web page
- Monthly fundraising tips & event updates

PENINSULA SPCA
peninsulaspca.com

Sponsored in part by:

FIGURE 14-18   Paws for a Cause Dog Walk & Festival Direct Mail Piece. *Source:* Used with permission of the Peninsula Society for the Prevention of Cruelty to Animals.

Because it is every marketer's goal to maximize profit on every activity, it is important to recognize the role that measuring and analyzing results plays in ensuring that tactics that are effective are repeated and tactics that are not effective are eliminated. It is also vital to recognize the importance of performing solid research to avoid investing in activities that are likely to fail.

At the end of the first year, Rowland and the PSPCA team raised more than $165,000 from marketing activities and projected raising over $250,000 in the second year. Just as important, however, is that the team's marketing efforts began the critical task of forming thousands of relationships with its community members—members who will become future donors, future volunteers, and hopefully, future families for the homeless animals of the Virginia Peninsula.

This case is dedicated to Tiger Spiller, who was adopted by the Spiller family during the writing of this textbook revision.

Case Discussion Questions

1. What other techniques could the PSPCA use to determine why some of its direct mail campaigns worked better than others?
2. What are other ways the PSPCA could use its database to achieve the two goals of its marketing plan?

3. Do you think direct and interactive marketing strategies and tactics have been effective for the PSPCA? Why or why not?

Notes

1. *The Power of Direct Marketing: ROI, Sales, Expenditures, and Employment in the U.S.,* 2006–2007 ed. (New York: Direct Marketing Association, 2007), p. 5.
2. Ibid.
3. Martin Baier, Kurtis M. Ruf, and Goutam Chakraborty (2002), *Contemporary Database Marketing: Concepts and Applications* (Homewood, IL: Racom Communications), pp. 192–194.
4. *The Power of Direct Marketing,* p. 68.
5. Ibid., p. 95.
6. Dirk Remley, "Relationship Marketing: Guaranteeing the Future," *Nonprofit World* 14, no. 5 (September/ October 1996), 15–16.
7. Adapted from Remley, "Relationship Marketing," pp. 13–16.
8. See http://www.bitc.org.uk/marketing.html, August 2000.
9. "Proving the Cause Marketing Is a Win-Win," Cause Marketing Forum, retrieved on May 21, 2008, http://www.causmarketingforum.com/page. asp?ID=345.
10. Hershell Gordon Lewis, "Direct Mail Fund Raising Tactics," *Fund Raising Management* 28, no. 5 (July 1997), 17.
11. "Record $300B Given to Charity," *Deseret News* (Salt Lake City) June 25, 2007, retrieved on March 24, 2008, http://findarticles.com/p/articles/ mi_qn4188/is_2007625ao_n19322258.
12. "AAFRC Trust for Philanthropy Giving USA 2005" in *Statistical Fact Book, 2006,* 28th ed. (New York: Direct Marketing Association 2006), p. 183.

13. Independent Sector, "Giving and Volunteering in the United States," 2002, retrieved May 21, 2008, http:// www.independentsector.org/programs/research/ GV01main.html.
14. Adapted from Bob Stone (1994), *Successful Direct Marketing Methods,* 5th ed. (Lincolnwood, IL: NTC Publishing Group), p. 168.
15. Ibid., p. 169.
16. Adapted from Rajan Selladurai, "8 Steps to Fundraising Success," *Nonprofit World* 16, no. 4 (1998), 17–19.
17. Bureau of Labor Statistics, "News," United States Department of Labor, January 23, 2008, retrieved on May 21, 2008, http://www.bls.gov/cps.
18. Corporation for National and Community Service, Office of Research and Policy Development (2007), *Volunteering in America: 2007 State Trends and Rankings in Civic Life,* Washington, DC, retrieved May 21, 2008, http://www. nationalservice.gov/ about/volunteering/states.asp.
19. Adapted from Lewis, "Direct Mail Fund Raising Tactics," p. 17.
20. "USPS Household Diary Study, 2005," in *Statistical Fact Book 2006,* 28th ed. (New York: Direct Marketing Association, 2006), p. 182.
21. A. Sargeant and J. McKenzie, "A Lifetime of Giving: An Analysis of Donor Lifetime Value," *West Malling, Charities Aid Foundation* (1998).
22. Adapted from Greg Gattuso, Elaine Santoro, and George R. Reis, "Notebook Open Hearts of Sponsors," *Fundraising Management* 27, no. 10 (1996), 10–11.

23. Adapted from Greg Gattuso, Elaine Santoro, and George Reis, "Summer Games Soar for Goodwill," *Fund Raising Management* 27, no. 10 (1996), 18–19.

24. Adapted from Greg Gattuso, Elaine Santoro, George Reis, "For the Sake of the Sport," *Fund Raising Management* 27, no. 10 (1996), 11.

25. "Charities Hope 9/11 Inspires 'E-Philanthropy'—Nation Contributes with a Quick Click," *USA Today Online,* March 19, 2002, p. 4d, retrieved on September 5, 2003, http://www.usatoday.com/usatonline/20020319/3950825s.htm.

26. Internet Nonprofit Center, http://www.nonprofits.org/fundraising.html, September 7, 2003.

27. "E-Donation Service Facilitates New Revenue Paths for Non-Profits," *Fund Raising Management* 31, no. 1 (2000), 10.

28. Ibid.

29. "Political Microtargeting," SourceWatch, 2008, retrieved on May 19, 2008, http://www.sourcewatch.or/index.php?title=Political_microtargeting.

30. "The 2008 Tools Campaign: Microtargeting," New Politics Institute, retrieved on April 29, 008, http://www.newpolitics.net/content_areas/new_tools_campaign/microtargeting.

31. Tom Agan, "Silent Marketing: Micro-targeting," Penn, Schoen and Berland Associates White Paper 2007, retrieved April 29, 2008, http://www.wpp.com/NR/rdonlyres/4D3A7EB2-9340-4A8D-A435-FDA01DD134DO/O/PSB_SilentMarketing_Mar07.pdf.

32. "2005 Profile of Convention and Visitor Bureaus," International Association of Convention and Visitor Bureaus, Washington DC, April 2005, retrieved on May 5, 2006, http://www.destinationmarketing.org.

33. Paul Seriff, "Measuring Travel & Tourism's Powerful Return on Investment: A Glimpse at the Other 9/10th of the Iceberg," Travel Industry Association of America, Washington, DC, 2005), retrieved on May 12, 2006, http://www.tia.org/marketing/roi_serff.html.

CASE 1:
MCDONALD GARDEN CENTER CASE

It was a wintry morning in early 2005. Pat Overton, marketing director for McDonald Garden Center (MGC), had arrived early to review the year's marketing plan.[1] There were several nagging concerns she just couldn't get out of her mind. "So much to do, so little time," she thought to herself. "You'd think that after 37 years in this business, I'd have seen it all. We offer the best products and personalized service. Our prices are competitive with other specialty garden centers. Yet each year, we lose more customers to the big box stores. This job just isn't getting any easier."

She sat back in her chair and surveyed the greenhouse adjacent to her office. Rows of dirt-filled trays were coming to life with tender, green seedlings. It wouldn't be long before those seedlings would start sprouting the fresh buds of spring. With the first flowers come the customers. It was her job to see that those customers kept coming.

Pat couldn't stop thinking about the decisions that had to be made—allocating the media mix, the future of the rewards program, growing the customer base. She decided to take a walk through the network of greenhouses and clear her mind before meeting with her promotions coordinator, Sherry Connell, and the team of associates that assists with marketing activities. Decisions would have to be made soon to be ready for the spring selling season.

THE COMPANY

MGC was founded in 1945 as a single retail garden center in Hampton, Virginia. Today it serves the entire Hampton Roads area from its original store as well as two additional retail locations. The Virginia Beach store on Independence Boulevard at Haygood is near a high-income neighborhood on a busy thoroughfare with high visibility. The Chesapeake location is on Portsmouth Boulevard on the west side of the city. Although this area is still somewhat rural with acres of farmland, city expansion is moving in that direction.

FIGURE MGC-1 McDonald Garden Center Logo.

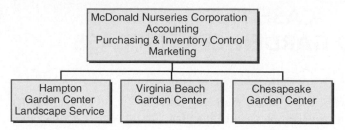

FIGURE MGC-2   **Organizational Structure of McDonald Nurseries Corporation.**

Each location operates as a strategic business unit and profit center (see Figure MGC-2). Its Web site, www.mcdonaldgardencenter.com, serves as an information and communication resource for the organization, offering advice, promoting workshops and seminars, and highlighting products. Given the perishability of the plants, there is no option to purchase products online.

The company is owned and operated by Eddie Anderson, a man with a passion for gardening who is dedicated to his customers and staff. Eddie and his crew strive to make MGC the premier garden center in Hampton Roads by offering a wide variety of high-quality products and services designed to enhance the lifestyle of customers for all seasons. MGC focuses on providing customers with the most informative, enjoyable, and successful shopping and gardening experiences possible.

Pat Overton describes herself as being "older than dirt" when it comes to marketing the garden center. Sherry and the staff refer to her as a guru. She's been in the industry since long before many of them were born. Eddie calls Pat and Sherry the dynamic duo and respects their zeal to know who the customers are and what they need. In this industry, strong customer relationships are critical to staying in business.

THE MGC RETAIL CUSTOMER

MGC serves both commercial and residential customers. The commercial business serves landscapers and is managed by a separate group from the Hampton location. The typical retail customer is female, 35 to 65 years of age, with mid to upper income levels. Customers are well educated, married with families, and own their homes. They also tend to be active (busy), civic-minded individuals who enjoy outdoor living and take great pride in their homes and gardens. MGC customers admit they willingly pay more for products because of the added value from the personalized service received.

Within the retail side of the business, MGC segments its residential customers by the types of products purchased. These subsegments include:

- **Collectibles**—Collectors of unique items like Department 56 Villages and Snowbabies.
- **Outdoor Living**—Purchasers of patio furniture, fountains, statues, and other outdoor decorations.
- **Indoor Plants**—Purchasers of houseplants and potted items.
- **Color Plants**—Purchasers of annuals and perennials for outdoor gardens, typically do-it-yourselfers.
- **Seed and Mulch**—Typically men who purchase lawn seed, fertilizer, peat moss, mulch, garden rock, and so on for home use.

PRODUCTS AND SERVICES

The diverse needs of the multiple retail segments MGC serves require an equally diverse line of products and services. In addition to indoor and outdoor plants, MGC also sells gifts and collectibles, seed, mulch and lawn care products, as well as an expansive selection of Christmas products and services. It produces many of the plants it sells to ensure their hardiness. Services range from delivery, gift cards, and garden advice to landscape design and installation, including tree planting and fountain set-up. Eddie sums up the philosophy of the company in one simple statement: "We know gardening and we share what we know."

Plants are an investment in the garden and home. Purchasing the best-quality plants ensures this investment. Plant production requires substantial resources—large areas protected from the elements, skilled staff, and lots of water. Despite substantial overhead costs, MGC prices are competitive with other garden centers and specialty stores in the area. However, its prices are usually higher than those of the big box retailers like Lowe's, Home Depot, and Wal-Mart. Pat laments that the balance among price, variety, and service becomes more difficult to maintain as the big box stores increase their garden products offerings.

THE GARDENING PRODUCTS INDUSTRY

In 2004, an estimated 84 million U.S. households participated in some form of do-it-yourself indoor or outdoor lawn and garden activity. This represents about 80 percent of all American households. Americans spent $32.1 billion in 2004. The increase in new home sales is presumed to be a major reason for the growth in gardening product sales over the past five years.

Garden seeds and plants was the largest sector within the industry in 2004. Hand tools and implements such as trowels, shovels, and spades, while the lowest in sales revenue, also experienced substantial growth. Much of the sales of garden and leisure equipment are attributed to the purchase of outdoor lawn furniture as homeowners seek to create beautiful outdoor environments to use and enjoy. Garden chemicals and fertilizers show the slowest growth, in part because of an overall market trend toward more organic ways to cultivate plants and lawns.

Retail sales of garden products are forecasted to grow to $40.8 billion by 2009. Steady growth is expected from 2005 through 2009, with overall annual sales increasing around 5 percent a year. Seeds and plants are expected to remain the largest sector, reaching sales of $12.9 billion by 2009. Buildings and leisure equipment is expected to grow to $9.9 billion, with growth coming from the purchase of luxury garden accents like high-end barbecues, fountains, sculptures, and accessories. Both power and hand tool sales are expected to grow at their current rates as well. Only chemicals and fertilizer sales will flatten, increasing only about 1.7 percent in the next five years.

Nationally, over half of all garden products are sold between April and June, typically in springtime. However, climatic spring occurs at different times of the year depending on geographic location. The country is divided into eight climate zones, representing the necessary plant hardiness and the start of the growing season. Figure MGC-3 indicates the sale of gardening products on a monthly basis.

RETAIL OUTLETS FOR GARDENING PRODUCTS

Homeowners shop for gardening products at a variety of retail outlets. Discount stores and home centers topped the list in 2004, with Home Depot achieving a 24 percent market share. Wal-Mart was second (18 percent), and Lowe's was third (10.5 percent). These top three retailers accounted

Month	Percent of Sales	Month	Percent of Sales
January	0.7	July	6.3
February	0.7	August	5.1
March	4.1	September	6.7
April	14.7	October	6.3
May	29.1	November	4.9
June	12.8	December	7.7

FIGURE MGC-3   Industry Sales by Month.

for over half of all residential gardening products sold in the United States. Price, more diverse product variety, and location were the primary reasons consumers shopped at these stores.

All garden supply stores accounted for 21 percent of sales in 2004, down from 23 percent in 2003. This category of retail outlet includes specialty garden retailers, the small, independent, local or regional chains like MGC. Customers who enjoy close, personal relationships and advice from more knowledgeable horticulturalists tend to shop at the smaller, locally owned garden supply stores. However, the composition of this category is about to change. Home Depot plans to open Landscape Supply stores, the first nationwide lawn and garden chain aimed at lawn care profession-als and gardening enthusiasts. This move is expected to cause more industry sales to shift to the gar-dening supply store category and make it even more difficult for the specialty garden retailers to hold their diminishing market share. With Hampton Roads estimated to account for between 0.5 and 0.7 percent of gardening products sales nationwide, the area appears to be a prime candidate for one of the new Landscape Supply stores.

THE TYPICAL GARDENER

The breadth of what is classified as gardening is extensive. For some, gardening means having a few potted plants on an apartment balcony. For others, it means various-sized plant and vegetable beds. Some of the most extravagant gardens are extensive spaces filled with plants, ponds, and furnishing.

On average, a U.S. household spent $449 on gardening products in 2004. This was up slightly from 2003, where the expenditures averaged $440 but down from 2002 where the typical household spent $466. Though practically all American households purchase gardening products, the ones that purchase more than the national average tend to be 45 years of age or older, college graduates, with an annual income of at least $50,000. Households in the Midwest and South tend to spend more on gardening activities than those in other parts of the country. The typical buyer is married, lives in a two-person household where both are either employed full-time or retired. Despite industry-wide efforts to involve children in gardening, those who spend the most on gardening products tend to have no children living at home. Men purchase more lawn seed, fertilizer, power tools, and mulch, and women purchase more plants, lawn decorations, and hand tools.

THE PROFESSIONAL LANDSCAPING BUSINESS

While the purchase of gardening products has increased over the past several years, so has residen-tial use of professional landscape and lawn care services. In 2004, 17.4 million households nation-wide spent an average of $556 with service providers in lieu of doing the work themselves. The typical residential user of landscaping service is 50 years of age or older, has a college degree, and has an annual household income of over $75,000. Research suggests that as homeowners get older and make more income, they are more likely to use professional landscaping companies to handle their lawn and garden maintenance needs.

The residential use of professional landscaping services differs by region of the country. Homeowners living in Southern states tend to rely on landscape professionals more so than elsewhere in the country. An estimated 24 percent of Southern households, including those in Hampton Roads, use outside service providers, compared with 16 percent nationwide. This trend is of particular concern to MGC because as the incomes of people in the area rise, so does the likelihood that they will opt to hire professional landscapers rather than do the work themselves. That means fewer retail sales.

SPECIAL EVENTS MARKETING AND PRE-REWARDS PROGRAM

MGC strives to portray an image of the area's premier, full-service garden specialist, having the most knowledgeable staff that offers sound advice, quality plants, and no-questions-asked guarantees. Pat, Sherry, and the marketing staff run several special events each year to highlight seasonal items and activities, as well as drive customers to its retail locations. Some of its big events include:

- **Outdoor Show.** Here customers can discover new products and services presented by local businesses, seeing everything from stir-fry cooking to elegant floral arrangements in a garden setting. This March event features over 80 vendor exhibits, displays, demonstrations, free seminars, activities, and a Kids' Corner.
- **A Butterfly Affair.** This annual event is held each May and includes live-action displays featuring crawling caterpillars and flying butterflies and the plants that attract them. Seminars and "how-to" classes by a butterfly specialist inform attendees of the butterfly life cycle and how to attract them to their yards.
- **Crepe Myrtle Festival.** This is one of MGC's oldest promotional events. "Myrtle Money" is distributed to customers who purchase products between May and July, redeemable at the festival in mid-July. The event features exhibits, booths, and refreshments.
- **Garden Fiesta.** This festival celebrates the spirit and color of the Southwest, complete with Mexican music, sombreros, piñatas, and fiesta balloons. The event is held in June and features seminars, how-to demonstrations, and activities for children.
- **Designer Days.** Consumers have the opportunity to make their garden visions come to life in August with access to landscape designers, how-to seminars, and speakers. A "visions" contest awards the creativity of several consumer do-it-yourself garden projects.
- **Grass Roots and the American Red Cross.** This cause-related event is held every Labor Day weekend. The focus is on fall lawn care, with educational programs and putt-putt golf for customers. A portion of the weekend's net sales benefits the American Red Cross.
- **Holiday Open House.** This November event features ideas, products, gifts, and time-saving decorating tips for the holiday season.

In addition to these annual events, MGC offers over 50 customer educational seminars throughout the year at each store. It distributes its *Greenleaves* newsletter to approximately 20,000 customers on its mailing list. In years past, most of its marketing budget was spent on promoting the annual events. Getting people to come to an event drives customer retail traffic to the stores.

For years, almost all promotional activities focused on the special events. As popular as the events were, MGC felt the growing pressures from the big box stores. Home Depot, Wal-Mart, and Lowe's used low price as a strategic weapon. The marketing budget at that time was 3.5 percent of

Media Type	Percent of Budget: Pre-Rewards Program Launch	Percent of Budget: Post-Rewards Program Launch
Newspaper	65	45
Broadcast (Television and Radio)	20	30
Direct Mail (including Newsletters)	10	22
Other	5	3
Total Budget	100	100

FIGURE MGC-4   Media Budget Allocation—Pre- and Post-Rewards Card Launch.
Source: McDonald Garden Center.

annual sales. Figure MGC-4 shows the percent of budget for the media mix before the *Garden Rewards* program was introduced.

THE GARDEN REWARDS PROGRAM

One day in late 2000, as Pat and Sherry strolled in the bodacious gardens of the Hampton store, they realized the company's existing marketing activities wouldn't continue to deliver the results achieved prior to the entry of the mass merchandisers. Pat lamented, "We just can't beat their prices."

Sherry noted, "And the cost of media just keeps going up. Cable TV has created so many viewing options for prospective customers, we can't afford to buy time on all those different stations to reach them. Who's to say they're even seeing our commercials?"

Television wasn't the only problematic media. With over 33 radio stations in the Hampton Roads area, it was especially difficult to select and expensive to buy enough ad time to reach prospective customers. The power of newspaper advertising was also diminishing as readership rates decreased due to people's busy schedules. As Pat and Sherry reviewed the media mix, they realized that most of their marketing activities were not measurable. They were "mass marketing" to the entire geographic market in the hope of reaching a select group of prospects. The media delivered impressions, but no one was sure of the response or the return on the promotional dollars.

Pat and Sherry were sure that the 80/20 principle applied to the company's customer base, but they had no way to identify or communicate with that most valued 20 percent. After extensive research, they determined a loyalty program would help the company establish stronger relationships with its best customers. A customer loyalty program would enable them to know the value of each customer and tailor product and service offering that fit their gardening activities.

Although a rewards program appeared to be a sound idea, it wasn't without challenges. Over the past few decades, several retailers have tried various means to build customer loyalty. Results were mixed. Those who were able to impact loyalty the most seemed to make their programs the focal point of all promotional efforts. To make this work, Pat and Sherry would have to integrate all existing marketing activities to reflect the importance of the new program. That meant MGC's newsletter, collectible program, Golden Gardeners program for senior citizens, business partner programs, coupons, and all future advertisements would have to be changed. A privacy policy would need to be established to let customers know of the company's commitment to their privacy. Despite the implementation complexities, Pat and Sherry decided to establish such a program.

The Garden Rewards program was launched in mid-April 2001. Membership was free to anyone and benefits included members-only price discounts, participation in special events, and various

FIGURE MGC-5 Garden Rewards Card and Promotional Materials.

use your card for these active membership benefits

- Discounts on selected plants and garden products
- Discounts on McDonald Garden Center brand items
- Savings on new or exclusive introductions
- Earn Points with each purchase *(see back for details)*
- Golden Gardeners Day
- Greenleaves newsletter subscription for active members*
- FREE local delivery on purchases over $1000
- FREE registration to seminars and workshops
- Selected special events & programs
- FREE pH soil testing
- Special Member Days
- Lost Key program
- No annual membership fee

* active members are those who have earned 50 points or more in the preceding year

FIGURE MGC-5 (continued)

program partnership opportunities. Pat and Sherry thought the cornerstone incentive would be the annual rewards attained by accumulating points. Figure MGC-5 shows the Garden Rewards card, list of benefits, and reward point awards.

Just prior to launch, all MGC employees were trained to get everybody "on board" with the program and change their mass media mentality to a one-on-one marketing mindset. The overall goals of the initiative were to identify current customers and their needs to serve them better. All customers were encouraged to become cardholders. Initial benchmarks were purposely set high—30 percent of all transactions would be recorded in the customer database through card use within the first two weeks of the program launch, and 60 percent of all transactions within the following six weeks.

Within six weeks of the launch, 15,375 customers signed up and used their card at least once. Over 42 percent used their cards two or more times. The data also revealed findings Pat never expected. For example, the maximum number of times a single card was used in the first six weeks was 26! About 7 percent of the cardholders had spent over $1,000 with their Garden Rewards card in the first six weeks of launching the program.

Within six months of the launch, 32,000 Garden Rewards cards had been issued. Over 28,000 cards had been used once and 15,173 cards were used two or more times. One card had been used a whopping 67 times! An anomaly? Not really. During that six-month timeframe, a water gardening customer used her card 55 times. In addition, overall transaction amounts were found to be higher among cardholders compared to the unidentified customers (see Figure MGC-6).

The Garden Rewards program enabled MGC to divert much of its marketing budget to more targeted media, and in doing so, increase overall profitability. Although the number of retail transactions

Retail Location	Average Transaction: Without Garden Rewards Card	Average Transaction: With Garden Rewards Card
Hampton	$35.15	$44.12
Chesapeake	$33.34	$42.52
Virginia Beach	$38.98	$48.40

FIGURE MGC-6 **Average Transaction Amounts—Garden Rewards Members versus Unidentified Customers.** *Source:* McDonald Garden Center.

was down in 2001 from the previous year, average revenue per transaction was up between $9 and $10. The net effect was a 2 percent increase in net profit for the year. The new focus on the loyalty program caused Pat and Sherry to also allocate more of the budget for broadcast media. Television spots would now focus on the benefits of membership in loyalty program and invite prospects to visit one of the stores to sign up. The last column in Figure MGC-4 indicates the revised budget allocation figures by media.

DECISION 1: KEEPING THE OFFER FRESH

In the three years since the launch of the Garden Rewards program, over 50,000 customers have obtained and used the card. The challenge Pat and Sherry face is continuing to identify new ways to keep the program fresh. The persistent question at every brainstorming session: "What more can we offer these people? What will entice the different customer segments to shop more frequently and spend more at our stores?"

Popular benefits previously introduced include:

- Two-for-one admission tickets for many of the area's educational and historical museums, including the Chrysler Museum, Endview Plantation, Lee Hall Mansion, Mariner's Museum, and Virginia Air & Space Center.
- Free local delivery of MGC purchases over $500.
- Bonus points on random days or for the purchase of specific products. (This benefit has proven especially successful in getting rid of excess inventory at the end of a season.)
- Advanced notices via e-mail for special events and promotions.
- Free pH soil testing service.
- Lost key program. (MGC supplies its *Garden Rewards* members with a coded keychain. Lost keys may be dropped into any mailbox by the finder, with MGC paying the postage for returning the keys to the owner.)

Sherry assembled ideas for five different postcard mailings in 2005–2006 and presented them to Pat. The projected costs as well as sample pieces are found in Figures MGC-7 and MGC-8.

Decision 2: Cleaning and Expanding the Customer Base

MGC's database currently holds 50,000 records with approximately 12,000 new customers signing up each year. The longer the company maintains the database, the greater the challenge of keeping customer records current. Knowing that 20 percent of Americans move each year, Pat fears the database has records of people who no longer live at the addresses on file. With a high percentage of military personnel living in the area, many who have moved may no longer be in the state.

FIGURE MGC-7   Samples of Possible 2005 Postcard Mailings with Associated Costs.

Both Pat and Sherry agree the records in the database had to be checked for currency and cleaned. The question was how? Once the outdated records were removed, how many "actives" would remain? Fearing the worst, they knew that in addition to efforts to retain existing customers, they would have to do something to attract new ones.

After much research and work with a list broker, they identified several list rental possibilities. But which ones will maximize response for a new customer offer? Figure MGC-9 provides details regarding several lists Pat and Sherry considered. Each list also had options for additional segmentation selections to pinpoint whom they thought would be the most likely customers. Lists could further be segmented by ZIP code (for an additional $5 per thousand), gender ($6 per thousand extra), state ($8 per thousand extra), income ($10 per thousand extra), education ($7 per thousand extra), and/or marital status ($8 per thousand extra).

In addition to list selection, they also had to determine an attractive offer. Sherry created two postcard offers to increase membership in the Garden Rewards program, one for free garden gloves, the other for a free geranium plant (see Figure MGC-10). Each offer was determined by looking at product inventory, availability, quantity, cost, season, and broad market appeal. Before making a final decision on the offer, Pat proposed a 500-piece test mailing of both to measure response rates. Each

Offer	Potential Segment	Quantity Mailed	Cost per Piece		
			Printing	*Postage*	*Redemption*
Cone-Crazy	Top 600 GR Members	600	$0.50	$0.37	$2.50
Garden Center of the Year	Top 350 GR Members	350	$0.50	$0.37	$2.50
Halloween	Top 500 GR Members	500	$0.50	$0.37	$5.00
Happy Birthday	GR customers who spent >$500 in the previous year	413	$0.84	$0.39	$2.50
Roses	Top 2000 GR Members	2,000	$0.50	$0.37	$6.25

GR = Garden Rewards

FIGURE MGC-8   Offer Details Table.   *Source:* McDonald Garden Center.

List	Description	Base Price	Minimum Quantity
American Gardener Magazine	Members of the American Horticultural Society. Avid and master gardeners, professional horticulturalists.	$100/M	5,000
American Private Golf Club Members	Serious golfers who play at private country clubs. Compiled from membership lists and prize recipients at golf events.	$95/M	5,000
Backyard Garden Design	Passionate, creative home gardeners. Subscribe to multiple home and garden publications	$85/M	5,000
Gardening Enthusiasts	Consumers with a love for gardening and a green thumb to prove it. From seeds to soil, these gardening buffs are open to offers that will help them enhance their gardens	$70/M	5,000
Hobby Enthusiast Network	Hobbyists with interesting ranging from gambling to gardening.	$70/M	5,000
Hispanic Hearth & Home	Individuals who want to improve, decorate, and landscape their property.	$85/M	5,000
Martha Stewart Living Gardening Enhanced	Affluent, paid subscribers who have expressed an interest in gardening. Upscale, well-educated women who love to garden and have the discretionary income to purchase garden products and services.	$105/M	7,500
New Homeowners	Compiled from public sources including county deed records. Updated monthly.	$64/M	5,000
Swimming Pool Owner Database	Free spending, fun loving consumers. Don't mind spending money on parties, landscaping, investments, home improvements or pool upkeep.	$70/M	5,000

FIGURE MGC-9   List Rental Options.   *Source:* NexMark, Inc. 2006.

mail piece cost $0.93 to produce at such limited quantities and $0.39 to mail first class. Garden glove fulfillment costs were estimated at $4, while the geranium plant fulfillment cost was $5.

SUMMARY OF THE DECISIONS

Pat returned to her office refreshed. Walking through the gardens always helped her clear her head. She sat down, opened her notebook, and made a list of the questions to cover with Sherry and the marketing staff during the upcoming meeting.

- What should we do to keep the Garden Rewards program fresh and enticing to get members to continue shopping at our stores?
- What level of response can we expect when targeting such small segments of customers like Sherry recommends? What will it cost us to generate that response?
- Of the five postcards Sherry recommended, are there one or two offers that look the most promising? Given the costs and quantities, what response rates are needed for the mailing to break even?
- How should we go about cleaning the database, and how many active records are likely to remain once the old ones are deleted?
- How should the Garden Rewards program database be segmented? Should we be treating customer segments differently?

FIGURE MGC-10   Samples of Potential Postcards for Customer Acquisition Program.

- Which of the lists identified look most promising for generating new Garden Rewards program members?
- Have we extinguished all the possibilities with what we have in-house? How might we prospect for new customers using our current customer database?
- If we do use one or more of these outside lists, should we add additional selects?
- Can we estimate which of the two offers Sherry created for new customer acquisition has the best chance of success? What are the response rates needed to break even with each of these options?
- Numbers aside, what do we expect the qualitative impact to be if we go with either of these offers?
- Given the highly competitive environment, are our growth aspirations realistic?

As Pat reviewed her list of questions, she realized the decisions she and her staff were about to make would impact the company for years to come. Just then, Sherry poked her head into the office. "You ready for us?" She asked. Pat replied, "Sure. Let's do it."

Bibliography

Enright, Michael and Heath McDonald, "The Melbourne Garden Nursery Industry: A Qualitative Review of Marketing and New Product Development Orientation in a Retail Environment," *Journal of Product and Brand Management,* 6, no. 3 (1997), 175–188.

Florkowski, W. and G. Landry, "An Economic Profile of the Professional Turfgrass and Landscape Industry in Georgia," *Georgia Agricultural Experiment Stations: University of Georgia* (December 2000).

"Garden Market Forecast: Retail Consumer Behavior" (2003). Unity Marketing, Stevens, PA. http://www.retailindustry.about.com.

"Garden Market Research" (2006). National Gardening Association. http://www.gardenresearch.com.

"Gardening Products in the USA," (October 2005). Euromonitor International.

Jerardo, Alberto, "Floriculture and Nursery Crops Outlook," *Electronic Outlook Report from the Economic Research Service,* U.S. Department of Agriculture, September 2005. www.ers.usda.gov.

Mosquera, Gabrielle, "Gardeners," *Target Magazine,* 26, no. 5 (May 2003), 65–66.

NextMark List Research Systems. (2006). http://www.nextmark.com.

"Population by State" (2006). U.S. Census Bureau, http://www.census.gov.

Note

1. This case has been coauthored by Lisa D. Spiller and Carol Scovotti. Some of the data provided by the company has been disguised and is not useful for research purposes. The authors thank Pat Overton and Sherry Connell for their help.

CASE 2:
COLDWELL BANKER PROFESSIONAL, REALTORS CASE

The Memorial Day weekend was just a few days away, which meant the 2007 summer residential selling season was in full swing.[1] However, as Mark Sarrett, general manager of Coldwell Banker Professional, Realtors (CBPRO), made his way down the hall in the company's Virginia Beach office, he noticed the network of glass-walled conference rooms were void of activity. A few years ago, those rooms as well as conference rooms in the 12 other offices of the CBPRO franchise were bustling with buyers, sellers, and agents closing deals on homes and condominiums. These days, only one or two of the rooms were occupied at any given time. "This market correction is killing us," he thought to himself. "Inventory is up, sales are down, and our agents are off doing their own thing without understanding how their actions affect the overall company. There has to be something we can do to pick up more market share." (Figure CB-1 shows the CBPRO logo.)

Mark pictured in Figure CB-2, has overall profit and loss responsibilities for the franchise's 13 offices in the greater Hampton Roads, Virginia, and northeastern North Carolina markets. A Certified Public Accountant by training, he had spent 18 of the past 20 years in commercial real estate. The past year and a half with CBPRO on the residential side was a new world for Mark. The

FIGURE CB-1 CBPRO Logo. *Source:* Used with permission of Coldwell Banker Professional, Realtors®.

FIGURE CB-2   Mark Sarrett, CBPRO
General Manager.

sales process for residential real estate was different than selling commercial property, and although he was well liked and respected by associates, a few questioned the value of his marketing initiatives for the residential marketplace. "That's not the way you sell a house" was a common response to many of Mark's franchise-wide marketing ideas.

All players in today's residential real estate industry face a host of challenges resulting from the recent market correction, rise in advertising rates for traditional media, and growth of Internet applications. One of the biggest difficulties is the nature of durable goods; when customers buy their homes, they effectively take themselves out of the market and destroy (or extensively delay) future demand. In addition, Mark was concerned about confusion emanating from the company name. Coldwell Banker was an internationally recognized brand, but many prospective customers in the franchise's service area were not aware of its market presence. His most difficult challenges were the lack of accountability of advertising dollars spent and viewing marketing expenditures as an investment rather than an expense.

Mark reached the break room at the end of the hall. As he filled his coffee cup, he thought, "There has to be a better way to market residential real estate. Right now we're eighth in sales and seventh in offers under contract in our service area. That's not good enough. In the next couple years I think we can be third. The question is, how do we get there? How do we increase our listings? Do we need more sales associates? How do we attract more buyers more quickly for the listings we have? Do we change our media strategy? How do we get independent agents who are paid on commissions to function together as a team?" As he pondered these questions, he returned to his office with a hot cup of coffee on a quest to put the bustle back into those empty conference rooms.

THE COMPANY

Colbert Coldwell founded a real estate company in 1906 as part of the efforts to rebuild San Francisco after the city was devastated by the earthquake that year. In 1914, Coldwell invited Benjamin A. Banker to become his partner, creating the organization now known as Coldwell Banker Real Estate Corporation. The company currently has 3,800 independently owned and operated residential and commercial real estate offices with over 126,000 sales associates in 35 countries.

FIGURE CB-3
Personal Retriever, Rusty.

Coldwell Banker is renowned for several industry firsts. It was the first real estate firm to attain a nationwide presence; the first national real estate brand with a Web site; one of the first with an interactive online property search tool, Personal Retriever, where visitors are guided through the listings by its trademark character, Rusty the Retriever (shown in Figure CB-3); and the first national real estate organization to offer online seller proposals. In addition, the company has received awards for Coldwell Banker Concierge Service, a program that helps homeowners find local contractors for home repair and renovation. Coldwell Banker Mortgage and a host of other services provide buyers and sellers with the help they need to complete a home sales transaction.

Nationally, Coldwell Banker is widely recognized as one of the premier real estate organizations. Recent research indicates the brand has over 90 percent recognition among recent home buyers and sellers. Brand recognition is perpetuated with national television campaigns, the Web site (www.coldwellbanker.com) that hosts 250,000 visitors a day, and public relation efforts that promote the company in broadcast, print, and electronic media. The goal of the corporation is to provide its franchise operations and their agents with the tools and support needed to develop profitable relationships with their customers. Through its "Celebrating 100 Years with 100 Homes campaign," Coldwell Banker gave back to communities across the country by sponsoring the construction of 100 new Habitat for Humanity homes.

CBPRO

CBPRO has been an independent franchisor of the Coldwell Banker brand since 2001, created through the merger of six independent real estate firms across Hampton Roads, Virginia. In the past six years, the company has grown to 13 offices with 299 agents. Its geographic area (see map featured in Figure CB-4) now starts at Richmond and extends south to northeastern North Carolina and the top of the Outer Banks. Though only a few years old, CBPRO ranked first in the service industry and second overall in the 2006 Virginia Chamber of Commerce Fantastic 50, which rewards the companies in Virginia for the highest growth.

The management believes that success results from the empowerment of its sales associates. To live up to its mission—"to be the premier real estate firm in the markets we serve, providing the highest quality service in an uncompromising professional and ethical environment that will empower our agents to grow professionally and personally"—the company provides proprietary services in addition to those available through the corporate. Customers (buyers and sellers) will find special offers on the CBPRO Web site (www.cb-pro.com). For sales associates, CBPRO offers creative and production services for the marketing materials needed throughout the sales process.

Since its inception, growth has been impressive. Between 2001 and 2004, record-breaking years for the sale of residential real estate, CBPRO sales rose 2,848 percent. In 2005, sales grew another 53 percent. Like the industry in general, sales flattened in 2006, down 2.5 percent. In 2007,

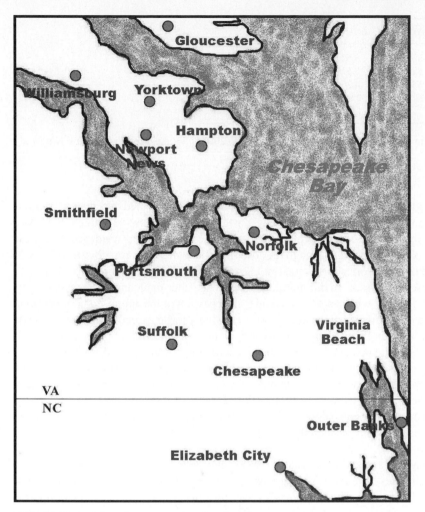

FIGURE CB-4   **Map of Hampton Roads, Virginia.**

sales were down 10.7 percent; however, sales under contract were up 16.4 percent from the previous year, suggesting that a rebound is forthcoming.

THE RESIDENTIAL REAL ESTATE INDUSTRY

The residential real estate industry has a significant impact on the overall GDP of the country. In good times it fuels consumer confidence and spending, causing the economy to grow. In bad times, it prompts the economy to plummet into a recession. The housing market today could be classified as "extremely volatile," with a major fluctuation arguably capable of causing a wide-scale recession.

In the first half of the decade (2000–2005), the country saw a surge of new and existing home sales. Homeowners came to expect their property values to increase at least 5 percent a year. After the stock market bubble burst at the beginning of the decade, housing appeared to be a "can't lose" investment. The Federal Reserve's ongoing reductions of interest rates were designed to stimulate the

Mortgage Rates	6/1/2004	6/1/2005	6/1/2006	5/1/2007
- 30-year fixed	6.28%	5.62%	6.67%	6.37%
- 15-year fixed	5.63%	5.52%	6.26%	6.06%
- 1-year ARM	3.98%	4.26%	5.68%	5.64%
Median Home Price	$215,700	$226,100	$243,200	$220,900 (4/2007)

FIGURE CB-5   Mortgage Rates and Median Home Prices 2004–2007.   *Source:* Freddie Mac and National Association of Realtors.

economy. They also made mortgages (seemingly) more affordable and prompted the creation of offerings like interest only and subprime loans. A recap of mortgage rates is found in Figure CB-5. As a result, a host of new buyers entered the marketplace, purchasing new and existing residences with little to no money down and bad credit ratings. Though the cost of the "dream home" rose, buyers felt it was still affordable because of the historically low interest rates and special mortgage offerings.

However, as interest rates rose, so did mortgage rates. The subprime loans with special 1 percent introductory rates, lenders' willingness to loan up to 100 percent of the appraised home's value, and the lack of concern about credit ratings have caused consumers who extended themselves to be in jeopardy of losing their homes. Many can no longer afford the cost of maintaining their adjustable mortgages. An estimated one in eight subprime loan holders are currently behind on their payments and in many cases, homes are worth less than the loan amounts. Consumers in the worst shape are those who purchased at the end of the bubble when prices were their highest and now need to sell. Today's buyer isn't willing to pay what homes sold for two or three years ago.

The pace of housing starts is also down 33 percent from its peak in January 2006. The slowdown in residential investments is considered to be one of the reasons for the lackluster 2.6 percent growth in GDP in 2006.

Today, lenders have tightened their standards on mortgage approvals, which is affecting home sales. Sales of existing homes have reached their slowest pace since June 2003, and unsold inventory continues to rise. This combination is a recipe for weaker prices as seen by the reduction in the median home prices experienced between 2006 and 2007.

What all these factors mean for the future of the residential real estate industry is subject to debate. According to economists at the National Association of Realtors, the current Pending Home Sales Index suggests sales will continue to decline but should eventually stabilize and level off. Other economists are not so optimistic. Given that Americans have $20 trillion in housing wealth, they suggest that a 10 percent price reduction would cause consumer spending to decline and send the economy into recession.

LOCAL COMPETITION

Primary competitors in the Hampton Roads market include the following companies:

- RE/MAX
- Long & Foster Realtors
- Rose & Womble Realty
- William E. Wood and Associates Realtors

- Prudential Decker Realty
- GSH Real Estate
- Wainwright Real Estate

As the real estate industry continues to evolve in the Hampton Roads area, so does the number of competitors. The leading real estate company in this area is William E. Wood and Associates. It began over 35 years ago and now has more than 20 locations in Virginia and North Carolina.

Rose & Womble Realty is the next largest real estate company in the area, conducting business solely in southern Virginia and northern North Carolina. It was established in 1998 with a merger of two of the top real estate companies in the region and is now the 36th largest independent realty company in the nation. Long and Foster Realtors is the third top contender with strong visibility and a solid reputation in the area.

Other leading competitors ahead of CBPRO include Prudential Decker Realty, RE/MAX Allegiance, Wainwright Real Estate, and GSH Real Estate. Each of these competitors offers a number of locations with many real estate agents offering quality real estate services in the Hampton Roads area.

THE RESIDENTIAL REAL ESTATE AGENT

The job of the real estate agent is to match customers with their desired residences. As the intermediary between buyer and seller, the agent works with his or her client from search or sale initiation through closing and beyond. Agents help buyers find and purchase residences as well as help existing property owners advertise and sell their homes. In some cases, an agent may represent both buyer and seller simultaneously.

Whether it's across town or across the country, moving is one of the most stressful activities a person undertakes. When a real estate agent works with a prospective buyer, he or she must first understand the customer's lifestyle preferences, neighborhood/community needs and desires, and budgetary guidelines. A buyer's representative should be familiar with an area's available housing inventory, and knowledgeable about the community (including neighborhood composition, services, schools, and property taxes) as well as the price and features of recently completed residential transactions in the area. The buyer's agent uses this knowledge base to find appropriate properties, set appointments for showing, visit properties with customers, and follow up with the seller agents with whom appointments were arranged. When buyers find a property they want to purchase, the agent completes the formal paperwork and submits the offer to the seller or his or her representative. The agent serves as the intermediary throughout the negotiation to the conclusion of the deal. Once an offer has been accepted, the agent helps the buyer arrange for property inspection, title search, financing, and other services that may be needed to complete the transaction.

When the agent works on behalf of the seller, he or she needs to discover the selling points and potential drawbacks of the residence, determine the appropriate target market, and figure out how to position the home for sale. The seller's agent should also understand local market conditions and available inventory movement to determine a competitive price. He or she completes all the necessary paperwork to list the home and gathers the data included on the Multiple Listings Service (MLS) database. The MLS is the shared database accessed by realtor subscribers nationwide and serves as a central information resource for available and recently sold property. The seller is also responsible for all advertising and promotion, arranging, showing and hosting open houses to sell the home. When a buyer extends an offer, the seller's agent works with the homeowner to negotiate a deal acceptable to all parties. He or she represents the seller through to the closing of the transaction.

Regardless of whether agents represent buyers or sellers, success depends on their understanding of people and their needs. They are inquisitive, good listeners capable of asking pertinent questions, and integrate what they learn about their customers with their community and inventory knowledge to negotiate deals that satisfy their customers' needs. They are knowledgeable and capable of handling the legalities and logistics of property transfers. In essence, they create and manage the conduit between residential buyers and sellers needed to complete property transactions.

The relationship between prospect and agent begins with the initial contact. This contact may result from the prospect contacting the agent directly or the company through phone, Internet, or stopping by the office. However, agents also solicit clients, either directly or through referrals. Thus, the residential real estate agent is also responsible for prospecting new business.

Technically an agent is an employee of the real estate company to which he or she is affiliated. However, the agent functions as an independent service provider. Typically, the company provides the marketing services and tools needed for real estate sales. In many cases, the agent pays a set fee for those services. The company also provides the agent with an office or desk, but again, the agent pays a fee to "rent" the space. CBPRO agents are provided with office space and basic promotional materials at no charge. Agents choose to work for a real estate company to offset the burdens of educational requirements, financial accounts, licenses, and infrastructure needed to operate a real estate company as well as take advantage of the benefits of strong brand recognition and the results of advertising campaigns.

A residential real estate agent is paid a commission on properties bought and sold. Arrangements vary by company and individual. No standard fees exist as that would be considered a violation of federal antitrust laws. However, like every industry, there are traditions. The typical commission paid to full-service real estate companies on the sale of homes is 6 percent of the purchase price, with half going to the buyer agency and half staying with the selling agency. The amount of commission maintained by the real estate firm is dependent on the level of support services provided and level of production of the agent. Some firms split commissions evenly between firm and salesperson. At CBPRO, new agents are paid 50 percent of the commission received by the firm. However, firms that offer less support may offer agents up to 90 percent of the commission received. In those cases, the agents are responsible for paying all operational and marketing expenses.

Given the nature of the agent/company relationship, it is not surprising that agents change affiliations relatively frequently. If successful agents find the arrangements with their existing employer unsatisfactory, there are plenty of competitors in the marketplace, and they can negotiate a better deal. At CBPRO, productivity is rewarded. The more an agent sells, the greater the percentage of commission the agent keeps without incurring additional marketing costs.

THE RESIDENTIAL REAL ESTATE CUSTOMER AND CBPRO

According to the 2006 National Association of Realtors Profile of Home Buyers and Sellers, the typical homebuyer was 41 years old, earned $71,800, and purchased a home costing $243,000 that was slightly larger than 1,800 square feet. These residential consumers searched eight weeks and visited nine homes prior to making a purchase decision. U.S. Census Bureau data indicate that married couples have the highest tendency to own homes. Over 84 percent of all married couples in the United States are homeowners. The percentage of single males or females owning one-person households is significantly lower. However, a recent trend in homeownership is emerging in that 24.8 percent of Americans aged 25 years or younger were homeowners in 2006, up from just 14.9 percent a decade ago. This trend may be due in part to increased higher education rates and the availability of mortgages with low interest rates. Another trend thought to influence home

Sale Price ($)	Listings Taken –Closed	% of Business	% of AGC	Buyer Controlled –Closed	% of Business	% of AGC	Number of Listings	% of Inventory
0–99,999	11	4.48	2.34	11	3.68	1.66	20	4.03
100,000–249,999	115	46.76	41.38	154	51.50	44.16	150	30.24
250,000–499,999	101	41.04	59.46	112	37.45	51.38	263	53.04
500,000–999,999	19	7.72	20.06	22	7.35	17.90	48	9.68
1 million–1,999,999	0	0	0	0	0	0	12	2.41
2 million–3,999,999	0	0	0	0	0	0	1	0.20
4 million+	0	0	0	0	0	0	2	0.40

AGC = Adjusted Gross Commission

FIGURE CB-6   CBPRO Sales and List Price Analysis Report, January–April 2007.   *Source:* Used with permission of Coldwell Banker Professional, Realtors®.

ownership among young adults is the increase in the number of younger real estate agents: A record 150,000 members of the National Association of Realtors are under 30 years old.

CBPRO targets repeat homebuyers, aged 35 to 54, who are more economically affluent. Unlike competitors in the area, CBPRO customers tend to be more sophisticated, be high-tech savvy, lead busy lives, be more highly educated, and are more actively involved in civic and community activities. Figure CB-6 indicates the prices of the homes bought and sold through CBPRO between January and April 2007, as well as the inventory of listings it maintained at that time.

DECISION PROBLEM: THE CHALLENGE

In light of the increasingly competitive U.S. real estate industry, coupled with residential real estate fluctuating with national economic conditions, and the narrowly defined target customer, CBPRO faces several distinct challenges. Mark clearly understands the need to create a synergy among the 13 CBPRO offices to demonstrate and enhance its market presence and increase the use of measurable marketing activities to justify the dollars spent. However, he also realizes that getting his agents to buy into that concept will be a formidable task.

When Mark joined the company, he spearheaded efforts to create a uniform image for the entire organization. Mark worked with the marketing support staff at franchise headquarters to create a logo, business card, and newspaper ad formats, as well as signage, Web site, direct mail, and even apparel design. Successful integrated marketing communications (IMC) campaigns require a strong and consistent message regardless of the customer touch point. He was confident a uniform image would help CBPRO build the brand recognition across the region it needed to continue to grow.

However, because residential real estate agents function as independent businesses, agents working in the 13 offices often design and create their own promotional materials. Mark has tried to convince the managers and agents of the advantage of a unified effort and promote more cooperative advertising among offices, but has been unsuccessful thus far. Figure CB-7 demonstrates a sample advertisement created by an individual office versus one designed by the franchise.

FIGURE CB-7 **Typical Newspaper Ad Created by CBPRO Franchise Headquarters.** *Source:* Used with permission of Coldwell Banker Professional, Realtors®.

DECISION 1: IMPROVING AND UNIFYING THE CBPRO BRAND LOCALLY

Mark began identifying specific issues he needed to address to get his agents on board to enhance the effectiveness of their branded marketing efforts. He thought his first task was to identify and document consumer perception about the brand. Are residential consumers aware that Coldwell Banker is a leading real estate company? What first comes to the consumer's mind when *Coldwell Banker* is mentioned? What can be done to improve the current level of visibility and market presence of CBPRO in its local market?

FIGURE CB-8　Coldwell Banker for Sale Sign.

Once Mark understood consumer perceptions about the brand, he saw his second task involving agent perceptions about the value of advertising cooperatives to promote the brand. How could he get the offices and agents to portray a more unified branding effort? He wondered what the role of Rusty the Retriever should be. How would greater use of this trademark character influence consumer behavior?

As Mark thought more deeply about his company's situation, he began reviewing and evaluating the current market situation and the arsenal of both national Coldwell Banker and local CBPRO marketing activities.

CBPRO pays a national franchise fee to its parent company, Coldwell Banker Real Estate Corporation. In 2006, the parent company aired a national TV campaign that was broadcast across all major networks and cable stations. In addition, it ran public relations efforts that resulted in over 552 million media impressions with an equivalent advertising value of over $30 million. Online and traditional media campaigns focused on promoting the Coldwell Banker brand and coldwellbanker.com as the destination to find out about open houses. The online Open House promotions on msn.com and Yahoo! resulted in over 300,000 people visiting the corporate Web site in just two days.

Beyond the national advertising campaign, local CBPRO marketing activities include newspaper advertising, including regular listings of properties for sale in the real estate sections and newspaper inserts; word-of-mouth and personal referrals; open house promotions; and the many marketing tools available via the CBPRO in-house marketing support agency, CB Net. This service provides creative and production services for the specialized marketing materials sales agents might use to promote themselves as a resource and get new clients or sell the properties they currently have listed. The materials that CB Net produces includes business cards, postcards, flyers, brochures, direct mail packages, promotional items, apparel, and signage (featured in Figure CB-8). It also offers personal Web site design services.

Strong brand awareness and image advertising campaigns have been implemented at the national level. However, the biggest challenge for CBPRO is leveraging that national brand awareness at the local level to drive consumer behavior to increase residential listings and sales. What are the most effective direct and interactive marketing strategies for CBPRO in penetrating the residential consumer market? Considering how consumers shop for real estate, how can CBPRO impact this trend and gain additional residential listings and clients?

DECISION 2: DRIVING MORE BUSINESS WITH ITS WEB SITE AND IMC CAMPAIGN

Mark was convinced that the Internet was the single most important tool for successfully competing in the residential real estate market, and he had plenty of statistics to back this up.

Mark was concerned about the expense and effectiveness of the traditional home listings placed in local newspapers. Old-fashioned listings just don't deliver anymore.

Given the target market he was trying to attract, he was convinced a strong CBPRO Web site was the way to grow market share. Results from previous research support his feelings.

- Over 20 million people browse real estate listings each month. In the past six years, real estate companies have increased their Internet presence through search engine marketing by 83 percent.
- According to a recent National Association of Realtors study, 75 percent of the people searching for homes on the Internet are considered "serious" buyers, and nearly half of those searching are prequalified for a mortgage loan. Of those who found the information they were looking for via the Internet, 33 percent requested more information from a realtor.
- In 2006, approximately 24 percent of actual home buyers used the Internet as part of their home search efforts. This is up from 15 percent in 2004, and 2 percent in 1997.
- Individuals who used Internet searches were more likely to use an agent to complete the home purchase than were non-Internet users (81 and 63 percent, respectively).
- The typical buyer searched homes for approximately eight weeks prior to purchasing a home, and most reported they found at least one home they wanted to view through an online listing.

However, as important as the Internet is today, the CBPRO Web site cannot be effective without an integrated marketing campaign to drive customer or potential client traffic to the company site and ultimately increase CBPRO sales and listings. Mark knew that he needed to come up with a big idea to project throughout online and offline channels. He thought that idea involved an IMC campaign.

He thought about what had to be considered—analysis of the current CBPRO marketing mix; determination of the most effective marketing and media plan with justification for each medium recommended and the overall strategy behind media utilization; as well as strategic decisions regarding CBPRO offers, positioning, message and media channels, testing, list rental, budget, and ROI projections. What should be included? What should be omitted?

Given an overall objective to drive brand awareness and consumer demand for CBPRO residential services, Mark knew it was important to stay open to any approach, provided it was logical, within budget (he allocated $120,000 for the brand building budget), and results were measurable. The traditional newspaper real estate listing ads were to be excluded from the IMC campaign. Replacing newspaper listings was probably too extreme in the eyes of the agents and office managers at this time. However, augmenting them with a branding campaign could be the first step to eventually eliminating them, provided the campaign delivers results.

There were lots of local media options that could be used. The *Virginia Pilot* and *Daily Press* were the two main newspapers CBPRO used on a regular basis. They could be used to help build the

Publication	Day Published	Cost per inch	Cost per ad
Yorktown Crier	Thursday	$ 9.30	$ 1,171.80
Gloucester Gazette	Thursday	$ 8.50	$ 1,071.00
VA Gazette	Thursday	$ 9.00	$ 1,134.00
Smithfield Times	Wednesday	$ 15.30	$ 1,927.80
	Saturday		
Norfolk Compass	Sunday	$ 27.00	$ 3,402.00
VA Beach Beacon	Thursday	$ 49.00	$ 6,174.00
	Sunday	64.00	8,064.00
	Combo rate	90.00	11,340.00
Chesapeake Clipper	Friday	$ 23.00	$ 2,898.00
	Sunday	29.00	3,654.00
	Combo rate	42.00	5,292.00
The Suffolk Sun	Thursday	$ 17.00	$ 2,142.00
	Sunday	22.00	2,772.00
	Combo rate	32.00	4,032.00
The VA Pilot	Mon–Wed	$ 112.00	$ 14,448.00
	Thurs–Sat	118.00	15,222.00
	Sunday	151.00	19,479.00
Daily Press	Mon–Thurs	$ 54.20	$ 6,829.20
	Fri & Sat	57.10	7,194.60
	Sunday	68.65	8,649.90
Oyster Pointer	Monthly	$ 16.39	$ 2,065.00

FIGURE CB-9   Print Publication Media Rates.   (Rates are based on standard, noncontracted, single full-page, 126 inch, 4-color ad.)

brand. In addition, a variety of local publications served the marketplace. Figure CB-9 provides current print publication advertising rates. Another media avenue was radio. Mark contemplated using radio ads because there are a number of local stations with listening audiences that effectively reach the CBPRO target market. Figure CB-10 lists local radio station advertising rates. Outdoor advertising was another medium that could be investigated. Based on the information provided by the CBPRO marketing department, the cost of one outdoor board on a highway location would be $6,500 per month. Creative and production of all advertisements in the campaign could be handled by CB Net so it wouldn't come out of the media budget.

Radio Station	Format	Cost per 60 second Spot Morning Drive Time
WPTE-FM The Point 94.9	Modern Adult Rock	$ 175.00
WVBW-FM The Wave 92.9	Adult Contemporary	$ 150.00
WGH-FM Eagle 97.3	Country Variety	$ 200.00
WAFX-FM The Fox 106.9	Classic Hits	$ 160.00
WPYA-FM BOB-FM 93.7	Adult Hits	$ 225.00
WTYD-FM The Tide 92.3	Williamsburg	$ 75.00
WBQK-FM Wbach 107.9	Classical	$ 45.00

FIGURE CB-10   Radio and Billboard Media Rates.

In addition to newspaper, radio, and billboard ads, Mark also thought direct mail might be a powerful medium to promote the brand and drive prospective buyers and sellers to the CBPRO Web site. But who should be targeted and what should be the message? He made a mental note, "Check NextMark.com for available lists and rental costs." Though CB Net could handle traditional post-cards and mailings, he saw innovative direct mail pieces involving enlarged and see-through post-cards (cost of production and mailing each postcard $2) as well as tube mailings (cost of production and mailing each tube $2.70) at the annual Direct Marketing Association Conference. Should he use traditional postcards that cost around $0.55 to create, produce, and mail, or should he go with one of these more eye-catching options that generate three to six times more response?

What should he keep? What should he eliminate? How can he get the agents on board with this company-wide IMC campaign? Given the budget, what kind of response rates would be needed to break even on such an IMC campaign? If CBPRO allocated 0.4 percent of the agency commissions maintained to this campaign, how many homes would need to be sold?

In addition to the IMC campaign, he wondered what should be done to improve the CBPRO Web site. How can the site be made more attractive and user-friendly? What additional links or applications should be included to become the "go to" site for the area's upscale residential prospects?

SUMMARY

Mark stared out his office window at the beautiful shores of Virginia Beach. The company had come a long way since its inception in 2001 and with sales under contract figures up, perhaps the market correction was nearing its end. Yet his head was filled with questions and concerns. The main challenges were formidable—developing the strategy to increase and enhance corporate brand image, establish itself as the leading real estate agency for the area's upscale residential customers, and increase sales and listings. What made accomplishing those objectives especially tricky was that not only did he have to accomplish these objectives with customers, he also had to convince CBPRO agents and office managers that a more unified branding effort was best for all involved. "I have to sell our associates as well as our customers," he thought to himself. Customers were changing the way they bought their homes, and Mark wanted CBPRO to be considered the de facto choice by upscale buyers and sellers in the area. As he packed his briefcase and prepared to leave the office to catch his son's baseball game, he knew that these issues couldn't wait. Something had to be done now.

Note

1. This case has been coauthored by Lisa D. Spiller and Carol Scovotti. Some of the data provided by the company has been disguised and is not useful for research purposes. The case authors thank Mark Sarrett for his help with this project.

APPENDIX A:
DEVELOPING A DIRECT AND INTERACTIVE MARKETING CAMPAIGN FEATURING THE MARTIN AGENCY

If you think it takes a Madison Avenue address to become a national success in advertising, think again . . . and meet The Martin Agency! The Martin Agency is an award-winning full-service advertising agency that is becoming well known for creating pop culture icons such as the GEICO gecko and GEICO's cavemen. In 2006, The Martin Agency was named one of *Advertising Age*'s top five agencies of the year. How did this successful company begin, and how does it create award-winning direct and interactive marketing campaigns? That's the topic of this appendix. We take a behind-the-scenes look at how The Martin Agency puts together award-winning campaigns for its clients. First, let's meet this famous advertising agency.

THE MARTIN AGENCY

The agency began in 1968 as a small shop doing mostly print work in a Southern city far removed from the sophisticated East and West Coast cosmopolitan centers of New York and Los Angeles. It is located in the heart of Richmond, Virginia's Shockoe Slip, a historic area of restored warehouses. The red-brick headquarters is set on a quaint cobblestone square, with a circular drive surrounding the water fountain that once was used by dray horses. Historic on the outside? You bet! But once you step inside the building it is bursting with energetic creative minds, high tech, contemporary furnishings, and fine art. This proves that in a wired world, geography doesn't really matter. The setting of The Martin Agency may be a bit subdued, but its staff of over 400 associates is certainly not.

The Martin Agency was founded by a couple of local ad executives, David Martin and George Woltz. They quickly snagged the bright talent of Harry Jacobs, who, in turn, recruited a young writer, Mike Hughes, to the company. Under this dynamic creative duo, the agency quickly became noticed. Its first national high-visibility campaign was the popular "Virginia Is for Lovers" in 1972. By 1981, the agency was ranked as one of *Advertising Age*'s top ten creative shops. In the 1990s, The Martin Agency moved beyond regional advertising, landing national accounts, such as Mercedes-Benz, Wrangler jeans, and Saab. Today, Hughes heads the company—as president and creative director. He is a creative giant in the industry. Recently, *Adweek* named him one of the "nine best creative directors in America" and the *Wall Street Journal* named him one of the country's "creative leaders." Hughes is joined at the helm by John B. Adams Jr., who is the agency's chairman and CEO. This dynamic duo may lead the agency, but it takes a brilliant, visionary, and hard-working staff to serve its clients in such fine, creative, and successful fashion. Today the agency's client list includes GEICO, UPS, Seiko, the Learning Channel, Discover Card, ESPN's X Games, B.F. Goodrich, Wal-Mart, and many others.

Now let's pretend that we are a new client of The Martin Agency and we have engaged them to plan and develop an award-winning direct and interactive marketing campaign for us. What will happen first? Whom will we meet? What's next? What series of stages will the campaign development take? How will we know whether it is a successful campaign? Let's explore the steps involved in planning and developing a direct and interactive marketing campaign via The Martin Agency.

CAMPAIGN DEVELOPMENT PROCESS

Initial Consultation

Welcome to The Martin Agency! Your initial meeting is about laying the foundation for a relationship that will produce great work that generates great results. Award-winning direct and interactive campaigns aren't stumbled on—it takes insightful and productive client and agency teams working together to hatch big ideas that motivate actions and elevate brands to a higher status. Like any personal relationship, the best relationships foster a high level of openness, trust, and respect.

Your initial meeting is with your agency ownership team, which is a seasoned group of agency leaders assigned specifically to your account. Ownership team members are from the areas of account management, strategic planning, media, and creative and provide the vision and direction for the account. A partner in the agency oversees the ownership team, looking over the account and providing you with senior-level accountability and the ability to marshal agency resources on your behalf.

What is covered in the first meeting? The opportunity for the brand. Every brand has an opportunity to extend itself from its current equity and grow, and the first meeting is focused on uncovering that opportunity. A large amount of data and knowledge are presented and discussed to come to a shared understanding of your company's business/category dynamics, current equity, core competencies, and any consumer insights you have. With a solid handle on the business and opportunities for your brand, the next step of campaign planning begins.

FIGURE A-1 **The Martin Agency.** *Source:* Used with permission of The Martin Agency, Inc.

FIGURE A-2   The Martin Agency Ownership Team.

Campaign Planning Meeting

Campaign development begins with establishing the best agency and client team for the task. The agency ownership team assigns an account director who is the main contact with your company and oversees the process of campaign development from beginning to end. In a full service agency, the account director manages all aspects of the relationship from making sure objectives are established to ensure the execution will achieve the best results.

At the campaign planning meeting, campaign goals are established, metrics for success are determined, potential target audiences are discussed, budget and timing are outlined, and the protocols for working together are defined. The discussion produces the necessary ingredients for a campaign strategy to be formed. It is exciting, with both agency and client teams embarking on a creative process that can have a monumental impact on your business.

Strategic Development

A direct and interactive marketing campaign needs to rise out of solid strategy. At this stage, you'll meet a strategic planner who, alongside key creative, media, and analytics staff, establishes the approach to reaching the campaign objective. Elements of a direct and interactive strategy include targeting, offer, and creative methods that are derived from insights about consumers and the category of your company. A test-then-rollout approach may also be considered.

Strategy development is often a collaborative process, so you are encouraged to share past strategies and their effectiveness, competitive strategies and positioning, data from an in-house database (if you have it) to lend support or challenge the strategic approach, and an understanding of operationally how a campaign might be deployed and who it might impact, for example, a sales force.

Market research is often conducted at this stage. Research helps inform the best strategic approach with the audience you're targeting. Research will reveal the strength of your brand, attitudes and perceptions, key drivers of use for your product, how the audience consumes media, and whether your strategy will likely produce the results you're looking for. Budgets and timing of research vary, so you can expect to talk through options that best fit the campaign strategy. Also at this stage, budgets are submitted and the expected return on that investment is projected.

Creative Development

Now the fun really begins. Direct and interactive creative development is as much of a science as it is an art form. The creative director will work with copywriters and art directors to bring out the strategy in a creative expression that prompts actions from the target audience. The creative director maintains a balance between using proven techniques and challenging old conventions.

The strategic planner and creative director will produce a document called a creative brief. This succinct document sets up the creative opportunity within the strategic direction and is what the copywriters and art directors use as a touchstone when coming up with great ideas. Brainstormed, then filtered ideas are refined for a creative presentation to your team.

Creative concepts are presented, complete with the rationale for why they will succeed. Creative directions are discussed and are often put into quantitative or qualitative testing to verify that the work will resonate with the target audience. In many instances, the creative is put into a live-market situation to determine its effectiveness with the offer and specific audiences the work is

FIGURE A-3   The Creative Development Process.

FIGURE A-4   The Creative Development Process.

intended to reach and create an action from. A creative idea is selected by both the agency and client team and the process shifts from idea generation to execution.

Campaign Execution

Creative ideas need to be delivered in targeted ways. This is where it all comes together. At this point, the media strategy turns into ideas for media execution that serve as the basis for a completed media plan. A media buyer will join the team along with a production manager to set the wheels in motion for the campaign to be executed.

This stage is all about the details. Schedules, checklists, specifications, and production all come together to produce a finished campaign. An account manager referees this process between your team and the agency team, making sure everything is taken care of. Any pretesting before roll-out will occur, with results poured back into the communications to refine it for optimization.

Meetings happen all along the way, typically with weekly status get-togethers where items are reviewed, approved, and sent to media for distribution. A communications lawyer makes sure there is no trademark or messaging issues, and the public relations department is put into action to generate buzz and excitement about the new work if it is an open-to-the-public campaign.

Tracking and Learning

Campaigns have the benefit of generating tangible results. Results are typically fed back into future strategies, testing, and execution. Leading this area will be The Martin Agency's director of analytics, who will not only report on the results of the campaign but also analyze it for optimization.

FIGURE A-5 Campaign Execution.

You'll see response rates, conversions, and a return on the investment calculation. Results are analyzed by segment, demographics, and past behavior. A campaign summary detailing all the results of what was learned is presented and kept handy. When the results are very strong, it may be eligible to win an industry award, such as a Direct Marketing Association ECHO (the Oscars of the direct marketing industry).

FIGURE A-6   A Patio Meeting at The Martin Agency.

Conclusion

The process of planning and developing a direct and interactive marketing campaign can take as little as four weeks or last as long as eight months, depending on client objectives and creative challenge. The key to developing a truly successful campaign is that it must meet your company's stated objectives. Is there fun in this process? Sure! But developing creative campaigns also takes a great deal of vision, research, and hard work. As you've seen from the process, it takes many talented people to create a successful direct and interactive marketing campaign. If you are thinking of a career with an advertising agency, such as The Martin Agency, please review Appendix B: Careers in Direct and Interactive Marketing. There we provide descriptions of the many different career positions available in direct and interactive marketing.

Note: The information contained in this appendix has been generously provided by The Martin Agency, Richmond, Virginia. The authors are grateful to the valuable ongoing contributions of the Martin Agency to higher education. We especially recognize Barbara Joynes, Partner, Integrated Services and J. P. LaFors, Vice-President/Account Director, for their work on this appendix.

APPENDIX B:
CAREERS IN DIRECT AND INTERACTIVE MARKETING

Select Direct and Interactive Marketing
   Career Positions and Descriptions
Careers in Direct and Interactive Marketing
   in Agencies

Direct and Interactive Marketing Career
   Resources

SELECT DIRECT AND INTERACTIVE MARKETING CAREER POSITIONS AND DESCRIPTIONS

Account Executive, Advertising Agency

Group Account Director, Advertising Agency

Account Supervisor, Advertising Agency

Account Executive, Advertising Agency

Group Account Director, Advertising Agency

Market Research Director

Marketing Manager Business Products/Services

Media Planner/Analyst

Marketing Manager Consumer Products/Services

Art Director, Catalog

Copywriter, Catalog

Catalog Marketing Manager, Consumer

Catalog Marketing Manager, Business-to-Business

Creative Director, Catalog

Catalog Circulation Manager

Catalog Marketing Director, Business-to-Business

Catalog Marketing Director, Consumer

Telesales Director, Outbound (B2B)

Telesales Director, Outbound (Consumer)

Telesales Director, Inbound

Telesales Manager, Inbound

Telesales Manager, Outbound (B2B)

Telesales Manager, Outbound (Consumer)

Circulation Director, Consumer Magazine

Creative Manager, Consumer Promotion

Circulation Manager, Trade Magazine

Circulation Manager, Newsletter

Marketing Manager, Internet

Search Engine Optimization Manager

Web Site Manager

Database Analyst

Database Director

List Manager, Corporate

Database Manager

Account Executive, Advertising Agency

The ambassador of an advertising agency in its relationship with clients, the Account Executive serves a triple role as the liaison officer, consummate marketing advisor, and eyes and ears of the agency's management team.

DUTIES   Assigned to specific clients, the Account Executive is responsible for advising the client, and the development and execution of programs designed by the agency, including direct mail, space ads, television, e-marketing, and in some agencies, catalogs. Works with creative directors, art directors and copywriters, media experts, market researchers, and production and traffic profession-als to insure maintenance of media schedule within budgetary guidelines. Responsible for reflecting client thoughts and the final acceptance of agency's program.

WHAT'S IT REALLY LIKE?   **Meet Dawn Duchene, an Account Director for Crossbow Group.** "I am responsible for meeting the needs of our clients. Working on everything from business strat-egy to creative to media, every day brings new challenges and rewards. The position allows me to develop close relationships with our clients to the point where I feel I am part of *their* marketing team. But because I am responsible for a diverse range of clients, I work on a variety of products and services to both consumers and businesses. This ensures each day is different than the one before. If you're interested in a career that offers various marketing opportunities across a range of industries, you may want to consider being an Account Director."

Group Account Director, Advertising Agency

The last word on the client accounts under his or her direction, this person has the final approval of all agency client projects. This person is the primary contact to senior-level marketing professionals on the client side, and must meet with expectations while ensuring the integrity of the agency's beliefs.

DUTIES   Oversee the development of the internal and client business strategy, build external rela-tionships while maintaining internal ones, develop expertise in a client's product/service and indus-try, oversee account reviews and analysis, participate in new business development and pitches, provide input for annual and quarterly revenue forecasts, negotiate contractual agreements between client and agency.

Account Supervisor, Advertising Agency

Account Supervisors rely on long days and their depth of knowledge for solving marketing problems for the agency's clients, maintaining a friendly and profitable relationship, and the supervision of Account Executives.

DUTIES   Responsible for development of the staff, day-to-day supervision and monitoring of agency account executives, and the strategic development and implementation of client programs within budgetary guidelines. Guides marketing, creative, media and production activities and participates in securing client approval of cost estimates. As a senior manager, participates in the acquisition of new clients as a member of the new business team. With a keen understanding of the realities of agency competition, insures maximum cost-effectiveness for clients and relentlessly pursues the achievement of client goals.

Market Research Director

Always in demand, even in the ancient epoch of the slide rule, the market research professional has risen in eminence with the development of the computer and analytical tools and now plays a leading role in all phases of direct marketing.

DUTIES   Responsible for evaluation, analysis, and implementation of research and statistical techniques to develop marketing insights and improve marketing plans, increase response rates, minimize credit risks, and decrease buyer attrition. Develops and initiates market segmentation programs using demographic, psychographic, and usage data. Conducts front- and back-end analysis and product performance measures. Tracks competitor mailing and product programs. Prepares reports for departmental needs. Presents forecasts to management. May supervise staff of manager(s) and analyst(s).

WHAT'S IT REALLY LIKE?   **Meet Chris Pritcher, Director of Strategic Analysis at Royall & Company.** "Interested in a fun and challenging job that requires a combination of skills, not just number crunching? That's what my job is all about. I was an engineering major in college, so you know I love math and science. But what's really fun about my current job is the fact that I use research and analysis every day to help our clients—to demonstrate the value of our programs and increase our understanding of what really works best when executing direct marketing campaigns for our clients. Along with a team of ten analysts, I examine results of hundreds of direct mail and e-mail campaigns, which inform our market segmentation and targeting, new product development, strategic planning, and more!"

Marketing Manager Business Products/Services

All businesses are consumers, but the reverse is not always true. Because there are fewer businesses, business marketers face great challenges in the marketplace, including, for one, continually finding new buyers for their products.

DUTIES   Responsible for the maximum penetration of a universe limited by the scope of the product, develops promotional direct marketing materials for the generation of profits. Supervises all testing and the creation of creative output ranging from, but not exclusive to, direct mail, card decks, bouncebacks, statement stuffers, billing inserts, as well as any e-marketing and response space advertising, generally in trade and business publications. Analyzes promotions and digests reports from research staff. Supervises assistants, decides on internal lists and external list recommendations. Maintains mailing schedules.

Media Planner/Analyst

Long after the lights have dimmed in other offices, this professional evaluates the past and ponders the future to ensure that the next direct marketing or telesales program achieves its goals, within an established budget.

DUTIES For the needs of the client, recommends the size and scope of myriad media options, including but not restricted to direct mail, space, TV, broadcast, coop vehicles, package inserts, and, more recently, cable and Internet promotions. Maintains current status reports of promotion budget, plans media schedules, and proposes new test vehicles and formats. Meets with list brokers, space salespeople, and other media vendors. Analyzes front- and back-end results on a timely basis, determines seasonal trends, and maintains an alertness for statistical inferences and variances in response rates.

Marketing Manager Consumer Products/Services

Hitting a target that's always shifting, demographically and geographically, is the specialty and challenge of the consumer direct marketer. Lifestyle changes, aging populations, and dual-income families impact all promotions.

DUTIES Responsible for the development of the budget. Determines the marketing position and pricing, directs creative department in production of a myriad of direct marketing promotional vehicles, including but not limited to direct mail, space advertisements, e-marketing efforts, free-standing inserts, bouncebacks, billing, and package inserts and even matchbook covers. Participates in the selection of product of services sold, credit and collection policies, list approval. Reviews results of front- and back-end analysis, sometimes presented by research department and uses information to improve profit picture.

Art Director, Catalog

Generally under intense time pressure, the Art Director gives the catalog its direction and aura. Also acts as the conciliator between the merchandising and marketing experts, a function that's never written on job specs.

DUTIES Responsible, under the leadership of the Creative Director, for the look and feel of a catalog, the Art Director constantly struggles with "square inch" formulas for space allocation made by marketing and merchandising executives. Designs with copy and, in the great majority of catalogs, photographic and/or graphic images, to make presentation of a three-dimensional product within the limited confines of a printed page. Also responsible for revisions and additions to an existing format or other promotional offering and in some cases the company Web site. Experienced with paper, type, photography, illustrations, and printing.

WHAT'S IT REALLY LIKE? **Meet David Russell, Art Director at Royall & Company.** "While my current job does not involve work with catalogs, specifically, much of what I do is similar to the description above. At Royall, I'm an integral part of a creative team that also includes a copywriter and Web designer. Together we conceptualize and develop the creative for marketing campaigns for direct mail, e-mail, and Web channels. As an Art Director, I am responsible for all of the visual aspects—the look and feel—of the creative we develop. This includes the format, design, typography, photography, and illustration, and creating visual hierarchy in the messaging that drives response. My typical day might include brainstorming with other creative team members to develop concepts to solve a strategic problem, presenting creative solutions to management or to clients, working with print production managers to find the most efficient production methods, or even traveling to visit a client as part of a sales effort. I enjoy being an art director because every day brings something new, it's creative and fun, and the work I do is crucial to the success of our marketing campaigns and our company."

Copywriter, Catalog

When consumers read what the catalog copywriter wrote, they feel you have found a solution, or captured a dream, as well as touched a product or smelled a fragrance. Copywriters know the power of words to create sales.

DUTIES   Working within the most stringent confines of inches, brings to life a valve, or a suit, or a book, without deviation from the specifications, the quality, essence, or contents of the product, often enhancing it with the benefits. Frequently working from a specifications sheet, writes for a printed page, often but not always accompanied by a photograph or illustration. Creates on paper (or in cyberspace) an image for the consumer at home or a buyer in the office. Details particulars of the product or the service offered in the catalog or Web site, and answers questions before they are asked, and with skill, reduces returns.

WHAT'S IT REALLY LIKE?   **Meet Chris Costello, freelance copywriter.** "Imagine having to tell a story, stay on brand, give relevant information about the product, and make the sale all in the space of about three sentences. Oh, and did I mention doing it hundreds of times for one catalog? To me, it's the biggest challenge you could have in marketing communications. TV spots? Easy. Print ads? Piece of cake. Direct mail? Please. And one other big benefit is that catalog writing skills translate to Web writing flawlessly. Deadlines are a reality in any copywriting job and this one's no different, but there's something exciting about putting the book to bed under a tight deadline, with everyone pulling together to make it happen."

Catalog Marketing Manager, Consumer

Working in a universe shifting in taste and lifestyle, the Consumer Catalog Manager is challenged daily to explore new marketing techniques and products. It's a fortuitous day when challenges don't come hourly.

DUTIES   With profit and loss responsibilities, develops short- and long-range marketing plans and goals, projecting sales, growth, and profit objectives. Determines pricing, directs creative output, supervises media including Web site and e-marketing efforts, list decisions, oversees telesales department, determines market research requirements, and maintains mailing schedules with production department. Vigilant for new products at trade shows and maintains contact with customer service for ideas in improving or adding to product line. Monitors market share ad competitive and noncompetitive "books."

Catalog Marketing Manager, Business-to-Business

Equivalent to product manager in a consumer package goods environment, the Marketing Manager for a catalog is responsible for day-to-day marketing, creative, and operations of one catalog. Or often, two, or three.

DUTIES Carries profit and loss responsibilities for a high-volume catalog or a number of smaller ones, generally under the guidance of the catalog marketing director. Develops and executes budget. Decides the positioning, theme, pricing, marketing approach, creative thrust, and media selection. Supervises production by internal or external facilities to ensure mailing schedules. Reviews fulfillment procedures to maintain expeditious delivery of customer orders. Confers with research department and is conversant and knowledgeable in recency/frequency/monetary analysis and its descendants.

Creative Director, Catalog

When dozens of products, in many instances hundreds, must be presented appealingly on a printed page to entice orders, you have an insight to the Herculean task facing the Creative Director of a catalog.

DUTIES Within the limits of a page and budgetary considerations, directs copywriters, art directors, traffic department, and often production in the theme, design, and execution of layouts for catalogs. Uses photography and/or illustrations to reflect and achieve marketing objectives. Frequently acts in the same function for multiple catalogs targeted at diverse market segments. Responsible for order forms, direct mail packages, space advertisements, television, Web sites, cable, packaging, corporate house organs, and ancillary creative materials, particularly if retail operations are involved.

WHAT'S IT REALLY LIKE? **Meet Dan Shaw, a freelance copywriter in Virginia.** "Pick up a random selection of catalogs and you'll find a range of "creative directions." Some use models in exotic settings, others use tabletop shots, still others build elaborate sets to showcase multiple products in one shot. Some even use illustrations. On the copy side, some use straightforward product descriptions, others tell stories, and some read like cocktail party conversations. What's the best? That's the job of the Creative Director to decide. Once I decide on which direction to head, executing against the vision is almost as difficult as creating the vision in the first place. Hiring just the right photographer or illustrator, striking the right balance between brand and product, and fitting it all in the most economical space, often results in late nights and weekends at work. But when the book comes together it's all worth it. And the best part? Seeing a catalog you've done sitting on someone's coffee table. The perfect balance between art, science, and marketing."

Catalog Circulation Manager

No business has a better understanding of the importance of acquiring new subscribers, and retaining the old, and their lifetime value, than does direct marketing. In this universe, the Circulation Manager rules.

DUTIES With creative insight, develops and tests many media, including direct mail packages, e-marketing efforts, list rentals and exchanges, space ads, statement stuffers, bouncebacks, package and freestanding inserts, and alternative media programs to acquire new customers. Responsibility for cost and profitability of acquisition efforts. Develops greater analysis and utilization of internal database. Establishes inquiry programs to develop circulation. Maintains contact and negotiates with list brokerage firms and list managers. Knowledgeable in merge-purge, enhancement techniques, and segmentation.

Catalog Marketing Director, Business-to-Business

Profit and loss responsibility for catalog sales to businesses, governments, and institutions, generally in a market niche or segment, with a range of propriety and distributory items. Continually seeks new markets.

DUTIES   Formulates budget and develops long- and short-term strategic marketing plans and policy. Supervises marketing managers and manages teams of creative, merchandising, list, production, research, customer service, and telesales professionals. Evaluates market share and monitors competition. Continually explores customer database to develop new products. Examines development of new markets by entry into markets defined by Standard Industrial Codes. Explores alternative media for customer acquisition. Monitors sales of ancillary products to broaden catalog or launch new ones.

Catalog Marketing Director, Consumer

This is the direct marketing executive charged with the profit and loss responsibilities for the company's sale of products and/or services by catalog to consumers at home. Enjoys dividing existing catalogs and conquering a new audience.

DUTIES   Prepares and executes corporate marketing plans, budgets, and short- and long-term strategies and pricing policy. Evaluates, tests, and retests new and old media. Assesses, develops, and tests new products to expand market share or introduce new catalogs or programs. Supervises department heads responsible for creative, merchandising, marketing, market research, lists and telesales, and reviews operations and fulfillment activities. Represents the corporation at industry functions. Keeps abreast of legislative and postal regulations as they affect catalogs or telesales and e-marketing efforts.

Telesales Director, Outbound (B2B)

From an ugly duckling into a beautiful swan, telesales has taken added importance and status as a marketing tool that profitably sells products and services to other businesses. A growing discipline with new players.

DUTIES   Complete marketing, strategic, and operational responsibility, including profit and loss, for integration of telesales into corporate marketing mix. Coordinates telesales with other method of sales and distribution. Monitors effectiveness of programs. Establishes personnel policies, training methodology, and motivation techniques. Directs sales activities toward meeting set goals. Supervises script and call guide strategies and performance ratios. Evaluates and recommends installation of new equipment. Responsible for facility planning, systems design, and cost control.

WHAT'S IT REALLY LIKE?   **Meet Tim Tribble, a teleservices professional with Progressive Impressions International.** "Getting the opportunity to offer your client base the next greatest product or advantage over their competition is like getting a letter from home with money in it. Being able to foster a competitive and goals-driven environment in your leadership group is an ever changing landscape typified by finding the right combination of support, encouragement, and recognition that they know how to do their job and to perform well under pressure to produce. Positioning your product by building your reputation instead of resting on it offers a new opportunity for your team and your organization to be successful with every new contact. Finding the right sweet spot and approach with your client list is like riding a never ending wave."

Telesales Director, Outbound (Consumer)

Calling consumers at home, at what may be an inconvenient time, is always delicate, but having them enjoy buying your product or service is the unique talent of the Telesales Director whose programs combine poise with sales.

DUTIES   Profit and loss responsibility for an outbound call center. Facility planning, equipment selecting, systems design, and cost control. Integrates telesales into total marketing mix and coordinates function with other avenues of sales and distribution. Establishes personnel policies, incentive or motivational plans, directs training activities, and establishes and maintains performance standards and records. Awareness of stress factors and methods to alleviate them. Manages the overall effectiveness of the department and produces progress and productivity reports for upper level management.

WHAT'S IT REALLY LIKE?   Meet Tim Tribble, a former outbound telesales director with Affina in Peoria, Illinois. "Building momentum and maintaining energy and morale in your leadership group across the floor is a full-time, demanding job; however, when all cylinders are firing and the floor's buzzing with excitement, it beats any high going. The role requires surrounding yourself with a strong, inspirational leadership team that knows how hard it is to sell a product on the phone, but is still fully committed to both the process and the belief that the very next sale will happen on this phone call. Sure it requires you wearing multiple hats and playing multiple roles based on the posture of the floor, but the potential for personal growth and financial incentive are great!"

Telesales Director, Inbound

The Inbound Department is often the only personal contact a company has with its customer. Everyone relies on this leader to keep customers loyal and happy to buy again, while monitoring productivity and morale.

DUTIES   Complete strategic and operations responsibility for the inbound division including the integration of the inbound function with order processing and fulfillment. Development of up-selling and cross-selling techniques and programs. Establishes acceptable levels of call handling, including rates for abandonment, busy signals, and time in queue. Responsible for scheduling, setting staff levels, and putting systems into place to measure and control allowable cost per order. Selection of telephone equipment, switches, line configurations, facility planning, and cost control.

WHAT'S IT REALLY LIKE?   Meet Tim Tribble, a former inbound telesales director with Affina. "By buying into the axiom that you never get a second chance to make a first impression and then working diligently to maintain that belief throughout the leadership staff, you can bring about an effective mindset change in the way your group perceives their roles. We are typically the first or last-ditch effort to relieve the frustration, remove the confusion, or simply be a sympathetic ear to the people that have or want to buy our products. We need to hold every contact sacred and genuinely ask ourselves, "Did we do everything that we could for the caller, when they needed our help?" With each contact we build and reinforce our brand and product image for reliability, empathy, and customer satisfaction, and that's why we take our roles so seriously. Where else do you get to be the hero or personal benefactor by simply knowing how and what needs to be supported for the products you offer."

Telesales Manager, Inbound

In the trenches with the troops, always alert to potential problems, acts as the eyes and ears of the order department to ensure proper staffing, without overstaffing, and maintains a professional atmosphere in a stressful environment.

DUTIES   Supervisory responsibility for a staff of Telesales Representatives (TSRs), often headed by supervisor(s), responsible for orders and inquiries. Implements and monitors the telesales order entry system and develops policies pertaining to fulfillment of orders. Oversees clerical and administrative support staffs. Responsible for the instruction of TSRs on product features and pricing. Schedules staff for optimum handling of incoming calls. Conducts performance reviews. Presents daily, weekly, and monthly reports on activity to management.

Telesales Manager, Outbound (B2B)

A three-star general in the sales department, the Telesales Manager works with the troops, ensuring their health, wealth, happiness, and contribution to the profits of the company. No day passes without a new challenge.

DUTIES   Responsible for planning, implementing, and managing the Telesales department and its programs. Duties include recruitment, training, and motivating staff in sales, sales techniques, and product awareness. Structures incentive and motivation programs to reduce turnover. Develops operational procedures. Monitors productivity standards and individual quotas. Directs list selection and analysis activities. Develops direct mail campaigns to support the Telesales effort and ensures cooperation and synergy between the department and the field sales force.

Telesales Manager, Outbound (Consumer)

Under the watchful eye of the Telesales Director, upper management, and the rest of the world, Telesales Managers who sell to the consumer at home watch their team with vigilance while reducing turnover and improving the bottom line.

DUTIES   Frequently conducted during the afternoon and evening hours, responsibilities focus on staffing, training, and monitoring the production of a sales force, comprised frequently of part-timers. Develops recruitment programs beyond "help-wanted" ads and adds to staff with candidates at shopping malls, college campuses, "open houses" and other nontraditional sources. Directs training and motivational sessions to improve productivity. Supervises scripts, develops and monitors budget, and recommends lists and direct marketing programs. Monitors calls to ensure quality standards.

WHAT'S IT REALLY LIKE?   **Meet Tim Tribble, a former telesales manager with Affina.** "With the advent of federal and state do not call/solicit legislation the pervasive attitude is to assume that these roles come with a heavy burden to shoulder and frankly, a negative connotation. I propose, however, that these changes offer a great opportunity for our industry to be very selective and appropriately deliberate in our approach to who we market to and whom we attempt to contact, because those who don't want to be called have been removed from our call lists. While the pace can be frenetic and harried, the role requires enjoying what you do and building the morale of the most important people in the building, the call floor staff and leadership. Each call is a new opportunity to reposition your product in the eyes of the consumer and to expand your current customer base while helping your group reach their professional and operational goals."

Circulation Director, Consumer Magazine

The marketing function in any organization represents one of life's supreme challenges, but when a company's every move is highlighted in the trade, and sometimes in the public press, the job takes on new dimensions. Enter the Circulation Director.

DUTIES   Part of a three-legged executive stool with the editor and advertising manager, the Circulation Director builds the base on which the publication thrives or flounders. A marketing professional with profit and loss responsibilities, determines circulation budget and long- and short-term strategy, and usually serves as an advisor and consultant to the editor and publisher. Responsible for the identification of the target audience, circulation acquisition, marketing policy and pricing adjustments, creative strategy and implementation, renewals, newsstand sales, fulfillment, and audits.

Creative Manager, Consumer Promotion

The amazing fecundity of the human mind is evident in the activities of the Circulation Manager, diligently seeking to make substantive inroads to build circulation through the use of every promotional vehicle.

DUTIES   Involved in acquisition and retention programs, and works with the circulation director and/or manager, plans and executes promotions, using all media, including direct mail, insert cars, gift subscriptions, take-ones, blow-in and bind-in cards, newsstand, television and space advertising, as well as e-marketing efforts. Tests and analyzes promotions. Deals with vendors to develop premiums. Frequently involved in list promotions to develop additional rental activity, including e-mail lists. Works with creative department and list specialists, computer service bureau, lettershops, and production departments to ensure scheduled mailings.

Circulation Manager, Trade Magazine

Squeezing blood from a stone is an easy task compared to the challenges handed to the Circulation Manager of trade magazines, competing for the advertising dollar. Of course, they are confined by audit regulations to a limited audience.

DUTIES   Yearly budget preparation and planning and execution of circulation acquisition programs, including creative, list selection, print orders and production and lettershop activities to ensure scheduled mailings. Front- and back-end analysis of promotions. Knowledge of audit regulations, generally BPA. Qualification and reverification of paid and/or nonpaid subscribers, preparation of audit materials for publisher's statement, and monitoring of telesales. Supervision of customer service and development of research information for editorial and advertising departments.

Circulation Manager, Newsletter

Each day the newsletter Circulation Manager goes home saying, "Well, at least we don't have to worry about advertisers." But that's small solace when you worry about renewals and new subscribers.

DUTIES   Full profit and loss responsibilities for single or multiple newsletters, generally highly specialized. Directs artists and copy writers, staff, and/or freelancers in the development of new packages for reader acquisition and renewal and billing series. Supervises production and in some cases Web site and Internet marketing efforts as well as letter-shop activities to ensure mailing schedules and fulfillment procedures. Heavily involved in the search for affinity lists, compiled or response, for expansion of markets. Proficient in the analysis of promotion results, pricing of publication(s), and postal regulations. Supervises the telesales activities.

Marketing Manager, Internet

The Internet channel is drawing many new recruits to the field of direct marketing. The traditional direct marketing manager's sibling, the Internet Marketing Manager, has emerged as a very desirable position managing a source that is growing by leaps and bounds. The opportunities afforded by the Internet channel in terms of cost efficiency, flexibility, and reactivity are just beginning to be fully recognized.

DUTIES   Access and use all relevant research and sales support tools to stay current in the online marketplace. Drive sales and customer retention through the Web site experience. Recommend product, content, and marketing programs to support company marketing plans. Monitor and report on the online sales and traffic results for the Web site. Build infrastructures and processes for enabling and executing Web contacts. Work closely with the marketing and IT teams to drive and execute various projects.

WHAT'S IT REALLY LIKE?   **Meet Nicole Spencer, Product Manager for Snagajob.com.** "When someone hears me say that I'm a 'Product Manager for a Web site company' they immediately say, 'Oh, I see. How interesting. Well, what do you really do?' At our company the Product Manager is a type of Internet Marketing Manager, someone who is bilingual, is a bit of gatekeeper, has a thirst for knowledge, is resourceful, and is able to organize, lead, manage, collaborate, communicate, and ensure continuity among cross-functional teams of people and processes. I need to understand the needs of the business and translate those requirements into acceptable geek-speak, or requirements documents and specifications, that a Web developer, software engineer, systems administrator, or quality assurance tester can understand so they have the information they need to get their jobs done. But it doesn't end there. I also need to back-translate the technical talk into business acumen or layman's terms that sales executives, marketing managers, customer service reps, and even external customers can understand. I am responsible for "the product," which includes every aspect of the Web site that a customer sees and experiences online. My primary goal is to deliver quality products and exceptional experiences that improve the way customers interact with the Web site, or any process related to the company's business, whether they are internal or external customers. If you have an entrepreneurial spirit with the drive to succeed by thinking outside of the box, researching, analyzing, interpreting, translating, working in cross-functional teams, and executing solutions, you should think about becoming an Internet Marketing Manager."

Search Engine Optimization Manager

Top ten positioning in search engines is the most effective form of online marketing. Mystery shrouds how to accomplish this. Enter the Search Engine Manager.

DUTIES   With the vast majority of all new visitors to a Web site originating from major search engines, it is essential that every business implement a search engine optimization marketing campaign that allows customers to find them ahead of the competition. The Search Engine Optimization Manager develops and maintains keyword phrases that have a high amount of search traffic, conducts site analysis to ensure the site is user-friendly and optimized, reviews text writing to maximize search engine ranking, and creates a program in which links are utilized. It takes skill and time to ensure that the Web site is ranked above competitors, while still achieving maximum return on investment.

WHAT'S IT REALLY LIKE?   **Meet Anne Richardson, owner of Channel Marketing.** "As the owner of an Internet Marketing company for nine years, a large part of my job is helping clients gain better visibility on the search engines. While there are some technical aspects to SEO, it is primarily a marketing function. Success in SEO is dependent on having good, optimized content. I spend a lot of time developing key word-focused content that is useful to human visitors, as well as search engine spiders. This content includes webpage text, articles, press releases, video, podcasts, blogs, and more. The Internet and search marketing are constantly evolving, so if you want a career where you will be challenged to continuously learn and use many skill sets, becoming an SEO Manager may be right for you."

Web Site Manager

The Web site is the storefront, or at least the corporate brochure, for the organization, and it takes a savvy professional to present it well. An effective Web Site Manager keeps them coming back again and again.

DUTIES   Responsible for developing and executing marketing communications focusing on building the company's Web site customer base. Responsible for growth of page impressions, unique users, Web subscribers, and registered users against target. Studies the analysis of site traffic and user surveys to gain understanding of customer purchase patterns. Responsible for the overall "look and feel" of the site and ensuring consistency with the company's brand image. Works closely with advertising technology vendors and partners to ensure advertising is delivered effectively and efficiently. Keeps abreast of Web-related developments and evaluates new revenue opportunities.

Database Analyst

At the right hand of the database manager, the Database Analyst knows the inner workings of the database like no other. The ability to manipulate raw data so that diverse audiences can use it is a special skill.

DUTIES   Responsible for interpreting information and reporting results. Compiling and analyzing metrics on customer file; responsible for queries to the operational system, data cleansing/hygiene, integration and data quality assurance. Recommends lists for internal decisions, pricing, positioning, and marketing. Evaluates and reports on data source, analysis of data, requests sample data, executes list hygiene plan, merge-purge literacy. Reports and recommends test strategies.

Knowledge of SAS or related programs. Responsible for database integrity issues, including NCOA, LACS, Telematch updates.

WHAT'S IT REALLY LIKE?   Meet Richard Tooker, Vice President/Solutions Architect for Knowledge Base Marketing. "The major advantage of this job is variety and challenge. It is likely that in any given week, you will be asked at least one question you've never answered before. Working through to the solution can often be quite rewarding. If you enjoy variety and a sense of accomplishment, you'll find this job very appealing. The primary drawback is that the work often has to be done in very tight timeframes. If deadlines don't bother you and you're okay with occasionally working some extra hours to finish on time, it shouldn't be a problem."

Database Director

Without the talents of this person, the database would be just a mountain of unrelated facts. It takes a professional with a special talent to make the information tell its story.

DUTIES   Oversees the development and implementation of database marketing operation solutions that support marketing and customer relationship management campaigns. Establishes corporate data strategy and strategic focus including written policies and procedures for database marketing. Oversees segmentation and targeting, including list strategy and media plan recommendations, matrix design and cell population, list purchases and merge-purge management, and developing technical specifications. Evaluates data vendors or internal staff capability for database enhancement, modeling, profiling, integrated database creation/management, and data warehousing.

List Manager, Corporate

Most professionals state that a direct mail promotion is comprised of three elements: creative, product, and list. For the list professional, the list comes first, second, and third, and then come creative and product, or product then creative.

DUTIES   Recommends lists for internal marketing decisions. Responsible for pricing, positioning, and marketing the rental of the house file to other firms. Liaison with clients and brokerage community to increase rentals of house lists. Direct execution of list promotions by direct mail, space, and personal visitations. Schedules, selects, and staffs trade shows. In some companies, also responsible for the list acquisition function, both response and compiled. Analyzes list performance, establishes merge-purge standards. Works with computer department, service bureau, and letter-shops.

WHAT'S IT REALLY LIKE?   Meet Brandy Palmer, Strategic Targeting Director with Royall & Company. "I am responsible for helping clients meet their targeting goals through the strategic use of lists. I spend most of my time communicating with clients, account executives, and list brokers. I provide knowledge-based campaign list recommendations to ensure lists are being used in best way possible. I am also heavily involved in analyzing data and using results to help improve list orders. I love being able to follow programs from start to finish and see how my knowledge and input has a positive impact on results. I find my work to be very rewarding as it is so vital to the success of a campaign. Even with the best creative and product, if you are not targeting the right people, your direct marketing simply will not work. Some skills that would help you succeed in this position include having great interpersonal and organizational skills, a keen attention to detail, and an aptitude for creative problem solving."

Database Manager

With few ancestors, but beginning a dynasty, the professional Database Manager has become the toast of all marketers and is wooed for the profits they bring.

DUTIES   Designs and enhances databases, in alliance with the marketing department and research professional, incorporating significant information including but not limited to customer psychographic and demographic attributes, purchasing patterns and preferences. Develops models, including response, predictive, conversion, and zip, providing insight for marketing decisions to increase sales, market share, and profitability. Expert at segmentation and list enhancement techniques. Ability to use information to gain meaningful insight into customer purchase motivation.

Salary Information

Crandall Associates, an executive recruiting firm, provided all of the career position descriptions included in the first section of this appendix. In addition, they can provide salary information for each of the above career positions.

Copies of the full salary guide with 60 functions and regional salary variations are available for $75 from Crandall Associates, 44 South Bayles Avenue, Suite 316, Port Washington, NY 11050, (516) 767-6800. The guide can be ordered online at www.crandallassociates.com.

All of the marketing professionals who provided personal career information and advice in this section of this appendix are members of the Interactive Marketing Institute (IMI) at Virginia Commonwealth University. Many are graduates of the IMI Professional Certification Program in Direct Marketing; others are members of its faculty and advisory boards.

IMI was founded in 1996 to provide professional development opportunities for the direct and interactive marketing community, and hundreds of direct marketing professionals have been awarded IMI's Certified Direct Marketer (CDM) distinction to date. Top practicing professionals, distinguished academic faculty, and many talented students bring an unparalleled depth of knowledge and experience to all IMI programs. Learn more about IMI opportunities online at www.IMI.vcu.edu.

Note: The information contained in this section of the Appendix has been generously provided by Crandall Associates, Washington, New York and the Interactive Marketing Institute (IMI) at Virginia Commonwealth University, Richmond, Virginia. The authors are grateful to Wendy Weber, President, Crandall Associates; and to Pam Kiecker, Executive Director, and Anne Schaeffer, Managing Director, both of the IMI, for their work on this Appendix section.

CAREERS IN DIRECT AND INTERACTIVE MARKETING IN AGENCIES

Whether you are interested in marketing, management, or finance, there is something for you in the direct and interactive agency industry. Agencies are businesses, just like any other. Although there are a lot of specialized functions unique to helping agencies create the work that they do, there are also many of the same career opportunities that you might find in any other industry:

- Human Resources: staffing, payroll, and benefits
- Accounting: billing, receivables, financial administration
- Facilities Management: everything from running the mail room to planning office parties
- Information Services: technology infrastructure

But what makes these jobs a little different in an agency environment is that they require an extra degree of *creativity*. When you are dealing with a very creative staff, the environment needs to be that much more creative (Facilities Management). Hiring and benefits needs to have that extra special touch (Human Resources). Connectivity to each other, clients, and what's going on in the world is key (Information Services). Sometimes you even need to figure out how to creatively finance the running of the business (Accounting).

Of course, there are many jobs that are unique to the way agencies work. Each agency may have different titles, but essentially the jobs fall into the following categories.

Account Management

Account Managers are the liaison between the client and the agency and are responsible for the agency's relationship with the client. Account Managers are expected to know their client's business inside-out.

Entry-level positions, such as Account Coordinators or Assistant Account Executives, are responsible for preparing competitive analyses, monitoring budgets, analyzing data, and developing monthly billing reports. Successful Account Managers will be strong in three areas as they grow through their careers: organizational skills, strategic thinking, and relationship skills, both with clients and within the agency.

Account Managers rely heavily on another function that helps move work through the agency. Project management, or traffic, it is a great place to start in an agency if you're not sure what you want to do, but you want to (1) learn how an agency works and (2) become familiar with all of the different departments. You will surely accomplish both of those as an Assistant Project Manager, because this job is responsible for scheduling the jobs an agency has to do, moving the work around the agency, and making sure everything stays on time. This role is vital to every agency, and the people who do it are super-organized and great motivators and negotiators.

Strategic Planning

Strategic Planners ensure that all strategic and creative initiatives undertaken by the agency on behalf of a client are strategically sound by incorporating a variety of tools, some qualitative and some quantitative. Planners review secondary research, design and implement primary research, and synthesize their findings. This helps them write sound creative "briefs," which guide the creative department in its idea generation.

Assistant Account Planners or Junior Planners are responsible for reviewing and synthesizing secondary research sources, drafting research proposals, learning to analyze quantitative data, and writing and editing reports. Planners must have excellent analytical, writing, and verbal skills, as well as the ability to present in a manner that influences and leads others around a great idea.

Increasingly, User Experience Planners, who use primary research to determine how consumers engage with online media to create the optimal consumer experience, are part of the planning department, as opposed to a separate interactive department. This makes a campaign much more holistic when planners are working together to think about all aspects of the work and what a consumer's experience will truly feel like.

Creative

Copywriter and Art Director are the two creative positions most people are familiar with. To get these positions in an agency, most entry-level hires probably went to a graduate or portfolio school to develop their "book" (a portfolio of work to demonstrate their creative capability). The

Copywriter and the Art Director are the ones who work on the agency's campaigns, the work that requires "concepts."

But there are other opportunities within a creative department where people with excellent technical skills can find entry-level opportunities (especially given the boom in the digital space):

Studio Artist: This position works with all graphics needs of the agency, especially those in 2D; requires proficiency in Quark, PhotoShop, and Illustrator and/or Freehand.

Digital Designer: Understands how a Web site comes together; is responsible for art concepts in the production of Web sites; has a basic understanding of HTML programming as it relates to design.

Flash Developer: Responsible for HTML and graphic production as it relates to programming e-mails, landing pages, and microsites. Should be conversant in action scripting, the latest version of Flash, click tagging for online banner ads, and file optimization.

HTML Programmer/Developer: Converts project specifications and statements to detailed logical charts for coding into computer language.

Interaction Designer: Helps ensure that the ideas of the art director are translated into workable ideas online; requires sound fundamentals in information architecture, but must also have a fresh enough design sense to keep all user interfaces and user experiences innovative while maximizing usability.

Media

As you've learned, the single most important thing in direct marketing is targeting, so the media department is a very important department. Very keen, strategic minds reside here. If you are interested in solving puzzles (where to find the prospect?), like to play with numbers (how much can I get for the fewest dollars?), and love to analyze and optimize (did it work? what worked best? how could it work better?), then media might be the right part of the agency for you.

Assistant Media Planners spend much of their day meeting with representatives of various media and list companies, doing research about those companies' offerings—learning about the demographics of the readers/watchers/listeners/mailing lists of those reps. These assistants are often given the responsibility to pull together the initial recommendation for how a client's budget should be allocated.

Assistant media buyers do the opposite of planning the purchases—they actually do the negotiating and buying! Assistants will be given smaller projects or markets, but they will place the buy, monitor its progress, track spending and results, optimize the buy, prepare reports, and resolve billing issues. (Note: In smaller agencies, the roles of planner and buyer are often combined.)

Analytics

The data analytics group is often closely tied to the media group in a direct and interactive agency, because so much of what is done is tied to results. While the senior management in an analytics group often consists of people with doctorate degrees, there are opportunities for entry-level candidates.

An entry-level analyst will compile and analyze data from secondary sources, as well help design and execute primary research. Enhanced computer skills will include knowledge of database software and statistical software.

Production

Last but not least are the terrific people who produce all of the work that has been created. Some of the work can be created digitally by the folks in the creative department. Other assets must be created either with in-house production resources or through outside resources.

The production department maintains a file of directors, photographers, film companies, printers, letter-shops, premium companies, box makers—anything and anybody that can help them produce whatever the creative department can dream up.

Assistant producers for video, art, events, branded content, and online create job dockets, prepare bid sheets, manage estimates as they come in, monitor status of jobs daily, create weekly status reports, coordinate with the talent department on talent releases, and manage billing (to cite a few responsibilities).

Talent payment coordinators maintain all broadcast agreements, prepare talent payment vouchers/authorizations, estimate reuse fees, and prepare talent contracts.

Note: The information contained in this section of the appendix has been generously provided by The Martin Agency, Richmond, Virginia. The authors are grateful to Barbara Joynes, Partner, Integrated Services at The Martin Agency for her work on this appendix section.

DIRECT AND INTERACTIVE MARKETING CAREER RESOURCES

Investigate the following resources to obtain additional information about direct and interactive marketing careers.

DMA Job Bank, http://www.the-dma.org/jobbank. This online resource offers job seekers and DMA member companies looking to fill positions, a state-of-the-art online job bank. It matches direct marketing employers and qualified candidates. It allows you to post a résumé and search for career positions. The job bank also contains articles with valuable links to job and career articles.

Other online resources include:

- CareerBuilder.com
- nytimes.com
- hotjobs.com

Note: The information contained in this final section of the appendix has been generously provided by the Direct Marketing Association (DMA) and the Direct Marketing Educational Foundation (DMEF). The authors are grateful to Anna Chernis of the DMA and Jeff Nesler of the DMEF for their assistance with the appendix, and to the DMA and DMEF for their constant support of and commitment to direct marketing education and career placement.

GLOSSARY

a posteriori after the fact.

a priori before the fact.

ad clicks the number of times a user "clicks" on an online ad, often measured as a function of time.

allowable margin (also known as advertising allowable) the amount of money that can be spent to get an order while still permitting some left over for media costs and the designated profit to be made.

alternative hypothesis the hypothesis that is determined when a null hypothesis is proven wrong.

annoyance in marketing terms, it is the way people feel when they receive too much unsolicited marketing communications.

automated numbering identification (ANI) identifies the phone number of the individual calling.

banner advertising the digital analog to print ads, targeting a broad audience with the goal of creating awareness about the product or service being promoted.

big idea the idea that becomes the company's logo, slogan, or tagline. It is the highlighted unique selling point or creative expression that is the focal point of a whole promotional campaign.

bingo card an insert or page of a magazine that is created by the publishers to provide a numeric listing of advertisers (also called an "information card").

bit the smallest unit of information that a computer understands; one electronic pulse.

blog Web sites that contain up-to-date, continuous information, which is posted for all viewers to read.

brand marketing marketing that boosts knowledge of a company or product's name, logo, or slogan.

branding refers to the use of a name, term, symbol, or design (or a combination of these) to identify a company's goods and services and to distinguish them from their competitors.

break even the point at which the gross profit on a unit sale equates to the cost of making that unit sale.

broadcast media television and radio that can be used as methods for direct response advertising.

business clusters reveal the impact of variables on the buying behavior of businesses located in these areas.

business-to-business (B2B) direct marketing the process of providing goods and services to industrial market intermediaries, as opposed to ultimate consumers.

call abandonment the number of callers in telemarketing that hang up before being serviced by a sales representative.

call center a dedicated team supported by various telephone technological resources to provide responses to customer inquiries.

catalog a multipage direct mail booklet that displays photographs and/or descriptive details of products/services along with prices and order details.

cause-related marketing a commercial activity by which businesses and charities or causes form a partnership with each other to market an image, product, or service for mutual benefit.

central limit theorem assures us that (in a number of random samples taken from a population) the sample means (response rates) tend to be normally distributed.

chi-square (χ^2) test a statistical technique for determining whether an observed difference between the test and the control in an experiment is significant.

chief privacy officer (CPO) a corporate officer whose responsibility it is to protect the sensitive information the corporation collects, from credit card accounts to health records.

circular a printed piece that augments the letter to provide additional information (often called a "folder" or "brochure").

classic format a direct mail package consisting of an outer envelope, letter, circular, order form, and a reply envelope.

clickstream the database created by the date-stamped and time-stamped, coded/interpreted, button-pushing events enacted by users of interactive media.

click-through rates the number of times a user clicks on an online ad, often measured as a function of time.

code of ethics a code that generally serves as a guideline for making ethical decisions.

cold calls a telemarketing term that indicates there is no existing relationship with or recognition of the direct marketer by the customer or potential customer.

collectivist culture a culture in which emphasis is placed on the group as a whole.

compiled lists prospect lists that have been generated by a third party or market research firm via directories, newspapers, public records, and so on. These individuals do not have a purchase response history.

confidence level the number of standard deviations from the mean in a normal distribution.

continuity selling offers that are continued on a regular (weekly, monthly, quarterly, annually) basis (also called "club offers").

contract manufacturing the process by which a company contracts a local manufacturer to produce goods for the company.

control group a group of subjects on which the experiment is not conducted.

conversion the movement of a prospective customer to a definite buying customer.

conversion rate the rate at which leads are converted into sales.

cookie an electronic tag on the consumer's computer that enables the Web site to follow consumers as they shop and recognize them on return visits.

cooperative mailings provide participants, usually noncompeting direct response advertisers, with opportunities to reduce mailing cost in reaching common prospects.

copy appeal the essential theme, which generally stems from fundamental human needs, of the whole promotion or campaign.

cost of goods sold all costs related to manufacturing or producing a good or service.

cost per inquiry (CPI) (also known as cost per lead, or CPL) promotion costs divided by the number of inquiries (people who responded but did not yet order).

cost per response (CPR) the total promotion budget divided by the total number of orders and/or inquiries received.

cost per viewer (CPV) the total promotion budget divided by the total number of people in the viewing audience.

coupon an offer by a manufacturer or retailer that includes an incentive for purchase of a product or service in the form of a specified price reduction.

cross-selling an important characteristic of direct marketing where new and related products (or even unrelated products) are offered to existing customers.

customer database a list of customer names to which additional information has been added in a systematic fashion.

customer lifetime value (CLTV) the discounted stream of revenue a customer will generate over the lifetime of his or her relationship or patronage with a company.

customer loyalty programs programs that encourage customer repeat purchases through program enrollment processes and the allocation of awards and/or benefits, sponsored by the organization or firm.

customer relationship management (CRM) a business strategy to select and manage customers to optimize value.

customer satisfaction the extent to which a firm fulfills a consumer's needs, desires, and expectations.

data mining the process of using statistical and mathematical techniques to extract customer information from the customer database to draw inferences about an individual customer's needs and predict future behavior.

database enhancement adding and overlaying information to records to better describe and understand the customer.

degrees of freedom the number of observations that are allowed to vary.

demographics identifiable and measurable statistics that describe the consumer population.

dependent variable a variable on whose outcome or effect the research is interested.

dialed number identification system (DNIS) a critical system that permits more efficient and effective call handling enabling any organization that has multiple toll-free or 900 numbers to differentiate incoming calls based on the number dialed by the caller.

direct investment the process whereby a company entering a foreign market acquires an existing company or forms a completely new company.

direct mail the leading printed medium that direct marketers use for direct response advertising.

direct marketing a database-driven interactive process of directly communicating with targeted customers or prospects using any medium to obtain a measurable response or transaction via one or multiple channels.

dry testing experimental research used to test a new product not yet available in the marketplace.

duties a tax charged by a government, especially on imports.

e-fulfillment the integration of people, processes, and technology to ensure customer satisfaction before, during, and after the online buying experience.

e-mail electronic communication that travels all over the world via the Internet but is not a part of the Web.

electronic commerce (e-commerce) the completion of buying and selling transactions online.

embedded ads ads that are designed to allow the viewer to receive additional information without having to link to other Web sites.

ethics a branch of philosophy, a system of human behavior concerned with morality: the rightness and wrongness of individual actions or deeds.

experiment a procedure designed to measure the effect of change (often called a "test" by direct marketers).

exporting when a company sells its products from its home base without any personnel physically located overseas.

fixed costs costs associated with a business that do not vary with production or number of units sold.

focus group interview a survey research tool where unstructured small groups (representative of appropriate market segments) converse in a relaxed environment about the subject of the research lead by a trained moderator.

frequency the number of ad insertions purchased in a specific communication vehicle within a specified time period.

fulfillment the act of carrying out a customer's expectations by sending the ordered product to the customer or delivering the service agreed upon.

Geographic Information System (GIS) a computer system capable of obtaining, storing, analyzing, and displaying geographically referenced information known according to position.

global market segmentation the practice of identifying particular segments, country groups, or individual consumer groups across countries of potential customers who display similar behaviors in buying.

Global Positioning System (GPS) a segmentation tool that associates latitude and longitude coordinates with street addresses.

gross domestic product (GDP) total market value of all final goods and services produced in a certain year within a nation's borders.

gross rating points a mathematical value computed by multiplying reach by frequency that measures the number of people exposed to an ad.

gross sales total sales made.

hits any online requests for data from a Web page or file.

hotline names the most recent names acquired by specific list owners, but there is no uniformity as to what chronological period "recent" describes.

house lists lists of an organization's own customers (active as well as inactive) and responders.

hypertext markup language (HTML) a simple coding system used to format documents for viewing by Web clients.

hypothesis testing an assertion about the value of the parameter of a variable (the researcher decides) on the basis of observed facts such as the relative response to a test of variation in advertising.

inbound calls a category of telemarketing where customers are placing calls to the organization to place an order, request more information or to obtain customer service.

identified users the demographic profile of either visitors or users of a site during a specified period of time.

independent variable a controllable factor in an experiment.

individualist culture a culture in which emphasis and value is in the individual.

industrial goods products that are generally used as raw materials or in the fabrication of other goods.

infomediaries companies that act as third parties by gathering personal information from a user and providing it to other sites with the user's approval.

infomercial a relatively long commercial in the format of a television program, to inform viewers of a featured product.

infrastructure is normally a leading indicator of economic development of a country and includes the essential services that support business activities.

input–output analysis derived from Census Bureau data, traces the distribution of goods from their origins to their destinations.

insert a popular form of print advertisement commonly used in a magazine or newspaper.

integrated order fulfillment a term based on the idea that the process of building and delivering products should not begin until after an order has been taken.

intellectual property products of the mind or ideas.

Internet a worldwide network of computers connected to one another to enable rapid transmission of data from one point to another reaching every country in the world.

Internet retailing a category of shopping that occurs through the Internet.

involvement devices devices used in direct response advertising to spur action by involving the reader; examples would be tokens, stamps, punch-outs, puzzles, and so on.

joint venture two or more investors join forces to conduct a business by sharing ownership and control.

key code a unique identifier placed on the response device or order form prior to mailing a promotional piece to track and measure results.

landing page Web pages where people are taken after clicking on an ad banner, a search engine result, or an e-mail link, or when they visit a special promotional URL.

law of large numbers assures us that (as sample size increases) the distribution of sample means concentrates closer to the true mean of the total population.

layout the positioning of copy and illustrations in print media to gain attention and direct the reader through the message in an intended sequence.

letter the principal element of the direct mail package that provides the primary means for communication and personalization.

licensee the foreign business that enters into an agreement and becomes authorized to manufacture or sell specific brand products in its country on behalf of a licensor.

licensing similar to franchising, local businesses become authorized to manufacture or sell specific brand products for another company.

licensor a company located in the home or domestic country that permits overseas manufacturing to occur.

lifetime value of a customer (LTV) the discounted stream of revenue a customer will generate over the lifetime of his or her relationship or patronage with a company (also called "customer lifetime value").

lift an amplified response rate due to selectively making an offer to only those market segments or clusters that are predicted to be most responsive.

limit of error describes the number of percentage points by which the researcher is allowed to comfortably miscalculate the actual response rate.

list brokers those who serve as intermediaries who bring list users and list owners together.

list compilers organizations that develop lists and data about them, often serving as their own list managers and brokers.

list managers managers who represent the interest of list owners and have authority and responsibility to be in contact with list brokers and list users on behalf of list owners.

list owners those who describe and acquire prospects (as market segments) who show potential of becoming customers.

management contracting the process whereby a contract is signed with local foreign people or the foreign government to manage the business in the country market.

market penetration the proportion of customers to some benchmark.

market segmentation a marketing strategy devised to attract and meet the needs of a specific submarket where the submarkets are homogeneous.

market segments placing people (customers or potential customers) into homogeneous groups based on certain attributes such as age, income, stage in the family life cycle, and so on.

match code abbreviated information about a customer record that is constructed so that each individual record can be matched, pairwise, with each other record.

mail order a transaction within a channel, characterized by the absence of a retail store or a salesperson; direct channel from producer to user.

matchback the procedure by which an order response is tracked back to the starting place (catalog or offer) from which it was generated.

mean arithmetic average; a measure of central tendency in a normal distribution.

media efficiency ratio (MER) a ratio that is calculated by dividing infomercial sales by the media cost.

merge-purge a computerized process used to identify and delete duplicate names/addresses within various lists.

micro-targeting the creation and direct delivery to customers of customized winning messages, proof points, and offers, and accurately predicting their impact.

mobile marketing marketing through cellular phones.

morals the judgment of the goodness or badness of human action and character.

motivations needs that compel a person to take action or behave in a certain way.

multibuyer an individual whose name/address appears on two or more response lists simultaneously.

multichannel distribution refers to a marketer using several competing channels of distribution to reach the same target customers.

negative option the shipment of a product is sent automatically unless the customer specifically requests that it not be.

net profit (also known as net profit margin) the amount of money the company retains after the fixed costs are subtracted from the gross revenues and before taxes.

nixie mail that has been returned by the U.S. Postal Service because it is undeliverable as addressed.

normal distribution completely determined by its two parameters: mean and standard deviation (bell-shaped curve).

North American Industry Classification System (NAICS) an industrial classification system using a six-digit code that focuses on production activities.

null hypothesis the statistical hypothesis that there is no difference between the means of the groups being compared.

offer the terms under which a specific product or service is promoted to the customer.

online panels online discussions marketers conduct with people who have agreed to talk about a selected topic over a period of time.

online social networking a marketing strategy that happens when a person or company publishes its information on an online social community.

optimization the process of improving Web site traffic through the use of search engines.

organic search engine optimization the process of improving the volume and quality of traffic to a Web site from search engines via natural or algorithmic search results for targeted keywords.

outbound calls a category of telemarketing where firms place calls to prospects or customers.

outsourcing a telemarketing term referring to the process of having all call center activities handled by an outside organization or a service bureau.

package inserts printed offers of products and services that arrive when the recipient receives an order that he or she had purchased.

packing slip a form or document that identifies the products to be included with the order.

pages a measure of the number of Web pages downloaded from a specific site at a particular time.

partner relationship management (PRM) the generation of greater value to customers through companies' cooperation and close work with partners in other companies or departments.

permission marketing the process of obtaining the consent of a customer before a company sends out online marketing communication to that customer via the Internet.

picking list a list identifying each item on an order list and serves as a routing guide to move the picker efficiently through a warehouse.

political micro-targeting combining groups of voters based on information about them accessible through databases and the Internet to target them with specific messages.

positioning a marketing strategy that enables marketers to understand how each consumer perceives a company's product or service based on important attributes (also known as "product positioning").

positive option the process whereby the customer must specifically request shipment of a product for each offer in a series.

predictive dialers advanced hardware systems that use machines to dial and connect a telemarketing call only when the computer detects a live human voice on the other end of the line.

preprinted inserts newspaper advertisements that are usually printed ahead of the newspaper production and are distributed with the newspaper.

price elasticity the relative change in demand for a product given the change in the price of the product.

price penetration a strategy used if the direct marketer wants to maximize sales volume.

price skimming a strategy used when the objective of the price is to generate the largest possible return on investment (ROI) where the price must be set at the highest possible level to "skim the cream" off the top of the market and only target a select number of consumers who can afford to buy the product/service.

primary data data collected specifically for the current research problem or need.

Privacy Act of 1974 an act that determined whether limits on what the federal government could do with personal information should be applied to the private sector as well.

privacy fundamentalists people who believe that they own their name, as well as all the information about themselves, and that no one else may use it without their permission.

privacy pragmatists people who look at the contact, offer, and the methods of data collection and apply a cost/benefit analysis to make a determination about a marketer's use of information.

privacy unconcerned those who literally do not care about the issue of privacy at all.

proactive telemarketing telemarketing in which the marketing communications are initiated by the company.

product differentiation a strategy that uses innovative design, packaging, and positioning to make a clear distinction between products and services serving a market segment.

product positioning a marketing strategy that enables marketers to understand how each consumer perceives a company's product or service based on important attributes (also called "positioning").

psychographics the study of lifestyles, habits, attitudes, beliefs, and value systems of individuals.

pull strategy the process whereby consumers seek out and demand information or products and services from the producer (also called "pull policy").

push strategy where information and marketing activities follow the normal path of distribution of a product—from the producer to intermediaries to the consumer (also called "push policy").

qualitative relating to or concerning explanations or reasons.

quantitative relating to number or quantity.

random assignment a component of a valid experiment that refers to the fact that both control and experiment group subjects must be assigned completely randomly so that differences between groups occur by chance alone.

random sample a sample in which every element of a population has an equal chance of being selected and differences occur by chance only.

reach the number of people exposed to a particular media vehicle carrying the ad.

reactive telemarketing type of telemarketing in which the customer initiates the marketing communications.

recency/frequency/monetary (R/F/M) a mathematical formula used to evaluate the value or sales potential of customers or prospects.

reference groups the people a consumer turns to for reinforcement.

reference individuals the people a consumer turns to for advice.

response device the part of the direct mail package that provides the means for action.

response lists lists of those who have responded to another direct marketer's offer.

return on investment (ROI) a popular tool of measurement in business, this is the net profit divided by the average amount invested in the company in one year.

right to confidentiality a consumer's right to specify to a given company that information that they freely provide should not be shared.

right to be informed includes the consumer's right to receive any and all pertinent or requested information.

right to privacy the ability of an individual to control the access others have to his or her personal information.

right to safety a right by the consumer to be protected from physical or psychological harm.

right to selection a consumer's right to choose or make decisions about his or her buying behavior.

run-of-paper advertisements (ROP) small advertisements that appear in the regular section of the newspaper where positioning of the ad is at the will of the newspaper.

salting the process whereby a direct marketer places decoys, which are either incorrect spellings or fictitious names, on a customer list to track and identify any misuse (also called "seeding").

sample size the number of observations in a sample, determined by first looking at two major considerations: (1) the cost of reaching the sample, and (2) the amount of information we need to make an efficient decision.

sampling a method of choosing observations from which we can predict estimations.

sampling errors errors that occur in market research due to nonrepresentative sample selection or a lack of randomness of the sample.

search engine an index of key words that enables Web browsers to find what they are looking for.

search engine marketing the whole set of techniques and strategies used to direct more visitors to marketing Web sites from search engines.

secondary data data collected originally for another purpose but may have relevance to the current research needs.

seeding the process whereby a direct marketer places decoys, which are either incorrect spellings or fictitious names, on a customer list to track and identify any misuse (also called "salting").

self-mailer any direct mail piece mailed without an envelope.

service bureaus groups that provide data processing, data mining, outsourcing, online analytical processing, and so on to support the interchange of lists and database information.

short messaging service (SMS) a technological breakthrough in telemarketing that provides alerts from direct marketers by delivering a text message to customers with cellular phones.

solo mailer direct mail pieces that promote a single product or limited group of related products.

source data the information contained in a customer database.

spam unsolicited e-mail messages.

split test a test where at least two samples are taken from the same list, each considered to be representative of the entire list, and used for package tests or to test the homogeneity of the list.

standard deviation the variance from the mean.

Standard Industrial Classification (SIC) System a four-digit coding system of industrial segments developed by the federal government.

stealth communications communications secrecy in that direct marketers can communicate with small market segments or individual customers without competitors or other customers having knowledge of it.

storyboard a series of illustrations that show the visual portion of a TV commercial.

stuffers printed offers of products and services that are inserted in the envelope with invoice or statement.

Sunday supplements mass circulation sections that are edited nationally but appear locally in the Sunday editions of many newspapers.

survey a research method in which data is gathered and hypotheses are tested using questionnaires.

syndication mailings mailings that offer a product to an established customer list.

T1 a giant pipeline or conduit through which a user may send multiple voice, data, or video signals.

take-one racks an alternative method of print distribution where the printed material is placed on a display rack.

telemarketing a medium that uses sophisticated telecommunications and information systems combined with personal selling and servicing skills to help companies keep in close contact with present and potential customers, increase sales, and enhance business productivity.

telephone script a call guide used by telemarketers to assist a telephone operator in communicating effectively with the prospect or customer.

test a term that direct marketers may use for experiment.

till-forbid (TF) an offer that prearranges continuous shipments on a specified basis and are renewed automatically until the customer instructs otherwise.

Topologically Integrated Geographic Encoding Referencing (TIGER) a system created by the Global Positioning System (GPS) and the Census Bureau, which, through use of latitude and longitude coordinates, identifies geographic locations that may be important for industry in the vicinity.

transactional data the information contained in a customer database.

Type I error results when the decision maker rejects the null hypothesis (even though it is true).

Type II error occurs when the decision maker accepts the null hypothesis (when it is not true).

unit margin (also known as unit contribution, unit profit, or trade margin) the amount of money each sale provides to cover fixed costs.

up-selling the promotion of more expensive products or services over the product or service originally discussed or purchased.

URL universal resource locator, otherwise known as your Internet address.

users a measurement of the number of different people or "unique visitors" who visit a particular site during a given period of time.

variable costs costs that vary with production and number of units sold.

violation in marketing terms, is the way people feel when they believe too much information about their personal lives is being exchanged between marketers without their knowledge and/or consent.

viral marketing a form of electronic word of mouth where e-mail messages are forwarded from one consumer to other consumers.

virtual enterprise a company that is primarily a marketing and customer service entity, with actual product development and distribution handled by a broad network of subcontractors.

visits count the total number of times a user accessed a particular site during a given period of time.

World Wide Web (Web) the portion of the Internet that has color, sound, graphics, animation, video, interactivity, and ways to move from one page to another.

INDEX